Additional Praise for

To Redeem One Person Is to Redeem the World

"[Hornstein] argues that Fromm-Reichmann's determ... ill patients cannot be divorced from her Judaism. She s... psychotherapy' as a kind of *tzedakah*, or giving, a relig... ...ιαι jus- tice. . . . Hornstein suggests the principle embedded in a... ...ext, that to redeem one person—to save a life—is to redeem the world."

—*New York Times Book Review*

"This first biography of Fromm-Reichmann is as thrilling and moving as Greenberg's now classic book [*I Never Promised You a Rose Garden*]. Thoroughly researched and elegantly written, Hornstein's biography details not only the psychoanalyst's life, per- sonal and professional relationships, and ideas, but also takes on broader issues . . . dazzling and provocative . . . a major biography."

—*Publishers Weekly*

"Hornstein's biography details a time when a group of mavericks, among the best and brightest in psychiatry. . . followed Freud in his courage and creativity rather than his behavior or in slavish devotion to particulars of his ideas. . . . Exemplary scholarship and lucid writing. . . . Reading [this book], we understand better where we are today, even as we close the institutions that shaped us."

—*Contemporary Psychology*

"This book tells of the pioneering work accomplished by one of the greatest of Freud's followers—a brilliant and knowing clinician who gave herself, heart and soul, to her exceedingly vulnerable patients to the point that her psychological wisdom, offered under difficult circumstances, became, over time, a courageous clinical witness: a kind of psychoanalytic soulfulness that has inspired so many of us these past years."

—Robert Coles, Harvard University, and Pulitzer Prize-winning author

"Gail Hornstein has written a definitive biography . . . [and] a gripping tale. . . . Frieda Fromm-Reichmann's optimism shone like a beacon in a very dark landscape. . . . This book . . . should be prescribed reading for all psychotherapists, psychoanalysts, and psychiatrists. Hornstein has not only produced a well-researched and fascinating biography, but has written it lucidly and well. It makes a compelling read and a salutary one."

—*Psychoanalysis and History*

"Hornstein's work reveals in absorbing detail who Frieda Fromm-Reichmann was both as a person and as a physician. . . . In spite of a biographer's natural sympathy for her subject, Hornstein retains a balanced perspective on this complicated person. . . . Her person and work deserve the close attention they receive in this provocative and emi- nently readable book."

—*Journal of Religion and Health*

"Through meticulous use of sources and delightfully lucid, unpretentious prose, Hornstein . . . recreates Fromm-Reichmann's social milieu and her distinctive piquant personality."

—*Kirkus Reviews*

TO REDEEM ONE PERSON

IS TO REDEEM THE WORLD

The Life of
Frieda Fromm-Reichmann

GAIL A. HORNSTEIN

Other Press • New York

First softcover printing 2005. ISBN 1-59051-183-2.

10 9 8 7 6 5 4 3 2 1

Library of Congress Cataloging-in-Publication Data

Hornstein, Gail A., 1951-
To redeem one person is to redeem the world : the life of Frieda
Fromm-Reichmann / by Gail A. Hornstein.
    p. cm.
Includes bibliographical references and index.
ISBN 1-59051-183-2 (pbk. : alk. paper) 1. Fromm-Reichmann, Frieda.
2. Psychiatrists--United States--Biography 3. Chestnut Lodge
(Psychiatric Hospital : Rockville, Md.)--History. I. Title.
RC438.6.F76H67 2005
616.89'0092--dc22

2005014218

In memory
of Barbara Rosenblum

Each one of us possesses a Holy Spark, but not every one exhibits it to the best advantage. It is like the diamond which cannot cast its luster if buried in the earth. But when disclosed in its appropriate setting, there is light, as from a diamond, in each one of us.

Rabbi Israel of Rizin

Contents

Prologue

There are no goals, only the goal . . . to lift up the fallen and to free the imprisoned . . . to work toward the redemption of the world.[1]

September 28, 1948. The evening was mild. The air, misted with the memory of rain, smelled of catalpa and breeze. Paths through the grounds at Chestnut Lodge were deep in shade, the broad-brimmed trees thick with birds and leaves. A family-owned asylum in the Maryland countryside, the Lodge was often mistaken for a country estate. No fences or gates enclosed the sweeping grounds, but patients did not try to leave. Those not on locked wards walked aimlessly along the paths, watching offices in the main building flare to light in the sudden dusk. It was the first evening in weeks that no one needed seclusion or restraint, and the hallways echoed with the sound of nurses unclenching their teeth.

From the heavily screened porches at the south end of each floor, a white clapboard cottage was visible just across the path. A lamp at its side window illumined a figure at the desk. Frieda Fromm-Reichmann sat heavily in an old leather chair, a half-smoked Chesterfield in one hand, black coffee in the other, drafts of the book she was struggling to finish scattered like leaves across her desk. In less than a month, she would be fifty-nine. It had been thirteen years since she had come to work at the Lodge, and on nights like this, she could imagine herself still in Heidelberg. War and the ironies of psychoanalytic history had made her—a woman, a Jew, a refugee—the most distinguished member of Chestnut Lodge's staff, but no American questioned her place. For three decades, she had chosen to work primarily in hospital settings and with the most disturbed patients. She still spent hours each week with people considered beyond reach by most psychiatrists, although seniority now permitted her to treat only those who particularly interested her. For the first time in six months, she had taken on a new patient, a young woman who was, at that moment, sitting silently on a locked ward pretending not to be terrified, unable to imagine the relationship that would transform her life.

At sixteen, Joanne Greenberg was one of the youngest patients ever admitted to the Lodge.[2] Her diagnosis of schizophrenia did not distinguish her from most others; every mental hospital in America was filled with schizophrenics in the late 1940s.[3] She had been seriously disturbed since the age of nine. Her behavior had the oddness we find so unsettling in mental patients—an embarrassing attentiveness to rules unknown to anyone else. Having finally become too strange to stay in school, she had been sent for an indeterminate stay at Chestnut Lodge.

There was little pattern to the strangeness, which frightened Greenberg's parents as much as the symptoms themselves. The pieces didn't seem to fit together. She refused to let anyone stand behind her, making for a slinking walk and a suspicious air. She claimed to smell odors and heard whispering from people who weren't there. She spoke aloud to them sometimes, in a language no one could recognize. She ate bits of paint or wood, pieces of string, movie tickets, unprepared gelatin. Lightning petrified her. Sudden stomach pains made her double over in agony, but doctors could find no physical cause for the attacks. The plodding gait and stringy hair gave her a dull awkwardness, which seemed at odds with the biting sarcasm that took the place of ordinary talk. There was no family history of mental illness, no obvious trauma in childhood. Yet when people met Joanne Greenberg, they knew something was terribly wrong with her, even though the look on her face made them want to leave before they found out what it was.

Hidden behind the flatness, however, were unmistakable sparks of someone still present. These were rare in a schizophrenic, except in one still a teenager. Psychosis is unrelenting anguish, a torment beyond most people's endurance, and those who end up as mental patients instead of suicides have found a way to blunt the edge. They pay a high price for this. As the lattice of lies, woven more and more tightly, blocks out the light, defenses turn parasitic, destroy the few remaining healthy parts, and then there is no way out.

Joanne Greenberg was too young to have reached that burned-out stage, but she was well on her way. Her absent stare had the look of someone "being beaten to death from the inside."[4] What made her different from a typical schizophrenic was that the battle was still taking place. Trickles of feeling seeped through the brittleness and appeared as expressions on her face. Her indifference had a studied quality, as if she weren't quite sure of it herself. People had yet to become interchangeable objects in her mind.

Frieda Fromm-Reichmann had built her reputation on the claim that no patient, however disturbed, was beyond the reach of psychotherapy. Even as a medical student, listening to wildly hallucinating patients as they screamed or raved, or sitting quietly by the beds of those who lay mute and unresponsive for days, she had been convinced that buried inside the avalanche of illness was a terrified person crying out for help. Her job was to do whatever was necessary to get that person out. She did not think of this as heroic or even particularly worthy of note; a physician's responsibility was to help patients, and she had chosen to do that work.

Frieda—almost everyone, even some patients, called her by her first name and it would be odd to refer to her in any other way—was legendary for her ability to gain the trust of even the most disturbed patient. But even she acknowledged that psychotherapy can work only if a person can stay present to the panic, at least a moment at a time. There has to be a tiny part of the mind that can separate itself from the terror long enough to see what it looks like. People who have reached the point of psychosis usually can't tolerate this; it feels too much like being in a collapsed mineshaft, told to crawl straight toward the danger just to see how bad it is. Literally paralyzed from years of fear, they choose the lesser evil, retreating to a place no one can reach.

Joanne Greenberg didn't end up like this. She began treatment with Frieda a week after arriving at Chestnut Lodge. Four years later, she was successfully attending college at nearby American University. Despite months on the disturbed ward, ripping her arms to shreds with jagged tin cans and crushing lighted cigarettes into the wounds, Greenberg made a recovery so complete she was able to marry, have children, and become an accomplished writer of novels and short stories.

It was highly unusual for a schizophrenic patient to recover at all, and the fact that Greenberg had been treated solely with psychotherapy—no drugs, shock, or any other biological methods—made her cure even more remarkable. But few people outside Chestnut Lodge knew of these events or would have believed them if they had. Frieda presented the case in disguised form in her book, *Principles of Intensive Psychotherapy,* and in various lectures to professional groups, but it was one among many clinical illustrations she used in the early 1950s, and she called no special attention to it. The successful outcome was satisfying to be sure, but it was also perplexing, and Frieda, always given to understatement, didn't endow it with any of the dramatic qualities it would later come to have.

In 1964, Greenberg published a "novel," *I Never Promised You a Rose Garden,* which presented a thinly fictionalized account of her illness, treatment, and cure. Frieda was dead by that point. Joanne used a pseudonym ("Hannah Green") to protect her family, but neither that detail nor the fact that the story portrayed real events was anywhere evident in the book. To the considerable surprise of Greenberg and her publisher, *Rose Garden* gained a huge following and has been continuously in print for thirty-five years. It has sold 5.7 million copies, been translated into a dozen languages, and been transmuted into a movie, a pop song, and a cultural cliché.

Mental patients hailed *Rose Garden,* psychiatrists denounced it, and it became the lightning rod for controversy about schizophrenia and its treatment. Eventually Joanne's and Frieda's identities were revealed, and they became one of those couples—like Freud and Dora, Breuer and Anna O., or Ferenczi and R.N.—that psychoanalysts revere like martyred saints.

Their story posed two fundamental questions, questions we still cannot answer today: Can relationship heal severe mental illness? and Why are psychiatrists the people fighting hardest against this idea?

Frieda Fromm-Reichmann would have been astonished by the adoring attitude that Greenberg's readers have taken toward her fictional incarnation, "Dr. Fried." She never saw herself as having special gifts as a therapist; she attributed her success with patients to commitment and diligence. Frieda always told people she had been a psychiatrist since earliest childhood. The eldest of three daughters in an Orthodox Jewish home, she had taken on responsibility for illusions of family harmony and was brilliant in the role. Like a simultaneous translator, listening past words to murmur, to the half glance, the tonality of a room, she interpreted everything everybody did with a grace that seemed effortless. Even as a toddler, she could execute this *pas de trois* so perfectly that neither of her parents knew she was doing it, and her vigilance transformed a thousand potentially incendiary moments into minor misunderstandings. Gliding back and forth between the sensitivities of her father and her mother's fierce control, Frieda learned to intuit a person's need the way dogs sense danger—with her whole body. Her own neediness went unnoticed, a sacrifice so complete it seemed deliberate.

From her earliest days as a psychiatrist, long before she had ever heard of Freud, Frieda had insisted that no matter how bizarre a patient's behavior, it had an unconscious meaning that could potentially be deciphered. This might take months, even years, but if the doctor could stand the uncertainty, the pattern would emerge. Interpretation wasn't the key, especially with psychotic patients, already prone to imbuing their actions with too much symbolic significance. Frieda's main technique was waiting, a method she deployed so skillfully it looked like magic.

Waiting was her forte, although this was sometimes hard to realize. Her indifference to politeness could seem impatient, but mainly she just couldn't stand to lie. This didn't always endear her to friends or colleagues, for whom her matter-of-factness could have too blunt an edge. But psychotics appreciated her directness more than they could say, and they rewarded her patience by revealing themselves.

Frieda's capacity to wait had been honed as a child, when she trained herself to expand to infinity the time she gave her parents to tire of misunderstanding. Medical school in Königsberg was one long act of patience, designed to prove that she and the handful of other women deserved to be there. Later, working at a Prussian army hospital during World War I, she learned from brain-injured soldiers what it was like to have a shell explode in your face and still be alive. Their muteness became her measure. When she took up treating schizophrenics in the 1920s, they seemed so intact by comparison that she found the work a pleasure. Most psychiatrists, accustomed to treating the "worried well," find the unbearably slow pace of therapy with psychotics intolerable. But Frieda could wait cheerfully through years of infinitesimal gain; the knowledge that recovery was anatomically possible was enough to keep her going. She could tolerate any behavior, no matter how disgusting or bizarre, so long as it seemed necessary to protect a vulnerable person. It was only when symptoms became ruses or habits that she started badgering patients to give them up and get better.

People were sometimes surprised to hear of Frieda's lack of pretense with patients, given how presumptuous she could be with everyone else. She would think nothing of calling colleagues on an hour's notice, announcing that she needed to be driven to a meeting or felt like playing with their child. She took for granted that her wishes would simply take precedence over whatever else was going on in their lives. But with patients she never pulled such stunts. To act willful or superior would risk mocking their pain. Frieda had an unerring eye for exploitation, and never used patients for her own ends.

She was willing to try practically anything that might help them, which was a great deal more than most other psychiatrists were willing to do. She saw one patient at ten o'clock at night because that's when he was most likely to talk. She took others on walks around hospital grounds, or to symphony concerts, or to country inns for lunch. Those too distraught to leave at the end of an hour were permitted to stay for two. If a patient was violent and couldn't be let off the ward, she went to his room or saw him in restraints, if necessary. "She would have swung from the chandelier like Tarzan if she thought it would help," Joanne Greenberg later observed. A colleague remarked, not admiringly, that Frieda's patients got better because she simply gave them no other choice.[5]

From earliest childhood, Frieda had been imbued with a deep sense of responsibility. No event, however insignificant, occurred in isolation; every act had implications for the lives of other people. The worldview of her Orthodox upbringing was embodied in this story, told by the great sixteenth-century rabbi Isaac Luria:

> During the process of creation, God's divine emanations were gathered together and stored in sacred vessels. But the vessels, unable to contain the light pouring into them, shattered, fragmenting the divine sparks, which fell to earth. The world became chaotic; nothing was in its proper realm. The task of human history and the responsibility of every Jew is to rescue the divine sparks and restore order to the world. This is the work known as *tikkun*. When it is fully accomplished, redemption will come to everyone.
>
> *Tikkun* is a collective task; no one person can perform it on his own. A divine spark is attached to each prayer, each charitable act, each moment of goodness. If a person fulfills her duty and strictly follows the ethical path, that spark is restored to its source in the divine realm. To assist another is to do God's work. To redeem one person is to redeem the world.[6]

Fields of medicine define themselves by the cases they take as prototypes, and psychiatry's hopelessness is painfully evident in the poor choices it has made. Perversely claiming only disorders that defy understanding or can't be treated, it has ended up with whatever has been seen as least curable in every historical period. For two centuries, psychiatrists have felt themselves unable to do much but pity their patients' deterioration.[7]

Yet a vocal minority has always opposed this nihilism. Frieda was one in a long line of rebels who refused to give up on patients, no matter how sick they were. There was William Tuke, the English Quaker, whose pioneering approach, "moral treatment," embodied the Quaker values of respect for the individual and the right of each patient, no matter how disturbed, to have the "spark of reason cherished within him." Tuke's asylum, the Retreat, founded in the northeast England town of York in 1796, became a model for humane treatment of mental patients across Europe and the United States. There was Philippe Pinel, the French physician, whose three decades of work at the Salpêtrière, the huge public hospital for women in Paris, brought the ideals of the French revolution to the treatment of mental illness. Pinel's personal, trusting relationship with his pauper patients and his rejection of all forms of coercion and restraint helped to define psychiatry as a field of medicine and recast insanity as a curable illness. A century later, Eugen Bleuler turned Zurich's Burghölzli clinic into an internationally recognized center for the treatment of psychosis. Introducing the term *schizophrenia* to highlight the splitting and dissociation he saw as fundamental to psychosis, Bleuler dedicated himself to developing psychotherapeutic approaches that could help even the sickest patients. Ernst Simmel, who in 1926 founded the first psychoanalytic hospital in the Berlin suburb of Tegel, demonstrated that even physical illnesses and addictions could be treated with psychotherapy. Historians have paid too little attention to these many dissenters, giving us a distorted image of psychiatrists and their work. Painting the rebels into the picture makes the whole field look radically different.[8]

For Frieda, treatment of mental illness was like physical therapy after stroke: a painstaking exercise in hope. Improvement was unpredictable, and was often followed by relapse or deterioration. Recovery, to the extent it was present, proceeded at an agonizingly slow pace. It was natural for the doctor to have periods of discouragement, even real despair, but he couldn't afford to give up, no matter how many setbacks there were. A patient had to have at least one person who could imagine the possibility of his getting well. Frieda thought the reason most psychiatrists failed at their work wasn't because their methods were ineffective, but because they gave up too soon. Their belief in their own potential to cure was so weak that as soon as they encountered a serious setback, they declared the illness "chronic" and abandoned the treatment. Unlike surgeons, who often do their best work when a patient is gravely ill, or oncologists, who pride themselves on creatively adapting their methods to the uniqueness of each case, psychiatrists tend to try one thing, which either works or doesn't.

Frieda accepted the fact that psychosis is often incomprehensible, but did the best she could with what she had. She neither promised miracles nor gave up on people who pleaded for her help. Instead, she improvised, like a doctor on a battlefield who has to keep going no matter what.

In praising a biography of Thomas Edison, one reviewer said it "demythologized the man and left the genius bigger than life." For Edison, who called genius "one percent inspiration and 99 percent perspiration," this is fitting praise.[9] It's equally descriptive of Frieda, a woman others called "gifted" but who thought of herself as simply "not lazy." With Edison, it doesn't make much difference whether we give the larger role to talent or to struggle; his successes can be measured in material terms. But for someone like Frieda, the question of genius becomes a moral one: if psychiatrists could cure psychotic patients by working harder, we'd have to start asking why they don't.

It sounds flattering to call a person gifted, but it's often a way of discounting what she does. If only "gifted" psychiatrists are successful, then nobody is to blame for the failures of the discipline. Psychiatrists can excuse their inadequacies the same way priests leaving seminary do: they can say they just weren't "called" to the work. But this dooms the field to impotence, a fact psychiatrists never seem to realize. By taking responsibility for her failures, Frieda claimed the right also to succeed; when a patient did well, she could attribute his improvement to their hard work together, not to some "spontaneous" cure.

This is not to say that talent doesn't exist. A person with perfect pitch isn't someone who just listens exceptionally hard. Natural abilities are clearly evident in fields from mathematics to track, and it's silly to pretend on grounds of democracy that they aren't. Frieda's intuitive ability was the psychic equivalent of perfect pitch. Reading transcripts of her sessions with schizophrenic patients or listening to tape recordings of her work, we stand amazed as she asks precisely the right question or says something exactly on the mark. There is an elegance to her creativity that sets it apart. Yet she herself insisted that any psychiatrist who worked as hard as she did could accomplish as much.

No one knows what causes mental illness or why some patients recover. At every point in psychiatry's history, there have been competing theories, each seen by its advocates as having stronger support than the others. Since most theories have held that psychotic patients are untreatable by any method, psychiatrists have increasingly avoided them, partly because they don't know how to help them and partly because they are frightened. It's comforting to think of therapists as less terrified by madness than the rest of us are, but in fact, people often embrace psychiatry as an amulet against their own fears, and nothing about the work reassures them. Most flee into private practice, to spend their days, as Freud once said, transforming neurotic suffering into ordinary unhappiness. The remaining few work in hospitals, facing an unending wave of patients so ill that it is difficult to conceive what might be done to help them.

Psychiatry's despair is so profound the field can scarcely be imagined without it, and it remains the only branch of medicine that discounts even the few successes it has had. There are scarcely any mental disorders with agreed-on causes or treatments, but those that do exist are no longer within psychiatry's purview. Some kinds of disturbance—like Alzheimer's disease or brain tumor—have been appropriated by the neighboring fields of neurology and neurosurgery. Others were abandoned by psychiatrists themselves— hysteria is an obvious example—when the politics surrounding their origins made them too risky to hold onto. Inexplicable disorders like schizophrenia stay a part of psychiatry's domain, but patients who manage to get better are called "spontaneous remissions," not treatment successes. The standard view of Greenberg's apparent "recovery" was that she had been misdiagnosed in the first place or would eventually relapse.

What psychiatrists don't realize is how often their failures result from their own fears. Patients whose therapists aren't afraid of craziness can risk being fully themselves. They don't need to sabotage the treatment. They can say what they need. They can let their doctors unwind the bandages and see the real wounds underneath.

Frieda's family were Orthodox German Jews, the kind who typically looked down on their uncultivated brethren from the *shtetls* of Eastern Europe. But she often heard Hasidic tales as a child, and was so taken by these stories— which, as Martin Buber says, use "the recital of a single incident to illuminate an entire destiny"—that she recounted her own clinical cases as if they were legends. A tale told of Rabbi Israel of Koznitz, famous for his "cures of the possessed," illustrates the simple power of improvisation that Frieda liked best:

A woman came to the rabbi and told him, sobbing, that she had been married a dozen years and had yet to bear a child. "What are you willing to do about it?" he asked her. She did not know how to reply. So the rabbi told her this tale. "My mother," he said, "was aging and still had no child. She heard that the Baal Shem Tov, the great Hasidic master, was stopping over in Apt in the course of a journey. She hurried to his inn and begged him to pray that she might give birth soon. "What are you willing to do about it?" he asked her. "My husband is a poor book-binder," she replied, "but I do have one fine thing that I shall give to the rabbi." She went home as fast as she could and fetched her good cape, which was carefully stowed away in a chest. But when she returned to the inn with it, the Baal Shem had already left for Mezbizh. She imme-diately set out after him. Since she had no money to ride, she walked from town to town with her cape until she came to where he was stay-ing. The Baal Shem took the cape and hung it on the wall. "It is well," he said. "My mother walked all the way back," said Rabbi Israel, "from town to town, until she reached Apt. A year later, I was born." The woman who had come to see him cried out: "I, too, will bring you my best cape so that I may have a child." The rabbi shook his head. "That won't work. You heard the story. My mother had no story to go by."[10]

Part of the reason it has been so easy for Frieda Fromm-Reichmann to be dis-placed by Greenberg's fictional Dr. Fried is that there are so few sources doc-umenting what she actually did. Indeed, for a person who lived practically her whole life in the twentieth century, astonishingly little is left of Frieda. Certain letters survive, along with some of her unpublished manuscripts and perhaps thirty photographs. There is a fragment of a recording where she reminisces to friends about life in Germany, taped the year before her death. There are scattered legal records—her medical license, divorce papers, last will and testament, death certificate. Notes and tape recordings of her treat-ment of certain key patients remain in the files at Chestnut Lodge. But prac-tically everything from the first two-thirds of her life was erased by Nazis and exile, like tracks on a beach when the wind is blowing hard. What re-mains is hearsay, from the decades-old memories of her one surviving rela-tive or the mythmaking of her friends. A dozen would-be biographers, uncertain how to pick their way through this scattered landscape, have criss-crossed each other's tracks so often that whatever path may once have ex-isted has long since worn away.

Frieda had her share in obscuring the trail, remaining close-mouthed with everyone during her lifetime and making friends promise to burn files at her death. Morrie Schwartz, the sociologist who practically lived at Chestnut

Lodge during the years he spent studying it in the 1940s, said he and his wife once spent a whole evening trying to get Frieda drunk to "get something out of her." It didn't work. "She wouldn't drink enough," said Schwartz, shaking his head.[11]

Relics of Frieda's life remain carefully preserved in homes all over the United States. Some—a painting that hung over her desk, the clock from her bedroom, chairs from her summer house in Santa Fe—are treated like ritual objects and proudly displayed. Others, like the emerald ring and the set of champagne glasses, are shown off only on special occasions, to the few still able to grasp their significance. It's as if Frieda herself has been dispersed, the fragments too charged to be kept all in one place. Even her cottage at Chestnut Lodge was still being described, forty years after her death, as a "magic, shrine-like place" in the minds of European psychiatrists.[12]

In some disciplines, it's an honor to become an icon, but in medicine, it's cause for suspicion. Doctors who seem larger than life do not inspire others to follow their lead. Their talents seem more like magical gifts than skills to be passed on to the next generation. This is particularly true in psychiatry, a field whose most powerful images come not from real events but from paintings or fiction: Pinel striking the shackles from the madwomen of Paris, Charcot hypnotizing a hysteric as if they were actors in a play. These aren't pedagogical examples; they are feats of amazement.[13] When Frieda's admirers depict her as St. Catherine, able to heal the afflicted with the power of her gaze, we lose sight of the woman whose fundamental commitment in life was simply to hard work.

Once *I Never Promised You a Rose Garden* appeared, the real-life Frieda became even further obscured. Published in 1964, seven years after Frieda's death, Greenberg's story became a source of inspiration for people all over the world who had no idea that serious mental illness could be cured. They didn't know Dr. Fried's real name, but it hardly mattered; the portrait was so accurate that even Frieda's sisters, reading the novel in translation, instantly recognized her. *Rose Garden* is a beautiful memorial to Frieda and an extraordinary testimony to her work, but by turning her into a fictional icon, it has made her seem even less real, a character in a novel, not a doctor with a systematic approach.

Biographers often struggle for a fresh view of subjects about whom much has been written, but trying to describe someone who vividly exists for most people as a fictional character is even more of a challenge. *Rose Garden* is based heavily on fact but it's also a novel, one written by a patient who was astounded at her own recovery and needed to reassure herself that it had actually happened.

That Frieda emerges as a saint in this narrative is unsurprising; the problem is to see beyond the glow of Greenberg's prose. The real Frieda did some extraordinary things, and they need to be appreciated for what they were. But she has been Dr. Fried for so long—even to those who knew her best—that her life already seems too invented to have happened. To reconstruct her now as a more complicated figure strikes her admirers as disloyalty or appropriation. Yet it is precisely because she was a real person that Frieda captures our attention and deserves broader interest.

I first read *Rose Garden* in 1966, in a cheap reprint with a mysterious Janus-faced figure on the front. I was fifteen years old. I had no idea that people weren't supposed to recover from schizophrenia or that there was anything controversial about treating them with psychotherapy. Ten years later, as a graduate student in psychology, I read *Principles of Intensive Psychotherapy* for a class. It seemed so humane, so pragmatic. I was impressed by Frieda's quiet confidence, her insistence that every patient was potentially reachable, her refusal to overstate her own accomplishments. A fellow student casually mentioned that Frieda was the one who had treated Greenberg. I read *Rose Garden* again, astonished that a patient could present her therapist's method with such accuracy and insightfulness.

Fifteen years later, when the very idea of psychotherapy with schizophrenics had been made to seem preposterous by a mental health establishment addicted to drug treatment, I became curious as to why so "absurd" a method would have been taken so seriously by someone as sensible as Frieda. I set out to recover the history of psychotherapy with schizophrenics, a topic strangely missing even from exhaustive accounts of psychiatry's development. I was completely unprepared for the outpouring of intense feelings this project immediately began to provoke from the historians and psychiatrists I contacted—people taking weeks to decide whether to let me interview them, insisting that the tape recorder be switched off at key moments, or whispering revelations and unearthing boxes of materials they had kept secret for forty years. Discussions of Frieda as a person seemed especially charged. There was an odd absence of any of the ordinary sorts of source materials and a constant, unnerving sense of erasure of most of the details of her life and work. People who had known her well were so protective of even the most innocuous facts that it was hard not to feel they were hiding some terrible secret about her; those who knew her only by reputation spun out elaborate speculations filled with spite and innuendo. The overly emotional response by both groups seemed far in excess of what was called for by a historical debate. I knew that the issue of treatment in psychiatry was controversial, but this didn't explain the air of mystery that seemed to surround even the most routine queries about Frieda's approach.

In no sense did I set out to write a biography. Indeed, for most of the ten years I worked on this project, I fought against the idea even of attempting one.[14] As I traveled across the United States and Europe, searching through archives and poring over hospital records and conducting interviews, I said over and over again that I wasn't interested in the details of Frieda's life so much as the historical significance of her work. I wanted to understand how an approach like hers had come to exist and why it had been repudiated and then literally expunged from the history books.

What I didn't understand was that when the very possibility of an idea ceases to seem believable, it becomes very difficult to talk about. I would tell people that I was studying the history of psychotherapy with schizophrenics, and they would give me a bewildered look and ask: "Is there one?" I was finally forced to the realization that the only way to get this idea taken seriously was to bring back the person who had embodied it most vividly.

But Frieda Fromm-Reichmann is a hard person to write about. Most people know her as a fictional character and would prefer her to remain one. A dozen prospective biographers had already given up when I began my work. Erich Fromm, Frieda's former husband, who outlived her by twenty years, rebuffed every researcher seeking information about their relationship. Most of her correspondence and other records were spirited out of her house the day after her death and remained locked in an attic in Richmond, Virginia, off limits to researchers. Those still alive who knew her personally had extraordinarily complicated memories about who she was. For a person who died more than forty years ago, Frieda still manages to exert powerful control over the lives of a surprising number of people.

So I cannot be the "courier" of a story that exists in fragmentary form in the written record, as Elisabeth Young-Bruehl describes herself in the preface to her biography of Anna Freud. Frieda did not leave neat parcels of correspondence, coded by year, the way Freud's methodical daughter did. Nor did she leave diaries from her youth like Karen Horney, or the draft of an autobiography as Melanie Klein did. I couldn't sit down with her for long talks over glasses of scotch the way Deirdre Bair did with Simone de Beauvoir.[15]

To write this book, I had to construct the story of Frieda's life, not simply assemble it from what was already there. I have had to depend on people's memories far more than most other biographers do, both to fill gaps in the written record and decipher the meaning of what does remain. If I had adhered to rules like not using information presented orally by only one source, Frieda's life would remain the secret it has been for all these years.

However, despite my oft-repeated insistence that no biography of Frieda was possible given the paucity of standard sources, and even if it were, I wasn't writing one, I did end up doing precisely those things a biographer would have done. Although I had to make a number of subjective judgments about what information was trustworthy and what was not, I exhaustively sought out all possible sources and tried to balance them judiciously against one another in what I wrote:

- I located every surviving letter, draft, note, record or tape recording written or spoken by Frieda or sent to her, and read all material not currently under seal.
- I read every secondary source that discussed, referred to, or even briefly mentioned Frieda or her work, including those filled with inaccuracies, lies, or diatribes.
- I searched every archive in the United States and Germany that could logically be expected to include correspondence or other material, however tangential, related to her life or work.
- I went to every place where she regularly spent time or lived (except Königsberg, too heavily destroyed by wartime bombing to be of use), locating whenever possible the specific buildings or neighborhoods relevant to the story and traveling the specific routes she took.
- I interviewed or corresponded with every person who knew her well enough to add substantive detail to my account, making a point to seek out those who disagreed with her ideas as well as those who supported them.
- I invariably gave priority to official records where they contradicted people's recollections or less reliable secondary sources (e.g., I took the date of Frieda's marriage from the legal transcript of her divorce proceedings rather than from Erich Fromm's biographer, who cites no source).
- I carefully evaluated the position of each participant in the events I describe, tried to balance it against other perspectives, and constructed accounts of very complex events like Frieda's death from a dozen vantage points.
- I got to know all the people who provided extensive oral recollections well enough to evaluate their particular weaknesses and strengths (e.g., some people's clinical insights were more trustworthy than their memory for dates; others gave reliable accounts only of events in which they themselves had participated).
- I took very seriously the fragmentary set of autobiographical reminis-

cences that Frieda taped the year before her death, both because the nuances of her phrasing and intonation allowed for a subtle understanding of the significance she accorded particular events, and because every detail that could be independently corroborated checked out.

- Similarly, I took the extensive information about Frieda's family provided to me by her niece (and only surviving relative) to be reliable because her memories were detailed and proved accurate whenever they could be checked against written sources (such as genealogies, published accounts of family reunions, and photographs, many of which she offered to me as documentation).

- Since there were many instances in which the details of Frieda's clinical work were preserved in multiple forms—progress notes as well as tape recordings, verbatim transcripts of therapy sessions or case conferences— and these demonstrated that Frieda was able to recall accurately a patient's precise words, in cases where only her notes existed, I took them as a reliable record of the dialogue. (In the one crucial instance where Frieda systematically changed the details of what had happened—the case of Mrs. E.—I analyze these variations in considerable detail.)

- Frieda's key role in the creation of Chestnut Lodge as the only hospital ever to specialize in the psychotherapy of psychotic patients is amply documented in hundreds of written records, so for this part of the story, I used interviews only to interpret more fully the primary source materials.

- The patients I discuss in detail all had extensive written records documenting their treatment: Frieda's clinical notes, correspondence, verbatim transcripts of case conferences, and in two key instances, tape recordings or verbatim transcripts of the therapy hours themselves. I have, of course, concealed or disguised the identities of these patients according to standard clinical practices, but all quoted statements are taken directly from tapes or transcripts.

- The one patient who is identified, Joanne Greenberg, talked with me extensively, and gave me access to all notes, drafts, and correspondence relevant to the writing of *Rose Garden,* as well as to its subsequent reception by patients, psychiatrists, and general readers over three decades.

Despite the paucity of written records concerning Frieda's youth and life in Germany, I did have access to an extraordinarily rich archive of her clinical work, including dozens of tape recordings and verbatim transcripts of her therapy hours with schizophrenic patients. Just as with any other case notes or physician records, scrupulous ethical standards govern my use of these materials. But their benefit cannot be overstated; they offer a rare glimpse of an artful therapist hard at work. No biographer of a psychoanalyst has ever had the advantage of literally being able to listen in on what was happening in the consulting room. In writing about an analyst like Frieda, known primarily for her clinical gifts, listening to the sessions themselves is a powerful experience.

I also had the benefit of being given completely free rein to wander into any office, basement, attic, or storeroom at Chestnut Lodge over a five-year period and read whatever I found there. Because the Lodge's archives were being created during precisely these years, I was allowed the pleasure of reading each manuscript, listening to each tape, and studying each photograph within a few months of its discovery. This is every biographer's dream: being handed the keys to a room filled with treasures and told simply to turn out the lights at the end of the evening. (Since I was on the grounds of a still-vibrant mental hospital, I was also told that if I wanted lunch or dinner in the cafeteria as a break from working, I should simply sign myself in under "guests.") Researchers who must rely on archives constructed according to someone else's plan have to spend a lot more time searching for what they need than I did.

I was fortunate as well in having gained the trust of so many of Frieda's colleagues and students as to become a general repository of memory for the group. People would start to recount stories from the 1940s, a time before I was born, and I would be so familiar with the details from what others had told me that we would end up reminiscing together. Because no one who knew Frieda in her youth was still alive when I began this work, I had to piece the story together from dozens of sources—some contradictory, and all partial. But because those I did interview were mostly psychoanalysts themselves—people who spend every day of their lives making sense of stray bits, moments of coincidence, subtleties of voice and tone—I had constant help in reaching that elusive goal Donald Spence calls "narrative truth."[16]

Frieda belongs to many people, and not all of them will find their preferred version highlighted in what I wrote. Nor is this a close chronological record of her daily life, partly because no diaries or appointment books have survived, but mostly because Frieda spent the bulk of her life behind the closed doors of her consulting room, treating patients.

The lives of psychoanalysts have become a source of fascination in a culture where therapists have replaced priests, and stripping away the layers of silence in which they have shrouded themselves seems tantalizing. But Frieda Fromm-Reichmann isn't like other psychoanalysts, especially the women. She wrote about schizophrenia, not femininity or children. She lived in mental institutions, not elegant apartments, and she devoted herself to patients who smeared feces or muttered incoherently or tried to attack her. Her

formative intellectual experiences took place on a ward for brain-injured soldiers, not in Freud's living room. She acted as if men and children were dis-
tractions, with no real place in a life like hers, dedicated to serious work. She
was an Orthodox Jew at a time of assimilation. In a field famous for "excom-
municating heretics" and given to interminable "civil wars," she took pains
never to disparage even her sharpest critics. And she had no interest in the
theoretical disputes that obsessed most of her analytic colleagues; curing patients was her consuming goal.

So here we have the life of a woman who denied that she had accomplished much, who most people think is a fictional character, whose intellectual legacy is ambiguous, and whose work stands in contradiction to
everything contemporary psychiatry believes in. Yet the ideal that guided her
life and work remains intensely powerful even in our jaded lives: "To redeem
one person is to redeem the world."

Psychologist Mary Gergen says we must "play at the shores of understanding" to tell the story of a life, building coherence gradually from the detritus
we find, sticking memories together with bits of shell from photographs,
struggling to keep ahead of the tides.[17] "The absence of the dead is their way
of appearing," said one biographer, and perhaps by closing our eyes we can
see beyond the lines.

Acknowledgments

Upon rereading one of her early books of essays, Janet Malcolm said they made her "think of someone trying to cut down a tree who has never done it before, isn't strong, has a dull axe, but is very stubborn." As I look back on my ten years of work on this project, her statement precisely describes my feelings. I started this book when I had neither the skill nor the background to finish it. At each step, I found talented, generous people who taught me what I needed to know, or steered me in a different direction, or patiently listened as I thrashed about. The book itself has had three completely different incarnations, so there are a great many people to thank for their help.

Abby Stewart first encouraged me to write about Frieda, and when I insisted that there were no source materials documenting her life or work, Abby told me to look harder.

My brilliant, imaginative colleagues at the Bunting Institute of Radcliffe College believed that I could learn to write in a way that did justice to the courage and complexity of the people I was studying. Verlyn Klinkenborg whacked away at the flaccid prose I had acquired from twenty years of social science writing until it shaped up. The members of the Women Writing Women's Lives seminar in New York inspired me to envisage biography as part of feminist work.

Flip Brophy of Sterling Lord Literistic and Susan Arellano, then of The Free Press, took a chance on me when none of us could say what kind of book this would turn out to be, and they stuck with me through years of uncertainty until I figured it out.

Mabel Peterson, who at the time I met her had just retired after forty years on the Chestnut Lodge staff, single-handedly created the archive on which most of the research is based. Without her painstaking efforts, this book would never have come to exist. I treasure the months we spent in those cramped basement storerooms, scrambling through attics, and piecing together lost stories. Her photographic memory, absolute integrity, and fascination with psychiatric history inspired me at every turn. I am deeply saddened that Mabel did not live to see this book in print.

No written acknowledgment can express my gratitude to Frieda's niece and only surviving close relative, Alisa Jacobson Fuchs, for helping to restore so much of Frieda's lost life in Germany, or to Joanne Greenberg, for so vividly recreating the feel of Frieda's clinical work. I am humbled by their trust and their generosity in sharing even very painful memories, and I hope that in some small measure, this book can repay the debt I owe to them. I also thank Joanne for allowing me to read and quote from the extraordinarily moving letters sent to her by readers of *Rose Garden*.

Sylvia Hoff Collins, Ann Silver, and Ursula Engel, whose earlier biographical efforts proved invaluable to my work, shared their ideas and materials, providing crucial—in some cases irreplaceable—sources and insights. I have deeply appreciated their generosity and encouragement, and although I don't agree with certain of their key ideas, my thinking has been powerfully shaped by the trail they blazed. I also gained a great deal from reading the dissertation on Frieda by Barbara Petratos.

Rusty Bullard gave me access to his father Dexter's papers and permission to use the Chestnut Lodge archives, with no questions asked, no drafts reviewed, and with a degree of trust and encouragement rarely seen in a private institution. His mother, Anne, in her nineties when I began my work, was unfailingly gracious, helpful, and supportive, and I am saddened that neither has lived to read this book. I thank Tony Bullard for granting permission to use the photographs of Frieda currently stored at the Lodge and for sharing his perspective on the issues I discuss. I am also extremely grateful to many, many members of the Lodge staff, too numerous to name, for their warmth and generosity during my many research trips. From clerks in the record room to library staff to groundsworkers, I never met a person there who didn't offer to help. I especially appreciated the many forms of assistance Elyce Brown provided after Mabel Peterson's death. Although I cannot personally thank the patients whose stories are told here, I am awed by their courage and fortitude in struggling with the agonies of mental illness.

The long list of people who graciously allowed me to interview them is included in the Notes, so I will not enumerate them here. I am deeply grateful for their trust and willingness to participate in lengthy and emotionally complex conversations, and for the many kindnesses they extended during my visits. One of the most moving parts of this research was meeting so many therapists who devoted their lives to treating schizophrenic patients. I shall never forget the power of their presence. The desire to pass on their stories before they were forever lost was one of the sustaining impulses of this work.

A number of people provided me with important sources, correspondence, documents, or access to the holders of such materials. I particularly thank Marvin Adland, Joanne Hatch Bruch, Don Burnham, Bob Cohen, Hannah Decker, Alisa Jacobson Fuchs, John Fort, Larry Friedman, Rainer Funk, Martin Niemöller, Sabine Richter, and Jane Weinberg.

My senior colleagues in the history of psychiatry and medicine—Barbara Rosenkrantz, John Burnham, and Gerry Grob—provided consultation, thoughtful critique, and invaluable suggestions over many years. Even though this has turned out to be a very different kind of book from the one they envisioned, I have welcomed their advice and learned a great deal from it. I am also extremely grateful to them for helping me to secure the many grants and fellowships that enabled the research. Gene Black, Danny Czitrom, Margaret Hunt, and Fran Malino also provided crucial advice regarding the interpretation of historical materials. Don Burnham used his blend of historical interest and Lodge experience to offer unique insights into the world of Washington psychiatry, and Lyndy Pye sensitively interpreted some of the complex clinical material.

Conversations with Karen Remmler and Holger Teschke allowed me to come to grips with my complicated feelings about Frieda's German origins, and I deeply appreciate their patience and gentle encouragement to visit Heidelberg and Berlin and become fascinated with a world that had long intimidated and frightened me. I am pleased to thank Bettina Brand-Claussen in Heidelberg for spending hours showing me the treasures of the Prinzhorn Collection and Harald Hahn for taking me through Frieda's house.

Karin Obermeier, Suzanne Owen, and Ilse Andrews translated many essential German sources, often under tight deadlines. I am grateful for their ingenuity in deciphering Frieda's impossible handwriting, and for the spirit of excitement they conveyed about the materials as they worked on them.

I could never have traveled to archives across the United States and Germany and sustained years of writing without the generous financial support of many organizations and institutions. With the deepest appreciation, I thank the National Library of Medicine for NIH Grant LM 05067; the National Endowment for the Humanities for a summer stipend and a year-long fellowship; the American Council of Learned Societies for a grant-in-aid of research; the American Philosophical Society for a research grant; and the Bunting Institute of Radcliffe College, the Marion and Jasper Whiting Foundation, and Mount Holyoke College for generous fellowships. I am very grateful to the Office of the Dean of Faculty and the Psychology and Education Department at Mount Holyoke for additional support, and to Janet Crosby and Gayle Higgins, in the department office, for dozens of forms of assistance with the research.

Halfway through this project, I developed a partial disability of my arms that prevented my typing or even writing in long-hand, and there is no way to convey my gratitude to the many physicians, physical therapists, and massage practitioners who made it possible for me to continue to work. For their extraordinary generosity, encouragement, and care, I thank Marilyn Pike, Dennis Pronowicz, Paula Murphy, Olga Broumas, Lenore Grubinger, and Michelina Craft. And without Marie Maes, Joan Dwight, Debbie Palmer, Joan Haddock, and Leela Sundquist, who transcribed interviews and typed hundreds of pages from my dictation and scribbled notes, this book simply could not have been written.

With great pleasure, I thank the staffs of the many archives and libraries where I was privileged to work: in Washington, the American Psychiatric Association, the Library of Congress, the National Archives, and the Washington Psychoanalytic Society and Institute; in New York, the Rare Books and Manuscripts Department and Oral History Research Office at Butler Library, Columbia University, the New York Psychoanalytic Society and Institute, the Manuscripts Division of the New York Public Library, and the William Alanson White Institute; in Rockville, Maryland, the Montgomery County Historical Society, Peerless Rockville, and the Rockville Public Library; in Boston, the Schlesinger Library at Radcliffe College, the Department of Special Collections, Mugar Library, Boston University, and the Countway Library of Medicine, Harvard University; in Houston, the Texas Medical Center Library; in Chicago, the Department of Special Collections, Regenstein Library, University of Chicago; in Baltimore, the Alan Mason Chesney Medical Archives at Johns Hopkins University; and in England, the Cambridge University Library. I also acknowledge with gratitude the special assistance of the interlibrary loan staff at Mount Holyoke College and Linda Callahan in the slide library, Marianne Duchardt at the Monroe County Public Library in Key West, Charles Niles at Boston University, and William Baxter at the American Psychiatric Association.

I have been extremely fortunate to have an enthusiastic, tireless, creative, and enterprising group of Mount Holyoke students as research assistants, and it is a pleasure to thank Jean Talbot, Leela Sundquist, Catherine Orland, Kristen Langworthy, and Winifred Connerton for the dozens of contributions, large and small, that they made to the project.

Many parts of this book were emotionally painful to write, and it helped a great deal to be in places filled with beauty as I worked. I thank the Rockefeller Foundation and the staff of the Villa Serbelloni in Bellagio, Italy, Tonie Strauss in Truro, Massachusetts, Judy Jack in Key West, and the Governing Body of Clare Hall, Cambridge University, for enabling my extended stays in these locations.

Lee Edwards, Barbara Rosenkrantz, and Elisabeth Young-Bruehl generously read previous drafts of the entire manuscript, and I am deeply indebted to them for their advice and recommendations, not all of which I heeded, but which were of unquestionable help in improving the quality of the final version. Philip Rappaport at The Free Press also made incisive suggestions at key moments, and his efficient colleagues have guided the publication process with good humor. I especially appreciated the attentive care Celia Knight and Will Morrison gave to the final preparations, and Joan Davis's thoughtful approach to constructing the index.

By precisely embodying Winnicott's definition of the good-enough analyst—"reliably there, on time, alive, breathing, preoccupied with the patient, and free from temper tantrums"—Ellen Keniston taught me things I could never have learned from any book.

Finally, for crucial conversations over many years and encouragement when I needed it most, I thank Lyndy Pye, Leigh Star, Ginny Valian, Andi Weisman, Alberto Sandoval, Cathy Riessman, Lee Edwards, Karen Remmler, Patty Pisanelli, Fran Malino, Gene Black, Bob Shilkret, Meryl Fingrutd, Sally Sutherland, Barbara Ehrenreich, Carole DeSanti, and my sister and brother, Lyn and David.

1

The Daughter

"When you come to a place where you have to go left or right,"
says Sister Ruth, "go straight ahead."[1]

Frieda was born on October 23, 1889, the same year as Hitler, a coincidence of fate that would have deep irony for her decades later. Kaiser Wilhelm I had just died at the age of ninety, having ruled Prussia and the newly unified German empire for her parents' entire lifetimes. His thirty-year-old grandson, Wilhelm II, was about to make his mark by driving the aging Bismarck from power. In the words of one observer, "Germany stood at perhaps her highest relative moment of political importance in the eyes of a respectful world."[2]

Pasteur was in his sixties, Lenin was nineteen, Einstein nine. Darwin and Marx had recently died. Queen Victoria had just celebrated a half-century on the British throne, and North and South Dakota were being welcomed into the union. Brahms was finishing his third symphony. Jane Addams was starting Hull-House. In no country in the world could women cast a vote.

Frieda spent her first eight years in Karlsruhe ("Karl's Retreat"), a small city just north of the Black Forest, near the border with France. Originally the hunting lodge of Karl Wilhelm, margrave of Baden-Durlach, the town had expanded after Karl built a castle for himself and turned his former hunting grounds into parks and gardens. As Germany's newest city (founded 1715), Karlsruhe was one of few to be explicitly planned. Its elegant layout in the shape of a fan—a design of "sublime simplicity and peculiarity"—had fourteen broad avenues radiating from the castle. By the nineteenth century,

Karlsruhe was flourishing, famous for its liberal atmosphere and "exquisite reputation in the fine arts."[3] Home to Germany's oldest technical institute (where Hertz discovered radio waves) and capital of Baden, it housed the state supreme courts and was known all over the region for its opera, theater, and first-rate museums.

Jews had flocked to Karlsruhe soon after its founding, attracted by the margrave's promise of equal privileges to anyone willing to settle there. By 1725, a synagogue, hospital, ritual bath, and burial ground had been built in one corner of the city; in 1783, declared no longer to be serfs, Jews began settling throughout the area. The edict of 1809 made Baden the first constitutionally accepted Jewish community in Germany, allowing far greater freedom and self-determination. The factional conflicts that plagued German Judaism throughout the nineteenth century were, however, clearly evident in Karlsruhe, and after a Reform temple with an organ and choir was built, the Orthodox members seceded in 1869 and founded the congregation where Frieda was named. At the time of her birth, Jews accounted for about 3 percent of the city's 80,000 inhabitants.[4]

No record survives of her parents' meeting, and descriptions of their marriage are tantalizingly incomplete. They were, however, both from deeply middle-class backgrounds. Adolf's family could trace its origins to 1555, the year Jews had been expelled from the town of Feuchtwangen in central Germany. Some had fled to Fürth, near Nuremberg, the closest Jewish community, and Adolf's grandfather, Seligmann Feuchtwanger, was born there in 1786. A successful silver merchant, Seligmann had little interest in business, and worked only as many hours each week as were absolutely necessary to keep his wife and children fed. Then he locked the doors of his shop and returned with joy and relief to studying the Talmud. According to family legend, on a particularly good week he was able to close on a Tuesday afternoon; a young couple who arrived to buy a wedding ring just as he was laying out his manuscripts were told: "Come back next Monday." Since Seligmann and his wife, Fanny Wassermann, had eighteen children, the family's lifestyle was necessarily modest. Fanny wore the black silk dress that had been part of her dowry to every festive occasion for decades, and some of the children slept in drawers pulled out each evening from a huge chest in the bedroom.[5]

Sophie Feuchtwanger, the ninth of these eighteen children, was Frieda's grandmother. Little is known of Moritz Reichmann, her grandfather, who died in 1869 at the age of forty-seven, leaving Sophie alone in Fürth with five young children. Frieda's father, Adolf, was ten at the time, and as the oldest boy, he was expected to leave school and go to work to help his mother. A sensitive child with a deep love of literature and music, Adolf was trauma-tized by the early death of his father. He often went without food to buy books, and he wished for the rest of his life that he could have devoted his life to study, the way his grandfather Seligmann did.

Frieda's mother, Klara Simon, was born in Lechenich near Düsseldorf in 1867. She had a far more fortunate and pampered background than Adolf. The ninth of ten children in a well-known Jewish family that could trace its history back to the Inquisition, Klara had a sense of entitlement that was well justified. Her father's ancestors, the Simons, had lived in France for several generations after the expulsion and were among the country's chief rabbis. After settling in Germany toward the end of the sixteenth century, they had distinguished themselves in business. Klara's mother, Amalie, had grown up in a similar family in Köln amid every advantage, and as a young woman had played piano duets with Clara Schumann. Amalie's arranged marriage to Ja-cob Simon, a well-to-do merchant, was considered an excellent match; her dowry included a dozen silver napkin rings, among other treasures.

Amalie and Jacob raised ten children, as well as a boy from Poland or-phaned in a pogrom. Amalie herself had been adopted in childhood by her mother's sister, and identified strongly with needy children. She also appar-ently never lost her gratitude for having been so well cared for, and was so devoted to her parents (who were really her aunt and uncle) that she insisted on living next door to them throughout all the years of her marriage. Re-membered for her elegant silk dresses and proper style, she raised Klara, her youngest daughter, to see comfort and order as existing side by side. Life in the large Simon household was pleasurable but never ostentatious. "If the bread was already spread with butter," one family member recalled, "you could not add jam, that would have been to indulge."

Klara was extremely close to her mother and remained so for her whole life, just as Amalie had been with her own parents. Klara's devotion, how-ever, bordered on the compulsive; after her mother's death, she never again wore anything but black, including even her underwear, necklaces, hats, and pocketbooks.[6]

Klara must have fallen in love with Adolf Reichmann; from an economic standpoint, he was a poor marriage prospect. Perhaps she was drawn to his gentle refinement. Or perhaps she recognized that he was sufficiently in awe of her to defer to all her wishes.

They were married on December 26, 1888, when Adolf was twenty-nine and Klara twenty-one. Frieda, beginning a life marked by obedience and careful planning, appeared precisely ten months later. Both parents were de-lighted with their healthy, blue-eyed, fair-skinned daughter, and her arrival was a major event in the huge extended family of Reichmanns and Simons, who numbered in the hundreds and were to be such important influences on Frieda's upbringing.[7]

Unlike various of his relatives who were bankers or prosperous merchants, Adolf ran a metalworks shop, selling "tools, iron and metal products, stoves and ovens, and kitchen and household products of all types." He had a partner, Naphtali Thalmann, and their business, called simply Reichmann & Thalmann, was on one corner of the shady Ludwigsplatz, four blocks from Karlsruhe's castle. The Reichmanns lived above the shop at Waldstrasse 40, a solid classicist building that the architect Christoph Arnold had built for himself in 1811. The location was ideal for both business and pleasure, on a quiet street near enough to the shopping district to be convenient for customers, yet only a few blocks from the art museum, the concert hall, the theater, and the botanical gardens. Frieda spent her early years frolicking amid the swans and peacocks that gathered at the shore of the ornamental lake beside the castle, or being taken for "the fresh air walks considered essential to health by generations of Germans" in the castle's spacious grounds, just down the street from her apartment.[8]

By all accounts, Adolf was a terrible businessman and dealt with his resentment at having to work at jobs he hated by failing at them. Although Karlsruhe was fast becoming a major industrial center and tools and machinery were among its principal products, Klara had to fill in as a cashier in the shop—a real indignity, given her upbringing—so the family could afford a housemaid in white cap and apron, "the indispensable pillar of middle-class respectability." Adolf's limited income also reflected the sacrifices necessitated by Orthodox practice. Having to close his business on approximately seventy Saturdays and Jewish holidays each year put him at considerable disadvantage vis-à-vis Christian competitors. As historian Mordechai Breuer notes: "In a world increasingly focusing on material gain and technology, on personal profit and pleasure, Jews who were Orthodox needed considerable courage and determination to turn their backs on so many amenities."[9]

Apart from Adolf's limitations as a provider, the marriage was apparently a happy one. He adored his smart and self-possessed wife, and happily let her make the family's key decisions. "He was terribly in love with her and terribly impressed by her," Frieda later observed, and Klara's "unflagging energy, sharp wit, and remarkable willpower" established her as the indisputable head of the household. Adolf was the soft-hearted one. Once, when a barefoot beggar came to the door, Adolf gave him the shoes he had been wearing and made do with his other pair. Years later, on a business trip, Adolf stopped by a lake to eat a sandwich. A man approached him, asking if he would like a ride on a boat. Adolf said no; he had to watch expenses. Urging him toward his best boat, the man cried out: "Do you think I would take a pfennig from the person who gave me his shoes still warm from his own feet? With those shoes, my whole life changed!"[10]

Frieda was a deeply wanted first child, remembered as "adorable, warm-hearted, friendly, clever, and always good—everything a mother could wish for!" Practically from birth, she demonstrated an extraordinary sensitivity to nuances of behavior, seeming always to know what was happening in the family without anyone telling her. One night, at the age of two, asked who should give her a bath and put her to bed—her mother or the young maid—she chose the maid. When Klara came in later to kiss her goodnight, Frieda whispered: "Mommy, naturally I wanted you to do it. But we must not hurt Ella's feelings!" From early in life, as Frieda's relatives were invariably to say, "she was understanding and responsible and saw to it that everyone was happy."[11]

Her primacy remained unchallenged by her younger sisters. Frieda was two and a half when the Reichmanns' second daughter, Grete, appeared. According to a story repeated for decades, Grete was so ugly that Klara told the wet nurse she ought to give her declarations of sympathy; the nurse suggested that Grete be baptized so she could later enter a convent. Shy, awkward, and lacking in confidence, Grete proved a poor second to her beautiful, talented older sister. "I was everything mother wanted," Frieda acknowledged matter-of-factly years later. Sturdy, resilient, and energetic like Klara, Frieda was clearly the favorite.[12]

Grete seemed resigned to her fate ("she knew how things were, and that was that") and retired to Frieda's shadow with good grace. She had a single, famous moment of rebellion, when seemingly without provocation, she slapped Frieda hard, right across the face. When Klara and Adolf demanded to know why she had done such a thing, Grete said she was fed up with Frieda's always being so perfect. (This event, much talked about over the years, was supposed to have been the only time in the history of the Reichmann family that one person ever hit another.)[13]

In 1895, when Frieda was six and Grete three, the Reichmanns moved to Königsberg, the farthest point in the sprawling German empire, more than 600 miles away. Klara's older sister, Trutta, had married a wealthy bank director there, and in the hope of enticing Klara to keep her company in lonely East Prussia and improve the Reichmanns' fortunes, Trutta had persuaded her husband to offer Adolf a position.

Königsberg was strikingly different from other parts of Germany. Perched on the shores of the Baltic Sea just south of Lithuania, its culture was far more similar to surrounding areas of Russia and Poland than it was to the German mainland. Founded in 1255 as a fortress of the Knights of the Teutonic Order, Königsberg was a major seaport, two and a half times the size of Karlsruhe, and for centuries Prussia's most important city.

Jews had been excluded from the region until the seventeenth century, and the first synagogue wasn't built until 1756, when about 300 Jews lived in the area. But a steady stream of Russian immigrants swelled the community to more than 5,000 by 1880, and its liberal intellectual traditions made Königsberg one of the centers of Jewish Enlightenment. There were Jewish students at the university as early as 1712, and later many became pupils of Kant. The city had a vibrant Orthodox community, and since George Marx, Klara's brother-in-law, was one of its most influential members, Adolf quickly rose to prominence within its ranks, becoming especially active in Marx's efforts to aid Jews fleeing the bloody pogroms in nearby Russia.[14]

In 1898, when Frieda was eight and a half and Grete was six, the youngest of the Reichmann daughters, Anna, was born in Königsberg.[15] Frieda, ever alert to events in the family, had figured out that Klara was pregnant but sensed this was one of those things children weren't supposed to know about. At the moment of Anna's birth, the girls heard a cry, and Grete exclaimed: "I think we have a new baby!" Considering it "the privilege of the parents to inform children of such a major event," Frieda responded: "Oh, no. You probably just heard some neighbor's child."[16]

Klara had a deep commitment to the principle of primogeniture, and throughout their childhoods, Grete and Anna were never allowed to contradict anything Frieda said. "Don't argue with her, she is the oldest," Klara would warn at the first sign of any dispute. She made similar outfits for the three girls, but Frieda's dresses always had an extra ruffle or an additional piece of embroidery or lace to mark her specialness. Frieda later claimed that she tried to prevent these inequalities—"God! How I tried to hinder my mother to make me a favorite"—but she clearly benefited from her advantaged status. Besides the extra privileges she was accorded, she also developed that confident sense of entitlement oldest children often gain from successfully outpacing their rivals. But her acute sensitivity made her painfully aware of the price Grete and Anna had to pay—"those two sisters of mine suffered terribly because I worked out to the dot exactly the way mother had dreamt it should be"—and in later life, Frieda clearly felt guilty for her special treatment. At the same time, she accepted without complaint the increasingly heavy responsibilities she was given. As one biographer put it: "Being always somewhat set apart as an authority figure became a way of life for Frieda from early on."[17]

She was, however, deeply protective of her sisters, especially Anna, who enjoyed her role as "papa's little pet" but needed a stronger defender than Adolf. In a story told over and over with many embellishments, Frieda and Anna were out on a walk one day somewhere in the country, when two large, angry goats suddenly started running straight toward them. Frieda grabbed each one by the horns and held them safely back from Anna until the farmer got there. (In another version, the animals are dogs, and Frieda throws herself between them and Anna, declaring: "You don't need to be afraid!")[18]

In photographs of the Reichmann girls as children, Frieda gazes directly at the camera, with sometimes the barest hint of a smile. She has clearly embraced her part as the adored child, eager to reflect her parents' pleasure back through her own eyes. Grete, by contrast, looks startled or dismayed, as if she realizes there is no way to win with Frieda there. In the one surviving picture of the three girls together—Frieda looks about fourteen, Grete perhaps twelve, Anna about six—Frieda is at the center, in front of the others. She and Grete are dressed identically; Anna's outfit is unclear. Frieda's face has the look of total determination she was to show in every photograph for the next fifty years. Grete looks retiring, seemingly satisfied to be behind. Anna's eyes are wide, as if she cannot quite grasp her place in that world.

Frieda's confidence and ambition were intensified by the many disappointments her parents had faced. Adolf, a man drawn to people and to learning, was forced by economic hardship into a career in business for which he was ill suited. Klara shared his love for music and the classics, and had trained as a teacher but was too conventional to work after marriage. With both her parents openly mourning their lost opportunities, their intense need for Frieda to succeed where they had not, coupled with her own devotion to their happiness, strengthened her desire to become whomever they most wanted.

The move to Königsberg at first did little to improve the family's fortunes. Adolf was installed in a position of financial responsibility at the bank owned by his wealthy brother-in-law, and failed miserably at his duties. Eventually, however, he was shifted to the job of personnel director, and for the first time in his life, found himself doing work that fit his natural talents. Attentive and warm to employees at every level, Adolf was respected and admired by the whole staff, and continued in this position for the rest of his life, to the satisfaction of everyone.[19]

The Reichmanns initially lived on the same street as the Marxes, and the two families saw each other constantly. As the bank became more influential, the Reichmanns moved to a comfortable seven-room apartment in a better neighborhood on the Glückstrasse, and the large Marx family took up residence in an elegant villa, complete with gardens, on the banks of the Pregel River. The children loved their ferry trips across the river, walks through the twisting, narrow streets of the old city to the castle, and games in the Königsgarten or the meadows along the Pregel. The Reichmann girls each had a "twin sister" about her age among the Marxes, as well as various "big brothers," famous for their teasing. Both sets of parents were close to all the children, providing to some extent a counterweight to the excesses of a nuclear family upbringing. Adolf is remembered especially for his "good hands," with countless children running to him at family gatherings clutching broken toys and pleading, "Uncle Adolf, fix this!"[20]

Thanks to George Marx's influence, the Reichmann family was catapulted to a position of respect in the Jewish community far beyond anything they could have achieved in Karlsruhe. As owner and manager of one of the largest banks in Königsberg, Marx was a *Kommerzienrat,* a business magnate, who played a decisive role in the development of the city's trade and industry. He was also one of the founders of the Adass Jisroel Orthodox synagogue and for years was a member of its governing body (to which he appointed Adolf as well as various other relatives). In addition to administering most affairs of the Jewish community—a huge job, involving supervision of synagogue officials, teachers in the religious school, kosher butchers, and cemetery inspectors, as well as the arbitration of whatever problems arose among members—Marx led a Talmud study group and arranged the financing of everything from the Jewish hospital to the summer synagogue in Cranz, a nearby Baltic sea resort where he and many of his fellow worshippers vacationed.[21]

It was in Königsberg that Emma Branies, then in her early twenties, joined the Reichmann household as maid, a position she was to hold for the next four decades. Anna, the baby, always thought of Emma as "hers," but the whole family adored her and treated her almost as one of them. In addition to caring for the children and the apartment, Emma also prepared the meals, a relief to everyone. (One of Klara's unconscious expressions of resentment at housewifery was to burn whatever she cooked.)

"Dear darling Emma," as she was always called, was hired just before Klara's last pregnancy. When Emma discovered a baby was on the way, she announced she was leaving; diapers and midnight feedings hadn't been advertised as part of the position. She was somehow persuaded to stay, and later always said that had she known the baby would be Anna, she wouldn't even have considered quitting. She treated Anna like her own child, confiding all her secrets to her, and molding her life to fit Anna's needs. It was Emma who made sure Anna did her homework and said her prayers before bed. It was

Emma who walked her to synagogue carrying her belongings on Shabbat. One day, Anna came home from school to find Emma sobbing in the kitchen. Pleading to know what was wrong, Anna finally got Emma to admit that she had just turned down an offer of marriage from a local tradesman. Asked why, she had cried out: "How could I leave you and the family?" Emma was careful to reproduce the Reichmanns' symbolic hierarchies. When she made toast in the mornings, she gave the first piece to Klara or Frieda, the best piece to Anna, "and if a slice got burned, she gave it a scrape and a wipe and that was for Adolf or Grete."[22]

Even with Emma's help, running an Orthodox household was a huge job, especially for a pampered youngest daughter like Klara. In addition to making all their own clothing and linens, women in turn-of-the-century Germany had to shop, cook, bake, preserve, and can. Coal stoves created constant grime and needed endless tending. Once made, clothing had to be mended and socks knitted. Keeping a kosher kitchen was practically a full-time job in itself. Cooking, baking, and cleaning for Shabbat could take a full day, and housecleaning for Pesach might begin in January. There were as well the myriad tasks of child rearing, after-school lessons, cultural education, and "emotional housework" always assigned to women.

In addition, the crucial job of maintaining family and social networks required elaborate handwritten letters and formal visits. Keeping household account books was also women's responsibility, with every cent of savings going directly to funds for children's lessons or daughters' dowries. When Klara helped Adolf in the shop in the early years of their marriage, this was on top of all her other duties.[23]

The family's daily life embodied the peculiar intensities of the middle class in late nineteenth-century Central Europe. What Freud was later to call the "oedipal drama"—the constant scrutiny of emotion, the rivalries, the enmeshed relationships between parents and children—formed the basic fabric of Frieda's upbringing (and that of every other psychoanalyst of her generation). Except during the hours when the children were in school and Adolf was at the bank, the family was together, typically in the same room. Evenings were spent with Adolf reading aloud from his large collection of German classics as Klara embroidered, or with the parents sitting contentedly as the girls sang and played the various musical instruments they were required to learn. ("Our children will be musical," Klara had told Adolf before any of them were born. "How do you know?" he asked. "They will be, I promise you that," Klara had replied firmly.) Frieda studied piano, Grete, the violin; Anna danced and sang and played a number of instruments. Frieda was sometimes out of tune, but her sisters "were never allowed to say a word about it—she was the oldest and that was that." Anna, by contrast, seemed to have real talent. "At the age of three," according to a story her daughter Alisa was to hear many times, "Anna climbed up on the piano stool and played with two hands a tune a man was playing outside on a hand organ."[24]

The girls, especially Frieda, were well aware of their role as the primary source of meaning in their parents' existence. "My daughters are my jewels," Adolf often said, reflecting both his love and his limited financial position. He and Klara adored their children and tried to be loving and sensitive parents, but their extraordinarily high expectations created intense pressures. The girls constantly strove to be as well mannered and as successful as they could possibly manage, with written resolutions made each year at Rosh Hashanah and the rest of the time spent struggling to improve. The constant push to excel put particular strain on Anna, never an especially good student. Even the most minor misbehavior earned Klara's look of disapproval, a punishment far worse in this intense household than any beating would have been.

Klara herself bore every difficulty with stoic silence and taught her daughters never to complain. Whatever her dissatisfactions with Adolf or the marriage, she was determined to set an example of strength for her daughters to emulate. Once there was an epidemic of head lice at school. Upset by the disgrace, the other mothers talked of nothing else for weeks. Klara kept quiet, except to say her girls were fine. Only years later did they learn the truth: as she combed their long hair on the balcony each morning, Klara had simply removed the lice one by one, without saying a word.[25]

The considerable dowry Klara had brought into the marriage added financial weight to the psychological power she already wielded. The fact that it was her family who had provided Adolf with a viable job, thus literally putting the food on the Reichmanns' table, further strengthened Klara's influence. In the outer world, women were literally seen but not heard—an address by a woman to the Chamber of Commerce in Karlsruhe in 1882 had been unprecedented—but in the family, women could have real autonomy. So long as they avoided any public challenge to their husbands' power, women like Klara who came from families of means could shape the domestic agenda.

Yet at the same time, they had to teach their daughters the obedient role so highly valued by the culture. Frieda clearly learned this lesson well. In a photograph of her as an adolescent, we see her in a studio setting, elaborately posed, her hands clasped ladylike in front of her, one foot positioned slightly behind the other. Her hair is piled on top of her head in turn-of-the-century elegance, and she is wearing an expensive-looking but unattractive white dress, shaped like a tent, with four rows of ruffles at the bottom, one across the chest and another in the shape of a flower directly over her left breast. (She must have been about twelve in this photo; the placement of the ruffles would have been obscene on an older woman.) Her shoes, of carefully polished leather, are laced to her ankles. With her head tilted slightly, her expression solemn, she looks, more than anything else, as if she is trying to be good.

The philosophy that guided Frieda's upbringing—and that of every other member of the nineteenth-century German middle class—was *Bildung,* cultivation, an inward process of development designed to lead to an enlightened existence. As historian Marion Kaplan writes: "In merging education with character formation, moral growth and self-improvement, *Bildung* described a cultured well-bred personality, an autonomous, harmonious person of refined manners, aesthetic appreciation, politeness and gentility. *Bildung* appealed to Jews because it could transcend differences of religion or nationality through the development of the individual personality." Ruth Gay notes that *Bildung* became a crucial means for Jews to demonstrate their identification with German values. "No home was complete without a piano, and children were set to learn instruments just as they were taught to read." Indeed, she continues, "even for Gentiles, the Jews became carriers of German culture, to whom quoting from the classics was as natural as breathing." For women, Kaplan adds, *Bildung* also meant "the creation of a model home life, a model family," in which Goethe and Schiller were always welcome at the dinner table.[26]

For children to acquire the requisite values to live appropriately in a world so highly cultured, disciplined study and aesthetic enjoyment were essential from earliest childhood. In the Reichmann household, the girls rose at 6:30 A.M. each day to practice their instruments before leaving for school at 8:00. They returned home for the main meal at midday; after school there were music lessons, Hebrew classes, and tutoring sessions with Klara to learn foreign languages. (Although the family was far from wealthy, money for study of any kind was always forthcoming. "A good education is worth more than any dowry" was Adolf's philosophy.) Hours of homework were expected, as was strict adherence to the many rituals of Orthodox practice, including daily prayers at which the whole family gathered. But the girls also enjoyed much merrymaking with the many cousins their age, and spent every vacation and summer holiday at the Marxes' seaside villa in Cranz, playing on the wide, sandy beach and composing elaborate skits with the other children and then staging them in the evenings for the adults. Like most other Orthodox Jews, the Reichmanns had few social contacts with Christians or even with their more assimilated co-religionists, who formed the bulk of Germany's Jewish population. Perhaps because of this insularity, the Reichmann girls experienced little overt anti-Semitism. Only once, on New Year's eve, did they recall a frightening moment. They had waited, full of excitement, to open the windows at midnight to hear the bells throughout the city. Everyone else on the block was joining in the same ritual. Suddenly, amid the shouts of "Happy New Year," came a drunken voice yelling, "Death to the Jews." They knew it wasn't directed at them personally, but it was unnerving nonetheless.[27]

The narrow social world of the German Jewish middle class made family ties even more important than they would already have been. In the evocative phrase of poet Heinrich Heine, the family was "the portable homeland" of the Jew. With no history of permanent membership in any regional or national group, Jews learned from an early age that the only people they could totally depend on were their relatives. This was especially true in Frieda's family, since Adolf was more emotionally involved in the daily lives of his children than men who had to travel extensively or work long hours in their businesses. His psychological sensitivity, coupled with his secure position in a family-owned bank, allowed Adolf to spend much more time at home than was typical even of Jewish men.[28]

The intensity of families like the Reichmanns was partly a reflection of broader social forces shaping German culture during this period. Compared to other European countries like France or England, industrialization had come very late to Germany, and as a consequence, had an unusually rapid and compressed character. Between the unification of the country in 1871 and World War I, the daily lives of most Germans—especially those living in cities, like the Reichmanns—were completely transformed. Adolf's shop in Karlsruhe was barely one generation removed from the work of the itinerant Jewish peddler, traveling from town to town, carrying his goods on his back. During a period of so much change, the family was imbued with even greater significance as a haven for men from the alienated world of business and as a crucial place of preparation for children about to enter a society utterly different from the one their parents had grown up in. Although these transformations were disturbing to formerly dominant groups like the Junkers of the Prussian aristocracy, they brought hope to the Jews, who saw the opportunity for greater integration into the broader society.[29]

Still, the dictates of Orthodox culture made for a circumscribed social world, especially for girls. In decided contrast to the artist Käthe Kollwitz, for example, who was born in a nearby Königsberg neighborhood two decades earlier, Frieda would never have been allowed to wander alone along the waterfront, watching the Russian and Lithuanian workers, their feet wrapped in rags, unloading the giant grain ships in the harbor. During the hours Kollwitz sat near taverns filled with drunken sailors, patiently sketching while knife fights went on inside, Frieda was ensconced behind the grilled partition of the women's section of Adass Jisroel synagogue, quietly learning her prayers under Klara's watchful gaze.

Years later, Frieda would laughingly remark that she had been a psychiatrist since the age of three. She didn't know this consciously until she entered analysis, but listening to people's secrets was something she had done since earliest childhood. Klara and Adolf had both begun confiding in their sensitive eldest daughter almost as soon as she could speak, and Frieda could absorb conflicts swirling around her without even realizing what she was doing. She recalled an emblematic moment, from about age four:

> My mother had surprised my father by having a friend of hers do a portrait of me. I looked quite cute. This was supposed to be a great treat for my father. But when he came home from work with a migraine, and went to lie down, he didn't notice the picture. [Mama] was miserable. Later on, he saw that he had disappointed her, and he was miserable, since he thought Klara came right behind the Lord. I explained them to each other. I explained to her that he was sick, what could he do? I explained to him that she would understand, and couldn't he look at it now? . . . That was how my psychiatric career began.[30]

When Frieda was nine, Klara became seriously deaf, an inherited condition that had worsened during her pregnancy with Anna. She was terribly worried about being able to bring up her daughters as attentively as she planned, and was horrified at the doctor's order that she have no more children. (She said she wanted six more, including at least one boy.) Overhearing her parents' anxious conversations from the next room, Frieda found it agonizing to see them suffering. Yet she also sensed their embarrassment and need for secrecy. For the next five years, as Klara struggled (through skillful lipreading) to maintain appearances, Frieda pretended not to notice which days her mother went to the otologist or where she hid the medicines that did her no good. The charade finally ended one day when Frieda was fourteen, as Klara, standing behind her daughter braiding her waist-long hair, had to admit she couldn't hear a word Frieda was saying. By then Frieda had totally mastered the art of knowing things without anyone's sensing what she was doing.

Dutiful to his wife and his religion, Adolf had occasional moments of rebellion, which Frieda also knew about but didn't reveal. Like every other Orthodox man, Adolf wore an *arba kanfos,* a small fringed prayer shawl, beneath his clothing. For some reason, he found this requirement "a little boring" and often ignored it. "He and the Lord had a very good relationship," Frieda recalled, and to Adolf, these lapses weren't important. Klara, however, enacting the traditional role of the Jewish wife as enforcer of piety, constantly worried about what would happen if Adolf were to be found improperly attired in the event of an accident. In general, Adolf had such strong principles that Klara nicknamed him "Zip," short for *Prinzip* ("principle"). Years later, when Frieda was in analysis, she decided that "Zip" had really been Klara's (unconscious) abbreviation of *Zipfel,* slang for "little penis."[31]

It was then that Frieda realized she had always seen Adolf through her mother's eyes. "I treated him as though he were a little dumbbell, which he wasn't," she said with embarrassment decades later. In public, Klara was deferential, like any good middle-class German Jewish wife; privately, however, her affection was tinged with contempt at Adolf's financial failures. Although Frieda was critical of her mother's standards, she was still insisting to friends in her sixties that Klara had "made it the most harmonious marriage you have ever seen. She did everything right, and it was the luckiest family you could think of."

This is an extraordinary statement for a psychoanalyst to make about her upbringing, but Frieda seemed oblivious to the ways she idealized her mother. She treated Klara's perfection like some kind of law of nature, simply part of the landscape of family existence. To have questioned her mother would have been tantamount to challenging her power, a possibility too foolish even to contemplate. "If my mama went with her forehead toward a wall," Frieda declared with wonder at the age of sixty-six, "the wall would give in." Even if Adolf had been brilliant, he couldn't have competed with this.[32]

Contemporary family therapists sometimes ask people to array their siblings and parents on a blank page, positioning them so as to indicate their relative psychological distances. Those who feel close are put near the center; those more distant displaced to the edges. Patterns suddenly fall into place, as people become stars in constellations, no longer individuals but parts of larger configurations. As unspoken alliances are revealed and estrangements made apparent, a child's siding with one parent against the other, or favoritism among siblings, emerges in stark relief on the page.

A diagram like this drawn in Frieda's hand would show Klara without question at the center. Adolf would be at one side, with Frieda occupying a jagged orbit in between them. Grete and Anna would be off somewhere in outer space. Every time Frieda rotated closer to Klara, she would occupy a bit more of the central sphere. When their combined intensity threatened to overwhelm Adolf completely, Frieda would float over in his direction and temporarily balance things. Her alliances with her father, although infrequent, provided an essential counterweight to Klara's power, creating a degree of harmony in the family that wouldn't have been possible otherwise. In later life, Frieda's colleagues would wonder how she managed to be on everyone's side and get what she wanted at the same time. They didn't understand that having mastered the art of wrapping her father around her little finger while embracing her mother with the other hand, Frieda could endear herself to people at cross purposes without even noticing what she was doing. No one in her family had the slightest idea that this would prove ideal training for a psychiatrist.

What stands out most powerfully about Frieda's childhood is the way she enacted the Orthodox Jewish values of obedience, study, and reverence for one's parents while simultaneously serving as the trusted adviser to all the adults. Acutely sensitive to the feelings of others, utterly devoted to her parents and protective of her younger sisters, Frieda became a person whose own needs were invisible and whose greatest desire was to heal.

2

The Student

The purpose of technique is to free the talent.[1]

Frieda was a brilliant student from an early age, and the more she excelled, the more she fueled the ambitions of both her parents. At age fifteen, however, her educational opportunities evaporated, as girls were still barred from *Gymnasium* in Königsberg, preventing her from further schooling. Insistent that her daughter not be thwarted by her sex as she herself had been, Klara appointed herself Frieda's tutor. Friends sent their daughters to join the sessions, and a virtual high school for girls was created in one room of the Reichmann apartment.[2]

Klara took for granted that Frieda would follow her path and train as a teacher, perhaps specializing in languages, a subject in which she had special talent. But Adolf, pouring his own stifled love of study into the eager mind of his eldest child, decreed that Frieda should prepare for medical school. He had an intuition that she would be good at such work, and a medical degree would prove to the world that his daughter had a full university education, not just a course of teacher training like her mother. (It would also ensure a steady income, should her lack of a dowry and family history of deafness limit her marriage prospects.) Klara, equally ambitious for Frieda but competitive with her in a way that Adolf simply wasn't, bitterly opposed this plan. She didn't want Frieda to end up a "revolutionary" like her Aunt Helene (Klara's older sister), who supported herself by writing books on socialism, traveled alone to England and Italy, and refused to marry.[3] Klara also clearly found it threatening to have a daughter who was smarter than she was.

"She'd kill me if she heard me say that," Frieda was still telling friends decades later, "but it was true and I knew it." Adolf could never bear to contradict his wife openly, and Frieda was still too young to take the entrance examinations, so the decision was put off for half a year until she was seventeen. She herself had little say about her future. "They decided. The time that I decided things [in my life] didn't come until much later."[4] But she was secretly grateful to her father for having uncharacteristically stood his ground, and she resolved to become a doctor he would be forever proud of.

Klara was furious at having failed to set the course of her daughter's future but knew she couldn't oppose her husband directly. So she enacted her resentment by insisting that Frieda use the six-month waiting period to master "domestic science." Sensing that this might be her last chance to turn Frieda into a proper young woman, Klara may also unconsciously have wanted her to suffer at least some of the indignities of her gender before escaping into the male world of medicine. Frieda spent the semester sewing, darning socks, and learning "the other female virtues." As a test, Klara required her to prepare an entire meal for the family and several guests with no errors. Frieda doubtless attacked these tasks with her usual verve; she also carefully emulated Klara's example and never again did anything for herself that she could pay a maid to do for her.[5]

Frieda finally entered medical school in 1908, the first year that women were admitted to advanced study in Prussian institutions. She continued to live at home, both because it was proper and because she needed to keep kosher.[6] Königsberg's university, the Albertina, was among the least distinguished places to study medicine; had she been a boy, Frieda would have been dispatched to Berlin or Heidelberg. Her classmates were mostly farmers' sons, and there were no more than four or five other women among the fifty entering students. Frieda stood out in every way, being younger, female, and Jewish, as well as about two heads shorter than the average Prussian boy. She wore the high-waisted Empire blouses and long skirts characteristic of the period but drew the line at corsets. ("I had my principles," she told friends proudly, decades later.) Frieda's ambition, carefully nurtured by both parents, served her well in medical school. "We had to prove that the girls could do it as well as the boys, and that the Jews could do it as well as the Gentiles, and that you could be short and [still] do it."[7]

Excelling as always, Frieda soon felt at home amid the fine Renaissance buildings of the university Kant had so loved, and she began to create a wider world for herself than either of her parents had ever known. Klara's response was ambivalent. She longed for her daughter to succeed where she had not, but "when I began to outshine her," Frieda laughingly recalled, "that caused a problem. That was not in the program." It would be forty years before Klara would say, at the age of eighty-three: "Frieda, I must at last admit it, you are smarter than I." Frieda was careful to avoid direct competition. Well into her sixties, she was still telling friends that any success she had in life was due to her mother's having arranged things "so wonderfully" for her.[8]

One thing she clearly absorbed from Klara was a single-minded determination to let nothing stand in her way. Physically tiny like Frieda (they were both less than five feet tall), Klara was seen as an all-powerful force by everyone who knew her. Even her body obeyed her. Klara was said never to have been sick a day in her life, and was so powerful a swimmer she supposedly once crossed the Rhine fully clothed. Frieda had an equally resilient constitution, rarely missing a day of school or work despite years of long hours and little sleep.[9]

Helene Simon, Klara's older sister, was also an inspiration. In 1895, at the age of thirty-two, she had refused to continue keeping house for her parents in Köln and had gone off to study economics and social policy at the newly founded University of London. An active socialist, she joined the Fabian Society and wrote exposés on factories and sweatshops, focusing special attention on conditions for women and children. She spent much of her time in the slums of the East End, experiencing firsthand "the blatant differences between fashionable London and the miserable wretches of the benches." Returning to Germany in 1897, Helene had moved to Berlin, studied at the university, and published biographies of Robert Owen, William Godwin, and Mary Wollstonecraft, as well as essays on school reform and women's work. By the time Frieda began her studies in Königsberg, Helene Simon was a well-known member of Berlin's feminist and leftist communities.[10]

Her relationships with her mother and aunt proved the ideal goad to Frieda's success in medical school. The seventy-year-old professor of anatomy had refused to allow women students even to enter his class; ordered to teach them or retire, he grudgingly let them sit in the back of the room. On Frieda's first day in class, he grabbed a piece of cadaver from a formaldehyde-filled beaker, strode up the aisle of the lecture hall, and shook it in her face. When she flinched, he bellowed: "I didn't tell you to come here with that bare neck of yours!" (Besides being a woman, Frieda was undignified, having refused to wear the stiff collar and whalebone corset considered proper for young ladies of her social class.) "I don't know why you came here anyway," he muttered. "The other girls, well, maybe they think they can catch someone. But my God, you are so young and so pretty. You don't have to come to anatomy class to get yourself a man!" As a final insult, he refused to allow the women to perform dissections with the rest of the class, saying their white uniforms looked too much like nightgowns and might distract the men. So, decades before air-conditioning, when male students did dissections in a cellar of the hospital in January, the women were forced to wait until summer vacation. "The stench was horrible," Frieda later admitted in the tone of a war-weary veteran, "but we survived somehow."[11]

Even examinations glorified the culture of men. Frieda never forgot one particular question concerning the esophagus, which could be answered correctly only by knowing the slang word for a Prussian fraternity ritual in which students drank themselves into a stupor and cut their faces with broken beer bottles.[12]

Frieda got her revenge for these indignities the way she always would: by quietly outdoing the men. Studying quickly and effortlessly, she excelled in every course and still had time for boyfriends and dances. Relatively free of Klara's control for the first time in her life, she plunged into a social world outside the family. This sometimes got her into trouble. When a friend of one of her professors saw her at the beach in Cranz a week before an examination, he was so enraged by her arrogance that he tried to bar her from taking the test. (Besides being a woman, at seventeen, Frieda was the youngest in her class. With her hair still in braids, clipped in neat rows behind her ears with tortoise-shell pins, she looked even younger, which seemed to incense her male colleagues further.)

In a photograph from that time, she sits at a table, appearing to read the thick book open before her, but clearly aware of the camera's glance. She is wearing a uniform that looks like a cross between a lab coat and a nurse's outfit. Her face seems small and plain; her hair is unstyled. She appears to be trying to occupy as little space as possible, the modesty of her downward glance studious rather than female.

Frieda's decision on a specialty provoked renewed debate in the family. She didn't want to do pediatrics, like "a nice little girl." She had so adored obstetrics that she irritated the nurses; unlike other medical students, who performed the delivery and left, Frieda wanted to stay and take care of the infants. (Even in her sixties, she was still bragging to friends about delivering forty-four babies in her first month's rotation.) But obstetrical work was physically awkward for a person as short as she, given the extensive reliance on forceps and other mechanical instruments.

She took up psychiatry after two dramatic events convinced her she had a knack for the work. One took place in her final year of medical school. Frieda was sitting with the other women in the back row of a huge amphitheater. A manic-depressive patient was being led down the aisle for that day's demonstration. (Turn-of-the-century medical instruction featured hapless patients forced to perform their symptoms on demand before hundreds of students.) As the man passed Frieda's seat, he blurted out excitely to her: *"Bertchen, Bertchen, hab ich dich endlich wieder!"* ("Bertie, Bertie, at last I find you again!") Frieda, who described herself as "extremely shy," was as astonished as everyone else by this outburst. But without realizing what she was doing, she turned to the patient.

> All shyness was gone. "It" said out of me—not I said, "It" said: "Yes, that's fine. I'm very glad too, but you know now the professor wants to talk to you. I'll come and see you later." I assure you "It" said this. I had no idea what to do.

Everyone gasped and pointed at her. They were even more amazed when, at the end of the lecture, Frieda stood up and declared: "I must go and see that man, I have promised him." Treating the ravings of a mental patient as meaningful communication was unheard of. "Who would say something to a crazy man, and then do it?" mused Frieda, stunned by her own iconoclasm. For so outrageous a thought to have come "from that little girl, that good daughter of her parents, that good niece of her uncles and aunts, I can't describe it. It was just amazing." She had been brought up with a deep respect for authority. ("Who was I, as compared with a great teacher?") Yet at the same time, she was overwhelmed by an intense feeling, which seemed to come out of nowhere and was entirely discrepant with her conscious experience, that said out of her mouth: "This I could do better!"[13]

The story made the rounds, eventually reaching Klara, who met Frieda at the door one day demanding: "Why didn't you tell me about that big stunt you made there?" Frieda had no answer. She had behaved literally without thinking. The experience remained so vivid for the rest of her life that she could tell people exactly what the patient had looked like and what words they had said to each other.

Something similar had happened a year earlier, during the externship medical students did after their sixth semester. In Munich for the term, Frieda had gone to a lecture by Emil Kraepelin, the most eminent psychiatrist in Europe. She was younger and even more in awe of authority than at the time of the Bertchen incident. Kraepelin was presenting an epileptic patient to a room of worshipful students. Frieda listened to him go on and on about "epileptic character" and the man's odd behavior, as though the patient weren't standing right there. Outraged by Kraepelin's insensitivity, she had suddenly heard those same words in her head: "This I could do better!"[14]

Later, as an intern at the University of Königsberg hospital, before psychotherapy was even taught in medicine, Frieda took to sitting by the beds of psychotic patients, just listening to them.[15] Sometimes she stayed all night. She couldn't understand their ravings but was absolutely convinced they meant something. (One of those she likely sat with was Hannah Arendt's father, Paul, who had been committed to that ward in 1911 with paresis, the insanity that resulted from tertiary syphilis. He died there, totally deteriorated, two years later.) Among Frieda's strongest memories of that period was the day a patient failed to remove his cap as the physician in charge approached his bed. Asked why, he said: "I can't. There are birds under my cap and they will fly away if I do." The whole ward erupted in laughter, but Frieda was horrified. "I was so mad I could have killed them. I knew it meant something. But at that time, one didn't yet know this. Kraepelin had said you can't treat schizophrenics because you can't understand the meaning of what they say. We only learned that later on, after Freud." But patients deeply appreciated Frieda's interest. "A prima donna couldn't [have left] with more gifts, more flowers, more things," she laughed years later, insisting that whatever success she had came solely from diligence.

When Frieda passed her medical boards, the whole family celebrated. At the party her parents held in her honor, her uncle George Marx toasted her. Then he turned to Adolf: "It's fine that she is now a physician. But how can you permit her to become an insane doctor?" To Frieda's astonishment, her father, who had never before stood up to his wealthy, powerful boss and brother-in-law, responded calmly: "I should have thought of that earlier. Once I agreed to let her study medicine, I gave up the right to decide for her what specialty to pursue." (Eventually Uncle George became one of Frieda's strongest supporters, loaning her the money to open a sanitarium and helping her to get started in private practice.)[16]

Frieda was in her mid-thirties before she understood that everything good that happened to her in life wasn't indirectly Klara's doing. Her mother's power seemed so absolute it was easy to believe in an invisible hand guiding her actions. Learning to rely on her own talents while simultaneously denying their existence proved a boon in Frieda's dealings with men; she could do whatever she wanted without threatening them.

She perfected the art of running things without being in charge during World War I, when she became administrator of a hospital for brain-injured soldiers, a position no woman could formally have held. Having completed psychiatric training, such as it was, in 1914, she was hoping to leave Königsberg for postgraduate study, perhaps in Berlin, where Aunt Helene lived. But when war broke out in August of that year, the head of the university's psychiatric hospital asked Frieda if she would stay on, to work at a neurological clinic he was hurriedly planning. An unprecedented number of brain injuries were resulting from the artillery fusillades and shell splinters of industrialized warfare, and physicians were scrambling to cope with casualties totally different from anything they had trained for.[17] "Now, I knew as much about brain injury as the man in the moon," Frieda recalled years later, "but I thought, well, if the director thinks I can do it, why, it might be very interesting. I'll learn it." So as brigades of singing soldiers marched through the streets of Königsberg on their way to battle, Frieda set off on visits to the two such clinics already in existence. On her return, she was installed as the unofficial head of the Königsberg unit. As a woman, Frieda could not be given an appointment in the Prussian military, so she was made an associate of the hospital and paid by the university. She started out with twenty beds in a converted schoolhouse and within a year was running a hundred-bed hospital for neurological patients of every description.[18]

Her position presented no problems until the day the military authorities announced they were planning an inspection. Frieda called her male supervisor, who was supposedly in charge of the unit, and said: "For heaven's sake, don't come in today." He had no idea what procedures were being used with any of the patients, and she didn't want him to be embarrassed in front of his superiors. When the tall, goose-stepping officers arrived at the gates, each a perfect specimen of the anti-Semitic, patriarchal Prussian army, they were greeted not by a young medic clicking his heels but by the tiny, Jewish Frieda in her white service outfit:

> Just poor little me, still with my braids over my ears and my tortoise-shell combs in my hair. I said to them: "The professor has asked me to apologize for him; he had to go to the Front. He has asked me to escort you around." Then I said: "Before I take you around, your Excellency—I had learned all the military ranks and did not make mistakes—I said, your such and such, won't you first come into the office? I would like to explain to you briefly what we are doing here." When I had talked long enough to make sure that they didn't understand a thing that was going on, I said: "Now, if you wish, we can make rounds."

Earlier in the day, in classic Frieda fashion, she had gone through each ward, telling the soldiers: "Boys, we have inspection today. You know it's a little problematic that I as a woman am working here for the Prussian army. It's up to you whether you want me or not. If you want me, then this hospital has to look as though you have the greatest disciplinarian in the world. If you don't want me, well . . . you know what to do." Frieda wasn't talking about a little straightening up; she was talking about the formal inspection of a Prussian military installation. Beds had to be straight enough to line up with a ruler. Patients had to be sitting with their arms folded in a certain way, dressed in their hospital uniforms, every button perfectly aligned, their slippers positioned at a ninety-degree angle to their beds. The blackboard above each bed listing the patient's condition had to have letters printed in exactly the same size. Apparently, "the boys," as Frieda liked to call them, were as fond of her as she was of them. "I don't think you could have found in the whole of Prussia a hospital which looked as reeking of good discipline as that one," she proudly told friends for the rest of her life.[19]

Frieda's satisfaction had little to do with her own accomplishments; she was focused solely on the welfare of her patients. She spent days memorizing the manual of psychiatric and neurological conditions until she could recite the disposition for each kind of case. ("I wanted to do right by my soldiers.") When her superiors made rounds, she would intone: "This man here suffers from category Z-25. According to Article 7-B, he will need hospitalization for three to six weeks," and so on down the line. Apparently this strategy worked. She later told colleagues, "I got everything I wanted for every man."

Even in that autocratic, masculine system, Frieda quietly found a way to adapt the rules to her needs. As an Orthodox Jew, she refused to hold clinic hours on Saturdays, thereby making hers the only army hospital in Prussian history where patients weren't treated on Shabbat. Eventually—she held this job for two years—everyone found out that Frieda was in charge, but as she recalled with amusement decades later: "You can go over the excellent records of two years and you will not find my name anywhere. It wasn't me. If you knew Prussia, and if you knew what I looked like, you would know how incredibly funny this was."[20]

She was determined to let nothing impede her work. When the Russian army surrounded Königsberg in the buildup to the famous battle of Tannenberg, women and children were ordered to evacuate. The trains were packed with panicked people (among them, Hannah Arendt and her mother) fleeing the city in advance of the ravaging Russian soldiers who had left a path of burned and plundered villages to the east. Adolf insisted that Frieda leave. She refused, furious at his overprotectiveness. "What! I'm in charge of a hospital for brain-injured soldiers. Suddenly I'm supposed to remember that I'm a poor female? No. That can't be done!" Later, when she was off on an inspection somewhere, the city came under siege. Her family was terrified. No trains were running, and communications were completely cut off with the rest of Germany. Then suddenly, plucky as ever, Frieda appeared. She had marched onto a troop train sending reinforcements to the Front, with a large white handkerchief tied around her arm, barking *"Sanitator"* (medic) to anyone who challenged her. She was greeted by the agonized screams of the Russian soldiers' horses dying in the swamps surrounding Königsberg, a sound Erich Maria Remarque called "unendurable, the moaning of the world, the martyred creation, wild with anguish, filled with terror and groaning."[21]

When a physician friend of hers became addicted to morphine and started missing work, Frieda did her shifts after finishing with her own patients. She often worked through the night, drinking cup after cup of black coffee to stay awake, taking a shower when morning came, and then starting all over again. "I earned my wrinkles honorably," she later said of this period, taking for granted, as always, that hard work was simply her duty. She kept up this pace for four years, as "the youth of Europe hurled themselves at one another" in what Käthe Kollwitz called "this frightful insanity."[22]

When the war finally ended, Frieda felt the need for more training in neurology, to supplement what she had learned from daily experience at the clinic. Her former professor Kurt Goldstein offered her a position as his assistant, so she moved to Frankfurt and spent two years studying and doing research at his institute. Between 1914 and 1920, she published twenty articles (eight coauthored with Goldstein or his colleagues), demonstrating a far greater mastery of neurological issues than most other physicians in Europe.[23]

This nonstop pace protected Frieda from the horrors of life in postwar Germany. Less than a day's drive from Frankfurt, tens of thousands of people were dying from hunger, cold, and deprivation as the defeated army retreated from the Western Front. The terrible "turnip winters" of 1916 and 1917 had already left most of the population with barely any heat or food. But in those freezing months in early 1919, when Communists seized power in Berlin and their leaders, Karl Liebknecht and Rosa Luxemburg, were beaten and then murdered by the rightwing Freikorps, when people all across Germany starved to death, Frieda, beginning a pattern she would continue for the rest of her life, cocooned herself inside a safe institution where she could concentrate on her work.

She had met Goldstein around 1913, toward the end of her medical training. Eleven years her senior, he had studied neuroanatomy, neurophysiology, and psychiatry with Germany's leading researchers. Goldstein supervised Frieda's M.D. thesis on visual perception in schizophrenics (which she had signed with her name and the required phrase, "a Jew from Silesia").[24] But soon after her graduation, he had left Königsberg for Frankfurt, to take up a position specially designed to blend his research and clinical interests. When war broke out soon after, he turned the Neurological Institute into the first hospital in the world devoted solely to the treatment and study of brain injury. Housing the largest number of neurological patients ever assembled in one place, Goldstein's center offered unprecedented training opportunities. Frieda was one of many who came to study and work with him in this period. Unlike other students, however, she arrived in Frankfurt having spent four years running her own clinic (a position for which Goldstein had probably recommended her), and could thus collaborate with him on research from the beginning.

The "irrationality" of brain injury had always baffled physicians. Symptoms could take an extraordinary variety of forms and often failed to correspond to known anatomical pathways. Casualties of war were even more puzzling, because the speed and trajectory of a bullet or a piece of shrapnel were completely unpredictable, creating what appeared to be a pattern of symptoms unique to each patient. Goldstein's wards were a bizarre mix: men compulsively laughing or crying, tilting their arms at odd angles, or walking in jerky, uncoordinated fashion. A patient might be mute and stuporous, or delirious and excitable. He might writhe in pain from a place where no wound could be found, or be utterly insensitive, smiling when stuck with pins during an examination. Abnormalities of temperature regulation made some patients shiver or sweat uncontrollably; an injury to the spine could cause paralysis, incontinence, or odd shuffling movements.

Goldstein's special interest was language difficulties, which often appeared so idiosyncratic as to defy categorization. One patient could write only if he squeezed his letters into a narrow band at the right margin. Another had to have paper with a certain kind of lines. There were patients who could read only if the words were printed in capitals, and others who failed to name letters but correctly identified words. One patient could read but couldn't spell; another used numbers correctly but not letters. Beyond the strangeness of the symptoms themselves, Goldstein was struck by a "characteristic peculiarity of these patients, that they are utterly *unaware of their deviation* from the normal."[25]

Meticulous studies of thousands of these soldiers—who were completely healthy except for their injuries, unlike the typical neurological patient afflicted with stroke or tumor—led Goldstein to reconceive radically the core assumptions of his discipline. He distinguished symptoms caused by the injury from those that expressed "the struggle of the changed personality to cope with demands it can no longer meet."[26] He drew attention to how patients altered their environments to avoid exposing their disabilities. He emphasized the extraordinary creativity of human beings forced to craft new solutions to problems and saw brain-injured people as particularly inventive.[27]

Most neurologists took just the opposite view, casting their patients as rigid and stereotypic. Goldstein thought this was because they were so distracted by the strangeness of the symptoms they couldn't see past them to the person underneath. By focusing on those capacities that remained intact even after severe injury, he embraced a flexible biology whose main characteristic was adaptation to change.

Searching for subtle abilities that might not be evident in ordinary behavior, Goldstein continually individualized his assessments. Observing the same patients for months, even years, sensitized him to minute variations. He examined every patient on many kinds of tasks, carefully noting whatever he said or did. "He never forgot that he addressed an individual, not a brain," remarked one appreciative student.[28] It was up to the physician, Goldstein insisted, to figure out what a patient could or couldn't do, not the patient's job to fit his symptoms to standardized measures.

He noticed, for example, that even minor variations in stimulus presentation could produce striking differences in response. With a tachistoscope (a device that limited exposure to a fraction of a second), the patient might show deficits not apparent under normal conditions. This made sense: longer exposures allowed the use of substitute methods; only with the T-scope would the underlying defect be revealed. Variations in instructions also proved significant. A patient suffering from apraxia (the inability to perform purposeful movements) might not be able to purse his lips when asked to do so, but could often whistle a tune (a meaningful action, well integrated into his behavioral repertoire). Like the Swiss psychologist Jean Piaget, who evolved a whole new theory of intelligence by analyzing *how* children solved problems, instead of counting the number of questions they correctly answered, Goldstein thought that brain injury was best understood by examining the totality of a patient's reaction, not simply whether he succeeded at an assigned task.

> Normal as well as abnormal reactions ("symptoms") are expressions of the organism's attempt to deal with demands of the environment. . . . Symptoms are *answers, given by the modified organism, to definite demands:* They are attempted solutions to problems derived on the one hand from the demands of the natural environment, and on the other from the special tasks imposed on the organism in the course of the examination.[29]

This approach led Goldstein to revise standard views of brain and mind completely. Analyzing a patient's response to his injuries instead of simply labeling his defects highlighted the central role of adaptation in neurological functioning. Even severely impaired patients found alternative solutions to problems, so long as they weren't overwhelmed by the "catastrophic anxiety" that kept them from experimenting. Patients were integrated organisms with goals and plans, not simply bundles of reflexes or automatons. They had a fundamental drive toward "self-actualization," leading them "to maintain a performance capacity on the highest possible level . . . and to use this new way of proceeding with great virtuosity."[30] Just because a patient's behavior was difficult to understand didn't mean he couldn't be treated. It was the physician's responsibility to meet the patient where he was and help him to confront the obstacles that now faced him.

> Sickness cannot be understood correctly if one assumes that it is something that befalls the individual from the outside. Our task is not simply to eliminate the disturbance or fight the effect of the sickness. Sickness seen from a higher aspect has to be considered as a disturbance of the relation between man and world, a disorder involving both.

Goldstein's nuanced observations made him skeptical of theory. "We may not be aware of the degree to which our preconceptions do violence to the facts we observe," he cautioned students. "Medicine is a kind of artistic enterprise mirroring the nature of man, which requires risk-taking and courage." Goldstein had an active interest in theory and drew heavily from Gestalt, psychoanalysis, and phenomenology, but "he was nobody's unconditional follower or apologist. . . . His approach was deliberately naive, setting the patient in the limelight and [casting himself] in the role of a teachable audience." Reflecting years later on this way of working, Goldstein remarked: "The holistic approach did not originate from any idea. It was forced upon me by concrete experience."[31]

This fascination with patients gave his Frankfurt clinic a unique vibrancy. Most neurological hospitals were depressing, hopeless places, where staff, horrified at the extent of their patients' injuries, spent as little time as possible on the wards. Goldstein's clinic, in contrast, was like a big family, where "patients, physicians, relatives, friends, and many citizens actively participated in the realization and maintenance of a serene and relaxed outlook." His warm supportiveness extended to his relationships with students and colleagues; for years, Goldstein teased Frieda about the "striking agraphia" that afflicted her only on Saturdays (when the dictates of Orthodox practice prevented her from writing notes).[32]

Frieda's whole approach to treatment emerged from her research with Goldstein, and it is impossible to understand her later work with psychotics without appreciating this fact. Years of daily contact with brain-injured patients accustomed her to so wide a range of symptoms that schizophrenia never seemed especially bizarre to her (as it did to most analysts, trained solely in work with outpatient neurotics). Goldstein's insistence that there was no such thing as "*the* brain-injured patient" made Frieda highly sensitive to individual differences, and his ingenuity at locating strengths in even the most severely impaired person taught her never to regard any one technique as sacrosanct. And because the patients in Goldstein's clinic had experienced traumas about which there was no ambiguity—unlike the many shell-shock victims being treated elsewhere, the "reality" of whose symptoms was contested both by physicians and military authorities—she never doubted that even the most mysterious behaviors had identifiable causes.

Goldstein's psychological approach to brain injury also taught Frieda to see past symptoms to the anxieties that lay underneath. Mutism or withdrawal might be ways to avoid fear; regression could be a desperate measure to feel more safe. However incapacitating these symptoms, they had to be understood as active attempts by an "integrated organism" to master his situation, not as meaningless reactions or "faulty wiring." Goldstein clearly saw the brain as hugely significant in mental functioning, but insisted that mechanistic ways of conceiving its functions were oversimplified.

The focus on gradual rehabilitation at the Frankfurt Institute also taught Frieda the importance of breaking long-term treatment goals into manageable units. She understood the patient's need to keep from feeling overwhelmed, and concentrated on building up his repertoire of normal behavior bit by bit. Goldstein's active, empathic response to patients, based on his nonverbal understanding of their needs, taught Frieda to trust her own instincts as a healer instead of hiding behind the persona of the dispassionate physician. If a patient felt hopeless and despaired of ever getting well, it was her responsibility to offer a "loan of conviction" that improvement might eventually occur.[33]

At a deeper, more personal level, Goldstein's emphasis on searching out the healthy parts of each patient, no matter how buried they might be, resonated with the Jewish view of redemption that had been instilled in Frieda since her youth. The notion of *tikkun,* hailed by ethicist Joseph Dan as "the most powerful idea ever presented in Jewish thought," ascribed responsibility to each individual to do her part to repair the rupture between God and human beings. Even the most mundane act had symbolic significance. As Dan explains: "Every deed (or misdeed) may decide the fate of the world. . . . There is no neutral ground. . . . If a man is idle for an hour, he has missed an opportunity to uplift a [divine] spark."[34]

So when Goldstein taught Frieda that even patients shot in the head could be helped by a doctor determined enough, she saw how she could perform her share of this redemptive work. Her responsibility was to aid the patient's struggle; whether he ultimately recovered was up to God. As a doctor, she could do only so much. Failing to take up the task, however, would have been morally irresponsible. There was a divine spark present in every act, and through the patient she could do her part to repair the world.

On a more unconscious level, Goldstein's idea of self-actualization allowed Frieda to see a force outside herself as bringing about the patient's cure. There were two simultaneous parts to this: the patient's drive to actualize himself fueled the work, and her assistance reflected God's hand, not her grandiosity. By attributing her striking early successes with patients to an external power rather than to her own talent, Frieda could avoid competing openly with her parents (especially Klara) while still confidently acknowledging that her patients had recovered.

After two years of work in Goldstein's clinic, Frieda was ready to practice medicine on her own. In 1920, she returned to Königsberg, both because it was near her family and because the leading Jewish psychiatrist there had died in the war. Beyond her enthusiasm for the work itself, she needed the income of a private practice. Her morphine addict friend was finding it increasingly difficult to care for her daughter, and Frieda had volunteered to take the child in until her friend was in better shape. There was a long tradition in her family of caring for those in need, and temporarily adopting a ten-year-old child didn't seem unusual. Klara, as always, arranged the details: "My mother found me a nice home and an office and a maid, in a nice part of the city where I could live with this girl and where I liked to work, and everything was hunky-dory," Frieda recalled.[35] The only problem was that she had no training in psychotherapy, a method that seemed more relevant to work with outpatients than the Kraepelinian diagnostics she had learned in medical school. One of the few physicians in Germany known to use psychotherapy on a regular basis was Johannes Heinrich (I. H.) Schultz, a professor at the University of Jena. Frieda wrote to Schultz, asking if she might train with him for two or three months. He agreed, but said he was leaving Jena to work at Heinrich Lahmann's sanitarium near Dresden; she would have to come there. Weisser Hirsch ("White Stag") was a famous spa in the mountains where wealthy people went to lose weight or follow Lahmann's natural healing methods. The treatment involved a combination of diet, massage, mineral baths, vigorous walks, and cutting wood in the fresh air; Schultz felt that psychotherapy would be a useful addition and was planning to introduce his approach, called autogenic training, into the regimen.[36]

Life at Weisser Hirsch was elegant and stylish, with theater, dances, and formal teas on the grounds. (It was a huge place as sanitaria went, with room for more than 300 patients.) Frieda was put off by the excess, but intended to stay only long enough to learn Schultz's method. (She had left the child with a friend in Frankfurt and promised to return within a few months.) However, shortly after her arrival, Schultz, like every other person Frieda was ever to work for, offered her a regular position on his staff. Frieda didn't especially like Schultz; he had "an anti-Semitic look," she thought, and later, in fact, he became a Nazi (a bit tricky, since his first wife was Jewish).[37] Besides, she had the child to think of. She couldn't very well live in that environment with a ten-year-old girl who wasn't her daughter. To her surprise, Schultz retorted, "Why not?" Frieda, still dubious, said she wouldn't fit in with the fancy clientele. And she kept kosher, which created yet more complications. "Tell them in the kitchen what you want, and they'll do it," Schultz insisted. (Lahmann had invented a special diet, and the sanitarium's wealthy patients were accustomed to having their whims catered to, so kosher cooking was easy to arrange.) Frieda was astounded—"here I was, a little girl, not at all elegant like them"—but she agreed to stay provided that the child could live with her, the food was kosher, and she didn't have to escort patients to the opera. For a person who had just spent six years with brain-injured soldiers, it was quite a change in atmosphere.

Years later, Frieda laughingly described Weisser Hirsch to friends in America:

> The patients had little blue books in which it was recorded how many baths they took each week, how many mornings they were to spend cutting wood, how many walks they were to take, how many times they were to see the doctor, etc. And everybody got a tip. The bathing master got a tip, and the masseuse got a tip, the head of the woodcutting machinery got a tip, and the doctor got a tip. The only difference was that the tip for the doctor was a little bigger. This was during [the terrible postwar] inflation and lots of people came from Hungary and Bohemia where they were better off. They also gave real gifts. I got a hat and dresses and all kinds of things.[38]

Having spent much of her childhood at the Marxes' villa, Frieda felt comfortable with wealthy people, so despite her contempt at the excesses of

Weisser Hirsch, she related easily to its clientele. She ended up staying four years, and her informal apprenticeship with Schultz reinforced and extended much of what she had learned in Goldstein's clinic.

Schultz's approach was based on research showing that certain psychosomatic illnesses could be relieved by systematic relaxation. (Asthma patients, for example, were taught to repeat the words: "My breathing is calm and regular." Those with high blood pressure said: "My head is clear and light. My heartbeat is calm and easy.") The assumption was that these "autohypnotic" exercises stimulated the brain's natural self-regulatory processes, creating a state physiologically opposite to anxiety and stress. Schultz called his method "autogenic training" to emphasize the patient's "self-generating" role in the treatment.[39]

This conception closely fit Goldstein's notion of self-actualization. The therapist wasn't curing the patient; she was helping to marshal the recuperative processes already present in his nervous system. Schultz's method encouraged Frieda to trust the nonverbal links between mind and body and to use metaphor as a way to reach symptoms. (Asthma patients who learned to say, "My chest is warm," for example, were symbolically inducing a state of relaxation, not literally increasing their body temperature.) Schultz also had a special interest in schizophrenics, particularly those in acute states. He didn't focus, as she later would, on the meaning of delusions or hallucinations, but his assumption that psychotics could be treated with the same methods as other patients clearly strengthened Frieda's commitment to such ideas.[40]

Although Schultz's idea of "psychotherapy" was more like what we would today call biofeedback or behavioral medicine, he did have an interest in the therapeutic relationship. He gave Frieda a few books on psychoanalysis to read, and encountering Freud's ideas on transference was tremendously exciting for her. "I had known from the first day I was in psychiatry that something funny went on in the doctor-patient relationship, but nobody seemed to know anything about it and nobody talked about it. . . . And this man [Freud] said he knew it happened!" She recalled an experience in the hospital in Königsberg that had always bothered her. A distinguished psychiatrist had told a long story about a hysterical patient who followed him wherever he went. Everyone thought this was hilarious, but Frieda knew it meant something "that patients got tied up with the doctor in a way that wasn't quite right." So now, discovering Freud years later, she realized that what she had always intuitively known to be important was something that could be systematically studied.[41]

Schultz didn't know much about psychoanalysis—and had in fact written several works on Freud that had been scathingly reviewed in analytic journals—but when Frieda said she wanted to go to Berlin for formal training, he gave her time off from Weisser Hirsch. ("Go tell them a few dreams if you want to" were his actual words.) This was in the early 1920s, years before an international association created a standardized curriculum for analytic institutes. Styles of practice varied enormously in different locations, and where one studied made a great deal of difference.[42] The Berlin group was known for its high standards and unconventionality, a combination that strongly resonated with Frieda's own inclinations.

Founded in 1910 by Karl Abraham, one of Freud's most brilliant early colleagues, the Berlin Psychoanalytic Institute had always been distinctive. Unlike analysts in Vienna, who tended to regard innovation as disloyalty to "the master," Abraham embraced a scientific spirit, welcoming ideas that challenged and extended the limits of psychoanalytic practice. Arguing that treatment ought to be available to the widest possible clientele, he opened a clinic offering free analyses to poor and working-class Berliners and encouraged efforts to treat psychotic patients. Abraham had spent six years of his own training working in hospital settings, including three years at the famous Burghölzli Clinic run by Eugen Bleuler and C. G. Jung, and at just the moment Frieda came to Berlin to study, he was engaged in pathbreaking work on schizophrenia and manic depression.

Abraham's institute also reflected the tolerant, socialist spirit of postwar Berlin, where psychoanalysis was part of the avant-garde, eliciting broad interest among intellectuals and critics. Unlike Vienna, whose stodgy atmosphere left analysts feeling isolated and threatened, attitudes in Berlin encouraged experiment. At the same time, Abraham's peculiarly rigid style of open-mindedness made training at his institute far more systematic than in Vienna (where even in the 1920s, one still became a student only at Freud's personal invitation and rules of technique were defined as whatever he happened to be doing). Abraham, in contrast, standardized both procedures and training, and imposed the first real framework for psychoanalytic education. His close relationship with Freud, and the tremendous respect in which he was held by the entire analytic community, allowed him the latitude to run his institute in his own fashion. Abraham trained some of the most gifted and innovative analysts of the next generation (including Melanie Klein, Wilhelm Reich, and Karen Horney), and the intellectual excitement in his classes and seminars was legendary. His sudden death in 1925 at the age of forty-eight was a terrible loss for psychoanalysis, but his guiding principles held sway long after his personal influence had waned.[43]

Frieda began her formal analytic training in 1923, while she was still on the staff of Weisser Hirsch. This was an especially exciting period for the

Berlin Institute. It had been the refuge for many in Ferenczi's circle forced to flee Budapest because of postwar anti-Semitism (Michael Balint, Franz Alexander, Sándor Radó), and it was attracting a gifted group of students from Britain (Alix Strachey, James and Edward Glover). Frieda learned a great deal from the classes, but the personal analysis she had begun with Wilhelm Wittenberg in Munich the year before had far more influence than the training analysis she was forced to undertake with Hanns Sachs. Abraham had introduced the rule that every candidate had to be analyzed by a member of the institute staff, and Sachs was responsible for all new students. (Originally a lawyer, he couldn't see patients at the hospital, so his colleagues made him the primary training analyst to augment his income. As one of Horney's biographers remarked, Sachs analyzed so many students in the 1920s "it sometimes seems impossible that [he] was only one person.")[44]

Many of the core tenets of Frieda's approach to psychoanalysis, especially her assumption that it could be successfully used with psychotic patients, were powerfully shaped by her training in Berlin. But she was never an active member of the institute community, probably because she commuted throughout the period of her studies, first from Weisser Hirsch and then, starting in 1924, from Heidelberg. Her extensive background in neurology also set her apart. Having already worked full time as a physician for a decade before beginning analytic training, she lacked the wide-eyed excitement of candidates fresh from medical school or converts from other disciplines. She wasn't looking to psychoanalysis for a new identity; it was a technique she saw as complementing what she had already learned in other settings.[45]

Frieda seems to have barely tolerated Sachs, a man who impressed people in such strikingly different ways as to be variously described as "gifted," "loquacious," an "intellectual monstrosity" and a "silent presence." His image as a bon vivant—with the love of good wines, witty conversation, and aesthetics that befit his Viennese upbringing—couldn't have been more at odds with Frieda's self-abnegating diligence. (In America years later, when she chose to live in a cottage on the grounds of a mental hospital, he bought an elegant home on Boston's Beacon Hill and kept an English butler.) She must also have found Sachs's worshipful attitude toward "the master" ridiculous; he had arranged the furniture in his Berlin consulting room so that patients lying on the couch "faced a portrait bust of Freud, standing on a high wooden pedestal."[46]

Sachs seems mostly to have taught Frieda how not to behave as an analyst. She frequently got migraines during their sessions, a symptom rich with potential significance (evoking her identification with her father, who had suffered from migraines throughout her childhood, as well as her transference hostility toward Sachs, neither of which seemed to attract his interest). On one particular day, the pain was especially intense, but Frieda, struggling to discover the unconscious meaning of her symptom, gamely kept free-associating. Suddenly, unable to control herself, she vomited all over the couch. Instead of interpreting the sadism inherent in this act or any other aspect of its significance, Sachs abruptly terminated the session, apparently concerned about his oriental rug. Frieda never forgave his insensitivity, and her own embrace of patients who smeared feces or pelted her with food during sessions can be seen as one of many ways she rejected Sachs's model of the dandified analyst.[47]

Ever politic, however, she did present as her qualifying paper for admission to the German Psychoanalytic Society an oedipally focused piece of cultural criticism of just the sort Sachs most favored.[48] Publishing this paper in *Imago,* the journal he edited, seems to have been her parting shot; she never again wrote anything remotely like this, and despite her generally oversolicitous attitude toward teachers, never cited Sachs in any of her subsequent work.

The person who did have a profound effect on Frieda's thinking during this period was her friend and colleague Georg Groddeck. The son of a small-town doctor who ran a healing spa, Groddeck had been exposed to heretical ideas about medicine since earliest childhood. His father's idol was the renegade Ernst Schweninger, Bismarck's personal physician, who disdained established techniques and adapted his methods to the idiosyncrasies of each patient. After his father's death and his own medical training, Groddeck himself went to study with Schweninger, who taught him "to doubt every claim he could not personally prove, to question every cure he could not duplicate, and to regard the physician as a mere catalyst, setting curative processes in motion."[49] Schweninger rarely used medication of any kind, relying instead on diet, exercise, hydrotherapy, and massage. (Groddeck had already discovered how powerful hands-on treatments could be, having stumbled on a form of massage that kept his father alive after a stroke by stimulating his breathing muscles.) Opening his own small sanitarium in Baden-Baden, Europe's famous spa town (where treatment of nervous disorders had long been a specialty), Groddeck developed a radical, imaginative approach designed to stimulate each patient's hidden reservoir of health.

Doctors all over Germany were soon sending him their most hopeless cases. "Groddeck didn't cure your illness," remarked one grateful patient. "He healed you." Frau A., a seventy-year-old woman who had been in agonizing pain from kidney disease and other ailments for years, was a famous instance. Groddeck prescribed a strange mixture of diet, arm baths, massage, and exercise, horrifying the proper Frau A. by performing the massage himself, kneeling on her abdomen. Too weak to protest, she had endured the regimen. Returning home a month later—twenty pounds lighter, entirely free of pain, and more energetic than she had been in years—she told her physician: "Groddeck is a lunatic, but he has cured me."[50]

At the age of fifty, having independently arrived at the idea that illness was not "a mechanical or chemical dysfunction of organs, but a creation, a symbol," Groddeck began to correspond with Freud, hoping to push psychoanalysis in more radical directions. If hysterics could "convert" their emotional conflicts to physical symptoms, Groddeck argued, then why couldn't so-called organic illnesses be treated analytically? "The It," as he called the unconscious, "expresses itself as much in pneumonia as in cancer or in a compulsion neurosis or in hysteria. . . . There are no basic differences," he told an incredulous Freud, "that force us to attempt psychoanalysis here and not there."[51]

Freud considered Groddeck brilliant and always acknowledged that his own concept of id was a "civilized, bourgeois, demystified" version of Groddeck's "It."[52] Most other analysts, however, thought Groddeck too out of control to be part of their movement. He enjoyed his status as the bad boy of psychoanalysis, snubbing the establishment by publishing his articles in a privately printed newsletter he titled the *Satanarium,* after the name a mischievous patient had given his clinic. Known for his focus on direct clinical experience rather than textbook abstraction, Groddeck once remarked to an analyst discoursing on Freudian method: "You talk a lot about anal eroticism; have you yourself ever looked at an anus?" Claiming that psychoanalysis could be used to treat cancer, tuberculosis, and heart disease, Groddeck said an illness was like a dream: it had a manifest appearance and an underlying, latent meaning. Physical disorders were no less symbolic than neuroses were; in both cases, the doctor needed to analyze how the It was being expressed and then interpret this meaning to the patient.

Groddeck's view of the unconscious was both more respectful and more optimistic than Freud's. Instead of conceiving it as a dangerous force that needed to be controlled, Groddeck saw it as a constructive ally that could create the conditions for the patient's recovery. Illness was a warning not to continue living in a particular way. But like any other symbolic communication, it had to be interpreted, and this was what the doctor could help to do.

Groddeck's only rule was to use whatever means were necessary—however extreme or unusual—to call forth the patient's inherent capacities for healing. Working tirelessly, seeing patients at all hours, six days a week, Groddeck thought of himself as a servant of the It, not an independent agent with an agenda of his own making. "It does not matter to therapy whether the doctor's action is correct or not," he wrote in a key clinical paper. "All that matters is that the patient should make use of this action in order to get himself well."[53] Psychotherapy was one of many methods that could be used; there was nothing sacred about its rules, no matter what analysts claimed.

Insisting that no patient was ever beyond hope, Groddeck told Freud in a letter: "Failure is due to the doctor. It is not inherent in the illness."[54] As one appreciative student later wrote: "He had astonishing success with patients suffering from chronic symptoms long since abandoned as non-curable by others. Those who were already mortally ill he would revive with his own courage, and side by side with them he would battle death to the very last moment."[55] Most analysts considered Groddeck crazy in the extremes to which he was willing to take these ideas (repeatedly urging Freud, for example, to come to Baden-Baden so his cancer of the jaw could be treated psychoanalytically). But rebels like Ferenczi, Horney, and Fromm hailed Groddeck as a genius—Ernst Simmel called him "a fanatic in the cause of healing"—and none admired his work more than Frieda.[56]

They met sometime in the 1920s, in circumstances unknown. When she and colleagues in Frankfurt and nearby Switzerland formed the Southwest German Psychoanalytic Working Group in 1930, they invited Groddeck to present one of the inaugural lectures. Frieda was personally closer to him than the others were, and often visited him in Baden-Baden after she moved to nearby Heidelberg. "Nothing that has been printed in psychoanalysis," Frieda wrote to him in 1933, "speaks to me so directly, at the same time both new and familiar, as your books." She called Groddeck's visits *the* center of my life in Heidelberg," and kept a supply of the American cigarettes to which he was addicted on hand to entice him to longer stays. The Swiss psychiatrist Medard Boss seemed clearly to be thinking of Frieda when he wrote in a tribute to Groddeck: "His great knowledge and impressive power drew many of the best minds around him, drawn as though by enchantment into the circle of his influence." Later, struggling to describe his impact on her during the tumultuous period right after Hitler took power, Frieda would tell Groddeck in a letter:

In times like these one draws up a kind of psychic balance sheet, and thus I have once again experienced, with deep gratitude, how infinitely much I have been able to learn from you—in terms of the keenness in listening and in intuition to all the forms of expression of the It, in terms of humility vis-à-vis irrationality, in terms of skepticism vis-à-vis science (all of this a woefully inadequate expression of the abundance of all that I am trying to encompass here), also at the core of my efforts, to serve people through therapy.[57]

Frieda never felt comfortable emulating Groddeck's outrageousness or thumbing her nose at the psychoanalytic establishment, as he constantly did. But she wholeheartedly embraced his iconoclasm, which, stripped of its excess, closely matched her own conception of illness. Groddeck's insistence that every patient was potentially capable of cure fit her own quieter ambition, and his unshakable faith in the healing powers of the organism reinforced much of what she had learned from Goldstein and Schultz. But more than anything else, Groddeck confirmed Frieda's belief that technique was merely a means to an end. The goal was to help the patient, not to stay loyal to any one method. As another admirer of Groddeck had noted: "The fate of his patients concerned him far more than that of his theories." And despite their striking differences—Groddeck a huge, powerful man arrogantly presenting himself as the doctor who must be instantly obeyed; Frieda a tiny, Jewish woman, casting herself as the eager student—she clearly felt within herself the same healing gift as he did. "Disease was his adversary, and he fought to win," wrote Groddeck's biographers, and Frieda shared his single-minded determination to battle the symptoms and rescue the patient from his illness.[58]

She never thought cancer could be cured with psychoanalysis as Groddeck grandiosely insisted. But she admired his refusal to work within established boundaries and felt emboldened by his experiments. Groddeck had always admitted his tendency to elide distinctions, telling Freud in a letter: "I do not see the boundaries between things, only their running into one another. That is a mistake, but also has its great advantages. Systematic minds need people like me as the pinch of pepper that perfects the dish." Too respectful of authority to challenge the rules directly herself, Frieda could use Groddeck's constant pushing at the limits to claim that her own innovations, which might otherwise have seemed radical, were only minor modifications.[59]

Throughout the 1920s, as Frieda moved from Goldstein's clinic to Weisser Hirsch and then to Berlin and Heidelberg, she began to forge a synthesis among the diverse perspectives she had studied. Imbued with what Arnold Zweig called "the spirit of the eternal student, which knows of the imperfection of knowledge and the high peaceful joy that comes from honoring great teachers," she tried to learn everything she could from each new experience.[60] By the time she started practicing on her own, two main principles governed her approach: using whatever worked with each individual and relying on a patient's own inherent capacity for healing to guide the treatment. Trusting her intuitions and believing deeply in the unconscious unity of body and mind, she began to evolve a unique clinical style that turned the therapeutic relationship into a fulcrum for change.

3

The Psychiatrist

Sopranos don't last as long as composers.[1]

Frieda can't be said to have developed a theory; rather, she forged a unique viewpoint merging ideas typically seen as unrelated. A follower of no school but a student of many, she drew on an unusually wide range of sources, combining them idiosyncratically, like a sculptor working with found objects or a chef creating bouillabaisse.

She was an empiricist in the literal sense of the word, deriving her theoretical commitments directly from experience. As she began to develop modes of treatment that seemed to work, she kept modifying her assumptions until they made sense of what she had observed. She never thought of this as iconoclasm or disloyalty to theory; she thought she was following the rules of scientific method—analyzing her results, revising her hypotheses, and then heading back to the lab. If a patient got worse or blamed her for his anguish, she treated these responses as data, like a pathologist confronting tumor cells among his specimens. Later, in America, she would take schizophrenic patients for drives in the country or to concerts in Washington, not to be gallant or do them a favor, but as experiments, designed to test her understanding of their behavior in diverse settings.

Like Goldstein, Frieda considered herself a scientist as much as a physician, and her approach to treatment has to be understood in this spirit. In "Contribution to the Psychopathology of Bronchial Asthma," for example, a paper she published in 1922 soon after leaving Frankfurt, she complained that asthma seemed to have "so varied and so diverse a nature as to offend modern scientific medical thinking." By failing to appreciate the "psy-chophysical unity" inherent in human life, she argued, physicians had vio-lated the principle of parsimony, the simplicity of explanation that was the ideal of every scientist.[2]

Key to Frieda's thinking during her early years as a psychiatrist was a view of the unconscious based on Groddeck's work. In a talk titled "The Body as a Means of Psychological Expression," for example, she reminded her audience of the well-known finding that fear or rage could shorten the co-agulation time of blood or increase heart rate and pulse. She noted that dozens of other physical symptoms—blushing, tremor in the hands, diar-rhea—were taken-for-granted signs of excitement or distress. "If mere ideas, fantasies, and perceptions" could produce such diverse reactions as sexual arousal, premenstrual tension, or paralysis, she continued, it made little sense to distinguish "physical" from "psychological."[3]

What makes Frieda's argument here so interesting is the way she inverted the standard logic of psychiatric thought. Most of her colleagues assumed that all mental symptoms had biological causes, identifiable in the case of "organic" conditions like brain tumor and not yet located in the so-called functional disorders like schizophrenia. Using precisely the same data, Frieda argued the opposite, suggesting that psychological causes for what appeared to be "brain disturbances" might someday be specified. She was being just as speculative here as her somatic colleagues, but in a field like psychiatry, where so little is known, theory has always been based as much on faith as on concrete data.[4]

This "collaboration between psyche and body" did not, however, require treatment using psychological means. With characteristic matter-of-factness, Frieda cited the case of a young girl with appendicitis whose inflammation seemed clearly related to unresolved fears. "Theoretically, she might lose her symptom if we analyzed it through," Frieda noted, but the inflamed appendix could not wait for interpretation; emergency surgery was the only appropri-ate treatment. "You can't overtake an express train with an ox wagon," Grod-deck's teacher Schweninger liked to say. In a sense, it didn't matter how the intervention was made. "Some kind of psychotherapy is more or less con-sciously part of every interpersonal relationship between doctor and patient," Frieda emphasized, making "even the success of an altogether organic treat-ment largely dependent on the doctor's psychological approach."[5]

Like her mainstream psychoanalytic colleagues, Frieda believed that the "choice of symptom" always carried unconscious meaning. In dermatologi-cal conditions, for example, the skin, which "touches the unfriendly outside world," becomes an "organ for expressing hostility." Paralysis of a limb could convey feelings of impotence; a coronary might signal unacknowl-edged rage. Just because the links between emotions and physical symptoms weren't always clear didn't mean that such connections didn't exist.

Even in cases of accident or epidemic disease, Frieda argued, a psycho-logical element might be present. "We have to ask why some people [in such circumstances] get cured rather quickly whereas the organism of other pa-tients seems to resist getting well." In choosing the term *organism* to describe the unified functioning of mind and body, she was again expressing her debt to Goldstein.

Throughout the 1930s, Frieda probed these issues, fascinated by patients with a "talent for expressing emotional experiences by means of the body." In a lecture to fellow analysts, she described the case of a woman who had suddenly risen from the couch exclaiming, "Oh, how my Jacob hurts!" Then, as if waking from this "dream work of the body," as Groddeck called such experiences, the patient had remarked: "I don't know what I meant in ex-pressing it that way. My left hip and thigh hurt terribly, like sciatica." Frieda suggested free associating to "Jacob." Suddenly the patient realized that like the biblical figure, who had injured his hip fighting with an angel, she too had been struggling for perfection:

> As soon as she found out about this unconscious determination for her sciatica attack and therefore for the name her unconscious chose for it by way of a contamination, the patient was suddenly altogether relieved of her symptoms. . . . This same patient [later] started growing some inches during and after her analysis even though she had already passed the age of physiological growth. We found out in the course of her analysis that hitherto she had not been allowed to grow, since in spite of her outstanding gifts, she dared not give in to her wish to be bigger—in the symbolic language of her body, to be taller than her small and mediocre parents and siblings were.

This "growth," Frieda stressed, was not simply the result of improved posture or greater self-esteem; it was "a real and measurable increase in her body's length."[6]

When Frieda called patients like this "talented," she wasn't being wry. Turning emotions into physical symptoms was an unconscious piece of artistry, something most people weren't capable of doing. Freud, following his teacher, Charcot, had acknowledged that certain patients seemed particu-larly drawn to "conversion," but he didn't see this as a "talent," the way Frieda did. Indeed, most psychoanalysts disparaged such patients as "primitive," because their "retreat" into physical symptoms made them resist psychological interpretations.

In contrast, Frieda took Ferenczi's and Groddeck's view that by "ventriloquizing," the body could convey what the mind denied. Gastrointestinal noises, for example, signified "the intestines talking about topics the organism was not ready to express by means of conscious language." Migraines communicated anger by clenching the muscles of the head. Fainting said a situation was too much to stand. Such bodily symptoms, Frieda argued, were no more "disguised" than anxieties or fears. In each case, the symbolic meaning of the symptom had to be analyzed, but physical complaints were no harder to interpret than behavioral ones.

Part of the reason most analysts didn't understand this, she continued, was that their view of the unconscious was too intellectualized. Instead of identifying with Freud's desire to control it ("where id once was, ego shall be," he had declared triumphantly), they ought to admit its powerful influence over their own minds (as he had bravely done in his early writings). Being an analyst meant having a *feeling* for the unconscious, an "inner belief" in its power, not "abstract lifeless knowledge . . . of its workings" in their patients' lives. Confronting irrationality and violence in one's own mind were terrifying, Frieda agreed, but this was the only way analysts could enter patients' experience. Even after decades of work as a therapist, she never lost her sense of wonder at the "trance-like state in which consciousness can listen with surprise to the talking of [its] deeper layers," enabling analyst and patient to hear their words as "belonging and not belonging" to their separate minds. Frieda urged analysts in private practice to take on at least a few psychotic patients, so they could experience interpretation as it was meant to be—an intense struggle for meaning, not an abstract exercise.[7]

Respecting the unconscious did not mean allowing patients to act out destructive feelings, either with the therapist or, in the case of hospitalized patients, on the ward. Like every other analyst, Frieda saw one of the primary goals of therapy as teaching patients that feelings were symbolic and didn't have to be literalized in action to be taken seriously. But in striking contrast to her classical colleagues, she insisted that enactment—via bodily symptoms or behavior—should be seen as a valid means of expression for patients too disturbed to verbalize their feelings. Frieda thought it was sadistic to punish patients for their symptoms; people who could communicate clearly to others didn't need psychiatric treatment.

She took for granted that the behavior of psychotics, in particular, would often be unintelligible to families and caregivers. But her fundamental assumption, repeated in every one of her papers, was that whatever patients "say and do makes sense to them, and part of it can be understood by us, just as a dream makes sense to the dreamer while dreamt [whether or not it is] understood by others or by the dreamer himself after awakening." The challenge of psychiatric work was to have "enough self assertion to afford the humility to take it without resentment and without any loss of security if you can't understand [a particular] communication." It wasn't the patient's job to make the therapist look good. "Let us keep in mind in our dealings with the psychotic," Frieda pointedly noted, that "it is not our prestige but the prestige of the patient which is at stake in the treatment."[8]

The therapist's primary responsibility was to offer hope. Using any means available, the therapist should seek to "awaken in [the patient] the conviction that he is not suffering from an incurable disease but from one which, in principle, he can be cured." As early as her 1922 paper on asthma, Frieda had suggested giving patients whose attacks were severe enough to require hospitalization a huge dose of chloral hydrate immediately on admission to provide "a suggestively potent psychological experience of an asthma-free period." She knew that sedatives like this would rapidly lose their effectiveness, but that was irrelevant. They "served excellently for a one-time interruption of the attack," thereby demonstrating that the doctor had treatments that worked. Frieda was even willing to ignore a patient's stated wishes if quick improvement might result. She ordered warm steam baths, for example, for a woman who arrived at the hospital in an "entirely unkempt state . . . [having] not taken a bath for years and [having] not washed herself for months."[9] She thought (correctly, as it turned out) that the patient's sudden increase in well-being might be the crucial first step in getting her to see herself as capable of improvement. Taking schizophrenic patients to concerts or to elegant country inns were means to the same end. Treating a chronic patient like a cultured person who could enjoy such diversions might remind him of who he had once been. The concerts wouldn't be any more curative than the chloral hydrate had been, but that wasn't the point; they might prove to the patient how strongly Frieda believed in his potential for recovery, which was her real aim.

Everything she had learned from Goldstein and Groddeck about patients' inherent healing capacities reinforced her own commitment to the practice of *tikkun.* By definition, the divine sparks were present in everyone; the challenge she set herself was to call them forth. Frieda was absolutely convinced that even the sickest patients had a natural resiliency that could help them heal. This "tendency toward order," as Goldstein called it, didn't need to be expressed in mystical terms; it was the same capacity that knit broken bones together or caused burned skin to peel. Although she never stressed the point as strongly as Groddeck or Jung did, Frieda clearly thought of the therapist primarily as a facilitator of the work. She couldn't heal a patient on her own, the way a surgeon could, but she could guide the patient toward the inner resources that lessened his need to stay ill. Later, in America, Frieda would embrace her friend Harry Stack Sullivan's image of the therapist as "participant observer" because it captured precisely this sense of being necessary but not sufficient. A patient couldn't recover simply because she willed him to; neither could he cure himself without help from her. Therapist and patient were collaborators, struggling toward a common goal, and it was her responsibility to convey her confidence in the ultimate success of the work. She gave this example:

> I had one patient who had been sick for five years . . . [and] did practically nothing but shout at me [for the year and a half that I had seen her] and abuse me and do it in such a noisy way that the whole hospital personnel felt they had to come to the rescue. But I was not afraid of her and thought she was not a dangerous person and said I would like to be alone with her. After this period of abuse she suddenly laughed, the first laugh I had heard in a year and a half and she said, "Well, I think it is enough now." The first thing she did was to say she was going to take a bath, go get some money and get some new clothes. This happened four years ago and she gets along all right. She recently said to me, "If you give a paper on schizophrenia, I wish you would use our experience."[10]

Because her fundamental loyalty was to the patient, not the method, Frieda departed whenever necessary from the standard rules of psychoanalytic technique. Here again, she was modeling herself on Goldstein and Groddeck, both of whom insisted that true physicians constantly individualized their approach. Every patient came to treatment with unique needs; to reduce him to a disease entity was an insult to his humanity and a sign of the doctor's lack of imagination. Treating a psychiatric illness wasn't like performing an appendectomy, and the physician's desire for certainty and routine couldn't be allowed to take precedence over the patient's needs.

By insisting that the right technique was the one that worked and not necessarily the one in the textbook, Frieda was allying herself with the viewpoint forcefully articulated by the Hungarian analyst Sándor Ferenczi. For decades, Ferenczi had been Freud's closest colleague, the one who joined him on the working vacations during which many of the key ideas of psychoanalysis were developed. The two men exchanged more than a thousand letters over a twenty-five-year period, and Freud had called Ferenczi a "master of analysis." Universally regarded as the most brilliant clinician of the early psychoanalytic movement, Ferenczi succeeded in treating the most difficult cases. However, by the early 1920s, he had become convinced that "analysis is not an instrument that functions independently of the person who uses it," and increasingly focused attention on the analyst's contribution to the therapeutic relationship. Ferenczi took on a large number of psychotic patients and introduced a series of technical modifications designed to create a safe, supportive environment in which they could reenact and work through their earliest traumas.[11]

Freud found all of this highly disturbing. He wanted the psychoanalytic context to be detached and scientific, like a laboratory or an operating room, with the analyst maintaining a "neutral" attitude. Ferenczi's active involvement with patients reminded him of Breuer's relationship with Anna O. or Jung's with Sabina Spielrein—the kinds of intense, eroticized transferences that had frightened Freud into developing a more controlled way of working. He was also deeply distressed by Ferenczi's claim that calling a patient "unanalyzable" was itself retraumatizing, and that failures were due to the therapist's countertransference difficulties, not the patient's resistance.

Frieda, on the other hand, deeply admired Ferenczi's willingness to do anything to help his patients. His student Clara Thompson later wrote: "Possessed of a genuine sympathy for all human suffering, [Ferenczi] approached each new case with an enthusiastic belief in his ability to help and in the worthwhileness of the patient. His efforts were tireless and his patience inexhaustible. He was never willing to admit that some mental diseases were incurable, but always said, 'Perhaps it is simply that we have not yet discovered the right method.'"[12] Similarly convinced that the onus was always on the analyst, Frieda welcomed Ferenczi's flexibility. She found many of his specific technical modifications extremely useful, especially his reliance on extended sessions to break through the defenses of very withdrawn patients, and his imitations of bodily movements as a way of understanding memories that couldn't be spoken. Most of all, she agreed with Ferenczi that admitting one's own mistakes could help the analyst to create a crucial contrast between therapy and the patient's past traumatic relationships.

In addition to poring over Ferenczi's clinical papers, Frieda spent time with him when he came to Groddeck's clinic for his frequent "therapeutic vacations." (So many of Ferenczi's colleagues emulated his example that Baden-Baden often had as many analysts in the summer as Wellfleet, on

Cape Cod, does today.) In 1927, when Ferenczi returned from lecturing in America, he spent an extended period with Groddeck, and Frieda came down from Heidelberg once a week for informal supervisory sessions. In a letter to Freud, Ferenczi called her "an astute and very analytically gifted person," quite a compliment from the man considered one of the psychoanalytic movement's greatest clinicians.[13]

Part of what linked Frieda so strongly to Ferenczi and Groddeck was her "respect for and belief in the patient." Rejecting the "pose of infallibility" that Freud had adopted to keep the patient's pathology at a distance, Frieda willingly admitted her own limitations. This allowed her to appreciate patients as talented people despite their difficulties, rather than dismissing them as "the rabble," as Freud had done.[14]

However, Ferenczi's admission that his own negative countertransference feelings could be a factor in the patient's resistance also encouraged Frieda's lifelong tendency to blame herself when things went wrong in her relationships. Up to a point, this was helpful because it protected patients from having to bear the burden of her inadequacies. But taken too far, this attitude of holding the doctor responsible for every treatment failure threatened to fill psychiatrists with so much guilt they became useless to their patients. Frieda was well aware of this danger; she constantly struggled to follow Ferenczi's lead and use countertransference feelings as a subtle source of information rather than a means of self-flagellation.

She was encouraged by Ferenczi's insistence that therapy with psychotics required modifying standard analytic methods. Although her detractors have always portrayed Frieda's "deviations" as extreme, she herself downplayed the differences, saying that she simply wanted to "change some accents in our doctrine of psychoanalytic technique in order to put more stress on certain parts which have not been emphasized enough, and to take not quite so seriously others."[15] Never wanting to be seen as a heretic in the psychoanalytic movement, she framed her ideas carefully to avoid being cast out like Adler or Jung.

Insisting that she never departed from the core axioms of Freud's approach—analyzing the unconscious, tracing symptoms to childhood conflicts, and emphasizing transference and resistance—Frieda identified herself with the mainstream whenever she could.[16] Her enthusiasm for techniques like free association remained undiminished. "Did you ever realize," she would often ask students, "what an ingenious deed of Freud's it was to make the demand to tell everything that comes into your mind? Do you realize what enormous courage it took to ask that from people who live within our culture which is so full of suppression and repression, and where nearly everybody lives under the continual strain of not telling undisguised what comes into his mind from fear of getting hostile reactions from his surroundings?" Later, in the wonderfully evocative phrasings of her early years as a speaker of English, Frieda would describe the "unbounded candidness" required of the patient—his need to talk "choicelessly" without regard for the analyst's reactions. Unlike most of her colleagues, who regarded free association more as a ritual than a source of amazement, Frieda urged students to appreciate the "intense relief" that this "audacious request" could offer to patients. She never minimized the extent to which psychotics found the unconscious terrifying, but insisted it was "the real source of our mind's productiveness." (At such moments, she sounded a lot like Groddeck or Jung, but she never pointed this out, lest she suffer the same "excommunication" they had experienced.)[17]

Whatever her critics might claim, Frieda saw many of her technical modifications as designed to foster precisely that merged state Freud considered crucial to analytic work. She strongly advised against taking notes, for example, because it interfered with the "free-floating attention" necessary to enter the patient's stream of consciousness. For the same reason, she opposed the rule that interpretations be given only in the last few minutes of a session. "Not talking to [the patient] on principle at a point where you feel you have to tell him something that is important is not advisable because it means that you have to make constant efforts to keep it in mind until the end of the hour and are not free to listen in a relaxed way to his further associations." If she had trouble understanding a patient, Frieda would follow Ferenczi's suggestion and "duplicate, actually or in imagination" his bodily movements. She often cited this example to show how useful such a technique could be:

A patient told me repeatedly that he wondered about a funny capacity he enjoyed: he was able to cross his legs not only once as we all do but twice, which he showed to me. I did not understand this physical expression until I tried to imitate it without succeeding but with the result that I got the impression that a person who is able to do that and to enjoy it may feel an intense love for himself. It just felt to me as if he wanted very eagerly to twice embrace himself. As soon as I talked to him about this suggestion he responded quickly saying: "Oh yes, I do love myself. One of my most beloved daydreams is to be able to [impregnate] myself. As a child, I tried again and again to put my own penis into my mouth, and today I still wish I could." Then he continued telling me about his disgust for women and started talking about his homosexuality as a consequence of his intense self-love, thus developing contents that were quite decisive for the further development of his treatment.[18]

Later, Joanne Greenberg would hail Frieda's talent as a "great natural actress," able "to show subtle gradations of approval or disapproval without committing herself to the force of a word."[19]

Transcending all details of method, however, was this fundamental rule: "to listen to whatever patients [say] without any moral valuation whatsoever." The only value in psychoanalysis, Frieda insisted, was "health and freedom," and it was the therapist's responsibility to help the patient "build up moral standards of his own independent of [those of] his analyst." This, she argued, was the real meaning of Freud's "analytic neutrality," the essential ingredient of effective treatment.[20]

Like every other analyst, Frieda saw transference as key to the process. She took the standard view that the sex of the analyst made little difference; transference was so automatic that patients simply projected whatever characteristics their therapists happened not to have. Similarly, she saw no barriers in a patient's age. She cited with obvious pleasure the example of a sixty-year-old woman whose intense transference had finally allowed her "to enjoy intercourse with her husband in the 30th year of their married life."[21]

However, from her earliest days as an analyst, Frieda saw oedipal issues as relatively unimportant, especially for the psychotic patients with whom she increasingly chose to work. This led her to an overall view of transference far broader than Freud's. Patients reenacted their conflicts in the treatment, but since these often had more to do with basic issues of trust than with sexuality, the transference took on added significance. "The compulsive repetition of ancient patterns of interpersonal relatedness," Frieda wrote, "deprives a person of the freedom to live and move about in the world of psychological reality, which should be his. . . . The transference experience, as the medium for regaining this freedom, becomes, if anything, even more important than it has always appeared."[22]

Freud's fundamental error, she argued, had been to see psychotic patients as incapable of developing a strong enough relationship with the therapist for treatment to succeed. If anything, she found such patients *more* likely to project their feelings than neurotics, making the transference more intense than Freud had described. In a key theoretical move for which she is never credited, Frieda was reconceiving the whole nature of the therapeutic relationship, claiming that Freud's oedipally based view not only failed to fit psychotic patients but was inadequate to capture the primitive nature of *every* analytic relationship.[23]

Privately, Frieda saw Freud's view as based less on his clinical experience than on his fear of losing control. She thought that was why he avoided treating schizophrenic patients and preferred short "didactic" analyses with students.[24] Yet she never rebutted him directly, as her colleague Karen Horney, for example, increasingly did. Rather, Frieda set about proposing a new set of rules that better suited the treatment process with psychotic patients. In a classic paper, "Transference Problems in Schizophrenics," she summarized the technique she had found most effective:

> The patient is asked neither to lie down nor to give free associations; both requests make no sense to [psychotics]. He should feel free to sit, lie on the floor, walk around, use any available chair, lie or sit on the couch. . . . If the patient feels that an hour of mutual friendly silence serves his purpose, he is welcome to remain silent. . . . Nothing matters except that the analyst permit the patient to feel comfortable and secure enough to give up his defensive narcissistic isolation and to use the physician for resuming contact with the world.[25]

The analyst's insecurities and fears, in other words, couldn't be allowed to sabotage the process. Psychotic patients had suffered long enough from the stigma of being "unanalyzable" because their therapists were too frightened to work with them.

More traditional analytic colleagues were infuriated by Frieda's claim that *their* problems, not the patient's, were what prevented effective work with those who were seriously disturbed. "If the schizophrenic's reactions are more stormy and seemingly unpredictable than those of the neurotic," she wrote, "I believe it to be due to the inevitable errors in the analyst's approach to the schizophrenic, of which he himself may be unaware, rather than to the unreliability of the patient's emotional response." She thought analysts ought to be able to tolerate these outbursts the way they would any transference reaction. Compulsively attempting to interpret a psychotic patient's every utterance, action, and feeling was simply another way to protect the therapist from the anguish of the work. "The psychoanalyst's job," Frieda reminded colleagues, quoting Freud, "is to help the patient, not to demonstrate how clever the doctor is."[26]

Insisting that "the less fear patients sense in the therapist, the less dangerous they are," she urged her colleagues to forge ahead, worry less about technical details, and focus on genuinely accepting the "fellow sufferer" who was appealing for their help. Successful work with psychotic patients depended less on abstract interpretation than on "sympathetic understanding and skillful handling" of the therapeutic relationship:

> The schizophrenic's emotional reactions toward the analyst have to be met with extreme care and caution. The love which the sensitive schizophrenic feels as he first emerges and his cautious acceptance of the analyst's warmth of interest are really most delicate and tender things. If the analyst deals unadroitly with the transference reactions of a psychoneurotic, it is bad enough, though as a rule not irreparable; but if he fails with a schizophrenic in meeting positive feeling by pointing it out, for instance, before the patient indicates that he is ready to discuss it, he may easily freeze to death what has just begun to grow and so destroy any further possibility of therapy.[27]

A fearless therapist was not, however, sufficient to gain a patient's trust and might even make him more suspicious. Frieda cited the case of a man she had seen at home in the evenings, after her secretary had left for the day. He had become more and more agitated at each session, until finally screaming one night: "Don't you realize I could knock you down and hurt you?" Frieda tried to reassure him that she wasn't frightened. In subsequent weeks, however, he turned openly assaultive—kicking her door and threatening to strike her. Frieda was forced to move their sessions to a seclusion room at the hospital. Only months later did she realize her error: instead of reassuring him that *she* wasn't afraid, she should have focused on how frightened *he* had been. Overwhelmed with being alone with her at night, he had been forced to resort to desperate measures. "Had I caught on immediately to the patient's anxiety," Frieda admitted, "he might have been spared the necessity of transforming it into overt psychotic symptomatology."[28]

Even stuporous patients, who appeared completely indifferent to everyone, were often terrified of their own potential violence. They ceased interacting, sometimes to the point of remaining motionless, as a crude, last-ditch attempt to keep themselves from hurting others. This extreme solution—preventing any part of the body from moving, to make sure the arms didn't strike out—showed the depth of the patient's terror, not his inaccessibility.

Just because a patient had no choice but to act out his symptoms didn't mean the therapist couldn't respond with words. A woman Frieda treated in the hospital urinated on the chair she knew Frieda would use when she arrived on the ward. Frieda told her "in no uncertain terms" how disgusted she was. This frankness later helped the patient to admit that her act had been "a planned expression of resentment," a way to punish her doctors for what she experienced as "excessive therapeutic pressure."[29]

Frieda called such thinking "prelogical," highlighting its similarities to other forms of "primitive" expression. "Magical thinking," she argued, is something we can all understand—our dreams are filled with it, and many of us cling to rituals we know to be absurd. "If you go through a ward and see [psychotic patients] sitting there doing nothing, you think: 'How can they stand it?' But they do not feel they are doing nothing, they are doing magical thinking. They believe what they think will have the connotation of actual happenings, like the primitive who, in thinking of shooting an arrow at the picture of an enemy, thinks that the enemy will die."[30] This overinvestment of meaning was part of why Frieda avoided interpretation with psychotic patients: they didn't need their behavior to be imbued with any greater significance. It mattered less, she argued, whether the therapist understood any particular action ("sometimes we have the good luck to understand them, sometimes not"), so long as he made clear that the behavior had meaning. Conversations with recovered patients also taught her that "no matter how disturbed the patient seems to be, he remembers everything that happened while he was sick," suggesting that interpretations could be made at a later point, when they might prove more useful.[31]

Frieda empathized with colleagues who thought psychosis had a biological cause. States like catatonia, for example, which prevented all speech or movement (sometimes even defecation) resembled Parkinson's disease or stroke far more than neurosis. She was as impressed by the subtleties of brain function as were her somatic colleagues—if anything, she was more impressed, given her years with Goldstein—but she was even more impressed by the powers of mind. So long as the causes of mental illness remained unknown, any approach that might reach the patient had to be tried. She cited the example of a woman who immediately deteriorated following minor scheduling modifications. "If I had to change an hour and the nurse failed to tell her," Frieda reported, "she would go into complete catatonic stupor." In this particular case, the psychic cause—the woman's terror at abandonment—happened to be especially clear; most cases weren't this obvious. But in medicine, even one instance counts as evidence, and rare events can still be instructive.

Frieda never assumed that every patient would recover, especially if the illness had reached the chronic stage. She was as pessimistic about catatonics as any other psychiatrist, once remarking: "It really looks like a dead person if it weren't for the fact that the eyes move about." But she took even the subtlest signs of improvement seriously, and thought it was presumptuous for anyone to claim he could tell in advance which patients would respond to a given treatment and which wouldn't. The day she figured out that changes in scheduling were what provoked stupor in that woman, she went to the ward, asked, "Didn't they tell you I would see you later today?" and with nurses and attendants gaping beside her, watched the stupor dissipate, like morning mist.[32]

"Psychotherapy with schizophrenics," Frieda acknowledged, "is hard and exacting work for both patients and therapists." Each psychiatrist had to find his own way to manage the stress. "I used to have strong feelings about technical details such as seeing patients only in the office, walking around with them, seeing them for non-scheduled interviews . . . now I consider [these details] unimportant," she said.[33] What was important was creating trust. Almost anything a patient might do during a session, short of actual violence, was tolerable so long as it facilitated the relationship. This was less heroic than it may sound. We all put up with repulsive or frightening behavior from people who are close to us; the only unusual thing about Frieda was that she let psychotic patients matter that much to her.

4

The Woman and the Jew

*What matters for the Jew is not his credo, nor his declared adher-
ence to an idea or a movement, but that he absorb his own truth,
that he live it, that he purify himself from the dross of foreign rule,
and that he find his way from division to unity.*[1]

During her years in Germany, Frieda's psychiatric work was an intrinsic
part of her commitment to Judaism. She talked of "serving people through
psychotherapy," clearly conceiving of treatment as a form of *tzedakah* (giving). She saw relationships with patients as embodying the respectful equal-
ity her friend Martin Buber was writing about in *I and Thou.* She constantly
sought ways to deepen her practice—both professional and religious—and
make it more personally meaningful and less ritualized.

Tzedakah had always been a crucial part of Jewish tradition, especially for
women. Giving to others in any form—charity, good works, community service—was seen as a means to social justice, as well as a way to help those
less fortunate. Performed correctly, *tzedakah* taught useful lessons to the
giver and caused the recipient no shame. It was a *mitzvah,* a blessing, for
each of them. Frieda's childhood was replete with examples of the joy of
selfless giving: her grandparents, Amalie and Jacob Simon, raising a boy or-
phaned in a pogrom alongside their own ten children; Adolf giving the shoes
still warm from his feet to the barefoot beggar and tirelessly working to help
Russian immigrants; George Marx supporting the Reichmann family (and financing most of Frieda's education). During World War I, Klara and her

women's group spent hundreds of hours aiding needy soldiers, and for years before that, she had taken Anna to hospitals and old-age homes on Sunday afternoons to play violin for shut-ins. Frieda's temporarily adopting the daughter of her morphine addict friend had been just one more example of the helpfulness her family had always considered fundamental to its religious and social values.

And although very few of the Jews who pursued academic or professional careers at the turn of the century were Orthodox, Frieda remained strictly observant despite the difficulties. She kept kosher throughout medical school and residency (riding home on the streetcar for most meals, bringing food to the hospital during long shifts), and refused to work on Shabbat in the army hospital, Goldstein's clinic, or Weisser Hirsch. Whether this adherence to Orthodox practice sprang from deep feeling or the desire to remain obedient to family traditions isn't clear. Frieda was intensely committed to being a "good daughter," and this was an obvious way of proving that working in the secular world hadn't compromised her values.[2]

But although she never hid her observance of Orthodox ritual from colleagues or patients, these practices in and of themselves were separate from her psychoanalytic work. In the early 1920s, however, Frieda brought these two strands of her life together in a utopian experiment others were to dub "the torahpeuticum."

Her first attempt to blend psychotherapy and Judaism took place at Weisser Hirsch. Having quickly become bored treating only patients she called, with fond frustration, "the wealthy fools," Frieda developed a scheme. Through her work in a local Zionist group, she had met a number of young people in the Dresden area who wanted therapy but couldn't pay for private treatment. She told her Weisser Hirsch patients that instead of giving her a small tip after each appointment (the way they did with the masseur or the woodcutter), they should subsidize sessions for these young Zionists. "I don't need a tip from you," she told her wealthy patients, "but not because I don't want money. I want plenty. I want more than you want to give me. Because there are lots of people who are just as sick as you were before you came and who cannot afford to come to Weisser Hirsch. In my free time I want to help them. So no gifts, and no little tips. But big tips are welcome, so I can do that work."[3]

Frieda put out the word, and members of the Blau Weiss—a Zionist youth group named for the colors of the Jewish flag—started showing up for therapy. She found them places to sleep near the sanitarium. She let them spend the day in her living quarters while she was off at work, and saved her leftovers from the previous day's meals so they wouldn't have to buy food. She imposed only one rule: by the time she returned from the office, everyone had to be out of her rooms, with things left in perfect condition. After a brief break for dinner, she scheduled sessions with these young people in the evenings. She charged no fee, asking only that they try to send her small amounts of money after they were well so she could treat others. As always, Frieda's energy seemed inexhaustible. She later told friends: "This meant a working day of eight hours for the hospital, and then eight hours with these people. Also, I wrote some papers. And then, of course, I had the child [of her friend, the addict]. And a vivid correspondence with the mother of the child and with her other relatives."[4]

For close to four years, this sanitarium within a sanitarium functioned as a model community, embodying the collective values of the Zionist movement. Patients helped each other in whatever ways they could: one would give Hebrew lessons, and another would mend his socks in return. "It was a perfect community with very good therapeutic results," Frieda told friends with pride, decades later. Even older members of the movement in Dresden started showing up for therapy. "I acted as a very nice *Jüdische* Mama for the whole crowd," Frieda laughed. She was like a Jewish Robin Hood, taking money from Weisser Hirsch patients and her own wealthy relatives and using it to help young activists and others who shared her commitment to advancing Jewish causes.

Eventually Schultz figured out what was going on, but like every other employer Frieda was ever to have, he didn't want to lose her. He told her she could see the Zionists in the office during the day along with her regular patients so she could have a little privacy in the evenings. (This was more than a gesture. Weisser Hirsch was a very elite place.) No one ever confused the two groups. "If somebody appeared at Weisser Hirsch who wasn't adequately dressed up," Frieda recalled with a smile, "somebody would come up to him and say: 'Oh, are you looking for Dr. Reichmann? You will find her over there.'"[5]

By 1924, however, she had had enough. It wasn't just the sixteen-hour days. After four years, she was feeling more and more frustrated by spending so much energy treating patients she cared little about, with not enough time left for those who really mattered.[6] So, imbued with the same independent spirit that fueled the ambitions of countless male psychiatrists of the period, Frieda decided to open her own sanitarium. She moved to Heidelberg, perhaps to be near Goldstein in Frankfurt, or because it was only a few miles from Karlsruhe, her birthplace. Like Hannah Arendt, who moved there the same year, Frieda was no doubt also "attracted by the cosmopolitan and liberal Heidelberg spirit known throughout Germany to be tolerant of innovation and experiment."[7]

Majestically set on both banks of the Neckar River, embraced by mountains, forests, and the glorious ruins of its sixteenth-century castle, Heidelberg ("the object of so many wanderings") was a real-life fairy tale. It was where Goethe fell in love and dueling became an art form, where Romberg set his operetta *The Student Prince* and Turner painted his most luminous landscapes. A timeless city, seeming to transcend any limit, it was home to Heidelberg Man half a million years ago, and an ancient funicular railway, transporting visitors a towering two thousand feet above the valley. Birthplace of the romantic movement and the German university, Heidelberg epitomized the beauty and culture Frieda loved, and the wistful longing that began increasingly to envelop her.

She bought a historic house in Neuenheim, an elegant residential area, on a street set high above the Philosopher's Walk, the city's panoramic vista. At various times a girls' boarding school, a research institute, and the headquarters of a battalion commander, the house had been known since the turn of the century as the Villa Cornelia. It sat grandly on a corner two blocks from the Mönchhofplatz with views of the castle from the upper windows, conveniently near a tram line but in a quiet area perfectly suited to Frieda's goal of creating a therapeutic community in the middle of an upper-middle-class neighborhood.[8]

She borrowed just enough money from Uncle George and her other wealthy relatives to make a down payment on the house. Schultz had paid Frieda well at Weisser Hirsch, but she had little salary left, partly because she was always giving money away and partly because the astronomical inflation of the early 1920s made it impossible to save anything. ("If you got paid on Monday," Frieda told incredulous American friends years later, "by Saturday the money was worthless. You had to take an hour off from work on Monday to spend it.")[9] The amount she borrowed wasn't enough to furnish the fifteen-room house, so the ever-pragmatic Frieda made a deal with Herr Pirsch, the previous owner, promising to pay him later if he would leave some of the furniture. She asked all her friends and relatives to give her whatever chairs, rugs, tablecloths, and silverware they could spare, and when she left Weisser Hirsch—"where I was a great success and considered a wonderful girl, after all, only an angel would adopt a child"—she told patients who wanted to give her farewell gifts to purchase the furniture from her rooms there and ship it to Heidelberg.[10]

Although she probably never thought of it in these terms, Frieda was symbolically acquiring a dowry to start her new life. It had long been the practice in German culture for a woman's family to provide all the linens, tableware, and furniture she needed to create a home. The custom in Judaism was for wealthy relatives to do this if the parents could not. Frieda certainly didn't announce her move to Heidelberg as an alternative to marriage, but buying a huge, expensive house on her own clearly carried this meaning, at least implicitly, cementing her bond to an independent existence.[11]

Beyond her desire to treat needy Jewish patients, Frieda's decision to open a sanitarium stemmed from her own powerful experiences in psychoanalysis. She had undertaken a personal analysis because Freud said transference could be understood only through direct experience. In addition to helping her learn about analysis firsthand, her work with Wittenberg had pushed Frieda toward a more mature appreciation of her talents. She had created a hundred-bed hospital for brain-injured soldiers practically on her own, published important papers with Goldstein, helped dozens of patients at Weisser Hirsch, and received an appointment as a university *Privatdozent* (an instructor position rarely awarded to women), yet she still had remarkably little sense of her efficacy as a person. "I was already kind of a somebody, but it didn't register because Mama was so great," she recalled without embarrassment forty years later. When Wittenberg remarked to her one day, "You know, you are a really productive and creative person," Frieda was stunned. "I thought I would fall down off the couch," she recalled, shaking her head. "I had never, never, never, never thought of myself in those terms."[12]

Analysis also forced Frieda to confront the significance of her parents' deafness and their strikingly different ways of responding to life's limitations. Klara, privately humiliated by even the hint of impairment or illness, put up a good front, as she did with every other challenge. For years, she simply denied her growing deafness; when it finally became obvious to everyone, she treated it with the good humor that had always been her saving grace. Living well into her eighties, deaf to an appreciable extent for fifty of those years, Klara just asked people to shout, or to write down what they wanted; if she still couldn't understand, she ignored them.

Adolf, far more sensitive and worried about people's opinions of him, agonized over the effect such an obvious hereditary taint might have on his daughters' marriage prospects. (Klara characteristically dismissed such concerns, saying that if the girls wanted husbands, they would have them.) Turn-of-the-century hearing aids were unwieldy, cumbersome devices, with dangling wires and strange crackles and whines. Adolf found them acutely embarrassing, but when he himself started to become deaf in his late fifties, he was forced to rely on them. His job as personnel director required him to lis-

ten carefully to people for hours each day, so he couldn't simply deny his difficulties. Desperately trying one contraption after another, his desk became so
cluttered with reinforcing telephones and extra enunciators "it looked like a
machine house." Still, he couldn't hear. Once a charming, outgoing person, he
became more and more isolated, easily hurt by imagined slights from friends
and colleagues. "He developed a little paranoid system around his deafness
and was terribly miserable," Frieda later remarked. "He had no reason really.
They all loved him. He was the kind of person everybody loved."[13]

Adolf apparently did not see things that way. On the morning of September
7, 1924, a Sunday, he went, as usual, to the bank. Like many other Orthodox
men, Adolf routinely worked on Sundays, since Saturday was Shabbat. His office was just a few steps above the first floor, not quite at mezzanine level. For
some reason, he went into the elevator, something he rarely had occasion to
do. There was an accident, witnessed by no one, and Adolf was found dead at
the bottom of the shaft. "There was no reason on God's earth that he should
have been in that elevator," Frieda was still telling friends decades later. Struggling to work through her feelings in analysis, she decided her father's death
had been an unconscious suicide. Sixty-five years old, almost completely
deaf, about to be forcibly retired from his job, it wasn't hard to imagine that he
had contributed in some way to the accident. Told that her husband's body had
been found without the required *arba kanfos,* Klara was said to have remarked
bitterly: "Didn't I predict it would happen?"[14]

Adolf's death (and his failure to wear the protective, ritual garment) had a
powerful, superstitious effect on the Reichmann family, vividly illustrating
how even highly cultured, educated people could harbor primitive fears of
punishment by God. For years afterward, none of the girls could ride in self-
service elevators, and for most of her life, Frieda got a migraine on her father's birthday. Adolf himself had suffered from migraines, but this was more
than simple identification. As Frieda was to note in a paper she herself published on the subject ten years after the "accident":

> Patients with migraine suffer from unresolved ambivalence; they cannot
> stand to be aware of their hostility against beloved persons. . . . [They]
> come from very cultured and somewhat conventional old families with a
> particularly strong solidarity within the family and a highly developed
> family pride. Within groups like these, aggression against one another is,
> as we know, extremely taboo. If one member of these families should
> dare to express hostility against another, he would be punished by exclu-
> sion, that is to say, by losing the protection of his family background,
> which means being abandoned in the struggle of life.[15]

Growing up in precisely such a family, with a father affectionately nick-named "the little dumbbell," migraines were an obvious way for Frieda to express her unconscious rage at an act as stupid as falling from an elevator. Her fear of "being abandoned in the struggle of life" would only intensify as she faced conflicts of her own.

Years later, Frieda would describe her surprise at Americans' refusal to believe in fate. They seemed to lack any sense of the tragic, any appreciation for how events not of their own making could radically reshape the trajectory of a life. But even Americans acknowledged their powerlessness over death. Clearly thinking of her own feelings about Adolf, Frieda said that one of the main reasons people blamed themselves when someone close to them died was that it gave them the illusion of more control. "If you can feel guilty, then you have had something to do with it. . . . If only you had done this or that . . . then he wouldn't have died. It takes care a little of this terrible narcissistic frustration that the Lord does it, whether you want it or not."[16] Having spent her whole life feeling responsible for other people's happiness, Frieda must have felt that letting her father die in so tragic a way was an unforgivable failure on her part.

A year after Adolf's death, in what one analyst has aptly termed "manic flight," Frieda began an affair with Erich Fromm.[17] Anna had been wed a scant four months after the accident, and Frieda may have been feeling some jealousy—carefully buried, of course—toward her youngest sister. She was also struggling to cope with a suddenly intensified relationship with Klara, the kind of overwhelming bond Adolf's presence had always shielded her from. And Frieda was thirty-six years old. Changing mores of the postwar period notwithstanding, she was dangerously close to passing marriageable age and becoming a permanent embarrassment to her family. Frieda may have been a modern, professional woman, but as historian Marion Kaplan reminds us, marriage had deep "symbolic and religious meaning, [as] one of the few crucial turning points where one affirmed or rejected one's group affiliation."[18]

Erich was the perfect choice for Frieda. He was charming and warm like Adolf, but brilliant, almost flashy, in ways her father never could have been. Erich also needed to be taken care of, a quality Frieda always found reassuring (in other people).

They met through Frieda's childhood friend Golde Ginsburg, who had been involved with Erich in the early 1920s. (She later went on to marry his friend, Leo Löwenthal.) Erich had studied in Heidelberg and had many ties there, and some of his closest friends were eager participants in Frieda's new sanitarium project. Yet even with all these overlapping friendships, no story survives of Frieda's and Erich's meeting. Despite the dozens of friends and colleagues they shared for the next thirty years, none ever learned anything about the marriage. One biographer claims to have seen a photograph of Frieda and Erich together in Italy; no photograph of the two of them, there or anywhere else, can now be located. "They were both very private people," say all their friends. But privacy is one thing; this is more like obliteration. And its reasons remain mysterious.

Erich was the adored only child of Naphtali and Rosa Krause Fromm, who both came from highly distinguished rabbinical families. Born in 1900 in Frankfurt—"the most famous of all Jewish communities in Germany"— Erich, like Frieda, grew up strictly Orthodox. His mother, he later said, was overprotective, his father distant, and he himself "an unbearable, neurotic child."[19] Erich was given an intense religious education from noted scholars and friends of the family, and groomed from an early age to carry on family tradition and become a scholar of the Talmud. In adolescence, however, he deviated slightly from this script by becoming a devotee of Rabbi Nehemiah Nobel, a brilliant, charismatic teacher who combined classical religious instruction with mysticism, philosophy, socialism, and psychoanalysis. Erich was one of a number of talented young men in Nobel's circle, a group that included Martin Buber, Franz Rosenzweig, Ernst Simon, and Löwenthal.[20]

After receiving his Ph.D. in sociology from the University of Heidelberg (in either 1922 or 1925; Fromm was so private a man biographers differ even on such basic facts), he joined Buber, Gershom Scholem, and others in the Freies Jüdisches Lehrhaus (Free Jewish Study House), the pioneering center for adult education Rosenzweig had founded in Frankfurt. Erich and several others in this group later went on to work together at the Institute of Social Research, one of the preeminent intellectual institutions in Germany, where he served as head of the section on social psychology.[21]

Fromm was a complex, highly reserved man, who all his life would be perceived in strikingly different ways by different people. The Reichmanns never considered him good enough for Frieda. One of her cousins later remarked disdainfully: "We thought his Zionism was phony, his religiosity was phony, his relationship to her was phony. He was just the opposite of what in my family was considered genuine." The Reichmanns especially ridiculed Erich's ecstatic style of praying, which they, equally Orthodox, considered exaggerated. (Perhaps he was taking his name too literally; *Fromm* means pious. Gershom Scholem said students in their circle jokingly used to pray: "Let me be like Erich Fromm, that I may to heaven come.")[22] Variously described by colleagues as "very authoritarian beneath his gentle surface," "a man of great pretensions and insufferable arrogance," "autocratic, shy, and brilliant," "exceptionally sincere," and a "power-driven prima donna," Fromm was especially attracted to older women. "A dependent prince who needed to be catered to," he seems to have gone directly from being his mother's darling into a series of relationships with women much his senior who doted on him. He knew precisely how to charm them, with an intense warmth and empathy that made them feel desirable and wanted.[23]

Erich was originally Frieda's patient, a fact known to every one of their students, friends, and colleagues but, by unspoken agreement, never discussed by anyone.[24] He was a handsome, cultured graduate student in his early twenties when they met; she was a dowdy thirty-six-year old with a decade of experience as a psychiatrist. They had an affair during the analysis, ended the treatment because of it, and later married to preserve appearances. Outwardly, Frieda was strikingly cavalier about all of this, later joking with friends: "I began to analyze him and then we fell in love. We stopped the analysis. That much sense we had!" Her inner feelings, however, were a lot more complicated.[25]

Psychoanalysis creates one of the most intense and ambiguous forms of relationship imaginable, and when it is literalized in actual sex, its fragile container explodes, usually in ways quite destructive for the patient. Of course, things were a lot looser in the analytic world of the 1920s, where people were constantly having affairs with their patients or marrying them.[26] We can't apply our own rigid rules to that world any more than we can call every relationship between a professor and student "sexual harassment." Besides, Frieda was never much of a classical analyst. Being naturally opaque, she didn't need a contrived neutrality for protection. Part of what let her work with psychotics was this inherent reserve, a barrier practically impervious even to extreme intrusions. Yet at a deeper level, she constantly blurred the boundaries of relationship. Erich may have been the only patient she actually had sex with or married, but throughout her adult life, Frieda routinely saw relatives for consultations, and her closest friends were all people she had treated at some point.[27]

Erich's specific means of seducing his analyst from the couch are best left to imagination, but he doesn't seem to have suffered many ill effects from the experience, except, of course, an increased narcissism. Accustomed to charming his mother and her friends, he may simply have plucked the matronly Frieda like a piece of ripe fruit. After years of embarrassment at Adolf's supposed intellectual weakness, she may have been too enthralled by Erich's showy brilliance to resist. The subjects he studied—philosophy, Hasidism, Marxist theory—were far more abstract and complicated than the medicine she had mastered. Perhaps Frieda was just swept away by finding a man who seemed so smart.

Later, she would make fun of Erich for having only a Ph.D. (real analysts had M.D.s), but she always admired his flair, his way with ideas. Too much the dutiful daughter to allow herself much intellectual boldness, Frieda was drawn to people who could challenge her. The Frieda who stood in awe of Groddeck's "wild analysis," who dissolved distinctions, who tried techniques no one else dared—that Frieda loved Erich's fondness for grand theory and his passionate engagement with the broad questions of human existence. Ultimately Erich turned out to be more glib than Frieda's other idols, but she respected his work, spoke of it with admiration, and often cited it in her own papers.[28] Erich, on the other hand, mentioned Frieda only once or twice in the hundreds of works he later published; his friends joked that his first book, *Escape from Freedom,* was really called "Escape from Frieda."

Aside from work, deep personal similarities in Frieda's and Erich's backgrounds drew them together. Both had fathers who worked as modest merchants but were unhappy in business and longed for lives of study, like their older relatives. Both had extremely powerful mothers who doted on them. Both came from strictly Orthodox homes where involvement in the Jewish community was highly valued. And both were struggling to find ways of holding on to the cherished Jewish traditions of their childhoods in the face of skepticism from their largely assimilationist colleagues. The ten-year difference in age and professional experience that separated Frieda and Erich when they met was nothing compared to the powerful bonds that joined them.

No one knew about their affair while it was taking place. People just assumed Erich was another of the young Jews Frieda was treating. (He seems to have visited her on various occasions at Weisser Hirsch, and their involvement may have started there.) His Talmud teacher talked fondly to her about "little Erich," suspecting nothing. Later it seemed natural that Frieda should have been seduced by his charms; everybody was a little in love with Erich: his female friends, Frieda's "adopted daughter," even her housekeeper in Heidelberg.[29]

But it wasn't shared ideas or charm that led Frieda and Erich to marry; it was middle-class propriety and the dictates of Orthodox Judaism. Having begun an affair, for whatever reason, they had to deal with the consequences. Yet although they hadn't set out to wed (Erich, always a ladies man, probably thought he was just having another fling), the arrangement benefited them both, at least initially: Erich got someone to dote on him, and Frieda got the political advantages of being a married woman.

The wedding took place in 1926, on May 14, at Klara's home in Königsberg.[30] Officiating was Julius Jacobowitz, the assistant rabbi at Adass Jisroel,
the Orthodox synagogue where the Reichmanns had worshipped for three
decades. Erich's parents were present, along with Klara; Adolf had died a
year and a half earlier. In a gesture of loyalty to her parents (or an unconscious expiation of guilt for her sexual acting out), Frieda went to the *mikveh*
for the ritual bath of purification required of Orthodox women. Her "perfection" as a daughter having been increasingly threatened by her failure to find
a husband, Frieda seems to have wanted the marriage to conform precisely to
a traditional script. However, few Jewish communities in East Prussia had
enough money for a decent *mikveh* (wealthy people were rarely observant),
and the water in this one was practically freezing. She got a tonsillitis so severe she almost couldn't be married (and later remarked, revealingly: "Even
if it had been warm, I would have gotten something"). At the end of a ceremony filled with joy and ambivalence for both bride and groom, Erich's father turned to Frieda with a big smile and exclaimed: "Now *you* can take care
of him!"[31]

And take care of him she did. Frieda treated Erich the way she treated
every other man: she admired his intellect, learned what she could from him,
and otherwise acted as if he were an amusing child for her to play with in
spare moments. Indulging his whims, expecting little or nothing in return,
she did everything she could to support his projects and encourage his ambitions. To us, this looks like a version of the good Jewish wife, freeing her
husband to study Talmud. To Frieda, however, it was a good bargain: she got
a man with her father's charm but more brains, who respected her indepen-
dence, never treated her like a helpmate, and happily let her be the provider
for both of them.

Erich began analytic training soon after their marriage—clearly the result
of Frieda's influence on him—but didn't feel he could let his conservative father know about it, so Frieda gave him a monthly "allowance" of 600
marks—half for him to live on and half to pay his analyst. (He followed her
lead and went at first to Wittenberg, then switched to Hanns Sachs at the Psychoanalytic Institute.) Erich commuted to Munich and Berlin for classes and
treatment, and to Frankfurt for work with his colleagues at the Institute of
Social Research. When he was home, he and Frieda had lively discussions
about psychoanalysis, Hasidism, and the potential role of therapy in social
change movements. Struggling to reconcile their continuing adherence to religious practice with the psychoanalytic claim that such behavior was neurotic compulsion, they provided a deep source of support to one another at a
time of considerable uncertainty. Like Frieda, Erich had a deep respect for

teachers, always calling himself a "pupil" of Freud even though he had never met him. And Erich shared Frieda's desire to keep the spirit of psychoanalysis alive in his work even as he departed from its more doctrinaire beliefs and practices.

Opening a treatment facility based on Orthodox principles was Frieda's attempt to forge a complex compromise among these conflicting values. Her Heidelberg sanitarium, like the informal one she had organized in the evenings at Weisser Hirsch, had an excellent reputation in the Jewish community and was seen (along with Rosenzweig's Lehrhaus) as a major institution of the self-renewal movement then sweeping through German Judaism. Frieda strongly agreed with the view, widespread in the Weimar period, that the emancipation of German Jews at the end of the nineteenth century had led to such overassimilation that there was now real danger of losing all sense of a unique history and identity. Building on the Zionist ideals of the Blau Weiss movement and the renaissance of Jewish art, music, and literature catalyzed by the work of Buber and others, institutions were springing up all over Germany in the 1920s seeking to revitalize Jewish culture. There were new journals, public libraries, and Hebrew schools, and novels, poems, paintings, plays, and musical compositions increasingly focused on Jewish themes. Rosenzweig's Free Jewish Study House, the most visible symbol of this movement, drew hundreds of students each semester to its adult education courses, study groups, and seminars. Jews of all ages and social strata were embracing Rosenzweig's philosophy of "New Learning," which called on students to work intensively in small groups, in a dynamic and egalitarian exchange with their teachers. Buber was writing *I and Thou* during this period, and it powerfully influenced their dialogue at the deepest level.[32]

Erich taught briefly at the Lehrhaus, as did his teacher, Rabbi Nobel, his close friends Leo Löwenthal and Gershom Scholem, and Frieda's cousin S. Y. Agnon (later, Israel's first literary Nobel laureate).[33] The strong sense of identity and community fostered by the Lehrhaus demonstrated the transformative potential of a new institution. Frieda's decision to create a sanitarium blending Jewish practice with psychoanalytic theory both paralleled and extended Rosenzweig's philosophy.[34]

Her idea, although utopian, was straightforward: if an individual could free himself from inhibitions and insecurities by bringing repressed memories into awareness, then perhaps the same approach could help to liberate the Jewish people from its painful legacies. Ritual practices didn't have to be compulsions performed in a rote way out of fear of punishment by God; they could be the basis for deep spirituality. This way of thinking combined the traditional Jewish focus on deeds as the evidence of true religiosity with the mystical notion of *kavanah,* intention, the "endowing of every act with a hidden significance directed toward God's destiny and the redemption of the world." By literally making her clinical work her religious practice, Frieda linked psychoanalysis and Judaism in a way that was considered truly radical. As Leo Löwenthal was later to note, analysis was regarded as "extreme and avant garde," and for intellectuals like Erich and Frieda to take it seriously was seen as tremendously significant in the Jewish community.[35]

Like all other social experiments, this one was extraordinarily exciting for a brief period. A number of people were attracted by Frieda's philosophy—quickly dubbed "torahpeutic" by the Zionist philosopher Gershom Scholem—and for several years in the mid-1920s, at least a dozen people lived communally in her large house at 15 Mönchhofstrasse. A number of others lived elsewhere in the area and joined the group each day for meals and therapy. Short texts from the Bible or other religious works were read and discussed at the long table in the beautiful wood-paneled dining room, and Erich often gave lectures on Jewish issues. After evening prayers, the group worked together to resolve whatever problems had arisen in their little community.

Frieda always cherished the memory of Adolf beaming at the head of the table during a particularly festive Shabbat dinner just before his death, as a roomful of people praised her vision of an Orthodox sanitarium. Adolf had been a little embarrassed that Klara's wealthy relatives had contributed all the money, and Frieda, worried that his wounded pride would lead him to refuse, hadn't asked his permission to approach them. But after he got over being hurt that she had gone behind his back (at a time when he was already highly suspicious because of his deafness), Adolf, as always, took pride in the achievements of his enterprising eldest daughter.

Besides the Jewish patients who formed the bulk of the community, there were a few Gentiles who came for the treatment (and were told they would simply have to "cope with the rest of it"). There were also some psychotic patients, admitted to augment Erich's training and because Frieda was committed to treating them. If a patient couldn't afford to pay, he bartered work for therapy. This made for some wild moments. "I analyzed the housekeeper, I analyzed the cook," Frieda laughed to friends years later, "and you can imagine what happened if they were in a phase of resistance!" But this model of therapy as a tool of political work, seamlessly connected with the rest of life, inspired a true egalitarianism. Money was a mere expedient. There were, of course, many expenses, and Erich, still a student at the Psychoanalytic Institute, was yet another drain on limited resources. But Frieda had strong entrepreneurial instincts and was constantly inventing ways to build her institution. "I'd sit in a room analyzing a patient, and I'd look around, and see oh, we need curtains for this room," she reminisced, "and as the next fee came in from somebody, I'd go buy those curtains." Thinking back on this period and many others in later years, she admitted: "I have always been very skillful in making money but never in having it."[36]

In addition to raising the funds for the sanitarium's upkeep and attending to every detail of its administration, Frieda analyzed all the patients. (Erich was still a student and wasn't allowed to practice independently.) The place was far more intense than even Chestnut Lodge would be: Frieda was the only analyst, and shared religion and ideology made relationships particularly intimate. Löwenthal, Erich's close friend and colleague, described the scene:

> The sanitarium was a kind of Jewish-psychoanalytic boarding school and hotel. An almost cultlike atmosphere prevailed there. Everyone, including me, was psychoanalyzed by Frieda. . . . The Judeo-religious atmosphere intermingled with the interest in psychoanalysis. Somehow, in my recollection, I sometimes link this syncretic coupling of the Jewish and psychoanalytic traditions with our later "marriage" of Marxist theory and psychoanalysis in the Institute [of Social Research in Frankfurt], which was to play such a great role in my intellectual life.[37]

In this sense, the fact that Erich had been her patient was totally unremarkable; Frieda analyzed everybody.

When friends later asked about Erich's contribution to the experiment, Frieda burst out laughing. "Oh, he helped. With words he helped fine. He would sit down and read the newspaper, and the girls who were supposed to be analyzed would help me move the furniture. . . . He was the spoiled only son of a German-Jewish family. He helped marvelously with ideas." This attitude didn't bother Frieda in the least. "I was a very active and energetic female myself, so it was all right. I got what I wanted—a very intelligent, very warm, very well-educated man who knew lots of things in another field from mine."[38]

Its utopian goals notwithstanding, the sanitarium ended up attracting people as much for its kosher food as for its philosophy. Rabbis from Frankfurt liked to visit on weekends, and various hangers-on, itinerant students, artists, and activists started gravitating to the house on Mönchhofstrasse, much as hippies and runaway teenagers would turn up at communes in the 1960s. Beyond the problems inherent in dealing with so motley a clientele, Frieda and Erich found themselves increasingly stymied by the contradictions of running an institution committed to practices their analytic colleagues considered neurotic. In 1927, they themselves published articles in Hanns Sachs's journal *Imago,* giving elaborate psychoanalytic critiques of Jewish ritual. Frieda analyzed the sexual significance of keeping kosher; Erich wrote on Shabbat and Yom Kippur. "That's how we announced we were through [with orthodoxy]," Frieda laughingly recalled, "in big style, like two real Jewish intellectuals!"[39]

Eventually, abstract analysis having proved insufficient, they decided to take more direct action. One Passover afternoon in 1928, Frieda and Erich went out alone, leaving behind a house filled with Jews fervently enacting the ancient practices forbidding the consumption of leavened foods. The hillsides along the Neckar River were wreathed in cherry blossom; the sun shone. They walked to a park far from the house, in a neighborhood where they knew no one, and sat down nervously on a bench. Then, with great ceremony, they unwrapped a loaf of bread they had purchased secretly and slowly ate the whole thing. Neither said a word. For all their sophistication, at some primitive level, they both expected to be struck by lightning or otherwise punished by God at that moment.[40]

To their astonishment, nothing happened. Later, Frieda would joke about the curse of *karet,* in which God "sets his face against he who violates his laws and cuts him off from his people," a punishment usually interpreted to mean childlessness or premature death, "dooming he and his line to extinction."[41] But her fear of being exiled as a heretic was deadly serious.

At first, they told no one of their sinful act, secretly eating the forbidden foods in private rituals designed to prove to each other their freedom from compulsion. (Choosing Passover, the holiday of liberation, as the occasion to make their break with tradition was clearly deliberate.) Frieda, then thirty-eight years old, was overwhelmed by the intensity of the experience. After a lifetime of stringent observance, every bite was an act of rebellion against her family and its centuries of orthodoxy. Later, she would develop a special love for lobster, oysters, and whatever else had previously been prohibited. But at the time, she could scarcely believe what she was doing and was practically sick every time she tasted *tref.* Erich became nauseous even at the sight of pork; Frieda liked to tease him by offering to make ham and eggs. They fantasized taking Wittenberg out for champagne to celebrate the end of Erich's analysis and asking him to teach them to eat oysters, but (significantly) he died before they had the opportunity.[42]

Frieda's fear of being cast out had powerful, superstitious effects that would last the rest of her life. She may have dismissed *karet* when, decades later, she told friends about that day in the park ("the punishment [for such sins] is that your family disappears from the universe, not that I believed that"), but clearly, at some level, she did in fact expect divine retribution. And well she should have. According to the very rabbinic traditions that Erich had studied every day for fifteen years, there are certain crimes considered deserving of the death penalty that lie outside the jurisdiction of any human court. Punishment for such crimes—which include eating leavened food on *Pesach* and a number of sexual transgressions—is supposed to come "without warning from the hand of God." This language has been variously interpreted to mean dying childless, dying prematurely, dying between the ages of fifty and sixty, or being denied a share of any future life (the "maximal punishment," since ordinary sinners, punished in this life, live on in the hereafter). Because, by definition, *karet* is inflicted for violations of Jewish law that occur in private without the presence of witnesses, only God is aware of the sin, and the timing of the punishment is left up to Him. For a person as dutiful as Frieda, who always described herself as "the good daughter of her parents, the good niece of her aunts and uncles," the person everyone could count on to do what was expected, a deliberate act of disobedience of this magnitude had to have deep psychic reverberations. And the fact that she had committed this sin with Erich, the person in her life most bound up with both sex and with orthodoxy, had to have imbued the event with even more complex meanings.

In the fall of that year, disillusioned enough to declare their attempt to blend psychoanalysis and orthodoxy a failure, they closed the sanitarium and sold the house. Frieda had to struggle to pay back the money she had borrowed (of the original 25,000 marks, 10,000 had been gifts, but the rest had to be returned to her relatives). With characteristic resourcefulness, she persuaded the house's new owner to let her rent several rooms where she could live and start a private practice. Besides needing to support herself and pay back the loans, Frieda again had Erich to worry about. He had just been diagnosed as having tuberculosis in both lungs and was being urged to go to Switzerland for treatment in Davos. Frieda paid all his medical bills for the first few months until he found a few analytic patients and could take care of himself.[43]

Years of Groddeck's influence had convinced her that tuberculosis, like every other illness, had psychic as well as biological causes. Erich vehemently denied this (even though he himself had given a lecture in Berlin in 1927 titled "Curing a Case of Pulmonary Tuberculosis During Psychoanalytic Treatment"). As Frieda began to act more like his analyst than his wife (two roles that had never really been separate to her), he grew increasingly angry. She wrote desperate letters to Groddeck begging him to intervene in Erich's "flight to Davos," until her husband's mounting hostility finally forced her to give up.[44] (She also, no doubt, recalled the time she had brought a patient to Groddeck for a consultation. The man had been told he had tuberculosis and needed to go to a sanitarium in Switzerland. Groddeck had examined him, and then told Frieda that a person who had to resort to getting tuberculosis to escape his family ought to leave.) Frieda visited Erich in Davos a number of times, and they exchanged frequent letters over the next several years, but they never again lived together. For all intents and purposes, their marriage ended sometime in 1930. When they were later forced to flee Germany, they left separately, divorcing once they had both established new lives in the United States.

Erich began an affair with Karen Horney during this period, complicating the situation. The three of them had overlapped during their years at the Berlin Psychoanalytic Institute, where Karen was on the faculty and Frieda and Erich were in training. Whether he began the affair as a way to leave Frieda or simply ended up as one of Horney's many conquests isn't clear.[45] Exchanging Frieda for Karen didn't help Erich to escape his mother (Horney was four years older than Frieda), but it certainly gave him a more sexualized version. And it exchanged his (formerly) Orthodox wife for a *shiksa* "with a roving eye," adding both excitement and punishment to the experience for the (formerly) pious Erich Fromm.[46]

Meanwhile, Frieda also started enacting her distress about the marriage and *karet* in a physical fashion. At just about the time Erich left for treatment in Davos, she began experiencing severe abdominal pains. As usual, she kept working. The next spring, she wrote to Groddeck that she had "chronic appendicitis" with "psychic determinants" that she had begun to analyze. "I have set myself the time of mid-July," she continued, "as the date until which I will accept that I am a woman who always has to deal with her body." If the symptoms didn't go away by then, she told Groddeck, she planned to consult an internist and try "to radically cure" herself during the summer vacation.[47]

But she was no more successful with her own symptoms than she had been with Erich's tuberculosis. On July 20, 1932, Frieda underwent surgery at the women's hospital in Basel, where a myoma, a benign tumor common in women, was removed from her uterus. She probably also had a hysterectomy.[48] She sent Groddeck a disjointed letter from the hospital, trying to piece together what had happened:

In the unconscious, I had to hold out for so long because [the] myoma that I had in the meantime constructed would only in mid-July—one year after the beginning of my husband's illness (my first noticeable symptoms occurred nine months after the beginning of his illness and his going away)—because, I wanted to say, that the myoma has only now attained the size and configuration of a child.

Eleven days ago I gave birth to it (i.e., I had it operated upon). As the doctor showed me the specimen two days later, as I had requested, I had to laugh about the power of the It that had fabricated a real child with a head, torso, formed limbs. And even though the "birth" was considered "major surgery," I've also recovered as quickly as a maternity case; today I was up for six hours, walking around in the garden, etc.

Unconsciously, in other words, Frieda had been pregnant with Erich's child, which, having grown inside her for nine months, was revealed to be a tumor. None of the intensely conflicted feelings she must have had about all this is made explicit. Later she would tell a friend in America that when she had expressed the desire for children early in the marriage, Erich had responded contemptuously: "Having a child is nothing; even a cow can do it." At the time of her operation, however, she simply told Groddeck how much she appreciated being "better able to understand its meaning through you," and cautioned him that everyone else thought she was having an appendectomy.[49]

Was this the punishment for her sin with Erich in the park that day? Had their union been divinely poisoned against a child? Was the extraordinary coincidence in the timing of their illnesses an unconscious statement about how destructive the marriage had been to both of them?

Or was this tumor-baby Frieda's punishment for something else? Something that had happened years earlier, something no one but her immediate family had ever known about. Something so terrible it was never spoken of, even by those who were aware of it.

It had happened in Königsberg, when Frieda was either a medical student or an intern. She had been walking home from the hospital one evening in late spring or early summer. The streets were not quite dark. Suddenly, out of nowhere, a madman, a "verrückter," grabbed her and threw her to the ground. He may have been a patient who knew her from the hospital; he may have been a stranger who encountered her at random. Frieda was raped. She may also have been beaten; the attack was said to be "brutal." What she did or said when she eventually reached home is unrecorded. All we know is that Klara was observed later that evening slowly and carefully mending the ripped, ragged underwear, which she gave back to Frieda and ordered her to wear.[50]

The intense humiliation of this experience—made even worse by Klara's sadistic denial and retribution—had to have been overwhelming for Frieda. For such a thing to happen to a Jewish girl from a good family was an abomination; for it to have happened before marriage was an unimaginable catastrophe. The force of Klara's buried rage at having failed to protect her perfect daughter from such a disaster—feelings that Frieda no doubt absorbed, as she did with everything in the family—had to have made Frieda's professional ambitions more urgent and her lonely suffering even more painful.

The whole experience was kept secret. Even Grete may not have known. (Anna, always "listening behind walls" like Frieda, took in what had happened without letting on that she knew.) For the shameful event never to have been spoken of in that puritanical family is one thing; for Frieda never to have revealed it to anyone for the rest of her life is something else again. The shame clearly made her more reserved, even with close friends, and intensified the already crushing weight of responsibility she considered it her duty to bear. Frieda always blamed herself for everything bad that ever happened. (Even in the one instance anyone can remember of her being assaulted by a patient, she insisted it was her fault. She had gone to the ward to see a young woman just transferred from another hospital. Frieda was in a hurry and didn't read the chart, which documented in detail the patient's history of violent outbursts. She asked some naive question about previous hospitalizations, and in response, the patient slugged her. Mortified by her own insensitivity, Frieda apologized "for not taking the time to adequately prepare.")[51] A person who considered herself responsible even for the violence of mental patients couldn't possibly have avoided blaming herself for something as dishonorable as being raped.

Perhaps Frieda eventually told Erich what had happened; perhaps not. We know nothing about their sexual relationship, and it seems unlikely that she ever had another lover after he departed. Various of her friends and would-be biographers regard this as a tragedy, but to Frieda, it was probably a great relief. She seemed to regard sexuality as an excess of youth, an indulgence ill suited to the soberness of adult responsibilities. Even in her thirties, Frieda appears in photographs dressed in a suit or dress of good fabric, carefully accented with jewelry, but looking strangely disembodied. She seemed to regard clothing solely as a marker of social class, something to prove she had been brought up well, unrelated to attractiveness. From a very early age, Frieda appeared frumpy, not so much because she lacked a sense of style as because she seemed never to inhabit her body.

Her colleague and patient Otto Will remembered being shocked by how asexual she seemed, even as an analyst. Soon after the start of his treatment, he reported a dream in which Frieda appeared as a beautiful woman, striking in appearance and very alluring to him. She dismissed the whole thing, saying it was "just a young man paying compliments to an old lady." (Will was in his forties at the time; Frieda was sixty.) He was stunned that a psychoanalyst could be so incapable of seeing herself as a sexual person that she couldn't even analyze a patient's dream in which she appeared in that form. At a theoretical level, Frieda downplayed the role of sexual factors in pathology, but this wasn't theory—this was denial.[52]

Since her relationships with men (other than Erich) weren't complicated by sex, Frieda could relax into a more comfortable role: that of muse. Starting with Goldstein and continuing through countless other friends and colleagues, she perfected the art of showing men off to their best advantage while choreographing events from behind the curtain. Frieda had mixed feelings about doing this. The part of her that had always deferred to Klara found it a relief to let someone else shine, and being brought up in an Orthodox world where "the public appearance of a woman in the day-to-day life of the congregation was unthinkable" made her most comfortable being supportive. But Frieda's own ambition and competitiveness also pushed her toward more dominant roles. In a compromise so exquisite it surely would have pleased Freud, she developed a way of "retreating into the limelight," thereby managing to satisfy both needs at the same time.[53] Frieda recalled the first time she had tried this. Goldstein had been out of town when one of his superiors made a surprise visit to the clinic. She told the head nurse: "Look, you go in there and say here comes the boss's associate. She looks very young and this and that and the other, but she isn't as young as she looks. And she's had some experience, and we know she does well with people, so just overcome your surprise and deal with her."[54]

Throughout her whole life, Frieda treated the men she worked with as charming children no matter what their age, and considered their occasional moments of brilliance as recompense for her indulgence. In public statements, she always gave men more than their due, treating her own accomplishments as derivative of theirs. Behind this deference she did what she wanted, overlooking the disjuncture as if it weren't there.

Being simultaneously self-effacing and confident allowed Frieda to accept power in a matter-of-fact way that would otherwise have been unseemly in a woman. The part of her that remained the obedient daughter, genuinely respectful of authority, made deferring to men effortless. And years of protecting Adolf's fragile pride left her exquisitely attuned to their vulnerabilities.

Unlike most other women, who resent having to coddle men, Frieda identified with their neediness, which meant she could let them take center stage without feeling exploited.

Horney was the exact opposite. Compulsively competitive with men but also extremely needy, she sexualized her conflicts by taking younger, less powerful men as lovers and then abandoning them when they challenged her power. Horney had none of Frieda's subtlety, a fact that Erich realized only after it was too late. As soon as he became a rival in the training institute Horney founded in New York, she fired him from the faculty and forbid students to study with him.[55] (These were the precise punishments meted out to her five years earlier by the Psychoanalytic Institute.) Horney could never have remarked, as Frieda once did in a tone entirely free of rancor, "I made it a job to do his job," as if there were nothing else to it. With a lot more energy than most other people, Frieda was used to doing the work of more than one person. She put in her time, then did as she pleased, which also kept everyone on her side, something Horney never learned to do.

Frieda understood the buried sadism in her attitude toward men. "I used to call them my victims," she once told a friend with a grim laugh. Yet as she herself admitted, "obviously I got great satisfaction from it, because I did it time and time again."[56] Freed from the guilt of elbowing men out of the way, she got the benefit of learning from some extraordinary people, who, aware only of her generosity, taught her far more than they realized.

Frieda was often impatient with men or disappointed by their failings, but the soft edge of contempt she inherited from Klara muted these feelings. In marrying Erich, she had satisfied her mother's deepest wish, choosing a man who posed no threat to her autonomy, and becoming his wife only after her own professional life was securely established. But a child with two parents is not solely the projection of one, and Adolf's need to be liked taught Frieda how to endear herself to men in the unthreatening way they admired.

"What can I do for you?" was the question she posed to every patient, student, colleague, and friend. The phrase perfectly embodied her desire to help, her arrogant assumption that she could, her focus on the other person, and her denial of her own neediness. Years of being the peacemaker in the family had given Frieda a genuine sense of pleasure in easing people's pain, and helping talented men was just one more way of being useful in the world. Thus, in striking contrast to Horney, who enjoyed humiliating men, Frieda made it look as if they were winning and then winked when their backs were turned. In this, she was merely following Klara, whose complete domination of the family was hidden by a screen of deference that made Adolf appear to be in charge.

So when Frieda talked about Klara's going with her forehead toward the wall and the wall giving in, she knew she was also describing herself. "Only I handle it better," she laughed to friends, "because I realize it's not so charming."[57] Klara, in some sense Frieda's first "victim," was therefore both a model and an example of what to avoid doing.

In the spring of 1924 when she had purchased the house on Mönchhofstrasse, Frieda was a single woman, an Orthodox Jew, and a psychoanalytic enthusiast, about to open a pioneering psychiatric institution. Six years later, she was a formerly married, no longer observant Jew, who had lost whatever chance she might have had to be a mother, and whose utopian experiment lay in ruins. Her father had died, her husband had left her, and she was living as a tenant in two rooms of the huge house she had once proudly owned. She was, if anything, even more deeply committed to psychoanalysis, aware of the irony that "the Jewish science" had been responsible for her break with orthodoxy.

Her deepest values, however, remained unchanged. Despite all the upheaval in her outer life, Frieda's main source of satisfaction still came from healing others. So long as she had patients to treat, she could feel she was being who she was meant to be. (As one of her Washington colleagues remarked years later: "I'm not a religious person, but I have to say that God made Frieda for helping patients.")[58] Marriage, motherhood, directing a sanitarium: they were all imagined lives she could do without. And although she had abandoned most of the daily rituals of Jewish life, Frieda's commitment to the ethical precepts of Judaism remained absolute. Foremost among these was *tikkun,* which continued to provide the source of meaning for all her work. Psychiatry would never just be Frieda's occupation; it was her way of contributing to the repair of the world.

There was also a more primitive quality to the power Judaism continued to have in her life. Religion and marriage may have been the realms where Frieda was most independent, where she freed herself most explicitly from the scripts others had laid out for her. But they were also the spheres where she was most haunted by guilt and fears of retribution for having violated laws centuries old.

It's hard to imagine what direction her life would have taken at that point had history not pushed her onto its own path. But Frieda's foray into private practice after nearly two decades of work in institutions would prove short-lived. And her terrifying fantasy of being cast out, forever cut off from her family and her people, would become real in ways she could never have imagined.

5

The Exile

Emigration is like a parachutist's jump. Either the parachute takes you gently down to earth or you crash to your death.[1]

The ordered pace of Frieda's life—like that of thousands of other German Jews—was abruptly broken by Hitler's rise to power in the early 1930s. She was living alone in Heidelberg after Erich had left, on one floor of the house on Mönchhofstrasse. Her mother, along with Grete, Aunt Helene, and Anna and her family, were all living together in a spacious apartment on Jenaerstrasse in Berlin's Wilmersdorf district. Grete had gotten a doctorate in musicology and was working as a music critic for the newspapers. She got free tickets to every concert, and she and Anna went to several performances together each week.[2] Helene, in her late sixties by that point, was still politically active and often held meetings in the large front room where the family played music together in the evenings. Their genteel but unassuming lifestyle on this quiet street in a heavily Jewish middle-class neighborhood seemed worlds away from the horrifying events that were about to engulf them.

Hans Jacobson, Anna's husband, was a physician who had long been active in antifascist work. Highly idealistic, he made no secret of his politics, and had once even refused to treat a patient at the hospital until he removed the swastika from his sleeve. On the night of February 27, 1933, less than a month after Hitler had gotten himself appointed chancellor, the Reichstag was set on fire by persons yet to be identified. By 11:00 that night, on the pretext that Communists were to blame, Nazis began swarming the streets rounding up dissidents. An informant told Hans he was on the list of those about to be arrested, and the Reichmann family began its long nightmare.

After a panicked consultation with Anna around midnight, Hans decided they had no choice but to try to escape immediately. They took their terrified daughter, Alisa, then six years old, to her kindergarten, where a sympathetic teacher agreed to hide her until morning. As storm troopers "methodically worked through the night like a keen blade flashing in the darkness . . . rousing bewildered men from their sleep and marching them away to captivity," Hans and Anna drove around for hours in the bitter cold, constantly switching from one taxi to another. Near dawn, as they passed a certain corner, the teacher jumped out of a different taxi, shoved Alisa in with her parents, and sent them off to the station right before the commuter train left for Danzig. Hans's goal was to get to any point in France. But it was too dangerous to travel directly; they hadn't had time to secure false papers, and every train was being searched, so they went first to Danzig and then by boat to France. Alisa was carefully instructed to say that she was on a holiday to visit relatives, should anyone ask. Mature beyond her years in the way children often are in times of turmoil, she knew this was a lie; her parents promised to tell her the truth once they reached safety. In Paris, Hans quietly explained that the Nazis were evil people who might have killed the whole family because of his political work. But she was never to say this. If anyone asked why they had left Germany, Alisa was to tell them: "We ran away because we're Jews."[3]

That terrible night of their escape from Berlin was the only time Alisa ever saw her grandmother weep. Refusing to acknowledge the danger they were in and clinging to her characteristic use of denial as a way to deal with every difficulty, Klara had tried to block their plan to leave. Sixty years later, Alisa could still hear her screaming at Hans from the balcony: "I won't let you take the child from me!"[4] But Hans was right. Five thousand dissidents disappeared that night, many sent to concentration camps.

Frieda was soon facing similar risks. The Nazi movement in Baden had been steadily increasing in strength since Hitler's enthusiastic welcome in 1927 at Heidelberg's *Stadthalle*. By 1931, Nazi rallies were drawing 150,000 people and SA men were parading in uniform through the streets. Nazi students were turning lectures by socialists and Jews at the university into violent brawls. When Hitler was named chancellor on January 30, 1933, the *Israelitische Gemeindeblatt* of Mannheim, the most important Jewish newspaper in the region, said the situation was "serious but with no reason for despair." Two months later, after Nazis seized control of the Baden government, Jews were removed from all state and municipal positions. Teachers were fired. The romantic streets of the *Altstadt* were filled with Brown Shirts

carrying revolvers and hand grenades. Doctors and lawyers began being kid-
napped from their offices and beaten or shot. It became unsafe to talk on the
telephone. On March 31, Heidelberg held its first official boycott of Jewish
businesses, and a month later, the head of the Nazi Medical Association called
on all "Germans" to stop seeking treatment from Jewish doctors. On May 17,
jeering crowds of students at Germany's oldest university held a book burning
in the ancient *Marktplatz* to rid the city of "anti-German propaganda and sub-
versive Jewish-Marxist literature."[5]

The writer Ernst Weiss described the terror of those first few months after
Hitler took power. "A monstrous, muddy flood of denunciations broke loose.
Fathers denounced their sons, sons their fathers, wives their husbands, in the
hope of gaining advantages from the new regime—or simply from a desire
for revenge, out of hate, out of the meanness of their nature."[6] Frieda's male
secretary was one of these people. Her maid discovered him searching her
files, desk, and living quarters whenever she wasn't in the house. Frieda had
been a consultant to the *Odenwald Schule,* and its headmaster was under suspicion for refusing to adopt the Nazi-ordered curriculum. When he suddenly
fled, taking his staff and all the Jewish children to Geneva, Frieda realized
that she and everyone else connected with him were now at risk.[7] Her colleagues at the Frankfurt Psychoanalytic Institute were also being accused of
"harboring Communists," a further threat. Like most other Orthodox Jews,
Frieda had few illusions about the willingness of German culture to tolerate
real assimilation and never felt the shocked surprise of less observant Jews
whose claims of "feeling so German" blinded them to the Nazis' real inten-
tions. She quickly grasped the danger she was in and decided to leave secretly for Strasbourg, pretending to be on a weekend trip. Anna's frightening
experience only a few months earlier had vividly demonstrated that speed
was essential and safety the only objective.

Having chosen Strasbourg because it was on the border, close enough for
her patients to travel to but in 1933 still part of France, Frieda prepared for an
immediate departure.[8] To keep from attracting attention at the checkpoint and
to make plausible her claim to be visiting for only a few days, she abandoned
the possessions of forty-four years and packed only two tiny suitcases. She
stuffed one with jewelry, clothing, and a few family photographs. The other
held recordings of the music she most treasured. The choices a person makes
in terrible moments like this are always intensely revealing, and for Frieda to
have decided to lug this huge stack of bulky, breakable 78s, easily weighing
fifty pounds, tells us how crucially defining the music of her childhood was
for her.

It is wrenching to imagine her hurried departure from that house saturated with the meanings and memories of a tumultuous decade. Unlike most other Jews who fled Germany in those years, there were no tearful good-byes to friends, no weeks of packing the huge wooden containers that would transport the tangible evidence of a former life elsewhere. Standing on the quiet, shady corner on Mönchhofstrasse, waiting for the taxi to take her to the *Bahnhof,* did Frieda gaze longingly at the upper windows thinking of an intimate moment with Erich early in their marriage, or a joyous Shabbat dinner in the "torahpeuticum," with friends and patients all gathered together? Or did this sudden rupture from certainty and comfort call forth darker images: Erich's leaving for Davos, being forced to sell the house, the weeks of worry about Anna. Riding past the familiar stores on Brückenstrasse, watching the trams cross the Neckar as students strolled idly along the riverbank below her, was Frieda distracted, tearful, numb, frightened? She never described these last moments in Heidelberg to anyone; they are obliterated now, like practically every other trace of her life there.

The short trip to Strasbourg must have been surreal. Less than a few hours from her house, a mere two miles inside what was then France, Strasbourg was a place where Frieda had gone for meetings with psychoanalytic colleagues, a place that evoked images of pleasant weekends, excellent wine, and her favorite local delicacy, white asparagus. It was spring. The carefully cultivated fields were a brilliant green. The disjunction between the softly rolling hills passing by her train window and the shouting Nazi officers scrutinizing identification cards at every stop must have felt totally disorienting. Then at Kehl, the last German town, a final, terrifying search of every passenger, and one minute later, the Rhine, and across it, the French border. The sudden safety must have been as incomprehensible as the terror of the brief journey.

Frieda took two rooms at a small hotel where she had once stayed for a meeting, intending to use one for a bedroom and the other to see patients. To her great joy, Hans soon got a job at a sanitarium in nearby Gübwiller, which offered meals and board, and Frieda was able to find a place close to her hotel where Anna and Alisa could live. They were all terribly anxious about being able to support themselves. France was then experiencing the worst effects of the worldwide depression; there were no jobs for citizens, much less for refugees. Anna was forced to sell her beloved violin for food. Eventually she got work as companion to a mentally disturbed girl, easing their money problems temporarily. But the girl was jealous of Alisa and pretended to get one of her "spells" whenever Anna paid any attention to her daughter. "The two of us started to hate each other," Alisa recalled, "until dear Frieda came to the rescue as usual."

Frieda moved her niece in with her. A cot was put in the bedroom, decorated with a balloon. "She was ever so good to me," said Alisa, "but during the time she saw patients in the other room, I had to stay in the bedroom with the toys she had given me and be so quiet that no one would know I was in there." In the evenings, Frieda secretly prepared food in the room to save money, using an electric kettle she kept hidden under a chair. Alisa remembers boiling spring potatoes and eating them with salt and butter, sitting on the beds.[9] Frieda made a few professional contacts in nearby Basel and even briefly joined the Swiss Psychoanalytic Society, but otherwise she kept a low profile. To her intense relief, almost all her Heidelberg patients had chosen to continue their analyses (commuting to see her by train), and the nine hours a day she was able to work provided enough funds to support herself and help Hans and Anna. The immersion in her patients' problems was also a welcome distraction. As an analyst trapped in Vienna during the 1930s recalled, "When the patient was talking, it could take away at least for a few hours the pressure and preoccupation one had with one's own safety."[10] Frieda's quickwittedness in leaving immediately and choosing Strasbourg was to prove crucial. Had she gone to Paris, like hundreds of other German-Jewish refugees, she would have been forced into a far more desperate search for work in a city already filled with unemployed French. And had she stayed in Heidelberg, she would likely have ended up deported to Gurs or Theresienstadt, with the rest of Baden's Jewish population.

Despite the constant tension of so precarious an existence, Strasbourg must have been a reassuring place for Frieda to end up in. An old university city like Heidelberg, its winding canals, delicate footbridges and cobblestone streets evoked a similar romanticism, with French refinement smoothing the hard German edges. Strasbourg's adaptability—molding itself to whatever ruling power happened to control Alsace in any given period—perfectly matched Frieda's own resilient spirit, and the subtle blend of French and German culture must have felt familiar, given her years in Baden. After an exhausting day of seeing patients, it's easy to picture Frieda taking a quiet walk and finding at least temporary solace in the softness of Strasbourg's curving streets. In a letter to Groddeck a few months after she had arrived, Frieda struggled to describe her feelings:

In this magnificent and timeless beauty, this untouchable expanse and serenity, my confusion, caused by the events and peril of my friends, and the helplessness of my heart regarding the behavior I had expected of my Aryan friends, has gradually dissipated. . . . I do not yet know how my life will develop, but somewhere I will find a sphere of activity, as well as the inner tranquility from which even longing can be productive.[11]

Frieda's close friendship with fellow analyst Gertrud Jacob provided a major source of comfort during this time of exile. Jacob is a shadowy figure, remembered by others mainly for her strangeness. But for Frieda, she was an intensely vivid presence, and their relationship, although brief, ranked in emotional significance second only to her bond with Erich.

Jacob was a psychoanalyst and an artist, best known for her portraits of psychotic patients, whose uncanny accuracy amazed everyone who saw them. The extraordinary sensitivity Jacob poured into these paintings was oddly absent from her daily interactions. "She hid behind a screen of aloofness," Frieda wrote in a tribute to her friend. "Those who were not close to her admired her self-contained and independent personality and the workings of her brilliant mind. They were impressed by dignified reserve and pride charmingly mixed with disarming naïveté and friendliness. . . . [unable to] surmise the depth and intensity of her intellectual and emotional life."

Jacob became a mirror for Frieda's deepest self, a mirror so etched with familiarity as to have almost no glare. Frieda could be herself with Jacob, a relaxed, unvigilant self that hardly anyone else even knew was there. This openness seemed to awaken Jacob. "Few knew of the blissful elation that she experienced upon gaining new scientific insight or upon finding an artistic expression for what she wanted to convey, or the sorrow when insight or expression eluded her," wrote Frieda. "Her ardent and uncompromising heart and mind burnt with indignation upon meeting with meanness or mendacity, in people or in causes."[12]

The similarities in the two women's lives had quickly created deep bonds. Almost exact contemporaries (Jacob was three years younger), they had grown up in the same kinds of Orthodox families, in which they played much the same role. Jacob was from Kiel, a Baltic seaport like Königsberg, and like Frieda, the eldest in a family of daughters (an even more intense position for Jacob, who had four younger sisters). From an early age, Jacob had been fascinated by emotions and the human mind, first studying portrait painting and then medicine, eventually settling on psychiatry as a way to combine both interests.

She had come to Heidelberg in March 1926 to complete her residency, and the two women may have met then. Or Frieda may first have encountered Jacob through her "uniquely expressive" portraits, which were exhibited at the psychiatric clinic at the University of Heidelberg and widely discussed among staff there. Frieda served as Jacob's training analyst from March 1929 to August 1930, and from the time Jacob left Germany in April 1933, the pattern of her movements precisely matches Frieda's. They seem to have been together for much of their two years as refugees.

Like Frieda, Jacob succeeded in arranging for many of her analytic patients from Germany to follow her to Alsace, and could support herself in private practice there. She also had a position at the sanitarium at Gübwiller where Frieda's brother-in-law Hans was later to work. The two women didn't live together during their time in Strasbourg, but they relied heavily on one another for support and spent most of their rare free time in one another's company.

In May 1934, word reached Frieda from Baden-Baden that Groddeck had suffered a severe heart attack. He was experiencing some kind of mental breakdown as well, insisting to anyone who would listen that Hitler was not himself anti-Semitic but "evil men around him" were conspiring to make it look like that. Groddeck had written several letters to Hitler trying to warn him of this plot. His open criticism of the regime had put him in danger of arrest, and friends were trying to persuade him to marshal his limited physical strength and leave the country, at least for a few months. To get him out of Germany without arousing his ire, Frieda arranged for the Swiss Psychoanalytic Society to invite him to lecture in Zurich. Groddeck delivered a dazzling talk, "Seeing Without Eyes," and then collapsed. Brought to Medard Boss's sanitarium in nearby Knonau, he rose up once more in manic glory. When Frieda visited him there a few days later, he greeted her warmly and then insisted she help him send a crucial message to Hitler. "Write, Frieda," he commanded. "The nurse won't take dictation from me. This must be written." For hours, Frieda sat quietly, recording his ravings. When the time came for her to leave, Groddeck was utterly spent, but could not be dissuaded from accompanying her to the train station. Climbing the hilly, wooded path to the village, he suddenly seemed to gain strength. They both knew they would never see each other again. The train came, Groddeck clasped her hand, stared at her with burning eyes and said: "All good things to you, Frieda." A few days later, he was dead.[13]

This was in June 1934. Later that year, Frieda traveled with Jacob to Palestine and spent some months there. They were both struggling to decide where to live. Even though Anna and her family were intending at that point to stay in France, the possibilities for permanent settlement seemed too insecure to Frieda to risk remaining there. (Here again, her intuitions turned out to be precisely accurate. Had she not chosen to leave Strasbourg, she would have been rounded up with the rest of the Jewish population and shipped to Auschwitz after the Nazis invaded.) Erich had just gone to the United States and could provide the necessary affidavit for Frieda to get a visa to go there.[14] She was intensely moved by the beauty of Palestine, but in the end, money proved the deciding factor. Palestine was a poor country filled with refugee doctors, and the chances of making a decent living were slim. With Adolf dead and her mother and sisters facing an uncertain future, Frieda knew she had to be the major source of support for everyone. It was the role she had always played, and she accepted it without hesitation. A cousin, orphaned in the 1920s, told a typical story: "I was staying with some aunt and things went wrong. To solve the problem of what to do with me, I was put on a train and sent to Heidelberg, where Frieda collected me and made me feel wanted. Whenever there was a problem anywhere in the family, Frieda was the address."[15]

She and Jacob arranged to sail for New York, with visas issued in March 1935 at the consulate in Haifa. Frieda sent a telegram to Erich, asking him to wire them the funds they would need to enter the United States. Somehow she and Jacob managed to make their way back to France, and Frieda said an agonizing goodbye to Anna on the pier in Cherbourg. They had no idea what course their lives would take or whether they would ever be together again.

Although Jacob wasn't family, she must again have been a consoling presence for Frieda during that melancholy voyage. They had booked third-class passage on the *S.S. Berengaria,* one of a number of former Hamburg-based luxury liners that Cunard had bought after World War I and renamed to get rid of their unpleasant Germanic associations. Among the largest ships in the world when it was launched twenty years earlier, the *Berengaria* had spacious decks for dancing, elegant dining rooms, and accommodations for nearly seven hundred passengers. Frieda and Jacob had neither the funds nor the desire to indulge themselves, and must have spent most of their time anxiously trying to imagine their lives in the United States. However, alert as always to useful learning opportunities, Frieda spent part of the long voyage carefully memorizing every curse word in the English language, after an American doctor on the ship told her this would prove indispensable for work with mental patients.

They docked in New York on April 16. In response to the immigration official's questions, Frieda and Jacob both declared themselves to be physicians, capable of reading and writing English, in possession of at least fifty dollars, and intending to take up permanent residence and eventually become citizens of the United States. For some unknown reason, they were both listed as being of the "German" race, unlike other Jewish refugees on the same ship identified as "Hebrew" despite their German addresses. Since it is highly unlikely that either Frieda or Jacob would have lied about their Jewishness and would never have been on a ship bound for America were it not for the fact of it, this "error" seems painfully ironic under the circumstances. After assuring the examining officer that neither of them had ever been "in a prison, an almshouse, or an institution for the care and treatment of the insane" (presumably as a patient), had never been deported, were not polygamists or anarchists, did not "believe in or advocate the overthrow by force or violence of the Government of the United States," and were in good health, "mental and physical," they were allowed to disembark. Frieda must have made an especially powerful impression during the questioning; the official listed her height as five feet seven inches, making her a full nine inches taller than she actually was.[16]

Jacob departed for the Park Plaza Hotel on Eighty-First Street, where the Psychoanalytic Institute (which had provided her affidavit) housed many of its new arrivals. Frieda went home with Erich, who was then living at 64 East Sixty-Sixth Street. Despite their four-year separation and the awkwardness of his having come to America at Karen Horney's behest, being reunited with Erich must have been intensely reassuring for Frieda. Whatever the failures of their marriage, they shared strong bonds of history and friendship, and had both been ripped away from comfortable lives under frightening circumstances. Having Erich to lean on in her first weeks in the United States, living in his apartment instead of being off alone in a hotel like Jacob, and for once, having him in the position of caregiver had to have eased some of the confusion and pain of this period of Frieda's exile. Erich had been in America for a year by that point, and besides being familiar with the myriad details of daily life in so different a culture, had crucial contacts in the psychoanalytic world and the broader émigré community.

Indeed, within two months of Frieda's arrival, he managed to get her a job that precisely fit her talents and background. In the throes of the Depression, when nine million Americans were unemployed and scores of formerly middle-class German Jews were forced to wash dishes or clean houses to keep from starving, Frieda became—thanks to Erich and her own resourcefulness—one of very few refugees from Nazi-occupied Europe to be spared any form of economic deprivation or struggle.[17]

However, neither Jacob nor Frieda had any real idea what awaited them when, in June 1935, they each left New York for temporary jobs—Jacob at Dr. Helen Coyle's sanitarium in Peoria, Illinois, and Frieda at a tiny place in Rockville, Maryland, called Chestnut Lodge.

6

Asylum

Exile contains redemption within itself, as seed contains the fruit. Right work and real diligence will bring out the hidden reward.[1]

It was June 26, 1935, a typically hot, steamy day in Washington, the city built on swamp. Arriving at Union Station on the afternoon train from New York, Frieda was met by a gracious woman with a soft Southern accent who said her name was Anne Bullard. Her husband, Dexter, the owner of Chestnut Lodge, was away at a meeting, so she had come to get Frieda. The elegance of the car was a bit intimidating, and some of Anne's words were hard to decipher, but smiling warmly and exuding European gentility, Frieda impressed her new boss's wife as a real lady. By the time they reached Rockville an hour later, their awkwardness had dissipated, and the two women spent the rest of the afternoon sitting under one of the large shade trees, sipping lemonade and getting acquainted. At one point, looking up at the porticoed balustrades of the main building, Frieda talked wistfully of how much the Lodge reminded her of her own sanitarium in Heidelberg. She met Dexter later that night, and for years afterward, he told people it had been "love at first sight."[2] Their attraction was political, more alliance than affair, and in many ways, they were an extremely odd pair. But they forged a remarkably successful partnership that provided what each most needed: for Dexter, a name to draw patients and staff, and for Frieda, a new home and a dream job.

Bullard could never have found an American with Frieda's range of talents and experience. She had worked with every kind of patient—wealthy neurotics, anguished young people, neurological cases, schizophrenics—and her training in Königsberg and Berlin was far superior to anything available in the United States. She had studied with some of the leading figures in German psychiatry and spent four years at Weisser Hirsch, a place whose clientele was much like that of the Lodge. And having designed and run her own sanitarium, she had indispensable insights into asylum management.

But on that June day in 1935, neither Dexter nor Frieda could possibly have realized how ideal a refuge Chestnut Lodge would be for her: intellectually radical yet socially proper, filled with warm family feeling yet deeply respectful of individual difference. She could run things without being in charge, arrange her daily life precisely as it suited her, and depend on the Bullards' "helpers" to deal with the dirty work. Dexter and Anne let her do anything she wanted, and she repaid their generosity by turning their struggling enterprise into an internationally recognized institution.

What made all this possible was the uncanny fit between Frieda's personality and the Lodge's eccentricities. A mental hospital unlike any other, with a history so picaresque it sounds like fiction, it was rooted in a world utterly alien to Frieda while embodying the precise ideals she most treasured. Had she landed anywhere else in America, she never could have had remotely as much influence.

The sign said simply "Chestnut Lodge." A person who turned into the long, curving driveway without knowing the kind of lodge it was wouldn't find out by looking. Until the 1940s, Montgomery Avenue was a quiet, rural road, and most of those passing the sweeping grounds assumed the Lodge was an inn of some sort. Well-dressed couples wandered in now and then asking what time lunch was served. Miss Simpson, the nurse, gently told them where they were, and it was a point of pride among staff not to laugh until the car had sped back onto the road.[3]

Chestnut Lodge was a family business, and every bit of it was suffused with the intensities of home. For many people, it *was* home. Dexter had grown up in the main building, and after he married Anne, moved to a house down the path. Most of his staff also lived on the grounds. The Lodge was the kind of place that drew people in. Even kitchen and maintenance workers stayed for decades and considered themselves part of the clan. The two Raymonds, for example, came from families (the Bakers and the Yateses) who worked for the Bullards so long they seemed like distant relations. Mabel Peterson supervised the front office for forty years and often spent more time with Dexter than she did with her husband, Al. The clerks in the record room could greet every patient by name, and the cook knew who liked their eggs over easy and who didn't. Equal parts plantation, rest home, company town, and tribe, the Lodge had the hothouse intensity that brought each one of them to life.

There would never have been a Chestnut Lodge if there hadn't been Bullards. A Bullard founded the place in 1910, and his descendants ran it for decades thereafter. A "psychiatric dynasty" like their friends the Menningers, the Bullards deliberately kept their operation on a smaller scale. But they were adept at protecting their interests, and no outsider, however skilled or ambitious, ever succeeded in loosening their grip on things. Unlike its main competitors—Austen Riggs in Stockbridge, Massachusetts, McLean in Boston, Sheppard Pratt in Towson, Maryland—the Lodge wasn't a nonprofit enterprise, administered by a board of directors. Profit-making hospitals may strike us as the jaded invention of postmodern greed, but in psychiatry, they have a long history. The Lodge was one of dozens of asylums that sprouted along the East Coast at the turn of the century, and for the Bullards, owning a mental hospital wasn't much different from any other family business.[4]

Not that they ever made much money from the Lodge. The medical staff always grumbled that the Bullards were getting rich off their hard work, but the family's money actually came from investments and real estate.[5] The staff, paid less than a third of what they could have made in private practice, had trouble believing this, but that's because the Bullards were so close-mouthed about finances. A visitor arriving on the grounds would not have felt in the presence of wealth. The Lodge was pleasant and well cared for, but unstylish. Everything seemed a bit duller green than it actually was. Yet the disarming openness, the feel of the family farm, made even hired hands treat the place as partly theirs.

The founding Bullard, Dexter's father, Ernest Luther, was a horse and buggy doctor with a stubborn streak. He had developed an interest in medicine early on (perhaps from hanging around Arlington House, his father's summer hotel, whose medicinal waters were a big draw) and in 1883, had graduated from Rush Medical College. Ernest worked briefly as a railroad surgeon and then opened a private practice in Waukesha, Wisconsin, before being elected to the state senate as a supporter of "Fighting Bob" La Follette, the progressive. When La Follette became Wisconsin's governor in 1901, he rewarded his friend Bullard with a plum appointment: the superintendency of a mental hospital. This was common practice at the time; since formal training in psychiatry did not yet exist in America, superintendents were selected for their political loyalty.

Ernest was a modestly confident man, no less qualified than most others, with a head for business and a belief in the benefits of rest. His institution, Wisconsin State Hospital for the Insane, stood as a tribute to 1850s optimism about mental illness. Perched dramatically on a bluff overlooking Lake Mendota, on what was said to be the most "beautiful and picturesque [site] in the whole state," it gave the citizens of Madison, in the capital, something to look up to as they gazed across the lake.[6]

Dexter, four years old at the time, fondly recalled living with mental patients as being as much fun as winter sleigh rides across the lake. His father's career at Mendota, however, proved short. It was difficult enough trying to manage hundreds of patients with only two assistants, but when the governor tried to pad the staff with cronies, Bullard resigned in disgust.

He decided to open his own hospital so he could really run things. The question was where. Ernest had vivid memories of the economy in Waukesha collapsing after the one steel mill in town had shut down, and he didn't want to put his asylum in an area with an unstable client base. Eventually he decided Washington, D.C. posed the least risk. Even in bad times, he reasoned, bureaucrats made sure their own jobs were safe. (Dexter, remarking years later on his father's perspicacity, noted dryly: "When there's a depression, ten thousand people flock to Washington to fight it.") After scouting for properties for two years, Ernest bought the Woodlawn, an abandoned hotel in Rockville, Maryland.[7]

In the mental hospital business, as in real estate, location is everything. Rockville proved an excellent choice: rural enough to feel like country yet close enough to Washington to count. For harried government workers, this was a seductive combination, and the town had one of the steadiest growth rates around.

Its history, however, was odd, and this was to have profound effects on the development of Chestnut Lodge. Rockville had begun as a bar—Owen's Ordinary, renamed Hungerford's Tavern in the 1770s—whose location at a crossing of the Georgetown-Frederick road provided a natural place for local tobacco farmers to meet. When the need arose for a more formal gathering site, they simply named their tavern the county seat. Eventually a courthouse was built nearby, but it was the town's reputation as a retreat that gave it a distinctive identity.

Washington was only sixteen miles away, and there was daily stagecoach service by the 1860s. In 1873, the B&O railroad extended its line, and developers started touting Rockville as a summer resort where sweltering bureaucrats with sixty cents and an hour to spare could escape the pleasures of living in a swamp. By 1890, promotional pamphlets were hailing "peerless Rockville" for its "clean, cool, and delicious water, no malaria, rarely a mos-

quito, ozone-rich air, groves of pine and hardwood, dashing streams of wa-
ter-rich vegetation, an abundant supply of fresh vegetables and produce, and
unapproached train service." The combination was said to leave the "mind
and body so refreshed as to enable a man to make more money [there] than
he otherwise would."[8] Travel from Washington became even easier when
electric trolleys started running alongside the trains.

The Woodlawn, Bullard's eventual asylum, was the town's best hotel.
Built in 1889, in a vernacular interpretation of Second Empire style, its
mansard roof, patterned brickwork, wrought-iron cresting, and turned
columns were of elegant design. Recessed French doors on the central pavil-
ion opened to a balcony of metalwork, and eighteen pedimented windows
graced the side dormers. The building was four stories tall, far grander in
scale than the area's other resorts. Its "immense breeze-filled porches"
proved an irresistible lure to urban dwellers seeking to escape "miasmic air,
epidemics, and [the roar of] pounding horses' hooves."[9]

Guests, many of them prominent Washingtonians, arrived by train, traveling the mile to the hotel in special carriages. (The east-facing facade was
made especially elaborate to ensure a good first impression.) The Woodlawn's activities quickly dominated Rockville's social scene, with stately
luncheons on the veranda, card games and concerts on the lawns, and soirees
and musicales in the ballroom. Guests marveled at the gas lighting, the state-
of-the-art plumbing, and the electric bell system connecting all forty rooms.
Like other hotels in town, the Woodlawn was open only in the spring and
summer, but in the Gay Nineties, this was enough for it to do well. The good
times ended about 1906, when a growing network of excursion trains permitted Washington fun seekers to roam farther afield. The Woodlawn's owner,
unable to pay the mortgage, was forced to put the property on the auction
block.[10] Ernest Bullard bought it two years later in an excellent deal. For
$7,100, he got the building (whose brickwork alone was valued at $8,000), as
well as eight acres of land, a windmill, carriage house, stable, ice house, and
a two-story laundry complete with servants' quarters.

About a thousand people then lived in Rockville year round. The local papers were running articles like "Praise for the Sardine," and you could buy a
Special Top buggy from the Probey Carriage Company for $50. People came
from miles around to the county fair, where, among other amusements, you
could "throw baseballs at some young colored boy paid to stick his head
through a piece of canvas . . . if you hit him, he dropped into a tub of water."
Rockville's landmark was the statue of the Confederate soldier. Believed to
be the northernmost monument of its kind, it had been erected in honor of the
"Heroes of Montgomery County, Maryland, That We Through Life May Not

Forget to Love the Thin Gray Line, 1861–1865." Many of Rockville's citizens had never forgiven Maryland for siding with the North, and well into the 1950s, weekly reports on Confederate groups were published in local newspapers.[11]

It took Ernest Bullard two years and thousands of dollars to transform the long-vacant Woodlawn into a mental hospital. Pipes were falling out of the walls, the porch was sagging, bricks hit workmen on the head, and the whole place seemed haunted. Bullard installed electric lights, central heating, and closets in every room. He had the whole building replumbed. His style was in no sense lavish, but compared to the county poorhouse in the middle of town, the only other place housing mental patients, Bullard's new asylum looked like a palace.

It was the summer of 1910 before he was finally able to move in, with wife Rosalie, twelve-year-old Dexter, and horse Ginger. Bullard had spent the months of waiting procuring the supplies he would need: huge tins of Horlick's Malt for fattening the anorexics, an electrotherapy machine for stimulating the depressed, paraldehyde for coaxing the agitated to sleep, and a Kelvinator that could freeze seven pans of ice ("endless winter for milk and cream"). He ordered copies of Walton's *Why Worry?* and Mitchell's *Fat and Blood* (the Bible of the rest cure movement), and arranged for a railroad car of coal (49 tons at $1.60 a ton) to make it through the first winter.[12]

Bullard decided to call the place "Chestnut Lodge" in honor of the hundred massive chestnut trees dotting the property, and because the name made his sanitarium sound like every other asylum on the East Coast.[13] He was entering the mental hospital business at an auspicious moment. The five preceding years had seen a 25 percent increase in the number of psychiatric patients, more than double the rate of increase in the U.S. population. This was partly the result of better diagnostic methods and partly an expansion of the categories of mental illness. State hospitals were filling up with people previously cared for at home: syphilitics, the senile elderly, and those afflicted with ailments like pellagra and epilepsy. Drug addictions and "sexual perversions" were also increasingly being defined as mental illnesses.[14] As proprietor of a private institution, Bullard had the luxury of taking only cases that interested him; he didn't have to deal with whoever was dumped on him the way he had at Mendota. Announcing his new enterprise to colleagues— on tasteful stationery with "Chestnut Lodge Sanitarium" in large, ornate script at the top, and the logo "For Mild Nervous and Mental Diseases" right underneath—he admitted his first patient on July 25, 1910. Within a year, the census had risen to a respectable six. From the very start, the Lodge was said to "enhance Rockville's reputation as a spa and health resort."[15]

Patients were mostly local. They suffered from "nerves" or vague physical ailments; many had the "liquor habit" or were morphine addicts. They had already tried standard remedies like Electric Brand Bitters, featured in advertisements for Vinson's, the drugstore down the street. (One pictured a locomotive about to run over a tiny man, with the caption: "STOP. THERE'S DEATH AHEAD if you allow yourself to get weak and listless, fagged out, debilitated and run down." Another showed a dark-skinned Indian next to the words: "This Dancing Savage is No Weakling. He has strength, vigor and endurance. . . . If you are weak, run-down, or sickly, [buy] Electric Brand Bitters.")[16] It was only a small step from tonics to a stay at Chestnut Lodge. Some people came for the rest cure, still in vogue at the time; others were sent away by relatives in need of a break. A few patients may simply have come out of nostalgia for the Woodlawn's resort days.

Ernest Bullard's business acumen was evident right away. Being in Rockville's fashionable West End attracted the well bred, and as the terminating point for the streetcar line from Washington, the Lodge had special cachet.[17] For five cents (six rides for a quarter), families could just pack their wayward ones onto the trolley and ask the conductor to deposit them at the asylum before he turned the cars around. This was especially helpful with alcoholics, who tended to fall asleep during the long ride. It may have been only sixteen miles from Washington to Rockville, but it seemed like sixty; the town was so sleepy that people always thought of the Lodge as a country retreat. Among the regulars in the early days was an alcoholic priest who had Bullard lock his clerical collar in the safe as he checked in. Carousing congressmen and judges snuck away from Washington for "vacations" to dry out; "nervous" women joined them for card games and relaxation. Rates were high at $25 a week and laundry was extra, but Bullard seemed to have no trouble filling the beds.[18]

Nor was it difficult to attract nursing staff. Hours were long—nurses got half a day off every other week and had to alternate on the night shift—but qualifications weren't extensive. Bullard hired any young woman who was "well mannered, neat in appearance, clean and orderly . . . in good health, industrious, kind and sympathetic [with] at least a common school education, and a liking for the work." He didn't disqualify those with prior "nervous disease" so long as they disclosed the particulars.[19]

Suitable attendants were harder to find; the pay was too low and the work too unpleasant. When Bullard was asked by a colleague about a woman he had once had on staff, he replied: "She was not particularly efficient . . . is not mentally alert and at times does rather queer things, [but] considering the difficulty of getting assistance of any kind, I would advise you to give her a trial not because of any special qualifications, but on the broad proposition that you can try anything once." These difficulties notwithstanding, Bullard never hired everyone who applied; he passed, for example, on the manager of a failed sanitarium from Pittsburgh, who pronounced his credentials "the best in the United States" and signed his letter "yours to command."[20]

Psychiatric treatment in turn-of-the-century America was minimal by any standard. One of the best descriptions comes from Victor Small, an assistant physician at a state hospital in the Midwest, whose memoir, *I Knew 3000 Lunatics,* is a classic of the period. On Small's first morning at work, he was telephoned by the nurse. "Mrs. G. is disturbed, doctor," Miss Stalling reported. Small had no idea what that meant. Hesitating, he asked: "What's disturbing her?" Miss Stalling was not amused. "I don't know what's disturbing her—she's just disturbed. What shall I do about it?" Small turned blankly to the physician who had been showing him around the ward. He snapped "give her two drams of paraldehyde and put her in seclusion," and Small rotely repeated his words. It was several weeks before he realized this constituted the entire treatment regimen. The only other option was castration, used occasionally for the "over-sexed." (Small felt uncomfortable with these operations—"I would as soon be a party to the cutting off of a man's head"—and appreciatively recounted the adventures of Hazel Webb, a nymphomaniac whose three-day "orgy" in an underground passageway produced the pregnancy that cured her distress.)[21]

Treatment at Chestnut Lodge was similar but more benign, as befit its status as a private asylum. Miss Simpson, the head nurse, and Libby Anderson, the Bullards' longtime cook, chatted with patients or organized games of bridge or billiards. When the weather was pleasant, everyone ambled outside for croquet or horseshoes on the front lawn. In many ways, the Woodlawn was still a spa. Ernest's ads in the *Washington Star,* which ran under a special heading of "sanitariums" created just for him, were right next to the resort column. The main difference between Bullard and the spa owners was that he offered a medical rationale for what he was doing. Like most other American physicians of the period, he assumed that people got better in asylums because attractive surroundings and an attentive staff restored the mind's natural balance. His publicity notices—sent to colleagues on discreet postcards, addressed by young Dexter in his best hand—read: "Many cases of mental disorder, neurasthenia and allied conditions, if taken in their incipiency, are quite amenable to sanitarium treatment." Warning that "undue delay often results in irreparable injury," Bullard declared: "This institution offers unsurpassed facilities for the care of *recent* cases."

In the early years, much of this seemed lost on his clientele, who regarded the Lodge as more spa than hospital. Bullard often sounded like a resort manager. In a chatty note to the relative of a patient who had just arrived, for example, he said: "Your sister did not care to take the front room as she thought the street cars might disturb her at night, so we [put her in] a quiet room on the east side of the house where she will get the morning sun." He welcomed patients who simply wanted a rest and those whose "stomach troubles" necessitated a better diet. Alcoholics came just to relax and escape temptation. Bullard sat them in lawn chairs in the sun to read, or on the back porch to catch the evening breeze. He prescribed long walks for those who didn't need to be in bed and sent reassuring letters to worried relatives: "Your husband eats and sleeps well, takes plenty of exercise . . . and when not walking, spends most of his time in the billiard room reading the papers, playing cards or swapping yarns with other patients." Convinced that good food and restful sleep were the keys to mental health, Bullard predicted confidently to one patient's brother that "when he begins to gain physically, he will have less mental distress." To relatives who proposed visits, he boosted local attractions ("The Chevy Chase Golf Links are about twenty minutes' ride from here on the trolley line. This is where President Taft performs and is one of the best golf courses in the country"). But when he felt he needed to discourage contact, Bullard set limits ("Visits from persons about whom patients have delusions are of course not advisable"). Aside from a few categories that were proscribed ("we do not take colored people . . . and are not prepared to care for violent patients"), he welcomed anyone who appeared.[22]

In the 1910s and early 1920s, Bullard rarely kept patients for long periods, although if they were improving, he might urge a longer stay. With alcoholics, the appeal sometimes went the other way. One relative pleaded, "Please try to keep him *as long* as you *can*." Bullard never sanctioned any form of deception to get people to the Lodge and cautioned families that while "patients are always under the watchful eyes of the attendants," he wouldn't keep them against their will unless they were committed. However, his attitude wasn't entirely laissez-faire. He warned an alcoholic who claimed he was going to town to buy a pair of shoes that "if he came back under the influence of liquor, night or day, I would not let him into the house."[23]

In letters to relatives, Bullard was careful to distinguish the Lodge from an "insane asylum," and certainly its style had little in common with the state hospital. Yet even in the early years, he welcomed patients whose symptoms were serious. To a man from West Virginia who wrote to ask if the Lodge would take his brother ("beside a nervous breakdown and melancholia he is troubled with catarrh in the head and bad digestion"), Bullard noted his "rather wide experience [at Mendota] in the treatment of [such] patients."[24]

Visitors would never have guessed that the place was a mental hospital unless they wandered into the back rooms, where patients too agitated for billiards were sprayed with hoses or immersed in huge tubs according to the regimens of hydrotherapy, centuries old. Bullard especially favored the cold wet sheet pack—in which the patient was placed naked on a bed and wrapped tightly in cold, wet sheets—because it simultaneously calmed and restrained. In the early years, such measures were sufficient. Not until the 1920s did Bullard attract sizable numbers of patients requiring more strenuous means. Even then, he was cautious. He contracted with the Human Restraint Company for several sets of wristlets and anklets, a leather binding lined with flannel and attached with a strap. If necessary, the hands of a violent patient were placed in a muff. Only the most unruly were put into straitjackets (from Nicholson of Baltimore, Dealers in Cotton Duck, Awning Stripes & Awning Supplies), which prevented any movement save useless thrashing. For those who required it, sedation was given, but never heavily and only in the evenings.[25]

A few of these methods sound a bit grim, but they were used sparingly and didn't detract from the bucolic atmosphere of the place. Huge chestnut trees arched across the broad paths, growing thick enough in some places to crowd out the grass. Every mental hospital of the day had some kind of farm, and the rolling fields beyond the main building were a luxuriant mix of vegetables and flowers. Red-brick Georgian mansions lined the nearby roads, and Southern gentlemen strolled the lawns with their families on summer Sundays. (As late as the 1990s, maps of Rockville were still labeling the property as "Bullard's Park.") Dexter called it "a lovely place to grow up."

Sons of mental hospital superintendents have often followed in their fathers' footsteps.[26] An only child, Dexter had grown up—first at Mendota and then at the Lodge—with patients as his playmates and babysitters, and he knew no other life. Patients were the people he was closest to: they taught him to play pool and whist, watched him mow the lawns, and feed the chickens mash (Park & Pollard's, "guaranteed to make hens lay or bust"). When the cook struggled to hoist the dumbwaiter to the fourth floor at lunchtime with Dexter hiding inside, it was patients who laughed at his antics. These experiences, so strange to our ears, were for him routine, and because of them he never learned to fear the insane. "Patients were not bizarre," he told a colleague years later, "they were part of my life from early on."[27]

The only time Dexter ever left the Lodge was when he went off to college, and even then he was home every summer. He enjoyed reciting his favorite line: "I was admitted to a state hospital at four, discharged at six, readmitted to a private hospital at twelve, and haven't gotten out yet."[28] After college at

Yale, medical school at Penn, and a wild internship in Hawaii (during which he tried unsuccessfully to persuade his father to relocate the Lodge to the islands), Dexter began his training in psychiatry. Despite mediocre grades and frequent probations, he was accepted for a residency at the famous Boston Psychopathic (known to its friends as "The Psycho"). But two months into the program, his father had a heart attack and called him home to help run the family business.

Dexter's lack of psychiatric training turned out to be the luckiest event of his life, and he later joked that Ernest's coronary had been deliberate. American psychiatry in the 1920s was a discipline so dismal it hardly warranted the name, and a student was lucky if he could tell a paranoid from a paretic by the time he finished training. The nineteenth-century presumption that insanity was an organic brain disorder still held sway, and cure was a concept rarely considered. Students memorized Kraepelin's diagnostic scheme, and then joined their teachers in wrangling about which symptoms were most extreme. The exercise, while sterile, had its egalitarian side: since no effective treatment existed for any category of disorder, patients from every walk of life enjoyed the same right to remain ill.

When Dexter returned to the Lodge in 1925, there were about 2,500 people living in Rockville. The Lodge had twenty beds. The head nurse got $80 a month and free board on the grounds. The cook and the two attendants made half that much and were off in town in rented rooms. Dexter moved back into his old bedroom on the first floor of the main building where he had lived since the age of eight, its walls still plastered with pennants from the sports teams he had once favored. He was right down the hall from his parents. The patients were upstairs. When he married Anne Wilson two years later, he moved to a house built specially for them, a hundred feet away.

"Little Lodge," as their house was quickly dubbed, was Ernest's first addition to the property, but it wouldn't be the last. The year after his son's marriage, he purchased a large tract of land adjoining the hospital, increasing the value of his investment and gaining several small houses that could become living quarters for an expanded staff.

Ernest's weakening heart required that he take a slower pace, so he appointed his son Assistant Physician and let him run the Lodge largely as he wished. For two years, they experimented with a system in which Dexter leased the hospital with his father as a kind of consultant; at the end of the trial period, Ernest resumed control, worried that his son was paying himself too much.[29] It was an apprenticeship of the old-fashioned kind, and it allowed Dexter to master subtleties of hospital management that his competitors never learned. With no board of directors to please and no legislature or governor to befriend, he could do anything he wanted so long as he kept the beds filled. Even in those first years, Dexter's unique approach to patients began to take shape: a no-nonsense flexibility that was as natural for him as it was unimaginable to most other physicians. Years later, recalling the lessons of that time in a simple way, Dexter said: "I learned that patients were quite capable of taking a large amount of straight talk, without too much explosiveness, and that they were not such fragile people after all."[30]

Dexter's interest in treatment went beyond anything his father had tried. Ernest was cautiously optimistic with patients, but Dexter was determined to find methods that really worked.[31] In the 1920s, the Lodge's treatment approach was still largely that of the spa. Inquirers were told the place was "situated amid fifteen acres of lawn and woodland," offering "an ideal environment for the building up of patients." That was all. Dexter's own letters hailed the "special attention given to diet" and the hydrotherapy department ("complete in every detail"), but beyond these niceties, there wasn't much else to brag about.[32]

The Bullards did try to keep up with the latest developments, hiring an occupational therapist as early as 1931, and using the "Behavior Chart" (Form 85, Hospital Standard Publishing Company, Baltimore) to keep track of forty-two specific actions, from "excreta decorates" to hallucinations. Such innovations did little to draw patients. The Lodge had to compete with popular crazes like the "music cure," which the *Montgomery County Sentinel* prescribed for any ill. ("Almost every mental trouble [can] be cured by suitable selections of classical music regularly administered. Jealousy, grief, overwork, homicidal mania, nervous breakdown, all [have] their corresponding air.")[33] The Bullards had to rely on alcoholics to keep up the census, along with other "nervous" types (stammerers, for some reason, were specifically excluded). By the late 1920s, though, patients were staying for longer periods, and rates, now figured by the month, had risen to $200, with laundry included.

In January 1931, enroute to a vacation in Florida, Ernest Bullard had another coronary and dropped dead on the train. A tribute read at the meeting of the District of Columbia Medical Society on February 3 proclaimed: "In honesty of endeavor and of opinion, in unfailing good humor and kindliness, in modest self-confidence, and especially in the common sense application of his broad knowledge of his specialty, none surpassed him."[34] With Ernest's death, all of Chestnut Lodge—patients, staff, buildings, and properties—passed to his thirty-three-year-old son.[35]

It was a bad time to be taking over a business. The Depression was deepening, and fewer and fewer people could afford private treatment. Dexter nervously watched other sanitaria go bankrupt all along the eastern seaboard, and wondered if his entire inheritance were about to disappear. Finally, Anne, an extraordinarily resourceful woman, proposed a deal: she would run the buildings, the farm, and the finances, and Dexter could concentrate on the clinical side. Maybe together they could make a go of things. She imposed only one condition: that he promise not to second-guess any of her decisions. This turned out to be an ideal arrangement, unique in psychiatry. Anne got a challenging job at which she excelled. Dexter got to do the work he loved, without having to worry about the details. (Whenever money caused tensions, he could just shrug and tell the staff: "You'll have to take that up with Anne.") As one of his colleagues was fond of noting: "Chestnut Lodge was the only hospital in the country where the business manager and the superintendent went to bed every night and talked things over."

Their combined efforts allowed the Bullards to eke their way through the early 1930s, but as the Depression grew worse, the census kept dropping. The Lodge looked as if it were about to join the ranks of most other sanitaria in the United States and quietly close. As a last, desperate measure, Anne asked the staff to take a pay cut to save their jobs. "Not a single soul left," she recalled proudly. Eventually more patients appeared, and she could restore salaries to their former level and pay everybody their back wages.[36]

Nothing in Anne Wilson's background presaged a future as business manager of a mental institution. Growing up in a prosperous home in nearby Kensington, Maryland, she had, like many other young women of her social class, attended Goucher College in Baltimore before marriage. Yet despite her privileged background, she thrived on hard work. Until the Bullards could afford a maintenance staff at the Lodge, Anne did everything from supervising the livestock to inspecting the linens. She had an elaborate system of penny-pinching that saved thousands of dollars and made the Lodge one of few sanitaria actually to expand during the 1930s. Anne did all the shopping herself to get the best prices. The fifteen-mile trip on dirt roads to the wholesale markets in Washington took at least an hour each way, but "we thought nothing of doing it two or three times a day if we had to in those days." She would climb into Dexter's mother's Pierce Arrow and return with bushel baskets of vegetables spilling out of the back seat. The sprawling Lodge farm provided everything from fruit to chickens (in the early days, before the Bullards could afford a tractor, a team of mules did all the plowing). Until sometime in the 1940s, laundry was sent out; then Anne decided to save even more money and built her own facility behind the main building. As a proper Southern woman, she never did kitchen work. A cook arrived at five o'clock each morning to light the wood stove and start breakfast for everybody.[37]

These frugal efforts paid off. As more and more of their competitors went out of business, Dexter hired an associate physician. He was determined to have more of a life than his father had—"Hell, in all those years, he never even took a vacation"—and the local medical students he paid to take call on nights and weekends weren't reliable enough. A fellow superintendent recommended Caroline Straughn from Western State Hospital in Virginia. Dexter wrote asking if she had any experience in psychotherapy, his newest passion. "There are 2,000 patients and four doctors at Western State," Straughn replied. "There isn't much time for psychotherapy." Bullard liked her honesty. Sight unseen, he hired her as the first member of his medical staff.

Straughn didn't last long. A year after her move to Rockville, she got married, and her husband insisted she quit the job. She did. Then he left her. The Bullards never found out what happened to her.[38] It was just as well that Straughn departed; she wouldn't have been able to contribute much to Dexter's evolving plan for a new kind of mental hospital.

In 1931, Anne gave birth to her second child and hired Raymond Baker as chief groundsworker. The property Ernest had purchased several years earlier included a house that had belonged to Raymond's grandfather, so for Baker, working for the Bullards meant never having to leave home. Several years later, when Anne and Dexter bought a vacation cottage on the shore in southern Maryland, they hired a cook who was a relative of Raymond. Through her, Anne got to know a number of other African-American families in the area. For decades, their relatives migrated to Rockville to work the Lodge fields or join the kitchen staff. These people were all blood relations like the Bullards, making the hospital's family atmosphere less and less symbolic.

Chestnut Lodge never promoted itself. Most asylums put paid notices in medical journals or sent out glossy postcards hailing their uniqueness. Alabama Bryce Insane Hospital in Tuscaloosa proclaimed itself "an institution of magnitude and a blessing for the unfortunate." Keeley Institute in Columbia, South Carolina, guaranteed its treatment ("a trial is all we ask to convince the most skeptical"). Fenwick Sanitarium in Abbeville, Louisiana, bragged about being "strictly ethical in its methods" and claimed mysteriously to "offer unusual advantages." Rumsey Sanitarium in Westfield, New York, called itself "the home of the chicken dinner." Lima State Hospital in Ohio, apparently lacking a more relevant selling point, listed its dimensions ("distance around building, 8,150 feet; approximately 70,000 cubic yards concrete, 12,800 tons reinforcing and structural steel, 6,000,000 face brick, 3,000 windows, 4,000 pieces of sash, 50,000 panes of glass, 37,000 feet of sash chain, 74 tons of sash weights, 122,890 feet of electric wire").[39]

The Bullards sent out announcements to mark special occasions, hinting at the homey atmosphere with artful line drawings and soothing photographs. For the opening of Little Lodge in 1927, for example, they used a card showing a doorway framed by trees, evoking the tasteful life of the country estate. A scene of the men's dayroom from the same period pictured a billiard table and easy chairs, a vase of fresh flowers, an oriental rug, and a pair of relaxing landscapes. (Heavy mesh screens on the windows were softened by ornamental woodwork and full-length draperies.) The photo of the main building that Ernest used as his 1930 Christmas card was so attractive as a snowy scene that the town of Rockville included it in promotional literature well into the 1980s. Dexter's fondness for beautiful cars added a dashing tone; a snapshot from the 1930s, for example, showed his Packard roadster nestled in a grove of sycamores.

In the broader context of psychiatric treatment in America, however, Chestnut Lodge was invisible. A 1934 survey reported that 174 state hospitals, many with thousands of beds, were caring for 300,000 patients. Twenty Veterans Administration hospitals housed 13,000 more. St. Elizabeths in downtown Washington had 4,600 patients. Even most private hospitals were far more substantial than the Lodge: Sheppard Pratt had 250 patients and a staff of 21 physicians, 80 nurses, and 100 attendants; McLean had 210 patients, 13 physicians, 220 nurses, and 50 attendants; and Austen Riggs had 40 patients, 6 physicians, and 6 nurses. Chestnut Lodge, in contrast, had 25 patients, 1 physician, 1 nurse, and 8 attendants. Of the other private sanitaria owned by individuals listed in the survey, two-thirds were larger than the Lodge.[40]

After his father's death, Dexter had given himself five years to decide the future of his hospital. Geography once again turned out to be crucial. By the 1930s, the Washington-Baltimore psychiatric community had become a home for renegades, and experiments were taking place all over the region.[41] Adolf Meyer was at Johns Hopkins teaching medical students to sit by the beds of psychotics until they could make sense of what their patients were trying to tell them. Harry Stack Sullivan was at Sheppard Pratt in nearby Towson, Maryland, running a special ward for schizophrenics and claiming recoveries in an astounding 85 percent. William Alanson White was in his twenty-eighth year as superintendent of St. Elizabeths, rounding out a career as psychiatry's most distinguished iconoclast by letting Edward Kempf try psychoanalysis with delusional patients.

Dexter had been warned to stay away from "filthy-minded analysts" by his professors in medical school. Had he inherited less of his father's shrewdness or been a less stubborn man, Chestnut Lodge might have ended up like most of its competitors, bankrupt by the mid-1930s. Instead, Bullard turned it into the only mental hospital in the world that specialized in psychoanalysis for psychotic patients.[42]

Sullivan and White had discussed this idea, and others had used psychotherapy with a few seriously disturbed cases, but no one had ever filled a whole hospital with schizophrenic patients and tried to treat them psychoanalytically.[43] Freud didn't believe his method worked with psychotics. Most American physicians in the 1930s didn't think it worked with anyone. They were busy experimenting with the new somatic treatments—insulin and metrazol shock, electroconvulsive therapy (ECT), and lobotomy—which seemed the best routes to a "scientific" psychiatry.

But Dexter Bullard could afford to be a maverick. He had no connection to the medical establishment. He didn't have to account to anyone but Anne for what he did. True, he had no training in psychotherapy or psychoanalysis, and he looked more like a fullback from a state university than a psychiatrist. But he owned the hospital and could do whatever he wanted, and what Dexter wanted most of all was to be different. Growing up among patients, feeling close to them all his life, he found it exasperating to see them "labeled and put on the shelf" with no real treatment. He had read a little Freud and decided "you couldn't have a special brand of psychology for one kind of person. . . . If Freud['s ideas] made sense for the neurotic, [they] had to make sense for the psychotic." His colleagues considered this logic naive, but Bullard ignored them and forged ahead. He hired Marjorie Jarvis, a local psychiatrist with some analytic training, and the two of them started "floundering around" to see what might work with seriously disturbed patients.[44]

This was in 1934. The Lodge had thirty beds. The place was like a small plantation, minus the slaves, with the Bullards up in the big house and their workers in shacks scattered around the grounds.[45] Anne and Dexter were prominent members of Rockville society, frequenting the teas and parties meriting mention in local newspapers. Their children were growing up at the Lodge just as Dexter had done, chasing each other through the trees and spending summer evenings riding bareback on the cows. (On the Fourth of July, the children's favorite, the Bullards shot off fireworks on the front lawn and hosted a huge picnic for staff, patients, and all the neighbors.)

Dexter's mother, Rosalie, in her eighties but still feisty, presided over every event from her rocking chair on the front porch of the main building. She kept an especially sharp eye on the nurses, whose rooms were right across the hall from hers. Patients were upstairs on the other three floors; only Marjorie Jarvis, the new analyst, lived in town. Neither she nor Dexter ever got a vacation, and their days off depended on finding local medical students willing to take call (for room and board and fifty dollars a month). Until Dexter started a training analysis with Ernest Hadley and had to go to Washington for the four weekly sessions, he could hardly ever leave the property.

One day in the spring of 1935, Hadley interrupted Bullard's free associations to ask if he would consider hiring the wife of his friend Erich Fromm, who had just escaped the Nazis and badly needed work. Dexter was in the midst of a period of resistance, and as he later put it, "wouldn't have given Hadley a nickel for Christ's head on a platter."[46] But a few months later, it dawned on him that if he let this refugee doctor fill in for the summer, he and Jarvis each could have a vacation. Frieda arrived at Chestnut Lodge in June 1935 as a two-month replacement. She ended up staying for two decades and totally transforming the place.

The summer of 1935 was a "poor year for haying," according to the local papers. Roosevelt was "strong with the masses," but housewives were rioting over high meat prices and staging pickets at the entrances to markets. Few women in America had access to advanced training of any kind, and the handful who were admitted to professional schools were being passed over for most positions. Frieda had absolutely no idea how lucky she was to find a job in the area of her specialty.

Rockville must have seemed like another planet to her. After forty-six years in urbane European cities, wrapped tightly inside a world of Jewish intellectuals, she suddenly found herself in a sleepy Confederate hamlet where Jews couldn't even buy homes. Montgomery County's "Newsiest Newspaper" was running articles on the proper use of bed coverings ("Blankets for summertime should be light in weight; heavy blankets are for wintry nights") and touting asphalt burial vaults ("Nothing to Rust! Eliminates that most detrimental feature—sweating"). At the Rockville Market and Dress Shop, ladies could buy new fall dresses (all sizes, $3.95) while stocking up on cookies of six varieties. The Rural Electric Administration was trying to convince farmers to wire their properties (only 10 percent of the thirty million rural residents in the United States had electrical service). Unemployed artists were being hired by the new Works Progress Administration to paint murals in post offices. Dr. Lloyd C. Shanklin, president of the United Brotherhood of Vegetarians, was touring with his invention, the odorless onion, and Parker Brothers was introducing Monopoly, its new board game. The Sandy Spring Colored Baseball Club ("We challenge any white team in Montgomery County") was playing the All Stars on summer Saturdays, and

Clark Gable was starring in *Mutiny on the Bounty*. The motormen had just stopped ringing their bells along Montgomery Avenue, their streetcars having been replaced by "modern and efficient buses." Fewer than two thousand people lived in Rockville in 1935, not quite twice the number Ernest Bullard had found when he got there twenty-seven years earlier.[47]

To Frieda, recently escaped from a Europe convulsed with fascism and epic national struggle, the place must have appeared utterly bizarre. Fortunately, she felt at home in a mental hospital anywhere, and simply hunkered down to work, oblivious to the peculiarities of life in small-town America. "Frieda was out of it," Joanne Greenberg was later to observe, "consciously, permanently out of it as though she were a Martian." Greenberg remembered the day ten years after Frieda's arrival when a patient turned in a false alarm. "The volunteer fire department came gonging through, yelling 'where's the fire!' These were folks who had to drop everything and leave their jobs in the middle of the day. When Frieda airily said to them, 'Oh, it's all right, you can go home now,' they wanted to tear her head off." Daily exigencies swirled invisibly around her, as if the logic of the asylum had displaced whatever knowledge she might once have had of ordinary living. Frieda could detect anti-Semitism even when it was slight, but remained curiously unaware that Rockville's blacks lived in slums called "Haiti" and "Monkey Run" less than a mile from her door. She was so blind to the realities of life in segregated Washington that when Raymond Yates, one of the Lodge's black workmen, drove her to a concert, she bought him a ticket, assuming he could join her.[48]

Frieda and Dexter couldn't have been more different. Partly it was the physical contrast between them; photographs of hulking Bullard and tiny Frieda can still make anyone laugh. But the utter disparity in their backgrounds was even more profound. Dexter came from a family that traced its origins in America back through ten generations, and he had the hale and hearty style of a man whose place in life had never been questioned. He found Frieda's European upbringing and psychological intensity mystifying, and she was the first Jew he had ever known personally. Her brilliance and sense of presence let her stand up to him in ways no one else dared, but having survived the loss of her entire former life, Frieda took few risks and constantly told Dexter and Anne how grateful she was to them for taking her in. She and Dexter worked together every day for the next twenty years, but their lives remained totally separate. He spent his favorite moments with his pals at the Rotary Club or sitting by the fireplace with a bottle of good bourbon. She spent her rare free time working, or at the symphony in Washington, or answering frightened letters from relatives and friends trapped in Europe, still alive only because she was supporting them.

In the one photograph that survives from Frieda's first months in the United States, she looks ravaged. Dressed entirely in black, she stares at the camera with an oddly averted glare. Her hair is uncurled, in the blunt cut of the refugee, and the crease in her forehead was so sharp the immigration official listed it as a scar. The lines that would later deepen the rest of her face are etched on the surface, as if their place were being marked out in this period. The look of tragedy, of desperate sadness that emanates from this face, the haunted look of having faced something unspeakable is what makes her look quintessentially like someone who has just fled the Nazis. There is also something so authentic about her gaze, so unlike the posed, frozen quality of other photographs, that makes her seem striking, even beautiful, in this one.

Frieda and Dexter did share an endless capacity for hard work and a great respect for each other's talents. For all the boldness of his ideas, Bullard was a superintendent, not a clinician. But he was a genius at attracting people smarter than he was and letting them experiment. Hiring Frieda was his first inspired move; his next was bringing Harry Stack Sullivan to the Lodge for a historic four-year seminar that taught a new way of conceptualizing mental illness. Sullivan's theoretical brilliance matched Frieda's clinical gifts, and the combination catapulted the Lodge to international prominence and attracted an extraordinarily talented group of young psychiatrists to its staff.

What made the Lodge distinctive was its treatment approach. Bullard had discovered in the early 1930s that people were willing to pay more for analytic therapy.[49] The mystique of psychoanalysis had captured Americans of a certain class, and while they were only a tiny percentage of the population, they were exactly the people who went to places like Chestnut Lodge. Dexter shared his father's business instincts and expertly carved a market niche. By the mid-1930s, he was hailing intensive psychotherapy as superior to other treatments, even for deep-seated problems like drug and alcohol addiction. He told Dr. George Kornegay of Kingston, North Carolina, for example, who inquired about treatment for morphinism, that the patient "must be brought to the point where the use of morphine is no longer needed as an escape from the conflicts of a poorly integrated personality." Without psychotherapy, he warned, "chemical or medicinal cures will not prove lastingly effective."[50] Bullard claimed that psychoanalysis also offered the best way to deal with difficult patients ("given a case in which the patient is too sick to make daily visits [to the physician], an institution in which psychoanalysis can come to the patient offers the most reasonable hope of success").[51]

Careful not to oversell his approach, he warned inquirers that "the ultimate value of psychoanalysis in the psychoses is not yet known." But Bullard was not above the occasional appeal to guilt ("for those relatives desirous of leaving no therapeutic stone unturned, [psychoanalysis] provides the most complete psychiatric study of a patient's capacities that it is possible to make").[52] He believed intensely in what he was doing and was convinced it made clinical sense. He was also shrewd enough to realize that if his sanitarium were to survive, he needed a service his competitors couldn't match. In the middle of the Depression, even Ernest Bullard's geographic brilliance wasn't enough. The Lodge needed a unique product to keep the beds filled.[53]

In a provocative study of private mental clinics, historian Edward Shorter argues that profit-making asylums have always relied on "patients, not doctors, to control admissions." If people aren't forced by the state to go to your hospital, something has to pull them in. There are only two real options for how to do this: by offering a unique form of treatment or by claiming the approach used is effective in a wider range of cases. Turning Chestnut Lodge into a psychoanalytic hospital allowed Bullard to do both simultaneously.[54]

But with barely any training, he could never have managed this on his own, which was why he greeted Frieda's arrival as a gift from God. Quickly realizing the market value of a senior, Berlin-trained analyst on his staff, Bullard energetically fought off all bids to steal Frieda from him. When she went out to the Midwest at the end of that first summer to give a talk and visit Gertrud Jacob, Karl Menninger offered to build her a house if she would stay and work at his family's clinic. (Europeans weren't eager to relocate to Kansas, which they considered a cultural wasteland, so the Menningers had to resort to special inducements.) Dexter quickly said he'd match the deal if Frieda came back to Chestnut Lodge.[55] The Bullards designed her "cottage" in the same colonial revival style as Rose Hill, the century-old mansion adjoining the hospital property they were renovating for their own family to live in.

So in early September 1935, Frieda returned to Rockville as a permanent member of the Lodge staff. Erich came down from New York for a weekend visit, and they agreed to continue their separate living arrangements. She told the Bullards she would put up with the awkward layout of her quarters so long as the cottage was built within the next few months. (Frieda's room on the first floor of the main building was next to the bathroom, and Dexter's mother had to squeeze past her bed in the middle of the night to get to the toilet.)

Frieda's long hours and constant efforts to fit in quickly endeared her to both Dexter and Anne. She cheerfully volunteered for night duty, throwing on a bathrobe and climbing the stairs whenever the nurses had a troublesome patient. She told Julia Waddell, hired that same year as nurse, chief housekeeper, and Anne's second-in-command: "I want to behave just like Ameri-

cans do. I don't want to be different." Julia, the first in a long line of depressed women who came to idolize Frieda, quickly began offering suggestions for attire at parties and the proper style for addressing invitations.
(Frieda knew she couldn't intuit the social customs of the Southern WASP
upper class.) As always, she provided reassurance in return. When Waddell's
husband was sent overseas after war broke out in Europe, Frieda declared
with characteristic certainty, "Never have any fear about whether he will be
back," and Julia stopped worrying. The Bullards also appreciated Frieda's
willingness to perfect her language skills. Unlike Hannah Arendt, for example, who upon her arrival in America sought "a job where she would not have
to rely on her still uncertain English," Frieda plunged into work requiring
mastery of linguistic subtleties, encouraging patients to correct her errors.[56]

In 1936, Frieda moved into her new home, a joyful occasion she celebrated with a large housewarming party. Friends and colleagues from New
York came down on the train or sent gifts, and although she was living in far
more modest circumstances than she had in Heidelberg, Frieda was deeply
touched by the outpouring of support for her "resettlement." Later, her friend
Hilde Bruch, herself a refugee, would nickname Frieda's cottage "the mousetrap" after hearing the saying, "The world will beat a path to your door if you
build a better mousetrap," an expression that perfectly epitomized the place
and sounded hilarious to their German ears.[57] The cottage was simultaneously Frieda's home and her office, a building owned by the Lodge (which
she formally rented), yet one always perceived as wholly hers. Its modest,
tasteful furnishings had a distinctly Old World feel, an odd mix with the clapboard construction and rural Maryland design. Built by Lodge carpenters in
less than five months, the cottage was the place that patients, students, colleagues, and friends most associated with Frieda. Living at the Lodge must
have felt comfortingly familiar to her—European psychiatrists were typically housed on hospital grounds—and Frieda considered it natural for patients to know their doctors' peccadilloes, much as students at small colleges
learn of their professors' love affairs.

From the outside, the cottage looked as though it belonged on a postcard
of a New England town (the Bullards actually did use a photograph of it
buried in snow on a Christmas card). The inside, however, was nothing like
Cape Cod. The place had been specifically designed for a psychiatrist to
work in (and was called simply "doctor's cottage" on the blueprints), giving
it certain unusual features, like a narrow office near the entrance for a secre-
tary-receptionist, and soundproof double doors on the consulting room. The
cabinets on the first floor had special locks to protect their contents from un-

ruly patients, and the front door had an extra device that could be fastened from the inside to deter unexpected "visitors."

Frieda was the only doctor ever to live there, and the place was soon being called "Fromm-Reichmann cottage" even on official maps of the grounds. Its decor reflected Frieda's utilitarian assumption that money was something to be used to help other people. Unlike fellow analyst Harry Stack Sullivan, who went through periods of lavish buying and elaborately redecorated five different residences in New York and Maryland, or Karen Horney, who lived in a double-sized apartment with a spectacular view of Central Park and was constantly purchasing new country houses for weekend escapes, Frieda lived in the same place, with the same furniture, for the twenty-two years she was in the United States. Even in the postwar period, when many émigré analysts of her age and social class settled into luxurious New York apartments or bought sprawling suburban homes, she remained in this cottage on hospital grounds. It wasn't that she lacked taste; she insisted on clothing of excellent material, disdained American costume jewelry as cheap looking, served meals on silver and crystal, and bought Mexican art. But ever since her days at Weisser Hirsch, Frieda had actively scorned the excesses of wealth. (During her many visits to Groddeck in Baden-Baden, she always teased him about practicing in a town famed for its elegant shops, neoclassical *kurhaus,* and a casino that Marlene Dietrich called "the most magnificent in the world.") Even when the Lodge began to fill up with patients who, as one colleague remarked, "could lie down on their beds and make more money in one day than we made in a month or a year," Frieda spent the rest of her life living in what they regarded as a "shanty."[58]

But she was happy there. She had grounds staff plant a large garden in the backyard, and the flowers were visible from the front hall. She kept liquor for parties in one of the cabinets with the special locks, along with large cans of her favorite white asparagus and the kosher dishes she reserved for visits from relatives. Eventually the Bullards built a screened porch onto the back of the cottage, and Frieda often sat there in the evenings to read or relax. If she had guests for dinner, she opened a folding table in the living room. With the main building less than a hundred yards away, she was always subliminally aware of whatever was happening on the wards, often telephoning nurses late at night to report a light left on or a wandering patient. "You'd think she was in charge of the housekeeping," said a colleague, shaking his head. He had no idea that living so close to patients made the Lodge feel like home to her.

This lack of separation between Frieda's personal life and hospital culture would later make her younger colleagues uncomfortable. "Everybody always knew where she was," Otto Will recalled. "Her car was there or it wasn't. Dexter's office was right across the way and his desk was right in front of the window—he could see exactly who came in and out of her door. . . . I don't think I could have stood that cottage." Will said he wished Frieda had bought a house in Bethesda and drove out to the Lodge during working hours. But Jarl Dyrud, Bullard's son-in-law, understood this difference between Frieda and the other doctors. "They were doing something that was not entirely themselves. They had to be somewhere else to be themselves, and Frieda didn't."[59] Having lost every other vestige of her former life, being a psychiatrist twenty-four hours a day was absolutely crucial to Frieda's psychic survival.

In her first few years at the Lodge, Frieda grew close to her colleague Marjorie Jarvis. (She and Frieda and Dexter constituted the entire medical staff in those days, so the two women naturally spent a lot of time together.) Bullard often made it sound as if Jarvis had only dabbled in analysis, but actually she had more training than most other Americans of the period (including a long analysis with Clara Thompson and a year of study in Budapest). Jarvis shared Frieda's interest in Ferenczi's work, and despite striking differences in the two women's backgrounds, Frieda cherished their friendship during this initial period of her "resettlement."

With her finely sculpted face and trained singing voice, Jarvis cut an elegant figure, carrying a carved cigarette holder, and once appearing at a Lodge party in a feather boa. Remembered by colleague Don Burnham for her "engaging vagueness," she was clearly able, when she felt like it, to zero in precisely on what a patient needed. She had an underlying strength despite a somewhat fragile exterior, like the delicate needlepoint chair in her office that Dexter, with his fullback build, for some reason liked to sit on.

Jarvis was divorced with a young child, and most of what we know of her comes from "Young Marjorie," as her daughter was still being called in her seventies. As the only child of a single, working mother, Marjorie was thrilled to be included in the "Lodge family" and spent hours frolicking with patients and Bullards. She especially loved formal dinners with the family (in their private dining room, just across from hydrotherapy), when Anne would press the foot buzzer and the maid would magically appear with the next course.

Jarvis, however, was frequently depressed and suffered from migraines, and Marjorie absorbed her anxiety, as intense, solitary children often end up doing. Sixty years later, she was still bitter at being "deserted for a whole year" while her mother studied in Europe, and spending much of her childhood in waiting rooms. As a single mother in the days before day care, Jarvis had no choice but to drag her daughter wherever she went. "When I was little I knew all the analysts on the eastern seaboard," Marjorie bragged, but it wasn't much compensation for the years of neglect. She did, however, remember certain fond moments, like the time Sullivan, surrounded by a roomful of sycophants waiting "to hear the word of God from his exalted lips," winked at Marjorie and launched into a description of how camel drivers tasted the urine of their animals to determine if they were pregnant.[60]

Jarvis had been on the staff for less than a year when Frieda, who had decades more experience in psychiatry and psychoanalysis, arrived as the summer replacement. Jarvis must have felt Frieda's seniority as something of a threat, despite Frieda's denigration of herself as the poor refugee, lucky to be rescued by the wealthy Americans. Marjorie remembers sitting on the front porch of the main building that first summer, telling stories about America and pretending to understand the heavily accented English of her mother's new colleague. Others recall the "Mutt and Jeff" contrast in their appearances, with dumpy Frieda at four feet ten inches and the elegant Jarvis standing close to six feet.

Jarvis took Frieda shopping and to concerts, and they looked quite dashing with their matching cigarette holders. Once, on a jaunt, they even tried one of Wilhelm Reich's orgone boxes. (Their reactions, alas, were unrecorded.) The two women were exactly the same age, and despite the disparities in their backgrounds—Jarvis was from a distinguished New England family—they shared the stigma that divorce and medical education carried for women in the 1930s.

For reasons no one seems to know, their friendship cooled after the war years. Perhaps Jarvis, who never thought very well of herself, envied Frieda's growing reputation. Perhaps Bullard's differential treatment created too much awkwardness between them. (Marjorie recalls her mother coming home from work one day announcing: "Dexter is going to allow me to practice at home and leave the staff of the Lodge." He probably didn't fire her, but he clearly didn't do anything to keep her.) Or Frieda may have lost patience with Jarvis's increasing narcissism. Colleagues recall her pressing students to do errands or otherwise cater to her. (She startled one analysand by telephoning before his scheduled hour to ask: "If you don't mind, would you pick up a pound of hamburger on your way over?").[61]

Frieda remained closer to Marjorie. If Jarvis had to go out of town, the girl would spend the night at the cottage, and sometimes, as a treat, Frieda would invite her over for a special meal. Marjorie remembered one day in particular, when Frieda served her a formal lunch in the backyard (actually serving was Edna Yates, the genteel, light-skinned wife of Raymond Yates, the Lodge carpenter, who worked as Frieda's maid in the early years). It was a scorching summer day. Frieda had instructed Edna to set the table with silver and crystal, and the glare of the Maryland sun off the heavy trays was blinding. "I was sitting there just dying, too shy and self-deprecating to say anything," Marjorie recalled years later. Automatically sensing her discomfort, Frieda simply rose from her chair, asked Edna to carry everything back in, and resumed eating with no comment.

By playing the older sister to Marjorie, as she was to do with the children of many of her other friends, Frieda could safely reenact her relationships with Grete and Anna without the guilt of actual responsibility. When Marjorie lashed out at Jarvis for not being there like other mothers when she came home from school, Frieda explained the difficult life of single women. She didn't always approve of her friend's actions (like the time Jarvis led her daughter past tier after tier of screaming men in a prison on her way to visit a former patient), but Frieda empathized with the hidden neediness of their relationship, so like hers with Klara.

Frieda gave Marjorie what she most longed for herself: intuitive understanding. Before Marjorie left for college, Frieda took her to one of Washington's fanciest shops for a going-away present. Marjorie wanted one of the stylish little cases women carried on trains in those days. Frieda immediately sensed which one she liked best and bought it, even though it was far more expensive than the others. "And I went off so proud with a pigskin case with this little pig embossed on the back as a kind of logo," said Marjorie wistfully. "I often wondered why this famous, busy person would pay attention to me," clearly grateful for Frieda's notice.

Once her situation at the Lodge seemed secure, Frieda began the process of applying to become a U.S. citizen.[62] She passed her medical boards in 1936—characteristically, on her first try—and got her American license. Then, to the great joy of her family, she managed to save enough money to travel to Europe in July of that year. In Interlaken, Switzerland (a neutral location where they could all meet in safety), she spent several weeks in an ecstatic reunion with Klara, Grete, Anna, and Alisa. Frieda told wonderful stories about the United States—"a country where everybody is friendly and people call each other by their first names"—and amused her family with definitions of unusual English phrases. Ever pragmatic, she also used the time to take a few driving lessons. Klara considered this an absurd luxury in the midst of the Depression, but Frieda explained that she couldn't live in

Rockville without a car; even the woman who cleaned her house owned an automobile. Klara was so relieved to have all three daughters together with her again that she bought them matching rings as a lasting memento, a deeply symbolic gesture that evoked the moment in Lessing's *Nathan the Wise,* one of her favorite German classics, where a father gives identical rings to his three sons. But Alisa remembered most vividly the painful leave-taking, with each of them departing for a different country and an uncertain future. "Anna and I were on a train. Frieda stood on the track waving goodbye. It all seemed such fun to me as a child. Suddenly I saw what looked like rain on Frieda's navy blue pleated blouse. Looking higher up, I saw where it came from. She stood smiling, but behind her glasses big silent terrible tears were rolling down."[63]

Frieda was to be totally cut off from her family for the next ten years, a time of war, struggle, and constant fear. In the brief period in the late 1930s when travel was still possible, Anna, Klara, and Grete did manage to see each other a few times, and once they spent Passover together somewhere in Luxembourg. Klara sent packages to help Anna's family, and Emma also visited while they were still in France. Horrified to find the Jacobsons packed into a dirty attic with no bathroom, Emma "immediately started cleaning and scrubbing everything, including Anna." They had so little food that Anna tried to eat a sandwich with bacon she found in Emma's suitcase; Emma, the Christian maid, snatched it away, saying she couldn't have food that wasn't kosher. (Anna had given up Orthodox practice years earlier, but Emma still ran a kosher home for Klara and Grete and apparently couldn't bring herself to violate its rules even under these circumstances.) The next time Emma visited, Hans had gotten a job and things were less tense, with outings in the German-speaking countryside in Alsace and a festive meal with the neighbors, prepared by Emma with special Königsberg delicacies.[64]

But as the 1930s wore on, Anna and Frieda both grew more and more frightened by Klara's refusal to leave Berlin. "Old trees can't be transplanted," she kept insisting, a painfully apt image for a person as stolid as she. Jews were forced to carry special identification cards and were subject to a range of daily humiliations, but Klara still had her old-age pension and life to her seemed little changed. Her blind denial of the danger put her whole family at risk and accentuated the stoicism with which she had met all of life's difficulties. She and Grete, Emma, and her sister Helene Simon were still living in the big apartment on Jenaerstrasse. Grete had lost her job and was frantic for them to leave, but felt powerless to challenge her mother's authority. Helene continued her political work clandestinely, sheltering persecuted friends and acquaintances who needed places to stay. But Klara's intransigence weakened her own good judgment, and at seventy-five, Helene didn't have the energy to fight her sister, the head of the household.[65]

By 1938, Jews were forbidden to enter theaters, concert halls, or museums; to sit on park benches; or to visit certain districts of the city. Fortunately, Emma was over forty-five and thus exempt from the Nuremberg law prohibiting "Aryans" under that age from working in Jewish households. After stores restricted their sales to "German" customers, Emma did all the shopping.

To Frieda's horror, even the terror of the November pogrom (cynically called *Kristallnacht* by the Nazis) failed to galvanize Klara. Throughout the day and night of November 9–10, 1938, in what the *New York Times,* in a front-page article, termed "a wave of destruction . . . unparalleled in Germany since the Thirty Years War" three centuries earlier, the Nazis sought to destroy all tangible evidence of Jewish culture. The streets of every German city "resounded to the shattering of shop windows falling to the pavement, the dull thud of furniture and fittings being pounded to pieces and the clamor of fire brigades rushing to burning shops and synagogues. . . . By nightfall, there was scarcely a Jewish shop, café, office or synagogue in the country that was not either wrecked, burned severely, or damaged." Jeering Nazis kicked in the doors of Jewish homes, demolishing furniture and paintings, and throwing crystal glasses by the handful out the windows. More than 200 Jews were murdered outright that day; 30,000 others were dragged from their houses—many without even being allowed to put on their shoes—and sent to concentration camps. Three hundred synagogues were burned to the ground or demolished, and 8,000 stores and businesses owned by Jews were vandalized or ruined within a twenty-four-hour period.[66] The synagogue where Klara had spent every Shabbat and holiday for more than a decade was totally destroyed. The *Times* ended its story with the ominous statement: "The Jews, who have now lost most of their possessions and livelihood, will either be thrown into the streets or put into ghettos and concentration camps, or impressed into labor brigades and put to work for the Third Reich, as the children of Israel were once before for the pharaohs." In Berlin, Klara shut herself in her room and stopped listening to news reports.

The following spring, a cousin in Belgium called Hans and Anna in France, itself a sign of emergency; telephoning from one country to another was prohibitively expensive and done only in the most dire circumstances. She implored them to do something, anything, to get Klara and the others out of Germany. Hans and Anna, who had been trying desperately for months to convince Klara to face what was happening, made one last effort, sending another relative to Berlin to try to impress the urgency of the situation upon her.[67]

Finally, late in the summer of 1939, barely weeks before war was declared, Klara and the others fled to England. By then it was almost impossible to get visas to enter the United States, so Frieda took advantage of the British government's brief moment of guilt and got them permission to wait in London until affidavits to go on to America could be secured. (Refugees weren't allowed to stay in England, only to pause there if they could prove they were "transmigrants.") Had Klara held out even a month longer, she and Grete and Helene would likely have ended up being marched through the streets of Berlin to the Grunewald tram station and loaded on the special trains that arrived at Auschwitz just as the gas was turned on.

Forbidden to take any money out of Germany and facing who knew what privations, Klara decided they should all have one last fling. In grand style—despite the humiliation of having the Nazi epithet "Sara" added to their names and watching as their passports were stamped with the large red "J"—the three of them traveled by airplane to London, "a very daring thing for an old lady," Klara later liked to tell people. They planned to stay there only as long as it took to get permission to join Frieda in the United States. Emma was left in Berlin. Klara had given her whatever money the Nazis hadn't extorted as "Reich flight tax," convinced that Emma would be more comfortable amid familiar surroundings than living as a refugee in America, unable to speak the language. Hans was furious and tried to force Klara to send Emma to them in France. "He feared a tragedy," Alisa recalled, "and how right he was. Emma died by the roadside, running away from Polish soldiers, in 1945."[68]

Hans took his wife and daughter to London as soon as Klara and the others arrived. Then, on the day before war broke out, he talked his way onto the last ship back to Paris "to do his duty" as a medical officer in the French army. Anna and Alisa would not see him again for more than six years.

Once war was declared, all travel was prohibited, and Klara and her family were trapped in England. Frieda took care of them, as she always had. Parcels of clothing started arriving regularly. "They all seemed new to us," Alisa recalled, "but Frieda explained that she could not use them anymore as she had been seen too often in them already, which one did not do in America. Probably she simply didn't want to hurt Hans's feelings." Every month, Frieda paid the rent at the boardinghouse in London where Grete, Klara, and Aunt Helene were living. She also supported a cousin and his wife and their four little sons crammed nearby in a rented room (and later managed to bring them to the United States). At one point during the war, Klara counted more than a dozen people being supported primarily by Frieda. According to Alisa, "there were probably even more, but this was the kind of thing Frieda never

wrote to the family in England about. The only time she mentioned something was when she praised a cousin for paying her back every month!"
(Having chosen early in life to "accept the hero role in the family," as one biographer put it, Frieda didn't need to draw attention to herself.)[69] Refugees
weren't allowed regular employment, so Grete and Anna worked at whatever
odd jobs they could manage to get. As soon as Alisa was legally permitted to
leave school, she also helped to supplement their meager income. "Poor
Frieda was very upset about this and wrote me long letters about the importance of an education, but I knew I was doing the right thing." Klara did what
she could to make money for "luxuries," which she refused to finance with
Frieda's funds. One of Alisa's clearest memories from that time was of her
grandmother giving her two pennies a week as spending money, which Klara
had earned by mending neighbors' socks. "She was an expert at mending,"
said Alisa, clearly thinking of that terrible night when Klara had silently re-
paired Frieda's torn underwear.[70]

At one point, Grete and Klara got a job making flashlight batteries, an
extremely messy job they did on the kitchen table. "They loved doing it," recalled Alisa, "as it was all for the war effort. Grete was also quite something—during the Blitz she stood on the rooftops of London buildings as a
fire watcher, a tin hat on her head!" Klara often visited Erich's mother, also
trapped in London. Mrs. Fromm, who clearly would have preferred that
Erich and Frieda stay married, was fond of all the Reichmanns. Alisa remembered her as "always very kind and warm," often giving gifts, most of
them pink, her favorite color. (Her presents of pink lingerie were famous in
the family.)

The British government had never intended to absorb the 40,000 Jewish
refugees it had allowed to enter the United Kingdom on their way to other
places and remained deeply insensitive to their feelings. After the outbreak of
war, all Germans, including the refugees, were declared "enemy aliens" and
forbidden to own maps, cameras, or radios lest they use them to spy for the
Nazis. Curfews were imposed, and people with German accents were often
denied food in shops. In 1940, increasingly worried about the danger of fifth
columnists, the government interned thousands of Germans on the Isle of
Man, housing Jewish refugees indiscriminately with Nazi sympathizers.
Those Jews who remained in London, like Klara and her family, were
warned by refugee groups not to speak German in public, to dress unobtru-
sively, and never to criticize anything English.

• • •

Off in America, Frieda had a much easier time adjusting. In a country of immigrants, it was considered natural for refugees to want to speak their native language, at least among themselves, and to retain cultural practices that reminded them of their former lives. Those who chose to become "Americans" could do so relatively easily, unlike refugees in Britain, who painfully learned the lesson that "you have to be born English to be English." But although she always felt grateful to the United States for sheltering her, Frieda was never really at home there, identifying at a profound level with Stefan Zweig's plaintive comment on his life as a displaced Viennese Jew: "I belong nowhere, and everywhere am a stranger, a guest at best."[71]

Burying her feelings, as always, in work, Frieda spent long hours seeing patients at the Lodge and in a private practice she had started. She was also a training analyst at the Washington-Baltimore Psychoanalytic Institute, and its elected president from 1939 to 1941.[72] Out of unconscious guilt at her own safety, or to distract herself from constant worry about friends and relatives still trapped in Europe, she kept taking on more and more patients. (She clearly also needed the money, given how many people she was supporting.)

In early 1936, Gertrud Jacob came to Rockville to live with her. Jacob had worked for several months at a sanitarium in Peoria soon after she and Frieda came to the United States, and had then accepted a position at the Menninger Clinic.[73] But Jacob had lasted only five months in Topeka. This was not for lack of skill—"her quick sensitiveness, her quiet reserve, her capable gifts both as an analyst and an artist deeply impressed everyone there"—it was because of illness. A severe attack of influenza had reactivated the tuberculosis Jacob had gotten from (heroically or absurdly) tube-feeding a patient with a fulminating pulmonary infection. When she grew too ill to work, she moved in with Frieda, who, tireless as ever, somehow managed to nurse Jacob through countless relapses while supporting all her relatives in Europe, carrying a full load of patients, and helping to run a hospital and a psychoanalytic institute.

Frieda had always, as an early biographer disparagingly put it, "taken in strays" (think of the daughter of her morphine addict friend from Königsberg), but to describe her life with Jacob in those terms is to utterly misread its meaning. The two women had been in America for less than a year when Jacob arrived in Rockville. Despite their both having gotten good jobs, they were living a precarious refugee existence. For Frieda to share her new home with Jacob—her closest friend in the United States, someone who knew her family and her whole world in Germany, now so painfully wrenched away—must have been extraordinarily comforting. (It must also have been an enormous reassurance to Jacob, who was alone in America and seriously ill. Even while still at Menninger, she had told Erich in a letter how lonely it was out there.) To imagine the two women puttering about the cottage together, speaking German to one another and relaxing at night in the heavy, over-stuffed chairs Erich had sent as a housewarming present—chairs far too big for the room, making it feel distinctly European—Frieda and Jacob seem a warm, supportive couple. And they shared a deeper bond as well—a word-less, magnetic draw to psychotic patients that others found so difficult to comprehend. Frieda clearly played her typical role of older sister in the rela-tionship, supporting Jacob financially and nursing her through repeated bouts of illness, but for once Frieda was deeply understood in return, which must have made all the difference.

Jacob was vulnerable enough to take care of, but gifted in ways Frieda's other women friends—Marjorie Jarvis, Edith Weigert, Hilde Bruch—simply weren't. Frieda had always been drawn to tormented artists, poring over bi-ographies of Schumann, Nijinsky, and van Gogh, fascinated by a talent that sprang from the same source as the anguish. Jacob was just such a person, and like Frieda, she had an intuitive understanding of psychosis, which gave their friendship a special depth and meaning. At one point, they even began writing a book together, for which Jacob did a series of paintings that each depicted a specific psychological state ("anxiety," "loneliness," "grandeur," "hostility"), and Frieda wrote accompanying profiles (which read like short stories but were based on actual cases).[74]

Most people found Jacob's portraits of psychotics unnerving; they were so eerily accurate, it felt as if the patient were in the room. Fifty years later, Anne Bullard could recall the painting that hung above Frieda's fireplace with such vividness that it still gave her a chill. But Frieda loved these por-traits—with their bold colors, so reminiscent of Kokoschka—more than any other art, and she hung them in every room of the cottage, rotating her col-lection periodically so as to better appreciate each one. After a day of work-ing with very sick patients, this was what she wanted to see on her walls.

For a brief period in the late 1930s, Jacob recovered sufficiently to treat a few Lodge patients. Bullard called her "an intelligent psychoanalytic theorist and a good psychiatric observer," whose contributions were "concise, clear, generous and helpful." Others, though, wondered if she were herself a former patient. Anne called her "manic" and strange, and was offended by the "sen-sation" Jacob created by painting a nude portrait of Katherine Weininger, the wife of a psychiatrist who had just joined the staff.[75]

Jacob presented a (presumably nonautobiographical) paper, "Notes on a

Manic Depressive," to the Washington-Baltimore Psychoanalytic Society in May 1938 and was appointed to the institute's training committee the following year.[76] But whatever career she might have had in America was cut short by repeated recurrences of tuberculosis. Frieda tried her on one medication after another (continuing Jacob's practice of sending the prescriptions to Erich in New York so he could get them at a discount), and dragged her to hospitals all over the United States. Finally, in the summer of 1939, just as Frieda was frantically struggling to get Klara and the others out of Berlin, she took Jacob to New Mexico in the hope that a drier climate might help. Frieda fell in love with the desert, so reminiscent of Palestine, and eventually bought a small vacation house in the hills overlooking Santa Fe. But at the end of that first summer, with Jacob still quite ill, she had to leave her in the care of friends and return to work in Rockville. Jacob regained enough strength that fall to treat a few private patients, and Frieda was reassured that the tuberculosis sanitarium nearby could provide further treatment if needed.

But in February, Jacob suffered another relapse. Her lungs were so obstructed that surgery was recommended. On April 15, 1940, in circumstances that are unclear, she died on the operating table at a hospital in Albuquerque. Frieda was in Maryland, two thousand miles away. The person who had shared her life for almost as long as Erich had been taken from her by the same disease that had ended her marriage a decade earlier.

Frieda was devastated. To have escaped the Nazis with Jacob, spent two years in exile with her, nursed her through countless bouts of illness and moved her to Santa Fe, only to have her suddenly die had to have overwhelmed Frieda with the sense of futility and helplessness she had spent her whole life trying to avoid. One friend recalls her as being so grief stricken she couldn't play the piano for months afterward. Others remember her compulsively talking about Jacob, even to people who barely knew her, and then spending fruitless months seeking to get her portraits published and shown. Except for managing to get photographs of a few of the paintings included in the obituaries that appeared in psychiatric journals, Frieda was unsuccessful in these efforts, which had to have made her feel even more useless. Finally, she resorted to a private exhibition of the paintings at the cottage (complete with printed invitations, formal viewing hours, and an admission charge, donated to the Red Cross). Jacob's portraits remained Frieda's most treasured possessions, the only items listed individually in her will, and still revered as priceless mementos by those who inherited them.

In a lengthy memorial statement Frieda published in the *Psychoanalytic Quarterly,* she hailed Jacob's "brilliant and intuitive mind, passionately set for truth and beauty." She vowed "that friends would [for]ever feel her loss and cherish the memory of her refined and discriminating personality." Frieda's colleague, Billy Silverberg, was so moved by Jacob's portraits that he published his own tribute:

> Repellent though some of these pictures may be, their subjects are no longer ugly, for Dr. Jacob's psychiatric art has made the chaotic distortions of personality presented by these people orderly and human. . . . These pictures are alive. . . . Their creator has seen behind the armor which physiognomies present, back to the very core which animates their subjects. With marvelous and unerring accuracy she shows us the instinctual springs of their personalities and also the poor, pathetic defenses against these and against the outside world that make these people what they are. . . . Yet they are far from being merely types. . . . The psychiatrist cannot only diagnose the maladies of these people as accurately from their portraits as he could from actual contact with them; he can also tell something of their individual stories.

Silverberg described an extraordinary afternoon he had spent with Frieda and Jacob free-associating to some of the paintings. The two women had "looked at each other in wild amaze," stunned at the accuracy of his intuitions. "This is truly art," Silverberg declared, "to see so deeply into the nature of a person that one understands that which the surface masks; to have the manual technics wherewith to convey the mask and what there is behind it to any who may have eyes to see."[77] It was this uncanny ability that had first drawn Frieda to Jacob, this capacity to humanize the "fellow sufferers" with whom they had each chosen to spend their lives. No one else would ever see into that part of Frieda as acutely as Jacob had.

Music, the core of Frieda's emotional life since childhood, became even more crucial during the terrible period right after Jacob's death, with war just beginning in Europe and her family trapped thousands of miles away. The case of recordings Frieda had lugged across the border to Strasbourg took pride of place in her Rockville living room, and after long hours treating patients, she would sink wearily into the overstuffed arms of one of Erich's chairs and let the old scratchy records recreate the genteel world so brutally ripped away from her. As a rare indulgence, Frieda had purchased a state-of-the-art hi-fi system soon after arriving in America, and she often traded records with Sullivan, whose love of classical music had been acquired not from childhood concerts and lessons like Frieda's, but from listening to player piano rolls in his thirties.

Frieda had pianos in both Santa Fe and Rockville (uprights, since both houses were so small), and she played often, both alone and with colleagues. Otto Will remembered lively Bach trios at the cottage, with him on flute and Leslie Farber playing violin. And there were relaxed evenings after seminars, with Frieda serving beer, Alfred Stanton picking out popular tunes on the piano, and everyone singing.[78]

But alone, Frieda would retreat to the German romanticism of her childhood, the music of domesticity, like Mendelssohn's "Songs Without Words," her favorite pieces. Dismissed by critics as "jam made with too much sugar," the songs are "simple character sketches," "folk melodies in evening dress," whose harmonies, "in every way traditional," have none of Chopin's inventiveness. But they are powerful evocations of mood, and this must have been what drew Frieda to them. With wards of screaming mental patients a hundred yards away and her family in a city besieged by nightly bombing raids, she could escape with her piano to "the well-appointed drawing room, the domestic circle," creating miniature mood pictures, "the poetic essence of a moment." Solo pieces written "for the ladies," the Songs Without Words were an intimate form of artistry that reflected Mendelssohn's distrust of wildness and provocation. Each "is a complete, well-proportioned and satisfying entity, presented as though in a finely carved frame. Abrupt endings, surprise effects . . . or similar practices of extravagant, autobiographic romanticism" have no place in them.

Frieda was especially fond of the song Mendelssohn's publisher had sentimentally entitled "Lost Happiness." Simple in texture, its wistful melody chopped into shorter and shorter units, giving a foreclosing feeling, the piece seems to climb toward something it never reaches. Wolf Weigert, son of Frieda's friend Edith, remembers her playing it so often he thought of it as "Frieda's song." To Weigert, the title was painfully apt: "She was married to Erich Fromm. I guess that was Frieda's lost happiness." The phrases of the piece, tumbling from her fingers again and again, must have felt intensely soothing, like moments in a lost life, echoing through the air.[79]

Her house in Santa Fe was also a refuge during this painful period. The desert has always evoked the deepest unconscious states; it was where Jesus had his visions, and where fourth-century monks retreated to pray, their asceticism fueling a piety we can barely imagine. It's no accident that the only property Frieda ever owned in the United States was a simple adobe dwelling in New Mexico. She went there every summer for a dozen years, to spend two months in the shadow of the red hills immortalized by Georgia

O'Keeffe. Frieda always said the landscape reminded her of Palestine, unsurprising for a mountain range named "Blood of Christ." People who have never been there think that O'Keeffe dramatized the color of those hills for artistic effect, but as soon as anyone sees them, they know that when the Indians called them blood, they weren't being metaphoric.

What makes the desert eerie is the silence. The air is so thin you can hear blades of grass rubbing against each other. The wind is alive. Bare hills bounce sound around in weird patterns; a bird half a mile off can startle you with its shriek. You start hearing sounds that aren't there, just to ease the stillness. Seeing things is next, at least for some people, and after that, there's no telling what will start to seem real.

Frieda was too down-to-earth for visions or otherworldly experience, but she was fascinated by people who could lose themselves in trance or ecstasy, and often went to Zuni dances or tribal ceremonies. She loved to walk through the pueblos, recreating ancient worlds amidst the ruins. Most of the time, though, she simply sat on her terrace, gazing out at the desert scrub, the mountains in the background, her thoughts far off.[80]

Back in Rockville, Frieda buried herself in work. As millions of Europeans were being slaughtered or forced into exile, when huge armies lined up against one another and national identities became paramount, Frieda focused, as always, on the individual. Hilde Bruch recalled her reaction to Pearl Harbor. Bruch, who lived in Baltimore at the time, traveled in a carpool with other analysts to a seminar Frieda held in her home on Monday evenings. "Then came the meeting on December 8, 1941 [the day Roosevelt issued his declaration of war]. The exodus to Rockville meant driving without headlights, but the two cars went just the same. This evening stands out vividly in my memory," Bruch later wrote. "Everybody talked about what he or she was going to do for the war effort, and everybody had grandiose ideas. Frieda said very quietly, 'I know what I'm going to do. I'll do what I know best. I'll do psychotherapy.'"[81]

And that's exactly what she did. Living a life, even in wartime, where she had people to attend to all her other needs, Frieda saw patients; she didn't, like other American women, stand in line for ration books, or roll bandages, or organize scrap metal drives.

Bruch added herself to the long list of people Frieda was already caring for. Bruch's whole family was still in Germany, subject to constant terror and threat of deportation, and Frieda was one of few colleagues who understood firsthand how agonizing this was. When Bruch asked Frieda if she could see her for therapy, Frieda squeezed her in every Wednesday, Saturday, and Sunday despite an already packed schedule, an arrangement that continued until the end of the war. For three of those years, Bruch also accompanied Frieda when she went away for the summer, to avoid breaks in the treatment. Although they had less personal contact during the period when Bruch was a patient, the two women stayed close friends for the rest of their lives. "We had many similarities in our living habits, in the ways we cooked, in what we ate, and in how we ran a household," Bruch recalled. "It is always surprising how much of one's intimate life is tied up with these everyday things." And they could speak German together, the language Ernst Weiss called "our whole life, all that remained to us . . . in which we thought, hoped, feared, calculated, remembered, and dreamed," now a forbidden tongue, the language of evil and violence.[82]

Frieda never suffered from serious depression the way Bruch and many of her other refugee friends did. But she was clearly distressed. Told about the concentration camps, she vomited and ran from the room. Like many German Jews, Frieda and her immediate family had managed to escape, but more than a hundred of her other relatives were murdered by the Nazis. Dozens more survived but lost everything.[83]

And during that terrible period in the late 1930s, when it still seemed possible to rescue people from the camps, Frieda spent hours interceding on behalf of friends and colleagues for the precious affidavits that literally meant the difference between life and death. She succeeded in many cases, but was tormented by the failures, especially Karl Landauer, her close colleague from Frankfurt. Despite her best efforts to find a position for him at the Menninger Clinic and a dozen desperate letters back and forth to her friend Max Horkheimer, who was working equally hard in New York trying to secure some other kind of job offer, Landauer perished in Bergen-Belsen. As Frieda would likely have done had she suffered the same fate, Landauer managed to provide psychotherapy to some fellow inmates before being tortured to death.[84]

In 1942, Frieda and Erich divorced, after technically having been married for sixteen years. She filed the case (standard practice for women in 1940s America) and appeared at the hearing. Erich paid the costs and was not present. The state of Maryland politely listed her as "over twenty-one years of age" (she was then fifty-two); Dexter and Marjorie Jarvis served as her witnesses. (Asked his occupation, Bullard responded: "I am a physician"; to the same question, Frieda answered, revealingly: "I am a psychiatrist.")[85]

She gave a characteristically matter-of-fact account of the marriage, saying that Erich had gone to Switzerland "on account of his health," and they had not "lived as man and wife" (the state's phrasing) since then. Frieda gave a terse "no" to such questions as: "Since you and your husband have been living in America, have you ever had sexual relations?" and "Has your husband contributed anything to your support since you have been in America?" Then, in an oblique reference to Erich's many affairs, she added: "In view of the fact that there is a difference in age of ten years [between us], I think it was quite evident that both parties would agree that neither of us felt like going on with married life."

They remained close friends, however, as they had since Heidelberg, visiting one another often in New York and Washington, moving in the same professional circles, and sharing many of the same friends and students. The year after the divorce, they worked closely together (with three other colleagues) to found a renegade psychoanalytic institute, much like the one they had started together in Frankfurt two decades earlier.

It was Erich who furnished Frieda's living room in Rockville, Erich who loaned her money when she needed it and served as a sounding board for her ideas. Dependent on him in America in ways she had never been during their marriage, he remained one of her true intimates. Gradually the "little Erich" Frieda had once made fun of turned into someone she seemed to idolize. Colleagues remember her giving the introduction at one of the many public lectures he gave in New York in the 1940s and being embarrassed by her effusiveness. Erich's subsequent marriages to two other women seemed to have little effect on Frieda's feelings; she wrote warm, chatty letters to both wives, and named Erich the executor of her will, thirty years after their separation. (As one of his biographers dryly noted: "It is probably no coincidence that neither Fromm's second or third wife was a psychoanalyst or appreciably older than he.") The curse of *karet* remained a powerful shadow in both their lives. Despite Erich's affairs and multiple marriages, neither he nor Frieda ever had a child.[86]

Her student Lawrence Kolb once made the intriguing comment that Frieda held the same values for Erich as she did for her psychotic patients. "When I inquired about the reasons for the divorce," Kolb recalled, "she said she felt it was only right for every individual to have the maximum opportunity to develop themselves freely. This comment, which might have been a rationalization, was nevertheless a remarkable statement [and precisely what] made it possible for her to work with schizophrenics. . . . She never forced her value system on patients, and she always taught that to students."[87]

• • •

When the war finally ended and travel restrictions were lifted, Frieda was eager for her mother and sisters to join her in America as they had intended. But Klara, always worried about being "a burden on Frieda," felt she was too old to make yet another move. She and Helene and Grete had gotten used to life in London's Finsbury Park, in a boardinghouse run by a German-Jewish family, filled with other refugees. It was hard enough for Klara, living in a foreign country in her old age, to understand through deaf ears an English so different from the one she had studied in school, decades earlier. She had learned to get by, giving people a warm smile, saying, "I'm deaf, please write it down on paper," and then handing over the pencil and little notebook she carried with her everywhere. (According to family legend, she once boarded a train with a sign around her neck that read: "Please put me out in Birmingham.") Grete, trying as always not to call attention to herself, struggled to hide her own increasing deafness by giving what she hoped was an answer to whatever had been asked, or changing the subject.[88]

When it became clear to Frieda that her efforts to bring her family to America were not succeeding, she got a special permit to travel by plane to visit them in England in December 1945. It was the first time they had seen one another in almost ten years, and despite the ravages of the Blitz still visible everywhere around them, the reunion was an intensely moving and joyful one. Through Sullivan's connections at the U.S. State Department, Frieda also got permission to bring Herbert Bruch, one of Hilde's few surviving relatives, back with her. Then thirteen years old, Herbert had spent the war in an English orphanage after his parents and sister were murdered in a concentration camp. Sullivan had arranged for him to join Hilde in Baltimore, but he wasn't permitted to travel unaccompanied. Herbert was so undernourished he looked no older than eight or nine, and the prospect of moving to a foreign country to live with an aunt he barely knew was terrifying. The moment he saw Frieda, however, he calmed down. She was as tiny as he was, and he reassured himself that all American doctors must be just his size. (Bruch, who was close to six feet tall, always appreciated Frieda's having inadvertently eased the transition for Herbert in a way she herself could never have done.)[89]

Frieda was intensely disappointed at not being able to bring her family to live with her, but was grateful that at least they were alive and well. Anna was back living in France, after a harrowing visit to Berlin right after the fighting ended, when Alisa, then sixteen, barely escaped being raped by marauding Russian soldiers, and Hans discovered that all his former patients had been exterminated as part of the Nazis' "euthanasia program."[90] Miraculously, however, Hans's sister, who had hidden in the subways during the entire war, had survived thanks to a Gentile woman who regularly left food for her in a tree hollow. After founding the Bureau for Prosecution of German War Criminal Physicians in Berlin, Hans returned to his work in France. In 1948, however, determined to make a new life, Alisa smuggled her way onto a ship bound for Palestine. Like dozens of other vessels, it was turned back because of the British blockade—"we saw Haifa from the sea but that was all"—but their daughter's action so impressed Hans and Anna that they decided to go together to the Holy Land. After an anguished stay in a camp for displaced persons in Cypress, they finally set sail on May 15, 1948, the day an independent state of Israel was declared. Eventually they settled on a *kibbutz*. Alisa, a "lonely only" child, felt the terrible burdens of her parents' lives. "They had wanted a dozen children," she recalled sadly, "but times were against them. They had a very hard life."[91]

Throughout all those years, no matter how pressed her schedule, Frieda wrote long letters to her mother and sisters, describing in rich detail everything that happened to her. She kept a Jewish calendar on her desk, knew precisely how long it took mail to reach England or Israel, and carefully sent each letter in time for it to be opened and read before Shabbat or the start of a holiday. She was "unbelievably loyal" to her family, recalled one relative, sending copies of her published papers even to distant cousins, not out of any sense of self-importance, but so they could "share in her life and accomplishments."[92]

But these efforts also reflected Frieda's lifelong struggle to hold on to a sense of Jewish identity in the aggressively secular (and sometimes anti-Semitic) medical worlds she chose to live in. Cut off from daily contact with anyone from her former life—unlike colleagues in New York, who could recreate the Old World within a large community of fellow refugees—Frieda had to settle for letters and occasional visits to break the isolation of living in Rockville. Having lost all vestiges of the warmth and closeness of those days in Heidelberg—first by Erich's leaving and then by her own forced exile—she had to confront war, Nazi terror, Jacob's death, and her family's suffering alone, and all within her first few years in the United States. Spending most of her time with very sick patients, living in an alien environment—totally different from the world exiles like Hannah Arendt made for themselves, "an atmosphere of German culture where the right quotation from Goethe was always at hand"[93]—Frieda plunged into developing new methods of treatment and creating a therapeutic community at Chestnut Lodge. In this sense, her partnership with Dexter Bullard was never just a job. It was her salvation and a way of ensuring a legacy for her work.

7

Improvising Method

*It is a safe rule to have no teaching without a patient for a text,
and the best teaching is that taught by the patient himself.*[1]

Portraits of four men hung above Frieda's desk at Chestnut Lodge: Kurt
Goldstein, Sigmund Freud, Georg Groddeck, and Harry Stack Sullivan. In
1950, when she published her major work, *Principles of Intensive Psychotherapy,* she dedicated it "To my teachers," followed (alphabetically) by these four
names. This wording was revealing, since she had never even met Freud, Groddeck and Sullivan were close friends, and Goldstein, her only actual teacher,
had supervised her work three decades earlier. "I want to show readers," Frieda
wrote to her editor, "that I am not sold on the teachings of any of the existing
and fighting psychiatric and psychoanalytic schools of thinking, but have en-
deavored to learn the best of [what these] four teachers stood for."[2]

She would have prevented a lot of misunderstanding had she made clear
that Goldstein, not Freud, was her most powerful influence. Analysts have always focused on Frieda's "deviations" from classical technique, but the key
to understanding her work is to see how Goldstein's studies of brain injury
provided the theoretical and moral framework for her whole approach to
treatment.

Frieda's 1942 paper on wartime psychotherapy provides key insights into her
thinking during these first years at Chestnut Lodge.[3] She took as her point of

departure the striking findings of colleagues in Britain, who had noted the extremely low incidence of psychiatric symptoms among civilian victims of the Blitz. A few people had needed sedation for brief periods, but if they were brought to a mobile unit right after the bombing and encouraged to express their feelings, even these victims had recovered "immediately and completely, no matter how severe the actual incident had been." Chronic disturbances occurred only among people unable to verbalize their terror.

Frieda argued that these findings precisely fit a psychoanalytic model of trauma. Millions of people faced violence and horror in their lives, yet few became psychotic. Therefore, it couldn't be the trauma itself that produced mental illness; it had to be the *repression* of the trauma—the cutting off of the event from subsequent experience (leaving it "an emotional foreign body at the bottom of our mental organism," in her characteristically awkward English wording).[4]

Trauma in the family, unlike that in war, couldn't be dealt with openly, making serious pathology far more likely to occur. A child could hardly be expected to express her rage or terror at rape or abuse if the "enemy" were her own parents. Repressing these feelings, often essential at the time, ultimately made the trauma more destructive by poisoning all the child's subsequent relationships.[5]

Casualties in a war that was invisible, psychotics were thus in the terrifying position of trying to protect themselves from dangers other people claimed weren't there. Imagine how frightening and bizarre it would be if everyone around you ignored the threats that came at you from all sides. Imagine how suspicious you would be of such people, how useless their reassurances would seem. Imagine how desperate you would feel as your frantic efforts to get anyone to pay attention to the terror continued to go unheard.

Even minor dangers can seem overwhelming if their effects are underlined. Someone alone in a house at night, frightened by an unexplained noise, startles at every sound. By morning, even the most stable person can be a trembling wreck. It doesn't matter whether the noises (even the original one) were actually a threat; the person *felt* they were, and that's what matters. A child abused at an early age might experience the babysitter's going home or the teacher's leaving the room as total abandonment. Years later, it might be hard to see this reaction as rooted in the original childhood trauma, but that didn't mean such links didn't exist. Frieda gave this example:

> I was walking around the grounds of our sanitarium with a [formerly] catatonic patient, who was at that time on very good terms with me. Suddenly he became frightened and tried to get away from me. I had no

idea why he did this. The next day I asked him about it. "We run away from fear of another rebuff," was his immediate reply. "This is the clue to each and every one of our reactions."[6]

Bizarre behavior, in other words, might be the only way a person could protect himself from being traumatized yet again. The more cryptic his behavior, the safer it might feel. One of Frieda's patients ridiculed her accent whenever he was angry with her. (This was in the early 1940s; he liked to call her "a Kraut" in front of other patients.) One day, after she made an interpretation he found useful, he asked, "Are you from Cambridge?" Frieda started to respond factually. Then she realized he was trying to compliment her, in an elaborately disguised manner that protected him from expressing the closeness he felt at that moment. "These experiences," Frieda declared, proved that the "seemingly meaningless and stereotyped actions of schizophrenics are meaningful, as are the rest of their communications." Most psychiatrists didn't know this because they spent so little time on the wards. Psychotic patients unconsciously colluded with their doctors' avoidance, "remaining cryptic and ambiguous" to protect themselves from the "danger of being misunderstood."[7] But they didn't get any better with physicians too insensitive to see through these defenses to the terrified, needy person underneath.

In a series of important papers published between 1939 and 1948, Frieda disputed the claim that schizophrenic patients were too "narcissistic" to be treated with psychoanalytic methods. Siding with a prominent minority in the analytic community (including Federn, Fenichel, Ferenczi, Abraham, and Fairbairn), she argued that no patient, however disturbed, was ever totally beyond the reach of psychotherapy. Traces of early relationship, "no matter how tenuous," could always be found, and these were sufficient to form a connection to the analyst. "There is," Frieda insisted, quoting Sullivan, "no developmental period when the human being exists outside the realm of interpersonal relatedness," which meant that no patient could be too regressed to form some kind of bond to his therapist.[8]

Instead of dismissing schizophrenic patients as untreatable, the way Freud felt the need to do, analysts ought to reach out to them. Desperately in need of closeness yet terrified by their own potential violence, psychotics were trapped in a vicious cycle that left them increasingly isolated. The question wasn't whether schizophrenic patients could be treated analytically, but whether psychoanalysts could stand up to the challenges of such work. Downplaying her disagreements with the mainstream as always, Frieda reminded colleagues that Freud had never actually opposed the treatment of psychotic patients; he had simply said that existing methods were inadequate to such a goal.[9]

Frieda's longstanding interest in transference and the dynamics of the therapeutic relationship, which dated from her experiences in medical school, drew her naturally to the "interpersonal" approach that Harry Stack Sullivan was developing in the late 1930s. Sullivan in fact became one of Frieda's closest friends in America, and his way of thinking confirmed and extended many of her own ideas. She met him soon after arriving—Erich and Sullivan moved in the same social circles and were very fond of one another—and it was at Frieda's urging that Sullivan was later brought to Chestnut Lodge to lead an extraordinary four-year seminar that powerfully shaped the ideology of the hospital.

Two people with backgrounds more different than Frieda and Sullivan can scarcely be imagined, but their intellectual debt to one another was profound and multilayered. Raised in upstate New York, the only surviving child of desperately poor Irish Catholic parents, Sullivan had grown up without electricity or plumbing on a farm so isolated he rarely saw a single person beyond the teachers and classmates at the tiny village school he attended, miles away. His two older brothers had died as infants, his mother had a mental breakdown when he was a toddler and disappeared for several years, and his farmer father drank heavily and rarely spoke to anyone. Considered a freak for his scholarly interests, the only close relationships Sullivan had in childhood were with the farm's cows and chickens. The year he graduated from high school, his county in New York State had a suicide rate more than twice that of the rest of the nation.

Sullivan attended Cornell University for two semesters, then vanished for several years during which he had a brief schizophrenic episode and was hospitalized under mysterious circumstances. He attended an unaccredited "diploma mill" medical school in Chicago, barely graduating, and then drifted around for several years doing odd jobs, often falsifying details of his background. An eccentric, difficult man who for the rest of his life would be fired from one job after another, Sullivan was given to extravagant, impractical tastes (drinking hundred-year-old French brandy, for example, when he was practically destitute). The contrast between his life and that of the cultured, European Frieda—doted on by every member of her large, intense Jewish family, encouraged in every scholarly pursuit, sought after by every employer, and utterly grounded in her own sanity—couldn't have been more dramatic.[10]

Yet they were drawn to one another by a powerful identification with "the lonely ones," the schizophrenic patients to whom they were each so devoted. Sullivan's background led naturally to this interest; Frieda's loneliness was more subtle—the isolation of being the person everyone depended on, never allowed any weaknesses of her own. Her far greater social skills smoothed his rough edges, and in this sense, Sullivan was yet one more man Frieda cared for. But they were very much kindred spirits, and their understanding of one another's neediness was nuanced and reassuring.

Sullivan's key ideas were developed at St. Elizabeths in the early 1920s. William Alanson White, the hospital's distinguished superintendent, had decided to take a chance on this strange young man who seemed to have such an uncanny way with mental patients. In the atmosphere of deep concern that White, "the great encourager," extended toward both staff and patients, Sullivan began to experiment with new ways of reaching schizophrenics. Powerfully influenced by his colleagues Lucile Dooley and Edward Kempf, who had been attempting psychoanalytic work with some of St. Elizabeths' most disturbed patients, Sullivan persuaded Ross McClure Chapman, the superintendent of Sheppard Pratt Hospital in nearby Towson, Maryland, to let him try out some of his most radical ideas.

On the experimental ward Sullivan established there, he tried to create an ideal environment in which young male patients experiencing their first schizophrenic break could have an experience of "benevolent intimacy" with the attendants hand-picked to serve as "chums," reinforcing a sense of shared humanity for all concerned. By the time Sullivan left Sheppard eight years later, he had become "a legend in both the clinical world and the world of the social sciences," whose therapeutic success with schizophrenic patients would inspire many younger psychiatrists.[11]

Sullivan's biographer has suggested that the extreme isolation and loneliness of his childhood may have helped to free him from any sense of loyalty to tradition or to family. Thus, he could much more easily strike out on his own than Frieda could, and this was clearly one of the qualities she most admired in him. Like Groddeck, Sullivan enjoyed thumbing his nose at the psychoanalytic establishment and was indifferent to whether people grasped what he was saying or agreed with him.

Frieda's colleagues always said that she "absorbed more of Sullivan's ideas than she needed to, making more of his contributions than they warranted," continuing a pattern of giving credit to powerful men for views she had independently arrived at years earlier. "She always deferred to him," one student recalled. "Even when announcing views that were just as much her own, she would preface her remarks by saying: 'As Dr. Sullivan has taught us . . . '"[12] His austere, convoluted style of writing differed sharply from her warm, unpretentious directness, and his anxieties about publishing (most of his work appeared posthumously) meant that many people first encountered Sullivan's "interpersonal psychiatry" from Frieda's writings.[13]

Yet she clearly loved learning a whole new language to describe what she already knew about working with schizophrenic patients, and was especially taken with Sullivan's image of psychotherapy as "participant observation." Both Frieda and her refugee friend Edith Weigert repeatedly told colleagues how happy they were to have found a new teacher in midlife. At times, however, Frieda got carried away, "admiring Sullivan extravagantly for characteristics he did not himself seem to value." Once, after she exclaimed, "he can hear the grass grow!" Sullivan dryly commented, "I'm not sure grass makes any noise when it's growing." But he deeply respected Frieda's own gifts, calling her "a clinician of extraordinary ability" and "emphatically recommending" that she be named to the highest rank in the American Psychiatric Association.[14]

Frieda especially appreciated Sullivan's focus on nonverbal communication, which reinforced ideas she had learned from Groddeck and Ferenczi. "Sullivan's genius was his capacity to pay attention," recalled Ben Weininger, an early Lodge colleague. This was much more than simple listening. Sullivan was like a Zen master, totally present to the patient. After years of treating schizophrenics himself and supervising the treatment of dozens of others, Bob Cohen, another Lodge colleague, declared: "More than anyone I have ever seen, Sullivan could sit down with someone who was unresponsive to everyone and somehow or other reach the person." Most psychiatrists were suspicious of such ability, but Frieda and Sullivan were both convinced that these "intuitive" aspects of therapist-patient interaction could be studied systematically. Sullivan was the first psychiatrist to tape-record therapy sessions for research purposes, and as early as the mid-1920s, he used a stenographer to make a verbatim transcript of interviews with patients.[15]

Being always "the outsider, the loner who lived mainly on the edge of things" drew Sullivan naturally to the sociological notion of "participant observer." In striking contrast to Freud, who thought of himself as a passive, blank screen onto whom the patient projected his unconscious wishes, Sullivan viewed the therapist's role more actively. Treatment wasn't "something done to the patient by the doctor; it was an interaction between two people engaged in an ongoing relationship." Insisting that his own reactions and feelings were a crucial part of the process, Sullivan "watched himself as well as the patient, observing what impact the patient had on him, and what effect his words, gestures, and tone had on the patient."[16] (Ferenczi had suggested much the same thing, and although Sullivan rarely cited anyone else's work, he always said Ferenczi's ideas were closest to his own way of thinking.)

This approach to therapy, especially with psychotic patients, dramatically changed the power dynamics of the relationship. It put the therapist in a less authoritarian position, and it empowered the patient to shape the direction of his own treatment. Sullivan sometimes enacted this literally, sitting "beside his patients, the better to hear (and not stare)" and conveying a feeling of being "on the patient's side" as they worked together. In arguing that the therapist was always a participant and not only an observer in the relationship, Sullivan was rejecting the mechanistic philosophy of science on which Freud had based his ideas, substituting a dynamic field theory where interaction was the unit of analysis.[17]

His own experiences of loneliness and respectful attitude toward patients led Sullivan to his key principle, the one-genus postulate: "We are all much more simply human than otherwise, be we happy and successful, contented and detached, miserable and mentally disordered, or whatever." He clearly wasn't the first to take this view. White, his mentor at St. Elizabeths, had long taught that "patients are very much more like the rest of us than they are different from us," and Frieda had learned the same thing from Goldstein. But Sullivan went further, making this postulate the foundation of his whole theory.[18]

For all his attentiveness to patients, however, Sullivan was "entirely unpredictable" with most other people, and could be "irritable, sarcastic, critical, demanding, aloof, and isolated." Students who remember his "profound and warm interest in his patients and his extremely gentle, tolerant, and understanding attitude toward them" recall him as caustic in supervision. His "fantastically complex" way of speaking and writing made it difficult to grasp what he was saying, and "he discouraged totally any sort of exchange that might resemble conversation." He told one student he had "barely missed being a charlatan" and routinely praised others for seeming schizophrenic. Frieda often found herself picking up the pieces after one of these episodes. Student after student recalls feeling humiliated or upset by Sullivan and going to her afterward to regain a sense of proportion. (Those whose supervisory sessions were held at his house in Bethesda also had to deal with Sullivan's five dogs, who intuited his feelings and bit the students who irritated him.)[19] And the same Sullivan who saw patients as "more simply human than otherwise" could be highly judgmental. Frieda was shocked when he repeatedly claimed, toward the end of the war, that the Nazis weren't human.

Frieda's father, Adolf
Reichmann, in the 1880s

Frieda's mother, Klara Simon,
around the time of her marriage
in 1888

Reichmann & Thalmann, Adolf's metalworks business in Karlsruhe, circa 1890.
Frieda was born in the family's apartment above the shop

Frieda (right), with her younger sister, Grete

Frieda (left) with one of her wealthy cousins, demonstrating the family's commitment to refinement and good taste

The Reichmann girls: Anna (left), Frieda (center), and Grete (right), enacting their respective roles of baby, authority, and dutiful middle child

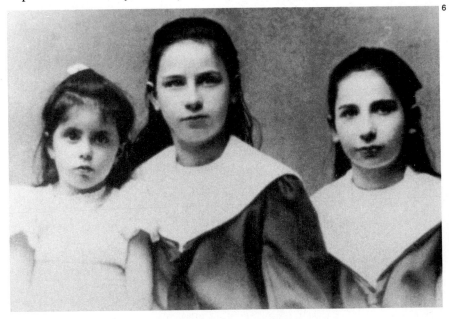

7

Königsberg, along the banks of the Pregel

8

The sanctuary of Adass Jisroel, the Orthodox synagogue in Königsberg where Frieda's family worshipped for decades. Its modest size and understated style contrasted sharply with Reform synagogues of the period, which could accommodate hundreds, even thousands, of worshippers and typically featured huge domes, imposing pillars, or intricate ornamentation.

The Königsberg villa of Frieda's uncle George Marx, the scene of many of her happiest childhood experiences

9

10

11

Frieda as a young woman, embodying the modest, obedient proprieties of the turn-of-the-century German-Jewish world in which she was raised

12

13

Frieda with hospital staff and (right)
as a pensive medical student

15

14

German troops in their trench at
the Eastern Front in World War
I. A stray piece of shrapnel or a
ricocheting bullet could have
quickly landed any one of them
in Frieda's Königsberg clinic for
brain-injured soldiers.

The resilience of soldiers in the midst of utter carnage, like these Germans at Vimy Ridge (1915), convinced Frieda that no patient, however traumatized, was beyond reach.

Erich Fromm, as a dashing
graduate student, circa 1922

17

18

Frieda in Heidelberg, around the
time she and Erich began their
affair, circa 1924

The elegant Heidelberg house
at Mönchhofstrasse 15 that
Frieda purchased in 1924 to
found her sanitarium

"Beyond Hope and Despair," one
of Gertrud Jacob's best-known
portraits of a psychotic patient

Dozens of her own relatives had been murdered in concentration camps and countless friends forced into exile, but she could not accept such a statement. It contradicted the fundamental axiom of her whole approach to mental illness.[20]

Since Sullivan had no interest in clarifying the relation of his ideas to classical psychoanalysis, Frieda was the one who ended up doing this. It was a natural role for her to play. She routinely blended views others saw as opposed or unrelated, and remaining a part of the analytic community was crucial to her sense of identity.

As always, she highlighted the underlying similarities, arguing that the interpersonal view was largely an extension of standard approaches. "It is to the immortal credit of Sigmund Freud," she wrote in a much-quoted passage, "that he was the first to understand and describe the psychotherapeutic process in terms of an interpersonal experience between patient and psychiatrist and . . . to study the personality of the psychiatrist, as well as that of the patient and their mutual interpersonal relationship."[21] Freud's failing lay simply in not taking this idea seriously enough.

In his own practice, Frieda always noted, Freud had been actively engaged with patients and acutely aware of his own part in the interaction. It was his fear of being tarred with the same brush as quacks who practiced "suggestion" that had led him to cast the analyst's role as a "neutral" observer. His followers had taken this prescription too literally, resulting in a view of the therapeutic relationship as sterile and artificial.

It was her rejection of this contrived neutrality as the frame within which transference took shape that marked Frieda's most striking departure from classical technique. There was nothing of the "blank screen" about her; she was always totally present. She saw most patients in her office at the cottage, with her dog next to her chair, the maid in the kitchen across the hall, and the secretary typing away on the other side of a thin wall. The phone rang constantly, with urgent calls often interrupting sessions, and in an emergency, she might even leave before the end of an hour. Frieda never disclosed personal details to patients and maintained a natural reserve, but knowing how terribly psychotics in particular suffered from dissembling, she made no attempt to hide her feelings.

Unlike Horney, who always emphasized her disagreements with Freud, Frieda framed her innovations as natural evolutions from his ideas. She argued that the migration of analysts to America during the Nazi years necessi-

tated changes in technique, changes Freud couldn't possibly have anticipated. No method as dependent on language and meaning as psychoanalysis
could be transplanted to so different a culture without requiring modification.
Having been forced at the age of forty-six to abandon assumptions she herself had taken for granted for years, Frieda was, like most other refugee analysts, initially overwhelmed by the strangeness of the American scene. Then,
with characteristic resourcefulness, she wrote a long paper, sorting out how
cultural factors affected analytic technique and reframing the transference relationship to fit the contours of the new situation. ("I may be able to show my
gratitude toward this country's hospitality," she told her audience, "by making some contribution toward the understanding of this problem.")[22]

Certain differences were striking but inconsequential, like the fact that
Americans didn't close the doors of rooms where they were working and
rarely spent their evenings debating philosophy, as Europeans liked to do.
But other attitudes had crucial significance for psychoanalytic practice. In
Central Europe, doctors belonged to a privileged class that included teachers,
employers, army officers, and kings—authorities to whom "one owed sub-
missive reverence and obedience." They were members of an intellectual
elite, who worked "for the sole purpose of helping their brethren," and whose
status was based on expertise, not income level. In a pioneering America,
however, values were different. Frieda recalled with amusement how she had
realized this:

> Shortly after I came to this country, I met a family with three lovely
> children. One of them showed the pondering reflective countenance of
> a little thinker. Intending to make a nice and friendly remark, I com-
> mented upon it by saying: "The child looks as though he might some-
> time in the future become a philosopher." Embarrassment spread
> among the group. I did not know why. Finally it was explained that my
> prognosis was not at all considered to be flattering.

Intellectuals, Frieda soon learned, were considered weaklings in America.
Physicians were purveyors of a service, for which they were hired by the hour.
She was shocked when one of her first patients, a salesman with little education, remarked appreciatively at the end of a session: "You and I are in sort of
the same business. Both of us have to study people and analyze their minds.
You want to sell them your ideas; I want to sell them my merchandise." In Europe, such a comment would have been unthinkable, but in a culture where
success was measured by prosperity and doctors made less money than many
businessmen, patients didn't have to be so deferential. Once she got over her

astonishment at the difference, Frieda decided American values actually facilitated treatment. Since the patient didn't mind "finding human weaknesses,
even neurotic symptoms, in his doctor," the analyst could more readily admit
errors and then correct them, instead of acting as if they were "affronts to [his]
dignity" as a physician.

Mass culture also put analysts and patients on a far more equal footing
than anything Freud had experienced. Everyone in America saw the same
movies, listened to the same radio shows, read the same magazines, smoked
the same cigarettes, bought clothing at the same stores, and drove the same
cars. Americans thought of themselves as members of groups and joined
them easily, with a gregarious openness completely unknown in Central Europe. "Pioneers and their descendants," Frieda observed, "cannot afford to be
enigmatic individuals concerned with complex personal conflicts."[23]

As a result, American patients showed little of the compulsive interest in
their analysts' private lives for which European patients were famous. An
American wouldn't wait for hours outside his analyst's house to see precisely
when and with whom she went out. He wasn't "passionately curious" about
the kind of coat she wore or whether she traveled by taxi, bus, or car. He
couldn't go to the local police station and look up his analyst's age and birth-
date, the date of her wedding, or her husband's age, or pore over her doctoral
thesis in a public library, the way any German could. Analytic patients everywhere were interested in their doctors, Frieda agreed, but Americans weren't
nearly as curious as their European counterparts, which inevitably changed
the dynamics of the transference relationship.

Although she retained the sense of entitlement typical of German doctors
of her age and social class, Frieda was far less pretentious than most other
émigrés. The obsessional strictures of analytic style had long irritated her,
and she was relieved to be able to act more naturally in informal America. To
shake hands with a patient for whom such a gesture might be highly meaningful, for example, seemed more likely to facilitate a genuinely therapeutic
relationship than the ritualized formality in which she had been trained.

American patients were also less likely to sexualize the transference, a difference Frieda found refreshing. Sexuality was more openly discussed than
in Germany (where even in the 1920s, one could still find female patients
who got bladder infections because they were too embarrassed to tell their fi-
ancés they had to go to the bathroom). American patients took for granted
that "like every grownup person, man or woman, married or single," analysts
had private lives that included sexuality. This made oedipal issues far less
dominant in the treatment.[24]

In response to these cultural differences, Frieda adapted her analytic style so as better to reflect American values, unlike many of her refugee colleagues, who clung to their Old World mannerisms (partly from nostalgia, partly because of their marketability). She thought it was irrational to reenact compulsively every detail of Freud's way of working, regardless of its sense or appropriateness. (Ferenczi had called analysts' refusal to adapt "counter-resistance," arguing that it could be just as much an impediment to treatment as countertransference.) Within a few years of arriving in the United States, Frieda shifted her chair from behind the couch "to a point level with and some distance away from its foot, where the patient could look at her or away with equal ease," claiming that this orientation facilitated therapy.[25] She pointed out matter-of-factly that Freud had positioned himself behind his patients only because he disliked "being stared at for eight hours a day." She, in contrast, enjoyed sitting face-to-face and found eye contact a highly useful source of information. Attacked for this "deviation" by classical colleagues, she retorted that such rules protected analysts more than they helped patients.[26] She cautioned students against "lonely, dissatisfied" therapists who unconsciously encouraged elaborate transference fantasies as a "substitute with impunity" for the inadequacies of their own lives. And she saw a constant focus on oedipal issues as a way for the psychiatrist to avoid "scrutinizing the tie-up between the patient and himself."[27]

Prohibiting contacts between therapist and patient outside treatment sessions, she continued, often had more to do with analysts' need for control than with therapeutic issues. Doctors had a right to privacy, but not if it was "glorified to bolster their own self-esteem." Besides, in working with psychotics, routine encounters around the hospital could be crucial in teaching patients the difference between reality and fantasy. (Imagine, she told students, how frightened and humiliated a disturbed person would feel if his therapist acted as if he didn't exist outside treatment sessions.)

Frieda understood that many analysts had stronger needs for protection than she did and thought it was fine for them to impose rules that made them feel safer so long as they didn't rationalize their own defenses as being for the good of the patient. Years of working with psychotics made her more attentive than most other analysts to her own safety, but she insisted this didn't require dissembling.

She encouraged colleagues to treat matters of scheduling in the same undefensive way. Analysts were busy people, who worked in a time-bound culture and needed to make a living. But cutting off an emotional outburst by a highly disturbed patient because it would help him "learn to deal with limits" was self-serving for the analyst and potentially harmful to the treatment. Frieda had firm boundaries and never allowed patients to exploit them, but when clinical needs dictated it, she adjusted her schedule, finding that even those inconvenienced by her lateness ultimately appreciated her willingness to adapt to the unpredictabilities of mental illness.

Although Frieda's most important contributions lay in the domain of technique, not theory, there is one now infamous idea for which she *is* known: that of the "schizophrenogenic mother." The notion that it is mothers who "generate" schizophrenia in their offspring is one of the most pernicious distortions of psychoanalytic theory, and it was Frieda's bad luck to be seen as its originator. The vehemence with which this notion has been attacked—and the number of people who know Frieda's name only in this context—suggest that it was a central idea in her work.[28] Actually she uses the term only once, in a parenthetical remark in a paper on transference written during her first years in America. A careful reader would find even this instance difficult to locate, buried as it is in a long paragraph about something else.[29]

Frieda would have been astonished at the uproar this concept later provoked. Struggling to adapt to American culture, highly sensitive to differences between Germany and the United States, she had simply taken note of certain aspects of the "mother role" in the two societies.[30] In the "distinctly patriarchal" family structure of Central Europe, she observed, the father "rules over his wife and children . . . and they, in turn, are very close to each other by virtue of their common fear" of him. In America, however, mothers and children are on different sides. "American women are not afraid of men, as European women are," Frieda continued, and the mother often takes the dominant role in family dynamics.[31] Since elementary school teachers in the United States are also typically women, American children grow up surrounded by powerful female figures. "The child's fear of his domineering mother," Frieda reasoned, could lead to mental illness in extreme cases. Mothers who were "imperious" or showed "unnecessary displays of authority" could create "feelings of insecurity, anxiety, and hatred in the mind of the dependent child which he may often not overcome for the rest of his life." Overly solicitous attitudes could be equally problematic if they served as a cover for "hidden domination." Citing numerous examples of the destructive effects of such attitudes, Frieda said that only unconditional love, given without regard for the child's behavior or the extent of his obedience, would provide the security he needed to develop as a separate person.[32]

For Frieda, the "schizophrenogenic mother" was a pathological exaggeration of a cultural type. She felt considerable sympathy for such women and never, as her critics have charged, blamed mothers in general for mental ill-ness. She often met with the parents of her own patients (sometimes traveling long distances to visit them), seeing them as victims of their own childhood conflicts, who, with appropriate understanding, could become allies in the treatment.[33] Indeed, at a deeper level, Frieda's discussion of mothers and their influence can be seen as her protest, albeit muted, against classical psycho-analytic views that gave primacy to fathers. Because she wrote so little about female psychology—in striking contrast to colleagues like Horney, Melanie Klein, and Clara Thompson—Frieda's thinking on such issues is easily mis-understood. However, to identify her solely with the schizophrenogenic mother is to render her critique of Freud's patriarchal assumptions invisible.

Frieda's appreciation of women's positive power clearly began in her own childhood. Klara's indomitable will shaped the Reichmann household into "the happiest family you could think of," and Aunt Helene Simon's political work offered a vivid example of women's effectiveness in the world. He-lene's explicitly feminist and socialist writings must also have impressed Frieda when she read them as a student. Taken together, these early experi-ences contradicted any notion of a universal male dominance.

Thus, when Frieda encountered J. J. Bachofen's and Robert Briffault's matriarchal views of history in Groddeck's writings, these ideas immediately resonated with her own way of thinking. Groddeck had long focused on the crucial symbolic significance of mothers in the development of human cul-ture and the unconscious of the individual. He critiqued Freud's single-minded emphasis on the father and often discussed the envy his male patients had of women's reproductive capacities (ideas that particularly impressed Horney, who elaborated them in greater detail in her own work).

Erich also had a deep interest in female power (rooted, no doubt, in his own early experiences with his doting mother and then reenacted in his many affairs with older women). He credited Bachofen's *Mother Right,* published in 1861, as one of the major influences on his thinking. The effects of the early matriarchal period on the unconscious of modern men and women be-came a focus for Erich's work in the early 1920s, and he continued to explore the special meaning of the bond to the mother in many of the books he later published in America.

So when Frieda wrote about the "mother role" in the 1940s and mentioned the "schizophrenogenic mother" as an example of female power taken to ex-cess, she was conceiving these ideas within the context of Groddeck's and Erich's work. She thought she was simply noting, once again, that Freud's exclusive focus on fathers and sons was too limited. She had no idea that in an America increasingly anxious about women's role, this idea would hit such a nerve.

One can certainly argue that whatever buried hostility lay in her offhand remark about "schizophrenogenic mothers" was Frieda's way of retaliating against Klara's domination. Having always felt that the love of her own mother was, to some extent, contingent on her being obedient, Frieda was clearly a person whose separate identity was threatened by a lack of unconditional love in her childhood. Part of her attraction to Groddeck and Sullivan was that they could strike out on their own in ways that she couldn't. But Frieda would also have been quick to credit her mother with providing the grounding for her healthy development. Klara may not have wanted a daughter who outshined her, but she clearly encouraged the fundamental autonomy that made Frieda so self-reliant. In warning against the danger of a "schizophrenogenic mother," Frieda was unconsciously praising her own mother for a sense of balance as much as she was lashing out at her for being controlling.

Frieda's critics often dismissed her therapeutic work with schizophrenic patients as a well-meaning but ultimately hopeless attempt to provide such people with the love they hadn't received in childhood. Frieda was caricatured as trying to be an "ideal mother" to her patients, gratifying their needs for closeness in ways no one else could. This stereotype was as much of a distortion as the "schizophrenogenic mother" attacks were.

Her Lodge colleague Alfred Stanton directly challenged these critics. He called Frieda's treatment style "touched with the austere" and said she explicitly rejected Federn's claim that establishing a positive transference was the main goal of treatment. Emphasizing that Frieda never did things for patients they could do for themselves—for example, interpreting behavior they unconsciously understood—Stanton said that she expected patients to work hard at therapy—as hard as she did.[34]

To make psychotherapy with schizophrenic patients better known in the field and to differentiate her own approach from those with which it was often confused, Frieda helped to publish an English translation of Gertrud Schwing's *A Way to the Soul of the Mentally Ill*. In her foreword, Frieda expressed her "joy and satisfaction" at having discovered "this truly human document of skill, knowledge, intuition and wisdom." She didn't explain how she had come upon Schwing's work and clearly didn't agree with all of her ideas, but Frieda did identify with Schwing's desire to rescue patients in "extreme and mortal danger." Kurt Eissler, who had witnessed Schwing's work in Vienna before his escape to America, noted in his introduction: "Like a medieval saint, she released the schizophrenics from their strait-jackets. Patients who had just been howling immediately quieted down when she turned toward them."[35]

Schwing had been drawn to illness and death since earliest childhood. "My concern was not just with any illness, but rather with the seemingly incurable ones. Lepers, those infected with the plague, the mentally ill, prisoners—these were the suffering human beings who lived in my heart." She thought of becoming a physician, but couldn't bear to wait through years of training. "My abiding wish was to be able to help instantly—*instantly and energetically!*" As a young woman, Schwing had some kind of personal collapse and was restored to health by a physician who later gave her a job in his father's clinic. She had no training of any kind, but was allowed to work alongside nurses treating the most disturbed patients. She eventually studied informally with Federn and in the late 1930s, treated schizophrenic patients at Pötzl's clinic at the University of Vienna. Forced to return to her native Switzerland after the *Anschluss,* she attempted to continue her work, but no one would hire her because of her lack of training. After her book was published, however, relatives of mental patients begged Schwing to take their loved ones out of hospitals and care for them. She brought some of these patients to live in her home; others she treated informally on psychiatric wards.

Schwing's technique was straightforward. She would go to the patient's room every day at the same hour and sit quietly near him. Eventually even those who were mute, violent, or otherwise unresponsive would "gain confidence and security from [this] abiding, resolute passivity" and describe the inner torment that kept them isolated. Schwing's case reports have the same miraculous quality as many of Frieda's: seemingly out of nowhere, the patient suddenly begins to speak, pouring out the feelings, wishes, and fears she had never before revealed to anyone. In some cases, Schwing treated patients like needy children—literally putting her arms around them, giving them candy, or bathing them. Her approach emphasized mutuality and a deep respect for suffering.

Schwing had the same fearlessness that was Frieda's major weapon in breaking through the defenses of very disturbed patients. With a young woman who had repeatedly swallowed needles and pieces of glass and who had smashed the windows in her hospital room despite being kept in three straitjackets, Schwing pleaded, "Look at me." When, to everyone's astonishment, the patient did, Schwing said: "There is so much sadness in you. I would like to be able to help you, may I try?" The woman began to weep. "Her defensive function having been overcome," she then talked openly of her feelings and experiences.[36]

Schwing thought Freud was right to see schizophrenia as a regression to the earliest stages of development, a retreat from relationships experienced as terrifying and dangerous. What he had failed to understand, Schwing argued, was that therapy could provide the reparative experience the patient craved. (Although she didn't point out the connection, she was taking much the same view as Ferenczi, whose student, Franz Alexander, later called therapy with such patients a "corrective emotional experience.")

Sounding remarkably like Frieda, Schwing said that a therapist must resolve his own unconscious conflicts before he could be useful to psychotic people. She acknowledged that no therapist could satisfy all of another person's needs, but said that admitting limitations candidly could earn the trust of even the sickest patient.

Schwing warned against trying to stop patients from performing bizarre rituals that didn't cause injury to anyone. Such behavior satisfied some need, and much so-called "negativism can be avoided if the staff do not constantly put themselves in the position of attempting to thwart the patient's action." For the same reason, Schwing never forced herself on patients. When they indicated (either verbally or nonverbally) that they didn't want contact, she withdrew, reasoning that if she respected the patient's wishes to be alone, he might later respect her desire for contact. Like Frieda, Schwing based the frequency of sessions on the quality of interaction. She might not see a patient for several days, then see him twice on the same day if he seemed particularly responsive. If a patient refused to eat, she didn't cajole him or discuss the symptom explicitly, but instead brought appetizing foods to the hospital (a gesture patients often greeted with surprise and pleasure).

For all her praise of Schwing's work, Frieda was careful to disassociate herself from the claim that therapy could provide psychotics with the love they lacked. Even the most disturbed patient senses "at least dimly," Frieda argued, "that his disaster cannot be solved by one person's offering him a type of acceptance otherwise not mutually obtainable in adult society." Indeed, such overtures might even be "experienced by the sensitive schizophrenic" as condescending. Physicians weren't substitute parents but "participating observers," helping the patient to come to terms with the realities of life as an adult.

The psychiatrist's job, Frieda insisted, was not to turn schizophrenics into "conforming good citizens." If such patients were able to find "their own sources of satisfaction and security, irrespective of the approval of their neighbors, of their families, and of public opinion," that was sufficient. Recovery couldn't be defined by the therapist's standards. In this sense, she noted, "schizophrenia is not an illness but a specific state of personality with its own ways of living."[37]

Frieda's fundamental belief in patients as collaborators led her to arrange for the reprinting of the first-person account of a schizophrenic man hospitalized in nineteenth-century Glasgow. This book, among the most evocative and brilliant descriptions of madness ever written, had long been out of print, and as Frieda began to concentrate more of her energies on teaching, she was increasingly frustrated by its inaccessibility as a resource for students.

The Philosophy of Insanity is perhaps the only patient narrative of mental illness that is as much textbook as memoir. The patient, who calls himself simply a "Late Inmate" of the Royal Asylum for Lunatics at Gartnavel, says he wrote out of a sense of responsibility to others, despite a concern that "the idea of doing good" might itself be one of his delusions. "I will neither have suffered nor written in vain," he says in the preface, "if my story arrests the hand armed with the suicidal knife, or sweeps aside the impious breath which would blow into flame that insane spark which, smoldering, lies in breast and brain of everyone."[38]

Throughout the 1940s, Frieda taught a course to therapists in training called "Assets of the Mentally Handicapped" (dubbed "the vitamin course" by students since it was numbered B-1 in the catalogue). This was not some grudging acknowledgment that psychotic people had skills. To Frieda, patients' disabilities were the source of sensitivities they might otherwise not have had. We can understand how blindness might help a person to hear more acutely or finely hone his sense of touch. Why is it so hard to see people with schizophrenia as "introspectively gifted," as Frieda claimed they were? She often had students read patients' accounts of illness to appreciate this point, and it was while searching for additional examples that she had stumbled on the Late Inmate's narrative. "How can I describe the humble admiration and the deeply moving surprise," she wrote in her introduction, "which I felt when reading that this unknown chronicler expressed as early as 1860 his conviction that the difference between the mentally healthy and the mentally disturbed is one of quantity only." No one, Frieda declared, "expressed the idea of the essential human likeness between mentally disturbed and emotional stable people more convincingly and in more beautiful lan-

guage than did this remarkable recovered psychotic in the middle of the nineteenth century."[39]

Writing at a time when madness was widely considered an incurable brain
disease, the Late Inmate had claimed: "The line which separates sanity from
insanity is invisible, and there are as many kinds and degrees of the disease
as there are sufferers." There could be no general rules that applied to all patients, "for what may be beneficial in one case may be hurtful in another, and
yet the symptoms in both cases be so nearly alike as to be almost undistin-
guishable. . . . Lunacy, like rain, falls upon the evil and the good."[40]

Fundamental to Frieda's model of therapy with people suffering from psychosis was a deep respect for the patient. "This is not a humanitarian or char-
itable hypothesis," she wrote, "but a scientific conviction."[41] She took for
granted that whatever was going on in a patient's mind made sense (at least
to him) and that bizarre behavior could always (potentially) be understood by
someone. Rose Spiegel, a younger colleague, remembered Frieda's knocking
on the door of one patient's room daily "for something like six months without his speaking to her, so that he would get to trust her persistence enough to
let her in." Like Groddeck, she often inherited cases that proved too difficult
for others. A patient who showed up for her session with Clara Thompson
carrying a loaded pistol, for example, was immediately referred to Frieda.[42]

This refusal to see any patient as beyond hope is strikingly evident in the
case of Miss S. Referred to Chestnut Lodge in 1939 after having been institutionalized for eighteen of her thirty-six years, Miss S. had been treated by
some of the best physicians in America. Nothing they tried seemed to have
the slightest effect on her. On admission, Miss S. sat with her head bent down
to her chest, eyes nearly closed, picking at her nails, looking hostile and suspicious. She failed to respond to inquiries of any kind and appeared to be hallucinating. Diagnosed as catatonic, Miss S. remained mute for months. Yet
Frieda described her "psychotherapeutic possibility" as "not unpromising."[43]

For two years, she saw Miss S. for five hour-long sessions each week. The
patient occasionally mumbled in a "voiceless speech" or laughed to herself.
Mostly she said nothing. Sometimes when Frieda sat near her, Miss S. would
grasp her fingers and hold them. On other days, Frieda wrote or read in an
adjoining chair, allowing the patient to feel her presence without the "constant obligation to be in contact." Every few months, Miss S. would say
something like, "Yes, I would love to," in response to Frieda's asking

whether she might like to sit on the porch rather than in the office for that session. Once, she greeted Frieda with, "Good morning, how are you?" When Frieda mused aloud about the conflicts Miss S. must have experienced in childhood, the patient sometimes blushed, cried, or perspired heavily. One Sunday afternoon, appearing at the cottage without warning, Miss S. walked through the unlocked front door right into the office. Frieda said she was sorry she had a previous obligation and "would have loved to stay if she had known in advance about the patient's visit." Miss S. responded, "Go to hell," and went back to her ward and her silence.

In a report to colleagues, Frieda agreed that progress in this case was extremely slow, but she insisted some change could be detected. In an effort to speed things up, however, she recommended giving Miss S. Benzedrine to increase her level of activity and/or sodium amytal to foster catharsis. Both were tried. The amytal seemed to have an immediate effect, making Miss S. "alert, active, and cooperative" and enabling her to "talk a little bit nearly every hour." But this wore off quickly, and the injections had to keep being administered.

Three years later, when Miss S.'s prognosis was listed by another Lodge physician as "guarded," Frieda told colleagues at a staff meeting: "I do feel we should be able to cure her." At this point, Miss S. had been institutionalized continuously for twenty-one years. She was still largely mute and hallucinating. She was also, as Frieda emphasized, "more friendly and seemingly happier" and appeared on time for sessions without having to be escorted. Frieda said she welcomed suggestions on how to "break the monotony of things" and admitted she was frustrated, but again concluded, "I still believe that something can be done for this patient."

Frieda made this statement in 1942, having worked as a psychiatrist for a quarter-century. She was neither so romantic nor so arrogant as to believe her efforts would always succeed. Indeed, to regard Frieda's dogged persistence with such patients as a sign of her grandiosity is to misunderstand her approach fundamentally. Frieda's refusal to give up on Miss S. came from a deep sense of humility; severe mental illness was so poorly understood that labeling a patient incurable seemed presumptuous to her. If, as she constantly stressed to Lodge colleagues, every patient was essentially a research subject, then who was she to declare the experiment over before all the data were in?[44]

Such a stance required fortitude and sometimes a reeducation of the patient. By the early 1940s, many of the people being referred to the Lodge had already been treated with biological methods at other places. They had no idea how to behave in psychotherapy. After shock treatment was unsuccessful with Mrs. B., for example, she was told by Walter Freeman (America's "dean of lobotomy") that she needed a brain operation. Admitted to the Lodge instead, she said she could not understand how "just sitting and talking could be a medical treatment." But after months of agitation, delusions, and violence, which Frieda patiently sat through—among other things, the patient repeatedly slapped her and called her a "fingerfucker"—Mrs. B. walked in to her session one day and asked: "How could you expect me to know how to talk? There was never anybody who talked with me the way you do, or who would have taken the time to listen."[45]

Frieda's younger colleagues were struck by how different her approach was from that of other analysts. Bob Cohen said that most therapists he knew quickly categorized the patient and were then "almost never puzzled" during the treatment. The patient in such an analysis was largely passive, Cohen noted, waiting to be "freed from his chains by a brilliant, powerful and beneficent figure." Frieda's style was precisely the opposite: "sharing the examination of successively deeper layers, with the patient often in the lead." Cohen said treatment with Frieda was like "actively finding one's way through a seemingly trackless wilderness with the help of a resourceful and fearless companion."[46]

This way of working, which Donald Schön calls "reflection-in-action," relies on a tacit knowledge that is "*in* the action" and can't be fully articulated, as when a baseball pitcher gets "a feel for the ball" or a jazz musician "finds the groove." The key to such "artistry," Schön argues, is an exploratory attitude. Shaping your next action to fit the unique contours of what is happening at that moment keeps your style deeply responsive, never rote or automatic. The problem, Schön notes, is that such "intuitive knowing is always richer in information than any description of it," making attempts to distill the principles of the practice or teach them to others only partly successful.[47] When Frieda urged patients to "take her along" into their experience, she was simultaneously conveying her humility about the complexities of mental illness, her willingness to let the patient guide the process, and her own unshakable belief in psychotherapy as "a mutual enterprise, if not a mutual adventure."[48] For Frieda, telling students to "make every hour with the patient a memorable experience" wasn't an attempt to impose perfectionistic standards; it was a way to stay open to possibility.

Psychiatry is a perverse field in many ways, but its abandonment of craft is surely among its most paradoxical features. Musicians and writers don't have trouble seeing talent and experience as equally important to their work. Even surgeons recognize that practice improves their skills. Aptitude is helpful, but there is also a great deal that can be learned from experience or from a good teacher.

The key to true artfulness is keeping an open mind. You have to enjoy playing around, making things up, ignoring rules that don't seem to fit the context you're in. A person who is defensive or cautious or too worried about making mistakes won't notice the subtleties in front of him; he'll be too wrapped up in himself to see what's there. When Frieda sat for hours by the beds of psychotic patients during medical school, murmuring a word of encouragement now and then just to keep them talking, she was like Jackson Pollock, flinging paint onto canvases to see if they ever became art. Achieving a particular goal wasn't as important as trying to learn. A chemist staring at a test tube behaving contrary to expectation has a choice: berate himself for his error, or discover something he didn't anticipate.

Frieda's inventiveness was never designed for shock value, like John Rosen's "direct analysis." A Philadelphia psychiatrist who never had formal training in psychoanalysis, Rosen believed in stunning his patients out of their symptoms. Disparaging classical psychoanalysis as too "indirect," he claimed his method produced faster success. Rosen sometimes spent ten to fifteen hours continuously with a patient, feeding him from a baby bottle or deliberately assuming the identity of a figure from one of his delusions. Relentlessly confronting schizophrenic patients in an effort to break through to the repressed material presumably producing their symptoms, Rosen would scream, threaten murder, or make remarks so sexually suggestive they shocked even close colleagues. "I wish I had breasts, then I would feed you like your mother should have," he told one patient. To a disheveled schizophrenic woman, he purred: "Don't you want to pretty yourself up? You're so lovely. I'd like to go upstairs and have intercourse with you."[49]

Rosen's defenders compared his technique to surgery, admitting that it was risky but might be necessary to save the patient. The analogy seems apt. Like surgery, direct analysis usually worked quickly or did nothing. As soon as the patient either snapped out of it or became chronic, Rosen lost interest. In this crucial sense, he and Frieda were opposites; her willingness to wait months for even the slightest response seemed useless to him.

Diplomatic as always, Frieda cited Rosen's work and discussed it respectfully, making it seem less crazy than it otherwise would. In general, though, she felt that his "method of shocking the patient out of his disturbed psychotic state, as it were, may create difficulties . . . which may interfere with the later course of treatment."[50] Yet there were clearly times when she went to

lengths most other therapists couldn't even conceive of. An especially striking example is worth quoting in full:

> A patient was subject to gravely disturbing persecutory delusions night
> after night. Powerful people of various nationalities were after him. He
> tried to escape being caught and pleaded with each of the persecutors in
> his own language. During the day this patient was in rational contact.
> There was no memory of his nightly delusions and therefore no possibil-
> ity of discussing them with him. The patient's only complaint was that
> he could not concentrate and that something interfered with the pursuit
> of his professional obligations. He did not know what it was except that
> he felt worn out and beaten down upon awakening in the morning, as
> though there had been some terribly frightening and trying experience
> during the night. A number of futile attempts were made to discuss the
> patient's delusions, about which the psychotherapist [clearly Frieda her-
> self] had been informed by the nurses' reports. The therapist finally de-
> cided to have the nurses awaken her at the time when the nightly
> delusional experience started, in order to make it possible for her to ob-
> serve the patient and to participate in his experience. With the therapist
> present, the patient got up and climbed from his bed to the bureau, from
> there to the wardrobe, and from there to one piece of furniture after an-
> other as though running from his persecutors, pleading with them alter-
> nately in English, French, German, and Hebrew. The psychiatrist
> followed him on his climbing excursion as best she could, trying to reas-
> sure him in whatever the language of the moment was by telling him that
> she did not see the persecutors but that, if and when she caught sight of
> them, she would try to protect him against them. After about fifteen or
> twenty minutes the patient quieted down, went to bed, and slept for the
> rest of the night. The psychiatrist's participation in the delusional expe-
> riences of the patient had to be repeated once or twice before she was
> successful in breaking through the wall which the patient had erected
> against their recall. After that the road was open for the application of
> [an] interpretive approach to the patient's persecutory delusions and to
> the severe states of anxiety which accompanied [them]. . . . Subse-
> quently, his rational communications could be worked through interpre-
> tively in connection with his delusional ideas, and both could be related
> to [his underlying] problems. After one and one-half years the patient
> was free from symptoms and left the hospital and the city where the psy-
> chiatrist lived to resume his professional work in his home town.[51]

We can only imagine the reaction of ward staff to the refined, ungainly Frieda, scrambling over pieces of furniture in pursuit of a wildly hallucinating patient, earnestly reassuring him in four languages that she would protect him from all threats, real or imagined. (If only someone had taken a photograph of the world-famous psychiatrist, demonstrating her technique of participant observation!) Yet however bizarre the image, Frieda's actions here were the result of weeks of careful reflection about how to access the patient's buried feelings. They were nothing like Rosen's seat-of-the-pants attempts to shock the patient into compliance.

A case that epitomizes the challenges Frieda faced in her early years at Chestnut Lodge was that of Dr. D., who alternated for more than a decade as a staff member and a patient. First admitted in 1934 after a previous stay at nearby Sheppard Pratt, Dr. D. was treated by Dexter Bullard in the days when he and Marjorie Jarvis were the only physicians. Dr. D. was discharged after two years, lived in Washington for a while, and then found work at a sanitarium in the South. She returned to Rockville in 1937 to enter analytic treatment with Frieda and was hired onto the Lodge staff a year later. Dr. D. was a highly effective therapist with certain patients, and both Frieda and Dexter grew quite fond of her.

But she had trouble staying on an even keel. In July 1939, Frieda wrote to a colleague at Sheppard and asked him, as a favor to her, to meet with Dr. D. to help her set aside "the ghosts of the past." He agreed, and two weeks later, Frieda sent a note of thanks: "All I can say in apologizing for the unpleasant task I ventured to impose on you is that we both are psychiatrists, and I took the same thing from this patient one hour or more every day for a solid 18 months." Dr. D. was clearly grateful for Frieda's efforts. "The fact that you really went [to Sheppard] with me and were not afraid to face this unpleasant situation takes all wind out of my sails," she said in a note. "There is no reason now not to try hard to get well. I'll stop thinking about the past, and settle down for good work."[52]

But things weren't that simple. Dr. D. remained confused about her role. Was she still a patient, dependent on Dexter and Frieda for all her needs, or was she their colleague, a professional equal? She wrote a letter to Bullard (scrawling at the top "Place? What does it matter? Sunday night, October 1, 1939") berating him for his patronizing attitude: "On the one hand, you have acted as if you wanted everyone to notice and observe what a savior you were of derelict me, while on the other hand, regretting it and being ashamed of your impetuous gesture last October when you asked me to say here. . . . What outstanding success have *REAL* members of your Staff made that I fall so far below them?" She lashed out at Bullard for making treatment with Frieda a condition of her employment and said she was "tired of having to feel so Damn grateful. . . . You pay me $15 a week (Frieda gets $100) and my 'food in my belly and a roof over my head'—the couch in the library!"

Frieda eventually decided the whole situation was too problematic and re-ferred Dr. D. to Lewis Hill in Baltimore. This made things worse. In 1944, in a confidential letter to Bullard (who was apparently paying Dr. D.'s therapy bills), Hill called her "without doubt the most difficult patient I have ever at-tempted to treat." Apologizing for "the failure," he continued: "I can't possi-bly accept further fees from you for a performance which I do not think she has ever regarded as therapeutic but merely as a way of staying in your good graces, and which I have come to believe is not therapeutic in its results."

A few months later, Dr. D. sent her own letter to Bullard. "Will you see me someday soon and tell me to my face why you have destroyed me as you have? . . . I know I was sent away as if a criminal, as if under a sentence, but by what authority do you own Rockville?" She said she was glad that one of the catatonic patients she had treated while on the staff was being sent else-where. ("You will miss the $10,000 Mrs. H. brought you each year now for almost five years, won't you?") She called Bullard's own abilities as a thera-pist "laughable and clumsy" and bitterly complained that he paid her less than his "kitchen boys."

Dexter's vacillations clearly didn't help matters. Threatening to sue him for "criminal negligence towards me as a patient and staff member," Dr. D. wrote in a letter also addressed to Hill, Frieda, and Ross Chapman (superin-tendent of Sheppard): "You should all be quite satisfied with your destruction of me. . . . This is your revenge on me, no doubt, because I have been a pa-tient and Psychiatrists and Analysts take revenge on patients." She blamed the four of them for making it impossible for her to be hired elsewhere. She seemed especially enraged at Bullard and his "quisling, Dr. Hill," repeatedly calling them "cruel" and saying (in the same seven-page, single-spaced let-ter): "You'd both paste down the wings of a butterfly and sit and watch it die an agonizing death, wouldn't you? That is what you both have done to me." Accusing Bullard of running the Lodge solely for the money, she ended with: "God forgive you, I cannot." Dr. D. eventually ended up in a state hospital.

Frieda seems to have played a dubious role in all of this. She tried to treat Dr. D. and then abandoned the effort (a striking departure from her usual diligence). Then she encouraged Bullard to let Dr. D. join the staff. (In Heidelberg, Frieda routinely hired patients as sanitarium workers.) Dr. D. did seem to exempt Frieda from many of her diatribes. Even in letters addressed to her along with the others, she never singled Frieda out for attack or abuse. Yet Frieda doesn't seem to have done much to help Dr. D. after having stopped seeing her for therapy, suggesting that there were patients too complicated even for Frieda to deal with.

But they were the exception. At the same time she was treating Dr. D. (and numerous others), Frieda took on two cases that were to rank among the most important in her whole career: Mrs. E., the patient who established her reputation in America, and Hermann Brunck, the man whose tragic suicide was forever to haunt her.

Mrs. E. was one of Frieda's first patients at the Lodge, part of the group Bullard had assigned to her before he left for vacation. Frieda wasn't even a regular staff member at that point; she was the summer replacement, a refugee doctor struggling to treat deeply disturbed patients in a language she herself had been speaking for only three months.

Mrs. E. was the kind of mental patient one reads about: filthy, uncontrollable, given to sudden fits of violence. She had threatened her children with a knife and been forcibly hospitalized. On the ward, she sang loudly in an indecipherable language, ripped off her clothes, defecated on the floor, and shrieked at anyone who came near her. After every known treatment was tried in three different hospitals to no effect, her doctors had her transferred to Chestnut Lodge.

The day Frieda met Mrs. E., the patient was singing loudly in a mixture of German, French, Italian, English, and a language she had invented. She danced naked around the ward with a towel she called Jesus Christ. She spat at the floor and crouched in the corner, singing to radiators. Screaming that the nurses were devils sent from hell to kill her, she scratched, bit, pinched, or spat at them whenever they got near her. She became especially violent when they wiped off the spit, screaming that her saliva formed the spiral wires along which the good ghosts would descend from heaven to protect her. Mrs. E. also spent a lot of time walking barefoot across her room in elaborate patterns, never allowing her feet to touch the dark spots on the linoleum. Sometimes she stood for hours in one place, causing her feet to swell to frightening proportions. When she was especially agitated or violent, she was put into a cold wet sheet pack. Further thrashing just warmed the sheets and tightened the cocoon around her.

Frieda often sat by Mrs. E.'s bed while she lay in pack. The patient was a psychoanalyst's dream: pouring out fears, wishes, fantasies, and delusions in an unending stream. The two of them must have seemed quite the pair, with Mrs. E. screaming lines of poetry or ranting about the good ghosts and the devils while Frieda sat quietly by her side taking notes.

On August 1, 1935, a day Frieda would later regard as one of the most significant in her psychiatric career, she dictated the following summary of her session with Mrs. E.

The patient has a pack, complains of it, the sheets are too cold, would be better to have a warm bath in a tub, or warm sheets.—(I promise to unpack her right arm, if she will sign some checks and documents).— "So it is John [her husband] who sent them?"—(Yes).—"Then it is alright, I will sign them." (I start unpacking her, cannot get along very well, tell her I will go and ask a nurse to help me).—"Oh, so you are afraid of me when I am unpacked, are you?"—(Not at all—I continue to unpack her myself).—She helps me by showing where the sheets are fixed and so on. When I bring the checks and other documents, she says she can't sign them "E." because she is "Mrs. A." [her delusional name]—(I say that the people who get the checks do not yet know the change of name).—"Yes, that is true."—So she signs them all without any further refusal.

Two weeks later, Frieda reported that Mrs. E. was noticeably better. She had stopped spitting on the floor, wore dresses, kept herself clean, and was occasionally observed knitting. One day she played the piano for the ward. She was taken out to sit on the lawn and didn't assault anyone. She enjoyed a visit from her son.[53]

Mrs. E.'s case is a classic of psychoanalysis, like Anna O. or Dora, which poses a key problem for clinical practice and then suggests its solution. The significance of her treatment for us, however, lies less in the drama of its success than in the beauty of its form—a blend of Frieda's intuitive leaps and the patient's genius for illness.

Like Breuer's Anna O. and Ferenczi's R.N., Mrs. E. was willing to take risks, to push the therapy to its limits, to do whatever was necessary to get better. She understood the fundamental requirement of successful treatment: helping the doctor to ferret out whatever will to health remained buried in the illness and urging it toward the goal of cure. Psychotherapy by definition is idiosyncratic to each case, but there are always two things present in a treatment that works: a patient willing to show her real needs and a therapist who can meet her where she is.

Rules of technique in psychoanalysis are invented at points of ambiguity, to help therapists feel their way along the edges of the unexplored. A patient who can tolerate the precariousness of such a place can sometimes help to show the way, much as moonlight, striking at the right angle, can guide a lost traveler through dense woods. This is what makes Anna O. and R.N. such powerful models: they were courageous enough to work right at the edge of the darkness.

Patients like this are desperate to have therapists who can bravely accompany them into the depths. Mental illness is exhausting. Having to add the burden of the therapist's fear can make it unendurable. Patients know they can't cure themselves. They need doctors who can bear witness to the terror and reclaim them from its power.

Many really gifted clinicians, like Ferenczi and Frieda, are unable fully to explain why they do certain things; they can only say what they tried. This is why Ferenczi's most important work is his *Clinical Diary* and Frieda's is a text, *Principles of Intensive Psychotherapy,* a diary of a different kind.

Like people with exceptional skill of any kind, therapists like this do what feels right at the moment, making subtle adjustments as they go along. Attending simultaneously to many levels, they trust their intuitions, letting the patient's unconscious mingle with their own. They allow themselves to be guided "by instinct," whether or not they can explain what this means. Freud was just the opposite—better at describing his method than using it. But his descriptions were so brilliant and seductive that analysts have come to value theory over clinical accomplishment. Frieda may have helped to heal her patients, sometimes even the sickest ones, but she couldn't explain how she did this, which is why Freud has followers and Frieda doesn't.

But she did have some extraordinary successes, and Mrs. E. is one of them. Recreating their work together, we see the naturalness of Frieda's talent and the grace of her moves. Yet like all her favorite clinical examples, Frieda made Mrs. E.'s case inspirational rather than didactic, more a parable than an achievement.

Through some mysterious process that began on that August day when she unwrapped Mrs. E. from the wet sheet pack, a process Frieda spent the rest of her life struggling to comprehend, the patient improved steadily to the point where she could be sent home. Reunited with her husband and children, she periodically sent notes updating her progress and remained in every respect a healthy woman. Among the many versions of this case Frieda later published, this one, from *Principles,* is particularly emblematic.

> Because of [the patient's] assaultiveness, she was seen in a pack for her interviews. One day I asked her, upon the superintendent's request, whether she would sign a check for us. (She had not been committed [by a court]; therefore, payments from her own funds for her stay in the hospital could only be made with her signature.) The patient declared that she would gladly sign the check if she were unpacked. As I went for the nurses to ask them to do so, some empathic notion for which I cannot give any account made me turn back towards the patient. I saw an expression of utter despair and discouragement on her face, which made me decide to unpack her myself. She was [later] capable of telling me that she considered my taking her out of the pack myself the starting point of her recovery. My doing so, in spite of her being much taller, heavier, and stronger than I, had the connotation for her that her doctor did not consider her to be too dangerous, that is "too bad" to emerge from her mental disorder.[54]

When Mrs. E. recovered so dramatically and in so short a time, she became Frieda's key fascination—the case she cited in dozens of articles and lectures for the rest of her life. Frieda didn't completely understand why unwrapping Mrs. E. from the wet sheet pack at that crucial moment was so decisive to her recovery, but the fact that it had happened was a powerful confirmation of her treatment philosophy.

However, this was a real case, not a miracle, and there were ups and downs, as there always are. A week after that moment in the pack, Mrs. E. resumed calling Frieda "Jean Jacques Rousseau" or "Dr. Dunton" and spewing out delusions about all three of them. (Dunton was the superintendent of one of the hospitals where she had previously been a patient; Mrs. E. had long been convinced he was in love with her.) Frieda tried to persuade her that she was neither Dunton nor Rousseau; Mrs. E. responded by saying she was the Virgin Mary and Frieda ought to kiss her. Frieda, ever matter of fact, said there were forty patients, and she couldn't give preference to one or kiss all forty.[55] Mrs. E. shot back: "But you *do* prefer me. Why not show them all?"

Therapists are always most fond of patients who get better, and Frieda was clearly taken with Mrs. E. She was like an early Joanne Greenberg: delusional, frequently out of control, but reachable, engaged, and capable of being symbolic. A patient who can think of her symptoms in terms of their meaning can become enough of an ally of the therapist to stay within reach. Analytic work can succeed only if the therapist is unafraid and the patient is willing.

Six months following the famous moment in the pack, Mrs. E. was discharged from the Lodge, totally recovered. She developed a warm and thoughtful relationship with Frieda and Bullard and suffered no further difficulties. As Frieda wrote in her discharge note, the patient is "altogether well ordered, orientated, and knows about the period of illness she went through."

Besides the fact that it occurred at all, the most remarkable feature of Mrs. E.'s recovery was her ability to go back and systematically explain to Frieda the meaning and origin of each of her symptoms. Frieda often told colleagues that psychotic patients understood their unconscious productions better than therapists did. But not even Frieda expected patients to conclude their treatment by interpreting each detail with extraordinary precision, as the doctor sat by, listening.

For example, Mrs. E. explained her frequent, loud singing to radiators, a symptom that had long puzzled the nurses, in a simple fashion:

> Once you told me that you liked my voice and my singing but that you disliked my singing during the night because it hindered you from sleeping. [This was when Frieda was living on the first floor of the main building, right below the patients.] I thought you made fun of me, and so I wished to sing during the night in spite of you and to interrupt your sleeping in order to have my revenge. That is the reason why you all thought that I directed my singing towards the radiator. I hoped if I would sing there it would creep down along the pipes and then you had to hear it downstairs.[56]

These are, of course, Frieda's words; Mrs. E.'s account may have varied slightly in tone. But the basic message cannot have been much different—Frieda's dictated notes were practically verbatim, and besides, no therapist could invent dialogue this perfect.[57]

Frieda was clearly impressed by Mrs. E.'s clinical acumen and repeatedly tested its limits. She asked the patient to explain why she had called her "Jean Jacques Rousseau" throughout one phase of the treatment. "It is so natural," Mrs. E. replied. "Jean Jacques Rousseau was a foreigner who made a great impression on me, and he wrote about pedagogy and knew about the human mind. You are another foreigner and you know about the human mind and also treat people. So of course I called you Jean Jacques Rousseau." Of course.

Frieda asked about Dr. Anderson, one of Mrs. E.'s previous therapists, a man she had been convinced was married to her. Her response was straight from Freud:

> He simply treated me in a very nice way, so I built up this phantasy about his being in love with me. But you see I know perfectly well now that was a phantasy. . . . But when you are sick you cannot control yourself, and here your passion comes up, and you know it is such a long time since my husband left, and he could not make love to me for a long time before he left. And Anderson looked very much like him.

Like a teacher with a dimwitted pupil, Mrs. E. patiently explicated the rest of her symptoms, as Frieda quietly took notes. One of Frieda's most endearing qualities was a generosity, extended equally to patients and colleagues, that allowed her to appreciate talent in any form. Frieda loved being a student and could turn almost anyone into a teacher; she thought it natural for patients to instruct her on how to do her job better. She could never understand why other psychiatrists denied themselves the pleasure of having their patients seem so astute.

There is no way to know whether Mrs. E.'s interpretations were retrospective inferences about the meaning of her symptoms or understandings she had glimpsed while still ill. Nor can we evaluate the accuracy of her explanations against any "objective" standard. But these caveats hold for Frieda's interpretations as well: therapist and patient either trust each other's judgments, or they don't. Logical proofs aren't what matters.

When Mrs. E. ran out of symptoms to interpret, she made suggestions for useful Lodge reforms:

> Don't make checked floors. You cannot imagine what that means to insane persons. It is quite a torture. You know the black and brown checked floor on 4th? I always thought black meant Hell and brown meant Heaven and so I had always to fight not to touch the black with my feet and only to touch the brown squares, and I had to spit on the black but not on the brown ones.

And recalling the intensity of her conviction that various men (doctors, as well as other patients) had been in love with her, Mrs. E. urged the Lodge to stop housing male and female patients on the same floor (a typical practice in the early years). "We should be protected from being seen by all these young men," Mrs. E. told the forty-six-year-old Frieda, herself acutely aware of the humiliations that a loss of dignity could bring. "Imagine what my sons would think," Mrs. E. continued, "if they knew that Mr. L. always saw me dancing around quite naked!"

She strongly criticized Frieda for having moved her to a less disturbed floor for a trial period:

> I think it was a mistake to take me downstairs and to tell me it was only for trying and you were not sure whether or not I could stay there. That made me feel that you did not feel secure about me. How can a patient get secure about herself if she feels that her doctor does not yet feel secure about her?

How, indeed?

Finally, near the end of Mrs. E.'s review of the treatment, Frieda asked: "Do you remember how I unpacked you once?" The patient's reply was immediate:

> Oh, sure I do, I wanted to try you out. I wanted to see whether or not you were a coward. Here you came and said you would unpack me. Then you said you could not and wanted to ask for help, and so I thought you were afraid to be alone with me when I was unpacked. I liked you very much because you finally did it without any help.

Psychiatrists have always ignored the contributions patients have made to technique, significantly handicapping progress in their field. Dozens of books have been written by recovered patients about mental illness and its treatment; dozens more lie abandoned, half-written, in desk drawers.[58] Countless other insights by patients lie buried, unacknowledged, in their therapists' publications and process notes. Given how baffled psychiatrists have always been about psychosis in particular, you'd think they'd want to learn something from people who have experienced it.

Mrs. E.'s insights were exceptionally lucid, with the elegance and simplicity to which psychoanalysts aspire in their own work. That these insights came from a woman who was, eight months earlier, delusional, violent, and defecating on the floor is what gives us pause. Mrs. E. just doesn't seem like a typical psychotic; she seems more like one of those coma patients who is later able to recall every word uttered in her hospital room during the days she was supposedly "unconscious." Of course, we have no idea how many other seriously disturbed patients might sound like Mrs. E. if they had doctors who thought enough of them to ask for their ideas.

From a certain angle—the one psychiatrists themselves are least likely to use—what stands out most sharply about the history of psychotherapy is how often patients have been the ones to guide innovations in technique. Over and over, patients tell the story of struggling to rise above their doctors' despair to get the help they need.[59] Breuer, for example, was utterly at a loss as to how to treat the hysterical Anna O.; she was the one who came up with the cartharsis of "chimney sweeping," reliving the trauma through words. Ferenczi's work with R. N. was repeatedly stalemated until she goaded him into the "mutual analysis" he found so threatening. Dora kept trying to get Freud to break out of the neat compartments of his method and see her symptoms as rebellion; it was his refusal to follow her lead that caused their work to fail.

Yet even when patients do manage to affect the course of treatment, they often have no way of documenting their contributions, so they remain unseen. Patient narratives are discredited by doctors in every branch of medicine, and mental illness, by definition, delegitimizes even further what patients say. Even those who recover and write detailed accounts of their illnesses can publish only in popular media; patients aren't allowed into psychiatric journals as authors, only as clinical illustrations. Patients may also have a hard time saying precisely what worked and what didn't. They often have a strong intuitive understanding of the treatment process, but being able to put this into words that other people can understand is not something most mental patients know how to do.

We can't speculate on how Mrs. E.'s narrative of her illness and treatment might have differed from Frieda's account. So far as we know, Mrs. E. was never moved to write one, a fact that may or may not be significant in itself. No matter how she framed her story, though, she would have had to see her recovery as dramatic and the experience in the pack an important moment.

Frieda may have been idealistic in imagining that every treatment could be as successful as her work with Mrs. E. But she was right to cite this case as often as she could; it was as clear-cut a recovery as any psychiatrist was likely to witness, and it provided support for her fundamental claim that even the most bizarre symptoms of psychosis could ultimately be understood. Mrs. E.'s recovery had an important symbolic benefit as well: it insulated Frieda from the full force of her equally dramatic failure later that same year, with a patient called Hermann Brunck.

Brunck was someone Frieda desperately wanted to help. His sudden psychotic break was straight out of a textbook, and he was intellectually gifted in ways that made psychotherapy seem the ideal treatment for him. But he got steadily worse during the time Frieda saw him, and was then sent away by his wife for shock treatment. A year after his breakdown, he killed himself.

What complicates Brunck's story—and allows us to use his real name—is the fact that his wife, Hope Hale Davis, later published a memoir indicting Frieda for his death. As the only public depiction of her clinical work that is entirely derogatory in tone, Davis's book forces us to confront a very different Frieda from the one we otherwise would have known.[60]

Brunck was an economist at the Labor Department when he was admitted to the Lodge in November 1935. His paranoia was so severe it threatened the physical safety of Davis and her three-year-old child. Brunck was brought to the Lodge specifically to be Frieda's patient; he wasn't simply assigned to her by Bullard or someone who just happened to end up hospitalized there.

He had emigrated from Germany a few years earlier and was finishing his dissertation when he met Davis. They were both active members of the Communist party and became lovers soon after joining the same secret cell. Like bit players in some McCarthyite drama, the group's members began infiltrating themselves into sensitive positions in the government. Only the clandestine nature of their actions differentiated these party members from dozens of other leftists in FDR's administration. Stalin's show trials were still a decade away, and thinking people all over the world were as attracted to Marx as they were to Freud.

In the summer of 1935, Brunck was asked to write the key chapter for a report on economic development being prepared by the Labor Department. Always an intense and complicated man, he found himself increasingly unable to complete the work as the deadline approached. He began to worry that his unfinished section would arouse the suspicion of his colleagues and threaten the secrecy of his political work.

Brunck's fears, initially somewhat out of proportion, quickly grew paranoic in scope. He fantasized about secret meetings among his colleagues and denunciation at a public trial. As he began raving all night, Davis grew increasingly frightened. Finally she called Florence Powdermaker, a New York psychoanalyst who had once been attracted to Brunck. After a two-day examination disguised as a weekend jaunt, Powdermaker recommended immediate hospitalization and treatment with Frieda.

A few days later, Davis tricked Brunck into the car and drove him out to Rockville. He knew she was lying about where they were going and tried to jump out the door. Frieda had been in America for less than six months at that point and had just been hired onto the regular staff of the Lodge. Being sent a patient as brilliant, cultured, and psychotic as Hermann Brunck was both a challenge and a compliment to her talents. His symptoms precisely fit her model of schizophrenia, and Bullard was so interested in having him as a patient that he agreed to charge Davis half the usual rate.

Brunck was actively delusional by the time he was admitted. He was also a gentleman, raised to conform to the perfections and proprieties of life in the (Christian) German middle class. Even in his most deteriorated states, Brunck struggled to retain the gallantries and polite gestures of that world, a world Frieda knew intimately but Davis, the daughter of midwestern evangelicals, found utterly alien.

Brunck quickly regressed to an animal-like state. He ate practically nothing and rarely slept. When the nurses came in to make the bed, they found him huddling naked in a corner, covered in his own excrement. Any patient would be humiliated by a deterioration this extreme, but Brunck, the former intellectual, found these insults to his dignity as much a source of anguish as the symptoms themselves.

Frieda was powerfully affected by her first session with Brunck and cited it in papers for the rest of her life. She had found him lying naked on the floor of his room. His mumbling droned incoherently; he continued to masturbate as if no one were there. She asked if he would speak up so she could make out his words. He gave no response. She moved closer, telling him quietly that she wasn't trying to be "aggressive against him" but simply wanted to find out what he needed. Brunck continued to mutter. She sat down on the floor next to him, saying she "hoped to understand him better." It was typical of Frieda to accommodate herself completely to a patient this disturbed. She took for granted that if he could control his behavior, he wouldn't be on a locked ward.

Brunck's response to Frieda's offer of help was striking and sudden. "He got quite awake," she recorded later in her notes, "with an ecstatic facial expression. He shouted half fearfully, half happily, 'No, you cannot do that for me, nobody can do that for me, that is impossible. You will run the same risk as I do. . . . I cannot accept it.'"[61]

Frieda was matter of fact. "I am perfectly willing to go with you through all the dangers of your sickness," she told Brunck, "and to be your comrade in overcoming them," an interesting choice of words for a patient who was an ardent Communist. Brunck took a blanket from the bed and covered himself, saying quietly to Frieda: "Even though I have sunk as low as an animal, I still know how to behave in the presence of a lady."[62] He looked startled, as if he had returned suddenly from some far off place.

In that one lucid moment, Frieda asked Brunck if he would drink some milk, since he hadn't eaten at all that day. He agreed, and she went down the hall to the ward kitchen, returning with a glass. Brunck grabbed it and threw it in her face. Then, as before, he returned from the terror and pleaded for forgiveness. He conversed thoughtfully with Frieda for several minutes. "He said he knows how sick he is," she later noted, "but cannot understand why he behaved so animal-like, not really knowing whether he still was supposed to be a human being."

Unfortunately, as this first session neared its close, Frieda had to tell Brunck she was about to leave for a week-long trip.[63] She apologized and promised she would see him the moment she returned. "He responded quite afraid and devotedly," she wrote later, saying: "Do you know what you tell me there? Do you know what it means that you say you leave for one week? In the condition I am in it may mean only one hour but it may also mean eternity." Frieda never forgot the look on Brunck's face as the once-elegant intellectual plaintively cried out to her as she left the room, "How can one fall down so deeply?"

Frieda understood that Brunck was terrified by not being able to trust anyone, even for a second. In the two minutes it had taken her to get the milk, he had lost all sense of who she was. She had become "one of them," the dangerous web of destroyers who threatened his existence.

A person that frightened is not a good candidate for psychotherapy. Although Frieda insisted that any patient could *potentially* form a workable transference, she acknowledged that this didn't always happen. Some patients were just too fragile to take hold of the treatment, like drowning victims too exhausted to grab the rope dangling just inches from their fingers. Hermann Brunck may have been such a person; there's no way for us to know from this distance.

For the rest of Brunck's story, we have to rely on Davis's account, which switches the focus to how she felt. There weren't any staff meetings at the Lodge in 1935—Bullard and Jarvis and Frieda just talked to each other when they needed to—and only the first several weeks of Frieda's notes seem to have been preserved.[64] Davis's memoir is stuffed with details, but her tone is so defensive she clearly seems to be hiding something. Frieda becomes the villain of her tale, with Brunck the martyred saint. She is simply a witness to the tragedy as it unfolded. The few Lodge records that survive contradict this account and suggest instead that Davis was actually the one calling the shots.[65]

Brunck's first weeks of hospitalization were marked by brief periods of clarity punctuating a steady decline. The intensity of his regression terrified Davis and Brunck's parents, but to Frieda, it was a hopeful sign. Open masturbation, defecating on the floor, mumbled threats, refusing to eat: these were standard signs of "decompensation," especially in patients who had been highly reserved. For Brunck, so total a regression may have been a huge relief, freeing him from the tensions of trying to balance secret communist exploits with a politically sensitive government position. And it may have offered "a period of rest in which his organism could gain a respite and marshall its resources against his emotional disorder," as Frieda later put it. At the same time, for a man as urbane and gentle as Brunck to have become practically bestial must have been humiliating beyond belief.

Frieda was less alarmed by Brunck's actions than by his increasingly bizarre delusions and fantasies. As the strands of betrayal and guilt twisted around one another more and more tightly, even innocuous acts became trapped in the web. He trusted almost nothing anyone said. A person who becomes psychotic always breaks at his weakest point, and for Brunck, the line between economic theory and conspiracy was becoming dangerously frayed. Psychoanalysts have long argued that people with seemingly opposite roles are unconsciously the same. Burglars and locksmiths, arsonists and firefighters, criminals and policemen: motivated by similar needs, they differ mainly in defensive strength. For Hermann Brunck, a man who had willingly joined an organization requiring him to spy on his closest friends, paranoia may have been too core a part of his personality ever to eradicate.

Before his breakdown, Brunck had imagined his colleagues conspiring to demote him or ridiculing his work. A few months into his hospitalization, he was accusing kitchen workers of sending coded messages in his food: the arrangement of muffins on a plate, for example, seemed to be their way of forcing him to visualize the position of his parents' genitals as they had sex.

For psychotherapy to work, a person has to trust his therapist enough to let her into his thoughts. Someone who is very paranoid can't risk doing this. He may not even experience his thoughts as his own; they may seem to arise from outside forces. In Clifford Beers's classic *A Mind That Found Itself*—perhaps the most famous account of madness ever written by a patient—Beers describes in agonizing detail how he grew so suspicious of his own perceptions that he couldn't decide whether the person claiming to be his brother was in fact he. For Hermann Brunck to have trusted an unknown therapist who claimed to want to "be his comrade" would have required an extraordinary leap of faith.

Frieda's attempts to convince Brunck that she was acting in his best interests were undermined by his wife's suspicions. Hoping to protect him from problems at home, Davis provided sanitized reports of what was happening and occasionally lied. Her constant obsessing about which things to reveal and which to hide eerily resembled Brunck's paranoia, and while he was psychotic and Davis clearly was not, their shared penchant for deception created a kind of collusion that can only have made him more frightened.

As Brunck deteriorated, Davis grew more desperate. At one point, she even persuaded Frieda to allow a conjugal visit. (Frieda didn't think what Brunck needed was sex, but Davis insisted, and Frieda decided it couldn't hurt.) Nothing much happened. Brunck managed the act, but found the effort exhausting. Davis settled for walks in the woods from then on. But when Brunck reached his eighth month at the Lodge and continued to decline, Davis became frantic. As she watched her already thin husband tighten his belt to where his ribs showed, she began to wonder whether Frieda really knew what she was doing.

Against Frieda's advice, Davis brought Brunck home for a weekend visit. (He had not been committed and could leave the hospital whenever his family wished.) At first, he seemed relieved to be back in familiar surroundings. Then in the middle of a tense but uneventful Sunday afternoon, he suddenly grabbed a kitchen knife and lunged so violently at Davis she had to fight him off to keep from being seriously wounded. After Brunck was returned to the Lodge by ambulance, Florence Powdermaker concluded gravely that he had really been trying to kill himself. (This was an interpretation shared by everyone but Davis, especially in the light of Brunck's shaving "accident" several weeks earlier, when he had almost slit his throat.) Back on the disturbed ward, Brunck began hallucinating, and his condition was downgraded from "poor" to "guarded."

Davis developed an intense desire to find a physical cause for Brunck's breakdown. She pleaded to a friend: "Can't there be a sort of adhesive that holds the parts of people together, a chemical that could be weakened, a disintegrating agent, resulting in illnesses like Hermann's?"[66] Her hope was answered by Manfred Sakel, an Austrian psychiatrist, whose controversial new method for treating psychosis was beginning to gain attention in America. Sakel had noticed that epileptic patients were rarely schizophrenic; he hypothesized that inducing "artificial epilepsy" might cure psychosis.

After various experiments, Sakel discovered that an overdose of insulin most reliably brought about the convulsions he was seeking. (Patients then entered a coma similar to what diabetics experience when their insulin levels fall too low.) Sakel's technique was, however, quite risky: overly intense convulsions could result in brain damage, and a coma that was not ended at precisely the right moment (via an injection of glucose) could kill the patient.

Davis learned that Sakel was planning to come to the United States and train the staff at a sanitarium in Ossining, New York (called, by coincidence,

Stony Lodge). She wanted Brunck to be transferred there immediately; Frieda thought it would be a terrible mistake to interrupt Brunck's treatment in the middle of the "therapeutic regression" she was convinced he was experiencing. Like Ferenczi, she saw the dissolution of a patient's defenses as potentially useful, so long as the process were carefully monitored within the protective structure of analytic treatment.

Frieda had seen methods like Sakel's come and go since medical school. She remembered psychotics being injected with malarial blood to induce high fevers or forced to inhale carbon dioxide to excite their nervous systems. She remembered continuous sleep treatment and barbiturate overdose, surgical removal of the teeth and ovarectomies. She knew that no matter how crazy a method might later appear, when it was first developed, it always had the support of at least some authorities in the field.

But sending Hermann Brunck off for insulin shock must have struck Frieda as particularly cruel.[67] Her years with Goldstein had brought her face to face with the agonies of assault to the brain. For a brilliant man like Brunck to be subjected to the daily terror of the "near-death experience" Sakel saw as therapeutic had to have seemed barbaric to her. Besides, she was convinced there was a real chance that psychotherapy could eventually help him.

In the climactic scene of Davis's memoir—a scene told with far more feeling than any of Brunck's anguish is described—Davis stormed into the cottage on a Saturday afternoon and accused Frieda of sabotage. Frieda was enraged at being confronted in her home, on her one day off. She threatened to call an attendant to have Davis removed bodily from the grounds. "As Frieda grew more emotional," Davis recalled, "I felt more deeply calm."

In Davis's account, which is all we have, Frieda finally broke down. She collapsed onto the sofa and began to sob uncontrollably. Davis was stunned: "The sounds kept coming, the amazing gulps and groans and snorting gasps, so incongruous from someone who lectured before international meetings." By "debasing herself" so completely, said Davis, Frieda revealed her essential "villainess."[68] She admitted having failed to send the referral report that Davis had requested, thereby blocking Brunck's transfer to Stony Lodge.

Should we believe this story? It contradicts every other description we have of Frieda, but even she must have had her limits. Despite Davis's deep investment in absolving herself of responsibility for Brunck's illness, many of her observations are astute and thoughtful. In the end, it doesn't really matter whether Frieda behaved as badly as Davis claims; she clearly tried to prevent Brunck's leaving her care. Perhaps she needed to prove to herself or to Bullard that she could succeed with so difficult a patient. Perhaps she identified too strongly with him. (In later accounts of his case, she often made Brunck's parents sound just like Adolf and Klara.) Any analyst who wrote as much about countertransference as Frieda did must have had some personal experience to draw on.

But Frieda's reluctance to send Brunck to Sakel could not, as Davis claims, have been due to some blind prejudice against somatic treatment. Davis didn't know anything about Frieda's background and clearly had no idea she had spent years working on neurological wards.[69] Having talked Brunck into marriage and joining the CP, Davis had ample reason to consider herself partly responsible for his breakdown. Putting all the blame on Frieda deflected attention from her own role and allowed Davis to ignore the tragedy that befell Brunck once he reached Ossining.

Severely paranoid by that time, he was repeatedly betrayed and humiliated by the staff at Stony Lodge. Sakel never showed up, but Bernard Glück, the superintendent, claimed that Brunck could be cured anyway within a few months. Instead, despite the elaborate security arrangements Glück boasted about (perhaps inspired by the hospital's neighbor, Sing Sing prison), Brunck hung himself in his room with his own belt.

Davis's memoir ends there. Brunck is no longer a man who went crazy in the 1930s; he is the symbol of "a whole generation of young believers whose lives were damaged by disillusionment in the Soviet Union's false promise." His suicide wasn't the desperate act of a schizophrenic; it was the "sacrifice" of an idealist to the cause for which he had long fought. And the tragedy of his death had nothing to do with Davis or Glück—it was Frieda's fault, since she was the one who was supposed to save him, and didn't.[70]

There is no way to know whether Brunck might eventually have recovered had he been allowed to remain in psychotherapy for a longer period. Frieda was realistic about the risks of suicide, cautioning students that a person intent on killing himself could always find a way, even on a locked ward. The prognosis for a patient as sick as Hermann Brunck was grim from any vantage point. We can appreciate Frieda's dogged attempts to reach him, even as we acknowledge that her efforts were of little use. In one respect, though, Davis was right: Frieda blamed herself for Brunck's demise. She knew she was one of the few people considered capable of treating a case like his, and she knew she hadn't reached him. Even if Brunck's suicide were precipitated by his despair at the barbarity of insulin shock, Frieda still felt indicted by his death.[71]

Chestnut Lodge records reveal an odd irony to this story: Frieda was actually Brunck's primary therapist for only the first few months of his hospitalization. Davis makes Frieda seem responsible for everything that happened:

for his extreme regression, for his failure to improve, even for his eventual suicide in Ossining. It turns out that Brunck had been reassigned early in the treatment to Frieda's younger colleague, Ben Weininger; it was thought that he might do better with a male therapist, and Weininger had just joined the staff.[72]

Lodge files also reveal dozens of lengthy letters from Davis to Frieda, describing Brunck's behavior prior to his hospitalization.[73] Calling herself "an amateur psychiatrist," Davis interprets every detail of her husband's actions (but not her own furtive note taking, which must have made the already paranoid Brunck extraordinarily anxious). These letters—addressed "Dear Dr. Frieda" (an expression Davis had heard Weininger use) and signed "Devotedly yours"—may have been Davis's attempt at a vicarious analysis. (She wrote at least once a week.) At a minimum, they document her constant effort to insert herself into her husband's treatment, a pattern quite opposite to the passive, "doctor-knows-best" attitude she attributes to herself in her book.

Davis's intense ambivalence toward Frieda is also painfully evident in these letters. She clearly saw both Frieda and Florence Powdermaker as rivals for Brunck's love. This intensified the insecurity she already felt toward Ernst Volkmann, Brunck's lifelong friend from Germany, with whom he had a relationship in many ways more intimate than his marriage. (During his most paranoid periods, Ernst was the only one whose loyalty Brunck never questioned.)[74] In Davis's memoir, published in 1994, she is openly jealous of Frieda's growing importance to Brunck, but in the letters she wrote sixty years earlier, she constantly remarked on how lucky she was to know Frieda and how much she enjoyed their talks.[75]

Davis's conflicted motivations notwithstanding, some of her charges do seem warranted. A note had to be sent in November 1936 apologizing for the delay in sending the referral report. A letter from Powdermaker in December urged Frieda to meet with her at the upcoming American Psychiatric Association meetings to "discuss the transference problems in the Brunck case."[76]

But if Brunck's story has a moral, it is unclear. Frieda never claimed she could successfully treat every psychotic; she would have regarded such a statement by anyone as pretentious and unwarranted. She did insist that even the most severely disturbed patient had the potential to get well, provided that he was able to enter fully into the treatment and had a doctor who wasn't frightened of his craziness. Frieda started to treat Brunck immediately following Mrs. E.'s dramatic recovery and may have felt especially optimistic about reaching somebody so ill. But Frieda didn't always listen to her own cautions, and her overdeveloped sense of responsibility often left her feeling like a failure when even the sickest patient didn't respond. She may well have convinced herself that she could have rescued Brunck from his anguish given adequate time and support. Therapists identify most strongly with people like themselves, and for a man of such brilliance and gentility to be destroyed at so promising a moment in his life must have seemed unbearably cruel to her. Perhaps no one could have saved Hermann Brunck, but Frieda must surely have wished that she were the one who could.

The treatment of patients as disturbed as Brunck or Mrs. E. (or any of the others Frieda took on throughout her career) couldn't have occurred outside the protected environment of a locked ward. In every one of her papers on technique, Frieda made clear that she assumed the work would take place within a structure that prevented patients from hurting themselves or others. This was the whole point of creating Chestnut Lodge: to enable people to do whatever they needed to recover themselves. But locking patients up was only the first step. The challenge was to design a hospital that could carry out psychotherapy with every patient who was seriously disturbed. No one knew how to do this in the 1930s when Frieda and Dexter started making up the rules.

Bullard's first article, "The Organization of Psychoanalytic Procedure in the Hospital," was exceptionally bold. Written in 1938 and clearly bearing Frieda's influence, he presented radical ideas as if they were obvious truths. "The common purpose of all psychiatric hospitals should be to secure for each patient the optimum conditions [for] recovery," Bullard declared, trying to embarrass his colleagues into turning their own asylums into places for treatment, instead of warehouses.

Optimum conditions imply first an environment in which the patient is regarded as a distinctive individual requiring sympathetic understanding of the difficulties which have brought him to the hospital and, equally as important, understanding of the difficulties which are keeping him there; second, an opportunity to reorient himself to these difficulties through psychotherapy; and third, a receptive attitude on the part of staff and personnel towards the way in which the patient expresses his hostility and need for friendship and security. . . . Obstacles should not be put in the way of the patient being as sick as need be. As the late beloved William A. White used to say so aptly, "Where can a person be crazy if not in the hospital?"[77]

Bullard knew that psychiatrists didn't use words like *recovery* in the 1930s, much less make this the goal of their work. They didn't treat patients like "distinctive individuals requiring sympathetic understanding," and they certainly didn't think of their institutions as contributing to the "difficulties" which kept patients ill. Yet a decade before the idea of a "therapeutic community" was popularized by sociologists, Bullard said he wanted Chestnut Lodge to be a place where patients could be "as sick as they needed."

The obstacles to such a goal, he insisted, were solely pragmatic. Physicians had to be analyzed to keep from being sucked into patients' unconscious conflicts. Nurses and attendants had to be trained to interpret subtle dynamics. He decried the paucity of centers where nurses could be analyzed "at fees commensurate with their salaries," and said he had personally financed the treatment of many of his own staff to improve their effectiveness. (Ultimately, of course, he passed this expense on to patients in the form of the higher rates he could then charge.)

What made a psychoanalytic hospital unique, Bullard argued, was that it offered "an environment in which [patients] may be sick and unpunished for it." Psychoanalysis "favored the exposure of psychopathology, not its suppression," so analytic hospitals were designed to tolerate far more craziness than the typical institution. Bullard recognized that allowing psychotics to plunge into the unconscious could "create disturbances very annoying to obsessional personalities among the staff," but said people should learn to deal with the anxiety or work elsewhere. "Roughly speaking," he said, his aim at Chestnut Lodge was "to provide a twenty-four hour environment as friendly and non-critical as is the analyst in the hour of treatment."

These were wildly idealistic goals, achievable only in the abstract. A patient who expressed "his hostilities, suspicions or neurotic love needs" had to be controlled. People couldn't be allowed to hurt themselves or wander off. Bullard tried to keep the therapist insulated from events on the ward by appointing a separate administrator, but in practice, these roles blurred. And he ended up being more autocratic than he wanted. When staff disagreed about what was best for a patient, he had to step in and make the decision.

The administrative physician may feel that all patients must be treated alike. This applies especially to privileges and to ways in which patients live out their patterns of getting into difficulties with others. The analyst on the other hand may rightly feel that an infraction of a standing rule may be a protest about something having to do with the analytic situation itself and calling for no outside interference until it can be worked through with the analyst.

Bullard advocated weekly staff meetings to deal frankly with such conflicts, even though making differences explicit sometimes made people angrier. (With acutely psychotic patients, however, one physician served as both therapist and administrator, to prevent the patient from becoming even more confused and agitated because of disagreements between his doctors.)

Bullard acknowledged that organizing a psychiatric institution so as to maximize the number of people simultaneously undergoing analysis created unique problems. "It is unfortunate but nevertheless a fact," he noted dryly, "that analyzed, analyzing and unanalyzed people do not always get along well together, for it is human to resent those who know more than we do, and to resent even more strongly those who imply that they do." Jealousies between nurses, common in any hospital, were likely to be "intensified to a rather acute degree" in such a setting. Young physicians in training analyses were likely to resent senior colleagues who were therapists but no longer patients themselves. And of course there were rivalries on the ward, especially among patients with the same analyst. Bullard claimed that these dynamics actually occurred in every institution; what made a psychoanalytic hospital unique was that they were explicitly interpreted. When every action by every person was seen as having unconscious meaning, even the most routine event could take on symbolic significance. Yet despite all these difficulties, Bullard insisted that his and Frieda's goal was to turn Chestnut Lodge into "what it [was] intended to be, namely, a haven of refuge for the sick and a therapeutic organization."[78]

This view was controversial even in analytic circles. The idea of a psychoanalytic hospital, born in the 1920s, had ended up meaning quite different things to different people. The key question was who ought to be analyzed: the patient or the institution. Ernst Simmel, who in 1926 had founded the world's first analytic hospital in the Berlin suburb of Tegel, argued for the individual; Will Menninger, in Topeka, thought the "analytic object" should be the institution.

For Simmel, psychoanalysis in a hospital was simply a way to extend the method to patients too sick to be treated in the office. Offended by the brutality of the typical asylum, which seemed to him largely designed to "satisfy the neurotic's tendency to self-punishment," Simmel thought analysts had a moral responsibility to use "the treasure of thirty years of research" to find better ways of treating seriously ill patients.

Relying on an early form of the argument Frieda would later develop in detail, Simmel saw reconceptualizing transference as the key issue. The patient would naturally view "the whole clinic as a kind of extension of the analyst's personality," so the hospital may as well exploit such feelings in the service of the treatment. Simmel argued for educating attendants in "the general principles of psychoanalysis" and using nurses as "an extra sense organ for the analyst." He quickly saw how such a situation might lead to splitting, with a patient expressing "tender impulses" toward the analyst and treating ward staff with hostility. But his ideal was for the clinic to function as a "hidden intrauterine existence," taking patients "into its sheltering arms, out of their neurotic misery." This did not, Simmel emphasized, mean allowing them "to lead a life of sybaritic luxury whilst nursing their symptoms." At Tegel, no sedatives allowed patients to dull their feelings and "no comforting encouragement from sentimental nurses or physicians helped them to deceive themselves" about the realities of their illnesses.[79]

Despite Freud's personal interest in Simmel's experiment, which he regarded as a pioneering treatment venture and as a potential site for training, it attracted few patients (unlike Frieda's Heidelberg sanitarium, which thrived during the same period). Freud contributed a considerable sum to try to save Tegel (and wrote numerous letters to others appealing for funds), but in 1931, Simmel's asylum had been forced to close, taking with it Freud's interest in the possibilities of treating psychosis.[80]

Off in America, Will Menninger was trying a different approach. He had great respect for Simmel, whom he had met on a tour of German facilities, but Menninger's ideas about analysis reflected his idiosyncratic blend of early Freud and midwestern pragmatism. Couching all his ideas in classical drive theory, Menninger argued that a psychoanalytic hospital ought to allow for the controlled expression of previously repressed impulses. Patients with conflicts centering on aggression, for example, were encouraged to "demolish a building, dig up sod in preparation for building a walk . . . punch the punching bag, drive golf balls, bowl [or] play football." Patients suffering from an excess of guilt were urged to engage in work that made them feel "debased," like scrubbing walls or cleaning bathrooms. Those lacking in love were given the opportunity to identify with persons of higher status. (One patient, for example, was told "to wear his coat to dinner so that he will appear dressed like the doctors.") A severely depressed minister was asked to translate a scientific monograph from German to English. "This he began at a period when he was still exhibiting tearful spells and had little interest in his environment. He worked solidly eight hours a day for four months, completing the job for his physician, and with it his recovery." Menninger saw "a program of activities to meet specific unconscious emotional needs" as more helpful than psychotherapy, so few patients at Topeka were treated individually.[81]

He took for granted that once the previously repressed impulse was out in the open, the underlying conflict would simply resolve itself. For example, one patient was sent off to spend frequent sessions "with the punching bag" and then, "to facilitate the transfer of aggression" from the bag to his family, "a face was drawn on the bag with chalk." Another patient was encouraged to "name her practice golf balls after her relatives and swing at them with all the pent-up hostility she felt towards these persons." (This idea came from Simmel, who had urged soldiers suffering shell shock following World War I to bayonet dummies representing their former officers.) Such "recreational therapy," Menninger argued, could help to "make reality more pleasant than the patient's illness."

Will Menninger had only a general reading knowledge of Freud's theory and no personal experience of analysis (having been delegated to run the hospital while his brother, Karl, went off to Chicago to be analyzed by Franz Alexander). He never questioned Freud's assumption that psychotic patients were beyond the reach of standard methods, and unlike Frieda and Bullard, stuck to a literal interpretation of drive theory. At the Menninger Clinic, psychoanalysis provided a scientific language to "package" practices already in effect; it was never a core part of the hospital's mission, as it was at the Lodge.[82]

Frieda basically agreed with Simmel that it was the patient, not the institution, who was being analyzed, but she had a far more ambitious idea of the kinds of patients who could be treated. Tegel had open wards and thus couldn't accept violent cases; Chestnut Lodge, in contrast, welcomed patients too sick to be admitted anywhere but the state hospital. For Frieda, the challenge was to make the institution sufficiently safe psychologically as well as physically for the patient to undergo a regression deep enough to work through the conflicts that had made him sick in the first place. Bullard was on the right track in saying the institution ought to act like "the analyst in the hour of treatment," but he had so little training or experience in psychoanalysis that Frieda knew it was up to her to figure out what this would actually mean.

She developed a complex view of the hospital's function that put clinical issues above every other concern. Patients certainly had rights, but Frieda thought it was irresponsible to act as if their needs for safety were identical to hers. Psychotics needed structured environments even when they couldn't ask for them. We don't defend children's freedom by letting them fend for themselves; we protect them from danger whether they want this or not.

In taking this view, Frieda was carefully trying to avoid the romantic excess later associated with R. D. Laing, whose experimental asylum in London, Kingsley Hall, dissolved in chaos. Embracing an existentialist philosophy that stressed the patient's autonomy and freedom, Laing created an institution in the Quaker tradition of the York Retreat. "Among us there was no staff, no patients, no locked doors, no psychiatric treatment to stop or change states of mind," Laing explained. "Kingsley Hall was a free-for-all space."[83]

Frieda saw such an attitude as irresponsible, a physician's abdication of the moral commitment to treat patients. She was like Laing in identifying with patients' anguish, but because she didn't resent authority the way he did, she could see how desperately psychotics needed someone to take care of them. The challenge was to find a balance between freedom and protection, a kind of "holding" that wasn't coercive.[84]

In a tightly argued paper titled "Problems of Therapeutic Management in a Psychoanalytic Hospital," Frieda laid out these issues. "How," she asked, "does the psychiatrist succeed in granting to the psychotic the right amount of privileges for the time of his hospitalization?" She took a clear stand against total freedom:

> Therapists may be inclined to counteract traumatic influences by giving [the psychotic patient] the gift of more freedom than [he] can handle. While it is most undesirable for the psychiatrist to create additional frustrations in a thwarted psychotic's life, he cannot undo the evil consequences of the past merely by safeguarding against their repetition.

For a seriously disturbed person, she argued, "freedom may mean nothing but an unbearable, compulsory burden." Doctors had to be careful not to impose their own values on patients:

> If the psychotic is protected from developing wishes for freedom which are of the psychiatrist's making, he will ask less frequently for privileges which he cannot handle, be spared the frustration of being granted privileges and having them withdrawn; also, the psychiatrist will make fewer errors in handling the patient's privileges.[85]

Frieda cautioned students not to turn therapy into missionary work. Plenty of people chose to live in protected environments—for example, the military or religious orders. Schizophrenic patients weren't that different; their needs for security were just more urgent.

At the same time, Frieda encouraged colleagues to offer patients as much freedom as they could handle and not to be "overconcerned . . . with [their] own prestige." If this made other staff nervous, so be it. Therapists had to focus on what was best for the patient. "Cooperation makes for smoothly running wards," she observed, "but is frequently the sign of a broken spirit." Even patients who had to have privileges rescinded sometimes took the fact of having had them as proof they might one day improve. Frieda acknowledged that some patients might cause problems or try to run away, but if mental hospitals were to be different from prisons, they had to run these risks.

Although she took for granted that all necessary precautions would be taken against violence, she constantly challenged assumptions about coercion and restraint. Once she removed an enraged woman from a seclusion room in the hope of encouraging contact. Suspicious, the patient had snarled: "I could kill you if I wanted to." Frieda had quietly replied: "It doesn't seem to me that this would help either of us." The patient gave her a long look and then began thoughtfully reflecting on her problems, to the astonishment of ward staff.

Frieda knew how to bring out the best in patients, which meant she saw a side of them that others couldn't even imagine. She thought psychiatrists who drugged their patients or kept them in restraints got what they asked for: people who were violent and out of control. By treating patients with the respect they would have gotten had they not been ill, her belief in their recovery became a realistic hope, not the delusion her critics sometimes made it appear. Frieda's attitude brought its own rewards. Seeing psychotic patients as acerbic commentators on hospital culture or witty, insightful analysts of conflicts among staff made work with them refreshing, even enjoyable, a fact that few outside the Lodge could even fathom.

At times, Frieda used the disarming combination of her tiny size and powerful presence to defuse tense situations. Dexter liked to tell this story:

> A patient was bitching, a huge paranoid man, angry with Frieda, angry with the Lodge, asserting he was God and nobody could tell him anything. Frieda, who was all of 4'10", smiled up at him after he stopped roaring and said: "You have my permission to be God."

Another angry man waved his cigar in her face and sneered: "How would you like *this,* Dr. Fromm-Reichmann?" Frieda reached into a drawer, pulled out a large box of cigars, and said offhandedly: "Just put it in here with the others."[86]

Like Ferenczi and Sullivan, Frieda said that a therapist couldn't be effective with psychotic patients if he were frightened of them. She understood why staff would feel this way, but urged them "to stay away from patients of whom they are afraid" to avoid intensifying their patients' anguish. If possible, the therapist should examine the "unconscious reasons for his anxiety" and try to overcome it. "The psychiatrist or the nurse [who] wants to continue work with a patient despite fear should speak about it with the patient. Once the therapist is aware and not ashamed of his fear, and is free to make it a topic of discussion with the patient, it [need] not interfere with his usefulness." She gave this example from her own experience:

> A patient hit me and asked me the next day whether or not I resented his having done so. My answer was that I did not mind his hitting me as such because I realized that he was too inarticulate to express, other than by action, the well-founded resentment he felt against me at the time. "However," I went on, "I do resent being hurt as everyone does; moreover, if I must watch lest I get hurt, my attention will be distracted from following with alertness the content of your communications." The patient responded by promising spontaneously not to hit me again, and he kept his promise despite several severely hostile phases through which he was still to progress.

Frieda dealt with issues of restraint in an equally pragmatic way:

> If it is the sincere conviction of the members of the staff that the function of the disturbed ward is only therapeutic, and by no means punitive, and if transfers to closed wards are administered exclusively for therapeutic reasons, hospital patients will have no feeling of humiliation, frustration or resentment, and will have no sense of discrimination or ostracism.

"Our patients," Frieda continued, to the likely amazement of her readers, "will at times ask voluntarily to be transferred temporarily to the disturbed ward, [if] they feel the need for protection from acting out uncontrollable destructive impulses against themselves or their fellow patients."[87]

A therapist could sabotage the treatment if his "inner attitude towards psychiatric symptomatology" made him recoil from patients. Acts like smearing feces, for example, were so repulsive that the patient could cease to appear human. Frieda admitted feeling this disgust herself; the difference was that she regarded it as indulgent and unprofessional, like a surgeon who refused to operate because a wound was fetid or covered with pus. She discovered that if she wore "worn out, long-sleeved washable dresses" with patients who smeared, she could focus on their humiliation instead of her own feelings. This change in attitude could significantly affect the treatment: sensing that she understood how vile they felt, patients didn't have to resort to using feces to convey their desperation.[88]

Frieda was fascinated by "administrative psychiatry," a field most analysts considered moribund. The image of the nineteenth-century superintendent, more occupied by plumbing problems than by patient care, had sent most of her contemporaries fleeing into private practice. But years of living on the grounds of mental hospitals, often in the same building as the patients, led Frieda to think of disturbed people as neighbors. She had always worked out her ideas about treatment in the context of institutions—from the army hospital in Königsberg to Goldstein's clinic, from Weisser Hirsch to the "torah-peuticum." She had been intrigued by the idea of using psychoanalytic principles to design an institution ever since Heidelberg, and Chestnut Lodge became the laboratory to test these ideas. Insisting that mental hospitals could be therapeutic communities—where every policy, every activity, every decision by every staff member was guided solely by clinical needs—Frieda argued that institutions could be agents of change helping people to get well and live in the world, just as therapy itself could.

She shared Ferenczi's assumption that "therapeutic regression" was what helped patients to work through their conflicts. But the regression that took place in a hospital was fundamentally different from what occurred outside, where the patient had to struggle to appear "normal" to keep from frightening his family and coworkers. In a hospital, being crazy wasn't something to avoid—it was the whole point of being there. Mental hospitals were among the most heavily stigmatized places on earth; the only reason a person ever voluntarily entered one was to have a place where he could act as crazy as he needed to.[89]

Most hospitals punished patients for doing this, which only made them worse. But a predictable structure—the "holding" British analyst D. W. Winnicott talked about—could avoid the dangers of both anarchy and arbitrariness. If the light in the nurses' station went out at exactly ten o'clock every night and the medication trays arrived at six, the world started to look like a place that sometimes made sense. Frieda took for granted that people who ended up in mental hospitals had childhoods that felt chaotic to them. They longed for rules. But the rules had to have a reason; they couldn't be blunt instruments to beat them into submission. When structure isn't coercive, it can feel intensely reassuring, especially to a person whose inner sense of order is shaky or nonexistent. As one Lodge patient later put it:

It was a relief not constantly having to be alert to the need for adjustment to treacherous inconsistencies and changes. . . . For a person already exhausted by illness and therapy, trust in the safety and sameness
of the milieu is paramount, like not moving the furniture in the house of
a blind person, or knowing the ground will be there when you're about
to take a step.[90]

For all its benefits, however, a psychoanalytic hospital had inherent contradictions. Patients were expected to express their deepest feelings, making
confidentiality critical; at the same time, disclosure was essential for the system to work. Staff had to be protected and patients accounted for. People
couldn't be allowed to disappear or hurt themselves. Frieda argued that these
tensions, while unavoidable, didn't necessarily undermine trust. "If he is sufficiently in contact with reality to give any thought to the problem," she
wrote, "a patient whose condition is serious enough to warrant hospitalization expects the joint therapeutic endeavors of the staff of the hospital, and
does not experience professional discussions of his case as violations."[91]

For this reason, she would have been violently opposed to current efforts
to protect a patient's right to privacy at the expense of something far more
important: his right to treatment. We don't leave accident victims lying unconscious in the street because they can't give written consent to being hospitalized. We expect emergency room personnel to do anything they can
think of to help patients—from cutting into their bodies to reporting on their
drug use. Mental patients are the only people allowed to "die with their rights
on," as some advocate groups have bitterly put it.

Frieda was no saint. She got exasperated and angry with patients. She
made many mistakes. But her boundaries were clear, and she never let people
take advantage of her. Every therapist, she warned colleagues, had to come to
"an unmasochistic awareness of the limits of his endurance." She didn't underestimate the stress and exhaustion of working with psychotics. But she refused to blame patients for their symptoms:

To remain alert, spontaneous and yet cautious continuously for many
hours with a rigid and poorly communicative person is an extremely fa-
tiguing experience. The psychiatrist should not avoid fatigue in the pursuit of his professional duties, but he must be able to keep free from
resentment toward the patient, and must learn to avoid undue expectations or demands as to therapeutic results.[92]

This meant very long days. "The limitation of psychoanalytic interviews to one-hour periods," she noted, "does not make sense to the psychotic who has no sense of time." With a far tighter schedule than most of her colleagues, Frieda didn't have hours to waste, but she took for granted that a physician's job was to respond to the needs of patients. "The decision as to when to terminate a psychotherapeutic interview," she wrote, clearly embarrassed at having to be so explicit, "should be determined by the patient's clinical needs in the judgment of the psychiatrist, not by a compulsive attitude about time." She gave this example:

> A thwarted, schizoid personality had gone for twenty years through several schizophrenic episodes. Once we talked without interruption for three hours. The patient was deeply moved, and was temporarily less rigid. "I wish somebody had talked to me that way twenty years ago; then I would not have turned out to be the person I am now," this rather inarticulate patient commented.

It was especially important to allow as much time as necessary for the initial interview. "The psychiatrist," Frieda stressed, "cannot take care of the responsibility of deciding the future course of events and the possibilities of bringing forth changes in another human being's life if he is pressed for time."[93]

Frieda clearly failed at setting unmasochistic limits for herself, a failure she never acknowledged and that probably shortened her life. Like Ferenczi and Groddeck, who both insisted on doing anything possible to help a patient, Frieda's expectations were extraordinarily high, and her students and colleagues sometimes felt burdened by them. But being unable to take one's own advice does not mean that advice is wrong. Frieda's constant sacrifices clearly helped her patients. And her work inspired a whole generation of young psychiatrists to try to create truly therapeutic environments for people assumed to be beyond reach.

8

Creating Chestnut Lodge

Meaning is never monogamous.[1]

"Chestnut Lodge," Miss F., a former patient, said wistfully, "was a place I got to like too much. Whenever I get depressed, I wish I could go back. It's my dream place."[2] It's hard to imagine a mental hospital as a dream place. But for people like Miss F., who came to the Lodge in the late 1940s, when Frieda's goal of creating a therapeutic community was most fully realized, being there was as transforming as being in college or the military.

The analogy to college isn't wholly symbolic. Hospitals like the Lodge often referred to former patients as "alumni" and described their grounds as "campuses," as if they were Smith or Amherst.[3] And Lodge patients were deeply loyal to their alma mater. When Clarence Schulz did a follow-up study of those admitted between 1948 and 1958, he found people rhapsodic about their hospital experiences. Even patients who didn't get better hailed Chestnut Lodge. Of course, some people were resentful or hated the place, but they weren't the majority, and to understand how this could possibly have been true, we have to get beyond our image of mental hospitals as snake pits or prisons.

The Lodge created loyalty through calculated risk, recreating the craziness of patients' families without the dangers. It let people be totally insane and still get better. Competing with large, public institutions that cost thousands of dollars less, Frieda and Bullard knew they could survive only by offering something patients couldn't get anywhere else. (And this was real money. Health insurance that covered hospitalization for mental illness wasn't widespread until the 1970s).[4] By definition, the Lodge had a devoted clientele; without it, the place would never have made it past the 1920s.

Part of this was image. People sustain only the places—be they schools, civic organizations, or asylums—that meet their expectations. Institutions recognize this and constantly seek to present themselves in the best light. However, since judgments of quality are relative, maintaining market share requires a flexible attitude. After years of decline in SAT scores, for example, the test was "revised" to make points per answer higher. This increased the average score and helped elite colleges stay looking competitive. (A key survival strategy, since the harder a place is to get in to, the higher the fees it can charge.) Using much the same logic, the Lodge counted practically any change as improvement, engendering loyalty from patients and families and justifying its high costs.

That Frieda and Bullard were able to create a truly psychoanalytic hospital with so disturbed a patient population is what makes their accomplishment so surprising. Except for their class background, patients at the Lodge were much like those at state hospitals.[5] Most had been married at some point.[6] There were more women than men. They came mostly from the local area (it wasn't until the mid-1940s that the Lodge had gained enough of a national reputation to attract sizable numbers of patients from elsewhere).[7] And in striking contrast to other private hospitals, patients at the Lodge were seriously ill, as sick as those in state institutions.[8] This meant a small number of people who stayed for long periods. Women tended to have especially long stays, a consequence perhaps of their greater fondness for talk therapy. (Patients from far away stayed the longest; families don't send a person to a hospital in a distant state unless she needs extended treatment.)[9] Yet despite a population that was mainly psychotic, the Lodge succeeded in presenting itself as a place where even the sickest patients could get better.[10]

And to a startling extent, patients valued being there. "When I left Chestnut Lodge," said one of those in Schulz's follow-up study, "I was not entirely appreciative of the place. Since then I have been to a snake pit [later identified as Menninger] which made the Lodge, in comparison, look like a golden palace."[11] Another man said leaving Chestnut Lodge was "the biggest disappointment of my life. . . . [It was] a tailor-made medical 'suit' that fitted me perfectly. My head-strong father disagreed . . . and his decision deprived me of the best chance offered in America for a recuperating mental patient. I still think my place is at Chestnut Lodge, or should be."[12]

Some of this praise was political, intended to preserve the option of readmission should it prove necessary. It was hard to get in to the Lodge, and patients knew that testimonials might later be useful. "The fact that I was able to go on and improve," declared one successful young man, "is a debt I owe [to] psychiatry as practiced at Chestnut Lodge."[13] Patients transferred to state hospitals were often particularly appreciative ("Chestnut Lodge is the best sanitarium I have ever known," said a man sent elsewhere).[14] "Other patients used to remark how their analysts asked questions or gave sodium amytal," wrote another. "I thought Dr. Stanton was very foolish not to try those methods with me. However, his sitting there waiting for me to talk, without the help of drugs, was by far the best treatment. . . . I could *never* say anything detrimental about Chestnut Lodge. . . . My three years of treatment [there] were more education than I could ever have received in four years of college."[15] A woman who had spent several years on the disturbed ward and later recovered wrote:

I regard my stay at Chestnut Lodge as having been of great benefit. It has left me with a greater desire to face things more squarely. . . . Sometimes, I feel that all the far-fetched fears and delusions I harbored in my mind, especially the first year of my stay (how one crazy thought brought on a chain of reactions and thoughts) *fell into a logical pattern*. . . . Some of the most terrifying moments of my entire life were spent there. . . . I saw things beyond what I dreamed possible. The mind is a wonderful thing.

Insisting that psychoanalysis had brought about her recovery, she urged the staff to offer lectures to patients so they could learn about analytic theory during their hospitalization.[16]

The Lodge's fundamental philosophy—"the patient is always right"—made for some bizarre moments, given how crazy people were, but it was a shrewd business strategy, and Bullard knew it. His father had been smart enough to locate his mental hospital in a resort hotel, and Dexter wasn't going to waste his capital. By 1940, the Woodlawn's elegance was fading— Doug Noble, hired that year, called it "attractive in a slightly decayed, nineteenth-century way"—and Bullard knew he had to find new ways to please patients.[17] If psychoanalysis worked better in the 1940s than soirees or bridge games, then he'd be the one to provide it, at better quality than any of his competitors.

From the moment of her arrival, Frieda was Bullard's prime asset and the key element of his expansion plan. As other sanitaria continued to go bankrupt up and down the East Coast, Frieda attracted so many patients and staff that business boomed at the Lodge. (She doubled Bullard's numbers in four years: in 1935, when Frieda arrived, the Lodge had twenty-five patients, two physicians and a few nurses; by 1939, there were forty-five patients, seven psychiatrists, five nurses, sixteen attendants, an occupational therapist, and a dozen housekeepers, maintenance men, and kitchen workers.) Besides allowing him to hire all these new staff, this windfall also let Dexter finish renovating Rose Hill, providing Anne and his four children with an elegant home and "higher-functioning" patients with comfortable, single rooms in the now-vacant Little Lodge. (Patients' fees didn't cover all the work at Rose Hill. Dexter's Aunt Lily was so horrified by his plan to install showers in all five bathrooms that she sent him $10,000 to make sure she could take a bath when she visited.)[18]

Frieda's reputation and Bullard's eye for talent drew an outstanding and diverse group of doctors to the staff, especially during the war. Some had entered psychiatry after years in general medicine, having simply been assigned to psychiatric units when the army ran out of trained physicians. The shock of seeing so many otherwise normal soldiers break down aroused their interest in mental illness. Harold Searles, later one of the best-known members of this group, always cited *Men Under Stress* as having more influence on his thinking than any psychoanalytic text. Published in 1945, this classic study by Grinker and Spiegel presented case after case of well-balanced, patriotic soldiers who were transformed into trembling invalids by combat terrors. Frieda's claim that schizophrenia was caused by similar traumas had powerful resonance for Searles and his colleagues. They were excited by the possibility that psychotic patients might recover by working through their conflicts, just as most soldiers did.

The startling incidence of psychosomatic illness in the military had also led many doctors to take mental factors more seriously. Martin Cooperman, for example—who described himself as having a "completely mechanistic orientation" before the war and a single-minded interest in cellular approaches to internal medicine—was so astounded by the number of psychosomatic cases in the navy that he decided he had to learn psychiatry. He chose psychoanalysis in particular because somatic methods like shock treatment seemed reckless. "When we treated diabetics in internal medicine," he explained, "we worried about one unit of insulin more or less. Suddenly with insulin coma treatment, you got a guy and shot him [up with] several hundred units. It scared the hell out of me."[19]

Washington was a leading center for psychiatric training, with some of the most distinguished figures in the field: Frieda, Sullivan, Adolf Meyer,

William Alanson White, Edward Kempf, Clara Thompson, Lewis Hill, Lucile Dooley. Physicians who found themselves in the nation's capital after discharge from military units could do residencies at the many mental hospitals in the area and pursue their research interests at any of a half-dozen universities or at the laboratories of the newly created National Institutes of Health in Bethesda.

American psychoanalysis was in its heyday right after the war, and training institutes had the excitement of Berlin in the 1920s (a quality that was to vanish completely within a decade). Young doctors needing a specialty in the suddenly competitive market of postwar medicine found psychoanalysis an excellent option. Americans felt frightened by an increasingly complex world, and psychoanalysis was being touted as the cure for every problem. Even mediocre analysts made a good living. And since institutes in the United States carried on the tradition of scheduling classes during evenings and weekends, a man could support himself (and his family) working full time at a hospital while the GI bill paid for all his training. Best of all, the generous insurance benefits offered to federal employees (the primary clientele for any Washington physician) covered 80 percent of the cost of psychotherapy, even four-hour-a-week psychoanalyses that went on for years. John Fort, one of the eager young men who came to work at Chestnut Lodge in this period, called Washington "a virtual lodestone for analytic patients."[20]

Besides Frieda, Bullard, and Marjorie Jarvis, the early Lodge staff included Edna Dyar (who had trained at St. Elizabeths) and Ben Weininger and Ralph Crowley (who had both done residencies at nearby Sheppard Pratt). In 1940, Doug Noble arrived after nine years at Sheppard and training at the Boston Psychopathic (where one of his fellow students was Manfred Bleuler, son of the director of Zurich's famed Burghölzli Clinic). Other Lodge staff hired before the war included Mabel Blake Cohen (who had a Ph.D. in physiology from the University of Chicago in addition to her degree in medicine), Bob Morse from the Menninger Clinic, and Alfred Stanton (who had done his residency at the prestigious New York Psychiatric Institute).

In 1943, Frieda and Bullard wooed David Rioch away from a position as professor and chair of neurology at Washington University in St. Louis. Then, in the years right after the war, a number of young physicians—including Herb Staveren, Marvin Adland, Otto Will, Don Bloch, Bob Kvarnes, and Don Jackson—came to the Lodge straight from internship or military service. In 1946, Bob Cohen arrived (like his wife, Mabel, he had a joint M.D.-Ph.D. from the University of Chicago, where he had studied with the eminent physiologist Ralph Gerard; later, he did residencies at both Phipps and Sheppard, and Frieda became his training analyst). Margaret Rioch was hired in 1947 as the first (and for years the only) psychologist. It was an unusually talented and energetic staff, willing to plunge into the work of helping Frieda to create a truly therapeutic community and to be brutally honest with one another. Otto Will recalled his first case conference: "I was shocked. I had never heard such direct confrontation between staff members." Even more startling, Frieda and Bullard seemed to thrive on the discord.[21]

Part of what made life at the Lodge so different from what these young doctors had experienced elsewhere was the example of nonelitist commitment set by both Frieda and Dexter. Bullard was at work every day by 8:00 A.M. and was available to anyone—physician, nurse, patient, groundsworker—who wanted to consult with him. Frieda never pulled rank; she did more than her share of the dirty work and saw patients late into the night and on weekends. Doug Noble remembered how inspiring he found this:

> She was always around. She was not tucked away by herself. Not only did she attend staff conferences regularly, but you'd see her in and out of her office all the time. You'd see her on the grounds. . . . She was very much of an equal, very much part of the organization, willing to play any part on the staff. She made no attempt whatever to use her position and her prestige to get out of the chores and drudgery that were a part of hospital work.

Staff who had trained at prestigious places were often taken aback by the lack of hierarchy. As Bob Cohen recalled: "We had come from the university and thought all knowledge came from the professor. Then to come here and see this dilapidated place, with Dexter looking like a fullback—it really took some getting used to."[22]

Frieda's goal of turning the Lodge into a psychoanalytic hospital capable of treating the most seriously disturbed patients was powerfully advanced by the historic seminar she arranged for Sullivan to offer. Because his framework for understanding schizophrenia was so provocative and because the whole Lodge staff became familiar with it simultaneously, it had a decisive influence on treatment philosophy. "Ideology is not equally important for all institutions," remarked the historian of one of the Lodge's failed siblings, but "if the institution is ambitious and aims at being special and unique, it can play a crucial role."[23] Chestnut Lodge was precisely such an institution, and since Frieda had long argued that classical analysis was inadequate to the task of understanding and treating psychosis, Sullivan's theory quickly became the dominant ideology.

He couldn't have had a more receptive audience. By the early 1940s, the Lodge had an unusually creative and dedicated staff, fascinated by Frieda's quest to figure out what psychoanalysis in a hospital might actually mean. They were all making up their jobs as they went along and were willing to try practically anything. (Patients often found this terrifying, and relatives were taken aback by the chaos, but mainstream psychiatry gave them so few choices they just put up with it.)

An institution that has no models becomes a magnet for mavericks. People came to work at the Lodge because they weren't afraid of craziness and were willing to experiment with new approaches. Embodying both Frieda's and Bullard's most radical view of themselves, Sullivan encouraged staff to forge ahead no matter what the obstacles.

His twice-weekly seminars (which took place from October 1942 to April 1946) were completely free-form. They were held in the evenings, in the basement rec room at Rose Hill, with Sullivan by the fireplace, a glass of bourbon close at hand, and the Bullards' great dane sprawled on the rug next to him. A roomful of people, exhausted from hours of treating very sick patients, found themselves revived by his brilliance. There was no structure, no timetable, no planned progression of topics. Sullivan simply talked for a while about whatever he wanted, and then everyone jumped in for discussion. Issues took shape only after countless arguments and digressions. No one quite knew where it was all heading, but excitement alone sustained the momentum. Despite surface differences, there was a profound commonality of viewpoint, with people talking very deeply to each other about things that really mattered. This was how psychoanalysis had begun—in Freud's living room, among colleagues who felt part of a daring experiment, and were struggling to make sense of their daily work with very troubled patients.

The Lodge of the 1940s—and the Washington analytic community more generally—was one of few places still like this. Psychoanalysis in New York and Boston was highly conservative. Freud had just died, and his transplanted Viennese colleagues felt it was their responsibility to codify his ideas. Change of any kind began to be actively thwarted. The Lodge offered a rare escape from the sterility and authoritarianism that was becoming characteristic of analytic training centers. You could plunge back into the unconscious, the place where it had all started, and understand psychoanalysis from the inside, the way Freud's original band of explorers had done. With Frieda and Sullivan egging them on, the staff felt freer and freer to experiment, and the Lodge became a kind of analytic think tank (like Austen Riggs in the 1950s, when David Rapaport and Erik Erikson were there). The contrast to the standard psychiatric hospital couldn't have been sharper. Don Bloch, who joined the staff right after the war, called Chestnut Lodge "a flourishing intellectual nursery" where physicians saw themselves as cryptographers, determined to break the madness code.[24]

Specializing in schizophrenia gave the Lodge a freedom that even Riggs didn't have. When physicians concentrate on cases others consider hopeless, no one expects them to accomplish much. They can try all sorts of experiments without pressure for quick results.[25] They can do outrageous things they couldn't get away with anywhere else. Because patients at the Lodge were so severely ill, even the tiniest success took on major proportions. A person might still have psychotic episodes, but if he stopped shitting on the floor, it might look like real progress to his relatives.

What Frieda most admired about Sullivan was that he made even the most difficult patient seem reachable. "Psychotherapy," he liked to say, "is just plain hard work," an idea with incredible appeal at Chestnut Lodge. If they just kept plugging along, staff heard him saying, they might see progress. If they worked exceptionally hard, they might even see recovery. This had been Frieda's credo since medical school, and having it trumpeted by someone as brilliant as Sullivan was thrilling for her. Not everybody was as impressed by him—Cooperman, for example, thought Sullivan was "just an arrogant son of a bitch"—but the power of his ideas was infectious. Sullivan's optimism about schizophrenic patients stimulated Frieda's and Bullard's natural hopefulness, and seeing psychotherapy as "plain hard work" fit their doggedness. "Just put two people together in the same room, often enough, over a long enough period of time," Dexter always said, "and something's bound to happen." Sometimes it even turned out to be what they wanted.[26]

Sullivan's influence on the Lodge was complicated. He clearly taught everyone, including Frieda and Dexter, an enormous amount and strengthened their commitment to very difficult work. But the same sensitivity that attuned Sullivan to schizophrenic patients made him a lightning rod for conflict. He could intuit angry feelings before they were even conscious and would then tell each person how the others felt. Having struggled against authority his whole life, he could take simmering feelings of resentment and throw kerosene on them. Fortunately, a shared love of bourbon drowned most of his and Bullard's feuds before they exploded; otherwise Sullivan could have done real damage to "the Lodge family."

The intense feelings he provoked lasted long after his death. When the Washington Psychoanalytic Institute was investigated in the 1950s for performing "wild analyses," Frieda bitterly remarked to Dexter that the attacks were revenge for their embrace of Sullivan. Besides his insistence that psychoanalysis could work with schizophrenic patients, he had enraged classical colleagues by refusing to acknowledge his debt to Freud. After Sullivan's death in 1949, psychoanalytic institutes literally removed his books from their shelves and (as befit a field whose similarities to a religious cult have long been noted) branded Frieda and everyone else associated with him as heretics. (However, as Bullard was fond of pointing out, "those who would jump down my throat most furiously still referred patients to us.")[27]

The adventurous spirits drawn to the Lodge cared little about approval from the hidebound psychoanalytic establishment. Analysts in Washington had long been considered anomalous because so many of them worked in hospitals and treated seriously disturbed patients. (Most analysts elsewhere worked only with outpatient neurotics.) "There was probably no place in the world where there was such a great gathering together of people interested in the understanding and care of psychotic patients," recalled Otto Will, who had worked at St. Elizabeths before coming to the Lodge. Alberta Szalita told an audience of young analysts in 1980: "I wish I could convey to you the extraordinary atmosphere that pervaded Chestnut Lodge when I joined the staff in July 1949. . . . [The place] was bursting with the ideas and struggles of a group of sharp-minded, brilliant people totally devoted to the challenging and difficult task of the treatment of schizophrenia. . . . It was impossible not to think and learn during each staff meeting." Margaret Rioch said people "were engaged in a pioneering venture" that was exhilarating despite its frustrations. Having so dedicated a staff had tangible benefits—by the early 1950s, Bullard had to put extra people on the switchboard to handle the flood of inquiries.[28]

To the casual observer, Chestnut Lodge was indistinguishable from siblings like McLean, Sheppard Pratt, and Austen Riggs, but in fact, it was a strikingly different kind of institution. Riggs, for example, while clearly psychoanalytic, was a "neurosis treatment center" with patients far less disturbed than those at the Lodge. Austen Fox Riggs, its founder, was a New York internist who had gone to rural Stockbridge, Massachusetts, to recover from tuberculosis. In the clear air of the Berkshires, Riggs had some kind of "emotional upheaval," which led to an interest in neurosis. Unlike Ernest Bullard, he didn't set out to found a hospital; rather, Riggs began treating patients informally during his own convalescence, and then after World War I, he turned his practice into a nonprofit corporation run from his house. Stock-bridge residents, in notable contrast to those in Rockville, actively opposed having "nervous patients" in their midst (a sign found outside the inn where patients boarded read: "Look, squirrels! The nuts are here!").

Austen Riggs persevered despite these problems, and by the 1920s, he was treating about forty patients, who each stayed in town for about a month. After his death, the place was reorganized as a foundation like the Menninger Clinic. An "open hospital" that never had a locked ward, Riggs attracted relatively young patients in the midst of what Erikson would later call an "identity crisis" (a concept he developed directly from work with them). Since such patients required little supervision, staff could devote much of their time to research and writing.[29] Of all the sibling institutions, Riggs was most like a college, with staff who acted like pampered faculty and patients who looked in books for answers to their problems. With a host of well-known analysts in its ranks, Riggs often attracted Lodge staff exhausted from treating much sicker patients.

Boston's McLean Hospital was a totally different kind of place. Founded a century before the Lodge, it had quickly grown too large to pay much attention to individual patients. (In 1854, for example, the year McLean's third physician was hired, the daily census was two hundred.) Around 1930, there was a brief flurry of interest in psychoanalysis, but with five times as many patients as the Lodge and a much smaller staff, there wasn't time for an approach that intensive. The superintendent seldom even made rounds, and physicians were lucky if they had a half-hour now and then to chat with an especially promising case.

In the early 1940s—when Frieda and Bullard were offering daily psychoanalysis to every one of their patients—McLean introduced three different kinds of shock treatment and started doing lobotomies. The staff prided themselves on being "medical men" (for example, always wearing white coats in group photographs, something physicians at the Lodge would have laughed at). Increasingly forced to rely on an upper-class clientele to keep its beds filled, McLean's nurses spent their time signing patients' mink coats in and out of storage and catering to their other whims. ("If the patient did not like the lamb we served for dinner and asked for lobster," explained a former steward, "we gave lobster. Appleton House was the Ritz Carlton.") Such an atmosphere was dispiriting to staff. Physicians "held no expectation that [patients] were going to be discharged from the hospital," and despite its elegance, McLean was primarily a custodial institution.[30]

Chestnut Lodge was also strikingly different from its closest competitor, Sheppard and Enoch Pratt Hospital in nearby Towson, Maryland. Opened twenty years before the Lodge, Sheppard was far richer, thanks to a sizable endowment from its founder, Baltimore merchant Moses Sheppard, and its major benefactor, philanthropist Enoch Pratt. Every detail had been designed for maximum comfort and attractiveness. The dining room had "furniture, silver, and general service resembling that of a well-conducted hotel." The grounds were laid out as a spacious park, complete with shuffleboard and golf; a landscape architect was brought from Boston to design harmonious walking paths. There was a chapel for religious services, a swimming pool, and a library more extensive than those in many small towns. (Such luxuries were nothing compared to English asylums like Ticehurst, which had a French chef and two hundred acres of "pleasure grounds, a pheasantry, an aviary of singing birds, a moss-house, a pagoda, a hermitage, and a bowling green.")[31]

A far more ambitious undertaking than the Lodge, Sheppard was treating more than a hundred patients by the end of its first decade. Neither Sheppard nor Pratt ever had any direct involvement in the running of the institution; like most general hospitals of the period, administration was left to a board of trustees and a hired superintendent.[32] At a time when few asylums offered any form of professional development, one of Sheppard's physicians was dispatched for training in the laboratories of Heidelberg, and staff were provided with research facilities and full accommodation.

They paid a price for these luxuries, however; their activities were controlled to an extent unimaginable at the Lodge. The superintendent was permitted to be absent from the institution for no more than twelve hours without formal consent from the president of the board. Assistant physicians, nurses, and attendants were required to live on the grounds and to be available at all hours. Even off-duty doctors had to account for their whereabouts. Staff behavior was rigidly prescribed—nurses, for example, were expected to rise when a physician entered the room, a practice that would have been considered ludicrous at the Lodge.

Patients were also required to conform to a tight schedule, utterly different from their laissez-faire life at the Lodge. William Rush Dunton, the founder of occupational therapy, was on Sheppard's staff for three decades and briskly moved patients through a standardized program of daily activities. However, despite the rigid rules, life at Sheppard was genteel, with none of the tumult so characteristic of the Lodge. Each week, a tea was held in the library; patients browsed among the two thousand books and magazines and conversed politely. A Cadillac was purchased for excursions to the country, and a "shopper" was hired to indulge patients' desires. (At Craig House, an even more indulgent institution near Beacon, New York, "patients were transported in chauffeur-driven limousines, and drank wine from the hospital's private vineyards.")[33]

Although Sheppard occasionally experimented with new forms of treatment, like Sullivan's special ward for schizophrenics, only a minority of patients were offered psychotherapy, and many of those admitted in the 1930s and 1940s received shock treatment. Sheppard didn't do lobotomies, but in striking contrast to the Lodge, it did admit a number of postoperative patients for follow-up care. (This was a huge market in the 1940s, when thousands of lobotomies were being performed; Bullard's willingness to go along with Frieda's rule of not admitting postoperative cases cost him a great deal in lost profits.)[34]

Yet despite its wealth and many advantages, Sheppard lacked the single most important asset of the Lodge: someone of Frieda's stature. There was nothing distinctive about its staff or approach; like McLean, lavish surroundings were its only draw. In 1949, Lewis Hill was recruited to try to fill this gap, and although he made a number of important contributions to the literature on schizophrenia, he was no Frieda. There was, however, a lot of overlap between the two places. Bullard's early hires (Ralph Crowley, Ben Weininger, Doug Noble) all came from Sheppard, and more than a dozen other staff worked at various times at both institutions. Staff tended to come to the Lodge during their young, energetic years, whereas patients often started out at Sheppard and got transferred to the Lodge when they didn't improve.[35]

An essential ingredient in the Lodge's success in creating itself as a unique kind of mental institution was Bullard's standing in the community. He wasn't anything like "all the other batty analysts running around," recalled Young Marjorie. "He was much more Southern, proper, bland, and dull." Dexter had grown up with the men who later became the judges, bank presidents, and elected officials of Rockville, and he remained closer to them than to his colleagues in medicine. He was a charter member of the Rockville Rotary Club and its second president. Tommy Anderson, the chief judge of the Maryland Supreme Court, was his childhood pal, and Dexter often joked that he knew so many lawyers and judges he could always count on having "friends at court." The heads of the local banks had all played ball with him as boys in the summer baseball league—one of the biggest chestnut trees on the Lodge grounds was first base—and like his father, Bullard was for decades a stockholder and a member of the board of directors of the largest bank. (Anne once sent a birthday check to her daughter signed simply "love, mother"; the bank cashed it with no problem.)[36]

The Lodge benefited in dozens of ways from Bullard's status as town father, allowing Frieda to design a mental hospital that she—a woman, a Jew, a refugee—could never have run on her own in 1940s America. Local officials protected Dexter whenever there was trouble, and the citizens of Rockville hailed their institution as a credit to the community. When patients wandered off the grounds—there were never any fences or gates—whoever found them would telephone the Bullards. "This is Mr. Jones down at the cleaners. Mrs. So and So is here. Would you like to come and pick her up, or shall I put her in a taxi?" Dexter remembered the time a lawyer pal of his called. "One of your patients is down at the tavern, acting pretty peculiar. I think we better look into it before we get into some trouble." Bullard checked to see who was missing; it turned out not to be a Lodge patient, just some town drunk. "But this was an example of the friendliness that helped us get along," he grinned. When another patient did run off, get drunk, steal a car from the local Ford dealer, and then crash it into a police car right in front of the police station, Ernie Thompson, the lieutenant on duty, just called Dexter and told him to "come get this fellow out of our hair and keep him at home where he belongs."[37]

Patients and their families were good business for Rockville: they took taxis, bought clothes, frequented local restaurants, and stayed in hotels. Neighbors rented rooms to those who recovered sufficiently to live off the wards, and nearby children never needed a playground; they had Lodge lawns. Jane Sween, who grew up across the street from Frieda, never thought of patients as a problem. "Sometimes they walked over and made strange noises while my father was mowing the lawn, but we never paid them much mind. I was more frightened of the Bullards' great danes than I was of the patients." In the 1940s, Doug Noble treated a man who had been an internationally ranked tennis player before his breakdown. Noble thought it would help him to play, but none of the other patients or staff were good enough. Dexter introduced him to a lawyer down the street who had a private court; he was delighted to have so excellent a partner, and their tournaments were famous in the neighborhood.

Bullard's relationship with the medical community had this same personal touch. Instead of advertising in professional journals, he relied on a private network of referrals. He and Anne went to the meetings of practically every medical society: the American Psychiatric, the Southern Psychiatric, the Central Psychiatric, the American Psychoanalytic, the AMA. They would rent a suite in whatever hotel was hosting the meeting, and fifty doctors and their wives would show up for free drinks and conviviality. "You meet a lot of people that way," Anne chuckled. Frieda also did her part, using charm rather than alcohol as lubrication. "Frieda was a great publicist," Dexter recalled appreciatively. "She would go to those meetings and talk up the Lodge in a way that I couldn't."[38]

This was the role she had played since her days with Goldstein. Designing an institution that embodied her ideals and then running it without technically being in charge was her preferred modus operandi. "Retreating into the limelight" kept Frieda from overtly competing with others (especially Klara), and serving as the muse to powerful men protected her from their misogyny. Although Frieda had clearly enjoyed having total charge of the "torahpeuticum," she also found it an enormous relief not to have to worry about paying the bills. With Dexter and Anne devoting full time to dealing with the details, Frieda could concentrate on clinical issues and attend only to those administrative matters that interested her. Bullard totally deferred to her judgment, and she made him look good, a pattern that precisely recapitulated the relationship of her parents. And just as Klara had created "the luckiest family you could think of," Frieda transformed the Lodge from an aging spa into a laboratory for treatment.

Her noncompetitive style of relating to colleagues allowed Frieda to work toward long-term goals she never could have achieved on her own. She knew that it was impossible for one person—even someone as indefatigable as she was—to do everything the institution needed. Collaborative relationships were essential if she were to succeed in creating a hospital close to her ideal. In dramatic contrast to someone like Horney, who was always elbowing other people out of her way, or Melanie Klein, who at every possible opportunity asserted the primacy of *her* work and *her* ideas, Frieda pioneered an alternative model of women's leadership. As usual, she was behind the curtain pulling the strings, but her willingness to accede to Sullivan or her younger Lodge colleagues when this advanced her broader goals was very real.[39]

It helped enormously that Bullard wasn't threatened by people smarter than he was. ("I have never known a person so free of jealousy of other people and their brains," as Alfred Stanton put it.) Martin Cooperman, who joined the staff after twenty years in the navy, said Bullard "had a peculiar type of style—allowing lots of freedom within boundaries. The boundary was almost always money. The freedom was to do whatever kind of treatment you wanted. . . . Dexter could take difference very well. He could have this whole gamut of people there, many of whom professed to hate him."[40] Like a college president who builds reputation with star faculty rather than fancy facilities, Bullard knew that to compete with places like McLean and Menninger, he had to offer higher-quality treatment, which meant hiring a staff more experienced than he was.[41]

Life at the Lodge was homey and pleasant, but there was none of the lavish style of a place like Sheppard. (For example, the wards weren't air-conditioned before the late 1940s. The main building, with four floors, had no elevator. A barn housed the occupational therapy department.) Yet salaries were excellent. Frieda got $240 a month in her first year, plus free room and board, and the assistance of a dozen Lodge "helpers." When Marvin Adland was at Sheppard in the mid-1940s, he was paid $100 a month, even though his analysis alone cost more than that. Bullard more than doubled his salary when he came to the Lodge after the war.[42]

Since the Lodge had no endowment like Sheppard and wasn't a nonprofit enterprise like McLean or Riggs, Bullard could never run a deficit or take more than an occasional patient at below-cost rates. Yet there was a limit to what even the wealthiest families were willing to pay. Thus, he found himself in precisely the same situation as the president of a university who can't support a high-quality faculty solely with tuition revenues. Bullard solved this problem precisely the same way university presidents do: he attracted a large number of younger staff and paid them low salaries labeled as "training stipends." Thus, like graduate students who teach courses for a fraction of what faculty would have to be paid to do the same work, Bullard got psychiatric residents to see his patients for far less than senior staff would. Since his philosophy of treatment dictated that staff themselves be analyzed, he made this a condition of employment, so they could take the costs of their analysis as a deduction on their taxes. After the war, when the National Institute of Mental Health was organized, Bullard used Riggs's strategy of getting federal training grants and paid part of the residents' salaries from these funds rather than his profits.[43]

Thus, like Harvard or Yale or the Mayo Clinic, the Lodge could bill itself as a teaching institution and claim to offer a much higher quality of treatment than it could afford. (Besides the low-paid doctors, the Bullards also padded their staff with student nurses.) They did not, however, seek to become like Menninger, one of the major sites for psychiatric training in the United States. The Bullards were convinced that Will and Karl, despite their reputation as "the Kennedys of psychiatry," had made a major mistake in allowing their institution to grow as large as it did. To accommodate so many training programs, Menninger had reorganized as a foundation, thereby turning control over to a board of directors instead of keeping it within the family. (By 1951, according to its own historian, Menninger was essentially a "factory" for producing mental health workers, with patient care secondary to its training function.) "I always felt sorry for the Menningers," Anne remarked, "because they kept making their hospital bigger and bigger, and so had to raise more and more money to support it. That's one thing we were saved from. We never became a business. The bottom line was never the important thing."[44]

Key to their strategy was wider recruiting. There weren't enough local patients wanting intensive psychotherapy; the Lodge had to appeal to the needs of families wherever they lived. Frieda's presence was the crucial ingredient in creating this larger client base. From the moment she arrived in the United States, psychiatrists familiar with her reputation in Europe started sending patients to the Lodge (Hermann Brunck was one of many in the mid-1930s; within five years, there were dozens of others). Frieda's claim that psychoanalysis could work with schizophrenics was also key to the Lodge's fiscal strategy. Patients who might have been quickly discharged from another hospital after shock or a lobotomy would stay at the Lodge for years; everyone knew that psychoanalysis was a slow process with many setbacks. But because it held out the promise of real recovery and not just an amelioration of symptoms, families were willing to finance much longer stays. And since Frieda held that regression was essential to the process of treatment, the fact that patients often appeared to get worse during the initial period of hospitalization could be persuasively presented to families as part of the cure (much as the side effects of chemotherapy are described to cancer patients).

Frieda's relationship with the Bullards was remarkably supportive and unconflicted, significantly easing her transition to America and creating the key conditions for the Lodge's success. They met each others' needs in complex ways: Frieda was older than Dexter, with the toughness of his adored mother; Anne had Klara's efficiency and determination, which Frieda found reassuring. Dexter was both good father and dutiful son to Frieda; she was his confidant, the only woman in his life who Anne found unthreatening.

They quickly forged an effective team. Frieda and Anne had great respect for each other's attention to detail and capacity for hard work. (Unlike other staff, Frieda always appreciated Anne's efforts to save money; having run a hospital herself, she never regarded frugality as petty.) Anne was well aware of her limits as Dexter's partner and gratefully acceded to Frieda on administrative and clinical matters. Frieda could tell Dexter off when necessary, both because she was older and more experienced, and because he was such a "mamma's boy" that deferring to her felt natural to him. Besides, Frieda was so artful in her criticism that by the end of the conversation, Dexter always thought that whatever she wanted had been his own idea.

Frieda used her influence to become "a kind of general spokesperson for patients' rights," subtly influencing Lodge policy to reflect her own values. If Bullard made a decision about a patient that other staff regarded as unfair, Frieda would smile and say, "I think I'll invite Dexter over for lunch," and the next day, the patient would have whatever was at issue. Otto Will called her "the conscience of the Lodge." Jarl Dyrud, Dexter's son-in-law and a longtime member of the medical staff, said they were a winning team: "Frieda was the front person, writing and giving lectures. Dexter met people and talked to them and made deals."[45] Frieda's total identification with the institution was apparent in any presentation she gave. The Lodge was never simply her affiliation; it was who she became.

In return for her endless hours of hard work and unwavering commitment to their family business, the Bullards treated Frieda "like royalty," and she was often referred to as "the queen of Chestnut Lodge." She was the only member of the staff allowed to arrange her working conditions precisely as she pleased—spending several months each summer in Santa Fe or Europe, later taking a year's sabbatical, assigned fewer and fewer patients as she got older to leave more time for writing and research. These privileges were never hidden from other staff and must sometimes have aroused their envy, but no one begrudged Frieda's special treatment. Her European training, her seniority, and her extraordinary success with severely disturbed patients put her in a different league. (It also helped that she worked incredibly hard, harder than the rest of them.) Even someone like Don Bloch, whose relationship with Bullard was so embattled he was eventually forced to leave the staff, called Frieda's and Dexter's partnership "a glorious story."[46]

These bonds were, however, strictly professional. Asked whether Frieda ever stopped by Rose Hill after dinner or on weekends, Anne looked perplexed, as if the idea had never occurred to her. "She didn't have time to do that; Frieda was too busy. She was a worker," Anne said with evident relief. "She would have liked to have analyzed me," Anne admitted, "but there was no way anybody was ever going to get hold of me!" The fact that Frieda wasn't trying to get hold of Dexter either made her safe in a way that other women on the staff never were.[47]

Frieda couldn't have felt personally close to the Bullards, no matter how allied their interests. The cultural differences between them were too profound. The urbane, Jewish intellectual world that had nurtured her for decades was utterly unlike sleepy, WASP Rockville. And arriving at the Lodge as she had—with those two tiny suitcases and a head filled with images of Nazis and exile—gave Frieda an awareness of hatred and loneliness that the Bullards, swaddled in Southern innocence, literally couldn't imagine. Asked about anti-Semitism in Rockville in those years, Anne said: "I never heard a word. We never had any here. You just didn't think about those things." (This was a town where formal covenants prevented Jews from buying homes.) A cousin of Frieda, himself a refugee, was always struck by her sense of vulnerability, of being a stranger, never really at home in her adopted country. He remembered how often she spoke of "her great luck" at being taken in by the Bullards and her gratitude toward them. Morrie Schwartz, the Jewish sociologist who worked at the Lodge in the late 1940s, was disgusted by how deferential Frieda still was, a decade after her arrival: "She worked her ass off for the Lodge but could never get free of her obsequiousness toward Dexter. It was like the Jew toward the Gentile. It made me sick."[48]

But Schwartz wasn't a refugee, and he had no idea how much Frieda's absorption into "the Lodge family" protected her from experiences of discrimination she otherwise would have faced. Cocooned in her cottage on the grounds, the exigencies of daily life taken care of by the Bullards and their minions, Frieda was sheltered from the anti-Semitism and anti-German sentiment of 1940s America. And the Bullards' status as one of Rockville's leading families created a shield that protected her wherever she went. (When she wanted to buy the house in Santa Fe, for example, Dexter personally arranged a loan with his pals at the bank.) Frieda was well aware that thanks to the Bullards, her life in America was far easier than that of many of her refugee colleagues. Leo Löwenthal, for example, her old friend from Frankfurt, tried to find a place near New York where he and his wife could take a vacation (in 1935, in the midst of the Depression, when resorts were starving for business). He was repeatedly turned away with the comment, "Jews won't feel comfortable here."[49]

Frieda's complicated feelings toward the Bullards are evident in the many letters she sent them from Santa Fe. (Dexter's birthday was in August, and Frieda was always away then, so in honor of the occasion, she would write a long letter, reflecting on whatever had happened at the Lodge the previous year.) She constantly thanked them for what they had done for her: giving her a job so soon after she had come to America, building the cottage, and "for the pleasure of working with and for you." She called Dexter's birthday "a day of joy and gratitude for me," and told Anne how much she appreciated "the many un-talked about small and great things you do all the year round for our cause which you have made your cause, too!"

Referring repeatedly to "your fields, your grounds" and her "devotion,"

Frieda never lost sight of who was in charge. Yet she also knew just how to charm Dexter into doing whatever she wanted. Deferentially requesting his permission to fence in the back yard of the cottage, for example, to protect her dog from being "exposed to positive and negative transferences of patients and personnel," Frieda noted parenthetically that she had already made arrangements for the work to be done. Another time, having told Dexter that she was "very grateful indeed" for his agreeing to build a carport along one side of the cottage, she went on to instruct him precisely where to site it to avoid darkening her office. "Remember, it is the room in which I spend on average 18 out of 24 hours," she noted, subtly reminding him what a valuable employee she was.[50]

In praise that was clearly heartfelt, welcome, and shrewd, Frieda never let Dexter forget his accomplishments (and her part in facilitating them). "Think of it," she marveled in 1945, "what has happened to your father's custodial care place for the old aged during the last 12 or 13 years, so that it became a training center for psychiatrists all over the country!" Her appreciative tone allowed her to raise touchy issues other staff could only rail about, and she managed to recast even the most difficult problems as opportunities for growth:

> Naturally enough, with the increase in reputation and responsibility the place has been endowed with, its shortcomings, unresolved problems etc. become more conspicuous and more painful to both of you, and to your friends and staff members who are devoted to the place. This discrepancy between our wished for achievements and our actual accomplishments gave us quite a bit of a hard time during the last months, Dexter, didn't it? But it is one of the assets and promises for further improvement that all such things can be verbalized at Ch. L., and so I think, and I am sure, you and Anne think, our struggling has been all to the good![51]

The Bullards, in turn, often consulted Frieda when problems arose, taking full advantage of her unique status—neither part of the family, nor quite on the level of other employees. In a style she helped to make standard at Lodge staff meetings, Frieda tinged her advice with psychoanalytic interpretation. For example, when Miss Simpson, the Bullards' longtime nurse, refused to take a paid vacation, Frieda wrote to Dexter:

> To my mind it is not up to her to decide whether or not you want to pay her for her vacation (which she did not take for many years). If she does

not want your money she can give it away—for charity or something, that is *her* business, just as it is *yours,* if you have decided to do so, to pay her, independently from her attitude. Besides, I think it is important to counteract masochistic indulgence by paying her. I hope she'll overcome the inevitable hurt in due time, and I shall be glad to do what I can to help her with it.[52]

Having run her own sanitarium, Frieda could also help Bullard think through complex administrative issues. When some of the younger Lodge physicians pressed to be relieved of night and weekend duty, she wrote a long letter carefully analyzing the institution's needs in these different circumstances. It might be all right, she advised Dexter, to hire interns for night duty, but Sundays were different:

There ought to be an experienced person around to talk with visiting relatives and physicians, at least until the new doctors have sat in on a number of sessions between older doctors and visitors, so that they are really indoctrinated regarding this important job. . . . Don't let us make our old mistake to let them go ahead entirely on their own steam, and then be disappointed that they don't do what goes with our philosophy.[53]

Just as she had once shuttled between Klara and Adolf, helping them to overlook each other's insensitivities, Frieda mediated between Bullard and his staff. During a period when Sullivan was going around trying to convince people that Dexter was exploiting them, for example, Frieda astutely interpreted the problem from every angle:

The present cycle in H.S.S.'s attitude toward Ch. L. is, of course, *partly* our fault, because we glorified him to a point which put a terrific strain on him, and it would have taken a God to live up to our expectations. On the other hand, it has, as we know, its main reasons in his personality difficulties, which won't change. So, we have to learn to take it into our stride, as long as some in our group are as devoted to and therefore as suggestible by him. [It is also], Dexter, the one painful handicap of yours, which has gotten you into trouble with your associates time and again! To my mind, there is no need to make the life-and-death issue of it which it has become at times, because you are always so very willing to see it as it occurs, and to get things straight.

Rather than urging Bullard to behave differently to ease tensions with the staff, Frieda encouraged him to change because it would make *him* feel better: "Lord, how I wish we could come to eliminate that [problem], because it would save you so much pain and trouble!"[54]

Frieda further endeared herself to the Bullards by serving as the Lodge's roving ambassador, bringing its unique philosophy to far greater prominence than it could otherwise ever have had. Besides all the papers she presented at professional meetings, she often gave seminars to the staff of other institutions. Frieda had always been a natural at public relations: her attentiveness to others made it easy to sense what would be most persuasive for each audience. Her classic paper "Therapeutic Management in a Psychoanalytic Hospital," for example, was first given to staff at Menninger; when she later published it in the *Psychoanalytic Quarterly,* she changed its tone, warning Dexter: "I have expressed myself on purpose in a somewhat more classical psychoanalytic language than we all use ordinarily," so as to present Lodge philosophy more effectively to an establishment audience.[55]

Frieda's devotion to Dexter and to the Lodge was all-consuming. She met with prospective donors to the Washington School of Psychiatry (a teaching institution she and Bullard and Sullivan had founded to advance their ideas) even during vacations, and arranged little seminars at her home in Santa Fe for people who might send referrals or give money. On the rare occasions when she thought she had mismanaged a case or otherwise done something she was not proud of, Frieda wrote a fond letter to Dexter, thanking "the superintendent" for being patient with his "director of psychotherapy," underlining her awareness that every aspect of her life in America depended on being his employee. But she also knew just how to get back into his good graces, praising his open-mindedness—"the great and lovable asset in your personality"—and telling him that he should be as proud of his "spiritual child, the sanitarium," as he was of his four real offspring.[56] This was clearly how she felt. For Frieda, Chestnut Lodge was the child she could safely give birth to, a substitute for all the losses she had suffered in Germany.

In the early years of their psychoanalytic experiment, Bullard and Frieda let their tiny band of adventurous doctors do anything they thought might help a patient. Ben Weininger, hired in 1936, discovered by trial and error that taking the initiative, interrupting dissociated statements, literally holding the patient's hand if necessary could stabilize even an actively psychotic person. Weininger recalled his first case:

She was a young woman with wild-looking, disheveled hair on the disturbed ward, walking here and there, occasionally shouting or talking incoherently. She had lived in this condition for two years. I had myself locked up in the room with her alone, where neither of us could escape until the hour was over. I did not use a watch since this kept me from being fully present. At the end of each hour the nurse's aide opened the door. I stood at one end of the wall. She stood at the opposite end near the window, shouting and talking as if she were addressing someone outside. Occasionally she turned and waved her hand, indicating that I should leave. Sometimes she spat in my direction. . . .

I was prepared to see her almost daily for years if necessary. After intermittently trying to drive me away for six months, she turned around and looked at me, eye to eye, as if seeing me for the first time. She moved toward me and, half way, I moved toward her and asked her to talk to me. We stood near each other, and she talked slowly for two hours. This continued for several days. Then I asked her to come meet me in my office. She reviewed her history, and several months later, she left the hospital. I continued to see her. Within a couple of years she married a divorced man who had three children. I kept in touch with her from time to time for the next ten years, and she did not have a recurrence.

Weininger found "Frieda's life and commitment catalytic, a contagious spark of energy and motivation" that inspired him to transcend his own limitations. "We assumed that every person in the hospital, no matter how many years he had been ill, had a chance to improve." With a patient who had practically bled to death after slitting his throat, convinced that his homosexuality doomed him to a lifetime of ostracism, Weininger became even bolder:

I asked the nurse to pack his things; I was going to take him on a vacation with me for the weekend. No questions were asked and we left on Saturday morning and returned Sunday evening. It was an uncomplicated overnight stay; we took walks, went sightseeing and talked. There was no sexual involvement. When I met him Monday morning, he was cheerful and had no complaints. He was clinically well. I saw him daily for the next several months, and he continued feeling well after he left the hospital. He came to see me from time to time to tell me how well things were going for him. He did not make another suicide attempt.[57]

Weininger's colleagues were equally imaginative. Otto Will once treated a very violent woman who suddenly hurled a chair at him. Frightened and angry, Will grabbed her and tried to push her back into her room. They both tripped, and he fell on top of her. She was perfectly quiet for a moment and then said: "Well, doctor, you have finally touched me." She was never assaultive toward anyone after that.

Months later, this same patient began smearing feces over herself. The nurses kept trying to clean her up before Will arrived for their therapy sessions, until he told them this wasn't necessary. (During the war, he had seen patients with open wounds being operated on in mud holes; a few feces were nothing by comparison.) Will got a bucket of water and sat the patient on a stool. He took off her soiled nightgown and carefully washed her. That was the last time she ever did anything self-destructive.[58]

Nurses played a key role on the staff and had much more autonomy than at other hospitals. They were encouraged to think for themselves and to bend or break rules when this seemed warranted. They did, however, pay a price for these privileges: having their motivations and personalities scrutinized just as closely as those of doctors.

In the late 1930s, the nursing staff consisted of a superintendent and two R.N.s, with five aides as assistants. Since there were three floors of patients (the top two "seriously disturbed"), staff were constantly moving from one ward to another to keep things under control. After a manic patient ripped the plumbing out of the wall and nurses survived several choking attempts, Bullard brought in a male aide as backup. Then, when an especially violent patient took a pin out of a wet sheet pack, held it over a nurse's heart, and threatened to kill her, a second male aide was hired to sleep in the building in case of nighttime emergencies.

Nurses worked twelve-hour shifts, with one day off in every ten. They did everything from keeping detailed records on patient behavior to scrubbing floors and calming distraught relatives. Frieda had appreciated the important role of nurses in the therapeutic process since her days with Goldstein, and Bullard was convinced they could rise to any challenge. Julia Waddell gave this example:

I came on duty one night and was told a patient was to be admitted. At nine o'clock the front doorbell rang. The medical student and I went to the door and a mother and her twenty-one year-old son were standing on the porch arguing. We took them to the Third Floor living room. . . . The son said, "Mother, I can't leave you here." The mother said, "I certainly wouldn't leave you in a place like this." I tried to break into the conversation, but very few words were directed to me. Which was the patient? I could not decide, so I kept them both all night. When I came in the next evening, neither was there.[59]

Frieda and Dexter made themselves available to patients twenty-four hours a day, setting an example other staff were long to emulate. People voluntarily worked overtime. Some therapists saw patients seven days a week, and nurses stayed on duty until they weren't needed ("We didn't punch clocks," one recalled proudly). When Frieda was hired, she cheerfully took call every other night (an easy load from her perspective, since she was living in the building and it was half the responsibility she had in Heidelberg). "It was a familiar sight," said Waddell, "to see her at 3:00 in the morning in her yellow-flowered robe, drinking coffee in the kitchen, telling us why the patients behaved as they did." When the staff grew larger, people sometimes colluded to keep things from Bullard. Waddell remembered one free-for-all on Fourth—"doctors ending up with cut arms, broken jaws, and nurses with broken legs and black eyes, blood on floors and walls"—and everybody rushing to clean up the place before Dexter made rounds.[60]

Nurses took part in much of the psychoanalytic education that went on at the Lodge. They were invited to presentations by Sullivan or Frieda ("an invaluable source of help and inspiration," declared Waddell), and therapists routinely took a few minutes after therapy sessions to fill them in on what was happening. Dexter and Frieda urged younger staff to respect the judgment of nurses, who spent twelve hours a day with patients and could often contribute essential insights to a case. (This attitude contrasted sharply with that of the Menningers, who treated their nurses as "hostesses of the ward" and never hired men because they lacked "maternal instinct.")[61]

Despite the high frequency of patient violence, surprisingly little force was used at the Lodge. Staff coped with behavior that would have caused panic at any other hospital "with an ease and apparent casualness mystifying to the outsider." Disciplinary measures often took the form of "help," "support," or "working out of difficulties" rather than restraint or intimidation. Physical force was used only as a last resort and even then was often so skillfully deployed that the patient felt minimally coerced:

When a patient became impulsively threatening or assaultive, the most effective procedure was for many of the personnel to gather around and stand between the patient and any other patients, with great care to avoid "cornering" the patient if possible, and simply to wait, often for several minutes. The threat of overpowering force, *available but not brought into action unless the patient attacked,* was almost uniformly successful in avoiding actual violence.[62]

Physicians also followed Dexter's and Frieda's example and went to the ward immediately to try to calm agitated patients so that restraint would be used only if absolutely necessary.

In the postwar period, nursing became more standardized. Shifts were reduced from twelve hours to eight, and maids were brought in to do the cleaning (to the great relief of the R.N.s). It was still extraordinarily intense to work at the Lodge. Nurses and attendants were frequently injured by assaultive patients, but were forbidden to exact the kinds of retribution common elsewhere. "Laughing at patients or symptoms was almost non-existent," Stanton and Schwartz later noted in their study of the Lodge, and "staring at patients, undisguised moral condemnation, disgust, or rejection were treated as problems of the staff."[63] As always, Frieda made herself available to staff experiencing difficulties and routinely analyzed nurses who wanted to work through their conflicts.

No patient—even on the disturbed ward—was forced to take sedation, adding to the intensity of nursing work. If a patient refused, a second attempt was made; if he refused again, the nurse was instructed to make a notation on the chart and to record the reason for refusal if she could ascertain it. (This clearly assumed both that there was a reason and that a nurse was likely to know it.)

Yet despite all the stress, people apparently had so much fun working at the Lodge that they had to be explicitly instructed not to "spend time on the [wards] when off duty unless assigned to the entertainment of patients." Nurses who lived on the grounds were cautioned that it was "not wise to entertain patients in your living quarters as your time off is allotted so that you may participate in recreation which relaxes you from your work."[64]

Because so many staff lived on the grounds, relationships between doctors and nurses were far closer and more informal than was typical at other hospitals. Margaret Ursell, who came as a head nurse after the war, recalled spending hours in the tiny, narrow kitchen on Fourth, talking to whatever doctor happened to be making rounds. Staff knew one another so well there was little need for formal notes; they just had a chat over coffee about the patients. Nurses went to staff meetings, said what they thought, and weren't intimidated by doctors the way nurses elsewhere often were. There was constant socializing together after work and much camaraderie between the two groups.

Staff saw themselves as part of an exciting but risky experiment. "You learned to depend an awful lot on hunches," Ursell recalled. "The more you could intuit what a patient needed, or whether he was about to be violent, the better off you were." (Later, when she worked at another hospital, she was disappointed by how inattentive to nuance the staff there were.) A tiny woman, Ursell could recall being frightened of a patient only once. Coming up the back stairs from Second to Third, she had just opened the door when a very paranoid man went for her throat. Caught off guard, she screamed, and somebody had to rescue her. (In classic Lodge fashion, she later said: "I think I asked for it.")

Ursell sought out work with those who were most disturbed. They had the greatest need, and their illnesses seemed the most "real" to her. "Schizophrenics," said Ursell, "knew what the world was really like. They didn't have any pretenses. Patients who weren't as sick didn't have the same spot in your heart." Needless to say, only certain kinds of people felt like this. Staff had to be creative and autonomous to succeed at the Lodge. Since rules about medications, diet, visits, restrictions, and so forth were never as standardized as they were at other hospitals, it was often up to nurses to decide for themselves where lines should be drawn. Ursell, who described herself as having "a very high tolerance for deviant behavior," loved the autonomy. Yet it was clearly difficult work. Thinking back over many years on the medical staff, Bob Cohen said: "I never found the Lodge a relaxed and happy place. I don't mean that it was grim and without humor, but the level of tension was high, and one had to protect oneself as best one could."[65]

Class differences between patients and staff also created animosities rarely seen at other institutions. Many patients came from families of wealth and treated the staff like the servants they had grown up with. "One of the paradoxes of working [at the Lodge]," Harold Searles remarked, "was that one could not afford to be treated there oneself." (At McLean, in contrast, doctors typically came from the same social strata as the patients.) Searles remembered the time Frieda invited several of her schizophrenic patients over for dinner and how appalled he was by their condescension toward her. These were women who had been on the disturbed ward of a mental hospital—in some cases for years—but were used to such elegance that the modesty of Frieda's living quarters seemed pitiable to them. When a nurse insisted that a difficult patient say "please" when he requested something, she was asked why it mattered so much to her. "You have to keep [your relationship with them] on a level where you aren't considered a low white trash servant," she responded. "We are here to help them, not to work for them." (In elegant English asylums like Ticehurst, expectations were quite the opposite. Attendants were required to "salute" patients and treat them with the deference appropriate to their class prerogatives. Footmen wore livery, and the dress of other employees was evaluated for its "smartness.") On Lodge wards, however, it hardly mattered who came from what background. All patients wore the same (mostly disheveled) clothing—even if they could afford mink stoles like their counterparts at McLean, they were too sick to wear them—and there was no black market for cigarettes or food the way there was in other hospitals.[66]

Lodge patients were not, however, expected to help with the cleaning or to do odd jobs, as was the custom in many other mental institutions, not only because this was seen as untherapeutic, but because it would have been demeaning to them. Asked what patients did with themselves other than seeing their psychotherapists, Ursell reported: "They had occupational therapy, they played the piano in the living room, they were taken out on walks, they played games, they gardened." After a moment she added, "They also sat around and hallucinated," as though this were one more diversion.[67]

To encourage social interaction, those patients "able to maintain socially acceptable standards of behavior and appearance" (whatever these were) ate in the Lodge dining room. (Patients too disturbed to leave the ward were served from trays in their rooms.) An elaborate system kept track of patients from the moment they left their rooms; those who could not be trusted to go directly to meals were "escorted." The silverware was carefully counted before and after each meal. Patients "with escape problems" were "specialled" by student nurses who remained glued to their sides at every moment. Staff were instructed "not to smoke while serving or to eat while patients are being served." However, if assigned by the dining room supervisor, staff could "join one or more patients and smoke, or have coffee or dessert, if these are indicated to make the patient more comfortable."

Standards were hardly those of Emily Post. So long as a patient could "assume responsibility for dressing and behaving somewhat appropriately," and "eat his food with a minimum amount of assistance or supervision," he was sent to the dining room. Policies were designed to make the experience therapeutic, like everything else at the Lodge. "The dining room might very well be a frightening venture to many patients until they become somewhat accustomed to the place," read one manual. "Nursing personnel should be prepared to accompany and eat with such patients until such time as the patients are able to be somewhat comfortable about going and eating adequately on their own initiative." Nurses were not simply to escort an anxious patient to the table and leave him to fend for himself. Patients who tended to isolate themselves were coaxed into conversation; those inclined to "be overactive and somewhat bizarre with their eating habits" were cautiously restrained. Those who "avoided balance in their food choices" were assisted in their selections. As always, staff were taught that this was yet one more opportunity for psychoanalytic interpretation and they should record relevant observations of a patient's eating behavior in the nursing notes.[68]

In keeping with the respectful attitude toward patients, family members bringing a relative to the Lodge were told that a detailed history was required on arrival, that this might require two separate appointments, and they should schedule their departures accordingly. (Relatives were always interviewed separately as well as together, "for whatever impressions may be gained as to their manner toward each other and the patient, relative dominance, areas of compatibility and incompatibility, and characteristics of which the patient's behavior may be a caricature.")

Families were cautioned that the Lodge expected them to "cooperate with the medical staff regarding the advisability, length, and frequency of visits." A thoughtfully worded statement read: "It has been our experience that visits shortly after admission are usually trying for both the patient and the family. Although individual circumstances naturally govern our advice in this regard, it is wisest to plan on an early parting." Patients were never required to see relatives. If a visitor arrived and the patient declined to see the person, the ward administrator, head nurse, or nursing supervisor politely explained the situation and barred the visitor. Relatives paid the bills and staff took pains to be cordial to them, but Lodge policies, of necessity, had to focus on the patient's feelings.[69] Frieda, as senior clinician, routinely reviewed each patient's progress, read the evaluations of his therapist and ward administrator, and tried to reassure worried relatives.

Although there were certainly many wealthy patients at the Lodge, Bullard excluded celebrities, seeing them as potentially disruptive to the "therapeutic community." He rarely took someone ahead of where they were on the waiting list, and when a colleague from Los Angeles called up whispering that she knew a movie star in need of treatment, he would say: "I'm sorry. Maybe we can take him in two or three months." A gossipy article in the Rockville newspaper claimed that the Lodge had turned down both Marilyn Monroe and Judy Garland, and that "kings, emperors, and titular heads [flew] in on their private planes for sessions at Chestnut," but Bullard laughed that off.[70]

Everyone at the Lodge—even typists and groundsworkers—knew the psychotherapy hour was sacrosanct. Nothing was ever allowed to interfere with it. (Frieda would give talks to nonclinical staff to explain things like this. As Mabel Peterson in the front office recalled: "We would gather on the grass behind the cottage and Frieda would sit on a little bench and talk to us about sick people and why they act the way they do.") "If the patient did not seek psychotherapy it was thrust on him," remarked one physician. "Patients were not permitted to leave the hospital during the scheduled hour," Stanton and Schwartz noted, "and patients who assaulted their therapists were sometimes placed in cold wet sheet packs while the therapist continued to see them. The protection of psychotherapy itself was so thoroughgoing that only the physician was permitted to interrupt it—a patient could not be too sick to see his therapist."[71]

Indeed, at Chestnut Lodge, "psychotherapy" and "treatment" were synonymous, and "even the most inarticulate or confused of new patients seemed to grasp [this] surprisingly easily." No one could recall a patient ever criticizing the hospital's refusal to use lobotomy, electroconvulsive therapy, or other somatic treatments. As Stanton and Schwartz were later to note: "Markedly dissatisfied patients who went to another hospital usually promptly returned, shocked by assumptions in the other institution." The interpersonal ethos also powerfully shaped patients' attitudes towards one another. "Each patient was given the privilege of living her illness in her own individual manner," and even those on the disturbed ward defended one another's rights to eccentricity or bizarreness.[72]

The whole point of being at the Lodge was to be in an environment where, as Bob Cohen put it, "the doctor has to adapt himself to the patient." His colleague Jan Foudraine gave this example:

A paranoid religious patient spent most of the hour prior to my vacation by keeping me at great distance. He inundated me with religious, lofty words. I was reduced to an immobile, silent spectator and there was no reciprocal feeling or involvement. I did not like to leave the patient like this, so I started, at the end of the hour, suddenly to intone, as if I were a fundamentalist preacher speaking to his congregation, saying, "And the Lord told unto me, go ye, Foudraine, to Florida; lie on the beach and enjoy thyself." And I said unto the Lord, "Lord, but what about Mr. Smith?" And the Lord said unto me: "Never mind Smith, go on vacation and enjoy thyself." The patient was shocked; he leaned forward and appeared off balance. He blushed. I had the initiative and knew that from this moment I would try to keep it. We looked at each other and the patient said in a soft voice, with definite emotion, "Doc, what did the Lord mean when he said, 'Never mind Smith?'" To this I responded by saying, "And I asked the Lord—Lord, what dost thou mean saying, 'Never mind Smith?' And the Lord said unto me, 'Vacation is vacation is vacation.'" The patient smiled as if he understood. There was now warmth between us and I stood up and walked toward him. I took the patient's face between my hands and the feeling between us was of a father and son. I said, "See you again, John—and don't sin." The patient put his hand on my arm and said, "I'll try," and had tears in his eyes. I walked off.

"People are always doing the best they can," Martin Cooperman noted. The Lodge's mission was to help them, not to defend some particular approach. Such flexibility was possible, however, only in an environment that supported it. The hospital, said Helm Stierlin, had to "become a kind of an institutionalized punching bag, which, in its totality, can take beatings from the patient which normally neither the therapist alone nor the people of the patient's usual environment would be able or willing to endure."[73]

As Frieda constantly emphasized, certain structural features had to be in place for a mental hospital to be truly therapeutic. Doctors had to like working with schizophrenic patients. They had to believe they could help them. They had to have a small enough case load to plunge in to the work. Young therapists had to be carefully supervised and adequately analyzed. There had to be a strong focus on research as a way of "promoting detachment and fostering an objective clarification of the relationship." If these conditions held, Stierlin argued, "the emphasis on the therapeutic relationship tends to energize the therapist and to sensitize him to . . . seemingly minute, hidden, and obscure aspects of the patient's behavior."[74]

This couldn't be carried too far. If the therapeutic relationship became "the yardstick against which every action of the patient is measured," nothing would ever be seen on its own terms. When the patient complained about the hospital or wanted to leave or became violent, everyone would ask: "What does this have to do with his therapy?" Stierlin thought that questions like these could be useful up to a point, but if they became the overriding focus, the therapist would become too anxious, appraise the situation less realistically, and be less understanding and helpful to the patient. As Stanton and Schwartz noted, there was a strong tendency at the Lodge to "fantasize life as one great psychoanalytic hour," an excess that Frieda's and Bullard's pragmatism couldn't always keep within bounds.[75]

Private hospitals, like private colleges, are incestuous, selective, and worried about their market niche. People who work in them are deeply affected by the experience, and those who purchase their services pay a lot of money just to be there. But a psychoanalytic hospital has an intensity all its own and can easily come to resemble a cult more than a college. With the actions of every file clerk, doctor, patient, and visitor subject to interpretation, significance becomes magnified beyond all proportion. To fill a hospital like that with schizophrenic patients was to turn it into a virtual hall of mirrors.

In a story that could well be true, Clarence Schulz drove to the Lodge on a Saturday, concerned about a young woman he was treating who had suddenly turned violent. Harold Searles ambled up as Schulz was getting his mail. "It's your countertransference anxiety that keeps you from being able to subdue that little girl," Searles remarked in passing. "You're a big guy. You ought to be able to take care of her." At that moment, the patient appeared at the end of the hall. She had an attendant clamped tightly to each arm and was about to explode. Wrenching herself free, she grabbed a chair and threw it through the nearest window. Schulz raced down the hall to ring for help. When he returned two minutes later, the patient had Searles pinned to the floor and was grinding her knee into his nose. As attendants struggled to pull her off, she grabbed Searles's tie and started choking him. His eyes bulging, he thrashed back and forth. "I looked on for a moment of self satisfaction," Schulz recalled with a smile, "and then I intervened. That was the kind of thing you got all the time from your colleagues. . . . that kind of free interpretation, unsolicited."[76]

Bob Cohen told a similar tale. During his residency at Sheppard, a patient tried to escape by wrapping herself in a rug and rolling down the hall to the front door, 200 feet away. A colleague of Cohen, experimenting with psychoanalysis, walked beside her, trying to elicit her feelings before she rolled out to the street. "This was such a fascinating approach I knew I wanted to learn more about it," said Cohen, explaining why he'd applied to work at the Lodge.[77]

Part of what made things so intense was that so many people were simultaneously being psychoanalyzed. This was true not only of doctors, who had to undergo an analysis as part of their training; at the Lodge, nurses, occupational therapists, and even some attendants were in treatment. When Frieda spoke of a therapeutic community, she wasn't being metaphoric. It was literally the case that practically everyone at the Lodge was a patient, a therapist, or both. It's hard enough to imagine working in a place filled with schizophrenics without also having coworkers crashing around in their own craziness. All of this analysis did make for an unparalleled degree of shared experience. At the Lodge, the average nurse or attendant had a depth of insight into patients' psychology that went beyond that of even senior psychiatrists at other institutions.

Sometime in the early 1940s, case conferences—held three times a week, and lasting at least several hours—began to be tape-recorded, with the verba-

tim transcript of each session (twenty to thirty single-spaced pages) distributed to the entire medical staff. These meetings were like everything else at
Chestnut Lodge: a kind of controlled free-for-all. (Searles compared the discussions to "the episode in Disney's *Fantasia* which shows the creation of
the world with volcanoes erupting.") People said whatever occurred to them.
If this offended someone or got too personal, these reactions became more
grist for the mill. Staff meetings were like batting practice. A doctor could
take a swing at anything that came his way, without having to worry about
the effect on patients. And since every word was being transcribed verbatim
and distributed, argument and interpretation could go on ad infinitum.

To create opportunities for even freer expression, the staff started meeting
twice a week in small groups (with four to six members who stayed together
for years) to focus on countertransference issues. "There was no assigned
topic," Bullard recalled. "Anybody could bring up anything they wanted. After you talked to the same people year after year, you really began to tell the
truth about what was going on in treatment and what your feelings were."

Sometimes all this interpretation paralyzed people when they had to make
quick decisions. In a famously revealing story, Raymond Baker, the Lodge
carpenter, was making repairs on one of the windows on the fourth floor of
the main building. When he went to get some supplies, a patient from the disturbed ward crawled out on the ledge that ran around the roof and threatened
to jump. A crowd of doctors and nurses gathered below, anxiously discussing
the appropriate response. While they deliberated, Raymond stuck his head
out a nearby window and called to the patient: "You can come in this way."
She took his outstretched hand, smiled pleasantly at the terrified therapists,
and went back to her room.[78]

Fortunately, most staff had enough of a sense of humor to appreciate the
absurdities of life at the Lodge. The annual physician follies parodied their
own excess, reassuring younger doctors that the place might not be quite as
crazy as it seemed. *Alice in Blunderland,* one classic performance, starred
Don Burnham sporting noticeably hairy legs and a long blonde wig. As Alice
presented a patient at the Mad Hatter's tea party (a case conference), his senior colleague, Frieda from Rockville, announced amid much bowing and
scraping that her intuitive abilities ("a kind of seventh sense") had allowed
her to cure the patient by zodiac repositioning. The whole staff joined together for the closing song:

> *Far from all neurotic clamor*
> *Like a faint mirage*
> *Stands our beloved alma mater*

Dear old Chestnut Lodge.
Now enlightened
By Fromm-Reichmann
We make our pledge to thee
To death we stand, as one strong band
Against shock therapy.

The cynics' scorn and criticism
Cannot our faith dislodge
Ever we'll defend the honor
Of our Chestnut Lodge
Ever zealous
Guardians jealous
We will always be
'Gainst those who hack, the frontal tract
By psychosurgery.

On the plains of Mount Olympus
The temple of the gods
Suffers by comparison
With our Chestnut Lodge
In towers ivory
With connivery
We plot conspiracy
To wage the fight, 'gainst all who might
With us dare disagree.

Another memorable production, based on the hit musical *Oklahoma,* featured Dexter crooning, "People will think we're in love," to Frieda, as Anne looked on, laughing. The occasional skits by office staff had more of an edge, with themes like the Bullards' money, Frieda's fame, the interminability of analysis, and, of course, the low pay.[79]

In addition to designing the Lodge's treatment program and teaching every term at several analytic institutes, Frieda supervised most of the younger staff, as well as dozens of other therapists. In her early years in the United States, these were mostly physicians, but after she and Sullivan organized the Washington School of Psychiatry, whose mission was to train nonmedical analysts excluded from the mainstream institutes, she also supervised many psychologists and social workers. The school had branches in both New York and Washington, and until Sullivan's death in 1949, he and Frieda commuted back and forth, seeing students in both places. She would take the night train up from Washington and hold supervisory sessions at the Dorset Hotel on Fifty-fourth Street or the Brewster on Eighty-sixth. She also kept an apartment on Connecticut Avenue in downtown Washington (so students from New York could come for sessions on weekends without having to travel out to Rockville) and spent a lot of time in Baltimore, where many of the trainees at the Psychoanalytic Institute lived. ("Every hour, a different young man would come up to her room at the Southern Hotel," Ted Lidz recalled with amusement. "After this had gone on for several months, the hotel management refused to give her a room.") Frieda considered all this supervision an essential part of her job and always made time for students, no matter how packed her schedule was. "If you needed an emergency consultation," Don Burnham recalled, she might say, "I've got to be downtown at such and such a time. Why don't you drive me down and we can talk about it on the way?"[80]

Frieda had no interest in "developing disciples who walked in her footsteps. . . . Her influence was expressed in helping each student to achieve the goals he'd set for himself." But she was a powerful model for many young psychiatrists. Silvano Arieti, later the author of a classic text on schizophrenia, wrote: "In an era when many thought that psychoanalytic treatment for the schizophrenic patient was hopeless, Frieda Fromm-Reichmann with her devotion and the originality and clarity of her thinking showed us that her treatment was not in vain, that her teaching was not in vain and we gathered around her to learn and to be inspired."[81]

Students appreciated her straightforward style. "She emphasized being useful to the patient," recalled Ralph Crowley, "and although she did not think psychoanalysis always had to be a grim business, she warned psychiatrists against painting the situation as less serious than it was, or giving any other sort of false reassurance." Crowley found it especially useful that Frieda "did not soft pedal actual mistakes or overlook the absence of significant material. She taught that if the psychoanalyst was secure and geared to the patient's needs," the relationship could survive even major lapses.[82]

Far more flexible than most of her colleagues, Frieda encouraged students to come to her for advice on a broad range of cases. "She was interested in anything that anyone had to suggest," Bob Cohen recalled appreciatively, and her willingness to do whatever was necessary to help the patient was legendary. Unlike Sullivan, who specialized in treating a very particular type of patient—young, male schizophrenics in the midst of their first psychotic break—Frieda had always been deeply interested in psychosomatic disorders, addictions, and every kind of serious mental illness.

"To listen and make sense of what seems absolutely incoherent requires great skill," said Beatrice Liebenberg, a social work student, recalling the pleasure of watching Frieda hone her intuitive edge. Doug Noble remembered her "extraordinary sensitivity" in making "every possible effort to understand the patient," and saw her interest in nonverbal communication, a topic largely unstudied in the 1940s, as a natural extension of her focus on subtleties of the therapeutic relationship. When Noble complained about a patient who was always criticizing him, Frieda said, "Well, she's showing you her positive feelings with her body, by gaining weight." Even more than Sullivan, universally considered to have an intuitive gift that was positively uncanny, "Frieda was willing to go out on a limb and say whatever she felt. She worked with her empathy; it didn't come from some tremendous theoretic framework."[83]

Noble was supervised by both Frieda and Sullivan, and found their styles strikingly different. "She had, of course, a great deal of confidence in her own abilities, and I sometimes felt put down in talking with her, as anybody would, but she was kind and not particularly sharp in the way Sullivan was. I was rather in awe of her." Noble especially appreciated Frieda's broad knowledge and interests, which allowed her, for example, to supervise his work with an alcoholic patient. "I couldn't imagine doing that with Harry Stack. He never would have agreed to it; he just wasn't interested in that kind of thing."

A person as intensely reliant on nonverbal cues as Frieda might have considered the distanced quality of supervisory work unappealing. Not so, recalled her friend Edith Weigert. "She gave her full presence to supervision, grasping with alertness the total situation, in all its complexities, which the student presented. She was able to put her finger on the gaps and evasions, the sore spots in the doctor-patient relation. Her criticisms seldom hurt, because they were usually so startlingly true and so adequate to the needs of both doctor and patient." As another colleague put it, Frieda "had a strength of personality which she seemed to assume everyone else possessed, or could possess." She neither "worried about hurting a fellow colleague's feelings, nor was she condescendingly gentle with her patients." Always scrutinizing her own feelings and motives, "she assumed a similar fortitude in her colleagues and dignified them through that assumption, interrogating them while implicitly believing that they too wanted their own defensive patterns to be revealed and then resolved." Psychologist Josephine Hilgard found par-

ticularly useful Frieda's direct injunctions, like "never, ever, turn your back
to a patient." Unlike Sullivan, whose scathing critiques often left students
trembling, Frieda's brisk encouragement seemed to embolden them. "I never
felt belittled by Frieda, even when I was quite insecure about what I was doing," recalled Hilgard. "One of [her] central principles was *answering* a patient's communication rather than *interpreting* it." Otto Will said Frieda
taught him "the acceptance of ambiguity" and the "confrontation of uncertainty," skills that allowed him to devote his life to psychotic patients.[84]

"One has to be something of a lion-tamer to work with schizophrenics,"
Frieda told Jarl Dyrud at a crucial moment. "You have to mean it." He was
treating a very violent patient and confessed in supervision: "I don't think I
can stand it. I'm too frightened." Frieda gave him a long look and then said
quietly: "Don't be afraid, you're not going to hurt her." During another session in which Dyrud seemed bored, Frieda told him: "Well, I know you're
tired of her, but she's tired of you, too." When Frieda told Rose Spiegel she'd
be able to handle a difficult situation and Spiegel protested, "But I'm not like
that," Frieda replied confidently, "You will be!"[85]

Her combination of bluntness and high expectations intimidated some students. When John Fort asked for help with a difficult Lodge patient who
came to therapy wearing dark glasses because he said the sun hurt his eyes,
Frieda suggested Fort say: "Eyes? Eye-balls? Balls? Is it your balls you are
worried about?" Fort told Frieda that *she* might be able to make such a comment, but he found the idea appalling. Another time, when he complained
about a chronic patient, Frieda admonished: "You must make each hour with
this woman a memorable experience." Feeling "awed and utterly inadequate"
to carry out such a dictum, Fort struggled on, discouraged and uncertain.

Clarence Schulz felt that Frieda put extraordinary pressure on students to
be as good a therapist as she was. "I had the feeling she was never satisfied,"
said Schulz. He admired her "tremendous clinical understanding" and ability
to predict "with uncanny accuracy" the next test result by the Lodge psychologist. "But when I would report on what I thought was a pretty good exchange," Schulz recalled, she would say: "What kept you from thinking thus
and so? Or asking about that?" There was no question, Schulz agreed, "that
she was way ahead of us, but I took this as a kind of pressure to be doing
more or accomplishing more" and resented it.

Frieda's refusal ever to give in to her own weaknesses and insistence on
maintaining a nonstop work pace—a style she had absorbed from her mother
in early childhood and took completely for granted—could dismay her younger
colleagues. Otto Will never forgot the time he was exhausted and disheartened
and called Frieda to say he couldn't come in that day; in a chilly tone she re-

sponded: "You are a doctor. This is your work. You are needed." Ashamed, Will reported for duty and never again tried to shirk his responsibilities.[86]

Students did find reassuring Frieda's view that other hospital staff could often be as important as physicians. She had learned from Goldstein never to underestimate the role of "ancillary personnel"—some of the earliest papers they wrote together were published in nursing journals—and she insisted that the therapy hour was only part of the treatment. Frieda always assumed that nurses and attendants were essential to patients' well-being, and if she heard someone screaming on the grounds, she would "telephone his ward and ask them to please give him whatever attention he needed at that moment."[87]

Because every detail of Lodge structure was designed (at least in theory) to benefit patients, a superficial "social adjustment" was never encouraged. Patients were expected to conform to rules that preserved the safety of themselves and others and, to a lesser extent, that of the furniture. But they were not punished—as they would have been at any other institution—for engaging in the very symptoms that had made them mental patients in the first place. Refusing to eat or smearing feces or masturbating openly didn't attract much attention at Chestnut Lodge. Staff were often repulsed or irritated by things patients did, but as long as they didn't actually hurt anyone else, the behavior got dealt with, and everybody went on. Since every act was subject to interpretation, the staff knew that their reactions were as likely to be analyzed as the patients' misbehavior.

Nurses certainly got angry, as they did at other hospitals, but they weren't allowed to use their anger to harass the people they were caring for. Patients were "invited but not pressed" to participate in hospital activities; only psychotherapy hours were mandatory. The assumption was that patients would do what was emotionally useful to them, and even if they were psychotic, their judgment was to be respected. Only three kinds of behavior warranted intervention no matter what the circumstances: threats of suicide or homicide, running away, or sex between patients.[88] Otherwise the Lodge allowed—sometimes even encouraged—patients to enact their craziness in whatever ways they chose.

This made for some trying moments. Miss N., a severely regressed woman who spent twenty years on the disturbed ward, flushed her underwear down every toilet she could find, often stopping up the hospital's plumbing system for hours. Patients were inconvenienced and maintenance workers grumbled, but this behavior was regarded as a sign of Miss N.'s illness and thus something to be interpreted, not outlawed. When patients threw food at each other or fought in the dayroom or got drunk on the grounds, the staff treated them like disobedient children from whom better behavior might be expected at some later time. If a patient did something that seemed to represent progress in working through a conflict, staff saw it as their responsibility to facilitate it, even if it was irritating or mildly destructive, so long as it didn't cause serious harm to anyone.

Suicidal patients were even permitted, up to a point, to express the rage or despair they clearly felt. Standard precautions were, of course, taken: transferring the patient to a locked ward, removing sharp objects, and checking on him every fifteen minutes, for example. But as Frieda stressed, "every psychiatrist knows that there is no absolute protection" against suicide. A person truly determined to end his own life will find the means to do so, even on a locked ward. Precautions were primarily a way to "keep alive what is left of the suicidal person's own tendencies towards life and health." In the same spirit, Frieda said that patients who refused to eat "should not be tube fed unless there is actual danger of starvation." Such brutal measures were justified only after every other possibility had been exhausted (leaving food with the patient for a longer period, replacing the ordinary meal with a sandwich, making the tray "especially attractive"). It didn't matter whether these extra efforts inconvenienced staff; if they helped the patient, they were worth it. "Patients who refuse food from fear of being poisoned," Frieda also noted, "may be induced to eat if the nurse or the psychiatrist invite themselves to share a meal."[89]

Violence was the exception. It was never allowed. Of course, this was less of a problem at the Lodge, where acting out by patients was typically seen as the fault of staff. At age ninety-two, thinking back over six decades, Anne Bullard declared: "We always felt that if a patient was screaming or abusive, there was something he needed." She never locked the doors of Rose Hill in all the years she lived there alone after Dexter's death, and couldn't remember even one time when a patient had broken in. "If you treat people with respect, they don't do things like that" was always her attitude.[90]

Frieda's philosophy that psychotherapy with psychotic patients could work only in a supportive context led her to strongly endorse Bullard's practice of separating the roles of ward administrator and therapist. This system of dual management later became the subject of many Lodge conferences and publications. John Fort emphasized the benefit of having two members of the staff intimately familiar with each case, able to help one another when necessary. However, Fort noted, since "competitiveness is often quite high in the best of therapists," a patient's own distortions could quickly turn tensions between his doctors into oedipal dramas. ("Two heads are often better than one," observed one of Fort's colleagues, "but not if they're used to butt each other with.")[91]

Part of the problem was structural. The therapist could do practically anything as part of treatment: see the patient in the office, take him for rides in the car, analyze his utterances, teach him to balance his checkbook. No one could define from the outside what constituted "therapy." But an administrator's decisions could be overruled by any number of people, and in irritation, he might retaliate by changing a patient's privileges without telling the therapist. ("This is the kind of thing that makes you go home at night and cry," said one physician. "The times that I have seen the worst damage done to my patients have been times when they were given freedom without my knowledge.") Disagreements were unavoidable: an administrator often had responsibility for as many as twenty patients, each of whom might have a different therapist, and it was not possible to communicate effectively with all of them. In one famous example, a patient smeared feces on the door to his therapist's office. The therapist went stomping off to the ward administrator demanding that something be done about it. The administrator said: "Now, let's see. Is this on the inside of the door or the outside? If it's on the inside, then it's therapy. If it's on the outside, it's administration."[92]

Frieda encouraged her colleagues to experiment with varying the number of therapists present in a treatment session, something she had learned years earlier from Goldstein. Jarl Dyrud and Margaret Rioch tried multiple therapy, where several therapists worked together (usually with a patient who had proved particularly problematic when seen individually). In most instances, two therapists were present, but sometimes there were three. ("It was our experience," Dyrud and Rioch noted dryly, that "*any* two of the three therapists worked together better and produced better results than when all three were present.") The multiple paradigm succeeded, to the extent that it did, because a therapist who became "tired, discouraged, bored, and angry with the monotonous rigidity and uncommunicativeness of the patient" had the support of another colleague during the session. For some patients, the addition of a second therapist stirred up so much anxiety that defenses were exaggerated, making them "easier for the original therapist to see and point out." Other patients found the presence of a male and female therapist to be particularly intense, allowing previously intractable problems concerned with sexuality to be directly addressed.

Even in instances where no appreciable progress occurred after the addition of a second (or third) therapist, Dyrud and Rioch argued that there were still benefits to the multiple therapy method. A therapist could be reassured that at least it wasn't his own behavior that was causing treatment to fail if a similar lack of response occurred with a colleague. And by creating optimal conditions for a patient to play one therapist off against the other, the method could also clarify difficult transference or countertransference issues.[93]

In the spirit of "let's try anything" so characteristic of the Lodge in the late 1940s, Frieda also experimented with treating schizophrenic patients in group therapy.[94] For some months, she met with five severely regressed women from the disturbed ward, plus head nurse Margaret Ursell and sociologist Morrie Schwartz. The group's discussions were colorful. When Frieda explained during the first session that they were getting together because "some of the problems we have are rather similar with all of us," Miss N., the patient famous for plugging up the toilets, responded: "I have a suggestion. Let us close the windows. It is warm in here and let us take off all our clothes." Frieda's interpretation—"it's true, then we would become even more aware of our similarities"—set the tone for later sessions.[95] As she struggled to get the group members to talk to one another, they cavorted around the room or sat groaning or hallucinating. One patient urinated on whatever chair she happened to sit on. Miss N. often recited passages from books. When Frieda made amused, self-critical remarks about her inability to get things going, the more withdrawn patients laughed heartily.

One day, having noticed that members of the group seemed to enjoy reading, Frieda suggested they do it together. (Perhaps she was recalling those many childhood evenings with Adolf reading aloud from Goethe.) As their text, she proposed her colleague George Preston's *Psychiatry for the Curious*. A few patients seemed attentive. One moaned. Miss N. spoke in French. Ursell concentrated on trying to keep order. When a patient who had urinated on the floor began chewing on the rag used to clean her up, Ursell asked Frieda if she should remove it. Frieda said: "Do as you like. My job is to try to understand why they do it."[96]

No matter how bizarre or seemingly nonsensical patients' behavior, Frieda took for granted that it had meaning. She repeatedly told the woman who spent the sessions groaning: "Mary, when it's a little louder, we'll stop and try to understand it." If Frieda had to be late for a session, she explained the reason, treating group members with the dignity she would have accorded friends or colleagues. If even the subtlest sign of improvement appeared, she highlighted it in the record and discussed it at the next session.

Schwartz, in contrast, thought the idea of group therapy with schizophrenics ridiculous.[97] But he did a good job recording the memorable moments, like the day Frieda read aloud from one of her own articles, while Miss N. ran around the room practically naked and another patient postured with a lampshade on her head. Frieda, as always, was doggedly persistent. She asked patients directly whether they understood what they were doing, and often commented on the subtlety of their actions (noting, for example, that even the most withdrawn members of the group conveyed that they were part of the conversation by moving a hand or moaning at regular intervals). She repeatedly stated her belief that patients had an easier time talking to one another than to doctors and that this was part of the rationale for the group's work. At one point, she invited a more verbal patient to join the sessions to see what effect this had. (Miss N., clearly jealous of the attention given to the new member, acted out even more than usual.) To call this experiment a success would be a stretch of the imagination; most of the time the patients appeared unresponsive to one another and to Frieda's efforts.

Another of her innovations of the 1940s were the programs of dance and psychodrama, instituted at the Lodge long before they became standard in other mental hospitals. Marian Chace, the founder of dance therapy, had taken several of Frieda's courses at the Washington School of Psychiatry, and Frieda persuaded her to come out to the Lodge on a regular basis to extend the ideas she had developed at St. Elizabeths. Ever since her days with Goldstein, Frieda had stressed nonverbal aspects of treatment and the involvement of staff other than psychiatrists.

Chace used a free form of enactment termed "spontaneous drama" to distinguish it from the "psychodrama" then being popularized by Jacob Moreno. In Moreno's version, the leader of the group imposes a tight structure, with preestablished scenes, assigned roles, and planned topics. In contrast, Chace was more improvisational. "Through the free but broadly controlled structure of the sessions," she later wrote, "the patients are able to come forth with their own specific needs and frustrations rather than those suggested by the leader." Even patients too disorganized to verbalize their feelings were active participants. "Much attention and tolerance is given to them when they do make an attempt to participate with a sudden sound or movement," Chace reported. "In general, the patients have *carte blanche.* They are allowed to set the scene, structure it, and choose the people with whom they wish to participate. . . . What is said is intensely real; actual feelings come out, and there is nothing artificial to hide behind." Since life at the Lodge was already so vivid, sessions labeled "psychodrama" weren't any more revealing of people's feelings than staff conferences or ward free-for-alls. But Chace noted that these formal enactments "created a climate in which patients can express intense emotions of even the most negative kind and yet experience a feeling of sharing with others."[98]

Other Lodge research projects analyzed how psychotherapy worked. Otto Will and Bob Cohen tape-recorded sessions to try to understand turning points in the interaction. They deliberately chose a random sample from an average case to focus on instead of highlighting a moment of crucial insight, as was the practice in most therapy research. The patient in their study was fully informed of the procedure; indeed, she could not help being aware of its every detail, since the crude equipment then available was so obtrusive that recording the session required her active participation. The tapes turned out to be of considerable use to both the patient and her physicians. At a point in the therapy where she frequently felt misunderstood, they became an ally, "something to back her up in the difficult dealings with a therapist who so often was found to be as severe, frightening, uncomprehending, and distant as her father."

Given the total privacy in which psychotherapy is conducted, the insecurity that therapists feel about their work (especially with disturbed patients), and the extreme rarity of subjecting it to open scrutiny by colleagues, Will and Cohen's decision to publish an hour in its entirety was courageous. Their interspersed commentary on the therapist's blunders and insensitivities further increased their vulnerability. After reading a draft of the article prior to publication, the patient commented:

> It is interesting, and you have brought out a great deal of detail about what has gone on. But there is a lot you have left out. You emphasize all the errors, what you think went wrong, and you don't say much about what went all right. There is a lot that has worked out pretty well, and you may be having some trouble in putting your finger on that part. . . . Sometimes you doctors don't seem to recognize the importance of the whole relationship and the feeling part that can't be expressed easily with talk.[99]

Beyond their humility about serious mental illness and their commitment to try anything that might work, staff embraced these experiments because they fit the general rebelliousness that had drawn them to the Lodge. As Stanton and Schwartz were later to note, "The staff felt that an insistence on formality was not the practice of psychiatry. They placed emphasis upon rapid decision on intuitive grounds, without systematic checks as to the effect of the decision; upon feelings rather than thoughts; upon spontaneity rather than planning. Those few who expressed or showed an occasional interest in the formalities in procedure were thought of as pedantic, legalistic, or frightened."[100]

Bullard clearly preferred a rowdy staff, and Frieda insisted that a lack of rigidity was an essential requirement of good therapy. As Morrie Schwartz once remarked: "These patients' greatest strength was being able to identify pretense and tell who was a bullshitter and who wasn't. . . . If you were very formal and conventional, you weren't going to get anywhere with them." He acknowledged the "fear of what might come from the unpredictable," but said that what attracted staff to the Lodge was "the fascination of this really strange, wonderful world with forms of human activity you could never find elsewhere."[101]

It wasn't only psychiatrists and nurses who felt this way. At Chestnut Lodge, even groundsworkers were inspired by the openness and flexibility. Stanley Wilcox, who spent four decades as Anne's "right-hand man," thought that "the philosophy of developing a deep personal relationship with each patient" made the Lodge a uniquely exciting place to work. Wilcox joined the staff on March 27, 1937. Asked how he could remember the exact date he said: "Oh, I'd never forget that."[102]

Stanley did practically anything. He grew cash crops of hay and corn, and a garden large enough to feed everyone. He raised hogs and cattle and ran a dairy that produced all the Lodge's milk. He took patients for walks or drove them to town to shop. He filled in as a fourth for bridge. He did all the maintenance work on Dexter's luxury cars, a major job in itself.

After the war, when the Lodge became a favored field placement for student nurses from the Bible belt, Stanley also became a bouncer, charged with trying to keep students' boyfriends off the grounds. (He was beaten up often by these boyfriends, never by a patient.) For years, before there was an elevator in the main building, Stanley also carried all the food, supplies, and laundry up four floors to each of the wards.

Presiding over all this from a large shack the Bullards built for him—still labeled "Stanley's house" on Lodge maps of the 1990s—he was like Dexter, Anne, and Frieda, always at work. The Bullards treated Stanley practically like a member of the family, an attitude clearly in their self-interest. "I was the cheapest maintenance man they ever had," he later said. "Since I lived on the grounds, I was on call all night long. Some of the things I did I think today would be illegal."

Like everyone else on the staff, Stanley was fond of many patients. He had quickly learned the Lodge credo: treat every patient with respect, no matter how bizarre the behavior. One woman called him "Stanley Hamburger" for a reason no one knew; he just smiled and politely answered. A former actress who often strolled the grounds searching for bright pieces of glass to sew into her dresses called him "Lord Herbert Gladstone" and he always replied, "How are you, your highness?" Asked if he ever thought of these rituals as parody, Stanley looked startled and said: "Hell, no. It was respect."

He was even fond of Miss N., despite her constant assaults on the plumbing system. "She was clearly part of the family," he recalled, although admittedly "a pain in the neck." Thinking back on some of her escapades, Stanley smiled. "Believe it or not, she was very charming in a lot of ways, very charming," quite a statement from the man who spent years crawling through sewers to undo her handiwork. (He once had to tunnel thirty feet deep, all the way out to the road, to clear out one of Miss N.'s messes, but this seemed not to diminish his fondness for her.)

The Bullards didn't seem to realize the depth of Stanley's commitment to them. He never forgot the day in 1940 when he was driving through town and a young woman asked for a ride. She turned out to be a new patient who had left without permission to go on a drinking binge. Dexter reprimanded him the next day: "It doesn't look good to relatives to have the employees taking patients out to bars." Stanley never made that mistake again, but Bullard's words stung. "I wasn't an employee," he said in a hurt tone fifty years later. "I was part of that hospital."

The medical staff did appreciate Stanley's way with patients, and those being sent home or transferred to distant hospitals often had him as their escort. (He remembered struggling with one particularly difficult man for twelve hours on a prop plane to San Francisco.) Another patient—whose scientific expertise was so specialized the army used to send a car to bring him into Washington during his rare lucid periods—eventually had to be sent to the state hospital. It was Stanley who listened to him cursing from the back seat the whole way over to Springfield.

Stanley was especially close to Frieda and found some excuse to see her practically every day. He brought her fresh flowers or drove her around to do errands. He helped clean up after her frequent parties and fixed the holes her dog chewed in the fence. He took her to Washington at least once a week for meetings or to catch a train for one of her many out-of-town lectures. To give her a place to relax, Stanley planted a large flower garden behind the cottage. "Frieda always wanted things done in a certain way," he recalled fondly, "but it was so easy to do what she wanted."

. . .

Frieda may have lived in a cottage for the twenty-two years she spent at the Lodge, but she always had both a secretary and a maid (in addition to free access to hospital staff). In all her years in Germany—when Adolf was barely making a living in the metalworks shop, during the terrible "turnip winters" of World War I, throughout her time in Heidelberg—someone had always been there to do the dirty work. At the Lodge, Frieda's maids didn't live with her (there wasn't room), but they did whatever was needed (and their availability was one of the reasons she liked living "on the plantation" rather than off somewhere in her own house). This wasn't an affectation: secretaries, maids, and workmen were simply part of the landscape of Frieda's life, and she took for granted that they would always be there when she needed them. She may have had inexhaustible energy, but even Frieda could never have done all the clinical and administrative work she did at the Lodge without these "helpers."

Mara Bowman, Frieda's secretary for several years, arrived as an unhappy student. Their needs matched perfectly: Bowman lacked direction, and Frieda, as always, was ready to take charge. "She was an unusually wonderful person," recalled Bowman years later, "and she sort of found this lost soul which was me." Initially, Bowman worked part time, typing the correspondence and reports that Frieda dictated in the five minutes between sessions. When, several months later, Bowman announced she couldn't live on the salary Frieda was paying her, Frieda, ever alert to opportunities to make her life easier while helping others, said: "Don't leave. I'll find things for you to do."[103]

Bowman took over the shopping and errands and the paying of household bills (with blank checks Frieda left on the desk—"she had total trust in me," Bowman proudly recalled). She took the dog to the kennel, mailed birthday presents to the children of Frieda's friends, and whatever else needed doing. "I think that's how somebody like that gets to be able to have a life in which they can be so attentive to people. They have somebody to take care of the details," mused Bowman, years later. Being white, Jewish, and middle class, Bowman was never asked to do cooking or cleaning. Those were jobs for the maid or the kitchen staff.

The boundaries of Frieda's relationship with Bowman, like all her other close bonds, grew fuzzier with time. She "checked out" Bowman's boyfriends at dinner, the way she did with her friends' children. She expressed her preferences regarding Bowman's intended marriage (not surprisingly, to an analyst). She gave advice on courses Bowman should take in night school and what books she should read. Initially Bowman appreciated all the attention, but eventually it became suffocating. Leaving the job after

two years to move to New York (on a date carefully selected to avoid incon-
venience to Frieda), Bowman felt a mixture of longing and relief. "I was too
attached to her," she admitted. "It was not good for me. I was so taken up by
her and her life that I wasn't living my own life." Asked whether this problem
was ever explicit between them, Bowman said: "No. We never discussed it, I
mean I did not have that kind of relationship with Frieda."

As an employer, though, Frieda was ideal. "She was enormously appreciative of everything I did," Bowman recalled, "a pleasure to work for." Like
everyone else in Frieda's life, Bowman "loved doing things for her. [She] was
sort of the ideal mother, the mother one never has because one's own mother
takes on another role. You have this fantasy mother somewhere else, and that's
really what Frieda was to me. . . . There are so many people that have gone
through my life that I have forgotten. But it's not possible to forget Frieda."

Donna Grimmer, who took over after Bowman's departure, was the only
one of Frieda's many secretaries to insist on a more formal relationship.
Grimmer called her "Dr. Fromm-Reichmann," never "Frieda," and resisted
all attempts to have her life restructured or her feelings pried into. Grimmer
was a local woman, married with several children, a Gentile with no particular interest in psychiatry, and this made it easier for her to maintain more distance. She worked Mondays, Thursdays, and Fridays, from 8:30 to 5:00,
primarily typing and answering the telephone. (Frieda got constant calls,
even during therapy hours.) Like Bowman, Grimmer also did the shopping,
picked up the dry cleaning, and ordered the food and liquor for Frieda's frequent parties.

After Grimmer had two babies in close succession, Frieda sat her down
for a chat about birth control. Grimmer said she was Catholic and didn't believe in using artificial methods. Frieda said: "Well, let me tell you how we
Jews think. The ten commandments were given to Moses, so men can't use
birth control, but they weren't given to women, so women can." Grimmer
thought this was crazy. "I just could not believe that anyone so brilliant could
believe such a distorted thing. It didn't make any sense. The real reason she
was having this talk with me," Grimmer remarked astutely, "was because she
didn't want me to quit to take care of all those babies."[104]

Grimmer recalled an awkward moment, when the black maid, a graduate
of Howard University, complained about being paid a dollar an hour, while
Grimmer, who had only a business school education, got twice that amount.
The maid—whose name, unsurprisingly, no one seems to recall—wouldn't
express her resentment directly to Frieda, so Grimmer joined the ranks of the
many people who absorbed hostility for her.

Although Grimmer resented Frieda's intrusiveness—"she was always trying to get me to borrow her books," she recalled with irritation—she found her "a very, very even-tempered and pleasant person. She was always very generous with me. I never, ever saw her angry." Frieda was not picky about details. "She usually just accepted what I gave her," including the typing, Grimmer's main responsibility. (On one occasion, however, Frieda dictated a letter to friends in Santa Fe, "Dear Dick and Jane" and Grimmer typed "Dear Jane and Dick." Frieda penned an apology under her signature, saying she "knew the man's name should come first," and told Grimmer she would "overlook" the error so long as it didn't happen again.) Frieda's heavy accent made dictation a challenge. Grimmer remembers looking up, startled, as she recorded in shorthand an inventory of items Frieda was packing to send to Anna in Israel. "One whale," Grimmer had written, before looking up to see Frieda holding a hat with a veil.

Grimmer was astonished when Frieda said she admired her willingness to work for a divorcée. "I guess she felt that my square upbringing and narrow outlook would make me judgmental about things like that. When I told her it didn't bother me she said she really appreciated it." Grimmer was more concerned about the tax deductions Frieda was taking for her dry cleaning. "She didn't wear a uniform, so to me, that didn't seem right." Frieda explained matter-of-factly that working with patients who routinely spat, pelted her with food, and smeared feces on her dresses made it perfectly appropriate to deduct cleaning costs.

One of the few things Frieda never asked anyone to do for her was select gifts for birthdays, Christmas, or other occasions (although she often sent her secretaries to have them wrapped or mailed). This was a natural part of her attentiveness, and people remember how invariably she made just the right choice. She often bought pottery or other Indian artifacts in Santa Fe, carefully saving them for an occasion when they would be especially apt, like the year she gave Dexter an engraved copper cigarette box for his birthday. If she were a guest in someone's home, she always sent a beautiful thank-you present. Frieda was an early devotee of mail-order catalogues, and in the years when the staff was still small, ordered a Christmas present for every single employee at the Lodge, as well as remembering the birthdays of dozens of colleagues and all her friends' children.

She was also extremely gracious as a hostess, with a style of entertaining that reflected an upbringing in which she "learned the social skills of the upper class while in the painful status of the poor relation."[105] She made a point of inviting people like Grimmer and her husband, not only fellow doctors, to the parties she held, and Lodge staff, who often helped clean up after these occasions, remembered the care Frieda took to make sure "nobody was sitting back in the corner alone." She hosted elegant receptions with oysters and champagne on special occasions, and if there were too many people to fit comfortably in the cottage, she held the event in a nearby restaurant, arranging personally for the place settings, the menu, and details of the decor.

Her years in America did little to soften the formality of her Old World ways. When a new physician joined the Lodge staff, Frieda would invite him over for a lunch of lamb chops (prepared by the maid), an invariant menu that was a source of much amusement among the younger doctors. ("Been to your lamb chop lunch yet?" they would quiz one another.) She ritualistically visited the home of each of her colleagues when their first child was born (as Klara had done in all the years in Königsberg) and carefully evaluated the potential spouses of her friends' children before giving her blessing.

Frieda was sometimes embarrassed by her unfamiliarity with American cultural practices, like the time a patient stole a bottle of ready-made martinis from the cottage and drank it on the ward ("anybody else would have known how to mix them, so the whole hospital could see that it came from me," she complained at a staff meeting). But her openness toward learning and her interest in cultural differences made Frieda's European ways seem more a part of her charm than a source of tension.

Like many other people who live alone, Frieda treated her dogs like spoiled children, doting on them in ways others found excessive. (This may also have reflected a childhood spent in Germany, a country where dogs are welcomed in hotels and restaurants and scamper about on trains and subways, rarely disciplined by their owners.) She had a succession of cocker spaniels beginning sometime in the 1940s, all descendants of a puppy Sullivan had given her from one of his dogs' litters. Like Sullivan, who kept all five of his dogs in the office with him, using them to detect subtle aspects of a patient's emotional state, Frieda's dog was constantly beside her. Except on brief lecturing trips, she took her everywhere, requiring drivers to "babysit" the dog during trips to Santa Fe, and arranging for her publisher's assistant to entertain her during editorial meetings in Chicago.

The same Frieda whose own meals were sent over from the Lodge kitchen or prepared by the maid spent hours personally cooking for the dog; Donna Grimmer said that when she came to work, "the place always smelled like chicken broth." The dog was allowed to behave as she pleased; various women recall her chewing the hem off their dresses during supervisory sessions. Frieda made it a point never to rebuke patients for outbursts of violence, but when one particularly aggressive man kicked her dog, she was so furious she threw him out of the house.

Sullivan once complained toward the end of his life that he knew no one but patients, and this was clearly a problem equally affecting Frieda. Having always been the confidante, the older sister, the responsible one, she never developed the capacity for peer relationships. One of her cousins remembers that even as a child, he was struck by Frieda's presence: "She was the oracle of the family, always in control, always in the limelight. Mutuality is not what I experienced." From her earliest days as a physician, relatives and close friends had sought her out for treatment, and there seemed to be no distinction between Frieda the person and Frieda the psychiatrist. As her Lodge colleague Margaret Rioch once put it: "You would never say about Frieda that she was not a caring person, but there was a particular quality to it that was totally unequal; Frieda helped you in the way she decided you needed help."[106]

When her friend Edith Weigert had a serious depression, Frieda went to her house every day. When it came time to leave for the summer, Frieda took Edith with her to Santa Fe. When her Lodge colleague Alberta Szalita arrived as a refugee from Poland, where her whole family had been murdered by Nazis, Frieda talked to her for fifteen minutes, then rose from her chair, walked to the phone, called a fellow analyst, and informed Szalita she had arranged therapy for her. ("I wasn't insulted by this," Szalita said later, "but I did think it was a pretty risky act on her part.") Lodge staff used to call Frieda the "Fuller brush woman" because once she metaphorically stuck her foot in the door, she made sure she wasn't turned away.[107]

"No one dared say 'no' to her," Margaret Ursell recalled with a mixture of admiration and dismay. "She had the ability to organize her world the way she wanted it," is how another colleague put it.[108] Frieda got Virginia Gunst, a wealthy Richmond housewife, to become her assistant and patron in just this way. Gunst attended a lecture series Frieda gave at the Washington School of Psychiatry in 1947 and went up at the end to express her appreciation. Frieda was preoccupied with finding someone to drive her to Santa Fe later that week for summer vacation; the friend who was supposed to accompany her had suddenly taken ill. After chatting politely with Gunst (whom she had never previously met), Frieda gave her a warm smile and asked, "Are you a good driver?" Gunst, taken aback, blurted out: "Well, I was head of the Army Motor Corps for four years during the war." Frieda was delighted. "Fine. We leave in four days. . . . Go home now and break the news to your nice husband and family. I do not believe they will object to your going with me or being away two weeks. You can take the train back to Washington." During the drive, Frieda asked Gunst if she knew how to type. Frieda had a lecture to give at Menninger the following week and said it would be "a tremendous help" if Gunst would prepare it from her dictation. Gunst agreed, later taking over the housekeeping and shopping and other errands. (Frieda found this highly amusing; as she told Dexter in a letter, "at home, she has three servants!") So began a decade-long relationship in which Gunst edited all of Frieda's written work, bought her expensive presents, and took care of whatever other details in her life weren't already being attended to by the secretary, the maid, or the Lodge staff. Like the wealthy relatives of Frieda's childhood, Gunst was a warm, supportive benefactor who helped her live beyond her means. Gunst said she forever appreciated "the opportunity to learn from Dr. Fromm-Reichmann's immense store of wisdom" and called their years together "a rare and wonderful experience."[109]

People always felt grateful for the chance to help Frieda, and she enjoyed being catered to. Since she did so little for herself, there were ample opportunities to step in. She was, for example, completely unmechanical. As Mabel Peterson once put it, "For Frieda, things either worked or they didn't; there was nothing in the middle." Whenever something didn't immediately function correctly, she would look beseechingly at whoever happened to be around, say, "What can we do?" and before she knew it, somebody had fixed it for her. She was such a frighteningly bad driver that people were always volunteering to take her wherever she needed to go. (Part of her problem was being so short. Stanley had to build a special seat to allow her to see over the steering wheel.) The owner of the beauty shop where Frieda had her hair done each week came running out as soon as he saw her car and parked it for her (lest she crash through his plate glass window). Frieda always thanked people warmly for helping her, but at some level took for granted that they got as much satisfaction from it as she did. (She assumed, for example, that she was doing the wealthy, idle Gunst a favor by giving her something useful to do with herself.)

For Frieda, there was never any contradiction between getting her own needs met and helping others. To her, this was what it meant to be a psychiatrist. What sometimes looked like arrogance was just her certainty that she knew what was needed. Her friends may not always have appreciated her efforts on their behalf, but they knew that the secret of Frieda's success with patients was that she simply never took no for an answer.

9

Joanne Greenberg

And what are facts, that we should imagine they have the power to explain the world to us?[1]

When Joanne Greenberg entered Frieda's life in September 1948, neither of them could possibly have guessed that their relationship would turn out to make psychiatric history. Compared to most other patients diagnosed as schizophrenic, Joanne was fortunate in being so young and having parents who could afford Chestnut Lodge. She also had the advantage of being brought there as soon as she needed help and permitted to stay for as long as proved necessary. But Chestnut Lodge alone couldn't have saved Joanne. Her real luck was to arrive in 1948, when Frieda had already become as good a therapist as she was ever going to be.

She had taken Joanne's case at a moment when she needed a challenge she could win. Frieda could not have made this explicit, but it is clear in retrospect. Thirty years of struggling to help people beyond reach had eroded even a confidence as legendary as hers, and the longing for some tangible evidence of success had become more urgent. As colleagues all over the country sent her the patients they found too sick to treat, she had fewer and fewer opportunities to act from her strengths. It wasn't arrogance or masochism that made Frieda keep taking these patients, just a weary acknowledgment that they had nowhere else to turn. She sensed that Joanne Greenberg was different in some fundamental way, and although she couldn't have explained how she knew this, she was grateful for the difference.

Joanne had been on the ward for several days before she was sent to see

Frieda the first time. We can imagine the scene. A student nurse, face carefully blank, appears suddenly on the ward and announces they are to leave.
Fumbling with the locks, she steers Joanne through a series of doors, down
the narrow staircase at the back of the building, and then outside, through an
unmarked exit at the rear. Joanne, blinking in the sudden sunlight, has no
chance to feel her way. For a moment, they are on a small path leading away
from the road. Then all at once the cottage appears, shuttered and white
framed like a Boston cape, tucked among low-growing pines. The absurdity
of such a house in such a place throws Joanne off, and the door opens before
she can think to knock.

A smiling housekeeper stands quietly, unfazed by the task of greeting
mental patients. Her dowdiness is flat against the bright wallpaper that
frames her. She is barely five feet tall. Her navy suit and silver brooch seem
oddly formal. Frieda has yet to appear. Joanne cannot decide what this
means. Suddenly the student nurse turns to leave, and after a moment of confusing silence, the housekeeper speaks. "I am the doctor," she says pleasantly. "Would you like to come in?"

Joanne is humiliated by the disguise and cannot understand how once
again, she has been tricked. The look on Frieda's face, a deliberate awareness, close to insistence, offers too little choice. Joanne stumbles in, following Frieda's few steps to an office down the hall. Heavy furniture clutters the
room. A black dog sleeps in a leather chair. The sound of a typewriter echoes
through double doors. Somewhere a telephone rings. Words are coming out
of Frieda's mouth, but her face is dissolving into the wall. Her tiny size
seems dangerous, a deception of yet another kind. Then, from inside the blur
come words: "Do you know why you are here?" The accent is thickly German yet musical; the tone is grave. Joanne cannot imagine what to say. The
silence inside her head begins to ricochet. Then something happens.[2]

Psychotherapy can't be described. We don't have a vocabulary for conversation that charged. Bringing two people together under conditions so abstruse and arbitrary that distance and embarrassment seem the inevitable
result, it somehow provokes the opposite. Trapped in a space where there is
nothing to lose, therapist and patient become adventurous in the strangeness,
in the totalizing quality of each other's presence, in an attention to nuance so
rigorous it is close to absurd. Intuitive leaps, once uncanny, become commonplace. Possibilities grow. Experiences too terrifying to acknowledge are
nudged toward the light. The analyst Leston Havens, struggling to describe
the "surprise of random mingling" between therapist and patient, talks of
things "made not by separate minds, but springing up in the common space"
between them.[3] Descriptions like this are useless. Of the hundreds of at-

tempts to say what psychotherapy is or does, none really takes us inside. We press our faces to the window, straining for a glimpse; we see the tendrils of the unconscious, entwining two people in its embrace.

If we could let ourselves believe that psychotherapy works, we wouldn't care whether it could be summarized. But unless we ourselves have watched, amazed, as it transformed our whole lives, we are likely to think of therapy as clichéd, something perhaps to be endured, but never chosen. To a person as frightened as Joanne Greenberg, it would have seemed like leaping off a precipice on the strength of someone else's say-so.

According to Lodge legend, when Frieda marched onto the disturbed ward, the whole floor suddenly calmed. Perhaps this is exaggerated. But the image captures the intensity of her presence, a force field so concentrated it absorbed the available energy surrounding it. Joanne later likened the scene to "the parting of the Red Sea," with nurses and attendants falling all over themselves as if Frieda were the queen, arriving at court. With patients, however, such theatrics disappeared. "As soon as she got down to business," Joanne recalled, "she changed. Almost visibly."[4] Frieda had an intuitive feel for the sociology of the mental hospital, where patients, already overwhelmed by their own craziness, are made to bear the burden of the staff's unconscious needs. Having spent her whole life defusing other people's tension, Frieda did it automatically, and patients appreciated the habit.

Joanne was seldom present during their first sessions together, her brittleness a concealed branch, ready to snap at Frieda's stumble. She couldn't believe that somebody so physically ungainly could navigate with such grace. When Frieda repeatedly evaded her traps, Joanne shifted to loud recitations of poetry in Irian, a secret language she had invented in childhood. She asked Frieda if the poems were good. Frieda had no idea; she couldn't understand any of the words. She asked Joanne to translate. (Actually what she said was: "Would you feel like translating?"[5] Frieda always wondered aloud whether people "felt like" doing what she wanted; this confused the effect of her Prussian style and gave demands a surprising, offhand touch.) Joanne translated the poems. Frieda seemed capable of tolerating more. A few months later, Joanne described the seven worlds of the Irian universe, a disclosure she had never risked with anyone before. Frieda, sensing the terror, made no sudden moves. "She is in a lower world," she told her colleagues, "and I am in a higher world. God knows when she will ever be able to come into the world [I am in]."[6]

Joanne could barely see past the years of silent suffering her parents had tried so hard to deny. Unable to convey the extent of her anguish, she had resorted to more and more desperate means of escape: disappearing into Iria, putting herself into "trance," doubling over with stomach cramps strong enough to distract everyone from the real pain. No one, least of all Joanne, doubted that these symptoms severely compromised her life. But without them, she would have been unrecognizable to herself. She was terrified that Frieda had some secret means of ripping these last few shreds of protection away from her. Frieda kept quietly insisting that some day Joanne would no longer need defenses; until then, she promised, she wouldn't touch them. "Her face lit up all over," Frieda later reported to her colleagues with an incredulity she rarely showed. "Every now and then, if one has the good luck to hit something which makes great sense to her, she would do that," Frieda went on, as if luck were what it took.[7] Joanne remembers very little of this first period of their work. "I subscribed to the theory that if you've seen one person, you've seen them all."[8]

One December morning, two months after the start of treatment, Frieda locked the cabinet in the second-floor guest room of the cottage where she kept patient records and walked quickly to the main building, a sheaf of papers tucked under one arm. She stopped briefly on the way to greet a patient she hadn't seen for several weeks. Entering the building through a side door, she arrived at a large room in the basement just as the staff meeting was getting underway. She was presenting Greenberg's case. Staff meetings at the Lodge were blunt affairs, and she knew she could count on her colleagues to say whatever occurred to them.

The men who sat around the table that December day—and they were men, except for Frieda and a few others—were of a caliber never again reached with such consistency at Chestnut Lodge. They had an aliveness, a way of being present to the work, even with very sick patients, that was all too rare in psychiatry. Psychoanalysis attracted a stellar group of Americans after the war—men who had been forced to make split-second decisions about other men's lives and were now ready for something nuanced and slow.[9] The Lodge allowed their imaginations full rein. It was one of the few places where they could get away with trying anything they thought might work, and they adored the openness.

They all dreamed of getting a patient like Joanne: articulate, capable even of wit, with florid symptoms that begged to be interpreted. Even at the most selective hospitals—and Chestnut Lodge in 1948 was as selective as Wellesley—most patients were not like this. Psychosis ground people down, no matter what their background, and when their illnesses became chronic, they lost whatever capacity for insight they might once have possessed. Many pa-

tients came to the Lodge as a last resort, after every other hospital had given
up on them, and even the most energetic therapist could see years go by without much tangible reward. The younger staff often listened to Frieda's presentations wondering whether there was any relation at all between their own
awkward efforts and what she was doing.

At most mental hospitals, cases are discussed with the patient present, so
the whole staff can ask questions and see the response. The practice became
popular in the nineteenth century, when medicine was taught didactically and
a patient's disease was "demonstrated" to an amphitheater of students, the
way neurological cases are sometimes "presented" today at grand rounds.
Mental patients find the questions terrifying and are humiliated by the dis-
play. At Chestnut Lodge, this was never done. The place was small enough
for everyone to know everyone else, and patients didn't have to be publicly
paraded to be visible to staff. Case conferences were intended to provide an
analysis of the patient's problems and set the therapist on the right path.
There were occasional outbursts, but they didn't come from schizophrenics.

Frieda began her presentation in a quietly authoritative tone. The sharp
crease in her forehead grew darker as she concentrated, leading some to mistake it for a scar. She made no attempt to dramatize Joanne's story or play up
the distinctiveness of the case. Her presentations were always understated,
with attention focused on the patient's strengths, not on her own interpretations. She moved quickly past Joanne's father, a successful lawyer whose career only partly contained the anger he had always felt. Joanne's mother got
the starring role. Frieda described her fantasy of becoming a professional
singer and its sacrifice to the tense exhaustion of keeping the family from
breaking apart. By the time she got to Joanne's younger sister—whose job
was to make it look like nothing was wrong—Frieda sounded as if she had
known these people for decades.

She gave Joanne's increasing isolation and bizarreness an ineluctable feel,
but then nothing ever turned out much differently from what Frieda expected.
The indiscriminacy of psychosis had long ago ceased to surprise her, the way
it still surprised her younger colleagues, who needed to believe good families
might somehow be spared. Frieda had lost her idealism in 1914, in the army
hospital near the Russian front, where men shot in trenches sat silently, parts
of their brains missing, and even the best Berlin background made no difference at all. To be sure, a patient like Joanne was not this bad off, but it was hard
to believe that damage inflicted so long ago could be completely undone. When
there is too much scar tissue or it is stretched too thin, the sutures of psychotherapy have nothing to attach to. In these cases, there might just as well be
part of the brain missing, and most psychiatrists simply talked as if there were.

Joanne was a puzzle. Despite the insidious development of her symptoms—the kind of gradual deterioration that had led Kraepelin to name schizophrenia "dementia praecox"—Joanne had certain qualities that set her apart. As Frieda presented the history, for instance, she noted that the details were "the way I got it from the patient, who has an incredible ability to report, with a vocabulary and an exquisite command of language which I have certainly never seen in a sixteen [year old] and very seldom in grown ups." This was not how schizophrenics were usually described, but Frieda was too taken by Joanne's gifts to notice her excess. Even in this first report, there is a quality of overpraise entirely absent from her summaries of other patients. Frieda seemed surprisingly unaware of this, as if Joanne's "lovely singing voice" or her being "exceedingly musically gifted" were simply facts of her existence.[10]

Part of what made Joanne different was that she could still take risks, an indulgence that psychotic patients could rarely afford. This brought out Frieda's natural playfulness, her willingness to explore. Frieda had an odd sense of fun, managing to find pleasure in the excavation of someone else's life, but it allowed her to rejoice in accomplishments she would have taken for granted in herself. Psychotherapy is like seduction, an algorithm of subtle signs, and no therapist can go faster or deeper than her patient will permit. Every time Joanne disappeared into Iria and Frieda pleaded, "Take me along with you; take me there; show it to me," they got to a level they hadn't reached before.[11] Frieda was careful never to pretend she knew what mental illness felt like, but she clearly wasn't too frightened to find out. She didn't romanticize the treatment or present it in magical ways, but she did insist its effects were real and its potential profound. When Joanne, in an early moment of despair, claimed therapy was impossible because "nobody can share anyone else's experience," Frieda said, "Of course not. [But if I can] . . . intensely participate in it . . . and come as near to it as I can, I can help you to understand it," which was something Joanne could conceive.[12]

Frieda's model of psychotherapy was mundane, more partnership than quest. The patient's responsibility was to open the door a crack. Her job was to slip in quietly and bear witness to whatever was there. It was an improvisation, a constant change of frame, responsive to the moment and to the feelings of each person. Performed with grace, the process could be extraordinarily moving for both therapist and patient. But if the balance was thrown off, the work of months could shatter in an instant, and the memory of what had once seemed possible made the suffering worse. It was this precariousness that made working with psychotic patients too painful for most therapists. It was bad enough to fail in the beginning, or with someone who couldn't be reached. But to work with a person for months or years, to be moved by a hundred moments of closeness and then have it all violently ripped away—this was more than most therapists could bear.

Frieda struggled to explain to her colleagues how Joanne's unpredictability increased the risk. As one of the few patients to avoid being hospitalized before coming to the Lodge, she didn't yet know how to behave. Division of labor has specialized every role, and the requirements for what sociologist Erving Goffman called the "career" of the mental patient are as detailed as those of any job.[13] Mental hospitals teach patients to enact their craziness in the forms that psychiatrists feel most comfortable with. Chronic patients serve as an object lesson. People quickly learn the most basic rule: the longer you stay on the ward, the sicker you are. Eventually, when staff stop imagining that you can ever recover, you become like a person blinded in childhood, unable to remember what seeing is like.

Joanne Greenberg was unusual in having the opposite problem: repeatedly being told she wasn't as sick as she really was. Her cultured, New York background encouraged the view that she might be "artistic" rather than crazy, and her parents had understandably preferred to believe this. But Frieda saw how destructive the dissembling had been, how it had caused Joanne to doubt her only reality—the sickness. Usually Frieda had to struggle to convince patients they still had the capacity to get well. She found the task of reassuring Joanne that she was seriously ill much easier to manage.

Joanne did her part by deteriorating dramatically soon after arriving. People often "decompensate" once they finally make it to a mental hospital—partly in relief, partly as a way to conform to their new role. Whatever its meaning, this sudden plunge into sickness terrifies relatives and gives a patient the bends. And yet there are some patients—Joanne was one—for whom exacerbation of illness is actually a sign of health. The paradox is only apparent: the symptoms, no longer encumbered by the constant distortion of being half held in, are finally able to have their say. Their sudden intensification, however frightening, confirms a truth the patient has always known. Joanne, being adolescent as well as psychotic, allowed herself the vivid, flamboyant symptoms textbook writers term "florid." She saw blood pouring from faucets, gates that locked behind her eyes; always there was the sound of voices, whispering and screaming inside her mind. The slight self-indulgence of these symptoms was enough to create a wedge into the fear. In the end, this is how psychotherapy works: by inserting a moment of hesitation between impulse and action, or between wish and fear, creating a space for doubt to slip in and compulsion to recede.

But every treatment has its own logic, and a therapist can't always glimpse a patient's deepest need. Somehow Frieda was able to sense that Joanne was attempting, in ways increasingly desperate and inscrutable, to express her self-loathing and desire for forgiveness. She also realized that her behavior seemed so frightening—to Joanne as well as to everyone else—because it was being literalized. By mistaking the symptoms for the illness, Joanne appeared to be nothing but the bizarre acts she felt compelled to perform. During one especially anguished period, for example, she repeatedly burned her arms with lighted cigarettes, a behavior her parents found horrifying. It seemed impossible to conceive such an act as meaningful. But Frieda saw the burning as purification, a ritual cleansing that couldn't be accomplished with ordinary means. This was why the charred, putrid flesh, so repulsive to others, was a relief to Joanne. Frieda never said things like this explicitly, even to a patient this verbal. Interpretation was distracting, especially with psychotics, whose tolerance for obfuscation was even lower than her own. Frieda just waited until the person felt less terrified and wanted to make sense for herself of what had gone on.

Joanne didn't require much waiting around. Something was always happening in the treatment, even at the beginning, although its meaning was rarely apparent to either of them. When Joanne came to session after session in the first few weeks overwhelmed by a state of confusion that made her unable to concentrate for more than a few moments, Frieda tried to get her to think about when this had started. "I don't know, I don't know," Joanne exploded. "I can't say. I'm just confused. Don't ask too many questions. That only makes it worse." Frieda waited a few weeks and tried another tack. She asked Joanne to go to Antilobia, the chief god in her Irian universe, and ask him to explain the secret of the confusion to both of them. Joanne was so startled by Frieda's seeming complicity with her hallucinatory world that she did as she was told. Most therapists have to struggle in the first months of treatment to get their patients to see them as different from everyone else. Frieda's patients had no trouble making the distinction. She behaved like no one they had ever known.

Patients often fantasize about being their therapist's favorite, even if they secretly believe that a good therapist wouldn't allow such a thing. In Joanne's case it wasn't fantasy; she *was* Frieda's favorite, and this colored every aspect of what transpired between them. The satisfactions of having a patient like Greenberg were obvious, but Frieda was also being pulled in deeper ways. There was something about Joanne that reminded her of herself at that age: the unruly hair, the loneliness of the oldest child, the wrench of expectation from a mother with too few satisfactions of her own. They took to each other in that way people call chemistry but is really physics—the perfect alignment of minds magnetized by the force of each other's need. For

Joanne, who spent most of her time so displaced from other people that they
were barely visible, "Frieda was real. She was always real. I didn't have to X
her out."[14] To Frieda, Joanne was many things, including a disturbed version
of herself she had managed thus far to keep hidden.

Their relationship was unusually close even at the beginning, a fact readily apparent to everyone at the Lodge. Frieda described Joanne's recitations
of poetry and her "dressing very neatly and carefully" for their early sessions
as if these were commonplace. This veneer of normality, however, quickly
dissolved, and after six weeks, few traces remained. Joanne became suspicious of staff and stopped changing her clothes. She mutilated her body in
ways that alarmed others. Patients began to avoid her, which at the Lodge
said a lot. What had initially made Joanne seem less disturbed than other patients turned out largely to be stronger defenses; when they finally crumbled,
she looked as crazy as the rest. Yet even as Joanne's behavior on the ward became more overtly psychotic, Frieda found her "always extremely willing to
talk . . . always willing to let me in on it."[15] It's a hopeful sign when a patient
stays connected to her therapist while fleeing from everybody else, and it was
a sign that Frieda's patients often showed. They found it reassuring that she
was so seldom distracted by symptoms, that even the most elaborate ruse
would fail to take her in. She would just offer a penetrating look and ask what
they were so frightened of.

Frieda was convinced that Joanne needed "a right type of relationship"
and set out to provide her with one. This was a radical formulation, given that
most psychiatrists saw psychotic patients as incapable of relationship at all.
Frieda escaped their pessimism by embracing a flexible sense of certainty
that left her tolerant of mistakes. She took for granted that a lot of schizophrenic behavior was inscrutable even to experienced therapists, but argued
that if doctors took every failure of understanding as a blow to their own omnipotence, the patient would feel attacked, and the work would go nowhere.
She set out to convince Joanne that although she was trying "like a devil" to
understand her, she would inevitably make errors. They didn't have to be catastrophic if Joanne would simply correct them and move on from there.

Joanne had no reason to believe any of this, and didn't. One day, early in
the treatment, Frieda asked whether she "felt like" writing down the important events of her childhood to clarify what had happened. Joanne agreed.
When Frieda asked for the description the next day, Joanne was silent. Minutes passed. Then she blurted out: "You sounded like the principal at that
school who kept saying you must do this or that and when I couldn't it was
terrible." Frieda responded, "What the heck, why don't you say so?" and
dropped the issue. Later, when Joanne screamed that Frieda was assaulting

her with accusations the way her father had always done, Frieda asked, non-plussed: "Why don't you tell me to shut up if it gets too much for you?"[16] Inside Joanne's incredulity was a hint of hope.

Like every other patient, she spent months testing Frieda in various ways. She spoke in Irian (her invented language), expecting ridicule. She disappeared into places Frieda couldn't follow, to see if she would be pursued. She railed against invasiveness and fought restraint of any kind. Frieda waited. She didn't pretend. It was a familiar struggle: finding a way into the terror without colluding in the sickness. She was interested in Iria and wanted Joanne to see that she was, but symptoms were subterfuges and had to be exposed for what they were.

Frieda sensed she was on the right track when Joanne began to talk about sex, a topic previously off limits. Being a mentally disturbed adolescent means being an outcast while everyone else explores. You don't learn even the most obvious things. Since you can't tell anyone you don't know, you end up with some strange ideas. Frieda described the mechanics of menstruation and talked enthusiastically about boys. She liked "explaining facts," defusing a charge that didn't have to be there. Joanne couldn't believe her straightforwardness, her ability to talk about absolutely everything in that tone of genuine interest. Frieda thought she was using the same techniques as every other analyst. Her colleagues thought she had a gift that few others possessed.

She and Joanne shared Jewish jokes during the sessions. Of course they didn't do this right away, but somehow the ground was there.[17] Even in the first months, Frieda felt something shifting. This happened so rarely with a psychotic patient that even Lodge colleagues didn't believe her when she said it, save for Margaret Rioch, the psychologist who had given Joanne a battery of tests and seen for herself that the responses weren't those typical of schizophrenia. There was a vividness, not attributable simply to adolescence, that colored Joanne's answers. In her report, Rioch had called her "an extremely interesting patient" with "fairly large areas . . . in which she functions 'normally.'" After analyzing the test results, Rioch had concluded: "Despite the operation of very severe repressive processes . . . there is still a great deal of liveliness of feeling, imagination, and enthusiasm in her which suggest a favorable outlook."[18] Rioch's ambivalent feelings toward Frieda kept her from publicly expressing agreement, but she was less surprised than other staff by Frieda's confidence in Joanne's potential health.

These hopes notwithstanding, Joanne was still quite ill. Later generations of psychiatrists, disturbed by the possibility that *I Never Promised You a Rose Garden* might be a true story, have claimed Greenberg wasn't really schizophrenic. They say her symptoms would be classified as less severe using current diagnostic schemes. But Frieda insisted that despite Joanne's talents, she was in fact schizophrenic, and others who interviewed her agreed. (As one physician later put it: "Frieda was no novice. She knew how to make a diagnosis.") It doesn't really matter which label we use; categorizing a person's mental state is mostly a question of judging how far removed she is. For Frieda to call Joanne "schizophrenic" meant she thought she was seriously incapacitated, "out of touch with reality," in the textbook phrase. People who are given that diagnosis today may seem crazier, but since our tolerance for insanity is also greater, the distance is probably proportional to what it was between Frieda and Joanne in 1948. Besides, the real question isn't so much whether Greenberg was "schizophrenic" as whether she was crazy enough for her recovery to matter.

Mental patients have their own hierarchies of illness and judge one another by the rank they are assigned. The sickest get special allowances, and this tempts some to exaggerate. But as David Rosenhan's famous study demonstrated, patients can always tell if someone is faking (unlike staff who are easily fooled). When Joanne was first admitted, some Lodge patients called her a rich girl who wasn't really that ill. Eventually, when she began ripping her arms to shreds with jagged tin cans and pushing lighted cigarettes into the wounds, they revised their assessments. Don Bloch, the psychiatrist who administered her floor, remembers Joanne "fitting in" as best one can be said to "fit" on a disturbed ward.[19]

Still, it can be argued that her symptoms seem "hysteric" or "borderline" rather than "schizophrenic," and clearly some of the things that happened between Frieda and Joanne don't sound typical of therapy with a psychotic patient. But to take Joanne's capacity for relatedness as evidence of a lack of disturbance is to diminish the power of what she and Frieda were able to accomplish. So few schizophrenic patients get treated by someone with the capacity to reach them on a deep level that we have no idea how many would respond as Joanne did if they had the chance. Psychiatry has tried its best to convince us that psychosis, by definition, is incurable and patients who respond aren't schizophrenic, but we could choose to believe otherwise, as Frieda clearly did.

A crucial moment early in Joanne's treatment came when she joined other patients in a spree of ripping up bedclothes and chair cushions and strewing the mess all over the ward. The nurses were furious and insisted that such destructiveness be put to an end. They didn't particularly care about the furniture, which is the concern staff in other hospitals would have had; it was the behavior itself that alarmed them and what that behavior meant. Joanne was convinced that some awful punishment would be meted out to her. But

Frieda was more interested in how she had felt. "It was wonderful," Joanne finally admitted, astonished by the question. "For once I had an experience of really sharing something with other people. But I know it was terrible," she rushed on, "and now you will hate me [and see that] I am a mean, ugly, fat louse-covered creature . . . and now everything [will be] over." Frieda responded pleasantly, "It's nice to have fun with other people sometimes, isn't it?"[20] Joanne was stunned. She couldn't understand how destructiveness could suddenly be acceptable; people had always hated her even when she had tried to be good.

What Frieda couldn't understand was why the intensity of her connection to Joanne wasn't producing more rapid amelioration of her symptoms. Concluding one of her presentations to colleagues in an embarrassed tone, Frieda wondered aloud about the possibility that such seeming psychological-mindedness might actually be defensive. Was Joanne one of those patients who enjoyed the process of therapy, but didn't really want to change? Was she using her capacity for metaphor and symbolic thought mainly to embroider her symptoms? Yet there was clearly a struggle going on inside her and a desperate reaching out for help. Eventually Frieda hypothesized that Joanne unconsciously believed that getting better would mean ceasing to recognize herself. Whenever this possibility edged closer, her symptoms worsened, and her illness got classified as more severe. It was as if the very fact of her bizarreness were comforting in itself, a sign to Joanne that she was still the monster she had always experienced herself to be.

Joanne's treatment lasted for more than four years, and this fundamental tension was present throughout the work. Could she recover and still be herself? Such a question is terrifying to anyone who has been mentally ill. To answer no is to destroy all hope. But the alternative seems an impossible wish. Freud liked to compare psychotherapy to surgery, saying it offered a way of excising the craziness while leaving the rest of the personality intact. But whatever Joanne's precise diagnosis, schizophrenic or not, she clearly shared the view of all other seriously disturbed patients—that change is potentially annihilating and recovery might simply cost too much.

A key turning point in the treatment followed Joanne's revelation that she had attempted to murder her infant sister. Five years old at the time, she had lifted the baby out of the crib, carried her to an open window, and was preparing to throw her out when she was suddenly interrupted by the screams of her mother. Working painstakingly through the details of this story over many months, Frieda finally convinced Joanne that no five year old could possibly have been strong enough to do such a thing, and what seemed clearly to be a memory must really have been a wish or a fantasy. When it subsequently emerged that Joanne's mother had left home for an extended period after a stillbirth, Frieda concluded that the abandonment Joanne had felt then had become fused with the rage she imagined her mother had directed at her for the "murder" of the real baby. Burning her arms with lighted cigarettes and engaging in other acts of mutilation were expressions of self-loathing and guilt for these early transgressions. When Joanne finally understood that she hadn't done the horrible things for which she was punishing herself, she was gradually able to stop being so self-destructive.

However, what remained unanalyzed throughout the four years of their work together was Frieda's treatment of Joanne as "special." Every time one of her colleagues pointed this out in a staff meeting, Frieda minimized the extent to which she was showing favoritism. The issue here wasn't simply a question of fairness; Joanne's mother had always considered her the "princess" of the family, and Frieda's recreating this role for Joanne in the hospital ran the risk of interfering with her therapy. In a staff discussion focused on Joanne's "narcissism," Margaret Rioch remarked pointedly to Frieda: "She gets it from you. You're always extolling her talents." Yet Frieda went on doing this despite repeated warnings from her colleagues. In a talk she gave at another hospital after the treatment was over, she described Joanne's penchant for poetry and insightfulness and then concluded: "You can see from the way she formulates things that she is indeed an unusually gifted girl." At some level, Frieda's own childhood specialness was being recreated, and she couldn't bear to break the spell.

Part of what endeared Joanne to Frieda was that she seemed far less ambivalent than most other patients about the hard work of therapy. "I've never seen anybody who deep down was so seriously concerned with really emerging from her illness and therefore, needing the doctor," Frieda noted in one report. A colleague thought part of the reason for this was obvious: Joanne identified Frieda with her powerful mother, and as he noted to the amused appreciation of other staff: "Frieda is the very powerful Mama at the Lodge." Besides being impressed with Joanne's artistic abilities, Frieda was especially taken with the creativity of Iria, her private language. "She built words which said in one word things which in English one had to express in many words," Frieda enthused, nostalgic for the compound nouns of her native German. "It reminds me of the words of Dr. Sullivan with all their hyphens in between. The way she expressed it, it was an attempt to get that in one word without hyphens."[21]

In 1953, Greenberg became an outpatient. She moved to an apartment, started dating, and attended college in Washington. Even Frieda seemed astounded by a recovery so complete. "It is very exciting to me," she told colleagues. "This is the first patient in my forty years of doing therapy who was schizophrenic but is not even schizoid now." Adding, "This means so much to me to have a brand new professional experience at my present stage of life," Frieda said it was crucial to understand what had actually transpired between them.[22] The therapy formally ended before Frieda's vacation that year, and Joanne went off to Aspen for summer classes. Signaling the shift in their relationship—and again illustrating Frieda's life-long penchant for blurring boundaries—she sent Joanne a program for the concert series there (which she herself had often attended) and invited her to Santa Fe during an upcoming sightseeing trip.[23]

By 1955, Joanne had graduated from college, married Albert Greenberg, and started a new life in Colorado. Years later, looking back on this complicated period in her life, she tried to describe it to Lodge staff:

> I had an awful lot of sorting out to do. . . . I didn't know the difference between symptoms and problems. I didn't have any social skills. I didn't know a lot of things. I didn't have much to build on. I confused a lot of things with a lot of other things. I wondered who [this Joanne] was who was getting A's in college and was talking to people and got summer jobs. Who is that? That scared the hell out of me. I didn't know who that was.[24]

She recalled several times after she was first discharged when she had to be rehospitalized for short periods to deal with the terror and strangeness of so much change. In a key lecture, Frieda later described this final period of the treatment:

> This patient emerged from a severe schizophrenic disturbance of many years' duration, for which she was finally hospitalized for two years at Chestnut Lodge and then treated as an ambulatory patient for another two years. Eventually she became free of her psychotic symptomatology except for the maintenance of one manifest symptom: she would hold on to the habit of pulling the skin off her heels to the point of habitually producing open wounds. No attempt at understanding the dynamics of this residual symptom clicked, until the patient developed one day an acute anxiety state in one of our psychotherapeutic interviews in response to my commenting on favorable "changes" that had taken place in her. After that, the main dynamic significance of the skin-pulling became suddenly clear to her and to me. "I am still surprised and sometimes a little anxious about the change which I have under-

gone," she said, "and about finding and maintaining the continuity and the identity between the girl who used to be so frightfully mixed up that she had to stay locked up on the disturbed ward of Chestnut Lodge, and the popular and academically successful college girl of today." The skin-pulling was . . . similar to another self-mutilating act of burning herself, which she repeatedly committed while acutely ill. . . . It made it possible to be ill and well at the same time, because it was only she who knew about the symptom which could be hidden from everybody else with whom she came in contact as a healthy person. After this discovery, the symptom eventually disappeared.[25]

As Joanne moved on to a life of her own, Frieda struggled to make sense of what had happened between them and to deal with her lingering countertransference feelings. She told colleagues in a staff meeting in 1955: "It is an intense satisfaction to help that girl grow up to be better endowed than I am. [It makes me think] I have done [what] I would have liked to teach my mother to do, in her way of handling my younger sisters." Asked whether she felt competitive with Joanne, she replied: "Sure, that girl is incredibly wellendowed. If you ask me, I am pleased about every new accomplishment that I see in her." Then, clearly thinking of what she herself had always wanted from Klara, Frieda added wistfully: "It is a little like a noncompetitive mother figure."[26] However, colleagues criticized this attitude, saying that Frieda had failed to allow Joanne to express her hostility. She had always seemed to have a completely positive transference, directing all her anger at herself (for example, by burning her arms repeatedly when Frieda left for an extended vacation). As one colleague put it: "She always reverted to making things hot for herself but not for you." Only during the last phase of the treatment, when Joanne developed the symptom of pulling the skin off her heels, did Frieda consider whether this might be a hostile response to her efforts to end the therapy.

Frieda seemed curiously unable to believe that her own actions, positive or negative, had helped to create the conditions for Joanne's recovery. In the talk she gave to colleagues at another hospital soon after the end of the treatment, she remarked:

If I present to you a patient with whom I was very lucky and where there was a real happy success, I don't mean to say that this always happens, because unfortunately it doesn't. But I mention this case first because I learned a lot from it and I hope you do too, and second because it's so encouraging to know it can be done, and we at Chestnut Lodge are convinced if we only were good enough, skillful enough, and knew enough, it could in principle be done with everybody.

After describing various of Joanne's symptoms and the ways they had worked through them, Frieda concluded: "Unlike [John] Rosen, who thinks the patient has to learn to think of a past mental illness as a foreign body to be terribly ashamed of, I feel the patient has to learn to accept the illness as an expression and part of herself and get befriended with it and integrate it like other experiences." She said she and Joanne had spent a number of sessions at the end of the treatment discussing what they each thought had been most helpful. She mentioned in passing the day she had remarked: "Getting well doesn't mean that your life thereafter will be a garden of roses. . . . [You have to] enjoy your rose garden when it is in bloom and take it in stride when it is not." Although Joanne hadn't believed this, she was impressed that Frieda took her seriously enough to tell her "such a horrible thing." The fact that they could each recall key moments in the treatment did not, however, enable Frieda to explain to her own satisfaction or anybody else's why Joanne had recovered so decisively.[27]

No one knows what makes an analytic couple great.[28] We recognize their names—Freud and Dora, Breuer and Anna O., Jung and Sabina Spielrein, Ferenczi and R.N. Psychoanalytic history has always been embodied in relationship, and these pairs have taught us what little we know about how therapy works.[29] Frieda and Joanne became the most famous couple in contemporary psychoanalysis, and we could learn a lot if we could explain why. Their work together was distinguished—even more so than that of the other classic pairs above—by its intense mutuality and its unambiguously good result. Yet Frieda was unable to explain what happened even though she tried many times, and Joanne's later fictionalized account leaves everything between the lines. The despair of contemporary psychiatry has so deformed their relationship that it now seems too successful to be real. They have become a kind of icon, a psychoanalytic Madonna and child, a yellowing photograph of a magical moment we can barely discern. We clutch the image like a talisman, unwilling to abandon the dream, as if all that stood between us and disbelief were Frieda and Joanne. Our anxiety about whether success such as theirs is possible obscures what they did. Most of all, it hides the fact of their coming together at a particular time and place, resonant with meaning and blotted now from view, and to see them at all, we must envision them in that world.

10

The Unredeemed

*If lunacy continues to increase as at present, the insane will be
in the majority, and, freeing themselves, will put the sane in
asylums.*[1]

Few mental patients were treated like Joanne. In the late 1940s, American psychiatrists spent most of their time worrying about competition from psychologists and social workers, whose ranks had been increasing dramatically since the war. State laws and a powerful medical establishment protected psychiatrists' right to administer somatic treatments, but there was no way to license "talk therapy" or prevent "lay practitioners" (as physicians called their competitors) from offering psychotherapy. This pushed psychiatrists to emphasize the biological bases of mental illness and to rely on those treatment methods which they alone were qualified to use.

The staggering number of patients in state hospitals had also intensified the demand for quick, inexpensive methods that could be applied on a mass scale.[2] With hundreds, even thousands of patients in each institution, psychiatrists were forced to concentrate on keeping track of people and attending to basic needs for food and shelter, not treatment. Overcrowded, deteriorating facilities led to squalor and sadism, making the situation even more hopeless. In May 1946, journalist Albert Maisel published a photo essay in *Life* magazine showing naked, frightened inmates in state hospitals, which he said had "degenerated into little more than concentration camps on the Belsen pattern." In several dozen articles in the New York newspaper *PM*, his colleague Albert Deutsch claimed: "I have seen animals better treated and more comfortably housed in zoos than are the mentally sick inmates of Detroit's institution." Crowding in some hospitals was so severe that elderly patients had to climb over one another's beds to get at the toilets, and cots were jammed into rooms never intended for patient use. By the early 1950s, mental patients occupied half of all U.S. hospital beds.[3]

Psychiatrists were utterly demoralized by this situation, and those who could manage to escape fled by droves into private practice, where they could concentrate on the "worried well." The rest of the profession, seeing no other choice, ended up, as historian Jack Pressman puts it, "settling upon a strategy of selling a vision of what psychiatry might accomplish if it were sufficiently medicalized."[4]

Their desire to be taken seriously by other physicians had long led psychiatrists to experiment with somatic treatments. Kraepelin's classic, *One Hundred Years of Psychiatry,* surveys dozens of nineteenth-century techniques. Tobacco enemas were used to free the blockages thought to cause nervous symptoms. Mustard plasters on the head and neck created suffering that helped the patient "regain consciousness of his true self." Ants or stinging nettles "forced [those] lost in the world of [the] imagination to adopt a new train of thought." The *bain de surprise,* in which the patient was suddenly dropped into a barrel of cold water, fostered a similarly revised attitude. Venesection and leeches rid the brain of excess blood. (As Pinel observed, however, "There was some doubt as to who was more insane, the one who ordered the blood-letting or the one subjected to the practice.") "The cruciform stance," in which patients were tied in a standing position with arms outstretched for eight to ten hours, induced fatigue and created "a feeling [of] respect for the doctor."[5]

By the beginning of the twentieth century, electrical stimulation had become the standard treatment for neurasthenia and depression, and hydrotherapy, an ancient remedy, had been extended to the "rain douche" and cold wet sheet pack. In 1927, Julius Wagner-Jauregg of Vienna was the first psychiatrist to be awarded the Nobel Prize in medicine, for inventing a treatment that injected mental patients with malaria-infected blood, to induce the high fevers thought to cure their psychoses.[6] Other somatic methods widely used in the 1920s and 1930s were forced inhalation of carbon dioxide, removal of the endocrine glands or ovaries, and "prolonged narcosis," in which patients were given massive doses of barbiturates to keep them comatose for several weeks. Schizophrenics were put into "mummy bags" with circulating refrigerants; blood drawn from horses was injected into their cerebrospinal fluid. More than fourteen hundred patients at the New Jersey State Hospital at

Trenton had their teeth, tonsils, stomach, colon, cervix, fallopian tubes, ovaries, or seminal vesicles removed after superintendent Henry Cotton proposed that toxins produced by bacteria in these areas caused a "focal infection" that spread to the brain and caused mental disturbance.[7]

But none of these methods could compete with the shock treatments of the 1930s.[8] Insulin coma, developed in 1933 by Manfred Sakel in Vienna (the technique Hermann Brunck was receiving at the time he killed himself) prescribed doses of insulin high enough to create a coma considered restorative. Metrazol shock treatment, introduced by Joseph Ladislas von Meduna in Hungary in 1935, substituted a synthetic form of camphor for the insulin. In ECT, developed by Ugo Cerletti and Lucio Bini in Italy in 1938, the easiest form of shock to learn and to use, a brief electrical current to the brain produced the convulsions. By 1942, more than 75,000 patients in the United States had been treated with at least one of these methods.[9]

The popular press went wild over shock, with enthusiastic articles appearing in *Time, Reader's Digest, Newsweek,* the *New Republic,* and *Scientific American.* In the same thrilling tones that greet every new approach in psychiatry, shock treatment was hailed as a miracle that could cure even the sickest patient. Its serious side effects—persistent memory loss, fractures produced by violent convulsions, brain damage if glucose were not administered quickly enough—were scarcely mentioned. Psychiatrists were so desperate that even A. A. Brill, founder of the New York Psychoanalytic Society and usually a critic of somatic therapies, declared that "schizophrenia is so hopeless, anything that holds out hope should be tried."[10] Since even ardent proponents of shock treatment admitted that it required repeated administration, patients were shocked over a period of weeks or months.

Psychiatrists liked these methods because they provided clear-cut solutions to intransigent problems. As Louis Casamajor told his colleagues in 1943: "One may question whether shock treatments do any good to the patients but there can be no doubt that they have done an enormous amount of good to psychiatry." At a symposium commemorating the contributions of Manfred Sakel, Ewen Cameron said his method had led to an

immense shift in our whole approach to the problem of schizophrenia. Our attitude now is one of determination, of the utilization of all possible therapeutic resources. It is an approach, above all things, of hope and of the expectation of success, and this shift in attitude is justified. Today, schizophrenia is no longer the formidable thing that it was prior to the introduction of the insulin treatment. Tomorrow is bright with hope. With success leading to confidence, and confidence to further success, the early future promises final victory over this long-dreaded and desperate disease.[11]

The fact that no one knew how these methods worked did little to diminish psychiatrists' enthusiasm for them. Nor did serious side effects. A standard manual for physicians noted: "We think that the possibility of persistent brain damage exists. . . . [However], in view of the gravity of a schizophrenic psychosis, it would appear that despite the possible occurrence of damage, the risk involved should not necessarily be regarded as prohibitive if there is a chance for improvement."[12] Until the late 1950s, when ECT was modified to prevent bone fractures, it was a violent method. The patient had to be physically restrained by several strong attendants, with a gag in his mouth to prevent dislocation of the jaw, and a spoon pressing down on his tongue so he wouldn't choke to death. The voltage was increased until a grand mal seizure occurred. The typical course involved twenty to sixty treatments, usually three a week. Some writers advocated ECT as a "maintenance treatment" given to chronic patients "at certain intervals over an indefinite period of time." Another suggested that a modified form of shock be given to children diagnosed with "preschizoid conditions" to prevent the development of psychosis.[13]

Psychosurgery, introduced by the Portuguese neurologist Egas Moniz in 1936, was quickly hailed as a breakthrough by psychiatrists all over the world. Moniz argued that severing the connections between regions of the brain thought to control emotion could eliminate symptoms like violence and depression. In no sense was psychosurgery a fringe method. Its major proponents in the United States were John Fulton, a Yale physiologist, and Walter Freeman, professor of neurology at George Washington University Medical School. Freeman and his colleague James Watts, a neurosurgeon, perfected their procedure on patients in Washington (many from middle-class families) and persisted despite serious technical difficulties (the type of blade they were using often broke off and lodged in the brain during the operation).

The theoretical rationale for lobotomy, like other somatic treatments, was unclear, but a prominent editorial in the *Psychiatric Quarterly* claimed the method was an advance despite its being "a stab in the dark." Lobotomy attracted enthusiastic reports in the *New York Times, Reader's Digest, Time, Life,* and *Newsweek,* and Harry Dannecker, a former patient, published a piece titled "Psychosurgery Cured Me" to much interest in *Coronet* magazine. "Worry has been cut out of their minds," claimed a 1941 *Saturday Evening Post* article written by the science editor of the *New York Times.* Freeman argued that the procedure was "not a radical operation," since by his estimate, "the frontal lobe comprises some 70 percent of the cerebrum, and in the average case [only] between 15 to 25 percent of the frontal association fibers are transected." By 1951, close to 20,000 lobotomies had been performed in the United States, and it was a lucrative sideline for many physicians.[14]

In the mid-1940s, however, Freeman recognized that even widespread use of psychosurgery would barely make a dent in the huge population of mental patients. The operation required a neurosurgeon and a number of support staff to care for patients during their long convalescence, luxuries lacking at state hospitals. So Freeman developed an alternative procedure called "transorbital lobotomy" in which a sharp instrument—he used an ice pick—was driven through the eye socket into the brain. In 1946, he described the method in a letter to one of his sons, then a college student:

I have also been trying out a sort of half-way stage between electroshock and prefrontal lobotomy on some of the patients. This consists of knocking them out with a shock and while they are under the "anesthetic" thrusting an ice pick up between the eyeball and the eyelid through the roof of the orbit actually into the frontal lobe of the brain and making the lateral cut by swinging the thing from side to side. . . . It seemed fairly easy, although definitely a disagreeable thing to watch. It remains to be seen how these cases hold up, but so far they have shown considerable relief of their symptoms, and only some of the minor behavior difficulties that follow lobotomy. They can even get up and go home within an hour or so.

Freeman was a neurologist, not a surgeon, but the overwhelmed superintendents of state hospitals couldn't worry about such details. As the demand for Freeman's services increased, he began taking trips around the country in a van with his sons, stopping at institutions along the way to perform the transorbital procedure, and then continuing on to scenic areas for hikes and camping. The method, he argued, was so "safe, simple, and quick" that a psychiatric resident could learn it in an afternoon. To demonstrate its efficiency, Freeman operated on 225 patients in twelve days—an average of nineteen per day. Neurosurgeons were horrified, and physicians fainted while witnessing the procedure. Even John Fulton, Freeman's long-time Yale colleague, said: "Why not use a shotgun? It would be quicker!"[15]

In 1949, Egas Moniz was awarded the Nobel Prize for inventing psychosurgery. The *New England Journal of Medicine* hailed his pioneering efforts, but lobotomy caused an angry split within psychiatry. In 1948, at the annual convention of the American Psychiatric Association, its advocates were openly attacked by more moderate colleagues, and in the only public political act of his career, Dexter Bullard stepped right into the middle.

Freeman and Bullard had known each other for years as members of Washington's small medical community. But Bullard and his colleagues at the Lodge were outraged by Freeman's cavalier attitudes about lobotomy. "Even if a patient is no longer able to paint pictures, write poetry, or compose music, he is, on the other hand, no longer ashamed to fetch and carry, to wait on table or make beds or empty cans," Freeman had written. Frieda and Sullivan found this appalling; to rob a patient of his capacity for insight and creativity were morally unacceptable acts for a physician. (As their friend Hilde Bruch bitterly remarked: "Don't forget that ten years after I graduated from medical school, German professors killed their patients.") When Charles Burlingame, a strong lobotomy advocate, became the official nominee for president of the APA, Bullard publicly opposed his candidacy. After an emotional debate, Burlingame lost the election by thirty-nine votes, and Chestnut Lodge, the only elite hospital never to use any of what historian Jack Pressman calls the "assault therapies," became a visible target of attack by mainstream psychiatrists and a last resort for many patients.[16]

The irony was that since psychotherapy and lobotomy were considered equally "extreme" treatments for psychosis, the same people were often referred for both procedures. "The best type of lobotomy patient," Freeman had noted, "was the one who had to be dragged into treatment kicking and screaming." Since from another perspective, such a person could be considered "spirited," it was little wonder that some of those for whom lobotomy was recommended ended up being sent instead to Frieda.

By the mid-1940s, most of those who came to the Lodge had already been unsuccessfully treated with one or more of the somatic methods. They were so "awesomely ill," as Harold Searles put it, that even Frieda stood little chance of reaching them. Miss N., the patient famous for stuffing her underwear down Lodge toilets, was one of these. Arriving at age twenty-nine, after four years in other hospitals, Miss N. remained at the Lodge for twenty years (until finally being sent elsewhere). With a diagnosis of "schizophrenia, hebephrenic type," she epitomized what Goffman called the "career mental patient." State hospital superintendents dismissed patients like her as being "formed from clay rejected by the potters," but a better image is a tree in a bonsai garden: stunted to fit the shallow contours of the pot in which it is forced to grow, but otherwise surprisingly robust. The dwarfing of Miss N.'s life was tragic; the energy and verve with which she pursued it were not.[17]

Becoming openly psychotic in late adolescence, she had time to absorb some of the values of the cultivated Jewish home in which she was raised. Unable to choose Vassar or Barnard because of her illness, Miss N. applied to become Adolf Meyer's personal patient. When he and his staff at Hopkins quickly lost interest, she sought transfer to the Lodge, where she did brilliantly. Fending off extraordinarily concerted attempts to help her, she created a warm, safe life in the place that felt most like home to her. Treated by many different therapists—including Frieda, at the peak of her career—Miss N. was so gifted at craziness that she got everyone at the Lodge to love her even as she resisted all their efforts to make her better. Unfortunately, being that good as a mental patient precluded any other existence.

It's hard for us to understand such a choice, but that's because we can't imagine being as unwanted as Miss N. She called herself a "miscarriage." Perhaps "unaborted child" would be a better description. Conceived at a time when her father was suffering severe losses in his business, Miss N. was born to a mother whose life felt totally precarious. In depression and rage, she withdrew—first from her husband and then from the daughter she had sought to refuse. From earliest childhood, Miss N. understood that she wasn't supposed to be there; her profound guilt at simply existing did little to soften her parents' hatred of her. They wore her as a crown of thorns, and she retaliated by escaping into a mental hospital and making them pay hundreds of thousands of dollars for her treatment and care. Probably not even the most heroic treatment could have saved her. Psychosis takes a long time to kill, but that doesn't mean it's not often fatal.

Miss N. had always been "difficult." Her parents said she was "lonely" and "always afraid," and "asked over and over whether she was adopted." For much of her childhood, she lived with her family in Europe. She tried music and painting but failed at both. Menstruation frightened her. There were a few "passes at jobs," but she never really worked. In her early twenties, having been forbidden to visit "a certain married woman who would talk freely to her of sexual matters," Miss N. "struck" her mother and was labeled "disturbed." Sent to a psychiatrist who urged her to become more independent, she traveled to the West Coast, intending to start over. She ended up in a mental institution near her parents, where she received metrazol and insulin shock.

Declared "much improved" by her doctors, Miss N. was discharged. She begged her parents to take her back. They did, but when she said she was afraid to return to the psychiatrist (the one who had pushed her to leave them), her parents sent her to Adolf Meyer. At his clinic at Hopkins, she received forty to fifty additional shock treatments (a combination of metrazol, insulin and ECT) and several months of psychotherapy, "without lasting improvement."

It is unclear whether Miss N. was ever treated by Meyer himself—the record lists two other doctors—but he clearly made a powerful impression on her. In an extraordinarily lucid letter she sent to her physicians, Miss N. wrote the following statement, quoted by Lodge staff every time they evaluated her:

I have some things that I want to discuss with Dr. Meyer about sociology and psychology. I want to tell him some things I have learned about life. It made me sick so that I had sexual and personality difficulties. I had insulin and metrazol. I could not coordinate my mind and body. I lost my mind. I want to be put under [his] direct care. I cannot understand the true reasons for my being here. Each time I think I have reached an exact explanation, I think differently again and wonder, am I not wrong? I think it has got something to do with my parents especially but I do not know what. Neither of them seem at all anxious to take me home with them and I don't think they are. That is not normal or natural for parents to feel that way and I don't really think they do. I want to come to you. I want to begin all over again and see what is the fundamental reason and cause for all this. I don't want to burden you with the problem that has been bothering so many people. I don't feel that it is my fault or that I am responsible and I want you to see really what really is and who really is and settle it in your way. I don't know the truth and each time I think I have found it out, I feel I am wrong again. It is not a very happy situation for me to be in.

I can think of several solutions that would solve it but the point is to use the right one. My first desire and wish was to take a child and from an emotional standpoint, I would be very happy. But I don't want any child's life made unhappy and I would consider it my duty towards this child to make it happy permanently. That would cure me. Another solution would be to go around the world, not staying any place any length of time and see all there is to see geographically, and it would be interesting. Or else just disappear or else ask them to kill me or else take my own life. I think I have lived through too much. I don't think I will take my own life. I am too strong. My body is far too healthy. No, the first solution I would want to use. The second I consider is right to use. The third one would be a cowardly escape. The fourth one is in your hands. Your opinion is of value.[18]

By the time she got to the Lodge five years later, Miss N. had become a textbook hebephrenic: chattering incessant gibberish in a sing-song voice, urinating on the floor, slicing her clothes into tiny strips, running naked around the ward. Hebephrenics are a caricature of craziness.[19] If they aren't careful, staff will quickly conclude they are too far gone to pay attention to. Miss N. never let that happen to her. She used her uncanny intuition and talent for mimicry to charm everyone from medical staff to maintenance men. Even when she developed the symptom of stuffing her underwear down toilets all over the hospital, people remained fond of her. Miss N. was fat, filthy, and frequently violent, but she was also an indisputable member of "the Lodge family."

Miss N.'s initial therapist was Dexter Bullard, but she was also part of Frieda's experiment in group therapy. Her contributions there were memorable. She read aloud from books or magazines, an activity the other patients enjoyed but which drove Frieda crazy. When Frieda became testy, Miss N. switched to acting as her assistant. She would turn to the most withdrawn patient—who often stared into space or urinated on the floor—and say in a warm tone, "Mary, why don't you join us and talk with us?"[20] Or, to set a positive example, Miss N. would exchange compliments with Frieda about clothes and hairstyles. If the telephone rang during one of the group's sessions, Miss N. would answer it in the polished tone of a receptionist. Ten minutes later, she might be taking off her clothes, cavorting around the room, or urinating or menstruating on whatever chair she happened to be sitting on. (The ever practical Frieda held these sessions in the main building, not at the cottage, for this reason.)

During Miss N.'s first few years at the Lodge, she clearly had a strong connection to Frieda, although Bullard was her therapist. In a group session where she seemed lucid but terribly anxious, Frieda asked: "Are you afraid you won't get well?" Miss N. said "Yes." Frieda said, "I hope that's not so—I heard you wanted to change therapists." Miss N. said: "Dr. Dexter Bullard said I could change. I could see you. He asked if I would like to change and I said yes." Frieda explained she had no hours open. Miss N. said: "I'll stop seeing doctors until you have some hours open—Dr. Bullard suggested you as a doctor and I said all right." Frieda again explained she couldn't take on new patients. Miss N. kept trying to persuade her. It was the most sustained interchange she had managed to have on any topic since her admission.

At the next group session, Miss N. moved a shelf so that it struck Frieda on the head. She yelled. Miss N. apologized. Frieda said angrily: "You knew what you were doing." Miss N. said: "No, I didn't. I'm really sorry, I didn't mean to do that. Your head is important." (Another patient, who rarely responded to anything, found this remark hilarious.) A week later, roaming nervously around the office throughout the session, Miss N. opened a closet. Brandishing a bottle of whiskey she found there, she declared: "Now all our problems are settled." Patients, nurse, Frieda, and Morrie Schwartz all burst out laughing. Miss N. adored being the center of attention.[21]

Bullard didn't accomplish much in Miss N.'s therapy, but like everyone else, he was impressed by her insightfulness. Once Miss N. bit a visiting psychiatrist, and when asked why, she said: "I bit him because I was afraid he would bite me." Bullard thought this was brilliant, given how sarcastic this man was.[22]

Miss N. was reassigned to Alberta Szalita, a refugee analyst from Poland and a close friend of Frieda. Szalita's entire family had been murdered by Nazis, but she retained a deep humanism and shared Frieda's gift for understanding very disturbed people. Szalita often took Miss N. for rides in the car to break the monotony of their sessions. In a staff meeting, she described one such day:

> I [had just] learned to drive and was a very poor driver, didn't feel too sure as a rule. That was during the time when I used to be quite irritated with her. She [would] switch what was possible to switch around, the window shields, the heater when it was hot, if the window was open she would climb out to the other side and I was always wondering if I would come back with her. Once we went in the direction of Washington. She said she wanted to turn to the left and I did, and came to a point where I had no idea whether we could get back to Rockville this way. . . . [We ended up] about eight or ten minutes' ride from the main road. She got frightened as I turned the car—it is quite awkward for me to make a U-turn—and took off one shoe, threw it out the window, then she threw out the other shoe, then she threw out her beret, then she took off her dress.[23] [No one at this meeting raised a question about these outings, which continued for several years.]

Szalita did anything she could think of to make contact with Miss N.: walks, rides, clothes shopping, speaking French. "Almost each hour there are a couple of sentences which represent a direct expression of her feelings," she reported to colleagues. "I do have the feeling that we have a better understanding of what is going on. She talks quite a lot about her lack of confidence, a certain amount about her fear." Szalita was moved when Miss N. told her: "You are the first person I have talked to in this way. I just don't know how to talk to people."

It was Szalita who finally figured out why Miss N. constantly destroyed her clothing. It was a way of taking revenge on her elegantly dressed mother, who gave Miss N. only cheap cast-offs. Flushing her clothes down the toilet and running around naked captured her humiliation and anger at being evidence of the abortion her mother wished she'd had. By expressing these feelings in a complicated, condensed way that her parents couldn't grasp, Miss N. forced them to take care of her in a style appropriate to their social class. Her actions also had unconscious resonance in a family where the children had always been encouraged to play nude around the house.

Unfortunately, these insights were lost when Szalita, whom Miss N. fondly called "Chiquita," left the Lodge and Frieda took over as therapist. Frieda always seemed utterly baffled by Miss N.'s destruction of her clothes, perhaps because she didn't go dress shopping with her the way Szalita did. Frieda also failed to understand that running around the ward naked was Miss N.'s way of showing that it felt like home to her.

Miss N.'s violence caused most people to withdraw from her. She felt humiliated by this behavior—calling herself "a criminal, insane, and a beast"—and was terrified she might kill someone. Once, when Szalita had to see her in a seclusion room, Miss N. "accidentally" locked the door, trapping both of them. Szalita was frightened at first, then decided to see what would happen. She asked Miss N.: "Do you want me to get them to open the door?" The patient said no. Szalita sat down. Miss N. took off the sturdy hospital outfit she was wearing and ripped it to bits. Then she started jumping around naked, screaming that a man was after her. She crouched down and urinated. Eventually her screams drew the attention of ward staff and a nurse let Szalita out, shaking her head.

The poignancy of Miss N.'s situation was apparent to everyone. Once, in an argument, another patient yelled at her, "Drop dead." Miss N. responded in a dull voice: "I am dead already for fifteen years." Yet even in her worst moments, she appeared to have some awareness of the needs of others. One young nurse recalled the day Miss N. "was in such a rage her face was black and her eyeballs were black. She wouldn't take the sedation and when I tried to give it to her, my hand was shaking, so she steadied my hand. Apparently, she appreciates a little honesty." At another hospital, Miss N. would likely have been lobotomized for being such a "management problem." (Even McLean dealt with "troublemakers" in this fashion.) And certainly people at the Lodge grew frustrated with her. After Miss N. attacked Bullard for the dozenth time, he threw her on the floor. Then he ordered her to get up and talk to him. Understanding the need for self-protection better than most other people, she never again hit him. "The amusing part is that some months later," Bullard told colleagues, "she said that I was too aggressive. I said, 'you mean the time I threw you on the floor?' She said, 'no, you talk too much.'"

Miss N. was fundamentally different from someone like Joanne Greenberg. For Miss N., recovering was much more frightening than staying in the hospital. She couldn't imagine being well and having anyone be kind to her. People at the Lodge seemed far more appreciative of her talents than anyone in her family was. (As Frieda noted in a staff meeting: "When she telephones, I have heard her say any number of times, 'I am talking from my residence in Maryland.'")[24] When Szalita told Miss N.'s parents that she spoke excellent French, occasionally discussed Shakespeare and Tolstoy, and might be the most intelligent of their five children, they were stunned. Nothing in their experience had ever suggested any of this.

In a classic example of what Gregory Bateson would later call a "double bind," Miss N.'s mother told her, "Anytime the doctors say that you can visit us at home, that will be fine." Then she called the ward administrator and said: "You know, doctor, we live on the sixth floor and there is a balcony out on the back and when she goes wandering out on that balcony, it makes me quite nervous. You know, we have to put things away and we have to get ready for her whenever she comes home. So, do what you think is best." As Frieda told colleagues: "These parents are only keeping together by virtue of the sorrow for this child that they have in common. . . . She is responsible for their marriage going on and it only continues if she stays sick. . . . She has to spend her life atoning for hating these parents to whom she was so unwelcome." Otto Will said this also happened on the ward. "She is getting [the staff] held together in the same way that she held the family together. We relate to her so repeatedly in that [fashion] we get stuck in it." Yet as Will remarked poignantly in an evaluation report: "It is notable that this patient, so long ill, has the great capacity to maintain the interest of others in her, and to awaken serious concern about her welfare. This capacity can continue to form a basis for useful therapeutic integrations, and argues well against the luxury of despair."[25]

In May 1953, Frieda decided to take Miss N. on as her patient. Given how well she already knew her by that point and how packed Frieda's schedule was, this was a clear sign of her faith in Miss N.'s potential. As Frieda told colleagues in a staff meeting:

> The patient and I both know that she is kind of standing at the sill of an open door to health and just cannot walk through, that she has worked

with a sufficient number of psychiatrists to know where they failed her so that she could not make the last step, and that she should tell me about these mistakes if she could, so that I would not repeat them. We would at least have only to cope with my own mistakes, about which she should tell me whenever she could as they occur.[26]

Miss N. was thrilled to be seeing Frieda at last and to have their sessions at the cottage instead of on the ward. To celebrate the end of their first hour together, she pushed the buzzer when Frieda wasn't looking, a signal to the secretary in the next room. When a nurse suddenly appeared at the door as if by magic to take Miss N. back to the ward, Frieda was astonished by so adroit a move.

An even more powerful moment came earlier in this session, when Frieda realized she couldn't hear Miss N. The patient was mumbling with her head turned away, the two conditions that most exacerbated Frieda's growing hearing difficulties. Although she always put on a show of being matter-of-fact about her limitations, Frieda was clearly humiliated when she couldn't hear patients. To Miss N., she merely remarked: "I have some hearing difficulties, but the doctors think using a hearing aid would be premature. Patients who want to get something out of me must cope with this and turn to me while talking." Miss N. made no response. "In an attempt to make our first interview a success," Frieda later told colleagues, "I walked over to where she was sitting, and without thinking of any implications, knelt down in front of her, for acoustic reasons." Frieda often sat on the floor next to patients too disturbed to get up, and if someone who muttered kept her head down, Frieda tried to position herself "more lowly" so she could make out what was being said. (These were all things she had done decades before she had hearing problems.) But this act stunned Miss N. She burst out: "Frieda, you should not kneel before me. If somebody should kneel, I should kneel before you." With studied nonchalance, she then moved to a chair right across from Frieda, remarking: "How silly that I didn't discover this chair before. It is so comfortable. I will use it from now on at all our visits." Whatever one says about the rest of their work together, this first hour was magnificent.

Most sessions were more mundane. Miss N. read aloud from newspapers or chatted nonstop about trivialities. Both left Frieda bored and irritated. Occasionally Miss N. would lock herself in the small bathroom next to the office and stuff her underwear down the toilet. Yet Frieda was clearly fond of Miss N. At a staff conference a year after they started therapy, she told colleagues: "Everybody calls this patient by her first name which we don't do here as a rule unless the patient specifically asks for it. I myself not only call her by her first name but I found myself the other day marking her in my appointment book with her first name which is so unusual for me that it deserves mention." She noted how much everyone at the Lodge appreciated Miss N.'s "incredible sense of humor" and clever observations.

Frieda described an emblematic moment from their work together. It was a hot day, and she had moved the session to her back porch. Miss N. started ordering her around and knocking over all the flower pots. Frieda said she didn't like to be "used as a door mat." Eventually Miss N. left. The next day, Frieda told her: "Look, you succeeded yesterday in getting me mad. That doesn't happen very easily, so something very special must have gone on that you succeeded in doing that. Do you think you were frightened of something?" Miss N. said, "Yes of course." Frieda asked what it was. The patient responded, Frieda told colleagues, "with a tone of voice as though I was the greatest dumbbell in the world since I didn't know this, that life is what she is afraid of." Miss N. went on: "Why do you try to make me change? I don't want to change." Frieda told her it was hard to understand choosing to live on the disturbed ward of a mental hospital instead of outside in the world. Miss N. said: "But Frieda, life here is secure and the outside is insecure." It would be hard to imagine a clearer summary of this case than that remark.

Frieda thought Miss N. was "eternally behaving somewhat like a frightened child," and symptoms like incontinence and destroying her clothing were the only ways she could exert power over anyone. "If she clutters up the toilet," Frieda told colleagues, "we have to call the handyman and he has to get it in order, and if she soils herself, we have to get her clean. This is her way of asserting herself."

One of Frieda's main goals in the therapy was to find more positive means for Miss N. to express herself. When she complained, "There is nothing of me in your house," and asked Frieda if she could keep her purse at the cottage ("I don't mean it as a gift, I just like to have something of me in this house"), Frieda agreed. The next day, Miss N. took back the purse, a pattern she repeated often. Yet despite all her efforts, Frieda had few illusions about Miss N. As she told colleagues: "This makes fifteen years in which she has intrigued a lot of people's interest and then made monkeys out of them. . . . Her attitude is anti-therapeutic. She talks it, she has learned the language, but she doesn't follow through one nickel's worth."

What especially annoyed Frieda was that Miss N.'s evasions seemed at some level to be deliberate. Frieda repeatedly told her to "cut out the monkey business," an intervention that momentarily made the meaning of whatever she was doing more apparent. For example, when Frieda expressed a lack of enthusiasm one day about taking Miss N. to an inn for lunch, the patient, clearly angry, began jabbering nonsensically. The next day, she announced that she was going with one of the patients on the ward, who, as Frieda noted, had "recently bitten her."

Sometimes when Frieda admitted a mistake and apologized, Miss N. would briefly become more coherent. But then, just as she had always done with Szalita, she would quickly retreat into craziness. Frieda often commented on this pattern. When the nurses confined Miss N. to the ward because of her violence, Frieda marched over and told her straight out that these outbursts were her way of staying in the hospital.[27]

Yet at other moments Miss N. seemed perfectly insightful about her symptoms. Asked why she had told a nurse that she had murdered Frieda, Miss N. replied airily: "Oh, I just said that to make it interesting. You know they are not as interested in what is going on between you and me as we are."[28] Comments like this kept Frieda engaged in the treatment and gave her hope that Miss N. might someday snap out of it. The patient was a true Skinnerian: she understood that by intermittently rewarding people's efforts, they wouldn't give up on her.

Hebephrenia has a strong hysterical component, so if the person can be made to feel less frightened, she might tone down the extremes enough to say what is terrifying her. In doing absolutely anything she could think of to make this happen, Frieda was like the relatives of some coma patients: assuming that at some level the patient was registering what went on even while "unconscious." Frieda's strategy had two main effects: it coaxed Miss N. to her highest possible level of functioning during their sessions, and it forced her into her most disorganized self back on the ward. In the end, whatever will to health Miss N. still had proved too fragile or deeply buried even for Frieda to call it forth.[29]

Yet the patient clearly enjoyed the more reciprocal adult relationship Frieda sought to create. At Miss N.'s request, they often went to lunch at elegant places in the Maryland countryside. Frieda told colleagues about their arrangement: "She takes me to the Olney Inn and I take her to Normandy Farm. In each place, whoever is hostess pays for the meal." On these occasions Miss N.'s class status triumphed over her symptoms: she never disrobed, urinated, or masturbated in restaurants.

The question was whether Miss N. was using her sensitivity to stay in the hospital rather than to gain insight into her illness. At a staff meeting, head nurse Margaret Ursell told this story: "I went in to her room some time ago and I was personally not feeling so well. It had nothing to do with her, nothing to do with the floor, but something to do with me. And when I came out of her room, I felt better. She did the right thing with me; she just sensed something and automatically did the right thing." David Shakow, a well-known schizophrenia researcher visiting from Austen Riggs, said it sounded to him as if Miss N. "is the therapist of the staff rather than you being the therapist for her. If she feels supported in [this role] perhaps that is one of the reasons why she won't leave here." Frieda agreed, noting how careful she had to be not to let the patient's attentiveness derail the therapy. "Oh, you seem depressed today," Miss N. would say, or, "Oh, you need the hearing aid today." Frieda said it was terribly hard not to get sucked in to this caretaking.[30]

Frieda's process notes are filled with examples of Miss N.'s thoughtfulness. Even in their first session, Frieda had noted her dog's greeting the patient "with a warmth and tenderness quite unusual towards a stranger." As a compliment, Frieda had told Miss N. that the dog did this "only if she is very fond of a person or if she feels there is a pleasant relationship between the person and myself." (Like Sullivan, Frieda used her dogs as radar, and they proved to be a highly reliable source of information.) And in this same hour, Miss N. had noted, "You and I, Frieda, have many similarities; we are both on the mildly depressed side," an extraordinarily insightful comment from so disturbed a patient.[31]

Frieda eventually decided to tape-record their sessions in the hope that this would lead to greater progress in the work.[32] She was becoming increasingly interested in nonverbal communication—in a patient's childhood and in therapy—and also wanted the tapes as data. Frieda understood that a patient can stay psychotic for a long time only by continually recreating her symptoms. The label "chronic" masks the active parts of this process, as if once manifest, a behavior continues on its own momentum. (One of Freud's greatest insights had been to recognize that symptoms require constant energy; we don't need to embrace his nineteenth-century physics to see this as a correct statement.) In recording her sessions with Miss N. and later analyzing filmed interactions with Bateson and his colleagues, Frieda was trying to figure out how patients managed what sociologists later called "the manufacture of madness." She thought that if she could catch them doing it at a particular moment, she might be able to slow the process down to understand how it worked.

The sixty tapes Frieda made of her sessions with Miss N. in 1954–1955 are among the few recordings ever made of psychotherapy with a chronic schizophrenic patient.[33] This creates an overwhelming desire to see them as representative of something—psychoanalysis, Frieda, schizophrenia, the 1950s. But psychotherapy is by definition idiosyncratic, specific to that particular relationship, the stage of the patient's illness, and the context where treatment takes place. Still, just as a single surviving vase provides a glimpse of an ancient world, these recorded moments in Miss N.'s treatment tell us an extraordinary amount.

We see nothing of the straightforward analytic work that marked Frieda's treatment of Joanne (which had ended only a few months before she took on Miss N.). Frieda acted as if she were the patient's host rather than her therapist. She offered her cigarettes, coffee, cookies, presents. They chatted of recent events and books they had read. They planned excursions to the country and shared memories of New York and Paris. Frieda was twenty-five years older than Miss N., who was forty at the time. They weren't exactly peers (among other things, Miss N. was far wealthier than Frieda), but they were both from old German-Jewish families, and there was enough similarity in their backgrounds to imagine them being friends in some other life.

The content of their sessions was often bizarre, although the form was conventional. Miss N. brought gifts of candy or flowers (usually picked from Frieda's garden on her way over), and Frieda proclaimed her "delight" at Miss N.'s "visits." But the patient's refusal to confront her problems was maddening. Miss N. spent many sessions reading aloud from comic strips in the newspaper, or reciting every advertisement. Frieda often resorted to "taking a nap" until the reading ended. "I'm like a dog," she told Miss N. "I can sleep with eyes open." Sometimes instead of ordering her to stop reading, Frieda appealed to the patient's vanity, pleading: "I don't want to spend the hour with some author but with you." Once she resorted to just a touch of ridicule: "You are like a clown in a circus. Not like a lady visiting with another lady. Like somebody who's frightened to be her real self. And why? (pause) She would have to tell me. I can't guess." The patient responded: "If you were my mother, I'd tell you to go to hell," an intensely revealing comment that Frieda inexplicably failed to pick up on.[34] Yet Miss N. was extremely careful not to push things too far. Frieda often marveled at her ability to sense the precise end of the hour so she could leave before Frieda threw her out. Even when their conversation had been completely incoherent, they parted pleasantly, with much politeness and warmth, as if they had just enjoyed tea and a chat.

Frieda tried the things that had worked with Joanne, but with Miss N. they had no effect. She would beg: "I'm not a mind reader. Take me with you." To Joanne, this had been reassuring; Miss N. just disappeared further into unreachability.[35] But she was careful never to vanish completely, interspersing enough thoughtful comments among the floods of nonsensical chattering to keep Frieda interested. The problem was that there didn't seem to be any particular relation between these moments of insight and anything Frieda said or did.

Yet in some sessions Miss N. behaved "like a perfect lady," as Frieda put it. They talked of furniture and decorating. Once the topic was winter resorts. Another day, discussing jewelry, Frieda remarked that she never wore earrings. "Do you think it's nice if someone has to wear a plug in her ear and then she draws attention to the ears with earrings? I think you would agree that really doesn't show good taste." Miss N. asked whether Frieda considered Charles Boyer handsome. She replied: "All I care about is whether they have decent health and a decent mind, that is what is handsome to me." Discussing smoking habits, Frieda said she used a cigarette holder so her fingers wouldn't get stained by nicotine. When Miss N. expressed interest, Frieda said she'd order one for her. (The patient requested an exact duplicate, which she proudly showed off to the ward.) But these attempts at a peer, adult relationship never worked for long. One day when Miss N. locked herself in the bathroom next to the office and began stopping up the toilet (which had just been unclogged from one of her previous adventures), Frieda piously announced through the door: "I will have to see you on the ward from now on. I gave you the privilege of being a guest here, but you were not able to respect my privileges as a hostess." The image of this hebephrenic patient—known for her violence, her frequent public urination, and her destruction of countless items of clothing—as Frieda's "guest" is an image that looks nuts, even at the Lodge.[36]

Yet Frieda clearly enjoyed chatting with Miss N. about hairstyles, clothes, movies, and books. She would end the session with, "Tomorrow, same time?" and the patient would respond, "I'll try to make it," as if they were in a *Kaffeeklatsch*. Inexplicably, however, Frieda failed to interpret Miss N.'s politeness and warmth as yet another part of her defensiveness. She also apparently failed to see how these "wonderful, perfectly ladylike visits" contributed to the patient's remaining in the hospital, making Frieda part of the same pathological system as Miss N.'s parents.

In one of their most moving hours together, Miss N. began singing a song. At first this irritated Frieda, then suddenly she said: "Say, maybe you could help me out. Do you know the song "My Bonnie is Over the Sea" or something like that?" Miss N. said: "My Body Lies Over the Ocean, My Body Lies Over the Sea." Frieda said that sounded like the one. The patient began to whistle it. Frieda asked: "Could you sing it for me? Then I could hear it better." Miss N. sang it, including every chorus. Frieda responded enthusiastically: "Oh, thank you. Sing it one more time so that I will really know it." Miss N. whistled the song. Frieda thanked her. She whistled it again. Frieda thanked her again. "Someone wanted me to sing a funny song, now I know one. Unfortunately, now we have to finish." Miss N. began singing the song again. Frieda joined her, not singing the words but humming along warmly and fitting her parting comments to the tune. "Here's your coat, here's your coat, thank you, thank you for teaching me the song." They said goodbye and Miss N. left. On the recording of this session, we can hear Frieda quietly singing the song to herself before the tape ends.[37]

Once, interrupting Miss N.'s chatter about nail polish, Frieda asked: "So, what's going on there in no man's land?" Miss N. answered: "Just the same as always. Never any different." There was a long silence. Then, in a voice that made clear her willingness to enter Miss N.'s image, Frieda asked: "Well, do you have any friends there?" Miss N. said: "No man." Frieda: "So you are all by yourself there?" Patient: "Yes." Frieda: "What are you doing? Do you have a home there?" For once, Miss N. didn't flee. "I have a couple of them." Frieda persisted. "Oh, describe them to me." As soon as Miss N. finished talking about one home, Frieda responded: "You said you had a couple of them, what about the others?" The patient went on. Frieda inquired about each room. It is absolutely clear from Miss N.'s tone that she is making up what she says as she goes along, telling yet another story to keep Frieda there with her. It's equally clear that to Frieda, it doesn't really matter whether the patient is recounting thoughts, fantasies, memories, or hallucinations—she is letting Frieda into her mental life. This is the ground on which psychotherapy takes shape; without it there is only surface change. As Miss N. detailed her various homes, it was possible to imagine her continuing long enough for Frieda to glimpse her real feelings, her intense loneliness. But she didn't go on. The next hour was like all the others.[38]

Yet Miss N. obviously felt close to Frieda, as she had with "Chiquita." Indeed, if this terribly disturbed woman can be said to have had any periods of normalcy, they occurred in sessions with the two of them. (Perhaps their European backgrounds helped; Miss N. associated her time abroad with both her happiest memories and her breakdown.) There is a warmth to her conversations with Frieda and Szalita that was entirely absent from her interactions with others. Even when she turned every sentence into maddening sing-song, a listener could tell she felt more relaxed and connected than she did on the ward. But compared to the intensity of her humiliation and terror, these feelings barely registered. It is painful, listening to a session that took place months after she started to see Frieda, to hear Miss N. suddenly announce halfway through the hour: "When you're ready to get rid of me just say it's time to go and I'll be glad to jump."[39] Aborting herself clearly seemed preferable to having Frieda get rid of her.

What is most difficult to understand is why Frieda persisted in believing Miss N. capable of perfect rationality, were this only to become an important enough goal. As Don Burnham later remarked: "I sometimes thought that Frieda approached the patient with the assumption that somewhere within, there was a little person or homunculus hiding behind a defensive mask or within a fortress of off-putting symptoms, and that her aim was to establish communication with that little person."[40] For example, one day Miss N. brought Frieda a crocheted holder she had made, and then blurted out (right in the middle of a long, nonsensical monologue delivered through the mumble of crunching cookies): "The next time I get angry or silly, you should remember I gave you this gift." Frieda assured her warmly that she would. Then, in a matter-of-fact tone, a tone one would use with someone capable of giving a straight answer, Frieda asked: "Do you know when you get these fits of anger what it has to do with? I don't really know *why* you get angry. Do you know?" Miss N. responded, "Uh, no," and turned to another topic. Frieda tried again, softly cajoling: "I asked you something first. You said no and your no was not very convincing." Miss N. responded: "Yes. Now is it convincing?" Frieda tried once more. "Now you say yes, that is, you *do* know when you get angry. Then tell me what the occasions are, because that's important for us." Miss N. began to chat about an upcoming social event. Frieda finally gave up.[41]

In the last surviving tape recording of their work together, the session of February 7, 1955, there is an incredibly poignant discussion of the "real" Miss N. Frieda talked wistfully of her hope that they could make this woman, so rarely present, "permanently the one that we see." Miss N. drew heavily on her cigarette and began to whistle. Then after a long pause she said: "When I look at you I know that you know a heck of a lot more than I have ever known, and I look at you to find out more. But I can't tell you that I have anything, and again I can't say that I haven't. Now would you please return the compliment and say that you learned something from me?" Frieda: "Yes I did." Miss N.: "What?" Frieda: "How a girl can prefer to be an emotional invalid . . . because she's afraid of taking her real self back again." Miss N. began to chat about her brother, who had visited the day before. Frieda pleaded with her: "You're pulling away. You could behave in treatment in such a way that we could figure this out." Frieda was convinced that buried in that gibberish was a rage too frightening to let anyone know about. "The other day when I said that if you stay in the hospital your father has to pay the big bills, you looked at me as though you wanted to kill me," she reminded Miss N. "You are no baby, you know you aren't kept here for nothing . . . without them getting anything in return for it. Now I think it would be quite justified if you made hard efforts to pull out of this."

Szalita once told another very disturbed patient at a moment like this that she had been sick long enough and needed to get better. That time, the directness worked, and the patient snapped out of it, the way people in the Middle Ages were sometimes said to do when thrown into snake pits. Unfortunately, this didn't work with Miss N. Like a prisoner of war willing to confess anything to prevent further torture, she discussed her potential recovery for the next half-hour in a way that made clear she would agree to any statement Frieda made, so long as she wasn't thrown out of the Lodge. She said one thing. Frieda said another. Miss N. said the opposite. When confronted with the difference between them, Miss N. said: "I mean just exactly what you mean." Frieda was exasperated: "Well, what *do* I mean?" Miss N. responded sweetly: "I don't know whatever you mean. You must mean well, and I mean well too. We both mean well." She began describing movies she had recently seen and an upcoming dental appointment. Frieda was silent. Then Miss N. said: "I have a little room up on the fourth floor if you want to see me some time. I moved from where you saw me before. I would like you to come there. You don't have anything of mine over here, in your closets or anywhere at all." The session ended with Miss N.'s cheerful goodbye. Whatever fantasy Frieda might have had about getting her out of the hospital dissolved audibly at that moment.[42]

A therapist who later tried to treat Miss N. called her "an extinct volcano with a few puffs of smoke going up now and then."[43] After twenty years at the Lodge, she ended up at Sheppard, where she managed to clog up the plumbing of the entire town and continued to demonstrate her remarkable ability to be treated by some of the most distinguished psychiatrists in America and to defy the best efforts of each one.

An even more painful failure for Frieda was Mr. R., a thirty year-old paranoid schizophrenic admitted in 1953. Unlike most other patients who came to the Lodge in that period, Mr. R. had received no somatic treatment during his two previous stays at hospitals in the Midwest. He had graduated from a well-known university and begun professional school; his breakdown hadn't occurred until his early twenties, a pattern typical in paranoia. He led a very isolated life, staying in the YMCA and having a lot of fantasy relationships. Claiming to be involved with a young woman on the staff of a hotel, he got into a fight with the manager and was arrested. His father got him off by promising to rehospitalize him.

Mr. R. was raised in a middle-class Jewish family in St. Louis, the only boy, with two older sisters. His father was intensely involved in every detail of his life, from his schoolwork to his girlfriends. Mr. R.'s mother seemed entirely absent, both in contacts with the Lodge and in her son's psychology.

Frieda saw Mr. R. at the same time she was treating Miss N. He was also seen in certain periods by her colleague Marvin Adland. Mr. R.'s relationship with Frieda was sullen and hostile. He showed up at her house at night and had to be forcibly removed by attendants. He repeatedly tried to attack her and masturbated during sessions. He kicked her dog, which especially upset Frieda. (Shouting that he could cause the dog "to become vicious toward strangers and patients," she threw him out of the house.)[44] Frieda was forced to move their therapy sessions to the main building after Bullard decided it wasn't safe for her to be alone with him. Mr. R. responded to this change by spitting in Frieda's face and then trying to strangle her.

When he wasn't overtly violent, Mr. R. was passively aggressive. He sat with his eyes closed and wore ear plugs to sessions. He rarely answered when Frieda spoke to him and mumbled despite her acknowledged hearing difficulties. Underlying all this belligerence was a connection equally intense for the two of them.

Their relationship had begun in more promising fashion. Brought to the Lodge against his will, from a great distance, Mr. R. arrived accompanied by detectives his father had hired to "make sure he was all right" during the preceding months. When Frieda first saw him, he seemed to have no idea where he was, blurting out questions about who ran the Lodge and whether Frieda was related to his previous doctors. The questions themselves made sense, but were interspersed among what appeared to be random comments—"I want to be at a place where they give me decent razors"—which made it hard to tell what he really wanted. Frieda gave a direct reply to every question, insisting on principle that patients were entitled to know basic facts about those treating them and how the hospital operated. She didn't give false reassurances and never resorted to euphemism. When Mr. R. said, "All I need is a rest and not all these screwballs on the ward," Frieda responded: "You know very well that this is not a place for rest, but a mental hospital, for treatment." When he asked if she were married and to whom, she told him the truth, commenting later in her notes: "He is encouraged to ask whatever he wants to know about me, since he is justified in wanting to be informed if he decides to go into the adventure of working with me."[45] When Mr. R. suddenly burst out, "You don't like me," and accused Frieda of lumping him with "other screwballs," she responded warmly: "I have spent 40 years of my life with 'screwballs' because I like them enough to be concerned about their misery." This seemed to reassure him. In a revealing interchange, he told her: "I was brought here against my will." She said: "And you are mad about it." He answered: "No. I am not mad but I am angry." By the end of this first session, Mr. R. had relaxed enough to compliment Frieda on her "nice office" and spend a few minutes "giggling together [with her] about the nurse reading magazines in the waiting room," forced to cool her heels while they continued talking beyond the scheduled hour.

Frieda was initially optimistic about Mr. R. She had just completed the last, outpatient phase of Joanne Greenberg's treatment and was struck by certain similarities between them. True, Mr. R. was paranoid (a far worse symptom than any of Joanne's), but he was highly verbal and had managed reasonably well for many more years than she had. Frieda was able to use interpretation often with Mr. R. and to rely on his ability to think conceptually (as she had with Joanne). Paranoia has a better prognosis than other types of schizophrenia, and Frieda thought Mr. R.'s fear and rage were close enough to the surface to be analyzed successfully and worked through.

Yet many of his comments were violent, and he frequently threatened both her and Bullard. Frieda tried to deal matter-of-factly with this. In one poignant moment, Mr. R. mentioned Rockefeller Center amid a flood of accusations and Frieda asked if he liked music. Clearly moved, he responded: "If you would have asked me that in the beginning instead of seeing my parents before you saw me, we would have gotten off to a better start." Frieda agreed, apologized for having failed to realize this, and said she hoped her understanding of his feelings was now more evident.

But things soon deteriorated, with Mr. R. alternating between the angry confrontation and sullen silence that were to mark his sessions with Frieda for the next several years. (We don't know much about the details, since most records from this period have disappeared.) In 1956, Marvin Adland, then the clinical director, asked colleagues whether the Lodge was "justified in continuing its efforts to treat this patient." Bullard wondered if he was suggesting there had been no progress. Adland replied: "I'll put it this way. I think Frieda feels *she* understands *him* better." So far as Adland could see, however, Mr. R. remained "the same isolated person . . . [whose] communications to [Frieda] are cryptic, symbolic, half-sentences which she feels she can intuitively make some sense out of." Adland adored Frieda (who was away at the time of this meeting) and in no sense meant this as an attack on her. But it must have sounded like one. Harold Searles, defending her from this rare slight, said Mr. R. was showing a classic pattern of therapeutic regression. A patient this ill could recover only by relaxing his defenses enough to let in some of his anguish. His appearing more disturbed was actually a sign of progress. Searles thought Mr. R. was "very definitely coming out of the woods" but hadn't yet "passed the turning point; the turn was coming on." He said Frieda had done "quite an impressive job" of getting him to be less assaultive.

But others wondered whether this was improvement or a sign of Mr. R.'s hopelessness. He had been at the Lodge for more than three years by that point. There had certainly been moments when he participated actively in treatment. He lashed out at his father and spoke of the voices that tormented him. But five minutes later, he would disappear into what Adland called "a silence that is more than just a silence—more than just a withholding of material—a very autistic, probably hallucinatory state."[46]

Since Adland was the clinical director and his concerns couldn't be ignored, a compromise was reached, and Mr. R. was made a research subject. From then on, his therapy hours with Frieda were tape-recorded, transcribed verbatim, and distributed to the entire medical staff. In addition, in response to formal written instructions from Bullard, she dictated "her impressions of the hours" in daily process notes. (To ensure the "freshness" of these impressions, a secretary was sent over immediately after each session to take her dictation.)[47] Frieda was confident of her abilities, but this intense scrutiny must have made her extremely anxious.

It clearly made Mr. R. worse. He spoke in cryptic phrases. Silences often lasted ten minutes. He was less assaultive than he had been when he first arrived, but there were still times when he tried to lift Frieda's skirt or touch her inappropriately. (On one such occasion, as she reported in her notes: "I finally gave him a light slap on his hand. He said in utter surprise, but without any sign of being hurt, 'you hurt me.' I answered, 'I didn't hurt you. I just gave you a light slap on your hand since you seem not to understand my verbal communications.'")[48]

They did, however, have their little rituals, like smoking cigarettes and eating candy together. Frieda, ever the analyst, let no detail pass uninterpreted. "If he is on fine terms with me," she told colleagues, "he has me light his cigarette; if he is on medium good terms with me, he takes the match out of my hand which I offer him; if he feels distant, he refuses and lights his own match." They also shared some classic Lodge moments. Once the window was open in the office where they met. It was January and very windy, and Frieda asked Mr. R. if he would mind closing it. He ignored her. She tried to do it herself, but was too short to reach the handle. "I did not want to give him the show to climb on a chair, because I didn't know whatever feelings or fantasies that might elicit in him," Frieda wrote in her notes, "so I put on my coat and wore it for the rest of the session."[49]

Since Mr. R. said so little, Frieda had to depend on subtleties of action, like whether he let her unwrap a piece of candy or called her "Frieda" rather than the more distant "Dr. Fromm-Reichmann." She often spoke as if expressions that appeared "for a second on his face" had an unambiguous meaning ("his face said . . ." was a frequent locution in her notes). In a session where Mr. R. seemed willing to take a cigarette only if she told him to, she remarked: "You want to be ordered to do pleasant things so that nobody will know how much you want them." He responded with "a big smile." She smiled back. He said, "I don't see anything funny about this" and blushed deeply. Then he wrinkled his forehead, Frieda later wrote, "as though trying to make this mimic confirmation undone. . . . [He is] mad, yet at the same time keeps a smiling expression on his face, especially around the eyes."[50]

Frieda was capable of noticing extraordinarily subtle communication, but it's impossible to know to what extent the patient concurred with her interpretations. (Greenberg would argue when she thought Frieda was wrong about something; Mr. R. never did this.) Once Frieda commented impatiently, "Oh, get it out," referring to some feeling she assumed he had, only to castigate herself immediately for "wording [this] invitation to talk in such a fool's way," which Mr. R. "would inevitably translate as an invitation to exhibit himself." After reading these notes, Don Burnham criticized Frieda's "assigning herself such a large area in what she assumes to be the patient's referential world." It was as if the constant scrutiny of their work together made Frieda unable to see any influence but hers. Even more problematic, the same Frieda who interpreted barely perceptible aspects of Mr. R.'s feelings ignored his repeated, explicit requests to get rid of the tape recorder. As Burnham noted, the microphone had become "a double bind—he is told he can pull it out if he wishes, but at the same time, whenever he does so he is criticized."[51]

Mr. R. constantly searched the room for hidden cameras, wires in the walls, or other means of spying on him. Frieda told him there were no such things, only the microphone in plain sight, but he never believed her. She seemed more sensitive to his persecutory feelings outside the therapy hour, for instance, taking care to ensure that Mr. R. didn't have escorts on the grounds, something that clearly upset him (hardly surprising, given his experience of being "escorted" by detectives during his journey to the Lodge).

Was it Frieda's own insecurity about the lack of progress in this treatment that kept her from challenging her colleagues' decision to tape the sessions? If she had simply told Adland and Bullard directly that tape-recording a highly suspicious patient against his stated wishes was ethically questionable and antitherapeutic, there is little doubt they would at least have reconsidered. Her failure to do this, and her repeated insensitivity to Mr. R.'s requests to unplug the microphone, poignantly illustrate how trapped Frieda became by the impossible expectations she and everyone else had for her.

Part of what makes psychotherapy with a paranoid person so difficult is that any hint of a warm and friendly relationship feels terrifying to him. The therapist is in a delicate position: needing to get close enough to be trusted but not being able to be open about this. In a general interview about her methods of treatment, Frieda talked at length about Mr. R., saying that things went better when she gave him "a good shout," thereby creating a sharp enough boundary for him to tolerate the anxiety of being there with her.[52] Instead of directly admitting her affection for him (as she did with Joanne and Miss N.), Frieda did little things for Mr. R. she thought would please him. She served him candy and complimented him on his clothes. After the Virginia Rounds he preferred were discontinued in the Rockville cigarette shop, she went to a special store in Washington and bought him some. But when he refused to respond to her overtures, she grew uncharacteristically irritated. His sitting with his eyes shut particularly got to her. "If you close [your eyes], it is like opening the door to apparitions and things like that," she snapped one day. "If you open them, it is to open the door to contact with a real person. Did you hear me? It's a prescription, for heaven's sake. You're talking with a doctor, or the doctor is talking with you, I should better say." Later in the same hour: "Hey, you are here with another person. You can withdraw into your shell all the rest of the day, but for heaven's sake, don't do it during this hour." Mr. R.'s repeated failure to respond to these injunctions seemed to have no effect on her.[53]

Frieda was equally impatient with his absences and frequent attempts to leave before the end of the session. Instead of focusing on how frightened Mr. R. clearly felt, she chastised him for not adhering to standard therapy practices. Once when he sent word that he wasn't going to show up that day, Frieda told the nurse that "he better get ready and quick." When ward staff said he was still in bed, Frieda announced she would be in his room in ten minutes (this was to give him time to get dressed if he wanted to). When they began to talk, Mr. R. said, "It takes a sucker to have these interviews," perhaps the greatest understatement ever made about their work together. Frieda replied: "Who is the sucker, you or I?" But for once, this didn't turn into another fruitless power struggle. Mr. R. said the reason he didn't want to come was that he had given up hope that he would ever get better. He said the Lodge was keeping him there for the money and he would never live outside a hospital. Frieda responded very seriously to all this, reminding Mr. R. "that he must leave the decision about whether or not it can be done to her, just as he would leave the decision about the need for an operation to the surgeon." She reiterated, as she always did when patients became discouraged, that the very fact she was making time to see him was proof of her belief in his ability to recover. The Lodge had a long waiting list, she continued, and didn't need to keep patients who couldn't benefit from its services.[54]

But this frank exchange was an exception; most of the time, they couldn't hear each other. Frieda often literally resorted to shouting to keep Mr. R. from walking out in the first five minutes. On one especially bad day, he returned for a short while, then left again. She ended up running awkwardly down the hall after him as he yelled: "I won't come back today and I won't come back any other day. Go to hell!"[55]

Frieda did take Mr. R.'s threats of violence seriously and was careful never to position herself so that he might injure her. For example, when he pressed her one day to unplug the microphone, she refused to do it until he sat down to avoid having her back to him. This was for his protection as well as hers; Frieda was convinced that psychotic patients could never trust therapists who let them lose control of themselves.

At a certain point, Mr. R. stopped eating and lost a lot of weight. This seemed to be a direct response to his father's having taunted him: "I pay all that money, and what are you doing—not eating your fill? Not taking advantage of what I pay for? You should eat as much as you can."[56] Having been forcibly brought to the Lodge—by detectives, no less—Mr. R. may have regarded the whole situation as his parents' way of punishing him. Refusing to allow Frieda or anyone else to have much effect on him may have been his only means of retaliating against them.

Her irritation at being his punching bag was exacerbated by the pressures she felt for success in this case. Frieda was famous by the 1950s, and foundations were offering her unsolicited grants to study patients like Mr. R. There was a huge interest in finding effective treatments for schizophrenia, and if it turned out that Frieda was onto something, people wanted to be able to say they had supported her (drug researchers were the other major beneficiaries of such hopes). Yet unsolicited grants can be a mixed blessing. They free recipients to do the things they're most interested in, but they also create incredible pressure for results at a point when there might not yet be any. Transforming her intuitions into testable hypotheses was not something that came easily to Frieda. She was philosophically an empiricist, absolutely convinced that one day it would be possible to explain precisely how psychotherapy worked. But she was a lot better at doing therapy than describing it, and psychiatry defined "success" as being on the cutting edge of theory, not helping patients. The fact that Frieda shared these values didn't help matters.[57]

She did, however, have the scientist's urge to turn every puzzle into a research project. Like Harold Searles's later treatment of Mrs. Douglas, her work with Mr. R. became more of an opportunity to learn than a way to help him. In both cases, the patient's lack of response to treatment made them especially useful as research subjects. One seldom studies successes in science; failures are far more likely to be instructive.

The intense scrutiny of her work with Mr. R., however, put so much pressure on Frieda that it inhibited her. She made fewer off-the-cuff moves, went more by the book; the contrast to her style with Greenberg couldn't have been starker. Clarence Schulz later said that Mr. R.'s case got so much attention at the Lodge that it started to be viewed as "the definitive treatment."[58] But for psychotherapy to work, the therapist has to feel relaxed and secure enough to improvise. Perhaps no one could have succeeded with Mr. R.—a patient who actively resisted treatment, whose illness was chronic, and whose relationship to everyone was sullen and hostile. But when Frieda found herself unable to do much with him, the added stress of having the sessions recorded, transcribed verbatim, and distributed to all her colleagues must have made the failure seem even worse. When Mr. R. protested the taping, she often said that *she* needed it regardless of whether he did, a painful sign of how anxious she was. Frieda had a flair for the dramatic, but being pushed into the spotlight seemed to make her want to run off the stage.

Ultimately she just trudged along. It was as if she had decided at some level that so long as she kept at it with her usual diligence, her colleagues wouldn't criticize her. At one point she described herself as a kind of postman, there "rain or shine" for their sessions, with every missed hour carefully made up. Mr. R. seemed to think his only duty was to sit there. He frequently kept his eyes closed or appeared for sessions wearing ear plugs. Although this was an act that fairly leaped from the couch—evoking Frieda's prominent, if ineffective hearing aids and Mr. R.'s complex feelings about them—astonishingly, neither she nor her colleagues ever commented on this. Frieda interpreted Mr. R.'s ear plugs only as one of his ways of "tuning her out."

Equally puzzling, she often acted as if Mr. R. were capable of understanding intricate details of scheduling even when his grasp of other events was clearly limited. Over and over in her articles on technique, Frieda instructed therapists to take a flexible attitude toward arranging sessions with schizophrenic patients because of the confused meanings that time may have for them. Yet when Mr. R. seemed unable to keep track of her complicated arrangement for making up hours missed because of her frequent out-of-town lecturing trips, she expressed only irritation. In one set of notes, for example, she made it sound as if his anger and confusion about these interruptions was completely unjustified; two pages later, she described him as too disorganized to light a cigarette.

Part of the reason Frieda was reluctant to give up on Mr. R. was that he was one of very few schizophrenic patients in the early 1950s never to have received shock or any other somatic treatment. This made him a "pure case" to assess the effects of psychotherapy. He was also fairly young, well educated, and verbal, all good indicators for a response to talk therapy. Despite Mr. R.'s persistent belief that the Lodge was primarily interested in making money off him, he was kept for some months at a below-cost rate when his family ran into financial difficulties.

The problem, as Adland noted in a staff meeting, was that Mr. R. had settled into a fixed pattern in which "there wasn't much anxiety available to him." For a patient to benefit from intensive psychotherapy, he has to be in enough anguish to want to change. But Frieda argued that Mr. R.'s constant acting out—especially his attempts to masturbate during sessions or attack her—were gestures, albeit distorted, of his desire for a closer relationship. And his fragmentary, jumbled speech was, she hypothesized, a way to convey the confusion he felt about his life. Frieda also emphasized the realistic basis for Mr. R.'s fears. Anyone with a father who hired detectives to follow them on dates would be frightened of relationship.[59] She thought that with time and steadfastness, he might come to realize that not everybody was out to get him (even people who were taping him against his wishes). Perhaps at some level, this paranoid young man also reminded her of Hermann Brunck, and she was both reenacting her feelings about him and atoning for that earlier failure by refusing to give up.

Psychiatry's most tragic truth is that psychosis is resistant to every form of treatment, and the longer a patient is ill, the less likely any method is to work. Physicians in state hospitals took this as justification for abandoning chronic cases, an attitude that was understandable given the overwhelming numbers of patients they had to deal with. But for Frieda, the more salient fact was that some patients *did* respond to treatment; even if their numbers were small, their existence couldn't be omitted from the picture. She thought it was frankly unethical for psychiatrists to act as if they could tell in advance whether a particular patient was likely to respond. This was a prediction no one, she included, was capable of making with any confidence.

Frieda wasn't the pollyanna her detractors have made her out to be. She readily acknowledged the poor prognosis of most schizophrenic patients and didn't expect to perform miracles in treatment. Her dogged persistence with a person like Mr. R. can easily be ridiculed as "madness on the couch," to use one recent phrase. But a more nuanced analysis raises difficult questions: What if Mr. R. were another Joanne Greenberg, with the potential to emerge from his illness and lead a productive life? It could take years for a psychosis to develop; why assume that a patient was beyond hope because he failed to show an immediate response? And once Frieda had taken Mr. R. on as her patient, wasn't she morally obligated to do whatever she could to try to reach him?

Frieda was a highly pragmatic woman, with a clear awareness of her own limitations and a long waiting list. We can stand back now and criticize her for wasting time with people like Miss N. and Mr. R., who resisted all her efforts and seemed only to get worse. But at the time, there was no way to know whether they would respond, and if either of them had improved to the point of being able to live outside a hospital, Frieda's treatment would have been seen as *both* humane and economical. Somatic treatments were quicker and cheaper than psychotherapy when they worked, but when they didn't, which was far more often than their advocates liked to admit, the costs, both psychic and financial, of keeping patients on back wards for the rest of their lives were enormous. For Frieda, several agonizing years spent trying to rescue someone from that fate was time well spent if there was even a chance that she might succeed.

11

The Luxury of Guilt

There is no obstacle that one cannot overcome, for the obstacle is only there for the sake of the will, and in reality there are no obstacles save in the spirit.[1]

In the heady days when Frieda first arrived in America and she and Dexter Bullard plunged into the pioneering work of creating a psychoanalytic hospital that could treat schizophrenics, the obstacles to this goal seemed solely pragmatic. They needed to attract a staff committed to hard work and open to experiment, willing to follow patients into the depths of their illness. And they needed to convince families already frightened by the craziness of their relatives that further regression—in the controlled environment of the Lodge—could be therapeutic.

By the mid-1940s, these goals had been reached to an extent that amazed Bullard's competitors. Applications poured in from staff at every level. Prospective patients waited months for a bed. Frieda's papers were cited as landmark contributions to the psychiatric literature, and Chestnut Lodge was hailed around the world as a place where even the sickest patients could be helped.

Within a decade, however, things began to deteriorate. More and more chronic patients were admitted. Staff became competitive and dispirited. Some of the best physicians left; others escaped into research or administration. There was constant tension over the Bullard family's ownership. Nurses on the disturbed ward found themselves having to work overtime because so many patients were violent; at one point some patients had to sleep in the ward's living room because there weren't enough rooms for everyone who needed to be locked up.

In 1953, "a polio-like virus" spread among the staff, affecting almost half the nurses and attendants. After examinations of spinal fluid proved negative and no one died, the "epidemic" was relabeled "hysteria." Head nurse Margaret Ursell recalled this difficult period: "We worked very hard, very long hours. I lived in Upper Cottage. We were too close. There was . . . there was too much. . . . I don't want to call it incest, but too much closeness. Later on, I had to move across the street. There was just too much intensity among the staff."[2]

Patient care was still highly individualized, but Frieda's personal influence on treatment style was weakened by an increasingly complex bureaucracy. Committees proliferated to the point that an "interdepartmental committee" had to be created just to keep track of things. New organizational structures were constantly being proposed, sometimes by internal Lodge task forces and sometimes by outside consultants hired specifically for this purpose. Energy that had previously gone into caring for patients was devoted to reports and procedures. The number of hours allocated to each patient per day was calculated to two decimal points, the dietary department started counting the number of meals served, and nurses tabulated the percentage of patients in cold wet sheet packs. As school children across America were being taught to "duck and cover," the Interdepartmental Committee was instructing staff and patients at Chestnut Lodge on civil defense procedures: "Lie flat on the floor next to the walls, facing Washington," read one manual (whether this had some specific health benefit or was a symbolic gesture, like facing Mecca, wasn't indicated).

Amid all the bureaucracy, people struggled to hold on to the psychoanalytic ethos. A ward administrator who recommended the firing of a nurse justified his request with a two-page, single-spaced account of his own anxieties and the symbolic significance of the events for all concerned. Therapists dictated reams of process notes on the details of analytic work. Every case conference was tape-recorded, transcribed verbatim, and circulated to the entire medical staff. Many patients had files three or four inches thick, and there seemed to be no limit to what was considered relevant. (One Lodge typist recalled sitting with her fingers poised over the typewriter keys ready to transcribe tapes of therapy hours and hearing nothing but the grunts of a mute woman.) Even the supervisor of the woodworking shop included psychoanalytic interpretations in her monthly reports.

In the broader psychiatric world of the 1950s, however, mental hospitals were increasingly being accused of promoting passivity, perpetuating pa-

tients' illnesses, and destroying their capacity to live in the world. "The institution," a British psychiatrist asserted, "has the power to mould patients into
the type best suited for its purpose. . . . For those who are predisposed, the
danger is most acute."[3]

So, in that spirit of experiment Frieda had always encouraged in her colleagues, Jan Foudraine decided to turn one of the Lodge's wards for chronic
schizophrenics into a model of independent living. He began with small
steps, like having nurses toss keys to patients so they could unlock a door
themselves, instead of waiting for staff to do it for them. He let patients who
wanted to help with routine ward duties answer telephones or distribute mail.
When shifts changed and nurses gave their report, Foudraine allowed patients to participate in these discussions if they so chose. (In the beginning,
staff were threatened by this, but eventually they came to appreciate the insightful contributions patients often made.) Nurses taught those who could
manage it to make their own beds and dress more attractively. Patients were
also encouraged to assist one another, giving them further opportunities to be
useful. (Sometimes staff who had "compulsive needs to help" opposed these
efforts, but patients seemed to appreciate being more independent.)

When Foudraine got carried away and renamed his ward a "school for living" and insisted patients refer to one another as "fellow students," the
process disintegrated. Patients were offended by his claim that "there was no
such thing as mental illness," and nurses resented his efforts to remold them
as "assistant educators." Psychiatrists visiting from other institutions asked
confidentially whether Foudraine was still in analysis. Eventually he realized
why his experiment had failed:

> To name a schizophrenic patient a "student" is denying his despair and
> serious incapacity. In denying his despair I was not only denying the
> extent of what was called his "psychopathology" but also my own de-
> spair about him. . . . I was acting as if I believed that these people would
> "straighten themselves out by telling them to shape up."

Yet for all his naiveté, Foudraine had put his finger on a crucial problem—
one that grew more acute throughout the 1950s. "The nearer a community
gets to the ideal," he reflected, "the more protected and secure one feels in it.
Despite efforts to counter this sheltered condition, the sense of security, of
being well taken care of, creeps in." If Frieda achieved her goal of creating a
truly therapeutic community, neither patients nor staff would ever want to
leave it.[4]

Alfred Stanton stepped into the middle of this paradox, setting into motion a series of events that forever changed the Lodge. Frustrated by Bullard's penchant for overturning his decisions and increasingly skeptical of psycho-analytic work with schizophrenics, Stanton began searching for alternative models of hospital treatment. In particular, he wanted to find a better way of conceptualizing the institution's role in the patient's illness.

Heavily influenced by social theorists of the Chicago school like George Herbert Mead (whose ideas Sullivan had always emphasized), Stanton argued that symptoms might be "a type of participation in the social process," not "entities residing within a person."[5] He took the bold step of hiring Morrie Schwartz, a Chicago-trained sociologist, to initiate a formal study of this process.

Working from the assumption that "at least some aspects of the disturbances of patients are a part of the functioning of the institution," Stanton and Schwartz hypothesized that Sullivan's extraordinarily high percentage of recoveries at Sheppard in the 1920s was a function not only of his clinical skill but of "the therapeutic effectiveness of an institution more adequately organized toward the achievement of its goals." Insisting that even the most disturbed patient was not psychotic at every moment, they suggested that variations in the severity of symptoms might be linked to events on the ward. Just as slips of the tongue could reveal the unconscious of an individual, the "mistakes" of an institution might have "a structure, a meaning, and at times a recognizable purpose."[6]

Armed with one of the first federal grants ever awarded in psychiatry, Stanton set out to transform the fourth floor from a disturbed ward to a social science laboratory. With Schwartz as a full-time sociological observer (whose thousands of pages of notes documented every detail of life at the Lodge), and a staff of research assistants, statisticians, and consultants, Stanton's project quickly became the largest, most systematic study of a mental hospital ever conducted.[7]

The most striking finding to emerge from the early stages of the research was that misunderstandings among staff—especially covert disagreements—could produce or aggravate a patient's symptoms. Even classic signs of psychosis—confusion, panic attacks, regression—could be directly linked to conflicts among staff. Since the participants in this collective process were never consciously aware of their part in it, the system continued despite its destructiveness. In other words, some of what appeared to be patients' craziness was really their response to problems on the ward. The power of this finding was dramatically illustrated when covert disagreements were brought out into the open (typically through the intervention of one of the re-

searchers), and a patient's symptom immediately disappeared, to the astonishment of everyone. Stanton and Schwartz argued that patients were essentially a "substitute channel of communication," expressing in action what
staff couldn't put into words. When disagreements were directly expressed,
patients no longer needed to do this.[8]

Even very severe symptoms like incontinence could be related to events
on the ward. Schwartz kept meticulous notes on several patients who frequently urinated or defecated in their rooms or on the hall, and demonstrated
conclusively that when their specific requests were met, they never did this.
Several of these patients were participants in Frieda's group therapy experiment, and in that context, their behavior was also noticeably different. As
Schwartz noted: "The attitude of the therapist was one of encouragement and
expectation that the patients could and would do better. Respect and consideration were shown for their needs. No sanctions were brought to bear for
their incontinence; instead an attempt was made to understand it. In this context incontinent behavior rarely occurred." It was when patients' needs were
ignored that regression was observed. "When the patient feels she doesn't
belong—is out of place in the social situation—she responds with an 'out-of-
place' participation." Sometimes the urination expressed anger, sometimes
sexual feelings; sometimes it was a substitute for crying or other forms of release. This finding had striking implications: rather than being an uncontrollable symptom of psychosis, incontinence functioned as a significant, albeit
obscure, "form of social participation."[9]

Since Stanton was administering the women's disturbed ward throughout
the period of the research, he could systematically show that much of the violence there could be stopped by appropriate changes in the social context.
Even collective disturbances, in which many patients on the ward simultaneously "exploded," turned out to have "a structure, which was shaped by all
the participants, representing a type of informal organization" temporarily
replacing the staff-imposed system.[10]

Stanton and Schwartz's research had a volatile effect on the Lodge. Their
sociological focus was a direct challenge to the psychoanalytic ethos, suggesting that patients needed a changed environment more than they needed
therapy. The study turned what had previously been personal grievances into
principled opposition, becoming the leading edge of an internal reform
movement. Staff meetings became so acrimonious that former Lodge physicians who had left for private practice had to be brought in to mediate. (Naturally, these sessions were recorded and transcribed for further analysis.)
Frieda was conveniently absent from these meetings (it was August and she

was in Santa Fe). Since even her best efforts at peacemaking would likely have had little effect, she was probably relieved to be spared the pain of watching the place she had so painstakingly constructed rip itself to shreds.

In one particularly difficult meeting, Herb Staveren accused the Lodge of holding on to patients "the way neurotic parents hung on to their children." Harold Searles said this showed the staff's own need for protection, for a secure cocoon in which to do very difficult work. But Staveren retorted that something more insidious was at work: the assumption that "people get worse before they can get better" was so strong that patients who didn't do this on their own had the Lodge do it for them. Jarl Dyrud, whose status as Bullard's son-in-law put him in an especially conflicted position, confessed that he had been more successful at the VA hospital than he had been at the Lodge. "I found upon coming out here that not only did I feel more under attack, more insecure, more threatened in general, I have also felt that my work with patients went downhill." The Lodge, Dyrud seemed to be saying, might simply be too intense a place to work.[11]

Staff clearly felt threatened. Even Mabel Cohen, whom everyone considered grounded and thoughtful, admitted: "I do think there is some chronic thing in the air around here that brings in that feeling of fault which is very poisonous." Searles thought this might be an expression of the staff's feelings of futility—since it was unacceptable to express anger toward patients, staff attacked one another. Expectations were so high and patients were so sick that the effort to treat them created impossible demands. As each staff member's insecurity mounted, he became less able to confide in colleagues and more competitive.

People increasingly behaved like squabbling siblings vying for Frieda's and Dexter's approbation. Their feelings of dependency were intensified by the fact that younger staff were themselves patients in analysis. A common response to disagreements in meetings was for someone to say: "Let's let each one take it up with his analyst." From Stanton's point of view, this was precisely the problem: people ignored the larger institutional issues and cast every difficulty in psychodynamic terms.[12]

Staff clearly felt trapped by their own expectations. They were supposed to be "perfect parents" who, according to "a legendary Lodge myth," were capable of curing their unloved schizophrenics. Given how sick most patients were and how little control staff had over fundamental structures of the hospital, it was no wonder they resorted, as Dyrud put it, to "talking psychodynamics out of the feeling of despair over doing anything about the reality situation."[13]

One of the staff's main sources of anxiety was not knowing what the criteria for evaluation were. This was by design: Frieda and Bullard had a very strong bias toward hiring people and then "letting them flounder and see what they actually did." They said they learned as much by seeing how the person "came through the floundering process" as by any standard measure. Since they didn't see experience in other psychiatric settings as a good predictor of success at the Lodge—both because the patients were so much sicker and because the psychoanalytic approach was so radically different— they made their best judgment about someone at the time they applied, and then waited to see what actually happened when they started work.

Frieda had taught Bullard to take the same attitude toward patients. "There isn't any way of assessing the potential prognosis of a patient except as observed *here,*" he insisted. This attitude openly conflicted with the wishes of most staff, who sought to admit patients based on their likelihood of benefiting from psychotherapy. But to Frieda and Dexter, this was irrelevant. "Our philosophy is that no patient is incurable; that is, the right person, the right therapist, can succeed with [that person]."[14]

These attitudes about patients and staff were consistent. People who seemed to have the potential to do good work were hired regardless of their track record elsewhere. Patients were admitted even if they hadn't responded to other treatments. Then the two groups were thrown together to see who could swim. A few did, but what more often happened was that patients tread water and staff drowned in their own guilt.

Bluntly put, the problem was that there was only one Frieda. Lodge staff in the 1950s were talented and deeply interested in work with very sick patients, but this didn't mean people knew what they were doing. They shared a commitment to the ideal that, in principle, every patient could be reached, but they differed widely in style, technique, and natural ability. And as Don Bloch pointed out in a staff meeting, structural forces kept people from working most efficiently:

For Dexter to be able to take nice young, fresh schizophrenics who will be out of the hospital in three to six months and then will need four years of outpatient treatment, he has to plan on having an outpatient department the size of a small town. . . . If we're going to keep the staff down to a moderate size, there has to be a fairly large proportion of chronic patients who don't get well fast. We have to have a fairly large proportion of patients who don't get well at all. Because if this hospital were filled with patients who were moved along so that you could treat new patients, we would in no time at all just simply be swamped; it would be impossible for us to keep the hospital open.

Bloch said that under such circumstances, it was better for evaluation criteria not to be explicit. "This condition of uncertainty and of things never being really clarified . . . enables me to conceal my grave errors."[15]

People constantly struggled to define their roles. Were they Bullard's employees or his symbolic sons? Were they parents to the patients or siblings to each other? Was Frieda their advocate or their mother? When things were going well, everybody wanted to be part of "the Lodge family," but when a crisis occurred—like the suicide or rape of a patient—there was a "collapse of the family group" and a sense of tremendous isolation. Just as patients were unconsciously frightened by their own omnipotence, the staff seemed terrified that they might be blamed for the failures that inevitably occurred. In one of her classic statements, Frieda pronounced guilt feelings "an unconstructive, paralyzing luxury, which should be discouraged in doctors as well as in their patients." This made people even more defensive: they couldn't succeed at their work, yet feeling guilty was a further sign of failure.[16]

Each staff member was left to find his own way of coping with the craziness of this situation. Some became overwhelmed and escaped to private practice or less stressful places like McLean or Austen Riggs. Dexter and Frieda set aside these feelings and focused on running the Lodge. Others defended against their own anguish by analyzing its meaning for the patient (Harold Searles was the master at this) or its implications for the hospital (Stanton's whole research project was an example of this). Whatever their individual responses, everyone on the staff participated in creating institutional structures—committees, subcommittees, research seminars, discussion groups—that could absorb and diffuse some of the intensity. These structures protected therapists from bearing the full brunt of their patients' pathology and gave everyone an enormous amount of busywork that helped to keep them from becoming completely overwhelmed. Although David Rioch often objected to this process of "institutionalizing individual problems," it was clearly essential in allowing staff to work for long periods with patients so seriously disturbed.[17]

At times, however, these defenses were so efficient they allowed ambitions to rise to absurd proportions. A therapist who complained that he was getting nowhere with a patient admitted as an "experiment in handling a lobotomy case" was told that a "time-out" from treatment might allow him to resume the work "from a fresh viewpoint."[18] Having embraced the principle that no patient was beyond hope, staff seemed unable to draw the line even at those for whom intensive psychotherapy was clearly inappropriate.

And yet, incredibly enough, people fought to stay on the staff. When a committee Harold Searles chaired in 1951 polled each individual regarding

his or her ideas about the the hospital and personal plans, six of the fifteen
full-time psychiatrists said they hoped to remain at Chestnut Lodge for five
years or more. The remaining nine said they would stay if certain changes
were made. "No one felt that they would have to leave because the Lodge
could not meet his or her needs." Searles said that when he went over these
results with Frieda, even she "expressed astonishment" at so uniformly positive a response.[19] But this surprising degree of commitment exposed an underlying irony of the institution's structure. It wasn't actually in Bullard's
interest to have a staff so satisfied that people stayed indefinitely. Indeed, this
would create an unresolvable conflict between financial interests and clinical
needs. Like Menninger and Riggs, the Lodge relied on a large number of
young physicians paid a fraction of what their more experienced colleagues
earned. The only way the place could afford to sustain so ambitious a treatment program was to have a few senior staff like Frieda who were paid at
higher levels (like tenured faculty) and a larger, relatively transient, younger
staff who stayed a few years and then moved on. One of the main dissatisfactions expressed in Searles's poll was the lack of sufficient time for research,
but from a financial perspective, it was not in Bullard's interest to provide
this (except for Frieda, who worked out a special arrangement in which she
worked only part-time on the clinical staff but received a full salary, with half
of her time going to research and writing).

Frieda's suggestions for change were, not surprisingly, conceived within
the status quo. She had no reason to oppose it and didn't, and Dexter relied
on her loyalty. Her working conditions were ideal: she was neither the owner
nor one of Bullard's scrapping sons. Her major suggestion in Searles's poll
was to allow physicians to write reports during working hours instead of having to do them at home.

The creation of the Chestnut Lodge Research Institute in 1955 was intended to dissipate some of the staff's resentment and respond to calls for a
more formal research program.[20] To allow the institute to receive grants from
the federal government, it was incorporated as a separate nonprofit entity.
(Dexter was still president and Anne was treasurer, with David Rioch appointed vice president to preserve appearances.)

This was a brilliant move on the Bullards' part. It solved some of their
most vexing problems and strengthened support for the Lodge's approach.
By establishing a tax-exempt aspect of their operation, the Bullards could get
sizable amounts of outside funding that would never have come to a family
business. And by not turning their whole hospital into a foundation, Anne
and Dexter retained a degree of control far greater than that of the Menningers. The Research Institute gave those Lodge psychiatrists Dexter

wanted to keep an appealing alternative to private practice. Most important, it allowed him to claim that the increasingly lengthy stays of Lodge patients were part of a long-term effort to understand psychotic illnesses, not simply a way for his family to build their profit base.

In a proposal to the Ford Foundation, Bullard recast the entire treatment program as part of the research effort. With the organized hindsight of the grant proposal writer, he said clinical work at the Lodge had for thirty years been "devoted to experiments with the psychoanalytic approach to the psychoses and to appraisal of its suitability and usefulness as a method of therapy." He made it sound as if Frieda had come specifically to pursue "clinical investigations of schizophrenia and, to a lesser degree, of the manic-depressive reactions." He said that in work with Sullivan and others, Lodge researchers had developed "a theory of communication which results from an intensive study of the psychotherapeutic process and the setting in which it takes place." Hailing "the freedom which Chestnut Lodge affords to staff members to pursue their research interests" and the extent to which they "have learned to tolerate an unusual degree of frankness in their exchanges with each other," Bullard portrayed the institute as uniquely suited to carry out a systematic program of psychiatric research. Beating out 200 other applicants and representing one of only four nonuniversity-based programs chosen for funding, he was awarded $250,000 over five years.[21]

At the heart of these struggles in the 1950s was a fundamental ambiguity in Lodge treatment philosophy. On the one hand, staff subscribed to Frieda's core assumption that no patient was ever beyond hope. As Bullard put it:

> As long as [he] can communicate anything, there is a possibility of effecting a change. One person may not be able to do it with this particular [patient], but as long as [he] is talking, there ought to be someone with whom, if he talks long enough, there is going to be a favorable change. That has been the fundamental philosophy or bullheadedness of keeping patients whether we have succeeded or not. . . . We don't know enough yet to be able to say why patients stay sick. Until we know that, we have no right to call them chronic and give up therapy.[22]

Yet refusing to give up conflicted with the natural desire of any physician for concrete results. In certain respects, standards were extremely low: so long as the patient was still talking, it remained possible he might improve. In a fond moment of recollection, Marvin Adland said, "We did look after each other. We protected each other. We listened to each other. And discussions were of a quality I rarely heard elsewhere. Sometimes we would laugh.

The conclusion after two hours of a staff conference would be, well, the patient is still breathing. Let's give it another few years."[23] Yet in other respects, expectations were unreachable. Lodge staff were being asked to cure the patients everyone else had given up on—not merely to patch them up and send them home, which would have been difficult enough, but to resolve the underlying problems that had made them ill in the first place.[24]

Martin Cooperman told this story. He was at a reception at Frieda's house and as the doctor on call, left for a while to attend to some crisis on the ward. When he returned, Frieda and Szalita were sitting by themselves talking nostalgically about the work. Szalita "waxed eloquent about treating regressed patients," recalling times when she had to see them in restraints because they were so disturbed, then later, seeing them progress to the point of coming to the office. Frieda burst out laughing: "How hungry we are for some little positive change! How good we feel about some tiny thing, but what are we really talking about here—a person who's still crazy, who is coming to your office on the grounds of a mental hospital with an escort." Cooperman always remembered this moment as an example of Frieda's sense of perspective and awareness that therapy was not "a nice simple mechanical something where you tighten up the screw and the bumper no longer rocks or makes a noise." But it also painfully illustrated how limited their successes often were. Working in an environment in which they were likely to fail and being implicitly encouraged to think of that failure as their own fault and never that of the patient was deeply disillusioning to staff. As one physician put it: "It's like being taught basic algebra and then being thrown into a nuclear physics laboratory and told to go to work. . . . People expect you to be able to do it."[25]

The increasing size of the Lodge also forced physicians to spend much of their time writing reports instead of treating patients. In striking contrast to the days of close, nonhierarchical relationships among staff, when doctors made time to come to the ward whenever they were needed, nurses in the 1950s complained that if they telephoned the physician on call at night, he would "snarl at them" and make clear he "didn't want to be bothered." More and more, interactions at the Lodge were like those in any complex bureaucracy, lacking the distinctive warmth and openness that had made them so effective in an earlier period. This was partly because there were so many disturbed patients, but it was also because staff were less confident that intensive psychotherapy could really work.[26]

· · ·

A major source of tension for all staff—doctors, social workers, nurses, typists, groundsworkers—were the Lodge's financial policies. Stanton and Schwartz had shown that problems about money often contributed to collective disturbances even when patients weren't aware of them. Since the Bullards insisted on keeping their affairs private—the only records to which the research team were denied access in their four years of work were financial—the staff were left to fantasize about how much each patient paid and what the hospital's profits were.

The actual situation was far different from what people imagined. In 1950, for example, 28 percent of all Lodge income went to nursing care, with an additional 22 percent going to salaries for physicians. And despite frequent rumors of patients being sent away as soon as they failed to pay their bills, there were a surprising number of below-cost cases. In 1951, when regular monthly rates were $950, some patients were paying as little as $125, and there was an average monthly loss of $4,000 from below-cost cases. One patient carried a debt of more than $9,000 without being discharged. Confidential memoranda in 1952 indicated that income from patients remained below budgeted amounts, but rather than charging higher rates or reducing the number of below-cost patients, the Finance Committee adopted such income-generating practices as raising the price of coffee for staff to ten cents for the second cup and imposing a charge of twenty dollars for outpatients who stayed overnight on the ward (the fee was reduced to ten dollars in certain cases). Annual gross income for the hospital was around $500,000 in this period, but net profits were only a tenth as much.

In 1958, Lew Garrison Coit, an investment analyst, was asked to assess the value of the Lodge. In the wonderful euphemisms of the financial world, Coit called "the nature of the business an uncommon one," and concluded in a statement far more prescient than he could ever have realized:

> As inflation continues, and taxes increase, the available funds of even the wealthy become restricted. As this takes place, more attention will be paid to public institutions. The prospective market for patients [at this] institution becomes even more limited, despite any desire on the part of families to secure this special care for their relatives. There is not, therefore, a mass market that is normally considered a desirable background for an earning asset. . . . Currently the inflationary forces are probably stronger than at any time in our history. We are becoming more and more of a socialistic state, and as we become more socialistic, we look to the State more and more for aid and assistance in welfare of all kinds.[27]

• • •

Frieda participated less and less in these struggles, and this whole period was an increasingly painful one for her. The psychoanalytic movement in America was openly battling over the question of what qualified as "real analysis," and she and the Washington-Baltimore Institute were among the first to be branded as "deviants." So at just the time that her major life accomplishment—creating the therapeutic community of the Lodge—was in danger of being dismissed as a failure, the field as a whole was being bitterly split.

This was the latest skirmish in an old war. Schisms had been part of psychoanalysis ever since Freud declared it to be as much a "movement" as a medical approach. Set up to function totally outside existing institutions, psychoanalysis had always had its own publishing houses, rules of membership, and approved doctrines. Freud's own feeling of ostracism from the Viennese medical establishment had made "loyalty to the persecuted leader" a key dynamic in the jockeying for power among his "followers." (These dynamics were so intense that Frieda's friend Edith Weigert remembered being plagued with guilt because she had once danced with Jung at an international conference while she was a student at the Berlin Institute.)[28]

Yet the same Freud who "excommunicated" those "disciples" who dared to disagree with him, called dissenters "immature," and pointed to their "unresolved oedipal rivalries," was also a dispassionate scientist, flexible in both technique and theory. These tensions in Freud's personality were continually recreated in analytic circles, leading to endless struggles about who had the right to wear the mantle of the "master." People like Frieda identified with the scientist in Freud and sought to emulate his systematic creativity. Others, especially refugee analysts in America, identified with his persecuted side and were always trying to protect "the pure gold of psychoanalysis" from contamination by "dissidents."

The problem was that no one could agree on how psychoanalysis should be defined or practiced. Freud had expelled Jung and Adler from the movement for failing to focus on sexual dynamics, but this wasn't a clear enough guideline to sort out other disputes. Freud's writings were like the Talmud, capable of being interpreted by each faction in support of its own views. This became painfully apparent in 1947, when the American Psychoanalytic Association appointed a committee to resolve fundamental issues. After four years of wrangling, its members issued a report that admitted, "It is impossible to find a definition of psychoanalysis that is acceptable to even a large group of members of the American Psychoanalytic Association."[29]

These issues came to a head when the explosive growth of training institutes after World War II required more uniformity in standards. The broad question, "What is psychoanalysis?" turned into, "Who can be an analyst?" "What curriculum should be taught to students?" and "When can a person graduate?" Since there were dozens of competing theoretical answers to these questions, operational criteria were simply imposed by legislative committees. Thus, seeing a patient a certain number of times a week, using the couch, remaining silent, having the work continue for a fixed number of hours over a specified period—these rules became the definition of "psychoanalysis." The problem was that Freud himself wasn't an "analyst" according to these criteria; he chatted with patients, lectured them, lent them money, saw them socially, or abruptly stopped seeing them. He also analyzed his own daughter (presumably requiring them to talk about her past and current sexual fantasies about him, an example of what Ferenczi called "re-traumatization in the psychoanalytic situation").

There was a special intensity to these debates because they centered on technique, the issue that had caused the split between Freud and Ferenczi, a rift so painful it had inflicted a permanent "trauma on the analytic world." The two men had been so close for so long and had broken so decisively that their colleagues came to see even brief discussions of technical issues as threatening to the integrity of the analytic community. And after Freud had accused Ferenczi of "an excessive zeal to cure," people who seemed more concerned with helping patients than preserving psychoanalytic purity were considered suspect, even pathological. (In his Freud biography, Ernest Jones had called Ferenczi "psychotic" and "delusional," setting the tone for the later denigration of "deviants." Jones did not, however, quote the source of Ferenczi's disturbance, the statement Freud had made to him: "Patients are nothing but riffraff. The only useful purposes they serve are to help us earn a living and to provide learning material. In any case, we cannot help them.")[30]

Since Frieda had been closely allied in Europe with Ferenczi and Groddeck and was obviously much more focused on helping patients than maintaining purity, she and the "radicals" she taught and supervised in Washington quickly became targets of attack by the conservatives in New York. As one of the members of the APA Board of Professional Standards complained: "There seems always to be a trend toward reducing training standards in the Washington-Baltimore area."[31] Clara Thompson and her colleagues at the William Alanson White Institute (who had all come from Washington or been trained by Frieda and Sullivan) were accused of not having enough "real" analysts on their staff to warrant being accredited. Egged on by her allies in New York, Jenny Waelder-Hall tried to get the more "classical" Baltimore analysts to split off, thereby isolating Frieda and Sullivan and their colleagues in Washington.

In addition to Frieda's flexibility in technique and her embrace of psychoanalytic methods to treat psychotic patients, what particularly enraged the conservatives was the welcome being given to psychologists and social workers by the "deviant" training centers. The New York Psychoanalytic Society appointed the Committee to Study Unauthorized Training and threatened to expel any member found guilty of educating nonphysicians (a move painfully reminiscent of laws that forbid the teaching of reading to African-Americans). Anonymous letters were circulated listing those accused of such "heresy," and an attorney advised the committee that it was well within its rights and didn't have to worry about libel issues. A letter sent to all members of the New York Society read: "Anyone who gives information of this sort [naming potential offenders] furthers the purposes of the Association and should be regarded as an informant, not an informer." Any member "who had relations with, or functioned in" groups like the White Institute was subject to immediate expulsion. "The lawlessness and danger inherent in indiscriminate training by unauthorized groups" warranted infringement on members' free speech. The 1953 annual report by the president of the society warned ominously of an "epidemic of improperly chosen, inadequately trained, self-appointed therapists who have infiltrated the community not only in New York but throughout the country."[32] In McCarthyite America, ferreting out "radicals" wasn't a job only for the government.

Despite occasional tensions within the Washington-Baltimore community, like those fomented by Waelder-Hall and her supporters, Frieda's approach remained the dominant perspective, so she was never in danger of being thrown out of her local institute, the way Thompson and Horney were in New York. She was also protected by the status of the Washington-Baltimore Society, one of the oldest in the United States, which couldn't easily be dismissed as a renegade center like the White Institute. There were also relatively few lay analysts in Washington, and much more openness to the idea of training nonphysicians (even by senior members of the institute), making for less internal strife than in other places.[33]

But the New York Society was the largest and most powerful voice in the American psychoanalytic movement, and its conservative agenda dominated national debates. When the *Journal of the American Medical Association* listed courses in psychiatry and psychoanalysis in one of its issues, the secretary of the APA wrote a letter of protest that three "irregular" groups had been included. When other institutes accused the New York group of being "monopolistic," its officers responded in a written statement sent to every analyst in the United States that "it is against the interests of psychoanalytic development to encourage groups which represent divergent theoretical viewpoints." There were occasional expressions of sadness about this increasing narrowness and rigidity—Martin Grotjahn said that "analytic training had become a kind of indoctrination instead of a learning experience," and Helene Deutsch famously remarked, "I feel like someone who has been working in an artist's studio and suddenly finds himself in a factory"—but there seemed to be no way of opposing the unyielding stand taken by analysts in New York.[34]

Frieda had complicated feelings about all of this. She thought it was silly to define psychoanalysis in terms of its methods when its goals (making sense of the unconscious, working through symptoms, analyzing the transference) were what was important. Yet, as always, she remained cordial even to her harshest critics. She didn't want the Lodge to be dragged into battles beyond those it was already forced to fight with somatic psychiatrists. Dexter was naive about psychoanalytic politics, and she knew it was her responsibility to protect their interests. (When Horney had dramatically resigned from the New York Institute in 1941—marching down Fifth Avenue with her supporters, singing "Go down, Moses, Let my people go"—Dexter had been invited to join her new opposition group. "I said sure," he recalled. "It was good for the sanitarium to belong to more organizations." Fortunately, he ran into Frieda before he sent in his dues. She said: "Wait a minute. You have no idea what's going on here. You don't want to be identified with these people right now." Chastened, he had declined the invitation and left such decisions to her from then on.)[35]

Frieda was not only much more tuned in to the intricacies of movement politics than Bullard was; they had deep personal meaning for her. Dexter was a typical American: he joined groups easily, assumed they would welcome him as a member, and didn't worry about what people thought of him. As a well-to-do Republican landowner, he didn't have to concern himself with issues of loyalty or ostracism. Frieda, in contrast—a Jew, a refugee, the proponent of a minority position within her professional reference group—was vulnerable in ways Dexter knew nothing about. She was also a woman, far more attuned to interpersonal dynamics and the subtle politics of discrediting.

As the former president of the Washington Psychoanalytic Society and one of its senior training analysts, Frieda also occupied a particularly prominent position. So when the Washington Institute was investigated by the Board of Professional Standards for its "deviance," when its candidates had their acceptance in the APA "deferred," when the institute's curriculum was criticized as inadequately "psychoanalytic," she took these attacks personally. This was a totally reasonable reaction; one of the inspectors announced that the general problem was that "Frieda hadn't really been analyzed" and was inflicting her own limitations on students.

She began being vilified at professional meetings. Harold Searles recalled a typical moment. Robert Waelder, a conservative member of the New York analytic establishment, was giving a talk at an APA conference. When he saw Frieda in the audience, he digressed from his prepared remarks to ridicule the idea of using analytic methods with psychotic patients. The whole audience started laughing. As Searles noted, "Waelder seemed totally out of touch with his callousness." At another APA meeting, Frieda was on a panel titled "Psychoanalysis and Dynamic Psychotherapy: Similarities and Differences." One of the other speakers was Edward Bibring, an especially orthodox member of the Boston Institute. As Bob Cohen recalled, "Bibring's only comment on Frieda's paper, in a voice trembling with rage, was the question, 'How can you consider yourself a psychoanalyst?'" When Frieda was invited to give the prestigious Academic Lecture at the American Psychiatric Association meetings, she was violently attacked for saying psychoanalytic methods could be used with schizophrenic patients. "It was crazy the way people went after her," said Marvin Adland. "They just couldn't let it go. They had to try to wipe her out. It wasn't a question of ignoring her; they had to prove she was wrong, to attack the basis of what she was saying."[36]

After Frieda's paper from the Bibring panel appeared in the official journal of the American Psychoanalytic Association, Kurt Eissler, the "dean" of New York analysts, published a rebuttal. Instead of disagreeing with the content of her remarks, he claimed that "refined observation" or "exact, scientific methods" would reveal the truth of his perspective. Frieda's approach, said Eissler, "was not parallel or equivalent to psychoanalysis. The essentials as well as the finer facets of the psychic apparatus are beyond the scope of [her] crude, common-sense psychology." Understanding the unconscious "requires self-discipline and adequate training," two qualities he obviously found lacking in Frieda.[37]

What seemed particularly to incense her critics was Frieda's use of insights from work with psychotics in her analyses of less disturbed patients. As Bob Cohen recalled:

I chaired the meeting of the Education Committee of the Washington Psychoanalytic Institute on the occasion of the first official visit from the American [Psychoanalytic Association]. The visitors expressed their concern about Frieda's preoccupation with countertransference. They felt that this reflected a deficiency in her training and a lack of understanding of psychoanalytic theory, and feared that many of us might be acting out our unanalyzed conflicts in similar fashion.[38]

Jenny Waelder-Hall, who had tried to instigate a split in the institute to put an end to such heresy, declared that many of the students "needed to be re-analyzed because Dr. Reichmann was so impressed by Sullivan and his ability to help the psychotic patient that she must have gotten the idea that if this worked so well in psychotics, it may work [just as well] with neurotics." Waelder-Hall made clear she didn't particularly care what Frieda did with schizophrenic patients, those of no concern to "real" analysts; it was her use of these unorthodox methods with neurotics—especially candidates in analytic training—that had to be stopped.[39]

Frieda felt deeply wounded by these attacks, a response best understood by her refugee friends. Alberta Szalita said Frieda "entertained fears of being identified as a heretic and cast out of the fraternity" of psychoanalysis, a terrifying prospect after her experiences with the Nazis. As Hilde Bruch once remarked: "I am a refugee from authoritarianism. I will not go into any group in which authoritarian attitudes determine who is allowed to speak and whose point of view is heard." Bruch said that having friends and family "disappear, many by death," made the experience of being professionally ostracized frightening to any refugee. She painfully recalled the "anguish" Frieda suffered when she presented her work at psychoanalytic meetings and was "told what she was doing was not analysis." Bruch said Frieda would invariably quote Freud's statement that any therapy that subscribed to three fundamental principles—childhood origin of symptoms, transference, and the reality of the unconscious—had the right to be called psychoanalytic.[40]

Yet while she admired Frieda's courage in expressing her own perspective despite constant criticism, even Bruch couldn't fully understand Frieda's feelings of vulnerability. "I recall myself saying: 'But why do you bother? If what you have to say is right, who cares?' Frieda would always say, 'I care.'" Part of what made these attacks so difficult was that Frieda herself took pains to avoid ad hominem arguments, always finding a diplomatic way to express disagreement with colleagues. As her friend Virginia Gunst noted, "Frieda showed a unique ability to learn from anyone in her field or other related fields if she had respect for their work, whether or not she liked or admired them personally." Her colleague Ruth Moulton added that unlike Sullivan, who completely discarded classical psychoanalytic concepts, Frieda "had some way of not looking down her nose at the orthodox yet blending it with the much more understandable interpersonal approach." Like Ferenczi (who despite his disagreements with Freud, remained a member of the International Psychoanalytic Association), Frieda would never have dreamed of organizing a splinter group, as Horney and others did.[41]

For Frieda, departures from mainstream ideas always had more to do with practical appropriateness than with tests of loyalty. Clarence Schulz liked to tell this story. Larry Kubie was once supervising a group of psychiatric residents at Sheppard. They were observing a patient being interviewed by another resident through a one-way mirror. The patient became increasingly disturbed and finally picked up a chair, threw it at the mirror, and ran off. The students started to rush to the aid of the therapist. "Kubie spread out his arms," Schulz smiled, "and said 'Don't go in there. You will interfere with the transference.'" Frieda would have considered such a display of purity ridiculous, said Schulz, and it was this flexibility her students most appreciated.[42]

She often seemed amazed at her colleagues' slavish imitation of Freud. In the paper Bibring found so objectionable, for example, she wrote:

> The remarkable capacity of Freud to promote and anticipate modifications and changes in psychoanalytic conceptualization and technique seems to me to be something we should all take to mind and emulate. Psychoanalysts should not put Freud unfairly on the pedestal of indiscriminate acceptance and adoration on which another great teacher of the nineteenth century, Karl Marx, was put by his disciples. Marx countered these attempts with his famous statement: "Moi, je ne suis pas Marxiste ("I am not a Marxist")."

Again and again, Frieda tried to make this same point, to no avail—that Freud was no Freudian, and it was silly for his followers to pretend otherwise. If they wanted to be like him, they should imitate his courage and creativity, not the literal details of behavior specific to a particular culture and historical moment, now long past.[43]

Since criticism was so much a part of the psychoanalytic movement, it is interesting to note people's strikingly different ways of responding to it. Freud cut off all contact with his critics but used their disagreement as a foil for working out his own ideas. Horney ended her relationship with the person and never again cited their work. Hilde Bruch lashed out in nasty personal letters but remained civil in public. Sullivan totally ignored his critics and appeared unaffected by anything they said. But Frieda took attacks personally and constantly tried to say whatever she meant in a less divisive way, not compromising her principles but doing anything other than that to keep the person in her good graces.

Revealingly, Erich's response was closest to hers. He was always trying to carve out some middle ground in polarized debates and ending up as an object of enmity for both sides. His wide popularity among the general public made his work even more suspect in professional circles. Karl Menninger, reviewing *Escape from Freedom* in the *Nation,* said Fromm "wrote as if he considered himself a psychoanalyst," an extraordinary statement from a man whose training was far less rigorous than Erich's and whose own books were best sellers. (As a "unique cross between a psychoanalytic heretic and a cultural celebrity," Fromm was clearly threatening to someone as insecure as Menninger.)[44]

This similarity in Frieda's and Erich's response to their critics was part of the legacy of their break with Orthodox Judaism. Having rejected the enactment of religious rituals that no longer felt meaningful or appropriate, they weren't about to embrace psychoanalytic rituals that seemed equally inauthentic. Erich explicitly made this link: in affirming the Biblical injunction against idolatry, he said that regarding "prescribed analytic techniques as sacrosanct" turned them into idols.[45] Yet just as both Frieda and Erich remained deeply respectful of Jewish tradition and tried to embody its principles in every aspect of their (secular) lives, they held fast to their fundamental identities as psychoanalysts. Calling themselves "pupils" of Freud (although neither of them had ever met him) fit this commitment to honor their ancestors by continuing to espouse their core ideals rather than imitating their actions. It also reflected their unconscious fear of being cast out; having already committed the crime of *karet,* they couldn't afford to take any further risks.

At a deeper level, Frieda's and Erich's attitudes about psychoanalytic orthodoxy directly reflected their religious upbringings. Loyalty to the community was a core value in Orthodox Judaism, but this was never interpreted as blind obedience. The Talmudic tradition stressed interpretation and questioning of sacred texts to get at their deeper meanings; simple repetition even of revered teachings was considered disrespectful of the Jews' search for true learning. And as historian Mordechai Breuer notes, the Orthodox regarded themselves as the "aristocracy of Judaism," embodying its real spirit.[46] So when Frieda cited Freud and declared that she was trying to live up to the ideals of psychoanalysis, this wasn't a clever rhetorical device intended to defuse criticism. She really meant it.

The lost world: cultured, urbane Heidelberg, complete with castle, circa 1920

Frieda's new home: rural Rockville, complete with Confederate statue, circa 1920

Chestnut Lodge Sanitarium, Rockville, Md.
Dr. E. L. Bullard, Supt.

24 Chestnut Lodge, 1930

Miss Simpson, head nurse, with the Lodge's stylish ambulance, 1930

25

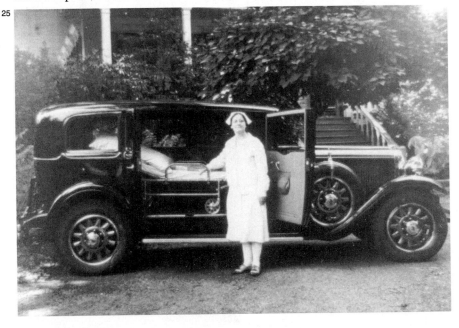

26

Frieda in the mid-1930s, shortly after arriving in the United States. The accumulated toll of her escape from the Nazis, two years of exile, and anxiety about the fate of her family, still trapped in Europe, are painfully evident.

27 A brief family reunion: (left to right) Grete, Klara, Frieda, Anna, and Alisa (in front) during their visit in neutral Switzerland (July 1936). Their strikingly unattractive appearances are testimony to the effects of exile and persecution.

28

29

Klara in old age, with her hearing aid and the little notepad she thrust at people when she couldn't make out what they were saying

Adolf in his sixties

30

Frieda's cottage on the grounds of Chestnut Lodge, where she spent her whole life in the United States

31

33

Her summer house in Santa Fe, the only property she ever owned in America

32

34

35

Dexter Bullard, in the 1950s

Anne Wilson Bullard, in the 1950s

Chestnut Lodge physicians in 1954: (back row, left to right) Milton Hendlich, Charles Baker, Norman Rintz, Joseph Coxe, William Welsh, Clarence Schulz, John Fort, Cecil Cullander, Jarl Dyrud, Robert Gibson; (front row, left to right) Otto Will, Donald Burnham, Marvin Adland, Dexter, Frieda, George Preston, Harold Searles

36

37

Frieda in her office at the cottage

Frieda (left) in the living room of the cottage, trying unsuccessfully to charm her sister Grete into moving to America, 1952

38

39

Relaxing with her beloved cocker spaniel, Munie, in the backyard

40

Frieda listening intently to someone in the 1950s

Psychoanalysts were embarrassed by their "civil wars," as Ernest Jones had named them, but seemed unable to keep from perpetuating them. In his presidential address to the APA in 1952, for example, Robert Knight said: "The spectacle . . . of a national association of physicians and scientists feuding with each other over training standards and practices . . . calling each other orthodox or deviant . . . is not an attractive one to say the least. Such terms belong to religious or to fanatical political movements and not to science and medicine . . . In the physical sciences, one does not squelch an Einstein by quoting passages from Newton . . . [nor] does one cease teaching Newton just because Einstein has gone further."[47]

Meanwhile, as Clara Thompson was later to note, while analysts were turning on one another, "their territory was being infringed on from outside. Anyone can buy a couch and use it. It requires no special skill to get a patient to lie on it." It hardly mattered how analysts defined their work; Americans got treatment from anyone who offered it. As Thompson warned: "Psychoanalytic groups can become so busy fighting one another that they fail to unite against the common enemy, the outright charlatan."[48]

Frieda's "deviations" from classical psychoanalytic practice got a strikingly similar response from her American colleagues as Melanie Klein's "heresy" was accorded in England during this same period. They had both introduced changes in technique after finding classical methods inadequate to treating new kinds of patients, and they both saw themselves as loyal members of the psychoanalytic community, carrying forward Freud's ideas.

But the consequences of Klein's technical innovations in child analysis were seen as much more dangerous for the long-term future of psychoanalysis than Frieda's modifications for treating schizophrenic patients. Child analysis was emerging as a separate subspecialty, for which particular training was deemed necessary. This meant that more people were affected by Klein's teachings, and the issue of how to train students—using her procedures or the less radical techniques of the other leading child analyst, Anna Freud—took on special urgency. Children were also of far greater concern to most analysts: they had their own, they were perceived as especially impressionable, and Freud had so many core ideas about them. Psychotics, in contrast, were people few analysts ever came into contact with or cared about.

So although Klein, like Frieda, never sought to create a split in her local institute or form her own group (the way Karen Horney did), Klein's ideas catalyzed enormous dissension in the British Psychoanalytic Institute. And

Klein's personal ruthlessness in discarding people who weren't totally loyal
to her—so unlike Frieda's cordial response even to sharp critics—meant that
she ended up as the de facto head of a warring group. In 1941, as Horney was
marching down Fifth Avenue singing, "Go down, Moses," and Klein was
"exhorting and deploying her troops, issuing commands, bullying, encouraging, unceasingly vigilant," Frieda was building Chestnut Lodge and serving
as the elected president of the Washington-Baltimore Psychoanalytic Institute.[49]

By the early 1950s, Frieda wearied of these battles and defended herself or
her Washington colleagues only when directly challenged. Her work load
was especially heavy in this period. In addition to all her Lodge duties and
private patients, she taught every semester at both the Washington School of
Psychiatry and the Psychoanalytic Institute. She also spent countless Saturday afternoons advising prospective students and helping to match them with
appropriate training analysts.

Frieda was now in her sixties, and increasingly lonely despite the satisfactions of work. The absence of any family nearby began to weigh more heavily on her. The long war years had, in contrast, drawn her mother and sisters
closer together, and they had learned to rely on one another rather than always looking to Frieda. Despite the many letters back and forth and the occasional visits, she had become more of a symbol than an actor in the life of
the family.

After Aunt Helene died in 1947 and Anna, Hans, and Alisa left for Israel,
Klara and Grete grew especially close. The only one of the three Reichmann
girls to remain Orthodox, Grete had long fantasized moving to Jerusalem
herself (and in fact kept a suitcase with clothes appropriate to that climate in
Anna's attic). But having "spent her life being a good daughter," Grete could
not bring herself to leave Klara, and once it became clear that the two of them
were not going to join Frieda in America, Grete stayed on in London. She
supported herself as a music teacher and spent most of her free time in the
British Museum, researching a book on music in the Biblical period. This
work was highly respected by colleagues; friends of Hilde Bruch's were en-
vious of her knowing "the great musicologist Grete Reichmann, who has a
sister somewhere in America."[50] Klara had long ago set aside the disappointments she had in Grete as a child, and their shared religious faith made for a
daily life rich in Jewish observance. When the boardinghouse where they had

lived during the war was turned into a home for the elderly, Grete was forced to move, but found a room a few blocks away so she could continue to share most of her time with her mother.

One Friday night in 1952, Klara fell down the stairs in her building. With the stoicism for which she had long been famous, she lay alone in the dark for some time rather than switch on the light and violate Shabbat restrictions. Eventually she was taken to the hospital with a broken arm and other injuries. This was the first time she had ever spent a day in bed, and it clearly signaled some profound shift. Klara died a week later, the indomitable force she had been for more than eighty years.

Frieda, stunned that her powerful mother would fail to triumph even over death, retreated further into herself and barely mentioned Klara even to close friends. In some kind of unconscious identification with her mother, she began to adopt denial, Klara's main defense. It didn't seem conceivable to Frieda that her mother would simply cease to exist.

She took for granted that Grete would now come to America to live with her. Grete, still longing for Israel, agreed to an initial visit. "Poor Frieda did her best to make Grete feel happy and at home," recalled Alisa. "They went on a holiday with the car to Frieda's little house in Santa Fe. Frieda hoped she would stay with her. There are wonderful pictures of Grete in America with her hair done up and all that goes with it." (Stanley Wilcox remembered driving them out to New Mexico, stopping at Jewish stores to buy food that Frieda would cook at the motel, the way she had done years earlier for Alisa in Strasbourg.) On their return to Rockville, Frieda hauled out the kosher dishes she had kept in her closet all those years. (The Adlands recalled Frieda's arriving unannounced to introduce Grete to them, necessitating an improvised meal of tuna salad on paper plates.) Grete visited relatives in New York she hadn't seen since the days in Berlin. "It all seemed great," recalled Alisa, "but she could not give up her dream of living in the Holy Land," a dream that had sustained her through fifteen years of war and deprivation.[51]

So for the first time in her life, Grete did what she wanted rather than following someone else's plan. She moved to Israel, not to a kibbutz like Anna, but to Jerusalem, where she could nourish her musical interests and remain Orthodox. Frieda, in her usual blithe determination to construct life in her own image, seemed oblivious to how bizarre it would have been for Grete to live with her on the grounds of a mental hospital, surrounded by the gentiles of sleepy Rockville.

Grete and Anna grew even closer to one another after Grete's move to Israel, and when Alisa eventually married and had children of her own, Grete was like a second grandmother to them. Although they lived in different parts of the country, Grete participated in every birthday party and important event in the life of Anna's family. The two sisters traveled together to Greece and Italy, and every summer Grete returned to London to research her book at the British Museum. But when she began to become deaf from the same hereditary condition that had plagued both her parents, she could no longer listen to music, a source of enormous sadness.[52]

Back in America, Frieda found herself struggling to deal with the increasing demands being forced on her. By the mid-1950s, the Lodge had become a place of last resort, where mainstream psychiatry dumped its failures and forgot about them. Having always drawn a more disturbed clientele than its competitors, the Lodge was filling up with patients who had spent years in a state hospital or VA center and whose families could afford to try one last measure. But by ending up mostly with chronic patients unlikely to respond to psychotherapy, the Lodge was undermining Frieda's whole philosophy.

For example, Mr. K., admitted in 1955 at the age of thirty-one, had already been in five other hospitals. Diagnosed with paranoid schizophrenia, he had been unsuccessfully treated with ECT and insulin shock, and was so agitated and delusional that he was given Thorazine on admission, a drug that had just come onto the market and was used at the Lodge only in extreme cases. Mr. K. remained on a locked ward for the next four years and was often so assaultive he had to be kept in a seclusion room. At one point, he refused to eat for days and had to be tube fed. Eventually, at the request of his father, he was transferred back to a VA clinic. Mr. K.'s leaving caused "strong mixed feelings, mainly of loss, of relief, and of failure" in his Lodge therapist.[53]

Miss Y. precisely illustrated the conflicts Stanton and Schwartz had highlighted. She too had been previously hospitalized and treated with insulin and ECT. But she came to the Lodge saying: "I look forward to the idea of intensive psychotherapy and hope it will let me discover what ails my living." Yet after spending her first weeks on the ward frolicking with a male patient, she did little but manipulate her physicians. Her ward administrator said she was "quite rebellious towards staff, took very poor care of her person and showed herself unable to plan realistically." Her therapist, on the other hand, thought she was doing well enough after several months to be discharged and treated on an outpatient basis.

The therapist prevailed and Miss Y. lived in town, but during her frequent depressions and manic episodes would be readmitted, for periods ranging from a day to a year. After eight Lodge hospitalizations, she wrote a formal letter to Bullard protesting her doctors' "vacillating decisions, unreasonable fits of temper and unwholesome demands on her."

Mr. O. was another patient whose stay was marked by constant conflict. He had been institutionalized since his teenage years. At his first hospital, he had received sixty insulin shock treatments and thirty ECT in less than four months and was considered a major "management problem." Sent to another institution, he escaped; his parents had to lie to get him to the Lodge.

During his admission interview, Mr. O. wanted to know "where the women were." A staff report several months later described him as "a boorish, insolent, offensive, demanding, litigious person." During testing by Margaret Rioch, the psychologist, he could give no association to the word "masturbate" and claimed not to know what a "vagina" was. An expert manipulator, Mr. O. got other patients to bring him TV sets, radios, and phonographs, which he promised to "repair" for them. His letters, filled with threats, often had to be censored. Yet he managed to elicit guilt rather than anger from staff; as his ward administrator noted, "he would be put in seclusion then accuse them of being punitive, and they were suckers for feeling sorry for him." After several years as an inpatient and some months living nearby while continuing his therapy, Mr. O. was finally sent back to a state hospital.

Mrs. T. was another typical patient of the 1950s. A mental health worker in the Midwest before her breakdown, she had twice been hospitalized and treated unsuccessfully with ECT. By the time she arrived at the Lodge, Mrs. T. was mute and confused, and she refused to eat or interact with anyone. She described her transfer as "abrupt" and was distraught at being a thousand miles away from her husband and children. After repeatedly smashing glass doors trying to escape, Mrs. T. was moved to the disturbed ward, where for the next six months, she regressed steadily, pulling out chunks of her hair and refusing to wear clothing. She constantly tried to force her way past the nurses into the elevator, and the only words she spoke were demands that she be sent to the airport. In a rare reflective moment, she pointed to her disheveled appearance and said to her therapist: "This is what the hospital has done to me."

Frieda was understandably dispirited by the unending wave of patients like these. She treated fewer and fewer of them herself, allowing the demands of teaching, supervision, research, and writing to absorb most of her waking hours. But she remained unalterably committed to her basic clinical philosophy: that no patient was beyond hope, and intensive psychotherapy offered the best chance for permanent cure.

Having always found patients' views a crucial source of information, she actively encouraged the Chestnut Lodge Research Institute to do follow-up studies that might help to demonstrate the value of the hospital's approach. No therapist, however empathic, could provide a detailed account of patient experience, and she was convinced that despite its struggles, the Lodge could still be successful in its mission.

Indeed, the results of Clarence Schulz's study in the late 1950s revealed enormously positive feelings on the part of many patients. More than 200 of his participants took the time to write narrative responses; they assumed (correctly) that such evaluations would be interpreted with the same attention to nuance as everything else at Chestnut Lodge. None seemed surprised that their views were being solicited, testimony in itself to the regard patients obviously felt.[54]

What stands out most clearly from these responses is the extraordinary number of patients who praised the Lodge.[55] Some said their relationship to the therapist had been most crucial. Others said the institution itself had been therapeutic. One woman, reflecting on her hospitalization seven years earlier, wrote:

> I consider being at Chestnut Lodge one of the most valuable experiences of my whole life. The treatment I received . . . is worth more to me than I can put into words. I am forever grateful for the way you treated me while I was there, as a person as well as in the actual treatment hours.[56]

Another former patient, who signed her response "B.S. from C.L.," wrote: "So many, many times during the ten years since I 'graduated' from Chestnut Lodge, I have thought with wonder and gratitude at the constant care and kindness I received from everyone while I was my most obstreperous and uncooperative self. . . . If ever any of my very dear friends needed care, I would try my best to have them go to your hospital."[57] A patient who had to terminate her treatment prematurely after she got pregnant said: "I felt incomplete for almost a year and spent some time searching for another analyst. . . . I wanted to be very sure I found someone of the same high caliber as the doctors at Chestnut Lodge. . . . I feel that the type [of treatment] I received there was the best kind that there is to be found anywhere for my psychoneurotic illness. I think that I might have been completely well if I could have completed [it]." Signing her letter "keep up your wonderful work," she urged the Lodge to maintain its psychoanalytic ethos.[58]

A patient who recovered sufficiently to resume his work as a physician answered the question, "How is your general ability to enjoy life?" with an enthusiastic, "Epicurean." He added: "I am pleased to recommend Chestnut Lodge," as if it were a restaurant his friends might want to visit. The wife of another patient wrote: "I feel like I never cease expressing my thanksgiving for all you, and those with you, have done for him. It has been nothing less than a miracle." She called Chestnut Lodge "a wonderful enterprise."[59] And these were all patients other hospitals had given up on, the ones likely to be stuck in a back ward or given a lobotomy.

A surprising number of patients criticized the Lodge for having discharged them too early (a far cry from the caricature of the place as a profit-making venture designed to milk patients out of every dollar). "My only suggestion about hospital procedure is that you should try to orient the patient a little bit more as to the problems he will face in getting back to the world of reality," one man wrote. "I could have benefited by about six months more at the Lodge, and I feel that at the time, in spite of my strong desire to get out, I could have been persuaded to stay."[60]

Of course, there were others who regarded confinement as destructive. One patient astutely commented: "I honestly do feel that if [people] are treated more realistically and constructively, they have a better chance to recover. . . . In ordinary living, if a person feels a little disturbed, he doesn't undress and get into wet sheets! I do feel there should be a closer correlation between living in an institution and living among the civilized world."[61] One woman, however, urged:

No patient should leave Chestnut Lodge without having spent some time on the 4th floor. . . . The life up there represents the inconveniences, the obstacles which call for intelligence to overcome, and the more than ordinary consideration of others sometimes necessary in living. To remain always on the 2nd floor or at Little Lodge is an unrealistic idea of living. It presents all of the sweet and none of the bitter. . . . Patients need to learn that even Santa Claus carries a whip. Besides, isn't it true that the fuller and more complete our experiences, the fuller individuals we become?[62]

And despite his months in seclusion, Mr. O., the expert manipulator, eventually recovered and wrote: "Chestnut Lodge was the only place that made an intelligent attempt to solve my problems." He even looked back to his time on the "violent ward" with some fondness. "We were a wild lot loaded with all kinds of energy and no ready outlet." He wondered if he had been given too much freedom, but said "no matter what you do to it, I'll probably always remember the Lodge and how it helped me."[63]

Yet although Frieda had clearly succeeded in attracting a staff notable for their hard work and adventurousness, even she had to admit that by the mid-1950s physicians at the Lodge were increasingly discouraged and uncertain. Psychotherapy with psychotics might be fascinating research, but when patients got worse, therapists lashed out at each other or blamed themselves. The hardest part was keeping a sense of proportion about the pace of the work. A patient who had been ill for years or been treated with five other methods before she got to the Lodge wasn't going to improve quickly, no matter how committed her therapist was.

Martin Cooperman told this story. He was treating a woman who was very regressed and had been on the fourth floor for months. When he first saw her, she was hanging from a screen on the outside porch. He took a chance and had her transferred to a more open ward. She perked up and began talking to him in their sessions. A month or two went by, and he started to think she was improving at last. Then one day she showed up in a totally deteriorated state, looking as bad as she had on that first day. Cooperman was devastated. Walking dejectedly over to the dining room, he ran into Frieda, who asked what was troubling him. He blurted out the story and said he had no idea what to do. Frieda gave him a long look and said: "Well, there's movement." It had never occurred to him to look at it like this. It mattered less whether the patient was up or down at any given moment than whether change was taking place. Forty years later, Cooperman called this "the single most important statement ever made to me about psychotherapy" and said it had given him the courage to go on working with psychotic patients.[64]

12

Public Acclaim

Details are confusing. It is only by selection, by elimination, by emphasis that we get at the real meaning of things.[1]

Brilliance is beguiling. Buried in every psychoanalyst is the wish to be a theorist like Freud. But Freud's genius lay as much in the elegance of his writing as in the content of his prose—he won the Goethe Prize for Literature, not the Nobel—and translating the unconscious into the vernacular is a talent too little known.

Compared to the work of her more abstruse colleagues, Frieda's writing seemed painfully literal. She wrote the way she did everything else: with matter-of-fact directness and an unwavering focus on the goal. She assumed that the point of writing was comprehension, not conceit, and did whatever she could think of to make her ideas clear. This earned her the contempt of many colleagues, but the fact that her books have been continuously in print since the 1950s proves she knew what she was doing.

During Frieda's lifetime, people often first encountered her ideas in spoken form. She lectured constantly to audiences in New York and Washington—often at public events open to anyone—and presented several papers each year at professional conferences. She was so short that she couldn't use a regular podium, so she stood on a box or platform, the microphone carefully adjusted to an angle low enough for her to reach. She knew precisely how to work an audience and could mesmerize the room. People remember how "artfully" she used her "unusually beautiful hands" as she spoke, how her spontaneity made the patient seem to be right there with her. "There was

drama in what she said," recalled one admirer, "but she was not dramatic."[2]
The engaging irony of her tiny size and huge ambition made attending her
lectures an unforgettable experience, and many of those who joined the
Lodge staff after the war were young doctors inspired by one of Frieda's
talks.

Although she was one of very few psychiatrists of her generation to still
use words like *cure*, Frieda never sought celebrity or disciples (like Klein or
Horney) or overstated the results of her work. Managing somehow to sound
grandiose and self-effacing at the same moment, she forced both students
and colleagues to wonder whether their own sickest patients might improve
if they followed her suggestions.

She thought of lectures as progress reports. Every claim was a hypothesis;
nothing was ever fixed or certain. Her style was confident yet nonauthoritar-
ian, a combination rare in medicine. When she talked about psychotherapy
with psychotic patients, her audience was often so incredulous at the very
idea they could hardly grasp what she was saying, but by the time she finished, they were persuaded—as much by her modesty and the strength of her
conviction as by the evidence she presented.

Frieda's publications had this same directness. She had an eye for the essential and left out everything else. Readers felt as if they were there beside
her, in the little office at the cottage or marching up the stairs to see some patient too violent to be let off the ward. For many, this straightforwardness
was endearing. Others found Frieda's style simplistic, her goals naive. Only
one analyst is allowed to be disarming, and his name is Freud.

We value opacity far more than we acknowledge, and we expect smart
people to be obscure. (How else to explain the phenomenal popularity of
someone like Stephen Hawking, a theoretical physicist who works on problems most people can't even name?) There's something alluring about ideas
we barely grasp; they confirm our sense that the world is a lot more complex
than any of us are capable of understanding.

Writing simply about something as incomprehensible as schizophrenia
discredited Frieda even more. Everyone knew that psychoses were extraordinarily complicated, perhaps even more confusing than eternal mysteries like
cancer or epilepsy. Yet Frieda wrote as if she understood her sickest patients,
the ones who had been thrown out of every other hospital and were considered unreachable by most psychiatrists. Unlike others who wrote primarily
on schizophrenia (Ferenczi, Groddeck, Searles), Frieda was never accused of
being crazy herself, but she was derided for being so direct. If something
wasn't clear, she said so; a childhood spent explaining one person to another
had left her painfully aware of the burden of secrets.

She had no interest in the kind of stylish writing that so captivated Freud. Her tone was often didactic, and even illustrations based on actual cases sounded contrived. When she wrote a series of character sketches in the 1930s to accompany Gertrud Jacob's portraits of psychotic patients, these supposedly fictional accounts were even more stilted. People recovered suddenly for unspecified reasons and often gave speeches to their doctors summarizing the meaning of their symptoms. Years later, a student who heard Frieda read one of these sketches in a seminar remembered being embarrassed by their heavy-handedness. Yet the very awkwardness of her Germanic constructions made her clinical results seem more convincing. An elegant style like Freud's raises the possibility of poetic license; one always wonders whether he might have embroidered the details to greater effect. Frieda, in contrast, was clearly telling the truth; her results were too surprising to have been invented. The irony is that *Principles of Intensive Psychotherapy,* the book she wrote to prove this point, convinced skeptics that "technique" was a feat only she could perform.

First published in 1950, *Principles* was based on years of lectures to students and distilled all of Frieda's key ideas into two hundred pages. Its style was so deceptively simple that the editor made her include a disclaimer in the preface saying that intensive psychotherapy couldn't be mastered just by reading this book.

Compared to the typical psychiatric textbook, *Principles* was unusual in many respects. Its first four chapters focused on the emotional requirements of the *therapist.* Only after making clear that the patient's pathology wasn't what determined the success of treatment did Frieda turn to standard issues like the initial interview, interpretation, contacts with relatives, and so on. In striking contrast to most other writers on technique, she also cited an exceptionally wide range of psychoanalytic authorities—from obvious ones like Freud, Abraham, and Jones, to "heretics" like Adler, Ferenczi, Jung, and Reich—reflecting her lifelong openness to learning from anyone. And despite the fact that *Principles* was a written text, Frieda's indebtedness to the oral tradition of the Hasidic legend was strikingly evident in all her clinical illustrations. "A story," said one of the Baal Shem Tov's disciples, "must be told in such a way that it constitutes help in itself," and this was clearly Frieda's intention. From the thousands of hours of psychotherapy she had done over three decades, she extracted the key moments that had shaped her approach. She didn't include long case histories describing the treatment of a few selected patients the way many analytic writers, following Freud, had done in their technical works. Rather, she used brief vignettes, which often sounded like parables, and left the moral implicit, as was the Jewish custom. As Buber noted:

The preponderance of the anecdote is primarily due to the general tendency of the Jewish Diaspora spirit to express the events of history and of the present in a pointed manner: Events are not merely seen and reported so as to signify something, but they are so cleanly hulled from the mass of the irrelevant and so arranged that the report culminates in a significant dictum.[3]

Some of the technical injunctions in *Principles* infuriated classical analysts, particularly Frieda's claim that patients should not be charged for missed sessions. "Psychiatric services are priceless if successful or worthless if they fail," she declared matter-of-factly, and while analysts were justified in insisting patients pay for services rendered regardless of their outcome, therapists weren't exempt from cultural norms. Other professionals weren't paid for work not done, and the idea of charging patients whether they appeared for a session was presumptuous. If this meant the analyst occasionally had an unused hour, this was to be celebrated. "To a productive personality," Frieda observed, "such free time may be of the essence."[4]

Principles of Intensive Psychotherapy was favorably reviewed across an unusually wide range of professional journals (in psychiatry, psychoanalysis, psychology, sociology, social work, and theology), as well as in the popular media.[5] Readers praised Frieda's "magnificent clarity and lucidity of exposition" and her "serene disregard of entrenched dogma and doctrine." The book was said to be "calm and objective in mood yet definite, confident, and provocative, indeed daring." Reviewer after reviewer hailed her "keen observations," "integrity," "penetrating" insights, and "the extreme dignity she extended to each patient." *Pulpit Digest* said it was "the outstanding work of the year." The *Quarterly Review of Biology* called it "amazingly helpful." Despite being a textbook, "the finest attribute of this practical and informative book," wrote one reviewer, "is that it conveys the most to those of greatest clinical experience." Frieda's colleague Billy Silverberg said she was one of few analysts to have the "courage to overcome the irrational anxieties" that had plagued writers of technical manuals since Freud had stated his aversion to them. Even the usually stodgy *Psychoanalytic Review* called Frieda "a natural-born teacher whose intent and meanings are crystal-clear." Kurt Goldstein, touched at finding his name among those to whom the book was dedicated, said her analysis of the requirements for effective therapy was "by far the best ever published." But the headline in the *Washington Post* took the prize: "Psychiatrist Bridges Gulf—The Neurotic Revealed as No Repulsive Alien."[6]

The few criticisms of *Principles* came from orthodox analysts, irritated by

Frieda's deviations from party doctrine, and from experimental psychologists, irked at her omission of their empirical findings. (These "deficiencies," sniffed Stanley Estes in the *Journal of Abnormal and Social Psychology,* demonstrate that "psychological analysis, being more comprehensive, precise, and conceptually adequate to the facts, will replace psychoanalysis.")[7]

Frieda's ideas about the causes and treatment of psychosis were derived primarily from work with schizophrenic patients, in contrast to theorists like Melanie Klein, who worked extensively with those suffering from manic depression. Frieda justified her almost interchangeable use of the terms *psychotic* and *schizophrenic* by suggesting a continuum of serious mental illnesses, with manic depression at the midpoint and schizophrenia at the extreme. Since schizophrenic patients far outnumbered all others in mental hospitals, she also argued that basing her approach on this group was most useful.

Beginning in the mid-1940s, Frieda undertook formal research on manic depression to test these assumptions. In a seminar she led at the Washington School of Psychiatry from 1944 to 1947 and in a study group that analyzed additional cases in the early 1950s, she worked with colleagues to develop a model of manic depression that could do justice to its unique features.[8]

Sharing the perception of many other psychiatrists (including Sullivan) that biological factors likely played a particularly important role in manic depression (a view still held), Frieda and her colleagues nevertheless cautioned against the "haphazard application of shock therapy and lobotomy, the effects of which still remain in the realm of speculation." They acknowledged that manic-depressive patients posed a special challenge to therapists. As their Washington colleague Lucile Dooley had found in a classic 1921 study, "the resistances of manic-depressive patients against analysis are even stronger than those of schizophrenics."[9]

In a monograph published in *Psychiatry* in 1954, Frieda's research group proposed a general model to explain this difference. At the earliest stage of development, they argued, there is intense closeness between mother and infant but little differentiation; as the infant matures, this primitive closeness diminishes, to be replaced by a bond in which self is experienced as separate from other. Schizophrenics, they hypothesized, were traumatized at an early point in this process, whereas manic depressives suffered disruptions in the later stages. This meant that a manic-depressive patient, although in some ways more "mature" than a schizophrenic, was nevertheless in the painful situation of having neither a close, identificatory relationship with the mother nor the capacity for a differentiated bond. As a result, he felt "particularly alone and consequently vulnerable to any threat of abandonment."

Manic-depressive patients ended up with a lot of acquaintances but few, if any, truly intimate relationships. The lively, witty exchanges of the manic patient gave the appearance of closeness, but there was no real exchange with others. "He is carrying out a relatively stereotyped social performance, which takes little or no account of the other person's traits and characteristics, while the other person, quite commonly, is allowing himself to be entertained and manipulated." Such patients often had one or two people in their lives with whom they were "extremely demanding . . . for love, attention, service, and possessions." They sought to control these people by "swallowing them up" to counteract intense feelings of "emptiness and need."[10]

These dynamics made establishing a workable bond with the therapist extremely difficult. Lacking the ability "for correct observation, registration, and report of interpersonal experiences," the manic depressive had little "talent for introspective observation and understanding." Such patients had a hard time even describing the problems in their relationships. Their reports "are peculiarly stereotyped, diagrammatic, and limited. There is a lack of subtlety, alertness for implications and refinement, and a tendency toward indiscriminate oversimplification." This style was strikingly different from the schizophrenic patient, "who notices nuances of expression and inflection, frequently in clear awareness, and then distorts their meaning." It was far easier for the therapist to correct a misinterpretation than to get the patient to appreciate subtleties he hadn't even noted in the first place.[11]

Therapy with manic depressives could, however, be effective if it were highly structured. Frieda recommended seeing the patient no more than three times a week and taking "a firm and consistent attitude of refusing to attempt to meet irrational demands from the beginning." To avoid the manipulativeness that made these patients such a trial to work with, she urged therapists to impose "a careful definition of limits and appropriate expression of disapproval when limits are violated." Frieda herself famously told one such patient "that it was against the rules for him to commit suicide, and, if he did so, she would discontinue the treatment!"[12]

But aside from this monograph and one other paper specifically focused on manic depression, Frieda concentrated most of her clinical efforts on schizophrenia and is clearly best known for her work in this area. At a major symposium on schizophrenia held in 1952, she presented an important revision of her earlier views.[13] The increased attention being given to countertransference, Frieda cautioned, was leading analysts to fetishize their mistakes, instead of seeing them as inevitable parts of the treatment process. She warned psychiatrists not to allow the task of monitoring their own emotional reactions to deteriorate into self-flagellation. "Guilt feelings," she repeated in that classic statement, "are an unconstructive, paralyzing luxury, which should be discouraged in doctors as well as in their patients." For therapists to become overwhelmed by their own inadequacies was just another way of avoiding the hard work of treating schizophrenics. Such patients, Frieda emphasized, weren't delicate flowers in danger of being retraumatized each time the therapist made a wrong move; they were partners in a slow, painful process that could ultimately help them, so long as their doctors didn't give up too soon.

Instead of spending so much time analyzing their own behavior, Frieda argued, therapists ought to concentrate on protecting psychotics from the excesses of their symptoms. "Schizophrenic patients loathe themselves for their hostile outbursts and do not respect the therapist who lets them get away with it," she stressed, after many recovered patients had told her so. Encouraging her colleagues to strive for "unqualified thriftiness in content interpretation," Frieda cited example after example where "listening alertly" with genuine interest had been the decisive factor in successful treatment.

Attending closely to nonverbal communication was key. Schizophrenic patients often expressed themselves in extremely subtle ways—for example, "by a change in posture and facial expression, which will be caught only by a very alert and sensitive observer." Dismissing Rosen's "direct analysis" as exhibitionism, Frieda said that the reason it worked with some patients was "because of the convincing, consistent intenseness of purpose, attitude, speech, and tone of voice with which he relates himself to them."[14]

In clear contrast to her own earlier view that therapists ought to do anything to facilitate contact with withdrawn patients, Frieda now argued that firm boundaries were necessary at every stage of treatment. She cautioned against "attempting to turn the strictly professional relationship into a pseudo-social one," and said that psychiatrists who felt "the temptation to try to reach a very disturbed schizophrenic by offering closeness, friendship, or love" should ask themselves whether their actions were motivated more by their own anxiety than by "an alleged concern for the patient." The same Frieda who in 1935 eased a frightened woman into therapy with coffee and cookies now insisted that "indirectness and sweetness" were not what patients needed. A seriously disturbed person should "be spoken to as one speaks to someone highly interpersonally sensitized," with all the respect such talents warranted.[15]

Frieda prescribed a scientific attitude to help therapists keep their focus. She told Lodge colleagues to think of "every patient with whom we do the type of extensive work we do at this hospital [as] a research project," and urged them not to add to patients' suffering with unrealistic expectations. Science was unpredictable. A failed treatment might yield insights that could help the next case. There was no way to know when a breakthrough might occur. In the short run, Frieda encouraged goals that were modest: to treat patients with respect and take their anguish seriously, so they wouldn't be forced to deteriorate to prove how sick they were. If psychotherapy helped, so much the better; at a minimum, it provided a chance to learn. In April 1943, at the height of an increasingly brutal war, she had told Lodge colleagues: "If our work tends to increase our decency in human relationships, it is of greatest importance at the present time . . . in counteracting the consequences of human indecency against which this country is fighting."[16]

In a 1954 talk to the American Psychiatric Association, Frieda gave a detailed summary of her revised approach. She had been invited to give the prestigious Academic Lecture that year and knew her audience would find the whole idea of psychotherapy with psychotics doubtful. Taking an uncharacteristically bold and uncompromising stand, she not only insisted that such work was possible, but argued that insights drawn from therapy with hospitalized patients applied equally to neuroses. "Anxiety plays a central role in all mental illnesses," she declared, making symptoms both "an expression of and a defense against anxiety and its underlying conflicts, regardless of the severity of the illness." As Dexter Bullard had long proclaimed: "You can't have one psychology for some people and a whole different psychology for others."

In laying out her argument, Frieda didn't mince words:

My experience during the last twenty years has been mainly with schizophrenic patients who came to our hospital in a state of severe psychotic disturbance, from which the majority emerged sooner or later under intensive dynamic psychotherapy. After their emergence, they continued treatment with the same psychiatrist through the years of their outwardly more quiet state of illness, with the aim of ultimate recovery with insight. During both phases the patients were seen for four to six regularly scheduled interviews per week, lasting one hour or longer. Sometimes relapses occurred. . . . As a rule, these relapses could be handled successfully if the psychiatrist himself did not become too frightened, too discouraged, or too narcissistically hurt by their occurrence.

The challenge was to help each patient find "a continuity . . . between the person as he manifested himself in the psychosis and the one he is after his recovery." Frieda cited Greenberg's skin pulling at the end of the treatment as a vivid illustration of this struggle.[17]

The key to success with severely disturbed patients, she emphasized, lay not so much in any one particular technique as in being less afraid and more willing to experiment. Frieda knew she was often as much in the dark as her mainstream colleagues were; she just wasn't as frightened by not knowing precisely where she was.

People who spend a lot of time walking in woods don't panic when they lose their way. This isn't necessarily because they have a better sense of direction; it's because they take for granted that each path eventually leads to a road. This is how Frieda thought of herself: not as a magician, but as a scout, guiding people through dense forests to a place where they could find their own way out.

To Heinz Kohut's classic question, "How does analysis cure?" Frieda had a clear answer: the relationship with the therapist heals the loneliness that lies at the root of all mental illness. A person can't act like others if he feels completely isolated. No matter what causes serious disturbance, relationship is what prevents complete breakdown. The therapist is like a plank laid across a rising creek; if the patient can let her bear his weight, she might help him cross to safety before it's too late.

The loneliness of mental illness, Frieda emphasized, is nothing like the solitude people seek at the ocean or to do creative work. It is a state of extraordinary anguish in which a person ceases to be able to imagine, much less experience, anyone else being able to enter his experience. Understanding this profound kind of loneliness was Frieda's life goal. Rarely speaking directly about politics or history, analyzing loneliness was her way of coming to grips with the horrors she had witnessed: the men gassed in trenches who screamed in their sleep, the schizophrenics who set fire to their bodies, the refugees who stumbled across a ruined Europe, terror in their eyes.

Drafting and redrafting a paper on loneliness that she could never finish, Frieda tried to make sense of these experiences. Usually an uncompulsive writer, she remained unsatisfied with this work and never published it. What we have is the version found in her desk after her death, edited slightly by Dexter Bullard. Combining "important psychoanalytic insight with an extraordinary aesthetic effect," it is a beautiful piece of writing, the closest she ever came to being profound.[18]

Frieda called loneliness "one of the least satisfactorily conceptualized psychological phenomena" and noted that it wasn't even mentioned in most psychiatric textbooks (a fact she found astonishing). Among the few analysts to write anything on the topic was Melanie Klein, and like Frieda, she had done this work late in life. Klein emphasized the unsatisfied longing for "an understanding without words," rooted in the earliest relationship with the mother. Frieda stressed the "incommunicable, isolated core—the corollary to our need for interpersonal intimacy."[19]

Struggling to articulate the experience of her psychotic patients—"the history of the lonely ones"—Frieda was painfully aware of the obstacles that faced her: "People who are in the grip of severe degrees of loneliness cannot talk about it; and people who have at some time in the past had such an experience can seldom do so either, for it is so frightening and uncanny in character that they try to dissociate the memory of what it was like, and even the fear of it." Psychiatrists, she admitted, "must resign themselves to describing [loneliness] in terms of people's defenses against it," like physicists portraying invisible particles in terms of the residual trace of their movements. Actually, Frieda noted, it was worse than this: defenses didn't appear until the "all-engulfing intensity" of the feeling decreased; the "naked horror" of real loneliness, "beyond anxiety and tension," made even defenses "seem out of reach."[20]

Faced with the irony of trying to write about something that, by her own admission, couldn't be described, Frieda did the best she could, relying on accounts by polar explorers, shipwrecked sailors, inmates in solitary confinement, and subjects in sensory deprivation experiments. In each of these situations, she noted, psychotic disintegration occurred if relationships weren't reinstated.[21]

Frieda urged psychiatrists to talk openly of their patients' loneliness and to create a space where both of them could explore such feelings. For patients too withdrawn to speak, "the doctor's mere presence" or statements like "I know" and "I am here" might begin to ease the isolation. The main obstacle to "therapy with the lonely," she argued, was the psychiatrist's inability to confront this terror in his own life. As a reviewer of her paper noted, "The fear of loneliness, the fear of being enveloped by that nameless state, may be what really makes people afraid of schizophrenic patients, makes them think of these patients as 'out of this world' or as a different species than the rest of us."[22]

Despite the increased tensions at the Lodge in the early 1950s, this period was an intellectually exciting one for Frieda. Her long-standing interest in intuition—dating from that famous moment with Mrs. E. in the pack in 1935—became the focus of formal investigation. Although Frieda had always held that intuition, like every other phenomenon of mental life, was capable of being studied scientifically, she didn't actually have a way to do this until the Social Research Fund gave her an unsolicited grant of $25,000 in 1952. Jumping at the chance to see fewer patients and concentrate on issues she had been thinking about for two decades, she organized four of her Lodge colleagues—Marvin Adland, Don Burnham, Harold Searles, and Alberta Szalita—into a research group. Frieda knew she was better at "being intuitive" than at explaining how the process worked. As Bullard had once observed, "Frieda as a therapist could do tricks that other people could not manage. Sullivan would coldly consider a proposition. If I say this, in the light of what the patient has said, what are the various possibilities that I can anticipate and which is more probable. And if I get this response, what is my next move . . . like a chess game. . . . Whereas Frieda would play it off the cuff . . . [asking] what does the patient make me feel . . . what does it probably mean, and then zero in on it."[23]

In the spring of 1953, midway through the first year of the grant, Frieda reported to the foundation on the clinical research she and the others had initiated. One study involved tape-recording therapy sessions with a schizophrenic patient and comparing her notes with the tapes to analyze specific "intuitive" moments. In another study, a recovered patient was asked to record her reactions to various phases of the treatment, and this account was then compared with Frieda's recall of the same events. Finally, in the most intensive study, one member of the group taped a sample of his sessions with a schizophrenic patient, and the other members recorded their intuitions about specific phases of the work. Summarizing their core assumptions, Frieda wrote:

"Intuition" is not a mysterious interpersonal process which uses extrasensory channels, nor does it require qualities outside of the known means of communication. Briefly sketched, we consider intuition to be the creative utilization of very alert, quick, sensitive and subtle perceptivity, the results of which are equally quickly tied up with memories from previous life experiences with other people and previous clinical experiences. . . . More frequently than not, these mental and emotional processes do not come to the person's awareness.[24]

This was an exceptionally talented group of researchers, and if anybody could have figured intuition out, they would have been the ones to do it. But the insurmountable difficulties of the task heightened each person's vulnerabilities, and working together became increasingly problematic. Early sessions were dominated by tense discussions of whose patient would be presented for group analysis. Narcissistic desires to show off competed with anxieties about being criticized. (As always, these arguments were themselves recorded, transcribed, and distributed to the group. The budget for typists at the Lodge in the 1950s must have been astronomical.) Frieda wanted Miss N. (then being treated by Szalita) to serve as their research subject. But after "swimming around in undefined areas, not trying to define the indefinable, but just going away from it," as Szalita put it, they ended up deciding that Don Burnham would present one of his patients.[25]

Since intuition didn't even exist as a topic in psychiatry until the advent of psychotherapy with schizophrenics, the group had little to guide its work.[26] Meeting together for two hours a week, they constantly had to struggle to get past the presumption that they were studying an "unexplainable, unaccountable, instinctive, extrasensual, supernatural, or magical type of knowledge."[27]

What made intuition seem so different from other ways of knowing was that it "erupts into the conscious mind in a ready-to-use form." This was particularly likely to happen in therapy with schizophrenic patients, where interchanges were already so spontaneous and imagistic, more like a "waking dream" than a conversation.[28] For intuition to be used creatively, the analyst couldn't become too anxious during the session. Psychosis was so threatening to the therapist's own sense of security that "listening with the third ear," as Theodore Reik famously called it, could be blocked entirely. But if the therapist could relax enough to enter the space of reverie where he and the patient were communicating on both conscious and unconscious levels, the meaning of what transpired between them might well be revealed in an intuitive moment.[29]

Frieda saw a clear connection to the problem of loneliness she had been struggling with. In one of the group's sessions, she commented:

> Not being able to understand somebody communicating with us connotes loneliness. If we don't understand, that touches our own possibilities of loneliness, and rather than accepting [that] there is this barrier of loneliness between the psychotic and us, we evade it and feel guilty. I think that the guilt feeling is an *evasion* of accepting the tragic facts of human loneliness.

Intuition, in contrast, could allow the therapist to seek out more positive elements. As another Lodge researcher was later to put it: "Intuition in a therapist is the goal-directed search, both inwardly and outwardly, for areas of healthy functioning and for specific impediments to the realization of these strivings in the other."[30]

Such formulations were, however, too abstract to be of much use in the therapy hour. As Frieda's group prepared to present its initial findings to the American Psychoanalytic Association, there was little to show for a year of work. In an unusually tense staff meeting where drafts of their papers were discussed with Lodge colleagues, the research was criticized as vague and unfocused. The papers didn't seem to be about intuition per se as about therapy in general. Trying to defend the group, Frieda noted: "This is our first attempt at getting into it. We should describe the problems we encountered—what prohibits or promotes intuition? It's like certain things cannot be defined in their own rights, it is too difficult, so we have to define them in terms of the promoting and inhibiting factors." But this didn't satisfy the objections people were raising. Clarence Schulz asked straight out whether the group felt it had learned anything about intuition itself. Searles, always given to countertransference interpretations, said that each person felt too guilty to respond to a question like that. By the end of the meeting, Frieda acknowledged that the papers said little about how intuition worked, but she still thought it was useful to talk about the pitfalls of trying to study so elusive a topic. Her insecurity and embarrassment about chairing a group that seemed to have so few tangible accomplishments was, however, less apparent in what she said than in what she was unable to articulate: most of her comments were uncharacteristically said in a voice so low that the transcriber had to leave them blank in her record of the meeting.[31]

The group presented their papers at the APA and then (with the exception of Adland) published them in the association's journal, but Frieda remained frustrated with their work. Years later, Don Burnham emphasized the tremendous pressure she was under—from the foundation providing the funds, from her fellow group members, from other Lodge staff, and from outside critics—to come up with a systematic explanation of how intuition functions in clinical contexts. Burnham wondered whether the push to be "scientific" made Frieda feel as if she had to be "an objective observer rather than a co-participant in the process or, even more contrary to her sense of individuality, a boundaryless non-entity in a field of forces."[32]

Frieda's uncertainty about her role in the "intuitive process" is clearly evident in her repeated attempts to explain that famous moment with Mrs. E. in the pack. Paradoxically, repetition seemed to make the event less clear; it was as if the better Frieda got at being a therapist, the less she could describe what she was doing.

Something closely scrutinized often appears more cryptic—details are seen from new angles, and boundaries get rewritten. But Frieda's accounts of her work with Mrs. E. don't just vary in detail; there are systematic changes

of meaning attributed to what went on. As she became more and more convinced that the case was paradigmatic of her whole approach, it took on even
greater significance. By the time Frieda had told the story for the tenth time,
it started to sound as if understanding that one moment with Mrs. E. in the
pack might hold the secret to psychosis. With stakes that high, it's not surprising that Frieda seemed less and less certain of what had actually happened.

The variations in how she recounted the event are, however, deeply interesting in themselves. We rarely have the opportunity to watch a doctor piecing together her account of a key case. "The clinical practice of narrative,"
historian John Harley Warner observes, hasn't typically been considered part
of doctors' work. "As we begin to recognize the day-by-day inscription of the
patient chart as itself a significant clinical activity," Warner continues, "we
begin to see the practice of writing as one among the practices of medicine."[33]
In the case of Mrs. E., Frieda's constant revising makes each description a
separate text. The repetitions, however, give the whole event a mythic tone,
as if it were one of her favorite Hasidic legends, the particular details of time
and place unimportant. The fact that Frieda always cited that one moment
with Mrs. E. in the wet sheet pack and no other part of the treatment intensi-
fies this effect, making that one moment seem the embodiment of her whole
approach.

Yet for all her eagerness to see patients as collaborators, even Frieda
seemed unwilling to grant them a central role. She clearly admired Mrs. E.'s
lucid insights about her illness but seemed to accord them less and less importance as the years went on. The more Frieda discussed this case, the more
she glossed over Mrs. E.'s contributions and emphasized her own role. Even
Mrs. E.'s explicit statements in the pack, so prominent in Frieda's original
notes, become increasingly invisible in her later accounts.

In the version of Mrs. E.'s case that Frieda published in *Principles,* she
writes: "Some empathic notion for which I cannot give any account made me
turn back toward the patient. I saw an expression of utter despair and discouragement on her face, which made me decide to unpack her myself." Notice what has happened in this retelling. A mysterious force has suddenly
slipped between therapist and patient. Frieda is no longer the agent of her actions; Mrs. E. doesn't directly express her needs. A diffuse "empathic notion" now controls the therapeutic action from some unseen place.[34]

In Frieda's original account—the notes she dictated in 1935, the day after
the session itself—Mrs. E. was far more energetic and involved. She challenged Frieda directly: "Oh, you are afraid of me when I am unpacked, are
you?" It was only after Frieda responded, "Not at all," that she set about un-

doing the pack herself. In the original version, no "expression of utter despair and discouragement" appeared on Mrs. E.'s face. Things that were once explicit and verbal have become cryptic forces, floating in the air.

Did Frieda change these details because she reinterpreted the meaning of the event, or because she recalled it differently at a distance of fifteen years? Perhaps she was imposing a finer grain of detail on her descriptions, especially of nonverbal communication, a topic she had known little about in 1935. We often remember an event differently when we learn a new way to describe it; memory is constantly being polished, its texture changed. But Frieda's revisions didn't simply add more detail; they transformed her into the primary actor, leaving Mrs. E. increasingly mute and afraid.

Frieda gave a still more complicated account of this moment in the paper she contributed to the intuition research group's symposium at the APA. Systematically studying the "intuitive process" for three years seemed to make the whole thing even more mystifying. So many new dynamics were now assumed to be present that it took Frieda three times as much space in 1955 to describe the moment with Mrs. E. as it had the day after it occurred.

This version (which turned out to be the last one she published) was by far the most convoluted and confused:

I had worked with a patient for a long period of time. Despite her assaultiveness a good mutual working relationship had been established. One day, while she was in a wet pack, I asked her whether she would be willing to give a legally needed signature. Her prompt answer was "if you unpack me." Turning away from the patient I walked toward the door of her room to go and ask the nurses to do so. On the verge of leaving the room I looked back at the patient without realizing why. I believed at the time, that as I looked back at her I caught the clue from the expression of disappointment and frustration, if not despair, on the patient's face, that "if you unpack me" meant me, and not the nurses. I came back and opened the pack single-handedly, and she gave me her signature. Later on the patient related this experience as having been the first step toward her recovery.

My turning around, without being motivated by conscious reasoning, yet with the subsequent realization that I had to unpack her without calling the nurses, was listed at the time as the result of an otherwise unexplainable, intuitive experience.

In the light of my further continuous experiences with schizophrenic patients as well as of my knowledge of my own personality, I feel today that there is good reason to assume that the non-verbal communication of the patient's wish to have me unpack her had preceded my turning toward the door. I now believe that I had initially tried to suppress or repress the visual impression of the patient's misery as a source of my intuitive grasp of what she wanted. . . . As I see it now, I [had] made a vain attempt to extricate myself from the demands of the patient and of my own professional conscience. At the last minute, I turned back to look at the patient, just before taking the step which might have meant failing her badly.[35]

Again, notice what has happened. The moment with Mrs. E., so simple and straightforward at the time it happened, has now become extraordinarily complicated and difficult to comprehend. What took a few seconds to transpire and (originally) a paragraph to describe now seems an enigma requiring the sustained work of many years to understand. Again, the event has been systematically altered. Again, there are changes in both Mrs. E.'s actions and Frieda's role. Originally the patient had explicitly helped, for example, by "showing where the sheets are fixed." Twenty years later, Frieda "opened the pack single-handedly." The Mrs. E. who once taunted Frieda, "Oh, so you are afraid of me when I am unpacked?" now doesn't speak. Once an active participant, Mrs. E. has now been reduced to cryptic glances and silent needs. Frieda becomes the main actor, and her potential failure the key issue at stake.[36]

These varying accounts are all equally "true," as are numerous others we might imagine. Had we witnessed the event ourselves, we may well have seen or remembered it in yet other ways. But even if we grant the inherent ambiguity of every interaction, especially with psychotic patients, we still have to wonder why Frieda's descriptions of this one changed so strikingly over time. In literary criticism, where creativity is everything, the discovery of many different versions of the same text is a cause for celebration; in psychiatry, where technique derives from precedent, such variations are problematic. With a patient as important as Mrs. E., they cause particular difficulty because Frieda's approach in this case clearly served as the model for all her subsequent work with psychotic patients. Failing to resolve these issues to her satisfaction, intuition remained both a challenging enigma and a source of frustration.

It is interesting to contrast Frieda's approach to these issues with that of her British colleagues, especially Melanie Klein. Instead of focusing on a cognitive process like intuition to explain the subtle dynamics of the therapeutic relationship, Klein emphasized the unconscious splits among the patient's "internal objects" and the transfer of unacceptable feelings into the analyst through "projective identification." On this view, it wasn't the therapist's active process of listening that was key; it was the movement of split-off contents between the unconscious of patient and therapist that shaped the quality of the interaction between them. Although both Frieda (following Sullivan) and Klein (like Fairbairn) were focused on the dynamics of relationship, Frieda concentrated on the overt interchange, whereas Klein was more concerned with the way internal parts of the patient's personality were connected or split off from one another.

This difference stemmed primarily from Frieda's lack of interest in metapsychology. Unlike Klein, who was fascinated by the relations among "internal objects" in a psychic world that existed only hypothetically, Frieda concentrated all her energies on the relationship with the patient actually sitting across from her. This was yet another reflection of an Orthodox Jewish upbringing that valued deeds more than theories. As Buber has noted, "Religious truth is not a conceptual abstraction but has existential relevance. . . . Words can only point the way. . . . Religious truth can be made adequately manifest only in the individual's or the community's life of religious actualization." Via completely different routes, however, Frieda and Klein both arrived at the same core conclusions: no patient was too disturbed to form a transference relationship to the analyst, and understanding the subtle dynamics of this relationship was essential to therapy with every patient.[37]

Given the many tensions she was experiencing at the Lodge in the early 1950s, it was with a great sense of relief that Frieda accepted the opportunity she was offered in spring 1955 for a year's sabbatical at the Ford Foundation's Center for Advanced Study in the Behavioral Sciences in Palo Alto, California. A fellowship at the center is a major honor—one does not apply; one is invited—and Frieda was the first woman and the first nonacademic to be chosen. After forty years of carrying a full load of patients as well as the heavy teaching, supervisory, and administrative responsibilities she had always taken on, the chance to concentrate on writing seemed like a gift from God. Doctors don't get sabbaticals, and being given one at this juncture— with *Principles* successfully published, Greenberg's treatment concluded, and an ambitious program of clinical research launched but stalemated— made the offer seem especially propitious. The center had the added allure of providing a chance to work with a talented group of peers, who could teach Frieda things in fields other than hers and who were not, like all her younger colleagues and students, people she was responsible for. It was like returning to those exhilarating days in the late 1920s, when she and Erich were part of the nascent Frankfurt Psychoanalytic Institute.

Frieda was especially excited by the value the center placed on interdisciplinary research. She had been invited the year before to become a member of the working group on communication organized by the Macy Foundation. (Of the thirteen members, whose fields ranged from anthropology to zoology, she and Margaret Mead were the only women.) The group's sessions, held every few months at countryside inns, were designed to foster sustained interchange on broad topics, transcending the limits of the traditional disciplinary conference. Frieda was especially stimulated by her conversations with ethologists like Konrad Lorenz and Niko Tinbergen, whose studies of animal communication seemed to her to offer provocative insights into the gestures and postures of the mute psychotic patient. To spend a whole year engaging in cross-disciplinary work with talented colleagues from every field of behavioral science felt particularly invigorating to Frieda at this point in her life.[38]

Before she left for Palo Alto, Frieda tried to figure out the most effective way to write up Greenberg's case. The therapy had been so collaborative it didn't feel right just to write a standard account. After exploring various options, Frieda finally hit on the idea of including both her perspective and Joanne's, in separate sections with commentary interspersed. Joanne's mother could contribute a third view, and Richard Frank, the psychiatrist who had treated Joanne as a child, could write a preface.

A clinical report constructed from these varying vantage points would have been truly innovative. Narratives about treatment in psychiatry, like those in all fields of medicine, typically provide only the physician's viewpoint. If patients want to give their version, they have to write for a popular audience; they don't have access to professional journals. For Frieda to have envisioned a case history that limited the authority of her perspective and put the patient and her mother on a par with doctors was unprecedented. Psychiatrists simply don't permit challenges to their own accounts of what worked and what didn't.[39]

When Frieda asked Joanne "if she felt like writing a summary of their work together," Joanne had no idea that this was an unusual request. As she later recalled:

> I was in college. I had done a lot of poetry and a lot of writing. Writing was what I did. So in a way this was a project in line with writing. . . . I worked in the morning before school. The whole problem was not to get sucked in by the sickness I was describing. . . . I set up a series of

hedges, so that right after I did the work every morning, I zipped off to school and sat with my friends for a half hour before class. I tried to objectify it, tried to put words on it. . . . I did it totally on my own. I was not in collaboration with [Frieda] at that time in any way. . . . I thought, I want to put this whole thing behind me. I never want to think about it again.[40]

Joanne completed a fifty-page draft, then graduated from college and moved to Colorado. She taught Latin etymology to sixth graders and began working on a novel, *The King's Persons*. A fictionalized version of a true event—the massacre of the Jews of York, England, in 1190—it was Greenberg's story only metaphorically, providing a useful psychic separation from her Lodge experiences. Yet the line between delusions and vibrant fiction remained thin. As Joanne told Frieda in a letter: "Sometimes I worry that it's unfair to make people who were once alive live again in a book as tongues of the author. . . . Sometimes they cry: 'What are you doing to us?'" She said she envied Frieda's clinical distance. "I think you are much more fortunate in your writing, because the wisdom which you unveil is all yours, and not borrowed words, or stolen."[41] (Frieda, of course, didn't consider her "wisdom" hers, any more than Joanne really thought her fiction belonged to others.)

Joanne's parents were supportive of Frieda's plan to publish the case (using the pseudonym "Evelyn Marcus" to identify their daughter). Toward the end of the treatment, Joanne's father, who had become so fond of Frieda that he referred to her with the Yiddish diminutive "Friedl," had declared: "Doctor, as long as this child was sick, we couldn't believe that she would get well. Now we [wonder] what could we do for psychiatry to show how grateful we are that she has made it. If you think it can help if you write this up, go to it. I don't want you to hold back anything you think is good to learn from."[42] So Frieda set off for California ready to write her section of the narrative and then juxtapose the various perspectives. En route, she attended Joanne's wedding to Albert Greenberg; Joanne remembers how "luminescent" Frieda looked.

Spectacularly set above the Stanford University campus, with views of San Francisco Bay and the Los Altos hills, the center was (and still is) an idyllic place to spend a year. Each office, built of redwood, has a glass wall looking out on a meticulously maintained property filled with walking paths and fruit trees. In a letter she sent to Kurt Goldstein soon after arriving, Frieda called it "indescribably beautiful, a dream come true, like the magic mountain without TB." Most extraordinary was the completely unstructured time, something she had never had in her whole life. "No strings are attached. You can think, you can look at your umbilicus, like the late Buddha and meditate; you can write; you can do as you please as long as you are sure that you will do something which will enhance your productivity." (Soon after she got there, Frieda went to the director and asked if her dog could accompany her to the office. He thought a moment and then responded: "Well, there is only one person who can know what the best conditions are for you, so if bringing your dog will help, by all means do it.") Then sixty-six years old, Frieda was intensely happy to have a break from seeing patients every hour; the staff of helpers ready to attend to her every need made it even more wonderful. And there were so many parties she had to force herself to limit social engagements to weekends.[43]

In her first weeks at the "think motel," as she later called it in a talk to Lodge colleagues, Frieda did feel somewhat insecure with the other "fellows." They all had blackboards in their offices, and their mathematical approach to behavioral science was completely foreign to her. With the same determination that she had memorized the military classification system in Königsberg or mastered anatomy in those sweltering summers in medical school, she decided she would learn it. (As she told herself: "If you weren't too old to accept this invitation, you can't hide behind being too old to learn the quantitative approach—now go to it.")[44] Fortunately, she soon realized that even if she spent the entire year trying to do this, she still wouldn't learn enough to use the new methods; instead, she plunged into a project for which she was far better suited.

Frieda organized an interdisciplinary research group with three other fellows: two anthropologists with strong interests in linguistics (Norman McQuown from the University of Chicago and Charles Hockett from Cornell) and her old friend and fellow psychiatrist Henry Brosin. They then recruited Gregory Bateson, ethnologist-in-residence at the nearby Palo Alto VA Hospital, and kinesiologist Ray Birdwhistell from Vanderbilt University to work with them. The group's "microanalysis" of an interview between a mother and her psychotic son would turn out to be one of the most widely discussed pieces of research in psychiatry, forming the basis for the "double-bind" theory of schizophrenia that Bateson and the others later popularized.

Frieda's remarkable ability to arrange life to suit her own needs and interests was once again apparent during her time at the center. It was she who enticed these researchers from different fields to collaborate, talking McQuown into setting aside the dictionary of American Indian language he was writing, getting Birdwhistell to come all the way from Louisville, and seducing Bateson, known for his prickliness and narcissism, to join a group effort. Frieda was convinced that her so-called gift for understanding schizophrenic patients was really an attentiveness to nonverbal communication. She thought that if the linguists could create a system for describing the subtle gestures, intonation, and movements that occurred in interaction, it would finally be possible to analyze "intuitive" aspects of the therapeutic process.

The group worked from filmed interviews that Bateson had previously recorded with families of schizophrenics. Their analyses were extraordinarily intensive—the linguist and kinesiologist initially spent six hours transcribing one second of interaction—creating fertile ground for tension and disagreement. Bateson later wrote that one of Frieda's "great contributions to this team was that we fought very little about matters which were not worth fighting about. One did not in Frieda's presence say things which one could recognize as second-rate. Perhaps even one's power to recognize the second-rate was in some way enhanced when she was around. It was not that she behaved didactically, but rather that her very presence insisted upon simplicity." This was quite a compliment from a man who remarked in the same paragraph: "Some of us are rigid, some of us want to be prima donnas, some of us rigidly want to be prima donnas."

And since Bateson was the interviewer in the film they were analyzing, there were many moments when the group interpreted his actions in ways he found embarrassing or painful. "At such times," he recalled, "Frieda extended a basic wide friendliness which made it easier for me to evaluate what was being said without those feelings of rejection which would otherwise make the comments unacceptable. It was not that she reassured by diminishing the force of the critical comment; what she did was lend that strength which enabled one to receive the comment."[45]

Henry Brosin remembered the team's work as "thrilling, with an abundance of ideas in constant flow." During the last three months Frieda was at the center, they sometimes spent fifteen hours a day poring over the data, analyzing every nuance of what had transpired between Bateson and the patient, as well as their own reactions to these observations.[46]

Midway through the year, Frieda gave a public lecture on her work at the Lodge, attended by a large and enthusiastic group of fellows and center staff as well as by colleagues from Stanford and San Francisco. One appreciative listener later wrote:

The large seminar room was packed. On the walls, paintings done by [Frieda's] patients were displayed. She spoke on her method of using psychotherapy with schizophrenics. The lecture conveyed to the lay-man the schizophrenic mind, its bizarre fantasy-reality, its strategy of evading other human beings. The listener got a glimpse into Frieda's predicament as a therapist, her subtle moves to draw the patient out of his shell, her attempts to strengthen any rudiments of normalcy, the way in which she transferred herself into his mode of existing—squatting on the floor beside him, if this was what he did—and shared his fantasies as long as this was beneficial to him, while all the time heedful to con-vey to him her deep concern and respect for him. . . . [She] talked about the uncertainties that haunt the therapist. Was a certain response of his right? Had the patient, emotionally or intellectually, been ready for it? Or did he feel hurt? . . . Can the therapist's intuition be fostered or im-proved? Can the laws by which intuition comes about be taught? At the end Frieda described the therapist's feeling of bliss when he becomes convinced that the patient is getting better. An unusually long, excited applause followed.

When members of the audience rushed up to praise "her remarkable lecture," Frieda shrugged off their responses. "Lucid? Convincing? After forty years of experience? What else do you expect?"[47]

She seemed equally unsurprised by the role she had taken on among the fellows. Despite her age and frumpy appearance, Frieda became a kind of shaman to the group, magnetically drawing people to her. Ray Birdwhistell recalled a classic moment:

> One night a cocktail party was given at the Center and a great number of very attractive young wives attended. Frieda arrived late, looked at the situation, took a rose out of the centerpiece, tucked it under her wristband, looked at it, looked around, and gradually most of the males in the place drifted over next to her.[48]

Throughout this year in Palo Alto, Frieda corresponded with Greenberg about their planned book. In a letter soon after arriving, she wrote, "It is per-fectly wonderful here and in a way it is just too bad that the status of our col-laboration does not make a trip of yours to California sufficiently necessary so that I could justify it before the Foundation." When Joanne went on an ex-tended honeymoon trip to Europe, Frieda wrote to her there. By April, how-ever, having not yet started her part of the manuscript, she turned to apologizing for having rushed Joanne to finish her section. As Frieda became more and more absorbed by her work with Bateson and Joanne settled into her new life in Colorado, their letters shifted from the book to warm exchanges about current experiences.[49]

Beyond the intoxications of life at the center, Frieda's difficulty in writing her report of Greenberg's case clearly reflected her uncertainty about how to explain the striking success of the treatment. Instead of boldly claiming so unambiguous an accomplishment, Frieda again seemed to see herself mainly as a hard worker, carrying out a plan set in motion by larger forces. She was extraordinarily pleased with the work she and Joanne had done together, but when it came to describing her own contribution to the process, Frieda couldn't seem to articulate what had made the therapy so productive. Perhaps the stakes were just too great. The last thing she needed was more people thinking of her work as some kind of private magic rather than the systematic application of methods available to other therapists.

So, revealingly, what Frieda did write during her year at the center was the introduction to a book titled *Progress in Psychotherapy,* which she was then editing with Jacob Moreno. The fullest expression of her lifelong commitment to open-mindedness and flexibility, this volume included chapters on every conceivable therapeutic approach, in the hope of bridging the divide between warring factions. The very fact of Frieda's agreeing to coedit the book with Moreno—a famously difficult man, whose own technique, psychodrama, was intensely narcissistic—demonstrated yet again her willingness to play the peacemaker and subordinate her needs to others. But spending six months of her precious year in Palo Alto toning down the strident claims of contributors whose views are now forgotten robbed Frieda of the time she needed to reflect on the complex dynamics of Greenberg's treatment. Instead of ending up as the author of what might well have become the best-known example of psychotherapy with a schizophrenic, she settled for coediting a compendium of other people's ideas.

In the expansive, relaxed climate of the center, Frieda did, however, allow herself to reflect on the meaning of some of her own life experiences. She spent many evenings in the comfortable carriage house adjoining the home of a former Lodge analyst where she had chosen to live for the year (a place strikingly like her own cottage in Rockville), reminiscing with friends about life in Germany. Leo Löwenthal, her old Frankfurt colleague, was also a fellow at the center that year, as was Jacob Marschak, a professor of economics in Heidelberg during her time there. Frieda invited Hilde Bruch, then in one of her depressed periods, to come out from New York for an extended visit, and in the warmth of this little German-speaking community she had created for herself, Frieda let go of some of her characteristic reserve. She allowed herself to be talked into taping memories of her early years, and the few fragments that survive give us priceless insight into those experiences. As she laughingly recounted the affair with Erich, spoke movingly of her guilt at her father's death, and bitterly recalled the behavior of her "Aryan" colleagues in the 1930s, Frieda's friends glimpsed for the first time the inner feelings that this deeply private woman suddenly seemed to want to speak of.

Frieda was also beginning the painful process of coming to terms with the thwarted life her mother had led. Dead only three years at that point, Klara was still an extraordinarily powerful presence in Frieda's mind. Having left it to Grete to take care of her all those years, Frieda now tried to make sense of what her real relationship with Klara had been. In many ways, she was living the life her mother had wished for herself—a life Klara's strength had made possible. Yet her mother's envy and resentment had been a barrier preventing the closeness Frieda had always craved. Outwardly, she had won the long-standing competition between them years earlier, but in her own mind, Klara was the omnipotent one and she merely a hard worker. Perhaps if her mother had died before Frieda were in her sixties, she could have come to appreciate in herself even a few of the unique talents others always attributed to her. Instead, clearly guilty at outdoing everyone in her family, especially her indomitable mother, Frieda buried her ideas inside the theories of others and disclaimed even obvious accomplishments. A forceful woman in so many ways, she struggled valiantly to unfortify her own mind, acting as if independent thought were dangerous and could be allowed into her work only in disguise. For Frieda, boldness and abandonment were just too intertwined to make striking out on her own seem safe enough to risk doing.[50]

Every treatment for schizophrenia is experimental, since effects are inconsistent and causes still unknown. Frieda was unusual in admitting this, unlike most of her colleagues, then or now. Although she would never have been so presumptuous as to link her work with that of Pasteur or Koch, she clearly identified with the long tradition in medicine that used the suffering of patients in the present to help those yet to come. In 1953, she received the Adolf Meyer Award from the Association for the Improvement of Mental Hospitals for her "distinguished contributions to the understanding of schizophrenia." In her acceptance speech, she emphasized how much remained to be learned.

Reviewing a book by her old Frankfurt colleague Walther Riese titled *The Conception of Disease,* Frieda derided physicians for being "inebriated" with the triumphs of bacteriology. It was hubris, she argued, to think that disease—"a part of human existence"—would ever be totally eradicated. Besides, pain and suffering weren't only destructive; they could, as Riese noted, "assume stimulating functions and open new roads, endowing the disturbed individual with unforeseen, though potentially pre-existing, gifts and abilities."[51]

Appreciating the darker side of human existence didn't make Frieda a pessimist, as it did Freud. She was more like Jung, seeing hate and redemption as natural processes, like the buildup and breakdown of cells, inseparable and equally necessary to life. This was why she never gave up on patients: not because she knew they would get better, but because the drive toward health was always there. This basic hopefulness, of course, had its own effects: by encouraging patients to concentrate on the work of healing (instead of proving to her that there was something left to save), their own desire to recover became clearer and more urgent.

Frieda could tolerate sitting across from her own craziness, which meant she didn't have to destroy those parts of herself that patients evoked. She had to be careful not to dissolve into them, but she could risk having little bits leak out. It's sanity's fragile container that is frightening, more than the contents inside. Most psychiatrists, concerned about their own clumsiness, can't risk even touching the glass. Frieda was physically stodgy, but her grace as a therapist was extraordinary, and colleagues found a thing of art. For patients, it was beyond art—a genuineness they had given up hoping for. It let them act more normally with her than with anyone else, and it let Frieda work with people who weren't nearly as frightening as her colleagues thought.

Difficult as this may be to believe now, what distinguished psychotherapy from every other method of treating psychosis in the 1930s and 1940s was the optimism of its approach. It might not work as fast as shock in relieving a patient's symptoms, but it held out the potential for a much more complete recovery later on. Families who had been told by mainstream psychiatrists that nothing could be done for their chronically ill relatives found psychotherapy an inspiring alternative, especially at the Lodge, where staff could report that some of their sickest patients were now leading productive lives. (Claims like these were regarded as delusional by many somatic psychiatrists. As historian Michael Clark observes, susceptibility to "psychotherapeutics" has itself often been seen as a form of mental illness.)[52]

Frieda was no ideologue. By conceiving of her work as research, she freed herself from the pressures of trying to find a quick fix and focused instead on long-term goals. Relaxing into the "effortless effort" Zen monks talk about—a concentration on the present moment so deep that the subtlest change can be noted—she kept going even when patients got worse. Alert to every nuance, attentive to variations often imperceptible to others, she felt her way forward through the darkness. An insight gained from one case might help the next, and bit by bit, she could imagine clearing a path wide enough for others to follow.

At a deeper level, one that Frieda never acknowledged to herself, this optimism offered no real protection from doubt. Her admirers have made it seem as if she somehow escaped the despair that plagued every physician who treated psychotic patients, but this is nonsensical. Her reluctance to claim credit even for successes like Mrs. E. or Greenberg and her habit of writing essentially the same paper over and over again show how hard it was for her to believe what she had accomplished. People remember Frieda as supremely confident, but she was far less certain of her skills than they were.

13

Private Decline

There is at least one spot in every dream at which it is unplumbable—a navel, as it were, that is its point of contact with the unknown.[1]

Frieda's year in Palo Alto marked a watershed in her life. For the first time, she had the experience of concentrating on a few things she really cared about, without the interruptions of emergencies on the ward, the needs of her students, trips to lecture or teach in other cities, or the dozens of requests for consultations or advice that constantly pressed on her. (In her first six months at the center, she refused thirty-two speaking invitations.) Having finally been able to work in a sustained way, she was understandably reluctant to give it up when it came time to return to Rockville.

During her absence, Dexter had been forced to find a way of running the Lodge without her for the first time in two decades. He and the staff consulted her by letter about crucial issues, and they all saw one another in Chicago for the meetings of the American Psychiatric Association, but inevitably people's responsibilities changed. So there was interest on both sides in examining what Frieda's role should be.

In a series of letters written while she was still in Palo Alto, various options were explored. The Ford Foundation grant had just been awarded, and Don Burnham, appointed director of research at a newly invigorated Chestnut Lodge Research Institute, was eager to have Frieda participate in the studies being planned. But she wasn't so sure this was what she wanted. As she noted in a letter to Dexter: "I was under the definite impression that we agreed in Chicago that I should not replace the time previously spent with practice by an equally rushed research program, but that you would make it possible for me to spend that part of my research time which I would not work under the Ford project working leisurely and doing my writing during the day rather than nights and weekends." She proposed being paid jointly by the Lodge and the Ford grant, and hinted that it was time for a more formal recognition of her seniority. As always, she took a conciliatory tone, concluding this part of the letter with reassurance: "We can talk about these details upon my return, and I know we shall find a mutually satisfactory solution as we always have. I just bring up the issue . . . because I believe it stands for the difference between a leisurely and peaceful working program and a time-bound rushed life for me." Yet even this minimal degree of assertion seemed to unsettle her. She wrote a postscript saying she felt uncomfortable with the letter upon rereading it, and wished that they could just talk together. (Dexter was on vacation and she didn't want to phone him.) Frieda seemed clearly ambivalent, even after twenty years, about distinguishing her own needs from those of the Lodge. Struggling to sort out these issues, she wrote to Burnham the same day, saying that what she most wanted was to "continue to investigate and write up the material I have [already] collected . . . in keeping with the present chronological and personal phase of my life." She again used the word *leisurely* (this time underlined) to describe the kind of research she envisioned.[2]

A week later, she wrote to Marvin Adland (who was both the clinical director and her closest personal friend on the staff) saying she would "love to hear" what he thought about the various proposals in his "mind of minds (an inadvertent Hebrewism!)." She realized that people's plans for her were well intentioned, but the idea of seeing fewer private patients and concentrating exclusively on Lodge projects made her nervous. "I feel a little reluctant to make myself entirely dependent on Chestnut Lodge for my living, which I have avoided for good reasons for twenty years," Frieda wrote. This was not because of the money, she told Adland, "but because of the element of control which this entails."

She was even more worried about something else. During the year in California, her hearing had gotten considerably worse. It had been deteriorating gradually for years, but after a severe bout of bronchitis in the spring of 1956, the deafness was more noticeable. Frieda told Adland in this same letter that it might well be that the nature of her work at the Lodge would depend on her hearing and not on whatever they planned. "I can get along in a person-to-person conversation in a quiet room as well as ever (with hearing aid)," she wrote, "but I don't know about the work with psychotics and I am handicapped in supervision because I cannot supervise recorded interviews unless they are transcribed." So if it turned out that private practice was her best option, she wanted this still to be possible. She was also concerned that her hearing might continue to worsen. "As you notice, I express it all rather tentatively because the adjustment to the new state of affairs is hard and makes me low spirited." She told Adland that she wouldn't really be able to tell until she was back in her ordinary environment and remarked with frustration that doctors she consulted in California had limited interest "in somebody who will make her final [hearing] aid decisions and adjustments three thousand miles from here." Thanking him warmly for "making my problems yours," she said she hoped he would tell her what he honestly thought.[3]

Frieda had complicated feelings about her deafness. Mara Bowman, her secretary in the early 1950s, remembers her "constantly fussing with her hearing aid. It was never working right. She was never happy with it." Even before the year in California, she had stopped going to big dinner parties. "They felt cruel to her," recalled Margaret Rioch. "Frieda was a converser, and it was really tough for her. She almost stopped going out unless there were just going to be one or two people." Marianne Marschak, the psychologist Frieda had befriended in Palo Alto, later wrote:

> In the lunch room of the Center, Frieda sat at a small table near the entrance. The buzz of voices in the more crowded part of the room, she explained, was picked up by her hearing aid as a confused, distressing noise. Her hearing had become worse recently, so that she could not follow a general conversation in a living room. Yet she would respond to an amusing topic with a smile on her face, in order not to dampen the spirits of the group.[4]

Losing her hearing was in many ways the worst thing that could have happened to Frieda, but she didn't think it unfair. Everyone suffered in some way, and this was hers. She had seen what it had been like for her parents and knew the feeling of being cut off from other people in a way that didn't show. Deafness was a terrible private sorrow for Frieda, but it was also a key source of insight into the isolation of her patients. Just as she had long argued that the suffering of many mentally ill artists was inextricably linked to their talents, we have to see Frieda's own disability as deeply connected to her intense desire to listen—to hear what people were saying at a level beyond words.

However, given that she was "strong deaf," suffering from a condition with a clear genetic component, we might well ask why she chose to become a psychoanalyst in the first place. With two deaf parents and a deaf aunt, she had every expectation that she would eventually lose her own hearing. And this was no subtle problem of old age: Klara was almost totally deaf by her thirties and Adolf by his late fifties. Nor had her parents borne their disabilities well. Adolf was ruined by his deafness, deeply miserable even before his mysterious accident in the elevator. Klara, stoic and determined, refused to let her limitations defeat her, but they clearly contributed to her massive use of denial as a response to every difficulty. When something threatened to disturb her deeply, she blocked it out of her experience. Frieda couldn't hide her disability in professional contexts the way Klara had done at home, but she did dissemble. Various people at the Lodge remember her catching only part of what was said but not asking for the comment to be repeated. She seemed to take Adolf's depressive attitude toward the problem. As her friend and former patient Jane Weinberg put it: "Frieda remembered how hearing aids didn't do anything to help her father, so she figured they wouldn't do much for her either." Given that thirty years separated Adolf's difficulties from hers—thirty years of extraordinary technological progress—this attitude, so unlike her usual scientific approach, clearly seemed defeatist.[5]

At one level, Frieda's decision to become a psychoanalyst—the only profession in the world where one spends hours every day listening to people who make little sense and are lying on a couch with their heads turned away—seems "counterphobic," running straight toward the thing she most feared. Why would she do this? To prove that she could escape her parents' fate? To express her family's tragedy unconsciously? To show how determined she could be? But as much as Frieda's deafness seems to cry out for interpretation, the real situation was probably less complicated. A person makes decisions about a career at a young age, when she feels invincible and able to cope with anything. What should Frieda have done: become a bookkeeper or a housewife in case thirty years later she had hearing difficulties? Whatever we choose to make of it, there is a painful irony here: Frieda's deafness was like Freud's cancer of the mouth, an affliction that robbed them of their defining part.

Being a psychoanalyst who couldn't hear symbolically reenacted the central tragedy of Frieda's life: her failure to cure her parents as a child. She was like Thomas Edison repeating, "Do you hear me?" into a paper cup attached with string to an invisible partner who never replied. Out of sheer persistence, Frieda kept yelling into her end, because every now and then some static or even a word or two made it through to the other side. For all the despair of her work with psychotic patients, Frieda found it sustaining partly because it replayed both the failures and the occasional successes of her struggles with Klara and Adolf.

These conflicts are painfully evident in Frieda's decision to resume treatment with Mr. R. when she returned from Palo Alto. His hostile mutterings were practically impossible for her to make out, and her inability to respond to the subtleties of what he was trying to communicate must have made both of them feel even more isolated. So why did she keep treating him? Although she had discerned some progress before she left—he had grounds privileges and saw her at the cottage—there was little warmth in their relationship, little that might have led her to look forward to resuming the work. Mr. R. was still unpredictably assaultive and largely unresponsive. It would have been easy to let Marvin Adland continue to see him.

But this is not what Frieda did, and her sessions with Mr. R. in the fall and winter of 1956–1957, tape-recorded and transcribed verbatim, for all her colleagues to scrutinize, are a caricature of the therapeutic process. Mr. R. spoke rarely and was belligerent when he did, spewing out angry comments that made no sense. He left sessions early or arrived late. Pauses of fifteen minutes were common. Frieda was seriously deaf by this point and missed much of what he said. Patients who loved her, like Miss N., sat close to her chair and looked directly at her when they spoke. Those who didn't sat across the room, looked away, and mumbled. Even when Frieda begged Mr. R. to repeat something, he ignored her. They had an occasional moment of closeness while companionably smoking together, but these respites lasted no more than a few minutes. The overall pattern was uncommunicative and hostile, and had to have been intensely frustrating for both of them.

Frieda was neither grandiose nor masochistic, and was famous for her good judgment. She made pragmatic choices about which patients to treat and which to refer to others. She didn't waste time—either hers or theirs. She could have seen any Lodge patient she chose when she returned from California, yet Mr. R. was the only one she wanted. She must have believed him still capable of change, or else she was more despairing by that point than anybody realized.

Competition may have been part of it. Adland had made it clear when he presented Mr. R. at a staff meeting during Frieda's absence that they were getting nowhere and had suggested sending Mr. R. to another hospital. He told Frieda in a letter: "I think I need to get clearer with myself on my feelings about having taken over [someone] who had worked with you." Frieda sent a sympathetic response: "Could it be that you talk a little bit too much and a little too warmly to him (and could that be because he was 'my' patient?)." Adland said he would keep at it. But Mr. R. became even more distant—leaving sessions after only a few minutes, wearing plugs in his ears, acting "exceedingly remote" on the ward.[6] So it may have been Adland's readiness to give up on Mr. R. that pushed Frieda into resuming the work. It was one thing to fail him on her own. But to allow Mr. R., who had been forced to switch to a new therapist in the middle of an already difficult treatment because she wanted a sabbatical, to be abandoned by someone else may have seemed intolerable. For a person as dutiful as Frieda to shirk responsibility was unthinkable. She may have felt too guilty not to take him back.

We know far more about Mr. R.'s treatment in the winter of 1957 than in any earlier period; more documents have survived, and there are tape recordings of many of these sessions. We can hear them with each other in hour after hour of unproductive work. As historical data, these materials are unparalleled; this is probably the only taped archive of psychotherapy with a patient diagnosed as paranoid schizophrenic. But as an illustration of Frieda's approach, these tapes are as much an indictment as anything else. The very act of tape-recording every hour with a man who was convinced people were talking about him behind his back seems a violent intrusion into his anguish.[7]

At every session, Mr. R. asked to have the recorder turned off. At every session, Frieda refused. She didn't refuse straight out; she refused the way a textbook psychoanalyst would—by making him feel guilty. She would say: "If it really bothers you, of course we can turn it off. But why don't you see how it is for a little while, and then if you really can't stand it, we'll turn it off." Mr. R. responded to this piece of psychic sabotage in the only ways he could: he talked nonsense, he came late, or he left abruptly in the middle of an hour. There would be a long silence, and then suddenly he would stand up, say, "I'm leaving," and be out the door before Frieda could say a word. Sometimes he came back fifteen minutes later; often he didn't. His leaving made Frieda furious. We can hear her on the tapes banging things around in the office and telephoning secretaries and nurses, demanding that he be located and brought back to her. Once she told him, "I came all the way over here to see you and you're not walking out." Two minutes later, when he did just that, we can hear her yelling, "God damn it!"

The complex relationship Frieda had to Mr. R.'s parents—in reality and in his fantasies—made things yet worse. They constantly pressed her to explain why it was taking so long to make their son better and were enraged at her for having left for a year. (Both Adland, the clinical director, and the social worker in charge of the case sent dozens of detailed letters documenting everything the Lodge was doing to try to help him, but his parents always blamed Frieda personally, just as Hope Hale Davis had with Hermann Brunck.) Not surprisingly, Mr. R. was sometimes confused about whether Frieda was a member of his family, speaking to her in a mixture of Yiddish and German, the languages of his parents. His feelings about her deafness were clearly tied up with anger at his father, who was in his seventies by that point and quite hard of hearing. When Frieda first got a hearing aid, Mr. R. wanted to see it and seemed very concerned about her. She poignantly asked if he would "prefer to change to another therapist without hearing difficulties." Then she decided that "if he wants me to hear him, he can talk loud enough so that I will understand him," a manipulative and hostile response to his ambivalence.

Amid all the tenseness and anger were moments that revealed the depth of their connection to one another. Ward staff reported that Mr. R. seemed visibly disappointed if Frieda had to cancel or postpone a session. He arrived carefully dressed in a shirt and tie, and on the rare occasions when he was ill groomed, she expressed her worry about him. At times, Mr. R. helpfully pointed out details that the technically inept Frieda had missed, like the microphone unplugged or the tape recorder not operating. (Given his hatred of the apparatus, this thoughtfulness seems especially touching.) Sometimes instead of yelling at him when he abruptly got up to leave, Frieda would say things like, "Stay; a man has the right to change his mind if he wants to." Once, when he spat out "I don't like that pose of yours—it's like a Southern belle," she said warmly, "An old German Jewess Southern belle? That *is* funny," and they both burst out laughing.

Perhaps they were in the midst of a particularly difficult period, or this was some conflict they eventually could have worked through. But it's hard to listen to these tapes and think that anything Frieda was doing made much sense therapeutically. We can understand how she might have been too frustrated or embarrassed by her limitations to stop seeing patients. (Think of all the old people who keep driving even when they're a menace on the roadways.) But a paranoid patient talking gibberish to a therapist who is rarely able to hear what he's saying does seem like a perversion of psychotherapy.

This wasn't the only domain where Frieda seemed to be "losing her edge," as one colleague tactfully put it. She hadn't "seemed herself" ever since her return from Palo Alto. She had been working for months on the paper on loneliness but didn't seem able to finish it. "Even though she was very anxious to publish this paper," her editorial assistant Virginia Gunst recalled, "unlike previous ones, this appeared to be a real effort." Psychologist Margaret Rioch said: "It was obvious there'd been a big change. She was miserable at being so deaf and even more lonely." Julia Waddell said she "began to get anxious about things." Don Bloch said that like a great athlete, Frieda seemed to be "losing her timing"; he noted that she was seriously injured by a patient for the first time in her life during this period. Otto Will wondered where she fit in to the new organization. It was almost as if the Lodge had outgrown her, with the young, ambitious men who now filled its ranks remaking it in their own image. "When you stay at an institution a long time," Will mused, "you're bound to feel somewhat anachronistic. I got the feeling she was just getting worn out, kind of ground down." The previous spring, Bullard had asked Will and Adland what Frieda was worth and what her title should be. Will was shocked. "How could you speak of Frieda in terms of monetary value? Frieda was Frieda. Whatever you could pay her, she should get."[8]

Mabel Peterson and Donna Grimmer both recalled her constantly asking them to speak from the next room so she could test her hearing. Other staff remember covering for her when she missed something, just as Frieda had done for Klara decades earlier. She went from one otologist to another, and they did her as little good as they had done for her mother. Thinking back to her early days at the Lodge, Frieda bitterly remarked to friends that she had been hired "through the back door." Unable to keep teaching, she asked Alberta Szalita to take over her seminar at the White Institute in New York. "I felt sorry for her," said Szalita. "She wanted me to do it, and I very gladly did, but it was clear that she was unhappy."

That winter, Frieda filed an affidavit with the German government for restitution of the property the Nazis had stolen from her rooms in the house on Mönchhofstrasse. When the check arrived, she tossed it on the desk, telling Donna Grimmer acidly: "It's nothing but a pittance." She was intensely aware of having fared better than others—fellow Heidelberg psychiatrist Josef Reis had died in Theresienstadt—but her usual optimism seemed to have left her.

In a photograph taken that year, Frieda stands in the kitchenette of the cottage. Dark trees are visible through the window behind her, and she is wearing a black dress that covers practically her entire body. Her deeply lined face stares past the camera. There is something flat in her expression that makes the pain seem even more intense. The formal look of her clothing—the earrings match the dress—contrasts sharply with the unguarded look on her face. She could not look more miserable, and for a woman as vain as Frieda to have allowed this picture to be taken reveals how despairing she must have felt.

At the end of January 1957, her dog, Munie, died after a brief illness. Frieda's constant companion for ten years—in Chicago, Santa Fe, Palo Alto, always next to her wherever she went—Munie's name, Sanskrit for "sage" or "the silent one," reflected her significance. When Jane Weinberg received a formal notice of the dog's death in the mail, she found it terribly painful.

Anne Bullard felt guilty that she had brushed the whole thing off. "When Frieda called to tell me what had happened," Anne said later, "I should have acted more upset."

Frieda apparently realized she was in bad shape, and according to one source, planned to consult with Larry Kubie. He had treated Virginia Gunst and Hilde Bruch, and was known as "a psychiatrist's psychiatrist": astute, committed to the highest standards, and meticulous about confidentiality. (During the years Kubie had lived in New York, he treated a lot of celebrities and was adept at keeping quiet about who he saw.)[9] Otto Will later sympathized with Frieda's plight: "I knew people who were very prominent who came from other cities to see Sullivan. It's too damned bad. Who do you go to when you get to that kind of position? When you feel depressed or isolated or unwanted and people are competing with you?"

Frieda had been invited to give the Karen Horney Memorial Lecture in New York that spring (a fitting irony, given their relationship), and when her old secretary, Mara Bowman, wrote to announce her upcoming marriage, Frieda said she looked forward to meeting her fiancé at the reception. She seemed to take particular pleasure in the fact that Bowman was marrying a psychiatrist, teasing her in a letter: "I smile and think, after all, Chestnut Lodge sold psychiatry and you to one another, didn't it? How skeptical you were in the beginning! I feel a little bit—and with great pleasure—like a kind of godmother to your engagement."

But these happy plans never materialized. Frieda became severely ill with flu right before the lecture and had to cancel the whole trip. Her convalescence was long and painful. As Donna Grimmer recalled: "She just didn't have her usual strength or vitality." Others noticed that she seemed to get exhausted easily. Anne Bullard was startled when Frieda said she often had to take sleeping pills at night and amphetamines to get up in the morning.

In April, Martin Buber, Frieda's old friend from Frankfurt, came to Washington to give a series of lectures. She didn't think she would be able to hear in a large auditorium, so she asked Buber if he would come out to the Lodge to visit her. This meeting was supposed to be a great secret. Buber later confided to a friend that Frieda was suffering a great deal and was preoccupied with never having had children. Jane Weinberg, sensing that she seemed unusually unhappy, offered to come from Chicago and take her away for a vacation somewhere. Frieda agreed that she needed a rest and went alone to Florida for a few weeks to try to get her strength back. She stayed at the Albion Inn on Sarasota Bay, in a quiet cottage near a small fishing village. Friends sent letters and get-well presents, and she wrote to Weinberg and Hilde Bruch to say how much this meant to her. When she returned to the

Lodge toward the end of April looking tanned and fit, Mabel Peterson remembered thinking that the old Frieda was finally back.

On April 25, Joanne Greenberg gave birth to her first child, David. She wrote Frieda an ecstatic letter saying that Albert had been there with her in the delivery room "to help share a joy too much for one person." She talked of how much she looked forward to the baby meeting Frieda, "his second grandmother," and told her not to "feel insulted that the generations have turned us both over one notch."[10]

On April 28, Marvin Adland's phone rang in the middle of a very hot Sunday afternoon. It was Edith Weigert. Frieda was supposed to come for lunch that day, but she hadn't showed up and Edith was concerned. "Why do they always call me?" Adland grumbled to himself in irritation. (At that point, he was associate medical director, Dexter's second-in-command, and people were constantly bothering him with trivial problems.) Adland told Edith he'd check on Frieda and drove the short distance from Chevy Chase to the cottage. He rang the bell. There was no answer. He dug out his master key and tried to unlock the door, but the chain was on from the inside and he couldn't get in. Suddenly apprehensive, Adland ran to get Raymond Baker and they came back with a pair of bolt cutters. They broke the chain and entered. Everything seemed normal. They went upstairs. Nothing unusual. Then they heard the water running. They opened the door to the bathroom. Frieda was in the bathtub, clearly dead. Adland turned off the faucet and told Raymond to leave. Then he called Dexter, who came over immediately. They called various other people. Eventually they called the police. "I know I should have called them first," Adland admitted, "but I didn't. I just couldn't."

The rumors about Frieda's death began at that moment. Telephones rang all over Washington and New York that afternoon, as stunned friends and colleagues tried to absorb what had happened. The details were unclear, which added to the speculation. She hadn't drowned; Adland said she was sitting up when he entered. But the circumstances were ambiguous. The police ordered an autopsy (which would have horrified Frieda—it is against Jewish law to desecrate a body). Finding evidence of advanced arteriosclerosis, Frank Broschart, the deputy medical examiner in Rockville, ruled that she had died of an acute coronary thrombosis. Frieda's closest friends were convinced she had killed herself.

The Bullards telephoned Anna in Israel. "She was so upset she couldn't understand what was being said," said Alisa, "so we had to call back. Telephoning another country was something unheard of in those days, so we went to a cousin's house who connected us. Anna and Grete were utterly devastated." They had been in the midst of planning a big reunion to coincide with Frieda's visit to Israel that summer. It seemed impossible that she had dropped dead. Women in their family were famously long-lived.

Dexter sent Joanne a telegram informing her of Frieda's death. Joanne's letter joyously announcing David's birth was returned to her unopened a week later by the post office.

The funeral was held on Wednesday, May 1, at Dexter and Anne's home on the grounds of Chestnut Lodge. Jane Weinberg came from Chicago; the Kasles, whose guest house Frieda had rented while at the center, flew in from Palo Alto. Erich and a dozen other colleagues and friends took the train down from New York. Joanne, still in the hospital after giving birth five days earlier, was too weak to travel from Colorado. Frieda had left specific instructions in the will found in her desk saying she wanted an Orthodox funeral. Adland had to scramble to make the arrangements since she was not a member of any local congregation. The Bullards left everything to him; they knew nothing of Jewish practices. There were far too many people to fit into the cottage, and although Anne felt reluctant to step in—"I wasn't her family, after all"—there didn't seem to be any other option. "I wasn't going to see Frieda buried from a completely strange place," Anne declared, vetoing the nearest Jewish funeral home. So the service was held at Rose Hill, which Morrie Schwartz called "one of the most gentile places I have ever been in."

The huge house was jammed. Young Marjorie said: "All I remember was how crowded it was." Many patients were present, along with the whole Lodge staff. The coffin was put in the dining room; people sat in rented chairs on the adjoining porch. Erich, wrapped in a prayer shawl and immersed in the ancient Hebrew psalms, sat with tears streaming down his face. Many others sobbed openly throughout the service. Mabel Peterson later told a friend: "It was my first experience with a Jewish funeral, and I found it very warm and meaningful. I liked not having loads of flowers, whose smell I usually find depressing." Burial was ten miles away in Mt. Lebanon Cemetery in Hyattsville, the nearest Jewish burial ground. Adland had explained that people would expect to come back to the house afterward, so Anne nervously tried to arrange things the way she thought proper. "We had food, sandwiches, and a lot of wine, which was what Marvin told us was appropriate." Dexter was more stunned than anyone had ever seen him, his hearty hospitality totally useless in that context.[11]

People were surprised that Frieda had made a point of wanting an Orthodox funeral, since she hadn't been observant during all her years in the United States. There was a certain resonance with Sullivan's death, eight years earlier. He had requested a formal Catholic ritual, complete with high mass and a gun salute at Arlington National Cemetery, which "was about the most opposite image you could have of this very modest and very open-minded and very liberal person," as Hilde Bruch recalled. But after she talked it over with friends, Bruch had decided it made sense: Sullivan had been so ostracized in psychoanalytic circles that he would want in death all the honors and recognition that were due him. In Frieda's case, it was the opposite. She clearly wanted to prove that she had remained, at some level, her parents' dutiful daughter and to atone for the sins she had committed.

In her will, she had appointed Erich and Virginia Gunst as joint executors. Apparently Frieda had never told Erich this, and he promptly had himself legally released from the responsibility. Anne and Dexter couldn't understand why Frieda had listed him in the first place—"We thought it was nutty," Anne recalled—oblivious to Frieda's deeply held conviction that on really crucial matters only Jews could be trusted.[12]

As it turned out, Frieda apparently had second thoughts about Erich herself. Her original will had been prepared in 1949 (by Virginia Gunst's attorney in Richmond). But at some subsequent date, she crossed out various lines in that document, including Erich's name, and penned a handwritten addendum specifying arrangements for disposing of her property, personal belongings, unpublished manuscripts, patient records, and Gertrud Jacob's paintings. The original will had included funds to be left to Klara, and since these were among the sections crossed out, it is likely that Frieda took the occasion of her mother's death in 1952 as the moment to prepare a new document. In July 1956, while she was still in Palo Alto, Gunst's lawyer sent her a revision incorporating all the handwritten changes. He included very precise instructions for how to ensure that the new will would be legally binding (including the requirement that she write her name as "Frieda Fromm"). She never did this, so at the time of her death, the old will remained in effect. On the day of Frieda's funeral, Erich and Virginia both legally removed themselves as executors. Erich further relinquished his right to any property or personal effects that might be awarded to him. He was paid one dollar to make this arrangement official and had no further role in the disposition of the estate.

However, despite having filed a similar petition, Virginia Gunst represented herself to the Bullards and all of Frieda's friends and colleagues as her executor. A few days after the funeral, she called Anne Bullard and asked if she could have the desk and rug she had recently given Frieda as a gift. Virginia was always buying Frieda expensive clothing and furniture, so this request seemed reasonable and Anne quickly agreed to it. She had no idea that the desk contained all of Frieda's private papers, correspondence, manuscripts, and financial records and that Virginia was thereby spiriting them off without anyone realizing it. When she later cleaned out the cottage, Virginia also took various storage boxes, including old photographs, letters, and other mementos of Frieda's life in Europe. That was the last anyone ever saw of them.[13]

Gunst, remembered as a tall, patrician lady from a distinguished Southern, Jewish family—and one of only a handful of Frieda's close friends never to have been her patient—arrived at the cottage unannounced one day soon after the funeral to supervise the dispersal of Frieda's belongings. She instructed Donna Grimmer to lay a sheet across the living room floor and to spread a number of small objects on it. Gunst then invited various of Frieda's friends and "helpers" to come in and take what they wanted. "I was very shocked," recalled Grimmer. "It was like people were vultures. I thought it was horrible. I felt like there should at least be a period of mourning or something like that before these things were disposed of. And here people were coming in saying 'oh, I want this' and 'I want that.'" Gunst gave Grimmer three or four chairs, the drapes from the office where she had worked, and a set of champagne glasses. (Gunst had looked carelessly at the glasses and said, "I don't need these. Do you want them?" Grimmer thought to herself: "I don't have any champagne glasses. I don't even have champagne. But I'll take them as a memento.") Hilde Bruch ended up with the clock from Frieda's bedroom (which symbolically passed to Joanne Greenberg after Bruch's death). Ruth and Ted Lidz got a painting that had hung over Frieda's desk. Jane Weinberg got a ring she had once admired (but she was denied the matching bracelet, which went to Gunst's daughter).[14]

In striking contrast to Erich's renunciation of any share in the estate, and despite her own personal wealth, Gunst took the half share stipulated in the original will. Stocks, bonds, and the other half of the assets were, according to Frieda's instructions, divided equally between Grete and Anna. There wasn't much else. Except for Frieda's piano and hi-fi set (each appraised at $100) and her silverware, seal fur jacket, and Persian lamb coat (appraised at $50 each), the remaining items in the cottage had little monetary value. (Years earlier, on a trip to New York, Frieda's colleague David Rioch had placed her traveling case containing all the jewelry she had smuggled out of Europe under the table in a restaurant, where it was stolen. At the time of her death, only a few items of significant value remained in her possession.)[15]

While Gunst was busy disposing of the tangible remainders of Frieda's existence, everybody else was obsessed with trying to figure out how she could possibly have died in the first place. She seemed, as a fellow poet remarked of Joseph Brodsky after his sudden death, like someone who "always existed in her friends' minds not just as a person but as some kind of principle of indestructibility."[16] Like Brodsky, who had died not of torture in the gulag but by chain smoking himself into a heart attack, Frieda seemed too heroic to have expired unceremoniously in a bathtub. True, she had worked fifteen hours a day for more than forty years, sustaining herself with cigarettes, black coffee, and hurried meals sent over from hospital cafeterias, and she had taken on all the burdens of her family, friends, and patients, but it still seemed inconceivable that this could finally have led her, at age sixty-seven, to drop dead of a heart attack.

The image of her alone and naked in the bathtub particularly tormented her friends. People began sorting through every moment they had spent with her during the eight months since her return from Palo Alto, searching for clues they had somehow missed. Donna Grimmer decided Frieda had never really recovered from the flu she had in April. "She just seemed to get weaker. She just was not well. But I certainly never thought that death was imminent." Head nurse Margaret Ursell said: "We had just seen her failing in front of us. She was failing. I saw it. So when she died, it suddenly made sense. And the particular way she died was how I thought it would happen."[17]

But the analysts focused on deeper interpretations. Marvin Adland thought back to the previous weekend, which Frieda had spent at his house. There had been a birthday party for one of his children, with lots of people coming and going. Adland was distracted. Later, he kept thinking that had he been more attentive to Frieda, he would have picked up on some subtle problem. Actually he felt that he *had* noticed something unconsciously, because when Edith Weigert called saying Frieda hadn't shown up for lunch, "I knew. I just knew. It immediately fell into place. The experience of the previous weekend suddenly came back to me." This was how Frieda had taught him to think. For years, he had arrived on the disturbed ward saying to himself: "If only I could do the right thing with this patient, if only I could intuit exactly what she needs at this moment . . ." Otto Will was filled with the same remorse. He had been out with Frieda the night before her death and had driven her home. On the way, he talked about a patient he was working with, a very stormy, easily upset woman. Frieda said to him: "I want you to be careful. I don't want you to get too involved." Had she been talking about keeping one's perspective in working with a difficult patient? Or had this been some kind of symbolic warning about his feelings toward her?

Frieda's closest friends began whispering to one another that she had killed herself. They agreed there was no direct evidence; she had not drowned, she had no injuries, and the autopsy had revealed no chemical substances in her bloodstream. But these details seemed irrelevant. If Frieda were going to commit suicide, she was subtle enough to do it more psychologically. There were rumors of a note. Two people were supposed to have read it. Both died without revealing what it said. One friend claimed Frieda had confided that she had "a heart problem" and had been warned not to take hot baths. People rebuked themselves for having somehow abandoned Frieda when she needed them most.

Otto Will was tortured by a memory of her at his house the night before. She had tried to play with his young son, who was one of her godchildren. The boy had run away from her. Will couldn't stop thinking about that moment. Frieda had tried to act as a "protective mother" to his son, and he had rejected her. "What comes again and again to my mind is the feeling of protection and understanding presence. That was Frieda. But I used to wonder—who the hell gave that to her?" Will was himself often resentful at her imperiousness, at the many times she called on short notice and asked him to drive her somewhere or otherwise attend to her whims. "I didn't like to say no. I wanted to be able to give her something. I felt that very strongly." But it wasn't enough, and Will blamed himself for failing her.

Other people blamed Dexter, saying he had worked Frieda too hard all those years, and it had finally caught up with her. Virginia Gunst seemed particularly angry at the Bullards. After disposing of Frieda's property, she severed ties with everyone at the Lodge.

Dexter was oblivious to all of this. Completely undone by Frieda's death, it was months before he could even speak of it. Initially, he thought he would go to Zurich to read the keynote address she was to have delivered at the International Congress for Psychiatry that summer, but in the end he couldn't summon the energy and sent Otto Will in his place. Many of Frieda's friends, former patients, and colleagues had sent condolence notes when they heard of her death; it was five months before Dexter could even send acknowledgments. In a form letter, he said sadly: "Things move along at the Lodge, but it isn't the same without her."[18]

The people closest to Frieda remained guilt stricken. They kept asking themselves why they hadn't seen how lonely she was, how much she needed them. In a memorial statement published a year later, Edith Weigert was still talking about the "waves of grief and sorrow" Frieda's friends, colleagues, students, and patients had experienced and how "deeply shaken" they were "by this sudden loss." There was almost a feeling of betrayal. How could Frieda have left them? "She had been so intensely alive!" Weigert wrote. "Her enjoyment of life seemed invincible."[19] Since Weigert, herself seriously depressed at many times, knew perfectly well that "deep shadows also fell across Frieda's rich life," her incredulity at her friend's dying clearly seemed to reflect her own guilt.

Again and again, people came back to the image of Frieda dying alone, without their having realized how needy she was. The layers of meaning attached to her death contrasted sharply with the opacity of her life, as if the suffering that lay under the private surface stood as a silent rebuke to all of them. And then there was the symbolic significance of her heart having given out. As an analyst ambivalent about Frieda's work remarked years later: "If she didn't kill herself, she should have." After Sullivan's lonely death in a Paris hotel room, there had been similar hints of suicide. In both cases, part of the appeal of this idea was that it resolved the ambiguity. Tragic as suicide may be, it has the advantage of being the only death that is deliberate and thus fully meaningful in the broader context of a person's life. In Frieda's case, the image of her naked in the bathtub seemed to add a vulnerability too excruciating to contemplate. If she had been alone but working at her desk, or marching over to see a patient on the disturbed ward, the emotional tone of the event would have been completely different. The particular form of a person's death provides the one fixed point in his or her life story, and there is an almost irresistible temptation to read back from that moment to everything that came before it.

Sigmund Freud's death has always been seen this way. He did commit suicide, assisted by Max Schur, his physician, the two of them having agreed years earlier that when Freud could no longer bear the pain of the cancer eating away at his jaw, Schur would give him a lethal injection of morphine at bedtime. Yet although this fact has long been widely known, Freud's death is never seen as submission. Somehow the fact that he had struggled for sixteen years with the agony and disfigurement of his illness, that it was a physical disease, and that he was in his eighties have made his death seem heroic. He was like a fallen soldier, assisted by his doctor on the battlefield, bravely fighting on until the last moment. Frieda, in contrast, was not, as far as anyone knew, physically ill. Her deafness made her more isolated, more lonely, more cut off from other people, but it didn't carry any threat of fatality. So her death seemed like a personal failing, a private secret veiled in ambiguity, a metaphor for her life, "ended but unfinished," as Dexter later wrote. She died alone, as she had lived alone, with no one, even those closest to her, privy to the circumstances.

Frieda herself would have had an entirely different view of her life's end, and it is crucial that we realize this. The year before her death, in the taped reminiscences she did in Palo Alto, she twice instructed her friends, using identical words: "If you want to know something for my epitaph, then I think we could say I wasn't lazy, and I had lots of fun, but of another type as compared with many other people. It was a very special type of fun." She laughed both times as she said this, and seemed clearly to enjoy the image.[20]

Frieda might even have viewed the timing of her death as unconsciously appropriate. In a family of unusually long-lived women—Klara, Grete, and Aunt Helene vigorous until their eighties, Anna into her nineties—Frieda died at sixty-seven. In this, she followed her father in a final act of devotion, and allowed her mother, who had died only five years before her, to win the longstanding competition between them. It was as if Frieda were saying to Klara: *see, even in death, I cannot outdo you; you are still the strongest.* Like Adolf, Frieda died alone, under somewhat mysterious circumstances, not fighting and stoic to the end, like her mother.

From beyond the grave, Frieda continued to have a powerful effect on people. Mara Bowman, her former secretary, returned from her honeymoon a month after the funeral to find a package in the mail, addressed in Frieda's ornate, impossible-to-read, Germanic hand. Bowman practically dropped the box, stunned that Frieda, in death, was still looking out for her. (The actual situation was less symbolic. Frieda had taken a gift she had purchased on one of her trips out west to a shop in Rockville and asked them to wrap it and send it as a wedding present. She had written out a note congratulating Bowman, left it with the gift, and died a day or two later. The owner felt he had no choice but to send it along to Bowman after the funeral.)

Several years later, when the Bullards turned Frieda's cottage into offices, Harold Searles got her bedroom. He often worked alone there late at night and on weekends. For several months, he felt haunted by her ghost, "a hostile and menacing presence, somewhere in the house." Eventually the ghost began to feel "loving and protective," and Searles relaxed and let it take care of him. He later said his unconscious hostility toward Frieda and his identification with her loneliness had led to the haunting.[21]

Jane Weinberg had a series of powerful dreams during this same period. In one, she was dead. She arrived in heaven, and there was Frieda. Weinberg asked her how she was. "Oh, it's very intense here," said Frieda. "I am the administrator of the Fourth District and I have to orchestrate the balance between good and evil in the entire district and I'm just exhausted by this."

Frieda's grave also became a charged place for many people. Julia Waddell and Anne Bullard became consumed with worry that she "was all by herself in that cemetery." (Neither of them had the faintest idea why being in a Jewish burial ground was so crucial to Frieda.) Anne decided to build a memorial garden on Lodge property and have Frieda reinterred there. Dexter understood Anne's desire to have Frieda near them but forcibly vetoed her

idea. "This is a mental hospital," he told her. "The patients wouldn't be able
to understand it. We can't have a cemetery here." Anne finally stopped badgering him, although for years afterward, she insisted it would have been better to have Frieda at the Lodge, where she belonged.[22] Marvin Adland
arranged for the gravesite next to Frieda's to be purchased by her estate, os-
tensibly to allow "more extensive plantings at a later time," but perhaps also
so she wouldn't end up lying for eternity next to a stranger. Various of
Frieda's later admirers made pilgrimages to the cemetery; one tried to plant a
rose garden by her headstone. Mr. R. visited her grave several times with Adland and was very moved by the experience, but it didn't keep him from ending up in a state hospital.

Frieda had been dead less than a month when the mythologizing began. At
the meeting of the Section on Psychotherapy of the American Psychiatric Association, a group she had chaired and helped to found, Jules Masserman and
Jacob Moreno delivered an extravagant eulogy:

> Each of us, perhaps by divine dispensation, has been fortunate enough
> to have known sometime in his life at least one being who possessed
> sufficient gentleness, warmth and grace to justify a renewal of faith in
> the essential goodness of mankind. We of the Section on Psychotherapy
> have been fortunate in having lived in especially close association with
> a universal friend who not only embodied all of these qualities, but
> added to them a wisdom, a skill and a humanitarian dedication that
> were the highest expressions of our own aspirations as physicians and
> psychiatrists. . . . None of us can or need add to Dr. Fromm-Reich-
> mann's memory in words; let us rededicate ourselves to the ideals she
> epitomized.[23]

In an editorial published a week after her death, the *Washington Post* called
her "the leading psychotherapist in the area" and one of the city's "most distinguished residents." The *Psychiatric Bulletin* made her sound like St.
Catherine: "strikingly successful in restoring even those schizophrenics who
had been for years in trance-like states."[24]

More thoughtful appreciations came from psychiatrists who identified
with Frieda's philosophy of treatment even though they hadn't personally
worked with her. Jean Baker Miller called Frieda "a giant in the psychoanalytic field," and said that "because of her understanding and genius for teaching others to understand people who had often been considered
unapproachable, she holds a special place in psychiatry and psychoanalysis."
Robert Coles called her "a hero of our time," one of the small group of clini-

cians "whose intelligence, compassion and above all, candor illuminate their deeds, their words and the failures they inevitably suffer." These are people, Coles continued, "whose labor is exceptional in the very special sense that it takes place in professional territory that is ignored, scorned or most often feared. . . . They cause their colleagues to see new things, go new places and most of all to feel less despair."[25]

But other colleagues began to vilify, ridicule, or belittle Frieda in ways they would never have dared when she was still living. Roy Grinker, thinking back on a lifetime in psychiatry, wrote patronizingly: "We are often impressed by the fact that enthusiastic individuals appear on the scene from time to time with initial goals that astonish us. Frieda Fromm-Reichmann, for example, felt at one time that she could cure schizophrenics." Leslie Farber, a one-time Lodge colleague, published and republished a fantasized account that made Frieda appear ridiculous. She had been treating a severely disturbed young man, claimed Farber, with whom it was difficult to communicate.

> One day, during a therapeutic hour, as this patient (mute, as usual) was sitting with Dr. Fromm-Reichmann in her office, she noticed that he was fingering his genitals with one hand that was crammed deep into the pocket of his trousers. It was also plain to her that he had an erection. She pondered this situation for a moment, then said to him, "If it will make you feel any better, please go ahead." Whereupon the young man unzipped his fly and proceeded to masturbate, while Dr. Fromm-Reichmann sat quietly across from him, her eyes down, her hands clasped in her lap.

Farber said that as a "marvelous hostess," Frieda was simply seeking to make the young man "more comfortable," and concluded, "Of course, he was trying to shock her and she was unshockable." Clearly, having failed to shock Frieda as he himself apparently wished to do, Farber invented this story to get back at her when she was no longer there to intimidate him. Otto Will, who had known Farber for years, was furious when he read this. The real story, said Will, was that Frieda had knocked on the patient's door, found him masturbating, and said she'd come back later.[26]

A more perverse example of exploiting Frieda for someone else's agenda was the pharmaceutical company that used her as a pin-up girl to sell its latest antipsychotic drug. Titled "Frieda Fromm-Reichmann on Anxiety," the promotional pamphlet that features her work was apparently sent to analysts reluctant to use medication. There is a bizarre picture of Frieda on the front cover, looking like a bad computer simulation of a photograph, which accentuates the angles of her face to make them look like the dueling scars of Heidelberg fraternity students after they rubbed salt into them.[27]

In the year after Frieda's death, her closest colleagues sought a more fitting memorial. Otto Will proposed a volume of selected papers, which the University of Chicago Press quickly agreed to publish, as it had done earlier with her textbook. Will made the initial decisions about which papers to include, then mysteriously ceased involvement with the project. Dexter became the editor. The beautiful memorial statement Edith Weigert had published in *Psychiatry* soon after Frieda's death was reprinted as an introduction, and all royalties from the volume were sent to Grete and Anna in Israel.

Appearing in 1959 under the title *Psychoanalysis and Psychotherapy,* the book includes most of the important articles Frieda published in the United States. (There is also a bibliography of her earlier German papers; a planned second volume of translations never materialized.) The book well illustrates the range of Frieda's interests—from general psychoanalytic technique to schizophrenia, psychosomatic illness to the cultural role of mothers. The paper on loneliness, found unfinished in her desk, was included as an epilogue.

Reviewers again praised Frieda's "penetrating insights," honesty, humane approach, and deep commitment to the most disturbed patients. A long piece in the *Saturday Review* hailed "her clarity of expression, and artful presentation of an intricately-patterned argument," and said the papers would be "of great interest to the general reader." Reviewers across a range of professional journals in psychology, psychiatry, and psychoanalysis praised her "sincerity and conviction," "the refreshing absence of ambiguity and confusion" in her style of writing, and "her exceptional sensitivity to the most delicate nuances of human behavior." Her "persuasive arguments for the unconverted" were called "gems of seductive reasoning." A "brilliant therapist who was intensely honest with herself," she "knew how to bridge the empty spaces between human beings." Even the *Psychoanalytic Quarterly* praised her willingness to "stand almost alone" against the objections of other analysts. The psychoanalytic mainstream, this reviewer commented, had finally caught up with her, proving the lasting worth of her contributions. Others hailed her "creative eagerness to seek out and utilize new ideas in the field up to the moment of her death," and even Roy Grinker, long a critic, wrote in the *Archives of General Psychiatry,* a journal known for its somatic bias, that Frieda's book represented "the major contributions of one of the most brilliant and intuitive workers in the most difficult area of psychiatry." Fifteen years later, when it came out in a new paperback edition, *Psychoanalysis and Psychotherapy* was said to be "revitalizing," with Frieda's emphasis on "looking for and encouraging in her patients the constructive and rewarding forces in their personalities" an essential reminder for every clinician.[28]

The main criticism, made by several reviewers, concerned the repetition of certain key clinical examples, particularly the moment with Mrs. E. in the pack. Although some redundancy was inevitable in a volume of papers written over a twenty-year span, reviewers were getting at a deeper issue. As Don Burnham later noted: "Frieda did seem fascinated by vital turning points, near epiphanies." He said her own account of choosing psychiatry as a specialty was similarly condensed into a few key dramatic moments, like the story of the patient exclaiming, "Bertchen, at last I find you again!" in the lecture hall in medical school. Clarence Schulz, thinking back over Frieda's constant repetition of the moment with Mrs. E., suggested that perhaps what had seemed so powerful was its concreteness—the sense that there was a "particular thing you could do that would be the turning point for the patient, and if you did it correctly, the patient would be cured." Schulz felt that Frieda spent her whole life searching for such moments. By describing them repeatedly to her students, she used them like parables, endlessly capable of inspiration. Burnham thought there might be a more personal dynamic here too. "All her life, Frieda was conflicted about authority and about occupying the role of authority herself," Burnham noted. "Was this way of describing and of thinking about her remarkable performance a way of handling her shyness and her wish-fear of grabbing the spotlight?"

> Somehow Frieda managed to be both in and out of the authority role. She was exquisitely sensitive to the down-putting aspects of the traditional social definition of the sick or patient role, with its connotations of passivity, dependence, need for help, and exemptions from such social responsibilities as work, etc. She conspicuously avoided using professional or arcane jargon with her patients, and even to a considerable extent in her professional writings. In her 1946 paper, "Remarks on the Philosophy of Mental Disorder," she deliberately chooses to refer to "mental disorder" rather than to "insanity," and she is openly critical of psychiatrists who "have greater respect for the society that pays their bills than for the patients who need their help and guidance."[29]

Burnham went on to make the provocative suggestion that Frieda, who always said her first choice of a specialty was obstetrics, may have seen her role as "a sort of midwife" to patients. Calling herself a "muse" to Goldstein and others may, Burnham suggested, have been "another way of compromising her conflict about being an authority."

Insisting that patients (especially psychotics) already understood the meaning of their symptoms similarly downplayed her role as a therapist. And Frieda's long-held view that any well-trained psychiatrist could be successful with seriously disturbed patients was another means, as Burnham put it, of "denying her special and probably unique importance." Although such attitudes clearly fit the emphasis on the patient's inherent healing qualities that she had learned from Goldstein and Groddeck, her penchant for thinking in these ways is, as Freud would say, "analyzable." She seemed to be modeling herself on the ancient role of the shaman, "the native healer who tries to come into contact with the part of the self that the person is not aware of," creating the conditions for "a new perspective that might help with the illness."[30]

Psychoanalysis and Psychotherapy brought Frieda's ideas to a wide professional audience; like *Principles of Intensive Psychotherapy,* it stayed continuously in print for decades. Both books became part of the standard curriculum in psychiatry, clinical psychology, and social work, and generations of students absorbed Frieda's methods from these works. But in the end, it wasn't her own writing that familiarized millions of people with Frieda's ideas. It was Joanne Greenberg's fictionalized account of their work together.

14

Rose Garden

The power of the survivor is the power of the presence in contradiction of what was possible.[1]

I Never Promised You a Rose Garden was never intended as a memorial to Frieda, and it didn't take on this meaning until years later and for reasons Joanne Greenberg couldn't possibly have anticipated. In the years just following Frieda's death, people vied to become her biographer. Some were close friends or colleagues eager to celebrate her accomplishments; others were opportunists hoping to expose the dirt they assumed to lie beneath her private surface. But one after another, they were forced to abandon their efforts. Virginia Gunst had all of Frieda's private papers locked up in her attic, and Erich told everyone who contacted him that he would actively block any biography being planned. And those who could perhaps have succeeded in writing about Frieda based on their own experience of her felt too competitive or guilty even to contemplate publishing anything.

So as the person with the purest sense of gratitude and the least negative feeling, Joanne Greenberg ended up being the one to preserve Frieda's memory. This is actually fitting: having spent her whole life trying to make patients' accounts of their illness and treatment more visible, and having always felt most "herself" with patients, Frieda became in death the person Joanne Greenberg created. But the fact that Joanne was writing about "Dr. Fried," the fictional therapist, not Frieda Fromm-Reichmann, the real person, meant that she was permanently enshrined as an icon, not a doctor known for her hard work.[2]

In 1964, the year of *Rose Garden*'s publication, it sold a few thousand copies, about average for a novel by an unknown author. Ten years later, sales were in the millions, and a movie with Anne Bancroft and Natalie Wood was being planned. Translations into more than a dozen languages brought the book to readers all over the world.[3] By the time "I never promised you a rose garden" started appearing as the punchline to *New Yorker* cartoons and in pop song lyrics, it had ceased being the title of Greenberg's novel and become a cultural artifact.

A story about a teenaged girl who burned her arms with lighted cigarettes and fantasized murdering her infant sister was not, in 1964, a story with broad appeal. The reason *Rose Garden* had so powerful an effect on so many people was that it proved anyone could go insane and sometimes, heroically, resume a normal existence.

"You did not read that book, you lived it," proclaimed the reviewer for the *Boston Globe*.[4] The symptoms of the main character, Deborah Blau, were bizarre, and people were repulsed and frightened by them, but the story was gripping and drew them in. Deborah's complete recovery from schizophrenia seemed miraculous, beyond anything readers thought possible. Yet when pressed to explain why they thought the book wasn't fiction, they said the story was "too real" to have been invented.

Today we are accustomed to the dissolve of truth to lie, but in 1964, if a story wasn't totally true, it got called "fiction." But good fiction is a simulation of the real, not a literalization, and Joanne Greenberg knew just how to balance the truth on its edges to make it more vivid.

Rose Garden was believable even to readers completely ignorant of mental illness. Events unfolded in the same abrupt and confusing ways they had in Greenberg's actual life, but the chaos was kept carefully below the surface of the prose. This let readers identify with Deborah's fear even as they recoiled from what she did. By the time she deteriorated to the point of real bizarreness halfway through the book, her actions seemed to make a certain sense. This was unnerving and fascinating at the same time, like seeing an accident on the highway and being unable to keep from staring at the blood.

The intelligence of Deborah's illness was disarming, but her wincing sharpness put people on edge. It was frightening to see insight and craziness so interconnected. And yet the fact of her disintegration was strangely reassuring; it affirmed a rationality readers desperately wanted to believe in. Her symptoms clearly had meaning, and her constant focus on the destructiveness of lying turned the book's existence into evidence of its truth.

What readers found most troubling were the contradictions of madness itself. The unconscious may have a logic, but it isn't Aristotelian. Feelings appear out of nowhere; behavior suddenly spins out of control. Acts that seem totally repugnant—like slashing your skin with razor blades—can feel comforting.

Yet strange as she was, people identified with Deborah Blau. Thirty years after the book came out, Greenberg was still getting letters saying, "I'm Debbie" or "You wrote that book about me." For other readers, Deborah became a metric against which to measure themselves; if she was crazy, then they were okay. And if she could get better, then maybe so could their sisters or fathers or wives.

Besides seeming so powerfully authentic, *Rose Garden* intrigued readers because its author's identity was so mysterious. It was impossible to tell how "Hannah Green" had come to know so much about mental illness. Was she the patient, the therapist, a relative, or a novelist with unusual insight? Reading *Rose Garden* was like reading a manual on explosives and not being able to tell if it had been written by a terrorist or the FBI.

The title page said simply "A Novel by Hannah Green." Nothing on the dust jacket hinted at pseudonym or memoir.[5] But readers are curious, and when *Rose Garden*'s fans went to the library to look up their favorite new author, they discovered she wasn't listed in any source. They started writing to the publisher to find out who she was. They were sent a form letter, which only made them more suspicious.

Rose Garden's fictional negligee turned it into an object of fantasy, as powerful for its secrets as for what it revealed. Readers could enter *Rose Garden* the way they entered a novel, free from irritating nonfictional questions like, "Is this true?" or "How could the author have known this?" Yet there was something so real about the story that readers were convinced it was based on fact.

Autobiography pays a price for literalness, even in this age of memoir. By extinguishing every flicker of doubt that it describes real events, it keeps us witness to someone else's experience. Fiction, by contrast, invites us inside. Having made its disclaimer, it can do as it pleases, even to the point of choosing to be almost totally accurate. We worry when historians or biographers rely on fictional devices to propel their narratives, but we seldom question novelists who label their books "fiction" and then tell us the truth.

A writer whose subject matter is frightening or violent does, however, need protective strategies to get inside her characters' lives. Joyce Carol Oates, for example, separates herself from the horrifying events she writes about by composing so rapidly and so compulsively that she never feels the fear or anguish.[6] Her most autobiographical novel, *Marya: A Life,* had to be written in self-contained sections and combined into a single work only afterward.[7] To write *Rose Garden,* Greenberg invented "hedges" to put some distance between her memories and the prose. By situating herself two steps away from the action—writing in the third person about someone named "Deborah Blau," and publishing under a pseudonym ("Hannah Green")—she could keep herself from being pulled back into the illness as she composed. Pushing for the book to be marketed as "fiction" created a further layer of separation.

Greenberg started writing *Rose Garden* during Adolf Eichmann's trial for Nazi war crimes. A friend, a survivor of Dachau, had commented: "People deal with an unbearable reality in one of two ways—they either push it away or they transform it." This was in 1961. Greenberg realized that in the ten years since she had left the Lodge, she had already begun to revise the memory of her illness; she wanted to bear witness before it was completely transformed. She was also irritated by the way madness was being lyricized in the 1960s by people like R. D. Laing. "I wanted to say there is such a thing as real mental illness and it is not romantic."[8] She wasn't trying to memorialize Frieda; the book was a testimony of her own experience.

Greenberg wrote *Rose Garden* the way she wrote a dozen other novels—in pencil, in a spiral-bound notebook from the drugstore, sitting propped up in bed. The fifty-page report she had written for Frieda as her contribution to their planned book served as a rough guide. Despite the intensity of the content, she had little trouble getting the words on the page. Asked later how she had encouraged her daughter's work, Joanne's mother laughed and said: "I didn't encourage her. You don't have to encourage Niagara Falls."[9]

Henry Holt and Co. paid $1,500 for *Rose Garden,* a decent advance for an unknown writer whose subject was likely to offend. It turned out to be one of their better investments; *Rose Garden*'s sales ultimately exceeded five million, with almost no marketing expenses. New American Library, which bought the paperback rights for $10,000 in 1964, has also made a huge profit, keeping the book continuously in print for more than three decades.

Greenberg's first editor, commenting on an early draft, said: "Since quite obviously you could not have written this story unless you were Deborah at one point, I think you have done an amazing job of telling the truth and yet covering [it] up." She had more trouble with Frieda. "I have very little feeling for her as a person . . . could you build Dr. Fried up?"[10] Joanne said this would be a problem, given Frieda's "assiduous playing-down of her own self and personality during the work." She was amused at the praise for Deborah's disguise. "When my mother read the manuscript, she burst into great gales of laughter at my paltry efforts."

In 1962, while Greenberg was still writing, Henry Holt merged with Rinehart & Winston, and her editor was let go. A young Christopher Lehmann-Haupt, fresh from a job at a tiny sports publishing house, was assigned responsibility for *Rose Garden*. Lehmann-Haupt had practically no editing experience—the two major books he had done at that point were *The Secret of Holing Putts* and *The Secret of Bowling Strikes*—but he threw himself into the work. A patient in psychoanalysis himself, he identified with Deborah and wanted the story to feel real to readers. "I was completely wrapped up in it for many months," he said later. "There were other books but nothing to that degree of intensity. . . . It was the one book that I could do something about that seemed worthwhile." Lehmann-Haupt, who soon left editing to become the daily book reviewer for the *New York Times,* said *Rose Garden* convinced him he needed other work: "That book is an exemplar of why I should not have been an editor. . . . I didn't know what was wrong and there were things that sounded clunky to me and so I just went to work line by line. . . . I didn't have the patience to figure out [how else to do it]."[11]

He and Greenberg spent months revising. (Their letters back and forth to each other, filled with minute detail, exceed forty single-spaced pages.) They were both convinced the story would be gripping for ordinary readers if it felt totally true to them. Literary considerations were allowed to shape pacing and tone, but reality dictated content at every turn. Some events were foreshortened, and a few of Greenberg's symptoms put into other characters, but Lehmann-Haupt insisted the illness be precisely accurate.

> The thing that struck me and the thing that I thought made it remarkable was the vividness of those characters. . . . Every detail had to be right, it couldn't be in any way vague. . . . I remember when I read the first page it wasn't clear who was sitting where and who was thinking what [and so I started there].

Greenberg was equally insistent that every nuance of the book's descriptions of Lodge life be exactly as she remembered. She corrected his use of the word *pain* to describe being strapped to a bed ("Chris, restraints are never sharp, and their effect is an ache later, not a pain"), and fixed his prepositions to reflect correct argot (he wrote: "Deborah was sitting on the corridor of the ward"; she said: "in all nuthouses I've ever heard of, the ward was the entire floorspace . . . you are 'on the ward' including all corridors, bathrooms, etc. . . . 'On the hall' is [another] idiom that any ex–mental patient will know"). When he inadvertently altered details that made a character's symptoms conflict with her diagnosis, she protested ("Chris, don't elide [this] . . . you are making her catatonic-schizophrenic. Anyone who knows beans about it will spot her as a paranoid").[12]

Their most interesting debate concerned the title. During most of its pre-publication existence, Greenberg called the book *The Little Maybe,* based on a moment in the story when a newly arrived patient, after years spent on the violent wards of other hospitals, looks around in astonishment and blurts out: "It's different here. I been lotsa joints, lotsa wards. What's here . . . there's more scared, more mad; pissin' on the floor and yellin'—but it's because of the maybe. It's because of the little, little maybe . . . the hope."[13] Greenberg loved this title, but everybody at Holt thought it sounded like the name of a children's book. After pointedly noting that *To Kill a Mockingbird* wasn't about hunting, she rejected *A Shadow of Hope, The Muted Cry, A Face on Each World,* and *The Tribunal,* among other suggested alternatives. It was Lehmann-Haupt who came up with *I Didn't Promise You a Rose Garden,* based on Dr. Fried's climactic line. Reviewers critiqued its clumsiness, far longer than was typical of titles at the time, but readers loved it, and its success as a cliché is testimony to Lehmann-Haupt's marketing instincts. (Greenberg and her family fondly call it "INPYARG" around the house.)

Until right before publication, *Rose Garden* was listed as autobiography in press kits. Holt was willing to allow Greenberg a pseudonym so long as the book was sold as nonfiction. However, insisting to Lehmann-Haupt that "it was written literary, it should go literary," Greenberg pressed for it to be re-classified as fiction. After trying halfheartedly to change her mind, he told his boss they had no choice but to accede to her wishes.[14] (Then they got Karl Menninger, the most famous psychiatrist in America, to declare in a prominent blurb on the cover: "I'm sure [the book] will have a good effect on lots of people who don't realize that this sort of exploration can be done and this sort of effect achieved.")[15] No one had any idea that the shifting ground on which the book rested—part truth and part fiction—would turn out to be its biggest draw, or that the pseudonym would intensify the effect by making it seem as if the author were hiding something.

Later, Greenberg would claim that she had given little thought to publishing under a false name. She felt pressured by her mother, who had spent years covering up the disgrace of the illness and hardly wanted it made public now that Joanne had recovered. Greenberg was also worried about her own two young children, her husband's reputation at work, and neighbors staring at her in the grocery store. Even her mother-in-law, she later told a friend, would have been "socially handicapped beyond remedy" were her real name to be used. R. D. Laing notwithstanding, it was a terrible stigma to be mentally ill in the 1960s.

But a person doesn't easily give up ownership of a book she has spent years writing. The literary critic Carolyn Heilbrun, recalling her own decision to adopt a pseudonym, talks of the "layers within layers of significance" inherent in such a decision, especially for women, too often forced into identities not of their own choosing. In creating "Amanda Cross," author of her mystery series, Heilbrun created a gutsy version of herself that had no place in her academic prose. For Joyce Carol Oates, who writes thrillers under the name "Rosamond Smith," a fictitious identity—widely known to be hers, with the same last name she uses in daily life—makes it possible to wall off a part of her personality.[16]

Writing in the third person about your own life is equally complicated. You create a character who has had your experiences but isn't you exactly. For Carolyn Heilbrun, this meant writing "on a level far below consciousness . . . to experience what I would not have had the courage to undertake in full awareness."[17] As Justin Kaplan remarked of his biographical subject: "It is not so easy as it may at first seem to say which of these, Mr. Clemens or Mark Twain, is the name his naked self answers to. It is the edgy traffic between these identities, and others, that engages our interest."[18]

Greenberg used three separate identities, and the "edgy traffic" between her, Deborah Blau, and Hannah Green created the ambiguity that gave *Rose Garden* its power. Readers didn't know Hannah Green was a borrowed name, but they sensed something fishy. Early reviews fed the speculation. *Rose Garden* just didn't seem novelistic enough to be so affecting.

What practically erased the line between fiction and case history was Dr. Fried. Deborah and Joanne are quite dissimilar in certain respects, but Dr. Fried and Frieda are identical. Of course, the portrait is idealized—it couldn't have been otherwise, written by Joanne—but every nuance is accurate (and confirmed by records of the case). Lodge staff and Frieda's students quickly saw through the "disguise," and Anna, coming upon the book in a store in Israel, recognized Frieda instantly, even from a translation. (Years later, when she decided that it wouldn't unnerve Joanne to receive a letter from the sister of her former therapist, Anna told her: "I want you to know how deeply grateful I am to you for the way you pictured Frieda, much better than *all* the snapshots I have of her.")[19]

Despite the thinness of the line separating Greenberg from her characters— or perhaps because of it—their relations were complex, like multiple personalities, only some of whom know of the others' existence. Joanne was the only one who knew everyone: Hannah, Deborah, Dr. Fried, Frieda. Hannah knew only Deborah and Dr. Fried, and they knew only each other. Frieda's sole relationship was with Joanne; she was dead before any of the others were invented.

Each figure served a purpose in Greenberg's mental life. Deborah provided the distance to allow her to recall painful details of her illness and hospitalization. Dr. Fried kept Frieda alive beyond the grave, a permanent "good mother." (Indeed, the dedication reads: "To My Mothers.") Hannah Green provided Joanne a way to be a writer and not just a former mental patient. This turned out to be important to a degree she couldn't have imagined; as the book started generating a more and more intense reaction from readers, "Hannah Green" was there as an intermediary to absorb some of the craziness.

But characters and pseudonymous selves often insist on living their own lives, independent of the author's plan. (Greenberg knows this firsthand. She once wrote a short story titled "That Bitch," in which characters she had edited out of other stories came back to berate her for murdering them.) Hannah Green and Deborah Blau may have started as "hedges" to give Greenberg the distance to write; once in existence, however, they developed relationships Greenberg couldn't have anticipated. With truth and fiction nestled inside one another like Russian eggs, readers could never quite tell where Joanne's life ended and Deborah's began. Nonfiction may have the ring of authenticity, but a thoughtfully written novel often feels more true.

In *Rose Garden,* the lines were fuzzy even for minor characters. In December 1963, late in the editing process, Greenberg suddenly realized that the delusional name she had invented for one of the women on the disturbed ward—The Wife of the Assassinated Ex-President of the United States— seemed an extraordinarily tasteless choice, given Kennedy's murder less than a month earlier. The book was already in galleys, so she was forced to create an alternative with the same number of letters, "The Secret First Wife of Edward VIII, Abdicated King of England." (Alert readers will note a number of places where the Wife of the Assassinated Ex-President—who Lehmann-Haupt called WOTAEX—managed to slip past the editor's pen.)

Rose Garden was published on April 16, 1964. Staff at Holt sent Greenberg a telegram wishing "they might have promised Hannah Green that rose garden—at least a part of it." Their wistfulness increased as the book failed to sell (in her third royalty period, June to December 1965, Greenberg got a check for $287.93). Her agent was unsuccessful in placing an excerpt in any of a half dozen magazines. Four years later, friends were still sending Greenberg condolence notes.[20]

Reviews, however, were many and varied. Some lamented the "unfortunate title" or dissected the dust jacket (which had a drawing of two Medusa figures with insanely intertwined hair; Lehmann-Haupt had insisted on hiring a special designer, Ellen Raskin, because he thought Holt's usual studio was boring). One reviewer saw psychoanalytic significance even in the book's binding ("smooth at the top and rough at the bottom, it echoes the double theme of the story").[21]

Those who focused on the content could hardly contain themselves. C. G. Gros, in *Best Sellers,* wrote: "The drama of Deborah's partnership with . . . the eminent and eminently human Dr. Fried . . . creates a novel about which it is impossible to become too enthusiastic." The *Chicago Tribune* called *Rose Garden* "a timely and timeless novel of authentic excellence," and *Newsday* said it was "a beautifully written book that adds a dimension of understanding not just of the mentally ill but of the real world they wish to reject." R. V. Cassill, in the *New York Times,* was effusive:

Hannah Green has done a marvelous job of dramatizing the internal warfare in a young psychotic. . . . With a courage that is sometimes breathtaking in its serene acceptance of risks, the author makes a faultless series of discriminations between the justifications for living in an evil and complex reality and the justifications for retreating into the security of madness.

Like a number of others, however, Cassill was suspicious. "Convincing and emotionally gripping as this novel is," he noted, "it falls a little short of being fictionally convincing." Brigid Brophy, in the *New Statesman* was blunter: "The book makes the impression of being only nominally a novel. Should it turn out to be a work of fiction, its value would vanish overnight." *Punch* referred to it as "Hannah Green's apparently autobiographical novel," and other reviewers went to unusual lengths to prove the book wasn't what it seemed.

Hannah Green is a pseudonym and *I Never Promised You a Rose Garden* is fictional experience rather than a novel. The distinction must be made because, absorbing though this book is, it lacks that indefinable and controversial quality recognized as creative work which a born novelist's imagination and skill produce from layers of thought, knowledge and time. . . . This is a case-history about insanity in general and schizophrenia in particular. It is a well-written, intensely moving and compassionately intelligent document.

It is difficult to appraise *I Never Promised You a Rose Garden* as a work of fiction, which is what Hannah Green (the pseudonym of a previously published fiction writer) chooses to call it. As a novel it is flawed, as nonfiction it is a painfully memorable case history told with great honesty.

This is more case history than novel. . . . The story is written in a thor-

oughly conventional novel form, but the author is, in fact, arguing a thesis, presenting evidence for a particular scientific, psychiatric theory. . . . The lumps of unassimilated abnormal psychology are irritating
esthetically, but Deborah Blau's suffering and slow healing are real.

No one explained why it mattered so much whether the book was fiction.[22]

Nor could reviewers agree on the image of therapy being portrayed. Dr.
Fried was variously labeled as "saintly," "trite and sentimental," and "brilliant." One reviewer, irritated by what she called the "pre-Freudian psychology," concluded: "The doctor's name, Dr. Fried, reads like a schizophrenic
pun itself, on *peace, freed* and *Freud.* If the doctor is remarkable, it is for her
moral honesty, of which the patient's own exceptional honesty can take advantage. The eventual cure is spontaneous." But others were more willing to
credit the therapy: "In Dr. Fried, [Greenberg] has conveyed a true portrait of
the analyst at work. . . . However, the two-steps-forward, one-step-backward
progression of Deborah surfacing to life lacks that tightness which fiction requires." One reviewer hailed the book as "a terrifying journey along which
Dr. Fried, a splendidly drawn character, guides the obstinate and displaced
Deborah through to reality . . . with a clarity seldom achieved." Another declared that "anyone who has wondered how therapy works can see it in action in this novel."

> The battle [Dr. Fried] and Deborah wage is nothing less than monu-
> mental. The sheer physical drudgery, the spiritual and mental exhaus-
> tion of plumbing the deeps of memory and experience are evoked in
> such simple language and engrossing style that Deborah's effort be-
> comes ours, Dr. Fried's hope is ours, and we share their final triumph
> with an empathy that is possible only in the finest fiction.[23]

Calling Deborah's experience "real to the point of pain," the *Charlotte Observer* said:

> The difference between this book and the myriad ones on insanity is the
> reader identification with the patient. You don't just read about cold
> packs, you experience one. You live personally in a mental patient's
> world without colors, just gray, and you feel the penetrating chill that
> has nothing to do with the weather.[24]

Others were gripped by the drama of the illness:

Miss Green (it is a pseudonym) has obviously written from experience rather than imagination. Her dramatization of schizophrenia is a brilliant and frightening thing. . . . [She shows us] that mental illness is an illness, subject to maddening and sudden setbacks, to harrowing crises, to blank plateaus—and to cure.[25]

Despite dozens of good reviews, *Rose Garden* sold poorly for a long time.[26] About five years after it was published, the paperback edition started being adopted as a text in high school and college classes, and sales soared. The publisher did nothing to bring this about; the book's popularity was spread entirely by word of mouth. Students brought it home to their parents; they pressed it on friends. Librarians put it on their recommended lists; nurses in mental hospitals gave it to patients. As more and more people read *Rose Garden,* curiosity about its author became even more intense. Holt began receiving scores of letters addressed to Hannah Green, motivated as much by a desire to find out who she was as to praise the book.

For readers who were themselves mental patients, the link to Deborah Blau wasn't symbolic. But for most people, it was the experience of being in therapy or feeling lonely or estranged that made Deborah seem like them. Readers intensely wanted to believe in the cure, because it was so hopeful and because it might be true. (If Hannah Green really had recovered, she could have authored the book.) Yet its very possibility cast into doubt everything they took for granted about mental illness.

The story's ending was messy, like a real life. In the final pages, Deborah leaves the hospital for part of each day to attend high school equivalency classes. Her confidence is shaky, but her behavior is no longer disturbed. Yet her life after a planned discharge is barely sketched. Readers begged Hannah Green to tell them what happened next, either in a letter or a sequel. (Greenberg said she had no interest in *"Bride of Rose Garden"* even though she knew it would sell.)[27]

Much of the speculation centered on "squat little Dr. Fried." She is "marvelous," wrote a reader convinced the character was Anna Freud. (The other most frequent guess was Karen Horney, a painful irony given her real relationship with Frieda.) One woman wrote: "I keep thinking Dr. Fried is Hannah Green—which of course is silly. She wouldn't have *time* to write a book." A young man who said his mother had been in mental hospitals all his life pleaded for anything that would bring him "closer to the book's reality . . . places to visit, the hospital, Dr. Fried . . . what does her house look like, her eyes, her handshake?"[28]

Others identified so intensely with the characters they lost any semblance of fiction. A young woman who said she had been "in love with a mentally ill boy" told Greenberg: "This may sound strange, but I feel I know and love Deborah very much. I feel very close to her and would love to be her friend."[29] Greenberg even got a letter from a "Dr. Royson," demanding to know how she had gotten his name (the most irritating psychiatrist in *Rose Garden* is called Royson). Many readers addressed their letters to "Deborah" or "Debbie." Others, certain that the author was Deborah's therapist, wrote to "Dr. Hannah Green," which always gave Joanne a laugh.

The intense curiosity about who wrote the book came from the need to know whether the cure was real. If Hannah Green were Deborah, the fact of her writing proved that schizophrenic patients could be healed. Deborah's fate became an imagined future that readers could hope for themselves. "It is not the hardest task to map Hell," one man wrote. "Surely the hardest task is to map the routes leading out of Hell. The awareness in this book is like a periscope, showing what is beyond the obstacles I am not tall enough to see over."[30]

One day, fifteen years after *Rose Garden* was published, Greenberg turned on the television in her Colorado living room and settled into a stack of ironing. Phil Donahue was interviewing a panel of psychiatrists. They were arguing about whether Hannah Green was hidden away on a locked ward somewhere or dead by suicide. Greenberg considered calling in just to say hello, but her husband, Albert, warned that if she did, she'd have to spend the next year appearing on talk shows, proving she didn't drool. Around this same time, a candidate for a job at Albert's clinic, trying to impress the staff, bragged of knowing "that *Rose Garden* girl on the back ward of a hospital in New York, hopelessly out of it."[31]

Greenberg found these rumors unsettling, although she understood their appeal. If she were dead or locked up somewhere, *Rose Garden* would be a novel, and psychiatrists would be off the hook. All the troubling questions the book raised about their failures would disappear into fiction. Instead, Greenberg started giving interviews and let Holt put her real name on the cover, which made things even more complex.

Giving up a pseudonym is at least as difficult as adopting one, and "Hannah Green" didn't just disappear on her own. Joanne did find it irksome that so many people assumed *Rose Garden* was the only book she ever wrote. And the more it was acclaimed, the less pressing the need for disguise felt. She was disturbed by some of the dreams she was having. In one, she was close to death after an accident, and someone asked if there was anything they should know and she said: "I've got a lost child somewhere." But it was discovering that there was a real Hannah Green that finally forced Greenberg to give the pseudonym up.

When she first heard that *Rose Garden* letters had been going to a writer in Manhattan, she was unnerved. "For some reason this bothered me terribly," Greenberg later told an interviewer.

I went around the house in a terrific funk for two days. And I remember one day while I was vacuuming, I realized what the whole bit was about. That I had really been terrified of being somebody else; somebody who's fought for identity as long as I have [doesn't want] to give it up. Without even knowing it, I had really been bothered by being Hannah Green. I didn't like it at all.[32]

Joanne wrote to the real Hannah Green, apologizing for the strange calls and letters. Green was frankly relieved to hear from her. Eventually after the two women met and as Joanne put it, "healed each other from what I had done," the thing became a private joke. But the pseudonym continued on its own. As Green recounted in a letter four years later:

Wherever I go, if a stranger approaches me with a worshipful expression in her eyes, I brace myself to say, No, it isn't I, and explain. . . . I have even been stopped—by someone who knew me slightly—in the middle of Seventh Avenue. . . . I've had phone calls for you too—one very creepy woman who was very persistent and really terrible trying to get your address . . . and another call from a sad, sweet young girl. She thought the book was about her, and I explained it was the story of the author, and later she wrote me a letter, saying that even though I wasn't the Hannah Green she admired, I seemed to be a warm person, and would I like to be her friend.[33]

There is no logical reason that printing "Joanne Greenberg" on the cover of *Rose Garden* should have made the book seem more true; it was still marketed as fiction, as it is today. If anything, using Greenberg's real name ought to have made her look more like a writer, since Holt started listing her other books on the back cover. But for many readers, this deepened the ambiguity: Greenberg clearly had an extraordinary imagination to be able to write so many different kinds of books, but there was still something about *Rose Garden* that set it apart.

As the book's fame grew, it spawned an odd array of spin-offs. A reader who said the story "haunted" her wrote a *Rose Garden* play. A high school teacher in Texas turned the book into reader's theater (complete with improvised food fights on the wards). One young woman wrote "a theme song," which she sent Greenberg, assuring her: "I have shown it to no one and I will not do so until you have heard and approved it." (A sample verse: "Though it was doubtful then/That you could ever win/Lost in a world of sin were you.") A Franciscan priest who sang in a folk group (this was the 1960s) wrote his own *Rose Garden* song. (In his version, Deborah is compared to a river, and sin is not mentioned.) Something about the book seemed to call forth music from its readers: a composer in Heidelberg sent Greenberg a "Yr-Suite for Reeds and Piano."[34]

Then, in 1970, a pop song that bizarrely rhymed "I never promised you a rose garden" with "I beg your pardon" burst onto the charts. Joe South (whose previous hits included "Down in the Boondocks") wrote the lyrics; the performer was Lynn Anderson.[35] The song hit number one on the country charts and made Anderson an international star.[36] (Greenberg didn't receive a penny from any of this, and several of her relatives suggested she sue, but she decided it wasn't worth it.)

The film version of *Rose Garden* was rumored for years before it appeared; readers started begging Greenberg for parts in the mid-1960s. Some insisted they were the real Deborah. A few claimed that only they could play Dr. Fried. (A pediatrician who said she simply had to be given the role listed as qualifications: "tiny, gray haired and plump, having spoken German as a child, and told I look like Helen Hayes.")[37] The film wasn't actually made until 1977. Greenberg had sold the rights for practically nothing when the book came out and had no subsequent involvement. Despite "virtually hundreds of requests" to repurchase them, nothing happened for a decade. Among those signed to play Deborah over the years were Mia Farrow, Tuesday Weld, Liza Minelli, and Natalie Wood. (Wood got too old for the part but refused to give it up, causing further delays.) Anne Bancroft and Estelle Parsons were each supposed to play Dr. Fried at various points.

Not being released until 1977 meant *Rose Garden* ended up being compared to *One Flew over the Cuckoo's Nest,* which had just won the Academy Award for best picture. But Jack Nicholson's outrageousness (which had nothing to do with real mental illness) made Greenberg's quiet agony seem boring. Vincent Canby reviewed the film favorably in the *New York Times,* and it won an award, but it had none of the haunting power or commercial success of the novel.[38]

The film version of *Rose Garden* did, however, have some disturbing features, like the complete erasure of the Jewish identity of its key characters. Frieda's and Joanne's relationship can't even be conceived without this crucial bond; it shaped every moment of their work together. Reviewers of the book didn't dwell on the implications of their being Jews in the late 1940s, but it was a fact often noted. In the film, "Deborah Blau" is renamed "Deborah Blake," and Bibi Andersson, a blonde, blue-eyed Swede is cast as Frieda. Chestnut Lodge, relocated to some unspecified, southern California setting, is filled with verdant groves of waving palm trees.[39]

Meanwhile, with no advertising or promotion, paperback sales of the book reached 5 million by 1977; among best sellers published between 1895 and 1975, *Rose Garden* was right between Dale Carnegie's *How to Win Friends and Influence People* and Thomas Harris's pop psych classic, *I'm O.K., You're O.K.*[40]

By this time, "I never promised you a rose garden" had entered the lexicon of cliché, serving as the perfect punch line to ironic moments. A *Doonesbury* strip that appeared during the peace talks to end the Vietnam War, for example, showed the U.S. president on the telephone with Le Duc Tho, Vietnam's chief negotiator. The president says:

> What can I do for you? . . . Yes, I'm sorry about the aid, but Congress has to act on that. . . . No, we haven't gone back on our pledge . . . Yes, I know about your schools and hospitals . . . but . . . but . . . LOOK, DUC THO, I NEVER PROMISED YOU A ROSE GARDEN!

A George Price cartoon in the *New Yorker* in the 1970s showed a couple dressed in rags, standing amid garbage and broken appliances. "I never promised you a rose garden," the husband intones as the wife gazes blankly around their hovel.[41]

Turning the key moment in Deborah's therapy into a joke helped lessen the intensity of feelings raised by the book. (Indeed, the fact that most people have no idea that the cliché comes directly from Greenberg's title means that there is no longer any danger of their feeling anything but bored amusement at hearing the phrase.) Since the words were actually those of Dr. Fried, the effect of the cliché was to trivialize the anguished struggle of a psychotic patient who was inching her way back toward the world. "After all," her caricature therapist seems to be saying in her climactic throwaway line, "I never promised you a rose garden." For Frieda's deep belief in the tragedy of mental illness to have been turned into this flip, Americanized silliness was an especially painful irony to those who knew her.

But people who read Greenberg's book after it became a best seller continued to be powerfully moved by the story's drama. This second wave of readers tried even more urgently to explain *Rose Garden*'s effect on them. Writing to Greenberg at 5:30 A.M., one man said: "I knew a blind woman & after knowing her for four years, she regained her sight. It was as if *I* had regained my sight & was able to *really see* things again. I can still see more clearly to this day. This is how your book effected [*sic*] me." Some insisted that even the gods in Deborah's delusionary world were actual people. "For me (and also my mother, who read the book, too)," wrote one man, "Anterrabae, Idat and the others gained real status as beings." He continued: "We own the book from which Debbie Blau took Anterrabae's image." (Debbie, a fictional character, is now so real she uses reference materials to construct her delusions.) And yet, even for a reader as taken in by the story as this man, ambiguities remained: "Is the book autobiographical, if I may be so blunt to ask?" suddenly ruptures the text of his letter.[42]

A number of readers wrote detailed accounts of how they had come upon *Rose Garden,* as if the specific circumstances might explain the intensity of their feelings. Others tallied the number of times they had read it, or said they carried it with them everywhere. One woman told Greenberg: "I reread chapters going over every thought of yours. . . . Eventually, I hope to fully comprehend every single line you have written."[43]

A woman who said she had been asked by the *New York Times Book Review* to write an article explaining the book's popularity sent Greenberg pages of questions. They started out thoughtfully ("its obvious literary merit would not explain [its special appeal to young people], nor would the fact that it is about a teen-ager"). Then her impatience took over: "I am sorry to dwell on your 'real identity,' but the book was so exquisite, it almost demands it. Why must you keep your identity a secret?"[44] This reader, like many others, seemed upset by the pseudonym, as if it signified some kind of denial of the book's message. For Greenberg, of course, "Hannah Green" served just the opposite function; by allowing *Rose Garden* to be written, she proved to Joanne that her cure had actually happened.

Many readers wrote for the titles of Dr. Fried's books or the location of her lectures. One man begged Holt to release her real name and address so that a relative of his, who "exhibits precisely the same symptoms as the character" in the novel, could be sent to her. "Treatment in many places has failed," he wrote, "and we are at our wits' end. The boy has now turned suicidal and violent and we want desperately to put him into the hands of someone who can finally cure him or ease his agony as soon as possible. Thus, we are exploring every avenue that even seems to offer an answer." That this included writing to the publishers of fictional works about mental illness testifies to the paucity of options psychiatry offered.[45]

Meeting Greenberg and thereby proving that the story was real desperately concerned many readers. Some said they would travel for hours or come on the bus; others pleaded that a conversation of even a few moments would be enough. "I told someone that the greatest desire of my life—next to serving God—was to meet you," wrote one young woman. Those who were frightened by their intense identification with Deborah thought meeting her might reassure them they weren't mentally ill. An anguished high school student wrote: "Most everything that happened to Deborah has happened to me or will happen in the future." But others seemed relieved just to know someone else shared their experience, like this man who told Greenberg:

> Thank you for writing your book *I Never Promised You a Rose Garden.* It makes me feel that you are real and alive and *there.* And just to know that there is *somebody out there* is enough to make a person want to stay alive, in the hope, always dying but not quite, that it is possible to be real to someone else and for them to be real in you. Thank you, just thank you.[46]

Reading *Rose Garden* was an even more powerful experience for those who were mentally ill. Many described the moment they had first come across the book, like this man, then in a state hospital:

> I was dubious. How, I wondered, could anyone write a novel about mental illness the way it ought to be written? I bought your book, however, and found that what I had thought was impossible had been achieved; the ephemeral moods and nuances of mental illness had been recorded and all the fears, aspirations, and frustrations—and the mute and urgent beauty of the sickness itself—were there.

Writing his letter after reading the book many times, he told Greenberg: "You have given me encouragement when I most needed it, and you have shown me beauty. You have filled a void and made me feel less lonely, and I want to thank you. God bless you." Patient after patient described being transformed by the book: "If you can make it, perhaps I can, too," as one put it.[47]

A patient labeled "improved" after treatment with ECT told Greenberg she had been "playing the part of the happy little moron, never letting life or anything vaguely resembling it, touch me." After reading *Rose Garden,* when "everything I had worked so hard to keep buried came soaring to the surface," she started psychotherapy: "My life has a completely different tone since you entered it. It is as though a dam has burst and an emotional and mental health has poured through and for *the first time in my life,* I look forward to the very strong possibility of a full and rich life."

Another patient, who began her letter saying, "I really feel as if I am writing to Deborah; she is as real to me as I am, whereas you are just sort of a name," told Greenberg:

> I read your book, and it gave me the courage to try—again. After eight re-admissions, it's pretty difficult. But the choice has been made. There is no alternative now—except to stick with it. Thank you—more than I can ever tell you. You have renewed some latent courage which I've managed to scrape together again for another go.

She ended her letter: "Thank you—whoever you are."

Another woman wrote: "I clung to *Rose Garden* during my own illness, reading and re-reading it many times, not as fiction, but as proof that I could endure. Not a small part of my ultimate cure was due to your book." Another said: "I wanted to prove to my therapist, just like Deborah did, that I had the willpower to be successful again."[48]

A mother wrote to say that she and her husband had decided to finance a longer stay in the hospital for their daughter because of the moment in the story when a patient, prematurely removed from the ward, kills herself and Deborah remarks with bitterness and wonder: "Her family didn't give her a chance, but mine . . . "[49]

Even patients never treated with psychotherapy identified powerfully with the book. A woman who said she had been "cured by means of a lobotomy" wrote to Holt to thank them. "Hannah Green," she said, had a "comprehension of life in a mental hospital" that was "astounding."[50]

Unlike most general readers, who wrote to praise the writing or the story's emotional power, patients were often motivated by concerns about Greenberg. One young woman pleaded: "Could you just send me a note to let me know you are 'alive and well' in Mexico City or wherever? . . . My psychiatrist tells me that you are Deborah Blau and Dr. Fried is the late Dr. Frieda Fromm-Reichmann. . . . I think perhaps my anxiety is just plain concern about you and an almost overpowering yearning to know how you are after all these years. . . . I am weeping now as I write this—both for what you suffered and for what I know about it first hand. Please let me know if you are still well." No amount of reassurance by others seemed to relieve this woman's fears: "My doctor says the book is a sequel to your illness since you wrote it yourself, but I am still disquieted." Another told Greenberg: "I suffered and I hope with all my heart that Deborah is safely out of Yr now."[51]

Many patients had an urgent need to know the recovery had held. "I just don't know how to approach you with what I want to ask of you," wrote one woman. "I know I have no right—absolutely none at all, to ask you this, but I have to at least try. Could I please, possibly, meet you? Just for a while, just to meet you and talk to you. . . . I am not exactly sure why I want to meet you; maybe just to make certain that you really do exist." Some of these former patients didn't care whether Greenberg actually answered their queries; the very fact of being able to write to her was proof in itself that she was a real person.[52]

Many conveyed with extraordinary precision how her experience matched theirs. "I read your book shortly after I had tried to kill myself," wrote one woman. "At that time I was calculating my deceits. That they would happen was the only conditional given in which I believed." Like every other patient, this woman knew the book wasn't a novel:

I find it almost inconceivable that anyone who had not experienced it could so accurately have described the sensation of being glassed in by seemingly impervious cold. Realizing the naiveté of the question, I still ask you: Does it ever really go away? . . . People have told me that Deborah Blau is a pseudonym for Hannah Green. Others have told me that Hannah Green is a pseudonym for the name of an analyst. Both assumptions give me a peculiar kind of hope. If it is the former, then it really must be possible to get well. If it is the latter, then it must be possible for someone to understand and feel the world of sickness so completely that the cold stops being the absolute intractable barrier that it seems. And in either case, there is more than fiction to Dr. Fried, isn't there?[53]

Some of these patients were identifying with Deborah herself, others with the brutality of mental hospitals. (That this brutality came through so clearly, even though Greenberg was describing the privileged atmosphere of the Lodge, painfully highlights the stigma of mental illness.) One former patient, struggling to express his appreciation to Greenberg for writing the book, went so far as to invent words in Yri, the secret language Deborah used when she was most frightened.[54]

A number of patients, especially young women, seemed confused about where their own identities left off and Deborah's started. Scrawling "IMPORTANT MAIL" across the front of her letter, one wrote:

My name is Deborah. I, like you were, am mentally disturbed. . . . I fell in love with Debby and her condition and I want to be like her. . . . I want to hide from this rotten life by being crazy. . . . I love Debbie—she was so good and I'm so bad. . . . Help me please. Your [sic] the real Debbie. You know how I feel. Tell me how to be like Debbie. How can I be crazy.

Another told Greenberg: "I'm writing you because I'm in trouble. You know me. You wrote the book *I Never Promised You a Rose Garden* about me." Also named Debbie, this young woman was among the handful of patients who assumed Greenberg was the therapist. She ended her letter with: "How much does it cost per visit for your therapy, and how would I go about making an appt. and what is the address of your office?"[55]

An actively psychotic young woman repeatedly sent letters from her hospital ward. At times, she seemed happy that Greenberg had recovered and asked: "Will you be my friend and my penpal?" But other letters angrily denounced "Hannah" for rejecting her: "You should be kind and sympathetic because you know what suffering is and now you are so well and had it so good." Sometimes she seemed confused about Greenberg's identity, asking: "Do you have the power to put someone into a mental hospital? Are you a doctor?" Yet she had managed to find out a great deal about the real Joanne; she knew the name of her husband, his occupation, and many other details of her current life. This patient's main question was painfully unanswerable: "Why did you go to Chestnut Lodge, the best and most expensive hospital, and I had to suffer in stinky state [institutions]?"[56]

Some patients intensified their identification with Deborah after their doctors said their cases were similar. One woman, whose therapist had heard Greenberg speak at his hospital, wrote: "He says I can get well like you did. . . . He respects you and he compared me to you." (She asked Greenberg to send her "the price of a hardback edition" of *Rose Garden,* saying she had read it several times in paperback, but needed "to have it in hardback, for security when I leave here.") Signing her letter "thank you for getting well," this young woman said Greenberg had given her the strength to leave the hospital.[57]

Other patients found their resemblance to Deborah frightening. A woman in her fifth year of hospitalization told Greenberg her doctor had just read a book "about a girl who seemed uncannily like me." When she read *Rose Garden* herself, she found the experience overwhelming, "because it was so true and because I had lived it myself thinking no one could ever understand, and yet someone had." The book forced her to confront the fundamental challenge of her illness: "I finally knew it was up to me to get well—not my doctor or the hospital or God or my world, just me." However, this woman became (understandably) unnerved when her therapist started dissolving any distinction between her life and Deborah's. Every time she "plagued [him] for reassurance that things would be better," he responded: "Ask Debbie." When she wondered what her future life might hold, he told her: "Debbie is married and has a family and is well and mostly happy." Not surprisingly, this patient began to think she was literally sharing Greenberg's existence:

"If we are truly as much alike as he says, perhaps one day I can write a sequel to *Rose Garden*." (Even the placement of her words on the page made vivid the erasure of this woman's identity. A person who saw her letter commented: "She writes 'I' as an almost vanishing dot, no taller than her lowercase letters, and separates it from the surrounding words with wide pools of empty space.")[58]

Many patients tried to use Deborah's experience to predict their own futures, but this was difficult since the book ended so inconclusively. Would Deborah have to grit her teeth at every moment against the old fears? Would she eventually suffer a relapse? Or had she really recovered, able to fully enter the world? A young woman who began her letter saying "I have never written to anyone outside my family before," begged for answers to the questions that terrified many patients:

> While you were at the hospital did you ever want to give up fighting to get well? Were you scared that maybe someday [Dr. Fried] would tell you you were going to stay at the hospital the rest of your life? Were you angry deep down inside because the people at the hospital wanted you to go home?

For this young woman, whose fear of remaining ill was matched by her fear of getting better, the idea of permanent recovery was alarming. Having spent most of her life in institutions, the state of wellness, "an almost pure abstraction," was potentially annihilating.[59]

Another patient, diagnosed as schizophrenic and recently discharged from the hospital, confessed that although she was doing well "according to all accounts," she was secretly "fighting to keep myself sick." A part of her longed to return to the hospital, the only place where she wasn't an alien. "My friends and family tell me my eyes are blank" she wrote to Greenberg. Terrified that some core strangeness set her apart from other people, she pleaded for answers:

> If you were completely cured of schizophrenia, did you lose some of your sensitivity; did you become more complacent and willing to accept the wrongs in the world—did the lack of schizophrenia make you more apathetic? (I don't think the withdrawal into schizophrenia is apathy—it is fighting in its own way.) Do schizophrenics ever get completely well, and like it?

Another young woman, overwhelmed by the impenetrable space that separated her from other students at her college, wrote:

> I just cannot help knowing the fact that I am different or not of
> them. . . . Most people do not know what it feels like to have no insides
> and be filled with smoke, or see things all in shades of grey, or two-di-
> mensionally, or feel like a whole room is talking about you, or that your
> very existence is on the verge of an inexplicable disintegration. There is
> a very great difference between the human world of day-to-day frustra-
> tions, loneliness, and feelings of insecurity, and the crazy world of im-
> minent chaos and confusion and destruction. The hardest thing for me
> to accept is that to most I will never be able to explain myself so that
> they will understand.

She ended her letter by asking: "When did you start feeling solid inside?
When did you stop intuitively expecting the world not to be a rose garden? . . . I am disappointed a thousand times a day."[60]

For patients who acknowledged that no one could predict what would happen to them, *Rose Garden* was less a source of revelation than a spur to action. One woman said: "The first time I read the book I was so frightened.
The second time upset me terribly, too, but after I read it again this week, I
gained hope and comfort." (She still worried about Hannah Green, though,
and begged for reassurance that she had remained well.)[61]

Greenberg answered every single one of these letters, just as she has answered every letter from readers of her other books for more than three
decades. She corresponded regularly with several former patients. One was
terrified by the striking similarities between her own symptoms and Deborah's. She too had gods like those in Yr, but hers were more vindictive. She
told Greenberg:

> I know now that my mind created them, and I now refer to them as "my
> mind," but that doesn't seem to lessen their power any. I keep reading
> your book over and over again, and sort of consider it my salvation
> from feeling totally futile. But my mind uses your book to its own ad-
> vantage, saying that it's a lie, that you didn't get well, and, more often,
> that even if it is true that it can't apply to me, because my evil is beyond
> anything psychological.

For this young woman, who felt as if she were simply "mismade," the possibility that Greenberg had actually recovered from schizophrenia was disturbing. "If someone seems evil or generally ruined like me," she wrote, "I can

feel on safe ground. But if they get well, it's like their 'sickness' was merely a hoax." Calling herself "just another person trying to borrow from your hard-earned sanity," she seemed embarrassed by the very fact of writing.[62]

Greenberg sent a complex reply. "You don't have to get well until you are ready and unless you want to. My sickness wasn't meant to prove anything to you and my getting well need not disturb you, although it does and I know it." She said she understood the terror: "It is as if the doctor is trying to make you leap out into utter darkness and fall 1,000 feet on his unsupported statement that there will be a world out there and that you will be caught, this despite the fact that you jumped daily for years and there was no catching, only falling."[63]

Years later, when Greenberg began working as an emergency medical technician in her mountaintop community, she came to a deeper understanding of these paradoxes of hope. Living nearest to the main road, she was often the first EMT to arrive at an accident scene. Once she sat waiting for an ambulance with a young man who had just been hit by a car. He was in excruciating pain and begged Greenberg to kill him. She was certain that if he had a gun at that moment, he would have shot himself. But Greenberg knew that in twenty minutes the pain medication would kick in, and in a few hours, he wouldn't feel much. In a year, the whole experience would be a story he could tell to friends. As they sat by the side of the road, she said: "I can see over this. You can't. I'm here to tell you that you'll get past it. You can't see it right at this moment but I can." This was the message *Rose Garden* had sent to so many mental patients, and it was a relief to Greenberg every time one of them heard.[64]

Literary critics had stranger responses to the book. In an article titled "The Archetype of Death and Renewal in *I Never Promised You a Rose Garden*," Ruth Diamond said the story was a "resurrection" and Deborah a "mythological hero" who reenacts the five stages of shamanic initiation—torture and violent dismemberment, the scraping away of flesh, the substitution of viscera, the retreat into hell, and the ascent into heaven. "When Deborah finally chooses the real world," said Diamond at the end of her overheated analysis, "she has completed an epic journey, as arduous and dangerous as any ancient hero's descent into death."[65]

Katherine Snipes's analysis in *Masterplots* was more straightforward. Noting that the roots of Deborah's illness are never made totally explicit, she said, "This lingering uncertainty lends plausibility to the story, for it avoids oversimplification." Snipes was intrigued by the idea of insanity as an "out of control" form of "the writer's craft." However, finding herself unable to distinguish Jungian archetypes or detect Freudian patterns in the characters, she concluded that the main strengths of *Rose Garden* are that it "does not romanticize mental illness" and lets the reader "see through the eyes and mind of the patient."[66]

Kary and Gary Wolfe managed to turn Dr. Fried into Jung's "wise old woman," but their main claim was that *Rose Garden* was itself an archetype for a new genre they called the "popular psychological narrative":

> Despite all its images of doom and confusion, *Rose Garden* is essentially comedic. There is from the outset a feeling of imminent resolution and hope; like the traditional fairy tale, elements of horror may be introduced as long as there is no overall feeling of despair. Part of this may be due to the journey motif, [which] naturally implies an end. . . . In the case of Deborah, this end is relative sanity . . . This movement, though not effortless, seems inevitable.[67]

Jeffrey Berman was the first of several critics to "discover" that *Rose Garden* described a case Frieda had discussed in her clinical writings. Noting that not even Freud had "anticipated the possibility that both patient and analyst might eventually write accounts of the same experience from different points of view, the narration of one complementing and perhaps contradicting the other," Berman triumphantly set out to compare Joanne's version with Frieda's. Praising *Rose Garden* as "one of the most psychologically sophisticated literary representations of mental illness" and calling it a "whodunit of the unconscious," he was especially taken with descriptions of Yr. "To imagine this self-created universe, the novelist uses mythological themes and symbols; a pantheon of dark gods, incantatory chants of seduction and damnation, metaphors of darkness and chaos, descent into an abyss, and a gradual reemergence into light. Deborah's gods have Latinate names, speak in Miltonic rhythms of defiance, and embody Dantesque horrors." At the same time, Berman argued, descriptions of the therapeutic process in *Rose Garden* were far more authentic than those in other fictional works on mental illness.

Yet despite his acknowledgment of their different perspectives, Berman complained that Joanne's account wasn't identical to Frieda's case illustrations. After perceptively noting the difficulties a patient faced when trying to imagine the analyst's internal experience, he concluded with irritation that "the restriction of the patient's imaginative freedom to enter into the analyst's character is helpful for therapy but harmful for literature."[68]

In the most elaborate literary analysis of *Rose Garden,* Evelyne Keitel contrasted it with other examples of "schizophrenic narrative." The "insistence on authenticity" characteristic of patient accounts was not, she argued, a desire to tell the truth but rather a device intended to create a certain effect in the reader. By capturing the fragmented sense of self so characteristic of contemporary life, schizophrenics offer a way to understand our divided selves. However, recovered patients like Greenberg are "boring" because their accounts are straightforward, chronological, and ordered, shedding no light on the postmodern experience. Keitel's analysis is focused solely on the reader:

> The aesthetic response to pathographical texts is characterized by certain ambivalent feelings which surface during the reading process; pleasure as well as a sense of oppression, paralysis and anxiety, those very feelings, in fact, that are called forth during a psychotic attack. . . . My hypothesis is that the fascination that emanates from reading psychopathographic texts arises from the fact that the rational and the irrational both participate in the reading process, that they come into conflict, that tensions arise and, consequently, erratic and unpredictable responses may occur.

Since the whole point of reading an account of madness is that it affords "the 'normal' person the chance of playing with these experiences . . . without having to face any of the dire intrapsychic consequences," Greenberg's orderly reconstruction of her illness doesn't satisfy this need for imagined chaos.

Keitel wants readers to experience vicariously the psychosis itself, "a dimension of experience in literature which remains closed to [them] in life."[69] But Greenberg's goal was entirely different: she wanted to announce the cure, not to bring others inside the illness. Having experienced madness firsthand, she never wished even a moment of that terror on anyone else. Keitel is like a person who goes to horror movies for a cheap thrill; Greenberg, a real torture victim, hopes others will never have to suffer as she did.

Lee Edwards has denounced the "imperialism" of such critics, who seek to "appropriate" psychosis in a way that does violence to the experience of patients: "[They] play with schizophrenia, toy with it, teasing out its discursive possibilities. . . . But when the self is seen purely as a text, its purity as text is reified, its terror as experience is lost." By creating "the study of the world without a self," Edwards argued, critics like Keitel ignore the agony of real schizophrenics, who long to "see a human face mirrored in [their own] shattered subjectivity."[70]

The response of most psychiatrists to *Rose Garden* was precisely opposite that of critics. Insisting that the story was a case history and unwilling to accept that Greenberg might have recovered without drugs or shock treatment, they felt the need to dispute her testimony. "I got better with plain old psychotherapy," as she put it, "so they fight on my bones." The insensitivity of many of these physicians was striking. Some telephoned Greenberg rather than troubling to write, a level of intrusiveness rare even among psychotic patients. Others sent her articles saying she had been misdiagnosed or might suffer a relapse. She understood their hostility—"I am standing in the way of the theory"—but it was still painful and bizarre to have to deal with these attacks.[71]

Lawrence Kubie, reviewing the book in the *Journal of Nervous and Mental Disease,* insisted Greenberg couldn't have been schizophrenic. He offered a variety of other possibilities (nonspecific brain damage, early toxic delirium) and used his own ability to come up with witty interpretations of Yr words as proof that they were "an array of puns and condensations . . . not the neologisms of the psychotic." Knowing full well that the book was no novel (he had worked at Sheppard and had many colleagues at the Lodge), he criticized Greenberg for failing to include data that would support his claims ("medical and surgical records of her condition at the time of [a childhood] operation and after, temperature charts, X-rays, clinical studies or EEG, and nursing notes describing her behavior"). The idea that she might want to represent her experience in literary form rather than as a case history seemed to infuriate him.

Kubie did not stop at a book review. He wrote a series of letters to Greenberg in care of her publisher and became increasingly arrogant and hostile when Holt refused his requests for her telephone number. After Greenberg wrote him a gracious reply, he started calling her. "He was arguing with me and arguing with me and arguing with me," Joanne recalled. When she politely disagreed with his interpretations in a subsequent written exchange, he kept insisting that only he could accurately characterize the meaning of her illness.[72]

Carol North and Remi Cadoret went to even greater lengths to "prove" Greenberg wrong. Writing in the *Archives of General Psychiatry,* they presented the results of an elaborate content analysis designed to show that "personal accounts of schizophrenia" were based on misunderstanding. North and Cadoret selected *Rose Garden* and four other such accounts and then dissected them page by page, comparing every symptom to criteria in the American Psychiatric Association's *Diagnostic and Statistical Manual of Mental Disorders*. According to this analysis, Deborah Blau, "the girl purported to be schizophrenic," was actually suffering from "somatization disorder." Castigating Greenberg for being "so vague" about her symptoms that it was difficult to categorize them using DSM-III, they blamed her and the other writers for "raising false hopes in people who have real schizophrenia or who have loved ones with it."[73]

One might wonder what would motivate two busy psychiatrists to spend hundreds of hours poring over narratives of recovered mental patients to invalidate them.[74] And to do so by demonstrating that their diagnoses failed to accord with DSM-III criteria is even more bewildering, since that edition wasn't published until 1980 and categories in previous versions were strikingly different (so patients hospitalized earlier couldn't possibly have been diagnosed using criteria that didn't yet exist). But what makes North and Cadoret's analysis truly bizarre is that in 1987, North published *Welcome, Silence: My Triumph over Schizophrenia,* a personal account of her own illness. In it, she reveals that Cadoret was her therapist and she had been miraculously cured by kidney dialysis (a technique she admitted worked in almost no other cases). Thus, the same Carol North who railed against "raising false hopes" and claimed that "dramatic accounts of cures or remissions in schizophrenia help perpetuate the concept that certain treatments are efficacious" was later guilty of precisely the same charges she had leveled at Greenberg, who had been treated with a far more widely accepted procedure. (As a further irony, North's publisher used *Rose Garden* to sell *Welcome, Silence,* claiming it was "even more moving for it is not only a *true* story . . . it has a happy ending.") After her recovery, North became a psychiatrist and has presumably spent her time persuading other patients not to write personal accounts of their treatments.[75]

A few analysts responded to *Rose Garden* by exaggerating its claims rather than disputing them. Gerald Schoenewolf, for example, in a chapter titled "Curing Schizophrenia," labeled the book a "case history written by the patient" and said it had turned Greenberg into "one of the most famous patients in psychoanalytic history." Distorting many details of the story to make it more heroic, Schoenewolf claimed the treatment was a "remarkable encounter between a great therapist and a great patient" whose relationship was marked by "special chemistry" and "magic." Repeatedly hailing the "extraordinary success" of the therapy, he made Greenberg's case seem as relevant to the ordinary treatment of schizophrenia as a brain transplant.[76]

Even Thomas McGlashan and Christopher Keats, two Lodge therapists who used Greenberg's case as one of four they studied in a retrospective analysis of the hospital's methods, called her "something of a diagnostic enigma." Although in their view she met DSM-III criteria for schizophrenia, there was something "evanescent" about Greenberg's symptoms that raised doubts about the proper categorization. The severity of her illness was affected by the degree of stress she felt at any given moment, and there was more variability across situations than was typical of true psychosis. In addition, although Greenberg's social interactions were clearly disturbed, she created a fantasy world "absolutely loaded with people," and thus never ceased being "actively related" even when totally withdrawn from "real" relationships. Frieda may have "guarded against unduly treating Joanne in a special way," McGlashan and Keats note, "but she was always a special patient, not only to Frieda but also to the entire institution."[77]

Thus, for Kubie, North, and other psychiatrists, the trouble with *Rose Garden* was that it wasn't literal enough—it didn't have the accuracy of diagnosis, symptoms, or test results they wished for. For critics like Keitel and the others, the problem with the book was that it wasn't literary enough—it was too accurate, too much like a case history, not novelistic. Yet for ordinary readers—those who had themselves experienced mental illness and those who had not—this ambiguity was precisely what made the book so powerful. By showing them the experience of madness without forcing them inside, and by proving in both the story and the fact of its having been written that it was possible to recover from serious mental illness, ordinary readers allowed themselves to believe that what Deborah and Dr. Fried had accomplished was worthy of celebration.

It is painful enough to see psychiatrists denying the possibility of their own success. They become nihilistic and grow to hate their work. But what made their discrediting of Greenberg's story especially destructive was that it pushed patients to give up their own last shreds of hope.

A young woman who had spent most of her life in mental hospitals movingly described her experiences with the book:

> I first read *Rose Garden* when I was about 13 years old. The first few times I read it I didn't understand it at all, couldn't have told you anything about it, yet it gave me this absorbed, exalted feeling, like being free, like finding something I'd buried a long time ago and forgotten, and then happened on again by accident. Even though I couldn't remember what the buried treasure was or why it was important, it made

me cry and made me happy for its forgotten associations.

The next thing I remember is battles, with people trying to get the book away from me, my father accusing me of trying to imitate it by acting crazy. . . . He and the nuns at school said I re-read *Rose Garden* too much, it was bad for me, and periodically took copies away. I either re-claimed the confiscated copy by doing some deed of school work or family duty or went and got a new one, if the task was impossible for me or the book was not meant to be returned at all, as sometimes was threatened. My dad threw a few copies in the trash. I never entirely understood their objections or their accusations regarding my behavior, since as far as I know, none of them ever bothered to read the book.

I read *Rose Garden* when I am lost and numb and especially, over the years, when I've been incarcerated at school or a hospital where the loneliness of not being understood was very strong, and the influence of others trying to impose their ideas has estranged me from even myself, and I doubted my own sanity, doubted my most deeply-held values and beliefs, doubted my identity, was reduced to sub-nothing nothingness by isolation with strenuous behavior-mod techniques, or stranded at a school where there was nothing to tell me I existed as the self I knew. *Rose Garden* gave me back, at these times, a language with which to address *myself.*

Years later, this young woman ended up a patient at Chestnut Lodge. She had no idea that the story had taken place there. Occasionally someone would make a cryptic comment, but generally *Rose Garden* "was a strangely undiscussed subject among patients at the Lodge." Then one day after McGlashan and Keats had published their account of Greenberg's treatment, people on the ward started talking about her:

I remember someone saying, "You know, now they think she was misdiagnosed. She was never schizo or borderline. Now they think she had some kind of hypochondriacal hysteria or something." Someone else said, "I guess if you had a doctor who was as devoted to you as Frieda was to her, you'd get well no matter what." End of discussion. Frieda was looked upon as a freak of nature—a doctor who cured—which was not likely to be duplicated in our time, and Ms. Greenberg was idolized, but then quickly discredited, and then there was nothing more to say.[78]

Several years later, unable to imagine that she herself might ever get better, this thoughtful, articulate young woman killed herself.

Greenberg identified strongly with people like this. In retrospect, it's easy to lose sight of the sense of fragility she had about her own life at the time she started to write. She wanted to call the book *The Little Maybe* to capture that precariousness. "I was not meant to be what I am, to do what I do," she later said. "I was meant to be half dead all my life, or fully dead, and a lot of people told me so." Her response to Clarence Schulz's follow-up study of Lodge patients was filled with amazement that events had taken so different a turn. But after *Rose Garden* was published, and especially after she started giving interviews, people tried to make it seem inevitable that she had gotten better, whereas for Greenberg and her family, it was a miracle.[79]

Although she probably couldn't have articulated it at the time, Joanne intuitively understood that she wasn't the real target of all the disputes about *Rose Garden;* it was Frieda. The reason it was so important to so many people to find out if Joanne were real was that she constituted the proof that Frieda's method worked. Furious that *Rose Garden* had resurrected the idea of psychotherapy with schizophrenics long after they thought it was dead, psychiatrists attacked the book because the real Frieda was no longer around for them to lash out at. What particularly drove them crazy was that Greenberg's novelistic license had made the treatment seem so believable to families and patients.

Psychiatrists thought Frieda was safely buried. But *Rose Garden* had not only brought her back to life; it made her totally heroic. How could real doctors compete with the magical Dr. Fried? Why should a patient trust them when they said there were no alternatives but drugs or shock treatment?

So every nasty thing that people didn't have the nerve to say to Frieda when she was still there being disarming got directed at Joanne (who, fortunately, had Albert to help her keep some perspective). Since psychiatry still had no answer to the problem of serious mental illness and few physicians could point to recoveries as clear as Joanne's, Frieda's ideas remained a threat.

But attacking *Rose Garden* didn't accomplish enough. For all its accuracy and symbolic weight, it remained the story of only one patient. To make totally sure that Frieda's approach didn't live on after her death, the work of her closest colleagues had to be discredited. This wasn't as easy as it sounded, since she cultivated no disciples and taught her students to think for themselves. However, there was one person who explicitly claimed "to be following in Frieda's footsteps," and that was Harold Searles.[80]

One of the energetic young physicians who joined the Lodge staff in the late 1940s, Searles had an unusual background for a psychiatrist. He had grown up in an "endemically anti-Semitic" small town in upstate New York, the only son of a "schizoid" mother and a "coarse, male chauvinist" father who ran a clothing store. Searles was told from an early age that if he became a doctor he'd "have the world by the balls." Ambitious for success, he went to college at Cornell and medical school at Harvard but kept asking himself: "How come I don't have the world by the balls?"

Openly admitting to having "narrowly avoided a schizophrenic break" in college, Searles chose to become a psychiatrist to avoid serving on the front lines during the war and because he had always identified strongly with mental patients. His dream was to be hired at the Lodge, but Bullard, concerned that Searles wasn't stable enough for the work, insisted he enter analysis first. Finally accepted onto the staff in 1949, Searles later said that his private criterion of success was not the lavishness of his home or the number of cars he owned but whether he could afford to be treated as a patient at Chestnut Lodge. (Earlier, when he was still in training at the Washington Psychoanalytic Institute, Searles said he had believed that any candidate who became psychotic would be treated for free at the Lodge.)

Searles went on to author dozens of papers and became internationally known for his work on countertransference and the merged, symbiotic relationship between therapists and schizophrenics. He revealed his own deepest wishes and feelings in his writings, and people often felt overwhelmed just reading his descriptions of therapy with psychotic patients. Searles was equally exhibitionistic in person: he traveled around the country demonstrating his ability to intuit schizophrenic dynamics by interviewing patients he had never seen before in front of audiences of stunned psychiatrists.

But there is a thin line between being able to tolerate craziness in one's patients and using them to stay connected to those feelings in oneself. Don Bloch, who became a family systems therapist after he left the Lodge, wondered whether Searles and his patients formed a relationship that offered "such a degree of protection or comfort or safety or refuge that neither of them could get out of it." It's no coincidence, Bloch and others have remarked, that Searles titled his most famous paper "The Patient as Therapist to his Analyst."[81]

Unlike Frieda, who identified with the shards of health that remained buried in her patients, Searles always seemed to gravitate toward their sickest parts. He talked openly of envying his patients' life at the Lodge, and often seemed so overly identified with their illness that he couldn't imagine them as any better than they were. His colleague John Fort noted that Searles invariably chose the most disturbed patients to work with. Openly speculating that Searles had some unconscious need to destroy the very thing he was trying to defend, Fort once told him straight out: "You're going to do more to set back the cause of psychotherapy with psychotic patients than anyone else" (because, having elected to work only with people who couldn't be reached, it would be impossible for him to succeed at the task). Searles seemed to need his patients to remain ill, either because this reassured him about his own sanity or because it aided his research. He admitted feeling guilty about this, a reaction that then became more grist for the work. In this respect, his contrast to Frieda, whose lack of envy toward her patients led her to see guilt feelings as a "luxury neither patient nor therapist can afford," couldn't have been sharper.[82]

These tensions are painfully evident in Searles's work with Mrs. Joan Douglas, the patient he treated for thirty-eight years. Mrs. Douglas (a pseudonym) was one of the most disturbed patients ever admitted to Chestnut Lodge. She had become overtly psychotic at the age of thirty-three, after the death of her mother. Mrs. Douglas had four young children, and when her behavior became increasingly delusional and chaotic, she was hospitalized for their protection as well as hers. After forty-two sessions of ECT and seventy insulin shocks to no effect, lobotomy was recommended. She was sent to the Lodge as a last-ditch alternative. Her first therapist quit in discouragement after a year "because of the proliferating, rather than lessening, state of her delusions, and her adamant resistance to treatment." As Searles later remarked: "His doing so was highly unusual behavior for a Lodge staff member, and one testimony of the formidable nature of her illness."[83]

Mrs. Douglas frequently assaulted both patients and staff. She was convinced that there were "doubles" of everyone, including herself. Rebuked for her violence, she protested: "Well, there are nine hundred and ninety-seven tertiary skillion women [i.e., doubles of herself] associated with Chestnut Lodge, so why should I be blamed for everything everybody did?" She claimed never to have had a mother or father and said her husband and children didn't exist. She seemed unable to differentiate between animate and inanimate, human and nonhuman, male and female, adults and children, ideas and persons, or fantasies and real events. She said surgeons had installed machinery inside her body and controlled her brain through a hole in her head. Once, when Searles mentioned her mind, she said: "You see, my mother *was* my mind."

Like other long-term Lodge patients, Mrs. Douglas became a fixture around the place and is remembered in strikingly different ways by different people. Some fondly recalled an early escapade when she escaped from the ward, went to Washington, rented a beautiful white horse (she was an expert rider), and rode up Pennsylvania Avenue to the gates of the White House demanding an audience with the president. Jarl Dyrud said he was able to have a perfectly rational conversation with Mrs. Douglas so long as he stood far enough away from her to allow her to feel comfortable in his presence. "We had this range of normal operation. I think I would have been inclined to work to develop that rather than burrow around in her insides." Ted Lidz had similar memories. "Mrs. Douglas was crazy as hell when she was with Searles, but at other times she seemed to be quite sane."[84]

Searles's work with Mrs. Douglas made even staff accustomed to long-term treatment uncomfortable. Martin Cooperman remembered a discussion in a supervision group he and Searles both participated in. It was the tenth year of Mrs. Douglas's treatment, and they spent the whole session talking about whether Searles ought to give her some kind of gift. "As I began to think about it," Cooperman recalled, "I realized it was an anniversary gift. He was celebrating an anniversary. He was celebrating their relationship. You don't end relationships that you celebrate." Other colleagues said that since Mrs. Douglas provided most of the material for Searles's publications, he would lose his most valuable source of data if he ended the therapy. Don Bloch was more pointed: "The patient pays the bill and it's nice to have patients who come three or four hours a week for so many years . . . you've got a retirement policy right there." Others talked of Searles using the treatment to feed his own "hunger for vilification."[85]

But the issue wasn't just the length of the treatment; it was the fact that Mrs. Douglas didn't seem to have improved to any appreciable extent. Many Lodge staff recalled treatments of Frieda's that had lasted for years; she always said patients should be seen as long as was necessary. But Jarl Dyrud summed up the crucial difference: "Harold's patients did not get better. Frieda's did." Otto Will wondered whether in the end, Searles and Mrs. Douglas would be buried together.[86]

For mainstream psychiatrists, attacking Searles became the perfect way to caricature the approach Frieda had pioneered. True, she had never held onto a patient for thirty-eight years, but maybe that was because she just hadn't lived long enough. To those outside the Lodge, Searles epitomized the absurdity of trying to reach people who were clearly beyond hope. The fact that his most famous patient spent her whole life in a mental hospital whereas Frieda's had married, raised two children, and become the successful author of fourteen books were details never mentioned by those who sought to tar her with Searles's failures.

Frieda spent her life struggling against the nihilism that kept psychiatrists from taking credit for the successes they did have. She may not have known precisely how to describe what worked, but she didn't discount those recoveries that occurred. Indeed, she took the view of physicians in most other fields: that breakthroughs in medicine often emerge from cases that don't conform to known rules. She would have been fascinated by a book published by Esther Goshen-Gottstein, an Israeli psychologist, about her husband's recovery after four months in deep coma.

Moshe, an internationally recognized linguist who spoke a dozen ancient and modern languages, failed to regain consciousness following a coronary bypass operation. Rodney Falk, an American cardiologist who knew him well, said that had Moshe been hospitalized in the United States, his complete lack of response would have led to the removal of life support. Yet although "no realistic hopes could be entertained for his recovery," Moshe was ultimately restored to a sophisticated level of functioning equal to that of his precoma existence. After rigorous rehabilitation efforts and "within eighteen months of his 'terminal' brain damage," the neurologist Oliver Sacks noted, "Professor Goshen-Gottstein had written two books and countless scholarly articles, attended conferences, lectured widely, and been appointed to visiting professorships at Harvard and Brandeis Universities." Sacks said that while "anecdotes of recovery exist, this is the first fully documented report of a 'return' from a deep coma where no return seemed possible."

Sacks and Falk both agreed that this was a completely atypical case, unprecedented in the neurological literature. Neither assumed that other coma patients would respond as Moshe did. Yet they insisted that his case contained useful lessons for the field. As Sacks wrote, "This book is much more than a mere report of an interesting (or even unique) case. It is an intensely human document of a man's suffering, fortitude, dignity, and recovery, and of the powers of care and faith which did so much to make his final triumph possible." In a powerful statement at the end of the book, Falk added:

> Whatever the reasons for Moshe's miraculous recovery, his story is a lesson in hope and in the marvelous devotion of a remarkable family. It is also a lesson in humility to me as a physician. Although I have never seen anything similar before or since (and I have experience of many such cases), it has altered my view of the word "hopeless."[87]

Every physician involved in this case or told about it afterward agreed that the length of the coma, the extent of deterioration, and the extraordinary recovery made it utterly unrepresentative. Yet none questioned that these things had in fact taken place.

The neurologists and cardiologists caring for Moshe Goshen-Gottstein did not take his uniqueness to mean that nothing could be learned about brain function from his experience. He was studied as intensively as transplant patients or very premature babies. No physician takes cases like this as representative; if anything, they are seen as revealing things that might never be learned from studying ordinary situations.

Yet psychiatrists take a case like Joanne Greenberg's and dismiss it out of hand, insisting that she either evidenced "spontaneous remission" or was misdiagnosed.[88] (Thirty years ago, many also said she would soon relapse, but since that never happened, this claim is no longer heard.) One of the strangest ironies of contemporary medicine is that doctors in other specialties are a lot more impressed by the powers of mind than psychiatrists are. Internists talk about the effects of "stress" and "lifestyle." Oncologists believe in a "will to survive." After their patients started flocking to acupuncturists and practitioners of "therapeutic touch," even surgeons admitted that methods they didn't understand sometimes worked. It's psychiatry, the field with the worst track record, that insists physical explanations are the only ones that count.

The reason all these debates about Frieda and her work occurred by proxy—with attention focused on people like Greenberg or Searles—was that Frieda existed as a real person only to those who had actually known her. To everybody else, she was Dr. Fried, the heroic therapist of *Rose Garden,* and however vivid she seemed in the book, she was still a character of fiction.

This was no accident. Once Greenberg's idealized portrait was out there, Frieda's students and colleagues didn't need to memorialize her. People who had contemplated (or begun) writing biographies abandoned their efforts, relieved at not having the onus of exposing her imperfections thrust upon them. Since the whole idea of psychotherapy with psychotic patients was increasingly under attack from biological psychiatrists, people who identified with Frieda's work felt that even hinting at any of her failings would simply be handing ammunition to her enemies.

But beyond these rational concerns lay deeper feelings. Everybody who knew Frieda—Erich, her friends, her students—was extraordinarily secretive about her, as if some inadvertent disclosure might be tantamount to destroying her. They said they wanted to protect her privacy, but there was more to it than this; somehow allowing even the tiniest cracks in her perfection to emerge made people feel as if they were betraying her.

A biographical subject participates in the relationship others have with her, and even those who are long dead projectively recreate whatever dynamics were most central in their psychology. Frieda spent her life cultivating opacity and remained unseen even to some of those who knew her best. We can explain this away as defensiveness, her way of protecting herself from the greater pain of being misunderstood. But she wasn't really as fragile as people fear, and we do her a disservice by refusing to allow her to be real.

Ironically, Joanne Greenberg was the person who best understood this. Having created the magical Dr. Fried, Joanne then spent years giving interviews describing her real relationship to Frieda and the details of the hard work they had done together. Just as she had written *Rose Garden* to preserve her own actual memories of illness, she actively sought to prevent mythologizing about Frieda. Joanne remembered a powerful moment near the end of the therapy when Frieda had her picture taken for some award. Incredulous when she saw the proofs, she had immediately telephoned the photographer. "What is this terrible blank face you have sent me?" He said: "Well, we retouched it as we do for all our patrons, taking out all those heavy lines that make people look so old." Frieda had commanded: "You put those lines right back in! I worked hard for every one of those lines, and I won't let you take away even one of them!"[89]

So years later, when Joanne was invited to give a talk at the White Institute (the New York training center Frieda and Erich had helped to found), she tried to describe the ways Frieda had encouraged modes of expression more positive than symptoms. "I had never examined this idea before—the thought that there might be forces inside a person independent of his illness which were working toward health . . . actually fighting the illness and contributing to creative growth," Joanne said. In a subsequent lecture, titled "Metaphor and the Treatment of Schizophrenia," she talked about how careful Frieda had been not to take psychotic behavior too literally:

> When I was sick, I was so terrified of saying the thing—whatever it was—that I used a series of hedges. Those hedges were metaphors, also dust-throwing devices, ropes from which I fondly hoped my damned therapist would hang her damned self. She was able, by means of those metaphors, to grab that rope and pull in until she got me at the other end. A me, who by that time, some years later, was willing to be more literal, or more direct.[90]

Joanne emphasized that however far they traveled in a session, Frieda always brought them back to the present, for example, making a point of recapping the main threads in the last few minutes. "We talked about such and such. You said this. I said that. And remember . . . (whatever the key point was in that hour). She'd ask: 'What happened?' She was very big on that." Most important, Joanne noted:

> She never fell for the metaphor when the metaphor was hallucinations. It's so easy to fall for that, to go with all those big symptoms, just like a beautiful bouquet. She didn't fall for any of that. Because way underneath there was the illness. That was her enemy. Not the hallucinations. She batted that stuff out of the way. She knew what was important, without, at the same time, denying me the use of my metaphors.

Joanne stressed that Frieda was far from perfect in the way she did these things. "We blundered around a lot. I remember a lot of mistakes that she made." She would just admit her errors and they'd go on.

> I would have the image all the time of blood coming out of faucets. She would say, "What does that mean?" She did not give me chemicals to keep blood from coming out of faucets. Another thing she didn't do was say it was wonderful and brilliant and creative that I had blood coming out of faucets. But she used it. And then declared that it was a metaphor. That it was being used for something else. That we were going to get to that. We were going for the hook, not the bait. And in doing that, she didn't have to descend to the literalism, to say this equals that.

The key to Frieda's approach, Joanne said, was flexibility. "She acted like a dancer acts, like a comedian acts, or a skier. You have to be nice and loose to ski, and you have to read the hill with your feet. That's what she did." Joanne talked about how helpful it had been for Frieda to tell dirty jokes in the middle of difficult therapy sessions. "There's something very healing about that. A form of play." But the key to all their work together was the sense of safety Frieda created. "The trouble with mental illness," Joanne emphasized, "is that it's drowning. You can't see above the water. You can't see what's past the pain. You have no height. What the patient needs is for you to be able to see over there, to see that there's a shoreline." Joanne thought it was crucial that Frieda never underestimated the intensity of the anguish, even as she held to a vision of the patient's humanity.

I once got into an argument with Karl Menninger in which he said,

"Well, it's all a matter of degree." And I said, "Yeah. If the difference in degree is the difference between a glass of water and the Atlantic ocean, it's a matter of degree. . . ." People like Laing wanted to blur the difference between sick and well because they look over that line and they see a human being on the other side. But that line is all sick people have to steer by. If you blot out the line, sick people have to draw it in again. Frieda knew that.

Greenberg understood that what has kept *Rose Garden* in print for more than thirty-five years is that it challenges our core assumptions about mental illness and allows us to believe in the potential for cure.[91] We are repelled by Deborah's craziness and want not to see it, yet her behavior makes enough sense that we can imagine her healed. Greenberg didn't know how to explain why her treatment worked any more than Frieda did, but she could *show* herself getting better, and thereby draw us in. By confronting us with the reality of recovery even from schizophrenia, the most frightening of all mental illnesses, Greenberg forces us to question our fundamental assumptions about madness and its treatment. And because she got better without drugs or shock or any of the other biological methods we have been taught to believe in, she highlights paradoxes that would otherwise remain hidden. Nothing about Deborah's story makes it seem as if she suffered from a brain disease; she was clearly saved by the Lodge's protection and Frieda's trust in her. *Rose Garden* raises the questions that make readers squirm: What if there are other Joanne Greenbergs out there? What if the person living in a cardboard box on the street was once like her, except that she had no Lodge to go to and no Frieda?

Joanne Greenberg never deteriorated as far as many schizophrenics do, but maybe that's because she got effective treatment before her illness reached the chronic stage. Since there's no way to know, she remains a thorn in psychiatry's side. *Rose Garden,* as Christopher Lehmann-Haupt mused, offers "a vision of a world that some people insist doesn't exist," and no matter what psychiatrists tell them, people want to believe in that world.[92]

Epilogue:
The Ambiguity of Hope

In the treatment of nervous cases, he is the best physician who is the most ingenious inspirer of hope.[1]

November 28, 1989. No seats were left. People were bunched by the doors of the auditorium, armed with notepads and lunches, scanning for a place to stand. Voices rose and fell amid the squeak of empty sandwich containers being crushed under chairs. Two women near the front laughed uproariously and pulled out appointment books to write something down. Several people called greetings across the aisles. An amiable, balding man picked his way to the front of the room, and suddenly there was no sound at all.

Alan Stone didn't usually draw a crowd. He was the only member of the Harvard faculty to have appointments in both law and medicine, but even in Cambridge, this wasn't celebrity. Neither his past presidency of the American Psychiatric Association nor his thesis on the psychology of football were widely known. The reason a hundred people left warm offices all over Boston on that November day wasn't Stone but his topic—"Is Psychoanalytic Psychiatry Malpractice?"—a question that appeared unseemly even to this group of doctors.

Stone wasn't there to talk about himself. He took his text from the life of Raphael Osheroff, an obscure nephrologist who had become psychiatry's newest symbol of controversy. Osheroff was not born to this role. He had grown up in Brooklyn, excelled in school—especially in music and art—and had many friends and an uneventful life. Until the age of forty, his balance sheet had resembled that of many Americans in the 1970s: two children, too much work, two divorces. It was after the birth of Osheroff's third child that the deterioration began. There must have been causes, but they were nebulous, as they are for most other people. Perhaps it was simply too many things happening at once. Osheroff's second wife had filed for custody of their children. The partners in his medical practice were pressuring him to sell the business. His third marriage was unraveling. Whatever the reasons for Osheroff's decline, its result was clear: a pervasive tension that made him unable to concentrate and threatened to consume his life. He began to drink, to take Valium, to pace incessantly. He saw a psychiatrist, who prescribed antidepressant medication. It had little effect; his anxiety grew to the point where he could barely work. He began having thoughts of suicide. Finally, on the advice of his therapist, Osheroff admitted himself to Chestnut Lodge.[2]

He arrived on January 2, 1979, a time of year when many psychiatric admissions occur. He spent the next six months pacing on a locked ward. Pacing isn't precisely the right word: what he did was propel himself up and down a narrow hall, relentlessly, for hundreds of hours, to the point where his feet ulcerated and turned black. Too agitated to eat, he lost forty pounds. He stopped shaving. He refused to bathe. By the time Osheroff had been at the Lodge for six months, it was no longer possible to think of him as a man with a $300,000-a-year medical practice and an elegant home in Alexandria. He looked more like a prisoner of war.

Osheroff felt demeaned by everything at the Lodge: his flapping shoes, his beltless pants, the once-an-hour cigarette doled out by a frightened student nurse. He knew these were standard suicide precautions, but he didn't care. He was a physician in a hospital; he couldn't understand why they were treating him like a mental patient. He told the staff his name was "Dr. Osheroff." They called him "Ray." Refusing to answer provoked more interpretation. The monotony maddened him; "group meetings" and psychotherapy sessions filled barely half the day. Osheroff could feel himself losing hold, and this terrified him more than anything else. The only way he could think to survive was to fight. Within a few months, he was fighting everything at Chestnut Lodge: having his telephone privileges restricted, being sent to group therapy, not being allowed to read his medical records. He knew he was outmatched, but fighting made him less frightened. Years later, in a bitter denunciation he wrote of the Lodge, Osheroff described that time as a "journey deeper and deeper into the depths of an inferno that Dante himself could never conceive of in his most tortured or creative moments." Calling the staff "captors" and the treatment "anti-therapy," he refused to cooperate with anyone. Osheroff was a voluntary patient and could have checked himself out whenever he chose. But he felt like a hostage and never even tried.

After seven months, having deteriorated to an alarming extent, Osheroff was persuaded by his mother and stepfather to transfer to Silver Hill, a private psychiatric hospital in New Canaan, Connecticut. He underwent a dramatic transformation there. Osheroff experienced Silver Hill as "elegant and beautiful," nothing like the "jail" he had just left. The staff called him "Doctor" and the patients looked like people he knew. He had a lovely room. Even the food was excellent. There was nothing to fight, no need to attack, and he began to feel more in control of himself. His physicians prescribed antidepressants, and this time they worked. After three months at Silver Hill, Osheroff had improved sufficiently to be discharged.

The life he returned to was in rubble. Having been a mental patient for almost a year, he had been declared legally incompetent. His hospital admitting privileges had been suspended. A colleague was usurping his medical practice. His children were forbidden to see him, and his third wife was gone. Compared to the life he had led a year earlier, these reverses were stunning, and there seemed to be nothing he could do about them.

Three years later, in 1982, Osheroff filed a malpractice suit against Chestnut Lodge. At the time, this was seen as a very odd thing to do. The Lodge was internationally known for its treatment of severe mental illness, and an argument that its care was substandard would have been hard to sustain. But Osheroff didn't make that claim. Nor did he charge ordinary malpractice—that a physician had failed to administer treatment for an identifiable illness, or had delivered that treatment in an incompetent way. Osheroff made a different argument: that it was the Lodge's *choice* of treatment—intensive psychotherapy—that had been at fault in his case. He claimed that had he been given drug treatment there as he had at Silver Hill, he never would have deteriorated as far as he did. Any hospital that insisted on using outmoded methods like psychoanalytic treatment, he charged, should be held negligent and required to pay damages.

A decade later, psychiatrists were packing an auditorium in Boston to hear Alan Stone explain what this would mean. Most of the audience was made up of psychoanalysts, and to say they were frightened would be an understatement. *Osheroff v. Chestnut Lodge* had just been settled out of court after years of wrangling. Osheroff had been given a cash settlement—no one knew its size—and both he and the Lodge had been enjoined from disclosing details of their agreement. This spawned endless debate, unconstrained by fact, about what had gone on behind the scenes. Alan Stone was trying to carve out a role as a neutral intermediary, which made him a target for everybody.

To this Boston audience filled with people he knew, Stone spoke without notes, pacing the room as if in court, warning darkly of "revenge by the biological psychiatrists."[3] Psychoanalysts had dominated American psychiatry for four decades, and although their fortunes were clearly on the wane, Stone was convinced that the only reason Osheroff had been able to put together a case against Chestnut Lodge was that three or four prominent, well-respected psychiatrists had defected to his side. Whether they had acted out of sympathy for Osheroff or to further their own ends was still being debated. Whatever their motivations, they had scored a huge win, thrusting the ambiguities of psychiatric treatment into unwelcome light.

Osheroff's most vocal supporter was Gerald Klerman, a psychiatrist at Cornell University Medical School and a longtime advocate of drug treatment, who had once headed the federal alcohol, drug abuse, and mental health administration. To Klerman, there was only one issue at stake: scientific evidence. "The psychiatrist," Klerman argued, "has a responsibility to use effective treatment" and the patient has a right to receive it.[4] Just because a minority of physicians still clung to a belief in psychotherapy did not warrant its use when other methods had stronger empirical support. For Klerman, the conclusion was clear: if a place like the Lodge "purports to be part of the medical world," it either "abides by the rules of evidence" or renounces its claim to be a hospital at all.[5] Stone retorted that Klerman's indictment was ideology, not science, since virtually all his claims "about psychotherapy apply with equal force to surgery and almost everything else that physicians do. . . . Much of what all physicians do has no demonstrated effectiveness."[6]

Central to Klerman's argument was the notion of a "standard of care," an agreed-on way to treat each illness that physicians in a given specialty are required to use. People who go to cardiologists with a symptom like chest pain, for example, are given a routine set of tests or medications; they aren't advised to take up croquet or eat more raisins. This is because cardiologists, like their colleagues in most areas of medicine, have reached consensus on how to treat the disorders they see every day. As a consequence, they are expected to adhere to these standards or risk being sued. Psychiatrists, in contrast, have never reached a consensus of this kind. Often they disagree even on fundamental aspects of a patient's case. Osheroff, for instance, was diagnosed at Chestnut Lodge as having a narcissistic personality disorder; at Silver Hill, he was treated for psychotic depression. The *Diagnostic and Statistical Manual of Mental Disorders* (DSM), published by the American Psychiatric Association, is supposed to prevent disagreements like this. But DSM is itself the subject of so much dispute that its categories are completely reconceived every ten years, and they are as much political compromises as they are descriptions of mental disease.[7]

Twenty minutes into his talk, Stone abruptly stopped pacing. He glared at a

woman in the front row who seemed to be writing down everything he was saying. "The trouble with Klerman," he resumed, pausing for effect, "is that he
wants to make DSM the Koran." A hundred analysts squirmed in their seats.
This was the last thing they wanted to hear. The mid-1970s revision of DSM
had all but erased forms of disturbance that could not be made to fit a biological model, and psychoanalysts were struggling for ground. If a patient's presenting problem couldn't be diagnosed in psychoanalytic terms, it was difficult
to claim analytic treatment was called for. As DSM categories came increasingly to resemble those of physical medicine, drug treatment edged closer to
becoming the standard of care, which meant that psychotherapy without medication, at least in severe cases, began to seem tantamount to malpractice.

Stone had to raise his voice to be heard above the whispering that spread
like goose flesh across the room. "Do you realize what this would mean?" he
asked, incredulous at his own words. "Every time something goes wrong in
therapy, or a patient gets worse or commits suicide or threatens someone,
you would be seen as negligent." People stopped whispering. There was a
moment of complete silence before Stone pushed on, relentless. "Think of
what this will do to the practice of psychotherapy. Think of what will happen
to hospitals. After a while, there won't even be places like Chestnut Lodge,
because the medical boards will refuse to approve institutions whose treatment lies outside the new standard of care."

At stake, Stone declared, was pluralism. "The Klermans of the world won't
recognize that there is a respectable minority in psychiatry who want to treat
patients differently from how they do. If you don't agree with them, you end up
being sued." Somewhere in the room a beeper went off, and a flustered resident
threw on his jacket and rushed to the door. Stone's voice turned wistful. "The
problem is, we no longer believe in Frieda Fromm-Reichmann. We don't believe in intensive psychotherapy for serious mental disturbance. We can't keep
selling *I Never Promised You a Rose Garden* to our patients."

The room had the stillness that follows impropriety, and Stone sensed he
had gone a step too far. Backtracking quickly, he declared "I myself believe
in Frieda Fromm-Reichmann," but it was clear that what he believed in was
her magic, not her method. He attributed her success with psychotics less to
a systematic approach than to an extraordinary gift for relating to very sick
people. "When the match between therapist and patient is right, with the
right chemistry, it's like falling in love," Stone mused. "She could do it with
those people. Most of us can't."

Osheroff's lawsuit was a reminder of psychiatry's despair. By embracing
only those disorders that defy understanding or can't be treated, psychiatrists
have allowed impotence to replace failure and made abdication their creed.[8]

They cover their hopelessness with a veil of verbiage about experimental treatments and breakthroughs in the limitless worlds of genetics and brain research. The blinding whiteness of the laboratory shields them from the fact that insanity isn't much better understood today than it was two hundred years ago, and most treatments eventually fail. Having colluded with legislators bent on saving money in emptying the state hospitals, sending most seriously ill patients off to nonexistent "community care," psychiatrists can't allow themselves to consider alternatives to biological models of mental illness that would open them to charges of moral negligence.[9]

The despair of Alan Stone's generation comes partly from disillusionment, which makes it worse. Stone and Klerman both entered psychiatry in the 1950s, when psychoanalysts ran the whole field—chairing the psychiatry departments of medical schools, designing the curricula, specifying the criteria for success. Stone and Klerman and their classmates were weaned on the pessimistic optimism that was Freud's greatest legacy: the belief that though true satisfaction may be beyond grasp, being insane does not, in principle, make one less likely to attain it. Trained to think of disturbed behavior not as disease but as defense, Stone's generation took for granted that somewhere under the layers of symptom and subterfuge was a terrorized person in desperate need of their help. It might take years of agonized struggle and extraordinary patience, but at least in theory, even the sickest person could be reached.

The problem for Stone and his colleagues came when they discovered they couldn't do what Frieda had done. They felt as though they had been duped, and their disillusionment was profound. Klerman was ambivalent about psychoanalysis to start with, and the more the field oversold itself, the angrier he got.[10] Most of his colleagues sealed over their despair by avoiding seriously disturbed patients; a schizophrenic shuffling into the room mumbling to himself felt too much like a kick in the face. The idea of doing psychotherapy with these people began to seem more and more cruel, and psychiatrists who once believed themselves capable of it felt their impotence turn to betrayal.

If there had been a context to talk about these feelings, they might not have become so destructive to the field. Instead, too many psychiatrists trained in the 1950s ended up hating very sick patients or abusing them. Some, overwhelmed with guilt at their own anger, turned to drugs or had "accidents." A few killed themselves.[11] Stone held on to his faith in psychotherapy by retreating into teaching and writing, the classic escapes from clinical work.[12] But he understood the bewilderment of colleagues who wondered how they could possibly have been suckered into treating people so clearly beyond hope.

There are some therapists who still treat seriously disturbed patients, but typically these are patients diagnosed as borderline rather than psychotic. To be sure, such people pose a real challenge, but doing psychotherapy with someone who can hold a job and live outside a hospital isn't the same as working with schizophrenics.[13]

When Alan Stone told a roomful of psychoanalysts in 1989 that they couldn't keep selling *I Never Promised You a Rose Garden* to their patients, he meant they should admit to no longer believing in it themselves. Novels have no place on the frontiers of pharmacology. If psychiatrists could convince themselves that psychosis is a neurological disease of unknown origins, they wouldn't even have to try to treat it. They could just make patients more comfortable until they succumb to their wounds.

In principle, this is a trade-off that could work. Many fields of medicine are largely palliative, and an aging population means there will soon be many more. The problem in psychiatry is that there have always been dissenters like Frieda, holding out for the possibility of real treatment. By refusing to subscribe to the pessimism that has long plagued the field, these rebels have robbed psychiatry of the limited consensus it might otherwise have had. As both sides parade their disagreements across the public stage, psychiatrists increasingly come to resemble politicians more than scientists.[14] But so long as incontrovertible evidence remains beyond their grasp, consensus can be achieved only by rhetorical means. Klerman's attempt to make Chestnut Lodge look like the last vestige of an "unscientific" psychiatry was just one of many efforts to portray biological methods as the new standard. This might have worked, had people like Stone not kept insisting on another side. Warfare in psychiatry, endemic for a hundred years, is finally dying out only because insurance companies have starved both sides into submission by refusing to pay for treatment of any kind.

Perhaps the only thing that can be confidently said about treating psychosis is that there has to be a fit between the patient's metaphor for the illness and the method used. For Frieda and Joanne, the treatment was a quest, a search for the answer to a tangled problem that could be revealed only by collaborative work. For Mary Barnes, who regressed almost to the point of infancy because she was convinced she had to "go down and come back up again," living in Kingsley Hall, a Laingian therapeutic community, was the only way to get better. As Greenberg once remarked, "Her metaphor was not mine. But it worked for her. For other people, the metaphor is that it's chemical, and therefore you're absolved. . . . You don't have to have any part in the process. . . . Some people say, 'I don't want to weave my own rope, I want it done for me. I want doctors to do it for me the way they did my appendix and my hernia.' "

For Carol North, kidney dialysis "removed some unidentified substance from the blood, presumably a chemical responsible for producing schizophrenic symptoms." North and her physician had a very specific image of what this toxic substance was and used a filter with tiny pores "because the molecules that are thought to cause schizophrenia are much smaller than those in kidney failure." Psychologist Norman Endler, whose psychotic depression felt unconnected to any life event, insisted that ECT was the only effective method. For Marie Cardinal, whose uncontrollable menstrual bleeding and hallucinations reflected a desperate struggle for "the words to say it," classical psychoanalysis was what worked. Paula Perlstein repeatedly sought psychosurgery because "cutting the medial tracts between the portions of the frontal lobe and the thalamus" was the "miracle" that relieved her suffering.[15]

It may well be, as has long been suggested, that there are many different kinds of schizophrenia or manic depression, each with a different cause, and differences in patient response reflect this variability. But since no one has ever come up with a reliable way of telling which patient is likely to respond to which treatment, such a claim has no practical import. Thousands of research studies and decades of work can still be summarized in one phrase: no treatment works for everybody, and every treatment works for some.

What Alan Stone's generation hasn't been able to do is hold on to their faith in themselves. In one of his more profound passages, Erich Fromm wrote:

> To have faith means to dare, to think the unthinkable, yet to act within the limits of the realistically possible; it is the paradoxical hope to expect the Messiah every day, yet not to lose heart when he has not come at the appointed hour. This hope is not passive and it is not patient; on the contrary, it is impatient and active, looking for every possibility of action within the realm of real possibilities.[16]

Physicians who work in neonatal intensive care units struggling to keep alive infants weighing less than two pounds at birth have this kind of faith; psychiatrists don't.[17]

Back in Boston, Stone finished his talk, and the room seemed to sigh. There was a moment of hesitation, close to longing, when something might still have been said. Then people began scurrying out, unable to resist the pull of paperwork and intake reports on their desks. A woman walked toward the front, as if she might ask a question, and stared intently at Stone. He didn't see her. She turned away. "He must be right about Frieda Fromm-Reichmann," she muttered, walking automatically toward the door. "He has to be right. Why wouldn't he be? But why, three decades after her death, does he feel he has to bury her all over again?"

Notes

Interviews with the following individuals are cited in the notes using the subject's last name. Interviews labeled "SHC" were conducted by Sylvia Hoff Collins, a previous biographer. Tape recordings and verbatim transcriptions of all interviews (except those of Kurt Eissler and Jane Weinberg, for which only detailed notes exist), currently in the possession of the author, will be deposited in the Library of Congress and, like all other Fromm-Reichmann materials there, sealed until 2021.

Marvin Adland, January 29, 1990 (Chevy Chase, MD); October 22, 1995 (by telephone)

Donald Bloch, January 22, 1993 (New York, NY)

Bryce Boyer, September 18, 1990 (Berkeley, CA)

Anne Bullard, March 20, 1992 (Rockville, MD); January 24, 1979 (SHC); March 26, 1986 (conducted by Ann-Louise S. Silver); June 23, 1988 (conducted by John Fort and Mabel Peterson)

Donald Burnham, January 19, 1988 (Bethesda, MD)

Robert Cohen, May 9, 1988 (Rockville, MD)

Martin Cooperman, June 25, 1992 (Stockbridge, MA)

Hope Hale Davis, March 15, 1990 (Cambridge, MA)

Jarl Dyrud, January 6, 1992 (Chicago, IL)

Marianne Horney Eckardt, July 3, 1990 (New York, NY)

Kurt Eissler, January 8, 1989 (New York, NY)

John Fort, May 9, 1988 (Rockville, MD)

Johanna Garfield, October 4, 1993 (New York, NY)

Joanne Greenberg, June 25, 1991 (Golden, CO); January 31, 1993 (by telephone); June 1985 (conducted by Laurice McAfee)

Donna Grimmer, November 14, 1990 (Rockville, MD)

Marjorie Jarvis Kehne, June 5, 1995 (Bethesda, MD)

Gerald Klerman, February 23, 1992 (New York, NY)

Christopher Lehmann-Haupt, October 1, 1995 (Riverdale, NY)

Ruth and Theodore Lidz, March 3, 1990 (Woodbridge, CT)

Beatrice Liebenberg, January 30, 1990 (Washington, DC)
Thomas McGlashan, October 5, 1989 (Rockville, MD)
Douglas Noble, February 17, 1979 (SHC)
Katherine Olinick, June 8, 1995 (Kensington, MD)
Margaret Rioch, January 17, 1988 (Chevy Chase, MD)
I. Rosenfeld, December 2, 1978 (SHC)
Clarence and Connie Schulz, May 9, 1990 (Towson, MD)
Mara Bowman Schwartz, July 2, 1990 (New York, NY)
Morris Schwartz, February 27, 1990 (Newton, MA)
Harold Searles, January 24, 1989 (Bethesda, MD)
Rose Spiegel, January 8, 1991 (New York, NY)
Alan Stone, June 5, 1992 (Cambridge, MA)
Alberta Szalita, December 5, 1989 (New York, NY)
Margaret Ursell, December 23, 1992 (Washington, DC)
Wolfgang Weigert, June 10, 1991 (Washington, DC)
Jane Weinberg, January 4, 1992 (Chicago, IL)
Stanley Wilcox, December 22, 1992 (Rockville, MD)
Otto Will, September 19, 1990 (Richmond, CA); December 28, 1978 (SHC)

Complete references for all published articles or books cited in the Notes can be
found in the Bibliography. Sources for unpublished or privately published materials,
lectures, and brief book reviews are listed in full in the Notes.

Source Abbreviations

AJF   Letters to author from Alisa Jacobson Fuchs, daughter of Fromm-Reich-
         mann's sister, Anna Jacobson, the only surviving close relative
APA   Archives of the American Psychiatric Association, Washington, D.C.
AT   Autobiographical tapes, recorded by Fromm-Reichmann in Palo Alto in
         1955–1956, transcribed by unknown friends (three tapes, twenty-five-page
         single-spaced typed transcript), CLA
CLA   Chestnut Lodge Archive, Rockville, Maryland
JG   Joanne Greenberg Collection, Department of Special Collections, Boston
         University, Boston
NT   Tape recordings of sessions with patient Miss N., CLA
OHC   Oral History Collection, Butler Library, Columbia University, New York
P   *Principles of Intensive Psychotherapy*
RT   Tape recordings or verbatim transcripts of sessions with patient Mr. R., CLA
Silver   Ann-Louise S. Silver (Ed.), *Psychoanalysis and Psychosis*
SP   *Psychoanalysis and Psychotherapy: Selected Papers of Frieda Fromm-
         Reichmann*
UCP   Records of the University of Chicago Press, Department of Special Collec-
         tions, Regenstein Library, University of Chicago, Chicago

PROLOGUE

1. Buber, *The Legend of the Baal-Shem,* pp. 33, 35.
2. "Greenberg" is her current, married name, not the name she had as a patient. But it is the name under which she is known for *Rose Garden,* so I have used Greenberg, rather than her maiden name, for consistency and privacy.
3. On characteristics of the mental patient population in the 1940s, see Gorman; and Grob, *From Asylum to Community.*
4. This is Greenberg's own phrase, in *I Never Promised You a Rose Garden,* p. 110.
5. Green, "In Praise of My Doctor—Frieda Fromm-Reichmann," p. 76; Rioch interview.
6. Dan, pp. 94–103.
7. The physicians responsible for treating mental illness have been variously known as "alienists," "nerve specialists," "neuropsychiatrists," and "neurologists"; the label "psychiatrist" came into usage only in the twentieth century. For reasons of simplification and clarity, and because "psychiatrist" was Frieda's own preferred term, I have used it throughout this book, even when referring to eighteenth- and nineteenth-century practitioners.
8. Tuke's work was carried on by his son Henry and grandson Samuel, making the family the prototype for the many psychiatric "dynasties." Pinel's focus on psychological causality was the first fundamental challenge within medicine to standard views of insanity as an incurable brain disease. Bleuler trained many of the men (C. G. Jung, Karl Abraham, Ludwig Binswanger, A. A. Brill, Ernest Jones) who went on to make major contributions to understanding the psychology of severe mental illness, and his *Textbook of Psychiatry* introduced generations of medical students to a dynamic alternative to Kraepelin's pessimism. Simmel had run a hospital for psychiatric casualties during World War I, and his commitment to broadening the scope of psychoanalysis to include institutionalized patients had a decisive influence on the development of the Berlin Psychoanalytic Institute.
9. David Gates, "Wizard of Menlo Park," *Newsweek,* March 20, 1995, p. 64 (review of Neil Baldwin, *Edison: Inventing the Century,* New York: Hyperion, 1995).
10. Buber, *Tales of the Hasidim,* p. 286.
11. Morris Schwartz interview. Schwartz was so enamored of revelation that he ended his life as the best-known dying man in America. His collected wisdom, published as *Letting Go: Morrie's Reflections on Living While Dying,* later became the basis for Mitch Albom's best-selling book, *Tuesdays with Morrie.*
12. Sven Randén and Hanna Sitter Randén, "Thoughts After the Chestnut Lodge Symposium," *ISPS Newsletter,* 1995, p. 2.
13. Despite its appeal as psychiatry's most mythic moment, Pinel did not actually strike the chains from the insane. For revised accounts of his work, see Goldstein, *Console and Classify* (pp. 72–119), and Weiner.
14. I wrote an entire article defending this decision and probing the ethical responsibilities of biographers and their subjects, especially when both are women. (See Hornstein, "The Ethics of Ambiguity.").
15. See Young-Bruehl, *Anna Freud;* Quinn; Grosskurth; and Bair.
16. See Spence.
17. Gergen, p. 128.

CHAPTER I. THE DAUGHTER

1. Norris, p. 159.
2. Bigelow, p. 107.
3. Dr. L. Schmieder, *Guide-Book to Heidelberg, Its Castle & Environs* (16th rev. ed.), printed by Dr. Johannes Hörning in Heidelberg, n.d. (ca. 1955), pp. 56–57.
4. See Schwab and Breuer for detailed histories of Orthodox Jews in Karlsruhe and other German cities.
5. Heinrich Feuchtwanger, "History," in *The Feuchtwanger Family* (Martin Feuchtwanger, Ed.), Tel Aviv: Edition Olympia, 1952, pp. 113–117. The novelist Lion Feuchtwanger and the many other distinguished members of this family were all direct relatives of Frieda.
6. All details of Adolf's childhood and Simon family history from AJF, September 20, November 23, 1992, August 30, 1993.
7. Hoff, "Frieda Fromm-Reichmann, the Early Years," pp. 115–121. For other brief descriptions of Frieda's early life, see Stevens and Gardner, pp. 205–208; Powell and Hoff, pp. 252–254; and Hoff, "Frieda Fromm-Reichmann," pp. 219–220.
8. Address books, Stadtarchiv Karlsruhe. I am deeply indebted to Martin Niemöller for locating this information, and to Ernst Otto Bräunche, director of the Stadtarchiv Karlsruhe, for making photographs of Reichmann & Thalmann available to me. The metal trade was one in which Orthodox Jews had long been particularly active (see Breuer, pp. 224–225). "Fresh air" from Young-Bruehl, *Hannah Arendt*, p. 13.
9. Hoff, "The Early Years," p. 116; Breuer, p. 36.
10. Hoff, "The Early Years," p. 116; AT, p. 6; AJF, November 23, 1992.
11. AJF, August 9, 1992.
12. AT, p. 4; Hoff, "The Early Years," p. 117. Since only the wealthiest Jewish families hired wet nurses, Klara clearly expected to live an upper-middle-class existence despite Adolf's financial limitations. (It is also possible that she was unable to nurse Grete herself and, in view of the distrust of bottle feeding prevalent at the time, had no alternative.)
13. AJF, August 9, 1991; September 20, 1992.
14. Jacoby, pp. 15, 57, 65.
15. Sylvia Hoff, an early biographer of Frieda, claims that Klara had a miscarriage in the years between Grete's and Anna's births: "Apparently it was a male fetus. It is remarkable for a Jewish family of that time that this event, the loss of their only male offspring, was always treated very lightly. In later years, Klara would laugh and say, 'It didn't want to be born because it was supposed to be called Moritz.' This was the name of Adolf's father, who had died in 1869" (Hoff, "The Early Years," p. 117). Hoff gives no source for this information, and it is impossible to assess its accuracy.
16. AT, p. 3; AJF, August 9, 1992.
17. AT, pp. 3–4; Hoff, "Frieda Fromm-Reichmann, M.D.," p. 76.
18. AJF, August 9, 1992; Weigert, "In Memoriam," p. 91.
19. Hoff, "The Early Years," p. 117.
20. AJF, November 23, 1992; speech by Grete Reichmann at family reunion, April 30, 1962, p. 1 of typed transcript. Scholem (p. 42) calls the Marxes "one of the most aristocratic Orthodox Jewish families in Germany."

21. See Jacoby for a detailed discussion of Marx's influence and responsibilities.
22. AJF, January 31, 1996.
23. I owe this entire description to Marion Kaplan's meticulous research. For a fuller portrait of the period, see her invaluable *The Making of the Jewish Middle Class.*
24. Hoff, "The Early Years," pp. 116–117; AJF, November 23, 1992.
25. AJF, April 21, 1993.
26. Kaplan, *The Making of the Jewish Middle Class,* pp. 8–9; Gay, pp. 182–188.
27. Hoff, "The Early Years," pp. 118–119; AJF, September 20, November 23, 1992. Jacoby (pp. 52–54) lists several notable instances of anti-Semitism in Königsberg, but these were relatively few and far between. See Schwab and Breuer on the insularity of the Orthodox community in Germany during this period.
28. Kaplan, "Priestess and Hausfrau."
29. In the Introduction to her book, Richarz provides a detailed overview of these events. For other useful histories of the German middle class and the Jewish community during this period, see Gay; Breuer; Kaplan; and Katz.
30. AT, p. 25.
31. Ibid., pp. 4–5.
32. Ibid., p. 4.

CHAPTER 2. THE STUDENT

1. Stanislavski.
2. Hoff, "The Early Years," p. 120. This "school" probably had no formal status, although when Frieda constructed her curriculum vita years later in America, she listed the years 1904–1907 under the heading *"Private Realgymnasialkurse des Vereins Frauenbildung, Frauenstudium,* Königsberg" (personnel file, CLA).
3. AT, p. 2; AJF, December 24, 1996.
4. AT, p. 6. Medical school entrance examinations were ordinarily given only in May, at the end of the *Gymnasium* term. The official in charge refused a request that Frieda be given the test a semester earlier, chiding her: "You are too young. Your father is a banker. Why can't he take care of you?" (Ibid., p. 22).
5. Ibid. It was unusual that Frieda learned to cook at all. Middle-class Germans always had live-in maids, and most had no idea what to do in a kitchen.
6. Even without the costs of room and board, Frieda's education was an expensive proposition. The curriculum in medicine required eleven semesters of study, and fees were higher than in any other field of study. Prussia was far more conservative in its policies toward educating women than other parts of Germany. Had Frieda still been in Karlsruhe in her adolescence, she could have attended the Girls' *Gymnasium,* taken the *Abitur,* and entered medical school as soon as she was ready. But she would still have faced considerable hostility from her male colleagues. As historian James C. Albisetti notes (p. 100): "It took a decade of uninterrupted agitation by German feminists to open the medical profession to women."
7. AT, p. 2.
8. Ibid., pp. 4, 22, 25.
9. Ibid., p. 5; Hoff, "Frieda Fromm-Reichmann, M.D.", p. 75.
10. Sassenberg, pp. 347–349.
11. AT, pp. 22–23.
12. Ibid., p. 23. Frieda's experiences in medical school were similar to those of other

pioneering Jewish women students, who routinely experienced far greater discrimination because of their gender than their religion. See Freidenreich's key papers on this topic.

13. AT, pp. 2–3, 24.
14. Ibid., pp. 23–24.
15. Like most other German medical students, Frieda interned in two different places, spending May–December 1913 at the University of Königsberg Psychiatric Hospital and January–June 1914 at the Municipal Hospital in the Berlin district of Moäbit.
16. Young-Bruehl, *Hannah Arendt,* pp. 17–20; AT, pp. 17, 25.
17. For a powerful account of this form of warfare and its attendant casualties, written from the perspective of the kinds of soldiers Frieda was soon treating, see Ernst Jünger's classic, *The Storm of Steel.*
18. In a somewhat overexuberant interpretation of Frieda's taped recollections of this period, Ann Silver has referred to her as "a major in the Prussian army," but there is no evidence of such an appointment.
19. AT, pp. 18–19.
20. Ibid., p. 20.
21. AJF, March 25, 1993; Young-Bruehl, *Hannah Arendt,* p. 21; Remarque, p. 62.
22. AT, p. 21; Kollwitz diary, p. 74.
23. For a complete list of these papers and a summary of their content, see Dyrud, "The Early Frieda."
24. Among Goldstein's primary teachers were Schaper and Edinger in neuroanatomy and Wernicke in psychiatry. See Dyrud, "The Early Frieda" for a summary of the M.D. thesis.
25. Goldstein, *Aftereffects of Brain Injuries in War,* p. 76 (emphasis in original).
26. Ibid., p. 69.
27. This attitude is epitomized today by the work of the neurologist Oliver Sacks, whose wide readership testifies to the popular appeal of such ideas. However, within neurology, such views have been highly controversial. For contrasting analyses of the history of the field, see Star; Blustein, *Preserve Your Love for Science;* and Harrington.
28. Riese, p. 25.
29. Goldstein, *The Organism,* p. 18 (emphasis in original).
30. Ibid., pp. 47, 244.
31. Ibid., p. 3; Goldstein, autobiography, p. 153; Riese, p. 28.
32. Riese, p. 25; Ursula Engel, "Frieda Fromm-Reichmann and the Heidelberg 'Thorapeutikum,'" p. 5 of typed draft. Goldstein's pioneering efforts were rewarded when he was named director of the Neurological Hospital and professor of neurology at the University of Berlin, the most prestigious post in German neurology. However, after less than three years in this position, Goldstein, like many other Jewish physicians, was jailed when Hitler assumed power and was released only after he promised to leave the country. He wrote *The Organism* during a year spent in a boardinghouse in Amsterdam waiting for an affidavit to enter the United States. He arrived in New York in 1935 and spent the next thirty years in a series of clinical and research positions created especially for him, extending his studies to schizophrenia and continuing a brilliant career in neurology and psychiatry until his death in 1965.
33. Petratos, "Development," p. 262; Dyrud, "The Early Frieda," p. 486.

34. Dan, pp. 98, 100.
35. AT, p. 7.
36. Among the people Schultz worked with at Weisser Hirsch was Hans Prinzhorn, later famous for his unique collection of artworks by mental patients. (See Brand-Claussen for a description of the collection.) Frieda was powerfully affected by Prinzhorn's work, which she got to know a great deal about later in the 1920s, when they were both in Heidelberg.
37. AT, p. 7. Schultz wasn't a deep believer in Nazi doctrine. Historian Geoffrey Cocks calls him "a clever opportunist whose patriotism and ambition for his profession made it natural for him to give lip-service to the regime" (p. 75). Schultz was politically astute enough to be appointed deputy director of the German Institute for Psychological Research and Psychotherapy, directed by Matthias Heinrich Göring (cousin of Hermann Göring, founder of the Gestapo and creator of the concentration camps). After psychoanalysis ("the Jewish science") was outlawed, the Göring Institute was the only place in Germany where psychotherapy was still permitted. (For a fuller account of the Institute and Schultz's career, see Cocks.) As Freud had commented in a letter to Ferenczi: "Abraham knows Schultz; he is very intelligent but devoid of all moral qualities" (Falzeder and Brabant, p. 262).
38. AT, p. 8; see also Shorter, "Private Clinics in Central Europe." As Shorter notes (p. 187), the regimen at Weisser Hirsch was something of a sham; patients on Lahmann's strict vegetarian diet would often "duck out to have a schnitzel at a nearby restaurant."
39. Lüthe and Schultz, pp. 1, 4–5, 177.
40. See Petratos, "Development," pp. 92–98, and "The European Teachers of Dr. Frieda Fromm-Reichmann."
41. AT, pp. 12, 22.
42. For contrasting perspectives on the history of psychoanalytic training, see Bergmann and Hartman; and Meisels and Shapiro.
43. As Sándor Radó was later to note: "The clinical spirit which Abraham established remained [even after his death]. And [his] was the Society which remained closest to medicine" (Bluma Swerdloff interview with Radó, April 6, 1963, OHC, p. 188 of typed transcript). For fuller discussions of Abraham and the Berlin Institute, see Alexander, Eisenstein and Grotjahn; Abraham and Freud; and Strachey and Strachey; for national comparisons, see Kurzweil.
44. Quinn, p. 269.
45. Most other candidates worked in hospitals as residents, so weren't yet able to treat patients independently. When they finished their shifts, they read or got together with fellow students before classes at the institute. Working full time at Weisser Hirsch and then running her own sanitarium in Heidelberg (where she treated every patient and was responsible for every detail of administration and financing) didn't leave Frieda much time to spend in cafés debating psychoanalytic theory. For a colorful account of the parties, masked balls, and other favored amusements of Berlin's psychoanalytic community during the 1920s, see Alix Strachey's letters in *Bloomsbury/Freud*.
46. Alexander, Eisenstein, and Grotjahn, p. 188; Edward Glover, oral history interview, August 1965, p. 11 of typed transcript (OHC).
47. Robert A. Cohen, introductory comments to "Frieda Fromm-Reichmann: A Seminar in the History of Psychiatry," American Academy of Psychoanalysis,

San Francisco, May 1980, on the tape recording but not the published version of his talk.

48. In 1926, the same year she became a member of the German Psychoanalytic Society, Frieda helped to found the group that would become, three years later, the Frankfurt Psychoanalytic Institute (formally named the Psychoanalytic Institute of Southwest Germany because it included colleagues from the whole region). The fourth analytic institute to be founded in Europe (after Berlin, Vienna, and London), the Frankfurt Institute was short-lived. In March 1933, its books were burned in public, a swastika was flown from its balcony, and its members fled. See Plänkers and Rothe for a detailed history.

49. Grossman and Grossman, p. 36.

50. Ibid., pp. 14, 46–47.

51. Ibid., p. 63; Groddeck, "Correspondence with Sigmund Freud," in *The Meaning of Illness,* p. 33.

52. Ibid., p. 93. See Groddeck, *The Book of the It,* for a fuller presentation of his view.

53. Groddeck, *The Meaning of Illness,* p. 210.

54. "Correspondence with Sigmund Freud," in ibid., p. 85.

55. M. Collins, Introduction to his English translation of Groddeck's *The World of Man,* p. 6.

56. Grossman and Grossman, p. 167.

57. Ibid., p. 197; FFR to GG, January 21, August 23, 1933. I am deeply indebted to Ursula Engel for making these and all other cited letters from Frieda to Groddeck available to me.

58. Collins, "Introduction," p. 28; Grossman and Grossman, p. 206.

59. "Correspondence with Sigmund Freud," in *The Meaning of Illness,* p. 64.

60. Gay, p. 238.

CHAPTER 3. THE PSYCHIATRIST

1. Ned Rorem, preconcert talk, First Congregational Church, Wellfleet, MA, August 11, 1995.

2. "Contribution to the Psychopathology of Bronchial Asthma" (1922), pp. 165, 168.

3. "The Body as a Means of Psychological Expression" (1936), p. 2 of typed transcript. In this paper and others like it, Frieda always cited texts like Cannon's *The Wisdom of the Body* and Dunbar's *Emotions and Bodily Changes* (classics in psychology and psychiatry, whose findings were uncontroversial), a rhetorical strategy that made her most radical ideas seem commonsensical.

4. Ironically, as psychiatrists become more and more committed to a solely biological view of mental illness, physicians in other specialties are increasingly impressed by the powers of mind. The popularity of Bill Moyers's book and television series, *Healing and the Mind*—and the dozens of other works relating "stress" to cancer, immune system breakdown, and heart disease—highlight this striking reversal in perspective. In "Body and Mind in Nineteenth-Century Medicine," historian Charles Rosenberg offers a useful framework within which to conceive these trends.

5. "The Body as a Means of Psychological Expression" (1936), pp. 13–14.
6. "Psychosomatic Reactions During Analysis" (1937), pp. 4–6 of typed transcript. This and other papers cited in this chapter, while delivered in English after Frieda arrived in America, are replete with examples from her work in Germany and clearly report on ideas she had arrived at years earlier.
7. Undated notes for a course on dream interpretation, pp. 3a, 7, 11 of typed draft (CLA). The pioneering American analyst Clarence Oberndorf shared Frieda's view that work with psychotic patients could be invaluable in psychoanalytic training. Reflecting on a lifetime of work in the field, Oberndorf wrote: "The study of the psychotic is probably the best means of convincing the novitiate in psychiatry of the truth of psychoanalytic mechanisms. In working with deteriorated psychotic patients the postulates of Freud become so obvious and undeniable that one who (like myself in 1909) still doubts the diagnostic as well as therapeutic value of psychoanalysis will be forced to admit the validity of psychoanalysis" (p. 87).
8. "Changes in Psychoanalytic Concepts During the Last Ten Years" (1943), pp. 2–3 of typed draft.
9. "Contribution to the Psychopathology of Bronchial Asthma" (1922), pp. 170–171.
10. "Psychopathology of Schizophrenia" (1942), p. 6 of typed transcript.
11. Haynal, "Freud and his Intellectual Environment," p. 35. See Dupont's invaluable edition of Ferenczi's *Clinical Diary* for a vivid sense of his therapeutic style.
12. Thompson, "Sándor Ferenczi, 1873–1933," p. 183.
13. Ferenczi to Freud, August 19, 1927. I am grateful to Ann Silver for bringing this passage from the as yet unpublished third volume of the Freud-Ferenczi correspondence to my attention.
14. Thompson, "Sándor Ferenczi," pp. 186, 190; Aron and Harris; Wolstein, "Ferenczi, Freud, and the Origins of American Interpersonal Relations."
15. Undated notes for a lecture on technique (ca. 1930s), p. 1 of typed draft (CLA).
16. "Four Basic Analytic and Dynamic Principles," ca. 1950s. As her authority, Frieda always cited this statement of Freud (from his 1914 paper "On the History of the Psychoanalytic Movement"): "It may thus be said that the theory of psychoanalysis is an attempt to account for two observed facts that strike one conspicuously and unexpectedly whenever an attempt is made to trace the symptoms of a neurotic back to their sources in his past life: the facts of transference and of resistance. Any line of investigation, no matter what its direction, which recognizes these two facts and takes them as the starting-point of its work may call itself psychoanalysis, though it arrives at results other than my own."
17. Undated notes for a lecture on technique, pp. 2–3 of typed draft. Frieda held strongly to the classical psychoanalytic view that the *contents* of the unconscious were equally frightening regardless of the patient's degree of disturbance; what distinguished psychotics from neurotics was that these contents were closer to consciousness. For a summary of Jung's view on this issue, see his *Memories, Dreams, Reflections.*
18. Undated notes for a lecture on technique, pp. 6, 11 of typed draft.
19. Green, p. 75.
20. Undated notes for a lecture on technique, p. 7.
21. "Transference" (1953), pp. 8–10.

22. Ibid., p. 6.
23. "Changes in Transference Concepts" (1945); notes for "Discussion—Transference," March 8, 1947, location and audience unknown (CLA).
24. By the 1920s, Freud's practice consisted almost entirely of analysts in training. As he wrote to Karl Abraham in 1924: "I hardly take patients now but only pupils" (Haynal, *Controversies in Psychoanalytic Method*, p. 9).
25. "Transference Problems in Schizophrenics" (1939), p. 123 of reprint in SP.
26. Ibid., p. 119; P, p. 19.
27. SP, p. 125.
28. "Psychotherapy of Schizophrenia" (1954), p. 200 of reprint in SP.
29. Ibid., p. 202.
30. "Psychopathology of Schizophrenia" (1942), paper presented in St. Louis (audience and occasion unknown), January 16, 1942, p. 4 of typed draft (CLA).
31. Ibid., p. 4. See also Burnham, Gladstone, and Gibson.
32. "Psychopathology of Schizophrenia" (1942), p. 5.
33. "Psychotherapy of Schizophrenia" (1954), p. 207.

CHAPTER 4. THE WOMAN AND THE JEW

1. Buber, "Judaism and the Jews," p. 21.
2. Both Kaplan, *The Making of the Jewish Middle Class*, and Breuer report that only 10 to 20 percent of German Jews were still Orthodox at the beginning of the twentieth century. An even smaller fraction of these became professionals.
3. AT, pp. 8–9.
4. Eventually the child returned to live with her mother. When she grew up, Frieda's "adopted daughter" married a psychoanalyst.
5. AT, p. 10.
6. According to Cocks, 1924 was also the year Schultz moved to Berlin, which may have been an added inducement for Frieda to leave at that particular time.
7. Young-Bruehl, *Hannah Arendt*, p. 66. However tolerant Heidelberg's spirit, it was also the home of Josef Goebbels and Albert Speer during this period, before they went on to become leaders of the Nazi movement. Frieda could probably see the Speer family's ornate house built into the side of the mountain above Heidelberg's castle from her upper windows.
8. Engel, "Frieda Fromm-Reichmann and the Heidelberg 'Thorapeutikum,'" p. 6 of typed draft. I am extremely grateful to Harald Hahn, the current owner of the house, for documentation of its history and a wonderful glimpse of its ambience and beauty.
9. In July 1923, at the beginning of the period of uncontrolled inflation, one dollar was worth 353,412 marks; two months later, it fell to 98 million marks; by November, the same dollar was worth 4.2 trillion marks (Brenner, p. 200). As Zweig (p. 312) remarked: "A pair of shoe laces cost more than a shoe had once cost, no, more than a fashionable store with two thousand pair of shoes had cost before; to repair a broken window more than the whole house had formerly cost, a book more than the printer's works with a hundred presses."
10. AT, p. 11.
11. See Kaplan, *The Making of the Jewish Middle Class*, on Jewish dowry practices.
12. AT, p. 12.

13. Ibid., p. 5.
14. Ibid., pp. 5–6.
15. Ibid., p. 6; "Contribution to the Psychogenesis of Migraine," pp. 283–289 of the reprint in SP. Frieda went on to note: "Migraine patients want to destroy . . . the brain and head, as the concrete representative of mental capacity. This mental castration of another person is not allowed and therefore, according to the analytically well-known unconscious mechanism, is turned back toward the patient himself; he does to himself by these means what he wanted to do to [the other], thus punishing himself for his forbidden tendencies" (p. 288).
16. AT, p. 1.
17. Ann Silver made this interpretation in "Frieda Fromm-Reichmann: Her Life Before Coming to the Lodge," paper presented to the Historical Committee of the Washington Psychoanalytic Institute, November 17, 1992.
18. Kaplan, *The Making of the Jewish Middle Class*, p. 116.
19. Erich's great-grandfather was the Würzburger Rav, Seligmann Bär Bamberger, one of the leading figures of nineteenth-century German Jewish orthodoxy (see Funk); "most famous of Jewish communities" from Scholem, p. 44; "unbearable, neurotic child" from Burston, p. 8.
20. Before coming to Frankfurt, Nobel had been the rabbi of the Orthodox synagogue Adass Jisroel in Königsberg, where the Reichmann family worshipped. Frieda was only eleven at the time and may not have recalled this fact when she met Nobel later with Erich in Frankfurt; however, her father and Uncle George were leading members of the congregation and likely knew Nobel well. Even as a child, Frieda may have been influenced by Nobel's famously spellbinding sermons. See Jacoby, p. 23.
21. For competing accounts of Fromm's background, see Burston, Funk, and Knapp. The definitive history of the Frankfurt Institute is Martin Jay's *The Dialectical Imagination*. On Fromm's specific role, see Burston, *The Legacy of Erich Fromm*, and McLaughlin, "Origin Myths in the Social Sciences."
22. Rosenfeld interview; Hoff, "The Early Years," p. 119; Knapp. The Reichmanns' attitude was typical of the Orthodox community. As historian Mordechai Breuer notes: "Excessive zeal in religious practice was frowned upon. If a worshipper in the synagogue rocked the upper part of his body fervently but all too vigorously back and forth, his neighbor might turn to him to say: 'Force, you know, won't get you up there'" (p. 12).
23. Paris, pp. 144–145.
24. I found it extraordinary that every person I interviewed knew this fact but claimed never to have discussed it.
25. AT, p. 16. While Frieda's marriage at thirty-six was very late by any measure, it was not that unusual for a woman physician. In Freidenreich's sample of 448 Jewish women receiving university educations in Germany during this period, 35 percent married after age thirty. See Freidenreich, "Emancipation Through Higher Education," paper presented to the Leo Baeck Institute, New York, February 26, 1992, p. 18.
26. A small sampling of analysts known to have married or had affairs with their patients would include Ferenczi, Jung, Groddeck, Horney, Stekel, Simmel, and Frink. There were doubtless many others.
27. Erich was even more prone to blur boundaries. Toward the end of the long affair he had with Karen Horney (which began during his marriage to Frieda), Erich

analyzed Horney's daughter, Marianne Horney Eckardt, herself later an analyst. This helped to bring about the breakup of his affair with Horney, but Eckardt has repeatedly talked of how helpful it was to be analyzed by someone who knew her complicated mother so well (Eckardt interview; Quinn, p. 368; McLaughlin, "Why Do Schools of Thought Fail?" p. 118).

28. Accused by both Freudians and Marxists of watering down complex theories "to write popular books that would make Americans feel good about themselves," Erich was derisively called the "Norman Vincent Peale of the left" by his colleagues at *Dissent* magazine. See McLaughlin, "Why Do Schools of Thought Fail?" (p. 125) and "How to Become a Forgotten Intellectual" (p. 226), and Burston's *The Legacy of Erich Fromm* for insightful analyses of Erich's many struggles.

29. AT, p. 13.

30. Funk, citing no source, claims the marriage took place on June 16, the anniversary of Erich's parents' marriage (Funk, *Erich Fromm Bildbiographie*, p. 61 of draft copy). Frieda and her lawyer in Rockville list the May 14 date on her divorce records, which I have taken to be the more reliable source.

31. AT, p. 13. Erich's father, despite being from a distinguished Frankfurt background, did not apparently see Frieda's childhood in Prussia as a problem (although it must have helped that she spent her first eight years in nearby Karlsruhe). In contrast, when Leo Löwenthal married Frieda's childhood friend Golde Ginsberg, Löwenthal's father refused to come to the wedding, declaring: "You're crazy! Königsberg, that's practically in Russia!" (Löwenthal, p. 207).

32. For detailed histories of the Lehrhaus and other aspects of the self-renewal movement, see Brenner, *The Renaissance of Jewish Culture* and Glatzer, "The Frankfort Lehrhaus." On the sanitarium experiment, see Blomert, "Das vergessene Sanatorium," and Engel, "Das Heidelberger 'Thorapeutikum.'"

33. Nobel was so charismatic a teacher that, according to Rosenzweig, "even on cold winter days 150 people would attend [his] class, some of them [arriving on] toboggans or skis" (Brenner, p. 237). Agnon, who had married Frieda's cousin Esther Marx, later became one of Israel's best-known authors (see Laor). Moses Marx, Esther's brother, although not himself a teacher at the Lehrhaus, was a publisher and bibliophile, with one of the largest private collections of Jewish books in Germany.

34. Unlike Rosenzweig and many other teachers at the Lehrhaus, who had been raised in assimilationist homes and were seeking to acquire knowledge of Jewish life they had lacked in childhood, Frieda and Erich were among the few participants with Orthodox backgrounds, which made the meaning of their involvement in the self-renewal movement quite different. They were seeking to deepen their practice of Judaism, not to initiate it. (See Brenner and Penslar for further discussion of these issues.)

35. Buber, *On Judaism,* pp. 48, 92–93; Löwenthal, p. 51; AT, p. 7. As Löwenthal notes, "Psychoanalysis was a despised and scorned science" in the 1920s. When Horkheimer allowed the institute Frieda and Erich later organized to hold its lectures in his building in Frankfurt, "the mere fact that a psychoanalytic institute was allowed to use rooms on a university campus was then almost a sensation."

36. AT, pp. 13–14.

37. Löwenthal, p. 26. Frieda did take on some younger psychiatrists as assistants—chief among them Friedrich Rothschild—but like Erich, none of them practiced

independently. Rothschild was brought in mainly to serve as a control case for Erich (FR to Ursula Engel, June 10, 1986).

38. AT, p. 14.

39. Ibid., p. 14. Frieda's paper, originally given at a meeting of the German Psycho-analytic Society to qualify for formal membership, is her only work analyzing sexual symbolism. Arguing that Jewish dietary laws are unconscious protections against incest, she describes several patients who, having abandoned such ritu-als, experienced a palpably heightened sexual tension in the presence of the for-bidden foods. One man (perhaps, as Petratos has suggested, a disguised version of Erich) got an erection every time he passed a butcher's shop and saw the dis-play of sausages (see Petratos, "Development," p. 134).

40. AT, p. 14.

41. Ibid.; Sarna; *Encyclopaedia Judaica; Oxford Dictionary of the Jewish Religion.*

42. AT, p. 15.

43. Ibid., pp. 14–15.

44. FFR to GG, September 27, October 16, 1931. Rainer Funk, Fromm's literary ex-ecutor, explicitly tying Erich's tuberculosis to his struggle to leave Frieda, says that once "the separation was internally completed," Erich left Davos, physically recovered (see Funk, *Erich Fromm Bildbiographie,* pp. 63–67 of draft copy). I am very grateful to Rainer Funk for sharing these materials with me prior to their publication.

45. The unconscious intensity of the conflict between Horney and Frieda was still strong enough in 1990 to cause one of Horney's biographers to repeatedly "for-get" appointments with me, even those she herself had arranged. Five years later, she confessed in a letter to enacting the unconscious guilt and rivalry Horney pre-sumably felt toward Frieda.

46. Eckardt interview; Paris, p. 144; "roving eye" from Quinn, p. 163. There is dis-agreement among sources as to precisely when Erich began his affair with Hor-ney. Quinn claims it was when they both came to Chicago; Paris says it was later, in New York. Eckardt and Funk agree with my view that it is more likely to have started in Germany and that Erich's following Horney to Chicago was the con-sequence, not the cause, of their involvement.

47. FFR to GG, July 31, 1932.

48. Many surgeons of the period preferred hysterectomy to myomectomy (the re-moval of the myoma alone) "because of the haemorrhage that occurs in my-omectomy, which could not be controlled without the use of blood transfusions." The only reason a surgeon would not have performed a hysterectomy on a woman with symptoms like Frieda's would have been that she explicitly refused, wanting to become pregnant. Mortality and morbidity were much greater fol-lowing myomectomy, so most surgeons in the 1930s recommended hysterec-tomy (see O'Dowd and Philipp, p. 412).

49. FFR to GG, July 31, 1932; Szalita interview.

50. AJF, March 25, April 21, 1993. Although Alisa heard this story from her mother, Anna, years later, its details precisely accord with what we know of Klara's be-havior in many other situations.

51. Ursell interview; Bloch interview.

52. Will interview. For one of many examples of Frieda's minimizing "the role of the sexual aspect in the patient's transference relationship with the analyst," see "Notes on the Mother Role in the Family Group" (1940), SP, p. 294.

53. This apt phrase is Liebenberg's, p. 91. On women in the Orthodox synagogue, see Breuer, p. 276.
54. AT, p. 17.
55. Paris, Quinn, and McLaughlin ("Why Do Schools of Thought Fail?") all give practically identical accounts of Horney's behavior with men in general and Erich in particular. As Quinn notes, Horney had herself remarked in a diary: "I have a wish to throw myself away, prostitute myself—give myself to any man at random." Horney had anonymous sex, adultery during her marriage, and sex with young analysts she was supervising. Quinn links this "desperate, driven quality of her quest for the right man" to Horney's subsequent writing on the "neurotic need for affection" (pp. 163, 166, 261).
56. AT, p. 17.
57. Ibid., p. 5.
58. Olinick interview.

Chapter 5. The Exile

1. Singer, p. 127.
2. Grete had begun working as a music critic in Königsberg, where she was also founder and director of a school for private music teachers (see Jacoby, p. 70).
3. AJF, October 24, 1995; Reed, p. 20.
4. AJF, October 24, 1995.
5. Grill, pp. 346–349; Leonhard; Giovannini, Bauer, and Mumm.
6. Weiss, p. 149.
7. AJF, October 24, 1995.
8. In the 1930s, Jews were allowed to take only ten marks out of Germany (about $2.50), and many who went directly to the United States arrived there destitute. It was not uncommon for intellectuals to end up in the most menial jobs simply to have money for food. In choosing Strasbourg, Frieda could complete the analyses of her Heidelberg patients and provide herself with a decent income.
9. Anna Jacobson to Joanne Greenberg, August 16, 1990; AJF, October 24, 1995.
10. Jenny Waelder-Hall, oral history interview by Archangelo D'Amore, Washington, D.C., December 8, 1973, p. 9 of typed transcript (archives of the Washington Psychoanalytic Society and Institute).
11. FFR to GG, August 23, 1933.
12. "In Memoriam: Gertrud Jacob, 1893–1940" (1940), p. 546.
13. Grossman and Grossman, pp. 196–197. See also Alexander, Eisenstein, and Grotjahn, p. 318; and Silver, "Frieda Fromm-Reichmann: Her Life Before Coming to the Lodge," p. 13.
14. According to McLaughlin, Erich went to the United States at the invitation of Horney, who tried to get him a position at the Chicago Psychoanalytic Institute, where she had gone to work with Franz Alexander. This situation didn't work out for either of them, and both ended up in New York soon after (see McLaughlin, "Why Do Schools of Thought Fail?," p. 117).
15. AJF, January 25, 1993.
16. Berengaria manifest, April 16, 1935, National Archives (New York office). I am grateful to Catherine Orland for locating these records.
17. In *Refugee Scholars in America,* Coser gives many examples of physicians and

academics who were unable to recreate successful lives for themselves in America or did so only after much difficulty. Burston (p. 19) recounts the painful story of Otto Fenichel, a distinguished German analyst who "died tragically of overwork, laboring fiercely to refurbish his medical credentials."

CHAPTER 6. ASYLUM

1. Newman, p. 97.
2. Anne Bullard interview with Sylvia Hoff Collins, January 24, 1979.
3. Mabel Peterson oral recollections, January 29, 1990.
4. In England, private "madhouses" had been run as profit-making businesses at least since the early seventeenth century, and in Germany and Austria, there were hundreds of them. See Parry-Jones; and Shorter, "Private Clinics in Central Europe."
5. Miscellaneous budget and financial records, 1910–1960 (CLA).
6. On Mendota State Hospital, see Ernest Luther Bullard, "The Care of the Insane in Wisconsin." For a broader context to these events, see Numbers and Leavitt.
7. Dexter M. Bullard, "Chestnut Lodge," talk presented to the Ontario Psychiatric Association, February 2, 1968, p. 2 of typed draft (CLA). The details of Ernest Bullard's life are based on his son's reminiscences. Among many nearly identical accounts, see DMB, "Chestnut Lodge—History and Philosophy," 1st Chestnut Lodge Annual Symposium, March 2, 1955, and DMB oral history interviews (conducted by Robert N. Butler, M.D.), 1963 (APA). See also Freeman, "The Bullards."
8. All details of Rockville history from the following publications of the Montgomery County (Maryland) Historical Society: Ray Eldon Hiebert and Richard K. MacMaster, *A Grateful Remembrance: The Story of Montgomery County Maryland* (1976); *Backward Glance: A Brief History of Rockville* (1983); "Chronological Record of Rockville Development" (1968); Mrs. Neal Fitzsimons, "Woodlawn Hotel—Chestnut Lodge Sanitarium—The Bullard Dynasty—Rose Hill," *The Montgomery County Story* (1974); "Peerless Rockville, 1890"; Eileen McGuckian, "Historic Rockville," *Gazette,* January 2, 1985.
9. Fitzsimons, p. 3.
10. Maryland Historical Trust State Historical Sites Inventory Form, May 1986, pp. 1–3. (The Woodlawn is listed in the National Register, so its history has been extensively documented.) "Network of excursion trains," from Fitzsimons, p. 4; "auction block," from Inventory, p. 5.
11. *Montgomery County Sentinel,* December 1, 8, 1911 (this and all subsequent *Sentinel* quotations from microfilm copies held by the City of Rockville Public Library); "All-America City," *Rampage,* November 17, 1971, Montgomery County Historical Society; DMB oral history interview with Jeanine Jeffs, May 1, 1975, p. 7 of typed transcript (CLA).
12. Miscellaneous bills and correspondence, 1909–1911 (CLA).
13. This was literally true. By 1934, there was a Stony Lodge (Ossining, New York), a Harlem Lodge (Catonsville, Maryland), a Westwood Lodge (Westwood, Massachusetts), and a Cedar Lodge (Wellesley, Massachusetts).
14. "Insanity Shows Big Increase," *Montgomery County Sentinel,* January 5, 1912. The most extensive account of this history is Grob, *Mental Illness and American*

Society, 1875–1940. See also Sicherman; Ackerknecht; and Rosenberg, "The Crisis in Psychiatric Legitimacy."

15. DMB, "Chestnut Lodge—History and Philosophy," p. 5; "Chronological Record of Rockville Development," p. 10.

16. *Montgomery County Sentinel,* December 1, 8, 1911.

17. The streetcar line had been extended in 1904 specifically to take guests out to the Woodlawn.

18. DMB Oral History with Butler, Interview 1, 1963, p. 8 (APA); "Chestnut Lodge—History and Philosophy," pp. 3–5. There was some variability in rates. Patients not requiring treatment, who came "merely for a rest," were charged $50 per month, and families could negotiate lower rates for long-term stays. Occasionally, in response to a particularly poignant plea, Bullard would take a patient for only a month or so at a reduced rate. In general, however, especially as compared to the rates at nearby boarding houses—which ranged from $7 to $10 a week—the Lodge was expensive from the beginning (miscellaneous letters, 1910–1911, to relatives and other inquirers, CLA).

19. ELB to Miss Eva Gray, January 12, 1911, Miss Grayce Sullivan, July 7, 1911 (CLA). These were essentially form letters, sent with minor variations to many others.

20. ELB to Joseph S. Shefloe, December 8, 1919, Leadre Publishing Co., April 18, 1919; George W. Quick to ELB, February 14, 1911 (CLA).

21. Small, pp. 77, 166–168. For detailed histories of therapeutics in this period, see Warner, *The Therapeutic Perspective;* Grob, *Mental Illness in American Society;* and Pressman.

22. ELB to Mr. GHK, January 28, 1910. (To protect the confidentiality of relatives of former patients, only their initials are used here.) ELB to Dr. AAS, January 8, 1913; Mr. GEH, June 29, 1912; Dr. EHM, July 20, 1911; Mrs. MFC, August 13, 1911; Miss SLC, July 26, 1911 (CLA).

23. For example, he wrote to Mr. GEH (August 10, 1912) regarding his brother: "The prospects for a cure are now more encouraging than they have been at any time since he came here, and I wish you could see your way to let him remain here until he gets well." Mrs. PM to ELB, December 18, 1912 (emphasis in original); ELB to Mr. GEH, May 23, 1912 (CLA).

24. Mr. JAH to ELB, May 15, 1912; ELB to Mr. JAH, May 16, 1912 (CLA).

25. DMB, "Chestnut Lodge—History and Philosophy," p. 6. Bullard drew up a commitment agreement that required patients to agree in advance to whatever methods he thought appropriate. ("I authorize [the physician in charge] to restrain me, if, in his judgment it may be necessary, in such manner as may seem advisable to him." Application for Treatment and Voluntary Commitment, May 1911, CLA.) Methods of restraint did not differ by sex, as had been the custom in Victorian hospitals in England, where special "velvet bracelets" were designed for unruly women (see MacKenzie, p. 142).

26. This pattern is common enough to have warranted a whole section titled "Psychiatric Dynasties" in Freeman's, *The Psychiatrist.*

27. DMB Oral History, Interview 2, 1963, p. 2 (APA). Manfred Bleuler makes a similar point about his upbringing; watching his father Eugen get up at 5:00 A.M. to work alongside the patients on the hospital's farm taught him to think of psychotic people as neighbors.

28. Freeman, p. 244.

29. His salary the first year was $250 per month; by the second year, it had doubled (DMB, "Chestnut Lodge—History and Philosophy," p. 12, CLA).
30. Freeman, p. 245.
31. Typical of Ernest Bullard was this quiet claim in a letter to the relative of a newly admitted patient: "In regard to her ultimate recovery, it is impossible to express an opinion at the present time further than to say that we can look for improvement with a good deal of confidence. The fact that this is her first attack is in her favor. Cases of this kind usually improve, not infrequently get quite well, but are liable to relapses" (ELB to Mr. HLM, April 7, 1911, CLA).
32. DMB to Miss EGR, May 10, 1930 (CLA).
33. *Montgomery County Sentinel,* October 16, 1925.
34. "In Memoriam, Ernest Luther Bullard, M.D.," presented before the Medical Society of the District of Columbia, February 3, 1931 (CLA).
35. This was the peculiar situation of every proprietary asylum. As the great Victorian psychiatrist John Conolly remarked: "The patients are transmitted, like stock in trade, from one member of the family to another, and from one generation to another; they come in youth to the father, they linger out their age with the son" (Parry-Jones, p. 84).
36. DMB, "Résumé of 45 years at Chestnut Lodge," presented at the annual CL symposium, October 31, 1969 (CLA); Anne Bullard interview.
37. A member of the Colonial Dames of America and the Chevy Chase Club, Anne went on to serve on the boards of dozens of civic organizations and was the first woman appointed "Man of the Year" by the Rockville Chamber of Commerce (Anne Bullard interview with John Fort and Mabel Peterson).
38. Bullard oral history interview, p. 32 (APA).
39. Postcards and other advertisements of sanitaria and asylums (CLA). None of these institutions went as far as some private asylums in the eighteenth century, which offered money-back guarantees to prospective clients ("No Cure, No Pay," read a number of the ads Parry-Jones reviews, pp. 102–105.)
40. Grimes, pp. 123–130.
41. On the history of Washington-Baltimore psychiatry, see Burnham, "Orthodoxy and Eclecticism in Psychoanalysis"; Douglas Noble and Donald L. Burnham, "History of the Washington Psychoanalytic Society and the Washington Psychoanalytic Institute, unpublished report, September 1969 (CLA); D'Amore; M. Engel; Lidz; Schulz, "Sullivan's Clinical Contribution During the Sheppard Pratt Era."
42. DMB, "Chestnut Lodge—History and Philosophy," p. 10 (CLA).
43. Schloss Tegel, Ernst Simmel's asylum outside Berlin, was the first psychoanalytic hospital, but it had open wards and never treated patients as disturbed as those at the Lodge. Institutions in the United States that employed psychoanalytic methods differed from the Lodge either by virtue of their eclecticism (Menninger and McLean, for instance, combined psychotherapy with shock and lobotomy) or by the restrictions they imposed on their clientele (Austen Riggs, for example, was psychoanalytic, but never admitted patients who required a locked ward). See Pressman; Bartemeier.
44. DMB, "Chestnut Lodge," p. 3; "Chestnut Lodge—History and Philosophy," p. 15 (CLA).
45. The fact that it was kitchen workers, and not patients, who were housed in shacks is a mark of the Lodge's well-paying clientele. Parry-Jones describes country

mansions in England converted to madhouses where poor patients were forced to live in stables and outbuildings, while those who could afford to pay resided in the house with the proprietor's family.

46. DMB Oral History, Interview 2, 1963, p. 20 (APA).

47. *Montgomery County Sentinel,* July 11, 18, August 1, 15, 22, September 5, 19, 1935.

48. Greenberg interviews; Kehne interview.

49. In 1935, for example, the custodial rate was $40 per week (this was for a double room; singles were $55), and the rate for "adjustive treatment" (what would now be called "supportive" psychotherapy) was $50 a week ($65 for a single), but psychoanalytic treatment cost $75 a week and up (data from miscellaneous admission letters, 1919–1936, CLA).

50. DMB to Dr. George E. Kornegay, December 14, 1933 (CLA). In response to an inquiry from Mr. RWD concerning his alcoholic brother, Bullard noted that "it is a matter of months, sometimes years, before permanent recovery may be reached. Relatives unwilling to take this long term view do better not to seek treatment of this type. As many of the factors leading to drinking are unconscious, the psychoanalytic approach has been the most encouraging in our experience, although all patients do not respond to psychoanalysis" (DMB to Mr. RWD, February 5, 1939, CLA).

51. DMB to Mrs. MR, June 9, 1934 (CLA).

52. DMB to Dr. Amanda Stoughton, November 23, 1934 (CLA). Bullard went on to talk admiringly of that "class of psychotic patients whose relatives appreciate the extent of the personality disorder and who realize that a social recovery such as is achieved by repression or by adjustive psychotherapy is but superficial at best and that real recovery comprehends the patient's reaching a thorough understanding of all the dynamics of the personality changes which have culminated in illness."

53. The quest for a unique treatment approach knew no limits. There was, for example, a highly successful movement in the 1920s and 1930s that used chiropractic methods to treat psychosis, an approach distinctive enough to keep several hospitals going throughout the Depression (see Quigley). There were also a number of sanitaria run by the Christian Science church offering "an atmosphere conducive to mind-healing" (see Hubner, p. 149).

54. Shorter, "Private Clinics in Central Europe," p. 160. Shorter's sample consisted of the 340 private asylums founded in Germany and Austria between 1890 and the start of the Nazi period. On similarities between proprietary psychiatric sanitaria in the United States and Europe during this period, see Ackerknecht; Grimes, part II; Abbott, chap. 3. Abbott's analysis of rates at psychiatric sanitaria in the United States from 1880 to 1930 shows the Lodge to be in the midrange for such institutions. As Abbott notes (p. 66), rates varied widely according to the services provided, but "sanitaria that lasted for at least ten years seemed to find stable markets."

55. There might also have been a technical reason for Frieda to live on hospital grounds when she first arrived—she had no American medical license. She took the exam that first year and was licensed by the state of New York in 1936. She was wise to turn down Menninger, which treated its women physicians as second-class citizens (see Friedman, p. 75).

56. Young-Bruehl, *Hannah Arendt,* p. 168.

57. Bruch, "Personal Reminiscences of Frieda Fromm-Reichmann," pp. 99–100, 102; FFR letters to Max Horkheimer, 1936.
58. Schulz interview; on Sullivan's and Horney's buying habits, see Perry and Quinn, respectively.
59. Dyrud, Burnham interviews; Otto Will interview with Sylvia Hoff Collins.
60. This and all subsequent statements attributed to Jarvis or "Young Marjorie" are from Kehne interview.
61. Burnham, Cohen interviews.
62. She became a citizen immediately following the required waiting period, receiving her naturalization papers from the District Court of the United States in Baltimore on April 14, 1941 (certificate No. 5011663, issued by the U.S. Immigration and Naturalization Service).
63. AJF, August 9, 1992.
64. Ibid., January 31, 1996.
65. Ibid. This was a typical attitude, especially among older Jews. Historian Claudia Koonz, in her classic study *Mothers in the Fatherland,* notes: "For every Jew who decided to emigrate before 1938, four calculated that they could continue to live in Germany, albeit at a reduced level of comfort and security" (p. 362).
66. Graml; Kaplan, *Between Dignity and Despair.*
67. AJF, August 30, 1993, October 24, 1995.
68. Ibid., January 31, 1996, July 17, 1998. After payment of the "Reich flight tax" and dozens of other fees, departing Jews were left with practically no assets. In 1934, losses averaged 60 percent; by 1939, when Klara and the others fled, 96 percent of preflight assets were being stolen by the Nazis (see Kwiet). Kaplan, *Between Dignity and Despair* (p. 131), describes the scene that Klara and her family were forced to endure: "In Berlin, the Gestapo set up a special 'one-stop' emigration bureau where 'the emigrating Jew was fleeced, totally and completely, in the manner of an assembly line.' When they entered they were 'still . . . the owner[s] of an apartment, perhaps a business, a bank account and some savings.' As they were pushed from section to section, 'one possession after the next was taken.' By the time they left, they had been 'reduced to . . . stateless beggar[s],' grasping one precious possession, an exit visa."
69. Petratos, "Development," p. 63. Erich also spent much of his income and energy in this period supporting relatives in Europe and desperately trying to get them affidavits to enter the United States, and sent money to Grete and Klara when they arrived in London. (The dozens of letters documenting his efforts are in the Fromm papers, New York Public Library.)
70. AJF, August 9, 1992.
71. Berghahn; Karpf; Zweig, p. vi.
72. Despite the considerably higher percentage of women in psychoanalysis as compared to other professions, they were still underrepresented in leadership roles, especially in U.S. institutes. The Washington-Baltimore Institute was strikingly atypical in this respect. In its first decade, it had three women presidents (Clara Thompson, 1930–1932; Lucile Dooley, 1933–1935, 1938–1939; and Frieda, 1939–1941). This was yet another reflection of the Washington psychiatric community's renegade status. On the general issue of women's participation, see Chodorow; N. Thompson.
73. Biographical information about Jacob from her two-page summary of background, experience, and training, submitted to the Menninger Clinic on October

1, 1935 (Menninger Archives, Historical Scrapbook, Vol. 22–22, used by permission of the Menninger Clinic); Frieda's obituary, "In Memoriam: Gertrud Jacob" (1940) and obituaries by the editors of the *Bulletin of the Menninger Clinic* (1940, *4,* 131) and Dexter Bullard (*Psychiatry,* 1940, *3,* 175). Also useful are Silverberg, "The Art of Dr. Gertrud Jacob, 1893–1940," and the interpretive notes accompanying Jacob's published portraits (*American Magazine of Art,* August 1937). Certain details of Jacob's life vary across these sources; I have used what seemed to be the most reliable information and am indebted to Lawrence Friedman for the crucial Menninger materials.

74. Complete drafts of seven of Frieda's profiles have survived (some of which are quite detailed), and the patients depicted are clearly indentifiable when compared to her case notes (CLA).

75. Bullard described Jacob as "joining the staff" in 1937, but it is not clear precisely what this means. Jacob was unable to pass the American medical boards, and thus could not get a license to practice in Maryland. In this, she was clearly not atypical; Else Pappenheim recalled that when she took the exam in Baltimore in the late 1930s, only four of seventy-five applicants passed (*American Psychoanalyst, 28,* No. 4, 1b, 2b.) Jacob's lack of a license may be part of the reason for Bullard's vagueness about her precise role on the Lodge staff (see his obituary of Jacob in *Psychiatry*).

76. Records of the Washington-Baltimore Psychoanalytic Society and Institute (APA).

77. Silverberg, p. 2.

78. Adland, Cohen, Will interviews.

79. Weigert interview. I am indebted to Ruth Solie for insights into Mendelssohn's work. For descriptions of the songs, see Marek; James Lyons, liner notes to the Westminster recording, No. XWN 18501; and Karl Schumann, liner notes to the Deutsche Grammophon recording, No. 2740104.

80. Frieda often invited friends and colleagues from the East to drive out with her to Santa Fe or to visit her there. I got very detailed descriptions from interviews with Bloch, Greenberg, Weigert, Weinberg, and Wilcox; see also Hilde Bruch oral history interview (APA). The house, much expanded by the architect to whom Frieda sold it in the early 1950s, is now the official residence of the president of St. John's College, Santa Fe.

81. Hilde Bruch, "Personal Reminiscences," p. 100. Franz Alexander had a more creative idea: he proposed that analysts contribute to the war effort by reporting to Washington on the morale of the civilian population, using "ideas culled from analytic patients on the couch" (oral history interview with Roy Grinker, APA).

82. Weiss, p. 185.

83. AJF, August 9, 1992. The published history of the Feuchtwanger family, which includes only Adolf's relatives, lists eighty individuals murdered by Nazis; the Simon family, which was equally large, must have had at least several dozen others (*The Feuchtwanger Family,* p. 127).

84. An important early contributor to analytic theory, Landauer fled to Amsterdam when Frieda left for Strasbourg, but did not go on to a safer country and was deported to Bergen-Belsen, where he died of starvation in January 1945 (see Plänkers and Rothe, pp. 105–106, 112–113; Bergmann and Hartman, pp. 59–61). I am grateful to Rainer Funk for providing copies of the correspondence between Frieda and Horkheimer.

85. Maryland State Archives, Annapolis, Box 525, File 10468.
86. Burston, p. 24; Anne Bullard, Spiegel, Szalita, and Weigert interviews.
87. Bluma Swerdloff interview with Lawrence Kolb, July 21, 1977, pp. 60–61 of typed transcript (OHC).
88. AJF, April 21, 1993; Hoff "The Early Years," p. 118.
89. Bruch, "Personal Reminiscences," p. 100; Joanne Hatch Bruch, *Unlocking the Golden Cage*. I am indebted to Joanne Bruch for her generous sharing of materials regarding Frieda's relationship with her husband Herbert.
90. AJF, September 20, 1992. On the Nazis' murder of mental patients, see Michael Burleigh's two detailed studies, *Death and Deliverance, and Ethics and Extermination*.
91. AJF, September 20, 1992.
92. Gunst, "Memoirs—Professional and Personal"; Sylvia Hoff interview with I. Rosenfeld (Frieda's cousin).
93. Young-Bruehl, *Hannah Arendt*, p. 197.

Chapter 7. Improvising Method

1. Sir William Osler, "On the Need of a Radical Reform in Our Methods of Teaching Medical Students" (1904), cited in Hunter, p. 27.
2. FFR to Rollin D. Hemens, Editor, University of Chicago Press, November 4, 1949 (UCP). In this same letter, Frieda expressed her concern that Hemens had been referring to the book as "*The* Principles of Intensive Psychotherapy," and urged omitting "The." It was, she stressed, "presumptuous" for any psychiatrist to try to "sum up (all) *the* principles of intensive psychotherapy" and she did not want to give the impression that she thought she could.
3. "Insight into Psychotic Mechanisms and Emergency Psychotherapy" (1943). In presenting her ideas, Frieda especially highlights the paper by Felix Brown of Oxford, "Civilian Psychiatric Air-raid Casualties," presented at the Southern Psychiatric Association, Nashville, Tennessee, 1940, and Gillespie's *Psychological Effects of War on Citizen and Soldier*.
4. "Insight into Psychotic Mechanisms" (1943), pp. 56–57. Later, Frieda would emphasize the "dissociation" of traumatic material (i.e., the "temporary barring from awareness") as being as important as repression in many cases of psychosis. (See "Four Basic Analytic and Dynamic Principles" ca. 1950s, p. 7.) This view is essentially similar to contemporary conceptions of posttraumatic stress and its attendant pathology (see Herman, for a detailed discussion of these issues).
5. Frieda saw repressed hostility as a central cause of most forms of mental disorder (see "Psychoanalytic Remarks on the Clinical Significance of Hostility," 1936, the first presentation she gave in the United States).
6. "A Preliminary Note on the Emotional Significance of Stereotypies *(sic)* in Schizophrenics" (1942), p. 131 of the version in SP (see also "Psychopathology of Schizophrenia," 1942).
7. "A Preliminary Note" (1942), pp. 130–132.
8. "Notes on the Development of Treatment of Schizophrenics by Psychoanalytic Psychotherapy" (1948), p. 162 of the version in SP. Frieda's views on treating psychotics had been strongly supported by her Frankfurt colleague Karl Landauer, who argued, as she did, that nonverbal communication often allowed the therapist to break through defenses that might otherwise preclude psychotherapy.

Other papers on this issue that Frieda wrote during this crucial first decade at Chestnut Lodge are: "Transference Problems in Schizophrenics" (1939) "Recent Advances in Psychoanalytic Therapy" (1941), "Psychoanalytic Psychotherapy with Psychotics" (1943), "Remarks on the Philosophy of Mental Disorder" (1946), and "Notes on Personal and Professional Requirements of a Psychotherapist" (1949).

9. In practically every paper Frieda wrote on the treatment of schizophrenia, she repeated Freud's claim that technical modifications might allow such patients to be analyzed successfully. She usually cited his 1904 "On Psychotherapy," where Freud wrote: "I do not regard it as by any means impossible that by suitable changes in the [psychoanalytic] method we may succeed in advancing beyond these hindrances—and so be able to initiate a psychotherapy of the psychoses."

10. All details of Sullivan's background from Perry, the most extensively researched account of his life and work.

11. Perry, p. 190.

12. Sylvia Collins interview with Douglas Noble; Hilgard, p. 230.

13. Among the collections of Sullivan's writings edited and published after his death, see *The Interpersonal Theory of Psychiatry* (1953), *Clinical Studies in Psychiatry* (1956), and *Schizophrenia as a Human Process* (1962). The only major work by Sullivan published during his lifetime was *Conceptions of Modern Psychiatry* (1940).

14. Fort interview; HSS to APA, April 2, 1943 (APA).

15. Weininger, "Chestnut Lodge—The Early Years," p. 508; Cohen interview; see also Schulz's two articles, "Sullivan's Influence on Sheppard Pratt" and "Sullivan's Clinical Contribution During the Sheppard Pratt Era—1923–1930."

16. Perry, p. 94; Schulz, "Sullivan's Clinical Contribution," p. 126; M. Green, p. 359.

17. Havens, "Harry Stack Sullivan's Contribution to Clinical Method," p. 362. In taking this view, Sullivan was allying himself with the perspective then gaining credence in physics that an observer could never stand completely outside the field of observation.

18. Perry, pp. 28, 122.

19. William W. Elgin, "Harry Stack Sullivan as I Remember Him," unpublished memorial statement, May 13, 1964; Mabel Blake Cohen, review of *The Contributions of Harry Stack Sullivan: A Symposium* (Patrick Mullahy, Ed.), *Psychiatry,* 1952, *18*, p. 339; Margaret J. Rioch, in O'Connell and Russo, pp. 176–177; Leslie Farber, "Harry Stack Sullivan and the American Dream," *Times Literary Supplement,* April 1, 1977, p. 386.

20. Stanton, "Frieda Fromm-Reichmann, M.D.," p. 124.

21. P, p. 3. Hilde Bruch later told an interviewer that she found it "nearly painful to read" those sections of *Principles* where Frieda attempts to show that Sullivan's ideas were compatible with Freud's. In Bruch's view, Frieda's intense need to remain loyal to both viewpoints led her to overstate the links between them (oral history interviews by Jane Preston and Hannah Decker, 1974–1975, p. 184 of typed transcript, APA).

22. "Notes on Some Cultural Differences Between the Attitude of American and European Psychoanalytic Patients and Physicians" (ca. 1939), p. 2.

23. Ibid., pp. 5–6, 15.

24. Frieda also found the content of oedipal dynamics different in America. The relatively unpatriarchal role of American fathers meant that power relations in the

family were significantly different from those assumed by classical theory. Fathers in American families were not the all-powerful, controlling figures Freud had described; patients were more likely to think of them as "confidants and friends," with mothers as the central authority. Fathers were often seen as benign and indulgent by American patients, and this naturally changed the kinds of transference feelings they projected in therapy. See "Notes on the Mother Role in the Family Group" (1940), a paper Frieda published several years after her arrival in the United States.

25. Cohen, "Notes on the Life and Work of Frieda Fromm-Reichmann," p. 92.

26. In 1989, Kurt Eissler, one of Freud's most ardent followers, was still so angry at Frieda for choosing not to sit behind the couch that he excoriated her as a "dried-up old schoolmarm" who had no respect for Freud's genius (Eissler interview). By that point, Frieda had been dead for thirty-two years, but this seemed not to diminish the force of Eissler's ire. He may have been especially sensitive to seating arrangements because Adler, the original "deviant," insisted on facing his patients as equals, as befit his socialist politics. This was not a new issue. Clarence Oberndorf recalled his incredulity at being told by a senior colleague in 1917: "If you watch the patient's feet as he lies on the couch and get accustomed to his tell-tale movements, these will reveal to you as much as his face" (Oberndorf, p. 123).

27. P, p. 100.

28. For recent examples of this attack literature, see Torrey; Hartwell; Neill; and Dolnick (esp. Chap. 5, "The Mother of the 'Schizophrenogenic Mother'"). These portrayals of Frieda are so filled with distortion and inaccuracy as to be barely recognizable, although it is striking that Dolnick decimates Frieda's ideas but seems to admire her as a person. Sayers, noting similarly exaggerated portrayals of Melanie Klein, remarks: "Klein has often been vilified as a monster for drawing attention—through her life and work—to the negative as well as the positive aspects of mothering" (p. 15).

29. The term *schizophrenogenic mother* does not even appear in the index to *Principles of Intensive Psychotherapy* (whose construction Frieda personally supervised) or her *Selected Papers* (which is extremely detailed and intended to highlight every important term and concept in her approach). Her one parenthetical mention occurs in "Notes on the Development of Treatment of Schizophrenics by Psychoanalytic Psychotherapy," 1948 (on p. 164 of the version in SP).

30. Unlike every other prominent woman analyst of her generation, Frieda published almost nothing on female psychology. Her decision to work at an army hospital during World War I and then to remain in institutional psychiatry for the rest of her career meant that she treated many more male patients than the typical analyst did. (Therapists in private practice always have more female than male patients, and the preference of many women for a female therapist means that women analysts see an even greater number. Male patients, on the other hand, often delay psychiatric treatment until they need hospitalization, so therapists on the staffs of institutions inevitably see more men than they otherwise would.) Frieda gave a few lectures on topics related to women—"Female Psychosexuality" (1936), "Notes on Some Cultural Differences Between the Attitude of American and European Psychoanalytic Patients and Physicians" (ca. 1939), and "Notes on the Mother Role in the Family Group" (1940)—but this last was the

414   Notes for Chapter 7, pages 133-141

only one she published. A brief talk she gave in 1950 as discussant of a paper by Clara Thompson was later published by Jean Baker Miller (under the title "On the Denial of Women's Sexual Pleasure"), and "Female Psychosexuality" was recently edited and published with an introduction by Ann-Louise S. Silver.

31. "Notes on the Mother Role" (1940), pp. 290–292, 297–298. Neither the fact that her own mother was an exception to these dynamics, nor the unconscious sadism inherent in writing about the destructiveness of powerful mothers while insisting that Klara was perfect are dealt with in this paper.

32. Almost identical claims are made today by analyst Alice Miller; they are hailed as brilliant by a generation that includes many children of "narcissistic" mothers. See, for example, her classic *The Drama of the Gifted Child.*

33. She included a whole chapter on "Contacts with Relatives" in *Principles,* urged respect for their feelings, and advised psychiatrists to "address [themselves] to patients' relatives more mindful of their potential assets than of their actual liabilities" (p. 224). For a more balanced analysis of the schizophrenogenic mother concept in the context of Frieda's nonjudgmental views of the feminine role, see Müller.

34. Stanton, "Frieda Fromm-Reichmann, M.D."

35. Foreword (by FFR) and Introduction to the English edition (by Eissler) of Schwing, pp. 9, 14, 16.

36. Ibid., pp. 13, 28, 34–35. For an approach that inspired Schwing's work, see Federn.

37. "Notes on the Development of Treatment of Schizophrenics by Psychoanalytic Psychotherapy" (1948), pp. 165, 173, 175.

38. "Late Inmate," p. ix.

39. FFR, "Introduction," *Philosophy of Insanity* (1947), pp. v–vi.

40. "Late Inmate," pp. 10, 76, 105. Among the many respects in which this narrative differs from hundreds of other patient accounts of mental illness is that it includes an appendix, in which the Late Inmate quotes extensively from autopsy reports of patients who died at his asylum (data clearly provided by his doctors). These detailed excerpts document the knowledge of the day regarding brain functioning and the causes of insanity, and make even more vivid the radically psychological thrust of his perspective.

41. P, pp. xi–xii.

42. Spiegel interview; Silver, "Frieda Fromm-Reichmann: Her Life Before Coming to the Lodge," paper presented at the meeting of the Historical Committee of the Washington Psychoanalytic Institute, November 17, 1992, p. 15 of typed draft.

43. These and all subsequent details of this case are taken from notes and reports by Frieda and other staff, January 20, 1939–February 18, 1942 (CLA).

44. In taking such views, Frieda was echoing Bleuler's classic critique of Kraepelin's pessimism. See, for example, Bleuler's paper, "The Prognosis of Dementia Praecox: The Group of Schizophrenias." For recent reevaluations of Kraepelin and a more complex historical view of his framework, see Havens, "Emil Kraepelin," and Berrios and Hauser.

45. FFR process notes, September 27, 1939 (CLA); "dean of lobotomy" from Pressman, p. 322.

46. Cohen, "Notes on the Life and Work," p. 98.

47. Schön, pp. 50, 54–55.

48. P, p. 45.

49. See English, Hampe, Bacon, and Settlage; and Rosen. Frieda's attitude toward Rosen was reminiscent of her response to Groddeck: she ignored the excess and appreciated the uncompromising dedication to treating very sick patients.

50. P, pp. 95–96. Peter Breggin, citing no documentary evidence, claims (p. 339) that in 1983, Rosen was forced to surrender his medical license "to avoid facing charges" for "physically and sexually assault[ing], virtually turn[ing] into a mental patient slave," one of his female patients, and that he repeated this pattern with other women. There is no way to evaluate this claim, but certainly Frieda never knew of such behavior. For a more heroic (slightly fictionalized) portrayal of Rosen, see Brand.

51. P, pp. 179–180.

52. These and all subsequent quotes are from letters in Dr. D.'s file, July 14, 1939–January 19, 1945 (CLA).

53. FFR process notes, July 29–August 25, 1935 (CLA).

54. P, pp. 29–30.

55. It is not clear which "40 patients" Frieda was referring to. The Lodge had only twenty-five to thirty beds in 1935, and of these, only some were Frieda's patients. She also had some private patients, and perhaps she was combining both groups. Or perhaps, in one of her slightly awkward uses of English, a language she had just begun speaking, she was simply using "forty" as a large number.

56. FFR process notes, December 10, 1935 (CLA).

57. Enough examples have survived of sessions with other patients where we have both Frieda's dictated notes and verbatim transcriptions or tape recordings of the hour that we can say with certainty that her notes typically preserved the patient's actual words. Frieda's concentration during treatment hours was apparently sufficient to allow her to commit to memory most of what the patient said.

58. More than 300 patient narratives of mental illness have been published in English alone, dating from as early as 1436. For a few examples of this huge literature, see Perceval, *A Narrative of the Treatment Experienced by a Gentleman, During a State of Mental Derangement;* Beers, *A Mind That Found Itself;* Hillyer, *Reluctantly Told;* Freeman, *Fight Against Fears;* Sechehaye, *Autobiography of a Schizophrenic Girl;* Schreber, *Memoirs of My Nervous Illness;* O'Brien, *Operators and Things: The Inner Life of a Schizophrenic;* Boisen, *Out of the Depths;* Stefan, *In Search of Sanity: The Journal of a Schizophrenic;* Benziger, *The Prison of My Mind;* Neary, *Whom the Gods Destroy;* Cardinal, *The Words to Say It;* Millett, *The Loony-bin Trip;* Styron, *Darkness Visible: A Memoir of Madness;* Kaysen, *Girl, Interrupted;* Jamison, *An Unquiet Mind: A Memoir of Moods and Madness.*

59. This history has yet to be told, since historians of medicine have been so closely identified with the interests of their clientele. John Harley Warner has been one of few to note how seldom the field has differentiated itself from the viewpoints of doctors themselves (see Warner, "The Fall and Rise of Professional Mystery"; Risse and Warner). In this respect, historians of medicine have been more conservative than their colleagues in other fields of history, who have allowed their fundamental assumptions to be called into question by the social movements of the 1960s. Writers of American history now bring the voices of the disenfranchised into even standard accounts, transforming our understanding of our country and its struggles. But giving African Americans or white women seats at the negotiating tables of history is not nearly as radical as allowing mental patients

into the room. Historians of psychiatry have yet to allow this, but their histories would be a great deal richer if they did. For further discussion of these issues, see Ellenberger; Scull, "Psychiatry and Its Historians" and "Psychiatry and Social Control"; Reaume; and Porter's "The Patient's View," and *A Social History of Madness: The World Through the Eyes of the Insane.*

60. Davis, *Great Day Coming.*
61. FFR process notes, December 27, 1935 (CLA).
62. "Transference Problems in Schizophrenics" (1939), p. 123.
63. This is a clear example of the difference between private practice and hospital work. No analyst in an office practice would see a seriously disturbed patient for the first time right before leaving on vacation. But an emergency admission to a hospital is different; the therapist sees the patient as soon as possible.
64. It's not possible to know for certain whether any more of her notes exist; many of Frieda's papers remain sealed or privately held.
65. Some reviewers of Davis's book, ignorant of the Lodge records, sensed the defensiveness in her tone. "The dissociation between what happens and her own part in it builds as the story continues," Gina Walker commented in the *Women's Review of Books* (April 7, 1995, p. 16).
66. Davis, *Great Day Coming,* p. 240.
67. There may have been a few experimental trials of insulin shock at the Lodge, but never regular use. Ralph Crowley, who joined the staff in the late 1930s, gave a report at the November 1937 meeting of the Virginia, Maryland, and District of Columbia Medical Society citing several such cases. However, it is not clear whether these patients were treated at the Lodge or at some prior institution where Crowley had worked (see Crowley, "Use of Insulin in Certain Psychiatric Disorders").
68. Davis, *Great Day Coming,* p. 274; Davis interview.
69. Davis's erroneous assumptions about Frieda's background are scattered throughout her memoir and the transcript of our interview. She seemed to have believed whatever Florence Powdermaker told her, with the same unquestioning acceptance that she believed Communist party doctrine or the Christian ideals of her mother.
70. Ibid., p. 337. Davis's publisher colludes in this process by using Frieda's name to sell Davis's book (the dust jacket calls Frieda "the heroine (under another name) of Joanna [*sic*] Greenberg's celebrated novel, *I Never Promised You a Rose Garden*). Reviewers joined Davis's denunciation. Jonathan Yardley, in the *Washington Post,* refers to Brunck's "mistreatment by the formidable psychiatrist Frieda Fromm-Reichmann, whose initial kindness . . . eventually turned into manipulation and deceit" (*Book World,* November 27, 1994, p. 3). George Scialabba, in the *Boston Globe,* calls Frieda's behavior "arrogant," "incompetent," and "despicable" and refers to her as "the odious Fromm-Reichmann" (November 20, 1994, p. B17). The *New Leader* said she was "patronizing" and hailed Davis's "non-idealized portrait" of a Frieda who had "appeared replete with halo in *Rose Garden*" (Daphne Merkin, "A Mysterious Love Affair," December 19, 1994, pp. 12–13). *Library Journal* decried Brunck's having become "the virtual prisoner of well-intentioned Freudian analysts" (January 1995, *120,* p. 110). Davis helped to pave the way for all this by describing Frieda as a "cult figure" in an article published several years before her book came out ("Looking Back at My Years in the Party," p. 11).

71. Several years after Brunck's death, Frieda used his case in a key article ("Transference Problems in Schizophrenics," 1939). In the middle of an intense account of their relationship and his progress in therapy, she abruptly ended with the words: "Unfortunately, he was removed from the sanitarium by his relatives" (p. 123). At times like this, Frieda seemed as interested in finding someone else to blame as Davis did.

72. It is not possible to determine precisely when Brunck began to see Weininger or whose decision the reassignment was. In particular, we cannot tell whether it was Frieda's clinical judgment or Bullard's administrative needs that led to the switch. Weininger is listed in Lodge records as arriving in 1936, but the day and month are not specified. Perhaps Bullard simply assigned Brunck to Weininger to divide the patients more equitably among an increased number of therapists, using the match of gender as an added justification. Or perhaps Frieda was frustrated by her lack of progress with Brunck and wanted to be freed from daily responsibility for him. Progress notes make clear the number of months Weininger treated Brunck and how many times a week they met, but these notes are undated, and there are too many alternative interpretations of their meaning to rule anything out.

73. Davis claims (*Great Day Coming*, p. 208) that Frieda refused to meet with Brunck's parents and thus relied on her for all background information. Lodge records make clear this was not the case.

74. Brunck and Volkmann had taken turns putting each other through college and graduate school, and Volkmann paid half the costs of Brunck's treatment at Chestnut Lodge.

75. Perhaps as a cover for her jealousy, Davis was strongly attached to a view of Frieda as married. She insisted in our interview that Frieda had not yet separated from Erich during the period of Brunck's treatment, despite my telling her that this had occurred more than five years earlier. When Davis's father-in-law informed her that Frieda had stayed with Erich during a visit to New York, she ended her letter to Frieda that week with an effusive "I so envy you going to your doctor Erich Fromm this weekend!" (Davis to FFR, May 25, 1936, CLA).

76. Powdermaker to FFR, December 4, 1936 (CLA). The intended recipient of the November letter is not clear from the copy in Brunck's Lodge file.

77. Bullard, "The Organization of Psychoanalytic Procedure," p. 679. For other key papers of Bullard, see "The Application of Psychoanalytic Psychiatry to the Psychoses," "Experiences in the Psychoanalytic Treatment of Psychotics," and "Problems of Clinical Administration."

78. Bullard, "The Organization of Psychoanalytic Procedure," pp. 698–701.

79. See Simmel's "The Psychoanalytic Sanatorium and the Psychoanalytic Movement," and "Psychoanalytic Treatment in a Sanatorium"; also see Bartemeier.

80. Freud's pessimism about treating psychotic patients is always taken as axiomatic of his approach. The historical data show, however, that it simply reflected his observations on work by Simmel and others, and was thus a far more limited empirical statement. Edith Weigert, who worked at Tegel early in her career, sees Freud's attitudes about psychotic patients as resulting largely from his lack of experience with them. Since leading positions in state hospitals or university clinics were closed to Jews, Weigert argues, Freud had little opportunity to come into contact with psychotic patients, except during his "vacations" in a cottage on the Tegel grounds (Weigert, *The Courage to Love*).

81. See Menninger's "Psychoanalytic Principles Applied to the Treatment of Hospitalized Patients," "Psychiatric Principles in Psychiatric Hospital Therapy," "Psychiatric Hospital Therapy Designed to Meet Unconscious Needs," "Psychoanalytic Interpretations of Patients' Reactions in Occupational Therapy," and Menninger and McColl, "Recreational Therapy as Applied in a Modern Psychiatric Hospital."

82. See Friedman, chap. 3 (especially p. 64).

83. Mullan, pp. 5–6, 172, 175. Laing grew up and studied medicine in Glasgow and was well aware of the method of "moral treatment" pioneered by the Tukes in York. The nonjudgmental "family" atmosphere at Kingsley Hall, and its fundamental mission to provide true asylum to people suffering from severe mental illness, place Laing's experimental community clearly in the tradition of the Retreat. (The complete lack of structure and 1960s counterculture values of Kingsley Hall were, however, utterly different from the ordered atmosphere of self-control favored by the Tukes.) For a detailed history of the York Retreat, see Digby; on the sociology of moral treatment and its connections to broader social movements in British society, see Scull, "Moral Treatment Reconsidered."

84. "Holding" is D. W. Winnicott's term for a safe environment, analogous to maternal care, where the patient can "reveal himself to himself," through trusting relationships with others (see *Home Is Where We Start From: Essays by a Psychoanalyst*). Laing eventually regarded his experiments with therapeutic communities as a bit of an embarrassment (see Mullan, chaps. 5, 6).

85. "Problems of Therapeutic Management in a Psychoanalytic Hospital" (1947), pp. 326–327; P, p. 63.

86. Fort, p. 249.

87. "Problems of Therapeutic Management" (1947), pp. 329–331; "Notes—Hospital Management," n.d. (CLA).

88. In their classic study of incontinence on a Lodge ward, Stanton and Schwartz show how "consistent acceptance and support and the wish to understand" on the part of staff dramatically decreased the incidence of such acting out (see Schwartz and Stanton).

89. Analysts like Bryce Boyer would later claim that schizophrenics could be treated as outpatients, using classical methods with no "parameters" (Boyer interview). These claims are widely contested, and Frieda would have been dubious that treatment under such conditions would allow for a regression intense enough to be effective. For a view of therapeutic communities that complements Frieda's, see Maxwell Jones.

90. Miss S. to author, July 25, 1992.

91. "Problems of Therapeutic Management" (1947), p. 337.

92. Ibid., p. 345.

93. Ibid., pp. 342, 344; P, p. 48.

CHAPTER 8. CREATING CHESTNUT LODGE

1. Sontag, "Writing Itself: On Roland Barthes," in Sontag, *A Barthes Reader*, p. xxiii.

2. Interview with Miss F., New York, October 4, 1993.

3. Austen Riggs is particularly taken with this language: both former patients and

staff are called "alumni," and patient "reunions" are held annually (a practice that would never have gone over as well with the far more disturbed clientele of the Lodge). Menninger is also fond of the collegiate image, referring to its grounds as "the campus."

4. McGuire, p. 6.

5. Since the Lodge's patient population had never been analyzed demographically and it was essential to characterize its key features to evaluate Frieda's success in creating a "therapeutic community," I constructed a sample using every tenth admission (as recorded in the patient register), from the founding of the hospital in 1910 until January 1, 1960 (a few years after Frieda's death). My sample consisted of 393 cases: 245 women and 148 men (the greater number of women reflecting the preponderance of female patients in mental hospitals generally, and the fact that significantly more women were admitted during the 1940s when most men were in military service and the Lodge couldn't find enough male attendants to staff male disturbed wards fully). Of the total sample, 309 cases were first admissions; 84 were readmissions. (There was a slight trend for women to predominate among the readmissions and men among the first admissions.) The distribution of cases across the five decades sampled was predictable: 39 cases (10 percent) were admitted during the years 1910–1919, 53 cases (14 percent) from 1920 to 1929, 113 cases (29 percent) from 1930 to 1939, 88 cases (22 percent) from 1940 to 1949, and 100 cases (25 percent) from 1950 to 1960.

6. Information about marital status was missing in many cases from the handwritten patient register (which constituted the only available source of data). Of the 235 cases for which information was listed, 140 (60 percent) were married at the time of admission, 24 (10 percent) were widowed, 9 (4 percent) were divorced, and 62 (26 percent) were single.

7. Locations were divided into four categories: "local," including Rockville and adjacent towns; "near," including places in Maryland, Virginia, and southern Pennsylvania that were within a few hours' drive; "distant," including places requiring a day's drive (thereby precluding frequent visits from relatives), like New York and Massachusetts; and "far," including locations 1,000 or more miles distant, like Chicago or California, requiring extended travel. Using these categories, the sample was distributed as follows: 60 cases (16 percent) were local, 248 (65 percent) were near, 43 (11 percent) were distant, and 32 (8 percent) were far (with 10 cases missing due to incomplete data). Analyzed by decade of admission, the distribution looked like this: 1910–1919—18 percent local, 77 percent near, 3 percent far; 1920–1929—8 percent local, 89 percent near, 2 percent distant; 1930–1939—2 percent local, 86 percent near, 8 percent distant, 2 percent far; 1940–1949—8 percent local, 46 percent near, 26 percent distant, 16 percent far; 1950–1959—40 percent local, 33 percent near, 10 percent distant, 15 percent far. (In the 1950s, many of those categorized as local were outpatients living in Rockville.) A chi-square analysis indicated that there were significantly more patients from distant/far locations in the 1940s than in any other decade ($p = 0.01$).

8. For 72 percent of the sample (282 cases), a diagnosis was listed in the patient register. The particular diagnostic labels varied, of course, as fashions changed in psychiatry. Each diagnosis could, however, be assigned to one of five general categories: neurosis, psychosis, sociopathy, drug/alcohol addiction, or organic disorder. Using these categories, the overall sample was diagnosed as follows: 133 (34 percent) psychotic, 66 (17 percent) neurotic, 56 (14 percent) drug/alcohol ad-

diction, 25 (6 percent) organic disorders, and 2 (0.5 percent) sociopathy. (Numbers do not add to 100 percent because of missing data.) Diagnoses varied over time, as would be expected: 1930–1939—15 percent neurotic, 24 percent psychotic, 32 percent drug/alcohol, 12 percent organic; 1940–1949—14 percent neurotic, 56 percent psychotic, 15 percent drug/alcohol, 1 percent sociopath, 6 percent organic; 1950–1959—36 percent neurotic, 54 percent psychotic, 5 percent drug/alcohol, 1 percent sociopath, 4 percent organic. (Numbers do not add to 100 percent because of missing data; patients admitted 1910–1929 had data too inconsistent to analyze.) Further analyses demonstrated that 56 percent of all organic cases were admitted in the 1930s; of the drug/alcohol addicts, 64 percent were admitted in the 1930s and 23 percent in the 1940s; and significantly more psychotics were admitted in the 1940s than in any other decade ($p < .01$).

9. Hospital stays were calculated in days from admission (with data for three cases missing). Findings were as follows: 28 patients (20 women, 8 men) stayed 1 day or less; 40 patients (16 women, 24 men) stayed 2–3 days; 47 patients (22 women, 25 men) stayed 4–7 days; 58 patients (28 women, 30 men) stayed 8–21 days; 39 patients (26 women, 13 men) stayed 22–40 days; 26 patients (18 women, 8 men) stayed 41–61 days; 29 patients (19 women, 10 men) stayed 62–90 days; 41 patients (32 women, 9 men) stayed 91–180 days; 34 patients (20 women, 14 men) stayed 181–365 days; 48 patients (42 women, 6 men) stayed 366 days or more. (Of this latter category, 35 had stays of more than 600 days, 23 had stays of more than 900 days, and 12 had stays ranging between 6 and 22 years.) A chi-square analysis indicated an effect for gender, with women spending significantly longer time in the hospital ($p < .001$). Men predominate in the categories of 2–3 days, 4–7 days, and 8–21 days, and there are more women in all the other categories. An analysis of variance comparing days in hospital indicated a main effect for location, with the distant/far group spending a much longer time in the hospital than the local/near group ($F = 32.45, p < .001$).

10. Of the 234 cases for whom a condition at discharge was listed, 13 (5 percent) were "recovered," 168 (72 percent) were "improved," and 18 (7 percent) were "unimproved." An additional 23 patients (10 percent) died while at the Lodge (this included deaths from all causes; in most cases, these were geriatric patients sent to the hospital because of senile organic disorders to which they eventually succumbed). Twelve patients in the sample (6 percent) were transferred to other hospitals. There were, not surprisingly, some variations over time: for patients admitted 1910–1919, 8 percent were categorized as recovered, 67 percent as improved, 3 percent as unimproved, and 8 percent died; for patients admitted 1920–1929, 6 percent recovered, 60 percent improved, 8 percent were unimproved, and 13 percent died; for patients admitted 1930–1939, 6 percent recovered, 48 percent improved, 5 percent were unimproved, 8 percent died, and 5 percent were transferred; for patients admitted 1940–1949, 19 percent improved, 1 percent were unimproved, 3 percent died, and 5 percent were transferred; for patients admitted 1950–1959, 39 percent improved, 6 percent were unimproved, 1 percent died, and 2 percent were transferred (numbers do not add to 100 percent because of missing data, and after 1940, many patients had such long stays that they weren't discharged in the same decade that they had been admitted). I thank Kristen Langworthy for her careful assistance in conducting these analyses and Barbara Rosenkrantz for suggesting this statistical profile of Lodge patients.

11. #3, pp. 1–2. This numbering system is mine. Since questionnaires from Schulz's follow-up study were randomly arranged in the Chestnut Lodge files, I alphabetized the 226 narrative responses, and then assigned numbers sequentially.
12. #28, pp. 1–2 (CLA).
13. #49, p. 2 (CLA).
14. #59, p. 2 (CLA).
15. #112, pp. 3–4 (CLA).
16. #168, pp. 1–2 (emphasis in original, CLA).
17. Douglas T. Noble, "Early Days at the Lodge," presented at the 9th Annual Chestnut Lodge Symposium, October 25, 1963.
18. Anne Bullard interview, p. 23.
19. Searles and Cooperman interviews; Grinker and Spiegel. According to historian Nathan Hale, when the United States entered the war in 1941, the army had only thirty-five psychiatrists, many not fully trained. Yet in the North African campaigns of 1942, for example, psychiatric cases amounted to 20 to 34 percent of all casualties. The army ended up training more than 1,000 psychiatrists, many of whom remained in the field after the war, especially in psychoanalysis (see Hale, *The Rise and Crisis of Psychoanalysis in the United States,* chaps. 11, 12, 15; also Grob, "World War II and American Psychiatry").
20. John Fort, "Notes for an Unpublished History of Chestnut Lodge," n.d. (probably mid-1980s). Ralph Nader's study group on mental health reported in 1974 that Washington had the highest per capita concentration of psychiatrists of any city in the country, due partly to the fact that federal insurance plans were still paying up to 80 percent of the cost of psychotherapy or psychoanalysis (see Chu and Trotter, p. 124). On psychoanalysis in America during this period, see Hale, "From Bergasse IX to Central Park West."
21. Will interview. I am deeply grateful to Don Burnham and Bob Cohen for helping to track down details of various staff members' backgrounds.
22. Sylvia Hoff interview with Douglas Noble; Cohen interview.
23. Stotland and Kobler, p. 10.
24. Bloch, pp. 63–64.
25. See Hornstein and Star.
26. Will and Cooperman interviews.
27. Bullard oral history interview, p. 15 (APA). Part of what prevented Sullivan from wrecking the Lodge was that Dexter was shrewd enough not to hire him onto the regular staff. Instead, by paying Sullivan as a consultant in a series of ad hoc arrangements, Dexter avoided being yet one more employer that Sullivan could rebel against.
28. Burnham, "Orthodoxy and Eclecticism in Psychoanalysis"; Will interview with Sylvia Hoff Collins; Schulz and Rioch interviews; Szalita, "Acceptance Speech on the Occasion of Receiving the Frieda Fromm-Reichmann Award."
29. Kubie, *The Riggs Story,* pp. 20, 82.
30. Sutton, pp. 75, 251; see also Pressman, pp. 245–252. Ironically, what eventually led McLean to change was Alfred Stanton's appointment as superintendent after a decade of work at the Lodge. Francis deMarneffe, then a physician on the staff, recalled his incredulity when Stanton defined psychotherapy "as sitting down with the patient in an appropriate setting, such as an office, and conducting psychotherapy for 50 minutes two, three, or four times a week. It had to be scheduled. . . . This was different from what it had been when, in the course of making

rounds, we as psychiatrists or residents had sat down for 15 or 20 minutes with a patient to talk about what he or she was doing. At the time, we had called that psychotherapy, but under the Stanton regime it certainly would not have been considered adequate" (Sutton, p. 274).

31. Forbush; MacKenzie, pp. 53, 183; see also Parry-Jones, p. 115.
32. For a detailed analysis of shifts in the administration and financing of American hospitals, see Rosenberg, *The Care of Strangers.*
33. Friedman, p. 38.
34. Frieda considered every psychotic patient potentially reachable by psychotherapy, but she drew the line at those whose capacity for insight had been destroyed by brain operations. Pressman's authoritative history of lobotomy reports that more than 20,000 such operations were performed in the United States between 1936 and the mid-1950s (see *Last Resort,* p. 2).
35. Physicians and psychologists who worked at both Sheppard and Chestnut Lodge include Marvin Adland, Grace Baker, Mabel Blake Cohen, Robert Cohen, Robert Gibson, Alexander Halperin, Robert Kvarnes, Ping-Nie Pao, Margaret Rioch, Clarence Schulz, Harold Searles, and Helm Stierlin.
36. Kehne interview; Bullard oral history interview, p. 35 (APA).
37. Bullard oral history interview, pp. 35–36 (APA).
38. Ibid., p. 21. Even as late as 1954, the Bullards declined proposals for a hospital brochure and continued to furnish information to inquirers by personal letter.
39. In "Women Who Lead," Ann Silver perceptively discusses Frieda's collaborative style in the light of historical and cultural changes in gender roles.
40. Alfred H. Stanton, remarks at the Chestnut Lodge Symposium, October 8, 1982; Cooperman interview.
41. Bullard's lack of competitiveness with his staff contrasted sharply with the Menninger brothers, both of whom felt threatened by the possibility that the distinguished refugees they had hired might eventually outshine them (see Friedman, esp. chaps. 5 and 9).
42. Dexter M. Bullard, "Chestnut Lodge—History and Philosophy," presented at the 1st annual Chestnut Lodge Symposium, March 2, 1955; Noble, "Early Days at the Lodge"; Rioch, "Dexter Bullard, Sr. and Chestnut Lodge," p. 2; Adland interview.
43. Bullard oral history interview with Robert Butler, 1964, interview number 5, p. 6 (APA); Bullard oral history interview with Jeanine Jeffs, May 22, 1975, p. 20 (CLA).
44. Interview with Anne Bullard. Many of the medical staff would disagree with Anne's view that the Lodge "never became a business." The Menningers' status as "the Kennedys of psychiatry" is from Friedman, p. xi; "factory" from p. 202.
45. Burnham and Dyrud interviews; Sylvia Hoff interview with Otto Will, December 28, 1978.
46. Bloch interview.
47. Ann Silver interview with Anne Bullard, March 26, 1986.
48. Sylvia Hoff interview with I. Rosenfeld, December 2, 1978; Ann Silver interview with Anne Bullard; Schwartz interview.
49. Löwenthal, p. 30. Frieda was extremely grateful to Dexter for helping her to buy the Santa Fe house, with "a simply gorgeous view of the city, the valley, and the mountains." She paid $6,000 in 1941, the only major purchase she made in her twenty-two years in the United States. Explaining to Dexter why she had no sav-

ings and needed a loan, Frieda referred matter-of-factly to supporting Gertrud Jacob and "maintaining 11 people in Europe, as well as some others whom I help out" (FFR to DMB, August 1941, CLA).

50. FFR to DMB and AWB, August 4, 1944, August 12, 1945 (CLA).
51. Ibid., August 12, 1945 (CLA).
52. Ibid.
53. FFR to DMB, August 10, 1946 (CLA).
54. Ibid.
55. Ibid., July 19, 1946 (CLA).
56. Ibid., August 13, 1948 (CLA).
57. Weininger, "Chestnut Lodge—The Early Years," in Silver, pp. 495–512; Weininger remembrance of Frieda (n.d.), p. 2 (CLA).
58. Will interview.
59. Julia Waddell, "The Evolution of Nursing Care at Chestnut Lodge," presented at the 1st annual Chestnut Lodge Symposium, March 2, 1955 (CLA).
60. Ibid.; Ursell interview; Stanton and Schwartz, p. 287.
61. Friedman, p. 75.
62. Stanton and Schwartz, pp. 280–281 (emphasis in original).
63. Ibid., p. 52.
64. "Chestnut Lodge Sanitarium—Conditions of Service and Welfare," n.d. (CLA).
65. Ursell interview; Robert A. Cohen, "Remarks at Dexter Bullard's Seventieth Birthday Celebration," Washington School of Psychiatry, October 4, 1968.
66. Langs and Searles, p. 89; Pressman, p. 245; Schwartz, "Patient Demands in a Mental Hospital Context," p. 253; MacKenzie, pp. 144, 183.
67. Ursell interveiw.
68. "Policy and Procedures Relative to the Dining Rooms," versions of May 1950 and October 1957 (CLA).
69. "Information for Relatives," n.d.; "Policy and Procedure on Patient Visitors," January 1950 (CLA).
70. Bullard oral history interview, p. 26 (APA).
71. Mabel Peterson oral recollections; Stanton and Schwartz, p. 74.
72. Stanton and Schwartz, pp. 172, 199.
73. Foudraine, "On Psychotherapeutic Technique with Chronic Schizophrenic Patients," staff conference, February 3, 1965, p. 17 of typed transcript; Adland, "Problems of Administrative Psychotherapy in Mental Hospitals"; Cohen, "The Hospital as a Therapeutic Instrument"; Cooperman, "Some Observations Regarding Psychoanalytic Psychotherapy in a Hospital Setting," p. 23; Stierlin, "Individual Therapy of Schizophrenic Patients and Hospital Structure," p. 340.
74. Stierlin, "Individual Therapy," p. 338; "Techniques of Psychotherapy in a Small Hospital," p. 102.
75. Stanton and Schwartz, p. 147; Schulz interview.
76. Schulz interview.
77. Cohen interview.
78. Searles interview; DMB, "Chestnut Lodge," talk presented to the Ontario Psychiatric Association, February 2, 1968; Burnham and Kehne interviews.
79. Miscellaneous scripts and photographs from follies and skits (CLA).
80. Noble and Burnham; Lidz and Burnham interviews.
81. Kolb oral history interview (OHC); Cohen, "Notes on the Life and Work of Frieda Fromm-Reichmann," p. 94; Arieti, p. 86.

82. Crowley, "Frieda Fromm-Reichmann: Recollections of a Student," p. 106; Crowley Biographical Statement, January 3, 1983, typed draft of a talk for an unknown audience, p. 5 (CLA).
83. Cohen, Liebenberg, Eckardt interviews; Sylvia Hoff Collins interview with Douglas Noble.
84. Noble interview; Weigert, "In Memoriam: Frieda Fromm-Reichmann, 1889–1957," p. 94; Silver and Freuer, pp. 25, 43; Hilgard, pp. 223–224, 226–227; Will, p. 132.
85. Dyrud, "The Early Frieda," p. 487; Dyrud and Spiegel interviews.
86. Fort, pp. 249–250; Schulz interview; Will, pp. 133–134.
87. Grimmer interview.
88. FFR, "Problems of Therapeutic Management in a Psychoanalytic Hospital," pp. 340–341.
89. Ibid., pp. 341-342.
90. Anne Bullard interview.
91. Dexter M. Bullard, "Chestnut Lodge," p. 6; Morse and Noble; John Fort, "Advantages of the Two Psychiatrist System in the Treatment of Hospitalized Psychiatric Patients," staff conference, February 10, 1965; Frederick Bram, "Still More Observations on Chestnut Lodge," staff conference, February 17, 1965 (CLA).
92. Staff conference, February 17, 1965; Schulz interview.
93. Dyrud and Rioch, pp. 22–23.
94. Like every other aspect of the hospital's "clinical research," these sessions are documented with verbatim notes (initially dictated by Frieda herself right afterward, and then for some months recorded during the hour by sociologist Morrie Schwartz, in CLA).
95. Notes of session of October 20, 1948 (CLA).
96. Notes of session of March 9, 1949 (CLA).
97. Schwartz interview.
98. Chace, pp. 122, 125, 128.
99. Will and Cohen, pp. 264, 281.
100. Stanton and Schwartz, pp. 38–39.
101. Schwartz interview.
102. This and all subsequent quoted statements from Wilcox interview.
103. This and all subsequent quoted statements from Mara Bowman Schwartz interview.
104. Grimmer interview.
105. Petratos, "Development," p. 59.
106. Sylvia Hoff interview with I. Rosenfeld; Rioch interview.
107. Szalita interview.
108. Ursell and Bloch interviews.
109. FFR to DMB, July 19, 1946 (CLA); Gunst, pp. 108-109.

Chapter 9. Joanne Greenberg

1. Oates, "Facts, Visions, Mysteries," p. 152.
2. This description is a reconstruction based on many sources: *Rose Garden,* Frieda's notes, the recollections of Lodge staff, and interviews with Greenberg.

3. Havens, *A Safe Place,* p. 26.
4. Laurice McAfee interview with Greenberg, June 1985, p. 3 of typed transcript (CLA). An edited version of some parts of this interview is published in Silver, *Psychoanalysis and Psychosis,* pp. 513–531.
5. FFR process notes, 1948 (CLA).
6. Minutes of staff conference, December 15, 1948, p. 3 of typed transcript (CLA).
7. Ibid., p. 7.
8. McAfee interview with Greenberg, p. 11.
9. John Huston's brilliant 1948 documentary, *Let There Be Light,* filmed at one of the army hospitals set up to deal with psychiatric casualties from the war, testifies to the toll that two-minute diagnoses and one-session treatments can take on young psychiatrists. Otto Will said that he had personally interviewed and classified more than 4,000 patients as a navy psychiatrist "but not spent more than a few minutes with any of them" (in Silver, p. 131).
10. Staff conference, pp. 1, 7.
11. McAfee interview with Greenberg, p. 70. Today most analysts are shocked by papers like Darlene Ehrenberg's "Playfulness in the Psychoanalytic Relationship," but that's all Frieda ever did.
12. Staff conference, p. 8.
13. Goffman; see also, Stanton and Schwartz, *The Mental Hospital,* chap. 10; Caudill, Redlich, Gilmon, and Brody; Braginsky, Braginsky, and Ring; Price and Denner; and Perrucci.
14. McAfee interview with Greenberg, p. 53.
15. Staff conference, p. 5.
16. Ibid., p. 6.
17. McAfee interview with Greenberg, p. 56.
18. "An extremely interesting patient," from staff conference, p. 11; other quoted statements from Margaret J. Rioch, Rorschach Test report, October 5, 1948, pp. 1–2 (CLA). Rioch's conclusion echoed that of every other evaluator, although each did concur with the diagnosis of schizophrenia. Hilde Bruch, for example, concluded her consultation report by saying, "There is every reason to expect that this girl will recover and eventually return home" (p. 2). An earlier report by Richard Frank, the psychoanalyst Greenberg had seen in outpatient treatment before her admission to the Lodge, concluded similarly: "Because of the resources still available in this girl, I consider the prognosis to be favorable" (Abstract, n.d., p. 3). These are not typical evaluations of a schizophrenic patient.
19. Bloch interview. Rosenhan's study, now familiar to every introductory psychology student, featured normal research assistants who faked their way into mental hospitals; only patients were reliably able to detect the identity of the "pseudopatients." See Rosenhan.
20. Staff conference, p. 10.
21. Minutes of staff meetings, November 22, 1950, April 8, 1953; FFR lecture at Ypsilanti Psychiatric Institute, December 1956, later published under the title "Frieda Fromm-Reichmann Discusses the 'Rose Garden' Case" (1982). Alberta Szalita, who had seen Joanne in a series of strikingly unsuccessful sessions during Frieda's vacation, was far less taken with Greenberg's creativity. She insisted to colleagues that Irian wasn't really a language, just "a poor set-up of some words that were similar to Armenian" that Greenberg had put together from having had Armenian friends. Szalita seemed irritated that Frieda ignored the fact

that Joanne translated the same words differently on different days and showed other inconsistencies in her use of this so-called language (minutes of staff meetings; Szalita interview).

22. Minutes of staff conference, April 8, 1953.
23. FFR to JG, July 7, 1953 (BU).
24. Joanne Greenberg, "Metaphor and the Treatment of Schizophrenia," videotaped talk to the Columbia Study Group, Columbia, MD, June 1986.
25. "Psychotherapy of Schizophrenia" (1954), SP, pp. 195–197.
26. Silver and Freuer, p. 35.
27. "Frieda Fromm-Reichmann Discusses the 'Rose Garden' Case." Some details of wording in my quotations are altered from the published version of this talk (which Hilde Bruch edited years later) to make them more consistent with the tape recording.
28. I first heard the phrase "analytic couple" in a talk by Owen Renik on countertransference enactment (Psychoanalytic Society of New England, East, Cambridge, MA, February 6, 1993). I don't know if it has an origin other than this.
29. Contemporary psychoanalysis has its own share of famous couples—Searles and Mrs. Douglas, Kohut and Mr. Z., Sampson/Weiss and Mrs. C.—and we still understand its practices primarily through this lens.

CHAPTER 10. THE UNREDEEMED

1. Editorial in *The Times* (London), April 5, 1877, in Scull, *Museums of Madness*.
2. In 1940, the total population of patients in state institutions across the United States was 410,000. By 1946, it was 446,000; by 1950, 512,000; and by 1955, 559,000. In 1947, each attendant in a state hospital was responsible for 12 to 30 patients; each nurse, 176 patients; and each psychiatrist, 250 to 500 patients. The idea of individual psychotherapy under such conditions seemed preposterous. The most detailed account of this history is Grob, *From Asylum to Community;* see also Pressman.
3. Grob, *From Asylum to Community,* pp. 71–76; Pressman, pp. 149–162. Mike Gorman, a journalist and lobbyist for the mentally ill, provocatively titled his call for better treatment *Every Other Bed.*
4. Pressman, p. 10.
5. Kraepelin, pp. 60–63, 86. Many of the founders of alternative medical systems were appalled by such "heroic treatments." Thus, in some respects, the advocates of "moral treatment" and psychotherapy were guided by similar concerns as homeopaths, chiropractors, and Christian Scientists (see Gevitz).
6. All details on somatic treatments from Pressman; Grob, *Mental Illness and American Society,* pp. 292-308; Valenstein, *Great and Desperate Cures;* and Braslow.
7. This was also a popular method in Britain. The well-known psychoanalyst Harry Guntrip had all his top teeth removed by an advocate of focal infection theory, and he suffered from the effects for the rest of his life (see Hughes, pp. 109–110).
8. The shock treatments of the twentieth century were updated versions of older ways of getting patients to "snap out of it"—hidden trapdoors in corridors that plunged the unsuspecting person into a cold bath, for example, and gyrating

chairs and swings that rotated patients at speeds up to 100 rpm (see Kraepelin, pp. 87–89; Scull, "The Domestication of Madness").

9. Kolb and Vogel.

10. Brill to William Alanson White, October 31, 1936, cited in Grob, *Mental Illness and American Society,* p. 298.

11. Casamajor, p. 607; Rinkel and Himwich, p. xxvi.

12. Jessner and Ryan, pp. 46, 56.

13. Kris, p. 80; Malzberg, p. 130.

14. Freeman and Watts, "Some Observations on Obsessive Tendencies Following Interruption of the Frontal Association Pathways," paper presented to the New York Neurological Society (later published in the *Journal of Nervous and Mental Disease*); quotation from Freeman's response to a question during the subsequent discussion (p. 233). According to Pressman, fees could run as high as $600 per operation (calculated in 1940s dollars), and a physician could do a number of lobotomies in a single day, further augmenting his profits.

15. By the late 1950s, medication replaced lobotomy as the major somatic treatment for mental illness, but the procedure continued under other names and is still used. All biographical details about Freeman from Valenstein and Pressman.

16. Grob, *From Asylum to Community,* pp. 34–35; Pressman, pp. 207, 365–367; Bruch oral history (APA).

17. "Clay rejected by the potters," from Pressman, p. 126. As noted in the Prologue, Miss N.'s case is heavily documented, with process notes from several therapists, verbatim transcripts of lengthy case conferences, and many tape recordings (all in CLA). Every quoted statement in what follows is taken directly from written or taped sources. All other information is from case conferences (disguised to protect confidentiality).

18. Minutes of staff conferences, August 2, 1943, October 28, 1959 (CLA).

19. In the current version of the *Diagnostic and Statistical Manual of Mental Disorders* (DSM-IV), the term *hebephrenia* is no longer used. The diagnosis for a patient like Miss N. is "schizophrenia, disorganized type." Only the label is different; the symptoms used to make the diagnosis are essentially unchanged from the 1930s.

20. Group therapy sessions of October 25, 27, 1948 (CLA).

21. Ibid., March 14, 16, 23, 1949 (CLA).

22. Donald Burnham interview with Dexter Bullard on the psychotherapy of schizophrenic patients, January 31, 1957, pp. 7–8 of typed draft (CLA).

23. Minutes of staff conference, March 22, 1950 (CLA). All subsequent details in this section from this and later cited staff conferences.

24. Ibid., February 23, 1953 (CLA).

25. Ibid., February 25, 1953, and Clinical Evaluation Committee, February 27, 1953 (CLA).

26. FFR process notes, May 22, 1953 (CLA). All quoted statements in this section from these notes and above-cited case conferences.

27. Ibid., November 16, 1953 (CLA).

28. Ibid., December 7, 1953 (CLA).

29. In certain respects, Miss N.'s strikingly different styles of action in therapy versus on the ward fit the pattern Burnham describes in "The Special-Problem Patient."

30. Minutes of staff conference, September 22, 1954 (CLA).

31. FFR process notes, May 22, 1953 (CLA).

32. Unlike most other tape-recorded material at the Lodge, these sessions were never typed up, probably because they were so filled with Miss N.'s gibberish that it would be practically impossible to transcribe them. All quoted statements in the section that follows are from my verbatim notes.

33. Searles's recordings of many years of therapy with the patient he calls "Mrs. Douglas" are among the few other examples of such an archive.

34. NT, session of January 12, 1954.

35. Ibid., January 19, 1954.

36. Ibid., January 22, October 4, November 29, 1954.

37. Ibid., November 22, 1954.

38. Ibid., January 22, 1954.

39. Ibid., September 3, 1954.

40. DLB to author, May 20, 1990.

41. NT, October 25, 1954.

42. Ibid., February 7, 1955.

43. Minutes of staff conference, October 28, 1959 (CLA).

44. FFR process notes, June 3, 1953 (CLA).

45. Ibid., February 6, 1953 (CLA).

46. Minutes of the Clinical Evaluation Committee, June 1, 1956 (CLA).

47. The memorandum Bullard sent to Frieda detailing these procedures—written, stilted, and formal—was nothing like their usual friendly exchanges. The whole situation of Mr. R.'s treatment seemed to create uncharacteristic tension in everyone.

48. FFR process notes, January 7, 1957 (CLA). I am deeply grateful to Don Burnham for providing me with a set of transcripts of Frieda's sessions with Mr. R. as well as the actual tapes of most of these sessions. For ease of reference, I have taken quoted statements in the following section from the typed transcripts.

49. Ibid., January 9, 11, 1957 (CLA).

50. Ibid., January 1, 1957; RT, sessions of January (CLA).

51. RT, January 22, 1957 (CLA); Burnham notes on January–February sessions, February 8, 1957 (courtesy of Don Burnham).

52. Donald L. Burnham, "Interview with Dr. Fromm-Reichmann Regarding Basic Assumptions About Schizophrenia and Psychotherapy," February 12, 1957 (CLA).

53. RT, session of February 4, 1957.

54. FFR process notes and RT, February 7, 1957.

55. FFR process notes, February 8, 1957 (CLA).

56. Minutes of staff conference, February 25, 1957 (CLA).

57. Peter Kramer wistfully reflects on these ironies in "Status for Psychiatrists Is Really Getting Inside a Head."

58. Schulz interview. Many other Lodge staff recall having this same view.

59. In a paper Lodge colleagues published a decade later, these realistic aspects of paranoia are systematically analyzed (see Artiss and Bullard).

CHAPTER 11. THE LUXURY OF GUILT

1. Rabbi Nachman of Bratzlav, in Buber, *The Tales of Rabbi Nachman*.
2. Alfred Friendly, "Epidemics Are Linked to Hysteria," *Washington Post,* January 6, 1970; Ursell interview.
3. Martin, pp. 1188–1189.
4. Foudraine, pp. 218, 301, 393.
5. Schwartz and Stanton, "A Social-Psychological Study of Incontinence," p. 399.
6. Stanton and Schwartz, *The Mental Hospital,* pp. 9, 12, 14, 19, 30.
7. Stanton and Schwartz's project was supported by grant MH51 from the newly created National Institute of Mental Health, supplemented by funds from the Chestnut Lodge Research Institute. The findings from the four-year study were published in their book and in a series of articles in psychiatry journals (see the Bibliography for complete references). Historian Nathan Hale, emphasizing the broad influence Stanton and Schwartz's work had on the profession, notes that theirs was one of the books most often recommended to psychiatric residents (see Hale, *The Rise and Crisis of Psychoanalysis,* p. 253).
8. Stanton and Schwartz, "The Management of a Type of Institutional Participation in Mental Illness."
9. Schwartz and Stanton, "A Social-Psychological Study of Incontinence."
10. Stanton and Schwartz, *The Mental Hospital,* p. 394.
11. Minutes of staff conference, August 30, 1950 (CLA).
12. As Stanton and Schwartz noted in their book (p. 39), whenever a structural problem arose in the institution, the senior staff would "discover some evidence of a 'personal problem,' 'transference problem,' or some other psychiatric difficulty . . . and avoid any action in the matter by suggesting or implying that more work was needed in the staff member's personal analysis."
13. Minutes of staff conference, September 8, 1950 (CLA).
14. Ibid., September 22, 1950 (CLA).
15. Ibid., pp. 13–14.
16. Summary of staff conference, November 24, 1950, p. 3 (CLA). On occasion, these meetings were summarized by a member of the clerical staff rather than tape-recorded. At Chestnut Lodge, even typists were sophisticated enough about psychoanalytic theory to take detailed notes of complex staff discussions. Frieda gave informal talks in her backyard to the nonmedical staff to increase their knowledge of key terms and concepts.
17. Ibid., p. 5.
18. Abstract of staff conference, December 8, 1950 (CLA).
19. Minutes and abstract of staff conference, March 23, 1951 (CLA).
20. The institute was incorporated in the state of Maryland on December 30, 1947, but its activities weren't significant until the mid-1950s.
21. Proposal to the Ford Foundation from the Chestnut Lodge Research Institute, Inc., 1955, pp. 1–4 (CLA).
22. Draft material from Stanton and Schwartz, titled "Formalities," n.d., probably early 1950s (CLA).
23. Adland interview.
24. Historian Nathan Hale notes the ambitiousness of these aims: "The goal of treatment at Chestnut Lodge was no less than radical recovery, an adjustment so secure that the patient was less likely to break down than he had been before he first

became ill. This was a stringent criterion and represented psychoanalytic ambition at its most impressive" (Hale, *The Rise and Crisis of Psychoanalysis,* p. 268).

25. Cooperman interview; George Darr, minutes of staff conference, September 22, 1950 (CLA).

26. Minutes of staff conference, June 27, 1955 (CLA).

27. Miscellaneous budget records; Lew Garrison Coit to James Parker Nolan, August 28, 1958 (CLA).

28. Edith Weigert oral history interview, June 13, 1973, p. 11 of typed transcript (archives of the Washington Psychoanalytic Society and Institute). Historians have disputed Freud's claim that his early works were ignored by the medical establishment (see, for example, Decker). The conflictual dynamics of the psychoanalytic movement are insightfully analyzed by Clara Thompson, "A Study of the Emotional Climate of Psychoanalytic Institutes," and Marianne Horney Eckardt, "Organizational Schisms in American Psychoanalysis."

29. Oberndorf, p. 234. Freud's own definition was broad and flexible, and people like Frieda always cited it as their authority: "Psychoanalysis is simply the study of processes of which we are unaware, of what for the sake of brevity we call the unconscious, by the free association technique of analyzing observable phenomena of transference and resistance" (ibid., p. 242).

30. "Trauma in the analytic world" from Balint, p. 152; "zeal to cure" from Bergmann, p. 154; "psychotic" and "delusional" from Ernest Jones, p. 176; "riffraff" from Haynal, *Controversies in Psychoanalytic Method,* p. 32. On Frieda's introduction of Ferenczi's ideas into the Washington psychoanalytic community, see Silver, "Countertransference, Ferenczi, and Washington, D.C."

31. Sara A. Bonnett, notes from meeting of September 26, 1951, Committee on Sponsoring New Groups (archives of the New York Psychoanalytic Institute).

32. Minutes of the Committee to Study Unauthorized Training, 1953; Report of the Subcommittee on Unaccredited Groups; Annual Report of the President of the New York Psychoanalytic Institute, April 21, 1953. These concerns had first arisen when émigré analysts had fled Nazi-occupied Europe. Since Freud adamantly supported the training of nonphysician analysts, there was panic in New York when it seemed as if its ranks were about to be diluted by an influx of "lay analysts." A memo from the Emergency Committee on Relief and Immigration, a body organized by the APA to try to cope with such problems, cautiously concluded that "if this incoming group is handled tactfully and generously, and if they can be convinced of the necessity of not continuing to train other laymen . . . American psychoanalysis has nothing to fear" (Emergency Committee report, June 1938).

33. The New York Psychoanalytic Society seemed obsessed throughout the 1940s with its lay members' power. The minutes of its December 18, 1945 meeting, for example, stress "the dangers of a possible coup by the lay members resulting in their eventual control of the Institute and its educational policies."

34. Robert P. Knight, secretary, American Psychoanalytic Association, to the New York Psychoanalytic Institute, July 28, 1944; Grotjahn cited in Burston, p. 19; Deutsch, p. 208.

35. Bullard oral history interview with Robert Butler, pp. 45–46 (CLA).

36. Adland and Searles interviews; Cohen, "Notes on the Life and Work of Frieda Fromm-Reichmann," p. 95. Yet the definition of *heresy* was clearly relative. As

historian Nathan Hale notes, Heinz Hartmann's quite striking revisions of classical theory were called "modifications," not "deviations," because he had been personally analyzed by Freud and thus considered part of the mainstream (Hale, *The Rise and Crisis of Psychoanalysis*, p. 235).

37. Eissler, pp. 314–317.
38. Cohen, "Notes on the Life and Work," p. 95.
39. Oral history interview with Jenny Waelder-Hall, December 8, 1973, p. 29 of typed transcript (archives of the Washington Psychoanalytic Society and Institute).
40. Szalita, "Acceptance Speech on the Occasion of Receiving the Frieda Fromm-Reichmann Award," p. 13; Hilde Bruch oral history interview, p. 75 of typed transcript (APA); Bruch, "Personal Reminiscences of Frieda Fromm-Reichmann," p. 104.
41. Gunst, "Memoirs," p. 112; Moulton, cited in Petratos, "Development," p. 344.
42. Schulz interview. Despite their differing degrees of analytic purity, Kubie and Frieda were close colleagues. At a symposium where he was the discussant of one of her papers, he commented: "Some meetings are both an artistic and a scientific pleasure. Such are meetings where Dr. Fromm-Reichmann is going to speak. I go to hear her with an expectation which I have only when I am to hear one other person in our field, namely Anna Freud; because their papers are always models of clarity and simplicity, with their roots firmly based in clinical data, and always with a theoretical presentation which grows out of that clinical data in a way that fills me with both aesthetic and scientific satisfaction" (quoted in Cohen, "Notes on the Life and Work," p. 96).
43. "Psychoanalytic and General Dynamic Conceptions of Theory and of Therapy: Differences and Similarities" (1954), p. 717.
44. McLaughlin, "Why Do Schools of Thought Fail?" pp. 123, 125. McLaughlin interestingly notes that Fromm was attacked (within Marxism) on precisely the same grounds as Frieda was. He cites a letter from Fromm's former colleagues in Frankfurt, Adorno and Horkheimer, in which they presented him as "sentimental," a dismissal remarkably similar to Eissler's of Frieda (see McLaughlin, "Origin Myths in the Social Sciences," p. 126).
45. Introductory remarks by Marianne Horney Eckardt to a reprint of Fromm's 1955 paper, "Remarks on the Problem of Free Association," in Stern et al., pp. 126 127.
46. Breuer, p. 36.
47. Eckardt, p. 158.
48. Thompson, "The Emotional Climate," pp. 56–67.
49. Grosskurth, p. 285.
50. Bruch to Anna Jacobson, November 21, 1980 (Bruch papers, Baylor University School of Medicine).
51. AJF, August 9, 1992; Wilcox and Adland interviews.
52. In 1973, at the age of eighty-one, Grete died very suddenly in London during one of her summer research trips, her book unfinished. Anna saw to it that she was buried in Jerusalem, as was her wish. Except for the painful years when Anna was nursing Hans, who suffered from the depression and paranoia caused by his increasingly severe Parkinson's disease, she lived contentedly with Alisa and her family on the kibbutz, surrounded by animals and grandchildren. Anna kept up a lively correspondence with friends and relatives all over the world—including

those she had met through Frieda, like Hilde Bruch and Joanne Greenberg—and died peacefully in 1994, at the age of ninety-six.

53. All descriptions of patients in this section from records in Lodge files (with identities disguised).

54. Schulz's total sample consisted of the 302 patients admitted to the Lodge for the first time during the period July 31, 1948, to June 30, 1958. (The only patients he eliminated were temporary emergency admissions and custodial geriatric cases.) Half the sample had previously been hospitalized elsewhere for at least six months, 18 percent of these for more than two years (one patient had been in a state hospital continuously for thirty years). Age at admission ranged from sixteen to sixty-nine, with 70 percent aged twenty to forty. Women composed 57 percent of the sample. Diagnoses varied across the spectrum of disorders warranting hospitalization, with 63 percent diagnosed as schizophrenic. Of the total sample of 302, 89 percent (268 patients) provided follow-up responses (one-third of the nonresponders had Lodge stays of less than one month). This extremely high response rate is itself an indication of patients' strong attachment to the Lodge. Of the 268 respondents, 226 sent narratives detailed enough to form the basis for my analysis. For a full report of his findings, see Schulz, "A Follow-Up Report on Admissions to Chestnut Lodge."

55. One might hypothesize that patients who sent positive evaluations would have been admitted with less severe diagnoses (and would thus have been more amenable to psychotherapy), but a detailed analysis demonstrated that this was not the case. Of the 226 patients who sent narrative responses, there were 98 whose individual diagnoses could be reliably identified. I categorized these diagnoses (using standard DSM criteria) on a 5-point scale as follows: 1 (less severe neuroses), 2 (severe neuroses), 3 (less severe personality disorders), 4 (severe personality disorders), and 5 (psychoses). The distribution of diagnoses for this subgroup of 98 was typical of Lodge patients in the 1940s and 1950s and closely matches Schulz's results for the entire sample of 302: 8 percent less severe neurotic, 14 percent severe neurotic, 2 percent less severe personality disorder, 13 percent severe personality disorder, 63 percent psychotic. To assess the relation between the severity of a patient's diagnosis and the nature of his or her evaluation of Chestnut Lodge, narrative responses were rated (by an independent judge) on a 5-point scale, where 1 = extremely negative evaluation, 3 = neutral evaluation, and 5 = extremely positive evaluation. Responses were highly skewed toward the positive end of the distribution, with 41 percent rated "extremely positive" and only 7 percent rated "extremely negative" (58 percent of the responses were rated either 4 or 5). A correlational analysis comparing severity of diagnosis with degree of positive evaluation revealed no relationship ($r^2 = .01$). Thus, of the subset of patients sending responses to the follow-up study for whom diagnoses could be determined (close to half the total group), most were extremely positive about Chestnut Lodge even though three-quarters of them had been very seriously disturbed during their hospitalization. I thank Jean Talbot for her careful assistance in conducting these analyses.

56. #115. These responses were alphabetized by the patient's last name and then numbered sequentially; the originals can be found (unalphabetized) in CLA.

57. #144, pp. 1–2.

58. #179, pp. 1–2.

59. #204, pp. 3–4.

60. #17, p. 2.
61. #168, p. 2.
62. #199, p. 3.
63. #165. For a perceptive account of a patient's experience at the Lodge from the perspective of his wife and family, see Naylor's (slightly fictionalized) *Crazy Love.*
64. Cooperman interview.

Chapter 12. Public Acclaim

1. "I Can't Sing, So I Paint! Says Ultra Realistic Artist; Art Is Not Photography—It Is Expression of Inner Life!: Miss O'Keeffe Explains Subjective Aspect of Her Work," *New York Sun,* December 5, 1922, p. 22.
2. Dexter Bullard, "At Chestnut Lodge," *WAW Newsletter,* Summer 1969, p. 8; Weigart, "In Memoriam," p. 94; Rosenfeld interview.
3. Buber, *Tales of the Hasidim,* pp. v, ix.
4. P, pp. 67–68.
5. Frieda herself thought the book had "special flavor as a human medical document" because of its focus on the relationship between therapist and patient, the satisfactions of working with psychotics, and above all, in its emphasis on the patient's "inherent motivation toward health." But when her editors decided to include endorsements on the cover from two better-known psychiatrists (Thomas French and Karl Menninger) in an effort to appeal to a broader audience, she was outraged by the "condescension this implied." She sent a telegram and a letter from Santa Fe and wired Bullard and other friends in the East—all to no avail. Her editors were convinced the book would sell to a general audience and thought the endorsements would help (FFR to Mary Alexander, University of Chicago Press, August 26, 1950; Paul Corbett, Sales Manager, to FFR, August 30, 1950, UCP). Incredibly, when asked by the publicity department for names of potential reviewers, Frieda listed Erich, saying that "he would be especially well qualified, since he is a sociologist and a psychoanalyst. He is also quoted repeatedly in the book." In this context, she apparently thought of him simply as a knowledgeable colleague, not her former husband (FFR to University of Chicago Press, August 24, 1950, UCP). She also volunteered Klara (then eighty-three years old) to do a German translation.
6. Victor W. Eisenstein, *Psychoanalytic Quarterly,* 1951, *20,* 300–303; O. H. Mowrer, *Psychological Bulletin,* 1951, *48,* 281–282; Kalman Selig, *International Journal of Group Psychotherapy,* 1951, *1,* 185; Seward Hiltner, *Pastoral Psychology,* 1951, *1,* 64–65; *Digest of Neurology and Psychiatry,* November 1950, 590; Wendell Muncie, *Quarterly Review of Biology,* September 1952; *Association for Family Living,* May 1951; *Pulpit Digest,* July 1951; Joseph Zinkin, *Psychoanalytic Review,* 1953, *40,* 378–380; William V. Silverberg, *Psychiatry,* 1951, *14,* 108–111; Kurt Goldstein, *American Journal of Psychotherapy,* October 1952, 782–786; Edith Weigert, *Washington Post,* December 10, 1950.
7. *Psychiatric Quarterly,* 1950, *24,* 834–836; Herbert C. Modlin, *Bulletin of the Menninger Clinic,* 1951, *15,* 195; Harold L. Raush and Allen T. Dittmann, *Journal of General Psychology,* 1952, *47,* 245–249; Stanley G. Estes, *Journal of Abnormal and Social Psychology,* 1951, *46,* 611–612.
8. The other members of the research group were Bob and Mabel Cohen, Edith

Weigert, and Grace Baker. They met at the Cohens' home for three or four hours every other Saturday during 1952 and 1953. Their monograph, "An Intensive Study of Twelve Cases of Manic Depressive Psychosis," was published in *Psychiatry* in 1954. An earlier paper by Frieda, "Intensive Psychotherapy of Manic-Depressives" (1949), also illustrates her approach to this issue.

9. "An Intensive Study," p. 230; see also Dooley.
10. "An Intensive Study" (1954), pp. 245, 249–251.
11. P, p. 87; "Intensive Psychotherapy of Manic-Depressives," p. 224; "An Intensive Study," p. 265.
12. "An Intensive Study," p. 270; Roger A. Mattson, "The Contributions of Frieda Fromm-Reichmann," paper presented at the Mayo Clinic, April 1969, p. 9 of typed draft (CLA).
13. "Some Aspects of Psychoanalytic Psychotherapy with Schizophrenics" (1952).
14. Ibid., pp. 179–180, 184.
15. Ibid., pp. 188–189.
16. "Changes in Psychoanalytic Concepts During the Last Ten Years," p. 16 of typed draft (CLA).
17. "Psychotherapy of Schizophrenia," pp. 196–197.
18. Chessick, p. 252.
19. "Loneliness," p. 306 of version reprinted in *Contemporary Psychoanalysis.* These links between Frieda and Klein are noted by Elizabeth Hegeman, "The Paradox of Loneliness: A Comment on Fromm-Reichmann's 'Loneliness,'" Ibid., pp. 364–367, and Alberta B. Szalita, "Some Thoughts on Dr. Fromm-Reichmann's Paper 'On loneliness,'" Chestnut Lodge Symposium, 1985. Melanie Klein's paper, "On the Sense of Loneliness," is in her collection *Our Adult World.*
20. "Loneliness," pp. 313, 316, 317.
21. Frieda argued that many of the phenomena categorized as "anxiety" (e.g., separation anxiety) were better described as loneliness or the fear of it. She saw psychiatrists as being so overwhelmingly focused on anxiety as to neglect the systematic study of other important emotional states, including grief, hope, pain, and envy, as well as the loneliness to which her own attention was drawn.
22. Ibid., p. 329; Allan T. Dittmann, review of *Psychoanalysis and Psychotherapy: Selected Papers of Frieda Fromm-Reichmann, Contemporary Psychology,* 1960, 366–367.
23. Bullard oral history interview by Robert Butler, 1963–64, interview 3 (July 29, 1964), p. 27 (APA).
24. FFR to Social Research Fund (later the Foundation's Fund for Research in Psychiatry), March 30, 1953 (CLA).
25. Minutes of session of August 27, 1952 (CLA).
26. Ann-Louise S. Silver, "A History of Intuition and Empathy: A Preliminary Report," paper presented to the American Academy of Psychoanalysis, January 22, 1988.
27. Szalita-Pemow, "The 'Intuitive Process' and Its Relation to Work with Schizophrenics," p. 7.
28. Ibid., pp. 9, 17.
29. "Clinical Significance of Intuitive Processes of the Psychoanalyst," pp. 85–86.
30. Silver, "A History of Intuition and Empathy," pp. 8–10.

31. Minutes of staff conference, October 30, 1953 (CLA).

32. DLB to author, January 30, 1996.

33. Warner, "The History of Science and the Sciences of Medicine," p. 191.

34. P, p. 30.

35. "Clinical Significance of the Intuitive Processes of the Psychoanalyst," pp. 82–84.

36. Frieda's original notes (dictated a day after the session) are themselves retrospective constructions, with their own inherent "inaccuracies." Statements and actions Frieda attributes to Mrs. E. in that account—for example, the statement "you are afraid of me when I am unpacked," or the patient's helping with the sheets—have to be seen as Frieda's extrapolations rather than things the patient "actually" did or didn't do. Each of Frieda's accounts reflected her understanding at that particular time; the fact that they became more complex and confusing illustrates the difficulty of describing something that was, in essence, too subtle to name. It is also possible that Frieda attributed actions or statements to the patient that she later decided were intuitions of hers.

37. Buber, *On Judaism*, p. 161. On the connections between Sullivan's "interpersonal theory" and Klein and Fairbairn's "object relations," see Guntrip.

38. For a report of the first year of the Macy group's meetings, which includes Frieda's specific comments linking animal communication to her work with psychotic patients, see Schaffner.

39. The later collaboration between psychiatrist Joseph Berke and patient Mary Barnes, published in 1971 as *Mary Barnes: Two Accounts of a Journey Through Madness,* comes closest to this. Ferenczi had also asked one of his patients to write an autobiography so he could present "the perspective of the patient" (see Rachman).

40. Greenberg interview.

41. JG to FFR, March 8, 1957 (BU).

42. "Frieda Fromm-Reichmann Discusses the 'Rose Garden' Case," p. 136.

43. FFR to KG, October 10, 1955 (Kurt Goldstein Papers, Rare Book and Manuscript Library, Columbia University); "My Year's Fellowship at the Center for Advanced Study in the Behavioral Sciences," pp. 2, 5, 7.

44. "My Year's Fellowship," p. 9.

45. Bateson, pp. 98–99.

46. This research group later went on to do a long-term project titled "The Natural History of an Interview," involving researchers from all over the country in the most intensive analysis of nonverbal communication ever attempted. The project continued for another decade and trained many of the people who would go on to lead the field (including William Condon, Adam Kendon, and Albert Scheflen). See Leeds-Hurwitz, "Frieda Fromm-Reichmann and the Natural History of an Interview" (Introduction by Henry W. Brosin), in Silver, pp. 95–127. The classic article on the double bind written by Bateson and others, as well as later commentaries on this concept, are presented in Berger.

47. Marschak, pp. 306–307.

48. Leeds-Hurwitz, p. 106.

49. FFR to JG, September 23, 1955; JG to FFR, Fall 1955; FFR to JG, December 14, 1955, April 23, 1956; JG to FFR, May 15, 1956; FFR to JG, June 6, July 26, August 22, October 18, 1956 (CLA).

50. I have discussed these dynamics in the context of biographers' ethical responsibilities to their subjects in "The Ethics of Ambiguity: Feminists Writing Women's Lives."
51. Review of Riese (1953), p. 413.
52. Clark, pp. 288–289.

CHAPTER 13. PRIVATE DECLINE

1. Sigmund Freud, *The Interpretation of Dreams,* p. 525.
2. FFR to DMB, June 21, 1956; FFR to DLB, June 21, 1956 (CLA).
3. FFR to MLA, August 1, 1956. I am deeply grateful to Marvin Adland for making his correspondence with Frieda available to me.
4. Bowman and Rioch interviews; Marschak, pp. 305–306.
5. Ursell, Bowman, Anne Bullard, and Weinberg interviews.
6. MLA to FFR, November 21, 1955; FFR to MLA, November 30, 1955; MLA to FFR, March 19, 1956. Contemporary theories in cognitive neuropsychology argue for an information overload in some schizophrenic patients, who are unable to filter out perceptual noise from the environment that other people barely attend to. Mr. R. was clearly expressing his anger and need to withdraw into his own protective space by constantly wearing ear plugs, but this may have served some perceptual function too.
7. Because there were verbatim transcripts for these sessions as well as the tapes themselves, my quotations in the following section are from the transcripts (CLA).
8. All quoted statements in this section are from interviews with the people named.
9. However, Kubie had another side, given to extravagant self-promotion, and after carefully protecting his celebrity patients during his lifetime, he donated his voluminous correspondence to the Library of Congress. Since his death, the dozens of letters in which he names these individuals have been there for any researcher to discover.
10. FFR to Mara Bowman, March 1, 1957; FFR to Hilde Bruch, April 8, 1957; FFR to Jane Weinberg, April 14, 1957; Mabel Peterson to Mara Bowman, July 5, 1957; Sylvia Hoff interview with Anne Bullard; interviews with Will, Grimmer, Wolfgang Weigert, Weinberg; JG to FFR, April 25, 1957.
11. Interviews with Adland, Will, Weinberg, Schwartz, Kehne, Grimmer, Olinick, Rioch, Anne Bullard; DMB to JG, April 29, 1957; AJF, October 24, 1995; Gunst, "Memoirs"; Hilde Bruch oral history (APA); Medical Examiner's Certificate of Death, Maryland State Department of Health, number 04222.
12. Anne Bullard interview; oral recollections of Pumphrey Funeral Home workers; Records, Case No. 10514, Orphans' Court of Montgomery County, MD.
13. Sylvia Hoff, an early biographer of Frieda, says Gunst showed her some of these materials, then stored in her attic in Richmond. She subsequently refused access to any other researcher and would not even answer queries about what was there. In 1996, after I sent numerous letters to her lawyers pleading with them to take steps to preserve these materials, they were donated to the Library of Congress, where they will remain under seal until 2021.
14. Grimmer, Greenberg, Lidz, Weinberg interviews. Gunst probably justified these actions by telling herself they were what Frieda would have wanted. In the ad-

dendum to the original will, Frieda had written: "The executors of this will, the owners of Chestnut Lodge (Dr. Dexter M. and Mrs. Anne W. Bullard), my other personal friends in this country and abroad, and such faithful hired helpers (maids, secretaries) who had worked for me at the time of and prior to my death, should be either invited to ask for and/or be given pieces of my personal, non-monetary property which they and/or the executors deem to be useful or of sentimental value to them. The people to whom this refers are known to the executors with regard to their relationship with me." Frieda specifically excluded from this disposition the paintings she owned by Gertrud Jacob and "personal clothes, coats, lingerie and underwear, photos and manuscripts."

15. Case 10514 records; Anne Bullard interview. To make as much money as possible available to Grete and Anna, the Bullards exercised their right to buy back the shares of Chestnut Lodge stock that Frieda had acquired and sent the proceeds to her sisters in Israel. The following year, when Hilde Bruch went to see them, she brought Grete and Anna the few pieces of jewelry that had been found, saving them the customs duties that would have lowered their value.

16. Seamus Heaney, "The Singer of Tales: On Joseph Brodsky," *New York Times Book Review,* March 3, 1996, p. 31.

17. All quoted statements in this section from interviews with the people named.

18. DMB to several dozen friends and colleagues of Frieda's, September 1957 (CLA).

19. Weigert, "In Memoriam."

20. AT, pp. 3, 16.

21. Bowman and Searles interviews; Searles, "Psychoanalytic Therapy with Cancer Patients," p. 175.

22. Anne Bullard interview with Sylvia Hoff, January 24, 1979.

23. Masserman and Moreno, p. vii.

24. Editorial page, *Washington Post,* May 7, 1957; "Frieda Fromm-Reichmann," *Psychiatric Bulletin,* Summer, 1958, 8.

25. J. B. Miller, p. 85; Coles, pp. 181–182.

26. Farber, pp. 191–192; Trilling, et al., pp. 102–104; Will interview.

27. Memorabilia (CLA).

28. The book was published in the United States in 1959 by the University of Chicago Press and in the United Kingdom by Cambridge University Press. Chicago issued a paperback edition in 1974 (UCP). Quotations from reviews are taken from Edward M. L. Burchard, "New Ways to Mend the Mind of Man," *Saturday Review,* November 28, 1959; Eugene B. Brody, *Journal of Nervous and Mental Disease,* 1960, *131,* 454-455; *Social Service Speaks,* Newsletter of the National Association of Social Workers, December 1959–January 1960, p. 6; Joost A. M. Meerloo, *American Journal of Psychotherapy,* 1960, *14,* 610–611; Edward E. Harkavy, *Psychoanalytic Quarterly,* 1960, *29,* 249–251; Robert A. Harper, "Tribute to a Distinguished Neo-Freudian," *Journal of Individual Psychology,* 1959, *15,* 105–106; Roy R. Grinker, *Archives of General Psychiatry,* 1960, *2,* 132–133; Neville Parker, *Australian Journal of Psychology,* 1960, *12,* 144–145; Frank Hladky, Jr., *American Journal of Psychoanalysis,* 1961, *21,* 294–297; Lawrence C. Kolb, *American Journal of Psychiatry,* October 1974.

29. Schulz interview; DLB to author, March 12, 1996.

30. Moyers, p. 329.

Chapter 14. Rose Garden

1. Fullard.
2. Frieda is hardly the only scientist to suffer this fate. For an insightful analysis of Michael Faraday's elevation to the status of prophet, see Cantor.
3. As of 1995, translations were: Japanese (where the title was "I Never Promised You a Tea Garden"), 1970; Norwegian, 1971; Portuguese, Chinese, Hebrew, Swedish, Spanish, Danish, German (with the subtitle, "Account of a Healing"), Dutch, 1973; Finnish, 1974; Italian, 1978; Polish, 1994.
4. Monica Dickens, "Irresistible Horror" (a review of Greenberg's *Rites of Passage*), *Boston Sunday Globe,* June 11, 1972, B-18.
5. Early drafts of the jacket copy, however, did just that: "This is the inner world of a girl who has lost touch with reality. . . . It is a book that holds out hope for all those who feel they must escape from the brutality of their extraordinary lives. No rose garden is promised to Deborah, not a world like the golden one she has invented for herself. She is slowly brought back to the real world, one that is often harsh and challenging. Deborah is a courageous person, poetically conceived by the author who brought her to life, but Deborah might still be any one of us. . . . Read as a novel, *I Never Promised You a Rose Garden* is an adventure that pits a girl against a part of herself. Read as a deeply meaningful revelation, a voyage into the depths of the human soul, it is an experience that no one can afford to miss."
6. Reviewers are often dismissive of Oates for her incessant production of new material (as of 1998, she had published thirty novels, eighteen collections of short stories, ten volumes of poetry, four plays, and six collections of essays; she estimated that an amount at least that size remained unpublished). This dismissiveness, clearly a defense against envy, makes less and less sense when one realizes the psychic costs of writing under such compulsion.
7. Creighton, p. 69.
8. Information about the writing of *Rose Garden* comes from my interviews with Greenberg, interviews with her by Lodge psychiatrist Laurice McAfee, and from these published sources: Stephen Rubin, "The Real Hannah Green's Rose Garden," *Denver Post,* May 30, 1971; Barbara Cook, "Sign Her Name . . . Joanne Greenberg," *Post-Bulletin,* February 20, 1973, p. 21; Vikki Porter, "She Never Promised a Rose Garden," *Colorado Springs Sun,* May 3, 1973, p. 9; and Catherine Behan, "A Rose by Another Name," *Denver Magazine,* July/August 1991, p. 49.
9. Margaret Carlin, "Author Dispels Myths of Writing," *Rocky Mountain News,* December 9, p. 44.
10. Jean Crawford to JG, June 5, 1962 (BU).
11. All quoted statements from Lehmann-Haupt from our interview.
12. JG to CLH, n.d.; CLH to JG, October 10, November 1, 1963. I am grateful to Christopher Lehmann-Haupt for allowing me to read and quote from the correspondence with Greenberg still in his possession.
13. *Rose Garden,* p. 107.
14. JG to CLH, n.d.; CLH to Howard Cady, August 12, 1963. Greenberg also resisted having the book advertised as a "first novel" (it may have been Hannah Green's first, but it wasn't hers), and was chagrined when a Holt marketer wanted to pro-

mote it as "a Jewish girl's rebellion against her mother" (JG to Louise Waller, December 27, 1963, BU).

15. Like most other blurbs, this took one remark out of context, making the evaluation seem far more positive. Menninger had actually written: "Several of us [at the Menninger Clinic] have read the manuscript of Hannah Green with mixed emotions. Frankly, it is a bit amateurish and not too convincing to me, but it's sincere and I'm sure it will have a good effect on lots of people who don't realize that this sort of exploration can be done and this sort of effect achieved" (KM to Arthur A. Cohen, January 6, 1964, BU).

16. The specific name chosen as the pseudonym is also significant. Oates's "Rosamond Smith" is a romantic feminization of her husband Raymond Smith's name, allowing her simultaneously to be him, a romance novel character, her married self, and a non–Joyce Carol Oates. In Greenberg's case, the pseudonym is as close as it can be to her actual name, with a first name that sounds more Jewish than Joanne. As Oates remarked in a paper titled "Pseudonymous Selves" (in *(Woman) Writer,* pp. 387–388): "When Walter Whitman, aged thirty-five, renamed himself 'Walt Whitman,' the gesture had the effect of cutting his life in two. . . . young David Henry Thoreau became 'Henry David Thoreau' as if to declare not only self-dependence but self-genesis. . . . though Eric Blair, prior to the publication of *Down and Out in Paris and London,* allowed his publisher to choose his pseudonym from several names Blair provided, 'George Orwell' shortly became the name by which he was known, even by friends: thus, 'George Orwell' the man, 'Eric Blair' an early and outgrown identity."

17. Heilbrun, pp. 110–111, 120.

18. Kaplan, p. 40.

19. Anna Jacobson to JG, "end of 1975" (BU). Frieda's secretary Donna Grimmer, who had typed Joanne's original treatment summary for Frieda to take to Palo Alto, recalled being struck by how *Rose Garden* "had not changed the facts one iota" (Grimmer interview).

20. Telegram, royalty statements, and condolence notes, all at BU. Greenberg is acutely aware of the fact that were *Rose Garden* to be published today, it would never be allowed to stay in print long enough to attract a following slowly, the way it did in the 1960s.

21. Virginia Sue Moore, "Mental Illness Theme of Fine Novel," *Daily Press* (Newport News, Virginia), May 24, 1964.

22. C. G. Gros, *Best Sellers,* May 1, 1964, pp. 49–50; Virginia Pasley, "A Dimension of Understanding," *Newsday,* 1964; R. V. Cassill, "A Locked Ward, a Desperate Search for Reality," *New York Times Book Review,* May 3, 1964, p. 36; Brigid Brophy, "An Yri Story," *New Statesman,* August 14, 1964, pp. 221–222; B. A. Young, "New Fiction and Old," *Punch* (London), August 19, 1964; "Out of the Snake Pit," *Spectator,* August 14, 1964; Haskel Frankel, "Alone in the Kingdom of Yr," *Saturday Review,* July 18, 1964, p. 40; Elizabeth Becker, "Novel Is Moving Psychiatric Document," *Houston Post,* April 26, 1964.

23. *Book Week,* May 3, 1964, p. 14; "Calling Mad Mad," *Times Literary Supplement,* August 13, 1964, p. 721; Wilma Dykeman, "Variations in the Human Condition," *Chicago Tribune, August* 26, 1964, p. 5; Brophy, "An Yri Story"; Frankel, "Alone in the Kingdom of Yr"; "Out of the Snake Pit"; Paula Clark, "Battle for Sanity," *Hartford Courant,* April 19, 1964.

24. *Charlotte Observer,* May 24, 1964. (Since it wasn't possible to run a photo of the mysterious Hannah Green, this review included a photo of the book jacket with the caption, "Unusual jacket design for unusual book.")

25. Mary McGrory, "A World of Her Own: A Good, New Novel," *Evening Star* (Washington, D.C.), April 26, 1964.

26. For example, in the royalty period ending December 31, 1966 (two and a half years after publication), Greenberg received $560.88 on sales of 850 copies (BU).

27. JG to SK, October 21, 1992 (BU). To protect the privacy of readers whose letters are discussed here, only their initials are used.

28. Mr. IL to JG, August 5, 1964 (BU). In early drafts, Frieda was called "Dr. Kraft-Rosen" and then "Dr. Weiss" (one of Joanne's friends commented regretfully, "Dr. Weiss, as a character, never quite triumphed over her perfection").

29. Ms. EB to JG, April 24, 1964 (BU). There were some strange inquiries about names, like the one from a woman convinced that Joanne was related to her, since, when combined, "Hannah Green" and "Deborah Blau" formed her name, "Greenblau."

30. Mr. SH to JG, April 21, 1965 (BU).

31. Greenberg interview.

32. McAfee interview with Greenberg, p. 529, of the edited version in Silver; Stephen E. Rubin, "Conversations with the Author of *I Never Promised You a Rose Garden,*" *Psychoanalytic Review,* 1972, *59,* p. 203.

33. Hannah Green to JG, July 11, 1966; Rubin, p. 203; Hannah Green to JG, April 28, 1970 (BU).

34. PR to JG, November 20, 1970; SR to JG, n.d. unsigned letter to JG, December 26, 1970; KE to JG, January 18, 1971; Ms. PH to JG, May 19, 1965, July 1965; Mr. MB to JG, May 2, 1968; Ms. HA to JG, December 10, 1991 (BU).

35. South seemed to have an attraction for works of psychology: "Games People Play," his Grammy Award winner, was titled after a popular book published in 1964 by Eric Berne (New York: Grove Press).

36. *The Comprehensive Country Music Encyclopedia* (New York: Country Music Magazine, 1994); Roger Lax and Frederick Smith, *The Great Song Thesaurus* (New York: Oxford University Press, 1989); Dave McAleer, *The All Music Book of Hot Singles* (San Francisco: Miller Freeman Books, 1994). "Rose Garden" won Anderson the 1971 award for Best Female Country Vocalist and was in the top ten on pop charts in both England and the United States.

37. Dr. HM to JG, February 6, 1969 (BU).

38. William Morris Agency to JG, July 27, 1965; Lois Wallace to JG, July 28, 1969 (BU); Vincent Canby, "Rose Garden Limns Dark Borders of Reality," *New York Times,* July 15, 1977, p. C10; Leslie Halliwell, *Halliwell's Film Guide* (9th ed.), New York: Harper & Row, 1989.

39. In his review, Canby noted the "absurdity" of Yr being portrayed as "a desert landscape inhabited by half-naked pagans whose origins could be comic books perused at some preliterate age." Among other bizarre attempts at "authenticity" were the subtitles used to "translate" Yr into English, and the kerchief Bibi Andersson wore around her hair (even indoors) to make her appear vaguely European.

40. Alice Payne Hackett and James Henry Burke, *80 Years of Best Sellers, 1895–1975* (New York: R. R. Bowker Co., 1977). Hackett and Burke used the

figure of 750,000 in hardcover sales or 2 million in paperback sales as their criterion for a "best seller."

41. Trudeau, April 16, 1974; Price, February 16, 1975 (*Washington Post* reprint of 1974 *New Yorker* original). In 1976, "Peanuts" cartoonist Charles Schulz published *I Never Promised You an Apple Orchard: The Collected Writings of Snoopy.*

42. Mr. PH to JG, n.d.; Mr. HS to JG, June 8, 1966 (BU).

43. Ms. VC to JG, April 17, 1969 (BU).

44. Ms. MK to JG, January 8, 1969 (BU).

45. Mr. LD to JG, July 30, 1969 (BU).

46. Ms. SB to JG, n.d.; Ms. BF to JG, August 3, 1967; Ms. WB to JG, August 21, 1969; Ms. TP to JG, November 15, 1970; Ms. BB to JG, February 24, 1992; BK to JG, n.d., emphasis in original (BU).

47. Mr. JG to JG, October 22, 1968; Ms. BL to JG, October 10, 1966 (BU).

48. Ms. HH to JG, November 14, 1968 (emphasis in original); Ms. PA to JG, July 13, 1966; Ms. CB to JG, October 24, 1971; Ms. IB to JG, August 5, 1992 (BU).

49. Ms. ML to JG, May 2, 1969 (BU).

50. Ms. BE to Holt, Rinehart & Winston, September 17, 1970 (BU).

51. Ms. JA to Hannah Green, June 12, 1968; Ms. CG to JG, July 9, 1968 (BU).

52. Ms. SC to JG, April 8, 1969; Ms. SC to Hannah Green, n.d. (a subsequent letter, written after Greenberg's reply, is dated May 17, 1972, BU).

53. Ms. SC to Hannah Green, n.d. (BU).

54. Mr. CVS to Hannah Green, n.d. (BU).

55. Ms. DM to Hannah Green, December 7, 1971; Ms. DC to JG, December 31, 1975 (BU).

56. Ms. PR to JG, June 18, July 19, 1970; February 12, December 17, 1971; March 3, 1972; and others, n.d. (BU).

57. Ms. SL to JG, April 20, 1975 (BU).

58. Ms. AP to Hannah Green, July 14, 1967 (BU); unpublished analysis by Jean Talbot, 1993, p. 12.

59. Ibid., p. 3.

60. Ms. BH to JG, March 28, 1967; Ms. SM to JG, September 29, 1975 (BU).

61. Ms. JA to Hannah Green, June 11, 1968 (BU).

62. Ms. N. to JG, May 11, 1971 (BU).

63. JG to Ms. N., n.d. (BU).

64. Telephone interview with Greenberg.

65. *Perspectives in Psychiatric Care,* 1975, *13,* pp. 21, 24.

66. Snipes, *Masterplots II* (Ed., Frank N. Magill). Englewood Cliffs, NJ: Salem Press, 1986, 769–773.

67. Wolfe and Wolfe, pp. 896–897, 905.

68. Berman, chap. 6 (pp. 154–176).

69. Keitel, pp. 6, 9, 30, 82–83, 118.

70. Edwards, pp. 28–29.

71. Behan, "A Rose by Another Name," p. 49; Greenberg interview.

72. Lawrence S. Kubie, *Journal of Nervous and Mental Disease,* 1966, *142,* 190–195; Kubie to Greenberg, August 4, 1967; Greenberg to Kubie, November 9, 1967; Kubie to Greenberg, November 28, 1967 (Kubie papers, Library of Congress); Greenberg interview.

73. North and Cadoret, pp. 133–137.

74. One might also wonder what would motivate a historian of psychiatry to take such a snide view of the suffering of mental patients that he would dismiss Greenberg's anguished account of her illness as "the supposed trauma" she experienced (see Shorter, *A History of Psychiatry,* p. 378).

75. North, *Welcome, Silence.*

76. Schoenewolf, pp. 59–77.

77. McGlashan and Keats, pp. 95, 108, 150.

78. Ms. S. to author, January 19, 1993.

79. Greenberg interview; JG response to Schulz follow-up study (CLA).

80. "Following in her footsteps," from Langs and Searles, p. 83. All subsequent quoted statements or biographical details about Searles from this source, pp. 7–19, 35–38.

81. Searles himself uses the term *exhibitionistic* (ibid., p. 10); other quotes from Bloch interview. Langs compares Searles's "symbiosis" to Melanie Klein's notion of "projective identification," and suggests that "one of the unconscious motives for becoming an analyst is to make pathological, inappropriate use of the patient as a container for our pathology," a statement with which Searles concurred (ibid., pp. 54–55). "The Patient as Therapist to his Analyst" is in Searles, *Countertransference and Related Subjects*, pp. 380–459.

82. Fort interview. See, for example, Searles's paper "Feeling of Guilt in the Psychoanalyst," in *Countertransference and Related Subjects.*

83. All details of Mrs. Douglas's history are from the version in Langs and Searles, pp. 188–195.

84. Szalita, Dyrud, Lidz interviews.

85. Boyer, Cooperman, Bloch, Morris Schwartz interviews; "hunger for vilification" from Schoenewolf, p. 146.

86. Dyrud, Will, Schulz, Weigert interviews.

87. Goshen-Gottstein, pp. ix–xi, 201–202.

88. There are, of course, many examples of neurologists refusing to believe atypical examples presented to them. Oliver Sacks, for instance, painfully describes the reception of his initial findings using L-DOPA with post-encephalitic patients: "Some colleagues insisted that such effects 'never' occurred; others that, even if they did, the matter should be kept quiet, lest it disturb 'the atmosphere of therapeutic optimism needed for the maximal efficiency of L-DOPA.'" After this outraged reaction, a "disapproving or uncomprehending silence," which one editor of a medical journal called a "strange mutism" kept Sacks's results from being taken seriously for years. He reports (with some pleasure) that the great Soviet neurologist A. R. Luria experienced the same "mutism" from his colleagues when he first published his famous case histories (see Sacks, foreword to the 1990 edition of *Awakenings,* pp. xxxii–xxxv).

89. Greenberg interview.

90. Hannah Green, "In Praise of My Doctor"; Greenberg, "Metaphor and the Treatment of Schizophrenia," videotaped talk to the Columbia (MD) Study Group, June 1986 (all quoted statements from my verbatim notes of tape).

91. *Rose Garden* has received no advertising from the publisher since 1964 (except immediately after the film's release); even the cover has not changed for twenty years.

92. Lehmann-Haupt interview.

EPILOGUE

1. Samuel Coleridge (1833), *Table Talk,* p. 331.
2. Information about Osheroff is taken from Malcolm, *Treatment Choices and Informed Consent,* the most detailed account of the case in the public domain. Malcolm draws heavily (especially in chap. 3) from Osheroff's unpublished autobiography, *A Symbolic Death,* and statements attributed to Osheroff are Malcolm's quotations from that work. For a more sensationalized account of the case, see Sandra G. Boodman, "The Mystery of Chestnut Lodge," *Washington Post Sunday Magazine,* October 8, 1989.
3. Alan Stone, "Is Psychoanalytic Psychiatry Malpractice?" Psychiatry Grand Rounds, Beth Israel Hospital, Boston, MA, November 28, 1989. All quoted statements from my verbatim notes.
4. Klerman, p. 417.
5. Klerman interview.
6. Stone, "Law, Science, and Psychiatric Malpractice," p. 424.
7. See Kutchins and Kirk on the history and politicization of the *DSM.*
8. For analyses of some of the boundary wars psychiatry has lost with its competitors, see Micale; Blustein, "New York Neurologists and the Specialization of American Medicine"; Burnham, *Paths into American Culture;* and Gifford.
9. The huge literature on so-called deinstitutionalization (which is really "trans-institutionalization," since many patients simply ended up in jails or prisons after the closing of the state hospitals) lies too far outside this discussion to be reviewed here (for summaries from a range of political perspectives on this issue, see Johnson; Isaac and Armat; Grob, *From Asylum to Community,* and "Mad, Homeless, and Unwanted"). Stone's "Conceptual Ambiguity and Morality in Modern Psychiatry" sketches the moral dimensions of the problem; Valenstein's *Blaming the Brain* and Ross and Pam's *Pseudoscience in Biological Psychiatry* critique the evidence for contemporary genetic and physiological models of mental illness. Sheehan's *Is There No Place on Earth for Me?* painfully illustrates these issues from the patient's perspective.
10. In our interview, Klerman did not hide the fact that he had been dropped as a student from two different analytic training institutes, and these humiliations clearly fueled his anger toward psychoanalysis.
11. Walter Freeman had to include two special chapters in his text *The Psychiatrist* to document the extent of self-destructiveness in his field. He presents data showing psychiatrists to be far more likely than other physicians to die of accidents or suicide.
12. In a famous paper, "The Retreat from Patients," Lawrence Kubie described how administration and teaching provide senior psychiatrists with an acceptable cover for avoiding contact with patients. "Hiding behind a defensive barrier of scorn and sometimes of venom against any kind of psychotherapy," retreating into research on brain tissue or seeing patients for five-minute medication appointments are, Kubie argued, psychiatrists' responses to their own guilt and impotence.
13. In his review of "borderline" disorders, Kernberg notes that this diagnosis emerged from the fuzzy set of categories previously used to describe those psychotic patients with a "better" prognosis (i.e., those labeled "preschizophrenic," "pseudoneurotic schizophrenic," "ambulatory schizophrenic," or "latent psychotic").

14. As the field of medicine most violently contested, psychiatry has difficulty gen-
     erating accounts of its past that are not themselves subject to attack. As two re-
     cent commentators have noted: "In no branch of the history of science or medicine
     has there been less interpretive consensus [than in psychiatry]. In few professions,
     inside or outside the sciences, has it been more difficult to demarcate the schol-
     arly, historical enterprise from urgent, present-day debates" (Porter and Micale,
     Introduction to *Discovering the History of Psychiatry,* p. 4). The fact that half the
     members of the American Association for the History of Medicine are themselves
     physicians is yet another reflection of the problem. Practitioners who write his-
     tory—and I speak from personal experience—always have an axe to grind. Even
     when they are critical of their fields, they retain the benefits of membership, and
     this inevitably colors what they say. As Porter and Micale aptly note, revisionist
     histories of psychiatry have "been no less rooted in social, political, and profes-
     sional circumstances than [those] they sought to displace" (p. 11).
15. Barnes and Berke; North; Endler; Cardinal; Isaac and Armat, pp. 189–191.
16. Fromm, p. 579.
17. As a society, we are also willing to allow insurance companies to pay hundreds
     of thousands of dollars to sustain such infants, whereas actively psychotic adults
     get practically no coverage.

Works of
Frieda Fromm-Reichmann

(*published and unpublished*) *cited in text or notes*
(*for a complete bibliography of her writings, see SP*)

1922   "Zur Psychopathologie des Asthma bronchiale," *Medizinische Klinik, 18,* 1090–1092. Originally presented October 23, 1921, at the meeting of the Central German Psychiatrists and Neurologists, Dresden. Later published in an English translation: "Contribution to the Psychopathology of Bronchial Asthma," *Journal of the Hillside Hospital,* 1966, *15,* 165–172.

1927   "Das Jüdische Speisritual," *Imago, 13,* 235–246. Later translated, edited, and published in English by Christopher T. Bever: "Jewish Food Rituals," *Journal of the American Academy of Psychoanalysis,* 1995, *23,* 7–17.

1936   "Psychoanalytic Remarks on the Clinical Significance of Hostility," *Medical Annals of the District of Columbia, 1936, 5.* Originally presented November 7, 1935, to the Section on Neurology and Psychiatry of the Maryland Psychiatric Society; reprinted in SP, 277–282.

1936   "Female Psychosexuality." Originally presented to a meeting of the Washington-Baltimore Psychoanalytic Society. Later published, with an introduction by Ann-Louise S. Silver, *Journal of the American Academy of Psychoanalysis,* 1995, *23,* 19–32.

1936   "The Body as a Means of Psychological Expression." Presented December 1936; audience and location unknown.

1937   "Contribution to the Psychogenesis of Migraine," *Psychoanalytic Review, 24.* Originally presented December 1935 to the American Psychoanalytic Association, Boston; reprinted in SP, 283–289.

1937   "Psychosomatic Reactions During Analysis." Presented to the American Psychoanalytic Association, 1937.

ca.   "Notes on Some Cultural Differences Between the Attitude of
1939   American and European Psychoanalytic Patients and Physicians." Audience and occasion unknown.

1939   "Transference Problems in Schizophrenics," *Psychoanalytic Quarterly, 8.*

Originally presented May 1939 at the American Psychoanalytic Association, Chicago; reprinted in SP, 117–128.

1940   "In Memoriam: Gertrud Jacob, 1893–1940," *Psychoanalytic Quarterly, 9,* 546–548.

1940   "Notes on the Mother Role in the Family Group," *Bulletin of the Menninger Clinic, 4.* Reprinted in SP, 290–305.

1941   "Recent Advances in Psychoanalytic Therapy," *Psychiatry, 4.* Originally presented to the Maryland Psychiatric Society, March 1941, Baltimore; reprinted in SP, 49–54.

1942   "A Preliminary Note on the Emotional Significance of Stereotypies [*sic*] in Schizophrenics," *Bulletin of the Forest Sanitarium, 1.* Reprinted in SP, pp. 129–132.

1942   "Psychopathology of Schizophrenia." Presented January 16, 1942, to an unknown audience, St. Louis.

1943   "Insight into Psychotic Mechanisms and Emergency Psychotherapy," *Medical Annals of the District of Columbia, 12.* Originally presented February 5, 1942, to the Section on Neurology and Psychiatry of the Maryland Psychiatric Society; reprinted in SP, 55–62.

1943   "Psychoanalytic Psychotherapy with Psychotics: The Influence of the Modifications in Technique on Present Trends in Psychoanalysis," *Psychiatry, 6,* 277–279. Originally presented to the American Psychoanalytic Association, May 11, 1943, Detroit; reprinted in SP, 133–136, and in *Advances in Psychiatry: Recent Developments in Interpersonal Relations,* (Mabel Blake Cohen, Ed.). New York: Norton, 1959, 153–158.

1943   "Changes in Psychoanalytic Concepts During the Last Ten Years." Presented April 13, 1943, to the medical, nursing, occupational therapy and secretarial staff at Chestnut Lodge.

1945   "Changes in Transference Concepts." Presented April 4, 1945, to the San Francisco Psychoanalytic Society, and October 3, 1946, to the Topeka Psychoanalytic Society.

1946   "Remarks on the Philosophy of Mental Disorder," *Psychiatry, 9.* Originally presented to the Society on the Study of Personality, New York Academy of Medicine, May 1, 1946; reprinted in SP, 3–24.

1947   "Problems of Therapeutic Management in a Psychoanalytic Hospital," *Psychoanalytic Quarterly, 16,* 325–356. Reprinted in SP, 137–159.

1947   Introduction to *The Philosophy of Insanity* by a Late Inmate of the Glasgow Royal Asylum for Lunatics at Gartnavel. New York: Greenberg.

1948   "Notes on the Development of Treatment of Schizophrenics by Psychoanalytic Psychotherapy," *Psychiatry, 11.* Reprinted in SP, 160–175.

1949   "Intensive Psychotherapy of Manic-Depressives," *Confinia Neurologica, 9.* Reprinted in SP, 221–226.

1949   "Notes on Personal and Professional Requirements of a Psychotherapist," *Psychiatry, 12.* Reprinted in SP, 63–87.

ca. 1950s   "Four Basic Analytic and Dynamic Principles." Occasion and audience unknown.

1950   "Discussion of Dr. Thompson's Paper," with Virginia Gunst, in *Proceedings of the Feminine Psychology Symposium* held by the Psychoanalytic Division, Department of Psychiatry, New York Medical College. Reprinted under the title "On the Denial of Women's Sexual Pleasure," in *Psychoanalysis and*

Women (Jean Baker Miller, Ed.). New York: Brunner/Mazel, 1973, 85–93.

1950   *Principles of Intensive Psychotherapy.* Chicago: University of Chicago Press.

1952   "Some Aspects of Psychoanalytic Psychotherapy with Schizophrenics," in *Psychotherapy with Schizophrenics: A Symposium* (Eugene B. Brody and Frederick C. Redlich, Eds.). New York: International Universities Press. Reprinted in SP, 176–193.

1953   "Transference." Presented February 21, 1953, to the Washington Psychoanalytic Society.

1953   Review of Riese, *The Conception of Disease*, in *Psychiatry, 16*, 413–414.

1954   "An Intensive Study of Twelve Cases of Manic Depressive Psychosis," with Mabel Blake Cohen, Grace Baker, Robert A. Cohen, and Edith V. Weigert, *Psychiatry, 17*, No. 2. Reprinted in SP, 227–274.

1954   "Psychotherapy of Schizophrenia," *American Journal of Psychiatry, 3.* Originally presented May 1954 as the Academic Lecture of the American Psychiatric Association, St. Louis; reprinted in SP, 194–209.

1954   Foreword to Schwing, *A Way to the Soul of the Mentally Ill.* New York: International Universities Press.

1954   "Psychoanalytic and General Dynamic Conceptions of Theory and of Therapy: Differences and Similarities," *Journal of the American Psychoanalytic Association, 2*, 711–721. Reprinted in SP, 105–113.

1954   "Assets of the Mentally Handicapped." Lecture course at the Washington School of Psychiatry; later published with an introduction by Ann-Louise S. Silver, *Journal of the American Academy of Psychoanalysis*, 1990, *18*, 47–72.

1955   "Clinical Significance of Intuitive Processes of the Psychoanalyst," *Journal of the American Psychoanalytic Association, 3*, 82–88.

1955   "Notes on the Psychiatric Aspects of Loneliness." Originally presented at the First Annual Chestnut Lodge Symposium, March 2, 1955; later edited and published by Dexter M. Bullard in SP, 325–336, and reprinted in *Contemporary Psychoanalysis*, 1990, *26*, 305–330.

1956   "My Year's Fellowship at the Center for Advanced Study in the Behavioral Sciences." Presented Fall 1956 at the 2nd Annual Chestnut Lodge Symposium.

1956   *Progress in Psychotherapy,* Ed. with J. L. Moreno. New York: Grune & Stratton.

1959   *Psychoanalysis and Psychotherapy: Selected Papers of Frieda Fromm-Reichmann* (Dexter M. Bullard, Ed.). Chicago: University of Chicago Press.

1982   "Frieda Fromm-Reichmann Discusses the 'Rose Garden' Case," *Psychiatry, 45*, 128–136. Originally presented December 1956 at the Ypsilanti Psychiatric Institute.

General Bibliography

Abbott, Andrew Delano. "The Emergence of American Psychiatry, 1880–1930." Ph.D. dissertation, University of Chicago, 1992.

Abraham, Hilda C., and Ernst L. Freud (Eds.). *The Letters of Sigmund Freud and Karl Abraham, 1907–1926.* New York: Basic Books, 1965.

Ackerknecht, E. H. "Private Institutions in the Genesis of Psychiatry." *Bulletin of the History of Medicine,* 1986, *60,* 387–395.

Adland, Marvin L. "Problems of Administrative Psychotherapy in Mental Hospitals." *Psychiatric Quarterly Supplement,* 1953, *27,* part 2, 264–271.

Albisetti, James C. "The Fight for Female Physicians in Imperial Germany." *Central European History,* 1982, *15,* 99–123.

Albom, Mitch. *Tuesdays with Morrie.* New York: Doubleday, 1997.

Alexander, Franz, Samuel Eisenstein, and Martin Grotjahn (Eds.). *Psychoanalytic Pioneers.* New York: Basic Books, 1966.

Arieti, Silvano. "Some Memories and Personal Views." *Contemporary Psychoanalysis,* 1968, *5,* 85–88.

Aron, Lewis, and Adrienne Harris (Eds.). *The Legacy of Sándor Ferenczi.* Hillsdale, NJ: Analytic Press, 1993.

Artiss, Kenneth L., and Dexter M. Bullard. "Paranoid Thinking in Everyday Life—The Function of Secrets and Disillusionment." *Academy of Medicine Bulletin,* 1965, *11,* 57–63.

Bair, Deirdre. *Simone de Beauvoir: A Biography.* New York: Simon & Schuster, 1990.

Balint, Michael. *The Basic Fault: Therapeutic Aspects of Regression.* London: Tavistock Publications, 1968.

Barnes, Mary, and Joseph Berke. *Mary Barnes: Two Accounts of a Journey Through Madness.* New York: Ballantine Books, 1971.

Bartemeier, Leo H. "An Historical Note on the Psychoanalytic Hospitals." *Psychiatric Journal of the University of Ottawa,* 1978, *3,* 77–79.

Bateson, Gregory. "Language and Psychotherapy—Frieda Fromm-Reichmann's Last Project." *Psychiatry,* 1958, *21,* 96–100.

Beers, Clifford W. *A Mind That Found Itself.* New York: Longmans, Green, 1908.

Benziger, Barbara Field. *The Prison of My Mind.* New York: Pocket Books, 1970.

Berger, Milton M. (Ed.). *Beyond the Double Bind: Communication and Family Systems, Theories, and Techniques with Schizophrenics.* New York: Brunner/Mazel, 1978.

Berghahn, Marion. *German-Jewish Refugees in England: The Ambiguities of Assimilation.* London: Macmillan, 1984.

Bergman, Martin S. "The Tragic Encounter Between Freud and Ferenczi and Its Impact on the History of Psychoanalysis." In *Ferenczi's Turn in Psychoanalysis* (Peter L. Rudnytsky, Antal Bókay, and Patrizia Giampieri-Deutsch, Eds.). New York: New York University Press, 1996.

Bergmann, Martin S., and Frank R. Hartman (Eds.). *The Evolution of Psychoanalytic Technique.* New York: Basic Books, 1976.

Berman, Jeffrey. *The Talking Cure: Literary Representations of Psychoanalysis.* New York: New York University Press, 1985.

Berrios, G. E., and R. Hauser. "The Early Development of Kraepelin's Ideas on Classification: A Conceptual History," *Psychological Medicine,* 1983, *18,* 813–821.

Bigelow, Poultney. *Prussian Memories, 1884–1914.* New York: Putnam, 1915.

Bleuler, Eugen. "The Prognosis of Dementia Praecox: The Group of Schizophrenias." In *The Clinical Roots of the Schizophrenia Concept* (John Cutting and Michael Shepherd, Eds.). New York: Cambridge University Press, 1987, 59–74.

"Manfred Bleuler." In *Psychiatrists on Psychiatry* (Michael Shepherd, Ed.). New York: Cambridge University Press, 1982, 1–13.

Bloch, Donald A. "Carl/a Auer: An Invention." In *Strange Encounters with Carl Auer* (Gunthard Weber and Fritz B. Simon, Eds.). New York: Norton, 1991, 63–68.

Blomert, Reinhard. "Das vergessene Sanatorium." In *Jüdisches Leben in Heidelberg* (Norbert Giovannini, Johannes Bauer, and Hans-Martin Mumm, Eds.). Heidelberg: Wunderhorn, 1992, 249–263.

Blustein, Bonnie Ellen. "New York Neurologists and the Specialization of American Medicine." *Bulletin of the History of Medicine,* 1979, *53,* 170–183.

Blustein, Bonnie Ellen. *Preserve Your Love for Science: The Life of William A. Hammond, American Neurologist.* Cambridge: Cambridge University Press, 1991.

Boisen, Anton. *Out of the Depths.* New York: Harper and Row, 1960.

Braginsky, Benjamin M., Dorothea D. Braginsky, and Kenneth Ring. *Methods of Madness.* New York: Holt, Rinehart & Winston, 1969.

Brand, Millen. *Savage Sleep.* New York: Crown Publishers, 1968.

Brand-Claussen, Bettina. "The Collection of Works of Art in the Psychiatric Clinic, Heidelberg—from the Beginnings until 1945." In *Beyond Reason: Art and Psychosis, Works from the Prinzhorn Collection.* London: Hayward Gallery, 1996, 7–23.

Braslow, Joel. *Mental Ills and Bodily Cures: Psychiatric Treatment in the First Half of the Twentieth Century.* Berkeley: University of California Press, 1997.

Breggin, Peter R. *Toxic Psychiatry.* New York: St. Martin's Press, 1991.

Brenner, Michael. *The Renaissance of Jewish Culture in Weimar Germany.* New Haven: Yale University Press, 1996.

Brenner, Michael and Derek J. Penslar (Eds.). *In Search of Jewish Community: Jewish Identities in Germany and Austria, 1918–1933.* Bloomington: Indiana University Press, 1998.

Breuer, Mordechai. *Modernity Within Tradition: The Social History of Orthodox Jewry in Imperial Germany* (Elizabeth Petuchowski, trans.). New York: Columbia University Press, 1992.

Bruch, Hilde. "Personal Reminiscences of Frieda Fromm-Reichmann." *Psychiatry,* 1982, *45,* 98–104.

Bruch, Joanne Hatch. *Unlocking the Golden Cage: An Intimate Biography of Hilde Bruch, M.D.* Carlsbad, CA: Gürze Books, 1996.

Buber, Martin. *Tales of the Hasidim: The Early Masters.* London: Thames and Hudson, 1956.

Buber, Martin. *The Legend of the Baal-Shem* (Maurice Friedman, trans.). London: East and West Library, 1956.

Buber, Martin. "Judaism and the Jews" (1911). In *On Judaism* (Nahum N. Glatzer, Ed.). New York: Schocken, 1967.

Buber, Martin (Ed.). *The Tales of Rabbi Nachman* (Maurice Friedman, trans.). London: Souvenir Press, 1974.

Bullard, Dexter M. "The Application of Psychoanalytic Psychiatry to the Psychoses." *Psychoanalytic Review,* 1939, *26,* 526–534.

Bullard, Dexter M. "Experiences in the Psychoanalytic Treatment of Psychotics." *Psychoanalytic Quarterly,* 1940, *9,* 493–504.

Bullard, Dexter M. "The Organization of Psychoanalytic Procedure in the Hospital." *Journal of Nervous and Mental Diseases,* 1940, *41,* 697–703.

Bullard, Dexter M. "Problems of Clinical Administration." *Bulletin of the Menninger Clinic,* 1952, *16.*

Bullard, Ernest Luther. "The Care of the Insane in Wisconsin." In *The Institutional Care of the Insane in the United States and Canada,* Vol. 3 (Henry M. Hurd, Ed.). Baltimore: Johns Hopkins University Press, 1916, 824–839.

Burleigh, Michael. *Death and Deliverance: "Euthanasia" in Germany, 1900–1945.* Cambridge: Cambridge University Press, 1994.

Burleigh, Michael. *Ethics and Extermination: Reflections on Nazi Genocide.* Cambridge: Cambridge University Press, 1997.

Burnham, Donald L. "The Special-Problem Patient: Victim or Agent of Splitting?" *Psychiatry,* 1966, *29,* 105–122.

Burnham, Donald L. "Orthodoxy and Eclecticism in Psychoanalysis: The Washington-Baltimore Experience." In *American Psychoanalysis: Origins and Development* (Jacques M. Quen and Eric T. Carlson, Eds.). New York: Brunner/Mazel, 1978, 87–108.

Burnham, Donald L., Arthur I. Gladstone, and Robert W. Gibson. *Schizophrenia and the Need-Fear Dilemma.* New York: International Universities Press, 1969.

Burnham, John C. *Paths into American Culture: Psychology, Medicine, and Morals.* Philadelphia: Temple University Press, 1988.

Burston, Daniel. *The Legacy of Erich Fromm.* Cambridge, MA: Harvard University Press, 1991.

Cannon, William B. *The Wisdom of the Body.* New York: Norton, 1939.

Cantor, Geoffrey. "The Scientist as Hero: Public Images of Michael Faraday." In *Telling Lives in Science: Essays on Scientific Biography* (Michael Shortland and Richard Yeo, Eds.). Cambridge: Cambridge University Press, 1996, 171–193.

Cardinal, Marie. *The Words to Say It.* Cambridge, MA: Van Vactor & Goodheart, 1983.

Casamajor, Louis. "Notes for an Intimate History of Neurology and Psychiatry in America." *Journal of Nervous and Mental Disease,* 1943, *98,* 600–608.

Caudill, William, Fredrick C. Redlich, Helen R. Gilmon, and E. B. Brody. "Social

Structure and Interaction Processes on a Psychiatric Ward." *American Journal of Orthopsychiatry,* 1952, *22,* 314–334.

Chace, Marian, with Judith R. Bunney. "Some Observations on the Psychodrama Sessions at Chestnut Lodge." In *Marian Chace: Her Papers* (Harris Chaiklin, Ed.). Columbia, MD: American Dance Therapy Association, 1975, 121–129.

Chessick, Richard D. *Great Ideas in Psychotherapy.* New York: Jason Aronson, 1977.

Chodorow, Nancy J. "Varieties of Leadership Among Early Women Psychoanalysts." In *Women Physicians in Leadership Roles* (Leah J. Dickstein and Carol C. Nadelson, Eds.). Washington, D.C.: American Psychiatric Press, 1986, 47–54.

Chu, Franklin D., and Sharland Trotter. *The Madness Establishment.* New York: Grossman, 1974.

Clark, Michael J. "The Rejection of Psychological Approaches to Mental Disorder in Late Nineteenth-Century British Psychiatry." In *Madhouses, Mad-doctors, and Madmen: The Social History of Psychiatry in the Victorian Era* (Andrew Scull, Ed.). Philadelphia: University of Pennsylvania Press, 1981, 271–312.

Cocks, Geoffrey. *Psychotherapy in the Third Reich: The Göring Institute.* New York: Oxford University Press, 1985.

Cohen, Robert A. "The Hospital as a Therapeutic Instrument." *Psychiatry,* 1958, *21,* 29–35.

Cohen, Robert A. "Notes on the Life and Work of Frieda Fromm-Reichmann." *Psychiatry,* 1982, *45,* 90–98.

Coleridge, Samuel. *Table Talk,* Vol. 1. (Carl Woodring, Ed.). Princeton: Princeton University Press, 1990.

Coles, Robert. "A Hero of Our Time." In *The Mind's Fate: A Psychiatrist Looks at His Profession.* Boston: Little, Brown, 1975, 181–185.

Cooperman, Martin. "Some Observations Regarding Psychoanalytic Psychotherapy in a Hospital Setting." *Psychiatric Hospital,* 1983, *14,* 21–28.

Coser, Lewis A. *Refugee Scholars in America: Their Impact and Their Experiences.* New Haven: Yale University Press, 1984.

Creighton, Joanne V. *Joyce Carol Oates: Novels of the Middle Years.* New York: Twayne Publishers, 1992.

Crowley, Ralph M. "Use of Insulin in Certain Psychiatric Disorders." *Virginia Medical Monthly,* November 1938.

Crowley, Ralph M. "Frieda Fromm-Reichmann: Recollections of a Student." *Psychiatry,* 1982, *45,* 105–106.

D'Amore, Archangelo R. T. (Ed.). *William Alanson White: The Washington Years, 1903–1937.* Publication No. 76-298. Washington: U.S. Department of Health, Education, and Welfare, 1976.

Dan, Joseph. *Jewish Mysticism and Jewish Ethics.* Seattle: University of Washington Press, 1986.

Davis, Hope Hale. "Looking Back at My Years in the Party." *New Leader,* February 11, 1980, 10–18.

Davis, Hope Hale. *Great Day Coming: A Memoir of the 1930s.* South Royalton, VT: Steerforth Press, 1994.

Decker, Hannah. *Freud in Germany: Revolution and Reaction in Science, 1893–1907.* New York: International Universities Press, 1977.

Deutsch, Helene. *Confrontations with Myself.* New York: Norton, 1973.

Digby, Anne. *Madness, Morality and Medicine: A Study of the York Retreat, 1796–1914.* Cambridge: Cambridge University Press, 1985.

Dolnick, Edward. *Madness on the Couch: Blaming the Victim in the Heyday of Psychoanalysis.* New York: Simon & Schuster, 1998.

Dooley, Lucile. "A Psychoanalytic Study of Manic Depressive Psychosis." *Psychoanalytic Review,* 1921, *8,* 37–72, 144–167.

Dunbar, H. Flanders. *Emotions and Bodily Changes.* New York: Columbia University Press, 1938.

Dupont, J. (Ed.). *The Clinical Diary of Sándor Ferenczi.* Cambridge, MA: Harvard University Press, 1988.

Dyrud, Jarl E. "The Early Frieda, and Traces of Her in Her Later Writings." In *Psychoanalysis and Psychosis* (Ann-Louise S. Silver, Ed.). Madison, CT: International Universities Press, 1989, 483–493.

Dyrud, Jarl E. and Margaret J. Rioch. "Multiple Therapy in the Treatment Program of a Mental Hospital." *Psychiatry,* 1953, *16,* 21–26.

Eckardt, Marianne Horney. "Organizational Schisms in American Psychoanalysis." In *American Psychoanalysis: Origins and Development* (Jacques M. Quen and Eric T. Carlson, Eds.). New York: Brunner/Mazel, 1978, 141–161.

Edwards, Lee R. "Schizophrenic Narrative." *Journal of Narrative Technique,* 1989, *19,* 25–30.

Ehrenberg, Darlene Bregman. "Playfulness in the Psychoanalytic Relationship." *Contemporary Psychoanalysis,* 1990, *26,* 74–95.

Eissler, K. R. "Some Comments on Psychoanalysis and Dynamic Psychiatry." *Journal of the American Psychoanalytic Association,* 1956, *4,* 314–317.

Ellenberger, Henri F. "Psychiatry and Its Unknown History." In *Beyond the Unconscious: Essays of Henri F. Ellenberger in the History of Psychiatry* (Mark S. Micale, Ed.). Princeton: Princeton University Press, 1993, 239–253.

Endler, Norman. *Holiday of Darkness.* New York: Wiley, 1982.

Engel, Milton. "Edward J. Kempf, M.D. (1885–1971) and the Introduction of Psychoanalysis into the Public Mental Hospital." Master's thesis, Johns Hopkins University, 1987.

Engel, Ursula. "Das Heidelberger 'Thorapeutikum,'" *PsA-Info-Nr.30,* March 1988, 4–16.

English, O. S., W. W. Hampe, C. L. Bacon, and C. F. Settlage. *Direct Analysis and Schizophrenia: Clinical Observations and Evaluations.* New York: Grune & Stratton, 1961.

Falzeder, Ernst, and Eva Brabant (Eds.). *The Correspondence of Sigmund Freud and Sándor Ferenczi,* Vol. 2, *1914–1919* (Peter T. Hoffer, trans.). Cambridge, MA: Harvard University Press, 1996.

Farber, Leslie. *The Ways of the Will.* New York: Basic Books, 1966.

Federn, Paul. *Ego Psychology and the Psychoses.* New York: Basic Books, 1952.

Forbush, Bliss. *The Sheppard & Enoch Pratt Hospital, 1853–1970: A History.* Philadelphia: Lippincott, 1971.

Fort, John P. "Present-day Treatment of Schizophrenia." In *Psychoanalysis and Psychosis* (Ann-Louise S. Silver, Ed.). Madison, CT: International Universities Press, 1989, 249–270.

Foudraine, Jan. *Not Made of Wood: A Psychiatrist Discovers His Own Profession.* New York: Macmillan, 1974.

Freeman, Lucy. *Fight Against Fears.* New York: Crown Publishers, 1951.

Freeman, Walter. "The Bullards." In *The Psychiatrist: Personalities and Patterns*. New York: Grune & Stratton, 1968, 243–248.

Freeman, Walter, and James W. Watts. "Some Observations on Obsessive Tendencies Following Interruption of the Frontal Association Pathways." *Journal of Nervous and Mental Disease*, 1938, *88*, 224–234.

Freidenreich, Harriet Pass. "Jewish Women Physicians in Central Europe in the Early Twentieth Century." *Contemporary Jewry*, 1996, *17*, 79–105.

Freidenreich, Harriet Pass. "Gender, Identity, and Community: Jewish University Women in Germany and Austria." In *In Search of Jewish Community: Jewish Identities in Germany and Austria, 1918–1933* (Michael Brenner and Derek J. Penslar, Eds.). Bloomington, IN: Indiana University Press, 1998, 154–175.

Freud, Sigmund. "On Psychotherapy" (1905). In *The Standard Edition of the Complete Psychological Works of Sigmund Freud* (James Strachey, trans.). London: Hogarth Press, *7*, 257–268.

Freud, Sigmund. "On the History of the Psychoanalytic Movement" (1914). In *The Standard Edition of the Complete Psychological Works of Sigmund Freud* (James Strachey, trans.). London: Hogarth Press, *14*, 7–66.

Freud, Sigmund. "On Narcissism" (1914). In *The Standard Edition of the Complete Psychological Works of Sigmund Freud* (James Strachey, trans.). London: Hogarth Press, *14*, 73–102.

Friedman, Lawrence J. *Menninger: The Family and the Clinic*. New York: Knopf, 1990.

Fromm, Erich. *The Anatomy of Human Destructiveness*. New York: Penguin Books, 1973.

Fullard, George. "Sculpture and Survival." *The Painter and Sculptor*, 1959, *2*.

Funk, Rainer. *Erich Fromm*. Hamburg: Rowohlt, 1983.

Gay, Ruth. *The Jews of Germany: A Historical Portrait*. New Haven: Yale University Press, 1992.

Gergen, Mary. "Life Stories: Pieces of a Dream." In *Telling Lives* (George Rosenwald and Richard Ochberg, Eds.). New Haven: Yale University Press, 1992.

Gevitz, Norman (Ed.). *Other Healers: Unorthodox Medicine in America*. Baltimore: Johns Hopkins University Press, 1988.

Gifford Jr., George E. (Ed.). *Psychoanalysis, Psychotherapy, and the New England Medical Scene, 1894–1944*. New York: Science History Publications, 1978.

Gillespie, R. D. *Psychological Effects of War on Citizen and Soldier*. New York: Norton, 1942.

Giovannini, Norbert, Johannes Bauer, and Hans-Martin Mumm. *Jüdisches Leben in Heidelberg: Studien zu einer unterbrochenen Geschichte*. Heidelberg: Wunderhorn, 1992.

Glatzer, Nahum N. "The Frankfort Lehrhaus." *Year Book of the Leo Baeck Institute*, 1959, *1*, 105–122.

Goffman, Erving. "The Moral Career of the Mental Patient." In *Asylums: Essays on the Social Situation of Mental Patients and Other Inmates*. Garden City, NY: Doubleday, 1961, 125–169.

Goldstein, Jan. *Console and Classify: The French Psychiatric Profession in the Nineteenth Century*. Cambridge: Cambridge University Press, 1987.

Goldstein, Kurt. *The Organism: A Holistic Approach to Biology Derived from Pathological Data in Man*. New York: American Book Company, 1939.

454 General Bibliography

Goldstein, Kurt. *Aftereffects of Brain Injuries in War: Their Evaluation and Treatment.* New York: Grune & Stratton, 1942.

"Kurt Goldstein." In *A History of Psychology in Autobiography* (Edwin G. Boring and Gardner Lindzey, Eds.). New York: Appleton-Century-Crofts, 1967, 145–166.

Gorman, Mike. *Every Other Bed.* New York: World Publishing Co., 1956.

Goshen-Gottstein, Esther. *Recalled to Life: The Story of a Coma.* New Haven: Yale University Press, 1990.

Graml, Hermann. *Antisemitism in the Third Reich.* Oxford: Blackwell, 1992.

Green, Hannah. "In Praise of My Doctor—Frieda Fromm-Reichmann." *Contemporary Psychoanalysis,* 1967, *4,* 73–77.

Green, Maurice R. "Sullivan's Participant Observation." *Contemporary Psychoanalysis,* 1977, *13,* 359.

Greenberg, Joanne. *I Never Promised You a Rose Garden.* New York: New American Library, 1964.

Grill, Johnpeter Horst. *The Nazi Movement in Baden, 1920–1945.* Chapel Hill: University of North Carolina Press, 1983.

Grimes, John Maurice. *Institutional Care of Mental Patients in the United States.* Chicago: The author, 1934.

Grinker, Roy R., and John P. Spiegel. *Men Under Stress.* Philadelphia: Blakeston, 1945.

Grob, Gerald N. *Mental Illness and American Society, 1875–1940.* Princeton: Princeton University Press, 1983.

Grob, Gerald N. "World War II and American Psychiatry." *Psychohistory Review,* 1990, *19,* 41–69.

Grob, Gerald N. *From Asylum to Community: Mental Health Policy in Modern America.* Princeton: Princeton University Press, 1991.

Grob, Gerald N. "Mad, Homeless, and Unwanted: A History of the Care of the Chronic Mentally Ill in America." *History of Psychiatry,* 1994, *17,* 541–558.

Groddeck, Georg. *The World of Man.* London: C. W. Daniel, 1934.

Groddeck, Georg. *The Book of the It.* London: Vision Press, 1950.

Groddeck, Georg. *The Meaning of Illness: Selected Psychoanalytic Writings.* New York: International Universities Press, 1977.

Grosskurth, Phyllis. *Melanie Klein: Her World and Her Work.* New York: Knopf, 1986.

Grossman, Carl M., and Sylva Grossman. *The Wild Analyst: The Life and Work of Georg Groddeck.* London: Barrie and Rockliff, 1965.

Gunst, Virginia. "Memoirs—Professional and Personal: A Decade with Frieda Fromm-Reichmann." *Psychiatry,* 1982, *45,* 107–114.

Guntrip, Harry. *Psychoanalytic Theory, Therapy, and the Self.* New York: Basic Books, 1971.

Hale, Jr., Nathan G. "From Bergasse XIX to Central Park West: The Americanization of Psychoanalysis, 1919–1940." *Journal of the History of the Behavioral Sciences,* 1978, *14,* 299–315.

Hale, Jr., Nathan G. *The Rise and Crisis of Psychoanalysis in the United States: Freud and the Americans, 1917–1985.* New York: Oxford University Press, 1995.

Harrington, Anne. *Medicine, Mind and the Double Brain: A Study in Nineteenth-Century Thought.* Princeton: Princeton University Press, 1987.

Hartwell, Carol Eadie. "The Schizophrenogenic Mother Concept in American Psychiatry." *Psychiatry,* 1996, *59,* 274–297.

Havens, Leston L. "Emil Kraepelin." *Journal of Nervous and Mental Disease*, 1965, *141*, 16–28.

Havens, Leston L. "Harry Stack Sullivan's Contribution to Clinical Method." *Contemporary Psychoanalysis*, 1977, *13*, 360–364.

Havens, Leston L. *A Safe Place*. New York: Ballantine Books, 1989.

Haynal, André. *Controversies in Psychoanalytic Method: From Freud and Ferenczi to Michael Balint*. New York: New York University Press, 1988.

Haynal, André. "Freud and his Intellectual Environment: The Case of Sándor Ferenczi." In *Ferenczi's Turn in Psychoanalysis* (Peter L. Rudnytsky, Antal Bókay, and Patrizia Giampieri-Deutsch, Eds.). New York: New York University Press, 1996.

Hegeman, Elizabeth. "The Paradox of Loneliness: A Comment on Fromm-Reichmann's 'Loneliness.'" *Contemporary Psychoanalysis*, 1990, *26*, 364–367.

Heilbrun, Carolyn. *Writing a Woman's Life*. New York: Norton, 1988.

Herman, Judith Lewis. *Trauma and Recovery*. New York: Basic Books, 1992.

Hilgard, Josephine R. "The Anniversary Syndrome as Related to Late-Appearing Mental Illnesses in Hospitalized Patients." In *Psychoanalysis and Psychosis* (Ann-Louise S. Silver, Ed.). Madison, CT: International Universities Press, 1989, 221–247.

Hillyer, Jane. *Reluctantly Told*. New York: Macmillan, 1926.

Hoff, Sylvia G. "Frieda Fromm-Reichmann." In *Dictionary of American Biography: Supplement Six (1956–1960)*, (J. A. Garraty, Ed.). New York: Scribner's, 1980, 219–220.

Hoff, Sylvia G. "Frieda Fromm-Reichmann, the Early Years." *Psychiatry*, 1982, *45*, 115–121.

Hoff, Sylvia G. "Frieda Fromm-Reichmann, M.D.: Pioneer in Psychiatry and Psychoanalysis." In *Women Physicians in Leadership Roles* (Leah J. Dickstein and Carol C. Nadelson, Eds.). Washington, D.C.: American Psychiatric Press, 1986, 73–77.

Hornstein, Gail A. "The Ethics of Ambiguity: Feminists Writing Women's Lives." In *Women Creating Lives: Identities, Resilience, and Resistance* (Carol E. Franz and Abigail J. Stewart, Eds.). Boulder, CO: Westview Press, 1994, 51–68.

Hornstein, G. A., and S. L. Star. "Universality Biases: How Theories About Human Nature Succeed." *Philosophy of the Social Sciences*, 1990, *20*, 421–436.

Hubner, Lewis. "The Function of Our Sanatoriums." *Christian Science Journal*, March 1974, *92*, 149–150.

Hughes, Judith M. *Reshaping the Psychoanalytic Domain: The Work of Melanie Klein, W. R. D. Fairbairn, and D. W. Winnicott*. Berkeley: University of California Press, 1989.

Hunter, Kathryn Montgomery. *Doctors' Stories*. Princeton: Princeton University Press, 1991.

Isaac, Rael Jean, and Virginia C. Armat. *Madness in the Streets: How Psychiatry and the Law Abandoned the Mentally Ill*. New York: Free Press, 1990.

Jacoby, Yoram K. *Jüdisches Leben in Königsberg/Pr. im 20. Jahrhundert*. Würzburg: Holzner Verlag, 1983.

Jamison, Kay Redfield. *An Unquiet Mind: A Memoir of Moods and Madness*. New York: Knopf, 1995.

Jay, Martin. *The Dialectical Imagination: A History of the Frankfurt School and the Institute of Social Research*. Boston: Little, Brown, 1973.

Jessner, Lucie, and V. Gerard Ryan. *Shock Treatment in Psychiatry: A Manual*. New York: Grune & Stratton, 1941.

Johnson, Ann Braden. *Out of Bedlam: The Truth About Deinstitutionalization*. New York: Basic Books, 1990.

Jones, Ernest. *The Life and Work of Sigmund Freud*, vol. 3. New York: Basic Books, 1957.

Jones, Maxwell. *The Therapeutic Community: A New Treatment Method in Psychiatry*. New York: Basic Books, 1953.

Jung, Carl G. *Memories, Dreams, Reflections*. New York: Random House, 1961.

Jünger, Ernst. *The Storm of Steel, from the Diary of a German Storm-Troop Officer on the Western Front* (Basil Creighton, trans.). New York: Howard Fertig, 1975 (orig. pub. 1921; 1st English ed. 1929).

Kaplan, Justin. "The Naked Self and Other Problems." In *Telling Lives: The Biographer's Art* (Marc Pachter, Ed.). Washington, D.C.: New Republic Books/National Portrait Gallery, 1979, 37–55.

Kaplan, Marion A. "Priestess and Hausfrau: Women and Tradition in the German-Jewish Family." In *The Jewish Family: Myths and Realities* (Steven M. Cohen and Paula E. Hyman, Eds.). New York: Holmes & Meier, 1986, 62–81.

Kaplan, Marion A. *The Making of the Jewish Middle Class: Women, Family, and Identity in Imperial Germany*. New York: Oxford University Press, 1991.

Kaplan, Marion A. *Between Dignity and Despair: Jewish Life in Nazi Germany*. New York: Oxford University Press, 1998.

Karpf, Anne. *The War After: Living with the Holocaust*. London: Random House, 1996.

Katz, Jacob. *Out of the Ghetto: The Social Background of Jewish Emancipation, 1770–1870*. New York: Schocken Books, 1978.

Kaysen, Susanna. *Girl, Interrupted*. New York: Random House, 1993.

Keitel, Evelyne. *Reading Psychosis: Readers, Texts, and Psychoanalysis* (Anthea Bell, trans.). New York: Blackwell, 1989.

Kernberg, Otto. *Borderline Conditions and Pathological Narcissism*. New York: Jason Aronson, 1975.

Klein, Melanie. "On the Sense of Loneliness." In *Our Adult World*. New York: Basic Books, 1963.

Klerman, Gerald L. "The Psychiatric Patient's Right to Effective Treatment: Implications of *Osheroff v. Chestnut Lodge*." *American Journal of Psychiatry*, 1990, *147*, 409–418.

Knapp, Gerhard P. *The Art of Living: Erich Fromm's Life and Works*. New York: Peter Lang, 1989.

Kolb, Lawrence, and Victor Vogel. "The Use of Shock Therapy in 305 Mental Hospitals." *American Journal of Psychiatry*, 1942, *99*, 90–100.

Kollwitz, Hans (Ed.). *The Diary and Letters of Käthe Kollwitz* (Richard and Clara Winston, trans.). Evanston, IL: Northwestern University Press, 1988.

Koonz, Claudia. *Mothers in the Fatherland*. New York: St. Martin's Press, 1987.

Kraepelin, Emil. *One Hundred Years of Psychiatry*. New York: Citadel Press, 1962.

Kramer, Peter. "Status for Psychiatrists Is Really Getting Inside a Head." *New York Times Sunday Magazine*, November 15, 1998, 92.

Kris, Elsie B. "The Convulsive Therapies: Technical and Clinical Considerations." In *Current Therapies of Personality Disorders* (Bernard Glueck, Ed.). New York: Grune & Stratton, 1946, 70–81.

Kubie, Lawrence S. *The Riggs Story: The Development of the Austen Riggs Center for the Study and Treatment of the Neuroses.* New York: Harper & Bros., 1960.

Kubie, Lawrence S. "The Retreat from Patients." *Archives of General Psychiatry,* 1971, *24,* 98–106.

Kurzweil, Edith. *The Freudians: A Comparative Perspective.* New Haven: Yale University Press, 1989.

Kutchins, Herb, and Stuart A Kirk. *Making Us Crazy: DSM, the Psychiatric Bible and the Creation of Mental Disorders.* New York: Free Press, 1997.

Kwiet, Konrad. "To Leave or Not to Leave: The German Jews at the Crossroads." In *November 1938: From "Reichskristallnacht" to Genocide* (Walter H. Pehle, Ed.). Oxford: Berg Publishers, 1991.

Langs, Robert, and Harold Searles. *Intrapsychic and Interpersonal Dimensions of Treatment: A Clinical Dialogue.* New York: Jason Aronson, 1980.

Laor, Dan. "Agnon in Germany, 1912–1924: A Chapter of a Biography." *Association for Jewish Studies,* 1993, *18,* 75–93.

Late Inmate of the Glasgow Royal Asylum for Lunatics at Gartnavel. *The Philosophy of Insanity.* New York: Greenberg, 1947.

Leeds-Hurwitz, Wendy. "Frieda Fromm-Reichmann and the Natural History of an Interview." In *Psychoanalysis and Psychosis* (Ann-Louise S. Silver, Ed.). Madison, CT: International Universities Press, 1989, 95–127.

Leonhard, Joachim-Felix (Ed.). *Bücherverbrennung: Zensur, Verbot, Vernichtung unter dem Nationalsozialismus in Heidelberg.* Heidelberg: Heidelberger Verlagsantalt und Drukere, 1983.

Lidz, Theodore. "Adolf Meyer and the Development of American Psychiatry." *American Journal of Psychiatry,* 1966, *123,* 320–332.

Liebenberg, Beatrice. "Fromm-Reichmann at the Washington School of Psychiatry." In *Psychoanalysis and Psychosis* (Ann-Louise S. Silver, Ed.). Madison, CT: International Universities Press, 1989, 91–94.

Löwenthal, Leo. *An Unmastered Past.* Berkeley: University of California Press, 1987.

Lüthe, Wolfgang, and J. H. Schultz. *Autogenic Methods,* Vol. 1. New York: Grune & Stratton, 1969.

McGlashan, Thomas H., and Christopher J. Keats. *Schizophrenia: Treatment, Process and Outcome.* Washington, D.C.: American Psychiatric Press, 1989.

McGuire, Thomas G. *Financing Psychotherapy.* Cambridge, MA: Ballinger, 1981.

McLaughlin, Neil G. "Origin Myths in the Social Sciences: Erich Fromm, the Frankfurt School, and the Emergence of Critical Theory." *Canadian Journal of Sociology,* 1999, *24,* 109–139.

McLaughlin, Neil G. "How to Become a Forgotten Intellectual: Intellectual Movements and the Rise and Fall of Erich Fromm." *Sociological Forum,* 1998, *13,* 215–246.

McLaughlin, Neil G. "Why Do Schools of Thought Fail? Neo-Freudianism as a Case Study in the Sociology of Knowledge." *Journal of the History of the Behavioral Sciences,* 1998, *34,* 113–134.

MacKenzie, Charlotte. *Psychiatry for the Rich: A History of Ticehurst Private Asylum, 1792–1917.* London: Routledge, 1992.

Malcolm, John. *Treatment Choices and Informed Consent.* Springfield, IL: Charles C. Thomas, 1988.

Malzberg, Benjamin. "Public Health Aspects of Insulin and Other Shock Therapies."

In *Current Therapies of Personality Disorders* (Bernard Glueck, Ed.). New York: Grune & Stratton, 1946, 117–131.

Marek, George R. *Gentle Genius: The Story of Felix Mendelssohn.* New York: Funk & Wagnalls, 1972.

Marschak, Marianne. "One Year Among the Behavioral Scientists: In Memory of Frieda Fromm-Reichmann." *Psychiatry,* 1960, *23,* 303–309.

Martin, Denis V. "Institutionalisation." *Lancet,* December 3, 1955, 1188–1190.

Masserman, Jules H., and Jacob L. Moreno (Eds.). *Progress in Psychotherapy, Volume 3: Techniques of Psychotherapy.* New York: Grune & Stratton, 1958.

Meisels, Murray, and Ester R. Shapiro (Eds.). *Tradition and Innovation in Psychoanalytic Education.* Hillsdale, NJ: Erlbaum, 1990.

Menninger, William C. "Psychiatric Hospital Therapy Designed to Meet Unconscious Needs." *American Journal of Psychiatry,* 1936–1937, *93,* 347–360.

Menninger, William C. "Psychoanalytic Principles Applied to the Treatment of Hospitalized Patients." *Bulletin of the Menninger Clinic,* 1937, *1,* 35–43.

Menninger, William C. "Psychoanalytic Interpretations of Patients' Reactions in Occupational Therapy, Recreational Therapy and Physiotherapy." *Bulletin of the Menninger Clinic,* 1937, *1,* 148–157.

Menninger, William C. "Psychiatric Principles in Psychiatric Hospital Therapy." *Southern Medical Journal,* 1939, *32,* 348–354.

Menninger, William C., and Isabelle McColl. "Recreational Therapy as Applied in a Modern Psychiatric Hospital." *Occupational Therapy and Rehabilitation,* 1937, *16,* 15–24.

Micale, Mark S. "On the 'Disappearance' of Hysteria: A Study in the Clinical Deconstruction of a Diagnosis." *Isis,* 1993, *84,* 496–526.

Miller, Alice. *The Drama of the Gifted Child* (Ruth Ward, trans.). New York: Basic Books, 1981.

Miller, Jean Baker (Ed.). *Psychoanalysis and Women.* New York: Penguin, 1973.

Millett, Kate. *The Loony-bin Trip.* New York: Simon & Schuster, 1990.

Morse, Robert T., and Douglas Noble. "Joint Endeavors of the Administrative Physician and Psychotherapist." *Psychiatric Quarterly,* 1942, *16,* 578–585.

Moyers, Bill. *Healing and the Mind.* New York: Doubleday, 1993.

Mullan, Bob. *Mad to Be Normal: Conversations with R. D. Laing.* London: Free Association Books, 1995.

Müller, Hartmut. "Frieda Fromm-Reichmanns Verständnis der Genese und Therapie der Schizophrenie." *PsA-Info-Nr. 30,* March 1988, 29–39.

Naylor, Phyllis. *Crazy Love: An Autobiographical Account of Marriage and Madness.* New York: Morrow, 1977.

Neary, John. *Whom the Gods Destroy.* NY: Atheneum, 1975.

Neill, John. "Whatever Became of the Schizophrenogic Mother?" *American Journal of Psychotherapy,* 1990, *44,* 499–505.

Newman, Louis I. *The Hasidic Anthology: Tales and Teachings of the Hasidim.* New York: Scribner's, 1934.

Norris, Kathleen. *Dakota: A Spiritual Geography.* New York: Ticknor & Fields, 1993.

North, Carol S. *Welcome, Silence: My Triumph over Schizophrenia.* New York: Avon Books, 1987.

North, Carol, and Remi Cadoret. "Diagnostic Discrepancy in Personal Accounts of Patients with 'Schizophrenia.'" *Archives of General Psychiatry,* 1981, *38,* 133–137.

Numbers, Ronald L., and Judith Walzer Leavitt (Eds.). *Wisconsin Medicine: Historical Perspectives*. Madison: University of Wisconsin Press, 1981.

O'Brien, Barbara. *Operators and Things: The Inner Life of a Schizophrenic*. New York:
Ace Books, 1958.

O'Connell, A. N., and N. F. Russo (Eds.). *Models of Achievement: Reflections of Eminent Women in Psychology*. New York: Columbia University Press, 1983.

O'Dowd, Michael J., and Elliot E. Philipp. *The History of Obstetrics and Gynaecology*.
New York: Parthenon, 1994.

Oates, Joyce Carol. *(Woman) Writer: Occasions and Opportunities*. New York: Dutton,
1988.

Oates, Joyce Carol. "Facts, Visions, Mysteries: My Father, Frederic Oates." In *Family
Portraits: Remembrances by Twenty Distinguished Writers* (Carolyn Anthony,
Ed.). New York: Penguin, 1989.

Oberndorf, Clarence P. *A History of Psychoanalysis in America*. New York: Harper &
Row, 1953.

Orr, Douglass W. "Transference and Countertransference: A Historical Survey." *Journal of the American Psychoanalytic Association*, 1954, *2*, 621–670.

Paris, Bernard J. *Karen Horney: A Psychoanalyst's Search for Self-Understanding*.
New Haven: Yale University Press, 1994.

Parry-Jones, W. L. *The Trade in Lunacy*. London: Routledge and Kegan Paul, 1972.

Perceval, John. *A Narrative of the Treatment Experienced by a Gentleman, During a
State of Mental Derangement*. London: Effingham Wilson, 1840.

Perrucci, Robert. *Circle of Madness*. Englewood Cliffs, NJ: Prentice-Hall, 1974.

Perry, Helen Swick. *Psychiatrist of America: The Life of Harry Stack Sullivan*. Cambridge, MA: Harvard University Press, 1982.

Petratos, Barbara Dionis. "The European Teachers of Dr. Frieda Fromm-Reichmann."
Journal of the American Academy of Psychoanalysis, 1990, *18*, 152–166.

Petratos, Barbara Dionis. "The Development of Dr. Frieda Fromm-Reichmann's Modified Psychoanalytic Techniques for the Treatment of Schizophrenia." Ph.D. dissertation, New York University, 1992.

Plänkers, Tomas, and Hans-Joachim Rothe. "You Know That Our Old Institute Was
Entirely Destroyed . . .? On the History of the Frankfurt Psychoanalytical Institute
(FPI), 1929–1933." *Psychoanalysis and History*, 1998, *1*, 103–114.

Porter, Roy. "The Patient's View: Doing Medical History from Below." *Theory and Society*, 1985, *14*, 175–198.

Porter, Roy. *A Social History of Madness: The World Through the Eyes of the Insane*.
New York: Weidenfeld & Nicolson, 1987.

Porter, Roy, and Mark S. Micale. "Introduction." In *Discovering the History of Psychiatry* (Mark S. Micale and Roy Porter, Eds.). New York: Oxford University
Press, 1994, 3–36.

Powell, R. C., and Sylvia G. Hoff. "Frieda Fromm-Reichmann." In *Notable American
Women, the Modern Period: A Biographical Dictionary* (B. Sicherman and C. H.
Green, Eds.). Cambridge, MA: Harvard University Press, 1980, 252–254.

Pressman, Jack D. *Last Resort: Psychosurgery and the Limits of Medicine*. Cambridge:
Cambridge University Press, 1998.

Price, Richard H., and Bruce Denner. *The Making of a Mental Patient*. New York: Holt,
Rinehart & Winston, 1973.

Quigley, W. Heath. "Pioneering Mental Health: Institutional Psychiatric Care in Chiropractic." *Chiropractic History*, 1983, *3*, 68–73.

Quinn, Susan. *A Mind of Her Own: The Life of Karen Horney.* Reading, MA: Addison-Wesley, 1988.

Rachman, Arnold Wm. "Ferenczi and Sexuality." In *The Legacy of Sándor Ferenczi* (Lewis Aron and Adrienne Harris, Eds.). Hillsdale, NJ: Analytic Press, 1993, 81–100.

Reaume, Geoffrey. "Keep Your Labels Off My Mind! or 'Now I am Going to Pretend I Am Craze but Dont Be a Bit Alarmed': Psychiatric History from the Patients' Perspectives." *Canadian Bulletin of Medical History,* 1994, *11,* 397–424.

Reed, Douglas. *The Burning of the Reichstag.* London: Victor Gollancz, 1934.

Remarque, Erich Maria. *All Quiet on the Western Front.* Boston: Little, Brown, 1929.

Richarz, Monika (Ed.). *Jewish Life in Germany: Memoirs from Three Centuries* (Stella P. Rosenfeld and Sidney Rosenfeld, trans.). Bloomington, IN: Indiana University Press, 1991.

Riese, Walther. "Kurt Goldstein—The Man and his Work." In *The Reach of Mind: Essays in Memory of Kurt Goldstein* (Marianne L. Simmel, Ed.). New York: Springer, 1968, 17–29.

Rinkel, Max, and Harold E. Himwich (Eds.). *Insulin Treatment in Psychiatry.* New York: Philosophical Library, 1959.

Rioch, David McK. "Dexter Bullard, Sr. and Chestnut Lodge." *Psychiatry,* 1984, *47,* 2.

Risse, Guenter B., and John Harley Warner. "Reconstructing Clinical Activities: Patient Records in Medical History." *Social History of Medicine,* 1992, *5,* 183–205.

Rosen, John N. *Direct Analysis: Selected Papers.* New York: Grune & Stratton, 1953.

Rosenberg, Charles E. "The Crisis in Psychiatric Legitimacy: Reflections on Psychiatry, Medicine, and Public Policy." In *American Psychiatry: Past, Present, and Future* (G. Kriegman, R. D. Gardner, and D. W. Abse, Eds.). Charlottesville, VA: University Press of Virginia, 1975, 135–148.

Rosenberg, Charles E. *The Care of Strangers: The Rise of America's Hospital System.* New York: Basic Books, 1987.

Rosenberg, Charles E. "Body and Mind in Nineteenth-Century Medicine: Some Clinical Origins of the Neurosis Construct." *Bulletin of the History of Medicine,* 1989, *63,* 185–197.

Rosenhan, David L. "On Being Sane in Insane Places." *Science,* 1973, *179,* 250–258.

Ross, Colin A., and Alvin Pam. *Pseudoscience in Biological Psychiatry.* New York: Wiley, 1995.

Sacks, Oliver. *Awakenings.* New York: HarperCollins, 1990.

Sarna, Nahumm. *The JPS Torah Commentary, Exodus 12:15.* New York: Jewish Publication Society, 1991.

Sassenberg, Marina. "Helene Simon." In *Jüdische Frauen im 19. und 20. Jahrhundert* (Jutta Dick and Marina Sassenberg, Eds.). Hamburg: Rowohlt, 1993, 347–349.

Sayers, Janet. *Mothers of Psychoanalysis.* New York: Norton, 1991.

Schaffner, Bertram (Ed.). *Group Processes.* Madison, NJ: Josiah Macy, Jr. Foundation, 1955.

Schoenewolf, Gerald. *Turning Points in Analytic Therapy: From Winnicott to Kernberg.* Northvale, NJ: Jason Aronson, 1990.

Scholem, Gershom. "How I Came to the Kabbalah." *Commentary,* 1980, *69,* 42.

Schön, Donald A. *The Reflective Practitioner: How Professionals Think in Action.* New York: Basic Books, 1983.

Schreber, Daniel Paul. *Memoirs of My Nervous Illness* (reprint edition). London: William Dawson & Sons, 1955.

Schulz, Clarence G. "A Follow-Up Report on Admissions to Chestnut Lodge." *Psychiatric Quarterly,* April 1963, 1–14.

Schulz, Clarence. "Sullivan's Clinical Contribution During the Sheppard Pratt Era—1923–1930." *Psychiatry,* 1978, *41,* 117–128.

Schulz, Clarence. "Sullivan's Influence on Sheppard Pratt." *Journal of the American Academy of Psychoanalysis,* 1987, *15,* 247–259.

Schwab, Hermann. *The History of Orthodox Jewry in Germany.* London: Mitre Press, 1950.

Schwartz, Morris S. "Patient Demands in a Mental Hospital Context." *Psychiatry,* 1957, *20,* 249–261.

Schwartz, Morris S. *Letting Go: Morrie's Reflections on Living While Dying.* New York: Walker, 1996.

Schwartz, Morris S., and Alfred H. Stanton. "A Social-Psychological Study of Incontinence." *Psychiatry,* 1950, *13,* 399–416.

Schwing, Gertrud. *A Way to the Soul of the Mentally Ill.* New York: International Universities Press, 1954.

Scull, Andrew. *Museums of Madness: The Social Organization of Insanity in Nineteenth-Century England.* London: Allen Lane, 1979.

Scull, Andrew. "Moral Treatment Reconsidered: Some Sociological Comments on an Episode in the History of British Psychiatry." In *Madhouses, Mad-Doctors, and Madmen: A Social History of Psychiatry in the Victorian Era* (Andrew Scull, Ed.). London: Athlone Press, 1981, 105–118.

Scull, Andrew. "The Domestication of Madness." *Medical History,* 1983, *27,* 233–248.

Scull, Andrew. "Psychiatry and Its Historians." *History of Psychiatry,* 1991, *2,* 239–250.

Scull, Andrew. "Psychiatry and Social Control in the Nineteenth and Twentieth Centuries." *History of Psychiatry,* 1991, *2,* 149–169.

Searles, Harold F. *Countertransference and Related Subjects: Selected Papers.* New York: International Universities Press, 1979.

Searles, Harold F. "Psychoanalytic Therapy with Cancer Patients: Some Speculations." In *Psychotherapeutic Treatment of Cancer Patients* (Jane G. Goldberg, Ed.). New York: Free Press, 1981, 167–181.

Sechehaye, Marguerite. *Autobiography of a Schizophrenic Girl.* New York: Grune & Stratton, 1951.

Sheehan, Susan. *Is There No Place on Earth for Me?* Boston: Houghton Mifflin, 1982.

Shorter, Edward. "Private Clinics in Central Europe, 1850–1933." *Social History of Medicine,* 1990, *3,* 160–195.

Shorter, Edward. *A History of Psychiatry.* New York: Wiley, 1997.

Sicherman, Barbara. *The Quest for Mental Health in America, 1880–1917.* New York: Arno Press, 1980.

Silver, Ann-Louise S. *Psychoanalysis and Psychosis.* Madison, CT: International Universities Press, 1989.

Silver, Ann-Louise S. "Countertransference, Ferenczi, and Washington, D.C." *Journal of the American Academy of Psychoanalysis,* 1993, *21,* 637–654.

Silver, Ann-Louise S. "Women Who Lead," *American Journal of Psychoanalysis,* 1996, *56,* 3–16.

Silver, Ann-Louise S., and Pollianne Curry Freuer. "Fromm-Reichmann's Contributions at Staff Conferences." In *Psychoanalysis and Psychosis* (Ann-Louise S. Silver, Ed.). Madison, CT: International Universities Press, 1989, 23–45.

Silverberg, William V. "The Art of Dr. Gertrud Jacob, 1893–1940." *Psychiatry,* 1941, *4,* 1–5.

Simmel, Ernst. "Psychoanalytic Treatment in a Sanatorium." *International Journal of Psychoanalysis,* 1929, *10,* 70–89.

Simmel, Ernst. "The Psychoanalytic Sanatorium and the Psychoanalytic Movement." *Bulletin of the Menninger Clinic,* 1937, *1,* 133–143.

Singer, Charlotte. "Diary of a Refugee." In *Women of Exile: German-Jewish Autobiographies Since 1933* (Andreas Lixl-Purcell, Ed.). Westport, CT: Greenwood Press, 1988.

Small, Victor R. *I Knew 3000 Lunatics.* New York: Farrar & Rinehart, 1935.

Sontag, Susan. "Writing Itself: On Roland Barthes." In *A Barthes Reader* (Susan Sontag, Ed.). New York: Hill and Wang, 1982.

Spence, Donald P. *Narrative Truth and Historical Truth: Meaning and Interpretation in Psychoanalysis.* New York: Norton, 1982.

Stanislavski, Constantin. *An Actor Prepares* (Elizabeth Reynolds Hapgood, trans.). New York: Routledge, 1936.

Stanton, Alfred H. "Frieda Fromm-Reichmann, M.D.: Her Impact on American Psychiatry." *Psychiatry,* 1982, *45,* 121–127.

Stanton, Alfred H., and Morris S. Schwartz. "The Management of a Type of Institutional Participation in Mental Illness." *Psychiatry,* 1949, *12,* 12–26.

Stanton, Alfred H., and Morris S. Schwartz. *The Mental Hospital: A Study of Institutional Participation in Psychiatric Illness and Treatment.* New York: Basic Books, 1954.

Star, Susan Leigh. *Regions of the Mind: Brain Research and the Quest for Scientific Certainty.* Stanford: Stanford University Press, 1989.

Stefan, Gregory. *In Search of Sanity: The Journal of a Schizophrenic.* New Hyde Park, NY: University Books, 1965.

Stern, Donnel B., Carola H. Mann, Stuart Kantor, and Gary Schlesinger (Eds.), *Pioneers of Interpersonal Psychoanalysis.* Hillsdale, NJ: Analytic Press, 1995.

Stevens, Gwendolyn, and Sheldon Gardner. *The Women of Psychology, Vol. I: Pioneers and Innovators.* Cambridge, MA: Schenkman Publishing Co., 1982.

Stierlin, Helm. "Individual Therapy of Schizophrenic Patients and Hospital Structure." In *Psychotherapy of the Psychoses* (Arthur Burton, Ed.). New York: Basic Books, 1961, 329–348.

Stierlin, Helm. "Techniques of Psychotherapy in a Small Hospital." *Bulletin of the Menninger Clinic,* 1963, *27,* 96–104.

Stone, Alan A. "Conceptual Ambiguity and Morality in Modern Psychiatry." *American Journal of Psychiatry,* 1980, *137,* 887–891.

Stone, Alan A. "Law, Science, and Psychiatric Malpractice: A Response to Klerman's Indictment of Psychoanalytic Psychiatry." *American Journal of Psychiatry,* 1990, *147,* 419–427.

Stotland, Ezra, and Arthur L. Kobler. *Life and Death of a Mental Hospital.* Seattle: University of Washington Press, 1965.

Strachey, James, and Alix Strachey. *Bloomsbury/Freud: The Letters of James and Alix Strachey, 1924–1925* (Perry Meisel and Walter V. Kendrick, Eds.). New York: Basic Books, 1985.

Styron, William. *Darkness Visible: A Memoir of Madness.* New York: Random House, 1990.

Sullivan, Harry Stack. *Conceptions of Modern Psychiatry.* New York: Norton, 1940.

Sullivan, Harry Stack. *The Interpersonal Theory of Psychiatry.* New York: Norton, 1953.

Sullivan, Harry Stack. *Clinical Studies in Psychiatry.* New York: Norton, 1956.

Sullivan, Harry Stack. *Schizophrenia as a Human Process.* New York: Norton, 1962.

Sutton, S. B. *Crossroads in Psychiatry: A History of the McLean Hospital.* Washington, D.C.: American Psychiatric Press, 1986.

Szalita, Alberta B. "Acceptance Speech on the Occasion of Receiving the Frieda Fromm-Reichmann Award." *Journal of the American Academy of Psychoanalysis,* 1981, *9,* 11–16.

Szalita-Pemow, Alberta B. "The 'Intuitive Process' and its Relation to Work with Schizophrenics." *Journal of the American Psychoanalytic Association,* 1955, *3,* 7–18.

Thompson, Clara M. "A Study of the Emotional Climate of Psychoanalytic Institutes." In *Interpersonal Psychoanalysis: Papers of Clara M. Thompson* (Maurice R. Green, Ed.). New York: Basic Books, 1964, 54–62.

Thompson, Clara M. "Sándor Ferenczi, 1873–1933." *Contemporary Psychoanalysis,* 1988, *24,* 182–195.

Thompson, Nellie L. "Early Women Psychoanalysts." *International Review of Psychoanalysis,* 1987, *14,* 391–407.

Tomes, Nancy. *A Generous Confidence: Thomas Story Kirkbride and the Art of Asylum-Keeping, 1840–1883.* Cambridge: Cambridge University Press, 1984.

Torrey, E. Fuller. *Surviving Schizophrenia: A Family Manual.* New York: Harper & Row, 1988.

Trilling, L., I. Howe, L. H. Farber, W. Hamilton, R. Orrill, and R. Boyers. "Sincerity and Authenticity: A Symposium." *Salmagundi,* 1978, *41,* 102–104.

Valenstein, Elliot S. *Great and Desperate Cures: The Rise and Decline of Psychosurgery and Other Radical Treatments for Mental Illness.* New York: Basic Books, 1986.

Valenstein, Elliot S. *Blaming the Brain.* New York: Free Press, 1998.

Warner, John Harley. *The Therapeutic Perspective: Medical Practice, Knowledge, and Identity in America, 1820–1885.* Cambridge, MA: Harvard University Press, 1986.

Warner, John Harley. "The Fall and Rise of Professional Mystery: Epistemology, Authority, and the Emergence of Laboratory Medicine in Nineteenth-century America." In *The Laboratory Revolution in Medicine* (A. Cunningham and P. Williams, Eds.). Cambridge: Cambridge University Press, 1991, 310–341.

Warner, John Harley. "The History of Science and the Sciences of Medicine." *Osiris,* 1995, *10,* 164–193.

Weigert, Edith. "In Memoriam: Frieda Fromm-Reichmann, 1889–1957." *Psychiatry,* 1958, *21,* 91–95.

Weigert, Edith. *The Courage to Love.* New Haven: Yale University Press, 1970.

Weiner, Dora B. " 'Le geste de Pinel': The History of a Psychiatric Myth." In *Discovering the History of Psychiatry* (Mark S. Micale and Roy Porter, Eds.). New York: Oxford University Press, 1994, 232–237.

Weininger, Benjamin I. "Psychotherapy During Convalescence from Psychosis." *Psychiatry,* 1938, *1,* 257–264.

Weininger, Benjamin I. "Chestnut Lodge—The Early Years: Krishnamurti and Buber." In *Psychoanalysis and Psychosis* (Ann-Louise S. Silver, Ed.). Madison, CT: International Universities Press, 1989, 495–512.

Weiss, Ernst. *The Eyewitness* (Ella R.W. McKee, trans.). London: Proteus, 1978.

Will, Otto Allen, Jr. "In Memory of Frieda." In *Psychoanalysis and Psychosis* (Ann-

Louise S. Silver, Ed.). Madison, CT: International Universities Press, 1989, 131–144.

Will, Otto A., and Robert A. Cohen. "A Report of a Recorded Interview in the Course of Psychotherapy." *Psychiatry,* 1953, *16,* 263–282.

Winnicott, D. W. *Home Is Where We Start From: Essays by a Psychoanalyst.* London: Pelican Books, 1987.

Wolfe, Kary K., and Gary K. Wolfe. "Metaphors of Madness: Popular Psychological Narratives." *Journal of Popular Culture,* 1976, *9,* 895–907.

Wolstein, Benjamin. "Ferenczi, Freud, and the Origins of American Interpersonal Relations." *Contemporary Psychoanalysis,* 1989, *25,* 672–685.

Wolstein, Benjamin (Ed.). *Essential Papers on Countertransference.* New York: New York University Press, 1988.

Young-Bruehl, Elisabeth. *Hannah Arendt: For Love of the World.* New Haven: Yale University Press, 1982.

Young-Bruehl, Elisabeth. *Anna Freud: A Biography.* New York: Summit Books, 1988.

Zwieg, Stefan. *The World of Yesterday.* London: Cassell, 1943.

Index

Photographic
Credits